INTELLECTUALS IN THE MODERN ISLAMIC WORLD

This book reconsiders the typology and history of intellectuals in the Islamic world in the modern and contemporary periods from the late nineteenth century to the present day.

Intellectuals in the Modern Islamic World distinguishes itself from other major studies on modern thought in Islam by examining this topic beyond the context of the Arabic world. The first section of this book concentrates on a journal, *al-Manār*, published between 1898 and 1935, and read by a wide range of audiences throughout the Islamic world, which inspired the imagination and arguments of local intellectuals in the first half of the twentieth century. The second part concentrates on the formation, transmission, and transformation of learning and authority, from the Middle East to Central and South Asia, through the twentieth century.

Providing a rich variety of case studies, by international authors of the most varied disciplinary scope, *Intellectuals in the Modern Islamic World* meets the highest academic requirements in a spirit of comparative vision and openness to the dynamism of contemporary societies of the Islamic world. As such, this book is essential reading for those with research interests in Islam and intellectual thought.

Stéphane A. Dudoignon is a research fellow at the National Center for Scientific Research (Paris).

Komatsu Hisao is a professor at the Graduate School of Humanities and Sociology, The University of Tokyo.

Kosugi Yasushi is a professor at the Graduate School of Asian and African Area Studies, Kyoto University.

NEW HORIZONS IN ISLAMIC STUDIES

Series editor:
Professor Sato Tsugitaka

The series New Horizons in Islamic Studies presents the fruitful results of Islamic Area Studies Project conducted in Japan during the years 1997–2001. The project has planned to do multidisciplinary research on the dynamism of Muslim societies in both the Islamic and non-Islamic worlds, considering the fact that areas with close ties to Islam now encompass the whole world. This series provides the newest knowledge on the subjects of "symbiosis and conflict in Muslim societies," "ports, merchants and cross-cultural exchange," and "democratization and popular movement in Islam." The readers will find multifarious, useful achievements gained through international joint research with high technology of geographic information systems about Islamic religion and civilization, particularly emphasizing comparative and historical approaches.

PERSIAN DOCUMENTS
Social history of Iran and Turan in the fifteenth–nineteenth centuries
Edited by Kondo Nobuaki

ISLAMIC AREA STUDIES WITH GEOGRAPHICAL INFORMATION SYSTEMS
Edited by Okabe Atsuyuki

MUSLIM SOCIETIES
Historical and comparative aspects
Edited by Sato Tsugitaka

INTELLECTUALS IN THE MODERN ISLAMIC WORLD
Transmission, transformation, communication
Edited by Stéphane A. Dudoignon, Komatsu Hisao, and Kosugi Yasushi

INTELLECTUALS IN THE MODERN ISLAMIC WORLD

Transmission, transformation, communication

Edited by
Stéphane A. Dudoignon,
Komatsu Hisao, and
Kosugi Yasushi

Routledge
Taylor & Francis Group
LONDON AND NEW YORK

First published 2006
by Routledge
2 Park Square, Milton Park, Abingdon, Oxon OX14 4RN

Simultaneously published in the USA and Canada
by Routledge
270 Madison Ave, New York, NY 10016

Routledge is an imprint of the Taylor & Francis Group, an informa business

Transferred to Digital Printing 2009

Typeset in Times New Roman by
Newgen Imaging Systems (P) Ltd, Chennai, India

British Library Cataloguing in Publication Data
A catalogue record for this book is available
from the British Library

Library of Congress Cataloging in Publication Data
A catalog record for this book has been requested

ISBN10: 0–415–36835–9 (hbk)
ISBN10: 0–415–54979–5 (pbk)
ISBN10: 0–203–02831–7 (ebk)

ISBN13: 978–0–415–36835–3 (hbk)
ISBN13: 978–0–415–54979–0 (pbk)
ISBN13: 978–0–203–02831–5 (ebk)

CONTENTS

PREFACE

Since the turn of the twenty-first century, the weight of the world of Islam, and its significance for humanity in general, have become strikingly apparent. In the aftermath of 9/11 there has been a spectacular increase in academic as well as public concern for the pursuit of inquiries into sociopolitical, economic, and intellectual dimensions of the world of Islam. The "Islamic Area Studies Project" (IASP), which was implemented by the Ministry of Education, Culture, Sports, Science and Technology (MEXT) of Japan during the last decade of the twentieth century, provided clear indications that foreshadowed the now universally recognized vital significance of these concerns.

From 1997 to 2002 the five-year IASP, consisting of six units, conducted interdisciplinary and cross-regional studies on the modern world of Islam. Among others, Unit 1 focused on the dynamism of thought and politics, and since 1999 this subgroup of ours aimed to analyze the evolution of contemporary thought. The essential question dealt with by this research subgroup can be summarized as follows.

Among the movements observable in the contemporary world of Islam one of the most outstanding issues is that of Islamic revivals. Far from being reduced to mere ideological phenomena, these revivals have been reflected in the most diverse political and social processes, in both Muslim-majority countries as well as in Muslim-background minorities throughout the world. Although based on the rich heritage of classical Islamic thought, these revivals reveal great changes in this tradition during the "long" twentieth century. What role should the Islamic world play in the twenty-first century? What significance will it embody in the future of humanity? In order to answer these questions one must understand holistically present-day Islamic revival movements.

We have endeavored to explore the ideas of major modern and contemporary thinkers from the world of Islam by making use of their texts. So doing, we were expecting to complement our comparative research between regions in order to elucidate the nature of twentieth-century Islamic thought and of the most varied Islamic revivalist movements. At the same time, we have tried to take into account the historical backgrounds and interregional influences that worked on various aspects and issues.

Over five years we conducted a number of seminars, workshops, and international conferences to discuss our common issues. Among various international conferences held by the IASP, two had special focus on the intellectual aspects of the modern Islamic world, namely "The Lighthouse of Modern Islam: *Al-Manār* (1898–1935) Revisited" in 1998, and "Intellectuals in Islam in the Twentieth Century: Situations, Discourses, Strategies" in 2000.

The former coincided with the one hundredth anniversary of the inception of the journal *al-Manār*. Its name, "The Lighthouse," indicates the aspirations of its founder and main contributor, Muhammad Rashid Rida, and of his colleagues, to provide intellectual illumination for the faithful throughout the world. Early twentieth-century Islam was perhaps approaching a low point, if compared with the ever expanding West, but in spite of that general impression of decay, or perhaps because of it, the "Manarists," who were associated with the journal, strove to stimulate a reinvigoration of Islam and of the world of Islam. The journal was published periodically until 1935, gathering information and opinions from, and disseminating them back to, the various parts of the world of Islam, from Java to Morocco. However, the journal was forgotten later as its authors' call was judged a failure, until the new tide of Islamic revival from the late 1960s onward proved the contrary. The conference held in Tokyo in 1998 was to evaluate the historical significance of the journal and to revive its value as a historical source, both on Islamic thought and on the social realities of the world of Islam in modern times.

While this conference singled out a particular medium at a particular moment in the history of Islam, the latter conference held in 2000 encompassed the entire range of the world of Islam with its diverse areas in culture and history, throughout the turbulent twentieth century. Its three sessions included: "Muslim Intellectuals in an Era of Transformation," "Modern/Contemporary Thought and Social Movements," and "Communicating Knowledge and Ideas: Networks and Media."

Intellectuals in the world of Islam were not only scholars, and men and women of letters, but also leaders and organizers of social movements. All of them had deep concerns about their own societies under the pressure of foreign domination and the mounting challenges of modernity. Though each had his/her own particular sociohistorical context, all of them endeavored to respond to the task of how a Muslim society in the new era of transition should develop itself, while each strove along the lines of his/her own particular orientation. The diversity and synchronicity of their thinking and works were impressive, and this conference was unique in its attempt to comprehend that diversity, as we usually see contemporary researchers and their work on Islamic thought focusing on the Middle East.

Having synthesized these two conferences with the fruits of later research into the current volume, the editors hope it will serve as an element for the mapping of the world of Islam through the twentieth century, which has been exceptionally significant in terms of social upheavals. Though not exhaustive in any sense, it will be a great satisfaction for us if these elements can serve further enquiries into the responses successively proposed by varied categories of intellectuals in the world of Islam to the question of how to live in the days of deepest transformation.

***

This volume aims to reconsider the typology and history of intellectuals in the Islamic world in the modern and contemporary periods, from the late nineteenth century to nowadays. Its two parts correspond to the two colloquia of which it provides the combined proceedings. While each chapter presents a separate regional case, with a historically and geographically different background, the two parts of the volume disclose commonalities, similarities, and intellectual echoes through comparative perspectives and identification of direct contacts.

Though numerous monographs and collective volumes on modern intellectual history of the Islamic world have been published, most deal with an individual region or country, and with more specific periods of time. Very few, if any, have tried to sketch direct intellectual exchanges between, for example, Egyptian and Indonesian reformist trends of the early twentieth century, or common features and differences in the modernization of Islamic scholarship between Cairo and rural locations in the Urals, in European and Asian Russia.

Last, this collective work proposes a unique contribution on the diachronic analysis of the modes of communication of information, learning, and authority throughout the Islamic world during the "long" twentieth century—from the international travel, teaching, and press activity of the late nineteenth-century activists to the early twenty-first-century upheavals produced by the generalization of elementary education and the diffusion of electronic medias.

In Chapter 1 of Part I of this volume, Kosugi Yasushi shows how the Islamic revival of the latter half of the twentieth century has stimulated a great deal of reflections among the students in the world of Islam about the role and function of Islam in the contemporary world. Being a pioneer or "the lighthouse" of modern Islam, as its name seems to suggest, the Journal *al-Manār* contributed substantially to later Islamic revivals. The journal contains an abundance of information on the world of Islam during its period of publication (1898–1935), as well as modern formulations of Islamic thought. This article reevaluates the journal in the light of more recent Islamic revivals, and advocates a renewed interest in the journal as a rich source for further historical studies. The author also touches upon the special role played by *al-Manār* in the field of Qurʾanic commentary.

In Chapter 2 David Commins explores why the "Manarists" had only a limited influence in Syria, by focusing on the conflict between the sultan's Islamic policy and the Manarist reformist movement in Syria. According to the author, Abdülhamid II succeeded in establishing an official version of Sunni Islam by utilizing popular Sufism and strengthening his own authority, while checking the Manarists through surveillance. It is more due to the Manarists' failure to win the sympathy of the conservative urban populace by criticizing Sufism influential among them as an obstacle to modernization.

Following the arguments by the major Manarist ideologues such as Muhammad ʻAbduh, Rafik al-ʻAzm, and Rashid Rida, Mahmoud Haddad then delineates the transformation of the Manarists' discourse. The Manarists had emerged as selective modernists who were inspired by modernization in the West and tried to fuse modern Western thinking with Islam, although in a later period they became critical of the West in the course of colonization by European powers and after the abolishment of the caliphate by secularist Turkey.

In Chapter 4, Kasuya Gen designates the fact that different Islamist currents such as traditionalism and modernism in the late Ottoman period were underlain by the endogenous themes shared with Westernism and Turkism of how to revitalize and modernize the Empire. Examining the works of Mehmed Âkif, a well-known pan-Islamist polygraph, the author points out that arguments of *al-Manār* led by the Arab ideologues were regarded as very provincial by him, and that their impact on the modernist Islamists in Turkey should not be overemphasized when we take into consideration the fact that there was incipient Ottoman Islamism endogenously emerging before Âkif.

Al-Manār's reach, however, extended far beyond the Muslim-majority world, up to the Turkic-speaking Muslim communities of the Middle Volga and the Western Urals in the north, and to the Malay-Indonesian archipelago in the east. Stéphane A. Dudoignon traces the role of an influential Tatar-Bashkir theologian from the southern Urals, Riza al-Din b. Fakhr al-Din (1859–1936), whose journal the *Šūrā* was one of the most significant enterprises of the "Muslim" autonomous press of Russia, from its foundation in 1908 to its suppression by the Bolsheviks in early 1918. Largely modeled on *al-Manār*, Riza al-Din's journal is contextualized within a network of madrasa colleges, of students returning from study at al-Azhar, and of multiple other autonomous journals of the Muslim communities of the Russian Empire. All of these actors participated in a vibrant discourse about society, relations with the Russian Christian state, and access to modernity. Rather than passively absorbing the reformist teachings of Afghani and ʻAbduh from *al-Manār*, the Islamic communities of these regions actively discussed their quest for an indigenous form of modernity.

Our exploration of Muslim minorities in non-Muslim imperial states continues eastward toward China. Contrary to other Muslim minorities such as the Uyghurs in Xinjiang, the Hui have tried to remain loyal to the Chinese State. The alleged hadith, "The love of *watan* is an article of faith" was strongly demonstrated among the Hui during the Japanese occupation of Eastern China, mainly through the *Yuehua* journal. Through this Islamic journal that was modeled on *al-Manār*, Matsumoto Masumi examines how they strove to be patriotic and nationalistic in modern terms, and how they have absorbed the influence of the Islamic reformers in Egypt, especially of *al-Manār*.

In Chapter 7 of Part I, Azyumardi Azra deals with journals as channels of transmission of modernist or reformist ideas from the Near-East, especially from Cairo and Mecca, to the Malay-Indonesian world. The author focuses in particular on how and by whom the influence of *al-Manār* was transformed into two indigenous journals, *al-Imām* and *al-Munīr*. Providing detailed biographical information of the editors and contributors of the journals, the author carves out the intellectual trends at the time, as well as the tensions between "young" reformists and "old" traditionalists.

***

The unprecedented expansion of the renewal movement throughout the world of Islam, of which the echoes of *al-Manār* bear testimony, had immediate effects in the fields of political thought. Whether there are indigenous roots of the constitutional theories and charters that were put forward in the Middle East and North Africa since the nineteenth to the beginning of the twentieth century is still open to debate. Stefan Reichmuth, comparing European and non-European constitutional movements and doctrines of this time, investigates the constitutional draft which was written in Morocco at the same period. It shows the strong interest of Islamic reformist scholars in local movements of opposition and constitutional reform, which had increased in response to European imperial encroachment. Despite its Utopian character, Murad's confidence in the Shari'a, as a source of dignity and a firm baseline for public consensus and political institution-building, reflects an important strand of Islamic political thought of the late nineteenth and early twentieth century.

A participant in the debates of this time, Shakib Arslan (1869–1946) is known as the most widely read Arab writer of the interwar period and the publisher of the French-language journal *La Nation Arabe*, that allowed him to reach Arab and non-Arab Muslims, Western policy makers, and anti-colonial activists, introducing concepts of the Arab world and the Islamic revival to new audiences. Raja Adal's article traces the members of Arslan's transnational network, looks into the manner in which it was constructed, and ultimately asks for its *raisons d'être* based on a systematic analysis of *La Nation Arabe*. Arslan's network can be seen as operating on three ideological plans, linking the intellectual currents of Arabism, Islamism, and anticolonialism.

Chapter 10, by Alexandre Popovic, takes into consideration the most representative Muslim intellectuals of Bosnia-Herzegovina in the twentieth century, amounting to about fifty names, and classifies them into specific groups according to their status, discourses, and strategies as well as by respective periods. Based on this overview, the author describes the main intellectual trends that appeared in the Muslim minority society in the course of a long and gradual period, covering the decline of the Ottoman Empire, the emergence of the South-Slav Kingdom, the establishment of the Communist Regime, and the post-Communist era followed by the civil war in 1992–1995.

For the Ismailis, the twentieth century will be regarded as a time of social and religious revival. After the long period of time from the fall of Alamut, the Ismailis have returned to the center stage of the Islamic world. They have constructed a worldwide NGO network called the Aga Khan Development Network (AKDN). As Nejima Susumu suggests, the AKDN is under the general control of the Imamat (office of the Imam), and the Ismailis are voluntarily working within the network. The NGO activities, involving hundreds of schools, hospitals, and universities, have produced thousands of highly educated Ismaili youth. Some of them have proceeded to religious studies, especially on Nasir Khusraw, the early theoretician of the Ismailiyya. The author shows how this intellectual phenomenon is giving a new character to the followers of the Aga Khan.

In a comprehensive analysis of reformist and nationalist movements among Chinese Muslim intellectuals during the period of turmoil from the late Qing to the beginning of the Communist era, Françoise Aubin investigates the cultural associations, the educational institutions in the Chinese language, and the press established by Muslim intellectuals. She points out that their movements played a decisive role in making the minority Muslims Chinese citizens, and in favoring an overall modernization of Islam in China. In the course of the twentieth century more than ever, Sino-Islam was an integral part of the world Islam as well as of Chinese culture.

After the Russo-Japanese War in 1904–1905, Muslim intellectuals had begun to have substantial interest in the emergence of modern Japan. Of these Muslim intellectuals, Abdurreshid Ibrahim (1857–1944) was among the most outstanding. He not only introduced Japan and Japanese people in detail to the broad Turkic Muslim audience through his extensive travels, by means of his journal, *The World of Islam: Spread of Islam in Japan*, but also made efforts in later life to establish a close relationship between the world of Islam and Japan based on his Pan-Islamic ideology and strategy. Komatsu Hisao provides a preliminary survey of his vision of modern Japan and presents basic information for further research on a comprehensive subject, Islam and Japan, the significance of which is clearly growing in the contemporary world.

In Chapter 14, Dale F. Eickelman criticizes previous modernization theory, through an analysis of the significant dynamism of relations between intellectuals and their publics in the contemporary world of Islam. Together with the emergence of new intellectuals lacking formal religious training, a new sense of public is emerging thanks to mass education and mass communication. Thinkers such as Fethullah Gülen, Muhammad Shahrur, and others are redrawing the boundaries of public and religious life in the Muslim-majority world by challenging religious authority. The author stresses that the Muslim-majority world is demonstrating a vigorous and increasingly diverse intellectual pluralism.

In these matters, thanks to its scope and hopefully to the precision of its individual contributions, the present volume has endeavored to become a landmark of comparative studies in human and social sciences of the modern and contemporary Islamic world. At the same time, it sketches perspectives for a further enlargement of these comparative approaches toward global appraisals of the place and role of different types and categories of intellectuals in such issues as alien domination (whether Western, Russian/Soviet, or Chinese), modernization, community- and nation-building, access to education and learning, from colonization to the current aftermath of the cold war. In the future, the systematization, in this spirit, of separate area studies should permit the appearance of comparative studies on the history of modern intellectuals in the Islamic world and in other cultural areas—in particular in Western, European, and North American societies.

***

We would not like to put the final dot to this short preface without expressing our deep gratitude to the MEXT and Japan Society for the Promotion of Science (JSPS), which provided our IASP with Grant-in-Aid for Creative Scientific Research, as well as to the Japan Foundation (Japan-Europe Support Program for Conferences and Symposiums) and to the Embassy of France in Japan, whose support and attention enabled the organization of our second conference "Intellectuals in Islam in the Twentieth Century: Situations, Discourses, Strategies" in Tokyo. Our thanks, however, would not be complete without mentioning our special gratitude to all the panelists and participants in our two conferences, especially to the first *al-Manār* conference session chairs Profs Nakamura Kojiro, Hachioshi Makoto, Nakanishi Hisae, Sakai Keiko, Kimura Yoshihiro, and Takeshita Masataka, as well as to the discussants Profs Oishi Takashi, Kagaya Kan, Nakamura Mitsuo, Usuki Akira, Tomita Kenji, and Naito Yosuke. Finally we wish to express our gratitude to the staff members of the IASP, especially Ms Nakamura Chihisa and Ms Shimizu Yuriko for organizing our two conferences as well as to our assistants Dr Sawae Fumiko and Dr Nejima Susumu for supporting our editing works.

Our special tribute goes to the late Professor Yusuf Ibish, who presented a paper on the significance of *al-Manār* in the first conference, and was to read a paper on a female Sufi saint of Palestinian origin in the second conference. Unfortunately, however, neither paper could be included in this volume due to his long illness and his death in January 2003.

CONTRIBUTORS

Raja Adal is a PhD candidate at the Department of History in Harvard University. His interest areas include comparative history of non-Western societies in the nineteenth and early twentieth centuries, concepts of time, and the formation of aesthetics consciousness. He is currently undertaking his doctoral research entitled "Aesthetic Consciousness and the Negotiation of Western Modernity: Fine Art Education in Egyptian and Japanese Elementary Schools, 1870–1930." He has published an Index of *La Nation Arabe* (2002) and "Methodological approach to the study of Shakib Arslan: Islamic thought and the Arab world in the interwar period" in *Asian and African Area Studies* 1 (in Japanese, 2001).

Françoise Aubin is an emeritus research director at the National Center for Scientific Research (Paris). She earned her PhD from the University of Paris (Faculty of Law) in 1964 for her thesis "Les soulèvements populaires en Chine du Nord entre 1214 et 1230." Currently she is conducting research on Chinese Islamic history in the nineteenth–twentieth centuries, post-communism in Mongolia, and history of Mongolian customary and written law. She is an editor of *Etudes Orientales*, 19–20 (2003), and the author of "Some Characteristics of Penal Legislation among the Mongols (13th–21st centuries)" in W. Johnson and I. F. Popova, eds, *Central Asian Law: An Historical Overview* (2004) and entries in *The Encyclopaedia of Islam*: "Taṣawwuf [in Chinese Islam]" in vol. VIII (1999), "Wali [in Chinese Islam]" In vol. XI (2002), and "Khatt" in Supplement 7–8 (2004).

Azyumardi Azra is the rector of Syarif Hidayatullah State Islamic University in Jakarta. He earned his PhD from the Department of History, Columbia University in 1992 for "Transmission of Islamic Reformism to Indonesia from the Middle East in the 17th and 18th centuries." He is continuing his research of Islamic movements in the premodern and modern Southeast Asia, and has published *The Origins of Islamic Reformism in Southeast Asia* (2004) and *Shari'a and Politics in Indonesia* (editor, 2003).

David D. Commins is the executive director of The Clarke Center, Dickinson College. His PhD from the University of Michigan (1985) concerned the Syrian

Salafi Movement in the late Ottoman era. His current research interest is in the history of Wahhabism and his recent publications are *Historical Dictionary of Syria* (2nd edition, 2004) and "Traditional Anti-Wahhabi Hanbalism in Nineteenth Century Arabia" in Y. Weisman, ed., *Ottoman Reform and Islamic Regeneration: Studies in Honor of Butrus Abu-Manneh* (2005).

Stéphane A. Dudoignon is a research fellow at the National Center for Scientific Research (Paris). He earned his PhD from the University of Paris III (Sorbonne-Nouvelle) in 1996. His areas of interest are the history and sociology of the spiritual and intellectual authorities of Islam in Russia, the Caucasus, and Central Asia from the eighteenth century to the present. He has recently edited *Devout Societies vs. Impious States?: Transmitting Islamic Learning in Russia, Central Asia and China, Through the Twentieth Century* (2004), and written "Faction Struggles among the Bukharan Ulama during the Colonial, the Revolutionary and the Early Soviet Periods (1868–1929): A Paradigm for History Writing?" in T. Sato, ed., *Muslim Societies. Historical and Comparative Aspects* (2004), and "From Ambivalence to Ambiguity? Some Paradigms of Policy Making in Tajikistan, since 1997" in L. de Martino, ed., *Tajikistan at a Crossroads: The Politics of Decentralization* (2004).

Dale F. Eickelman is a Ralph and Richard Lazarus Professor of Anthropology and Human Relations at Dartmouth College. He earned his PhD from the University of Chicago in 1971 for "Moroccan Islam: Tradition and Society in a Regional Pilgrimage Center, 1870–1970" (published 1976). His recent research themes are religious intellectuals and the new media in Muslim-majority societies, and he is a coeditor of *Public Islam and the Common Good* (2004) and *New Media in the Muslim World: The Emerging Public Sphere* (2nd edition, 2003). He has also published *The Middle East and Central Asia: An Anthropological Approach* (4th edition, 2001).

Mahmoud Haddad is the chairperson of the Department of History, University of Balamand in Lebanon. He earned his PhD from Columbia University in 1989. He is currently researching the social and intellectual history of late Ottoman Syria, and the results are published as "A Brief History of Lebanon, Syria, and Iraq in the Twentieth Century" in Volume VIII of *The History of the Scientific and Cultural Development of Humanity* (2004), "The Ideas of Amir Shakib Arslan before and after the Collapse of the Ottoman Empire" in N. Yavari, L. G. Potter, J. R. Oppenheim, and R. W. Bulliet, eds, *Views From the Edge: Essays in Honor of Richard W. Bulliet* (2004), and "The Impact of Foreign Missionaries on the Muslim Community in Geographical Syria in the Nineteenth and Early Twentieth Century" in R. Simon and E. Tejirian, eds, *Altruism and Imperialism: Western Cultural and Religious Missions in the Middle East* (2003).

Kasuya Gen is a lecturer at Nihon University, Tokyo. His current research interest is in secularism and Islamism in Turkey in the late Ottoman and early

Republican periods. He has published articles such as "Pan-Islamic policy of the Turkish nationalists in the War of Independence period" in *Studies in Humanities and Social Sciences* (in Japanese, 1999), "The boundary of the *millet* in the construction of the Turkish Republic" in K. Sakai, ed., *Nationalism and Islam: Antagonism or Conformity?* (in Japanese, 2001), and "Islamic currents in Turkey: Said Nursi and Fethullah Gülen" in Y. Kosugi and H. Komatsu, eds, *Contemporary Islamic Thought and Political Movements* (in Japanese, 2003).

Komatsu Hisao is a professor at the Graduate School of Humanities and Sociology, The University of Tokyo. His current theme is Modern History of Central Asia. He is a coeditor of *Research Trends in Modern Central Eurasian Studies* (with S.A. Dudoignon, 2003), and *Islam in Politics in Russia and Central Asia (Early 18th to Late 20th Centuries)* (2001), and an author of "The Andijan Uprising Reconsidered" in T. Sato, ed., *Muslim Societies: Historical and Comparative Aspects* (2003).

Kosugi Yasushi is a professor at the Graduate School of Asian and African Area Studies, Kyoto University. He earned his LL.D. on political systems, law, and Islam in the contemporary Middle East from Kyoto University (1999). He is a coeditor of *Readings from Islamic Political Thought* (in Arabic, 2000), *Iwanami Dictionary of Islam* (in Japanese, 2002), and *Contemporary Islamic Thought and Political Movements* (in Japanese, 2003), and the author of *The Islamic World* (in Japanese, 1998), *Muhammad: Visiting the Sources of Islam* (in Japanese, 2002) and *The Study of the Islamic World* (in Japanese, 2006).

Matsumoto Masumi is a professor at Keiwa College, Niigata. She earned her PhD from Niigata University in 1997 in the field of modern Chinese history. Currently she is interested in Protestant missions to Muslims and Islamic awakening in China. She has recently published "Sino-Muslims' Identity and Thoughts during the Anti-Japanese War—Impact of the Middle East on Islamic Revival and Reform in China" in *Annual Report of JAMES* 18/2 (2003), "Islamic New Cultural Movement in China" in Y. Kosugi and H. Komatsu, eds, *Contemporary Islamic Thought and Political Movements* (in Japanese, 2003), and "An Aspect of Islamic Revival in International City Shanghai" in Editorial Committee, ed., *Plural Perspectives on the Sino-Japan Relations* (in Chinese, 2002).

Nejima Susumu is an associate professor at the Faculty of Regional Development Studies in Toyo University. His PhD is from the Graduate University for Advanced Studies (1999) for his dissertation "Islam and NGO: Ismaili Community in the Northern Pakistan and Aga Khan Foundation" (published in Japanese, 2002). He continues researches on Islam and NGOs, fair trade and culture. He has recently published as a coeditor *Contemporary Pakistan: Ethnicity, Nation and State* (in Japanese, 2004), and an article "Refreshments in Pakistan and Islamic Philanthropy: Rooh Afza of

Hamdard" in M. Takada, Y. Kurita, and CDI, eds, *Cultural Anthropology of Refreshments* (in Japanese, 2004).

Alexandre Popovic is an emeritus senior research fellow at the National Center for Scientific Research in France. Currently he is conducting research on Muslim communities in the Balkans from such perspectives as history, culture, mystical order, magic, and Muslim press. Among his recent publications are "A propos de la magie chez les musulmans des Balkans" in V. Bouillier and C. Servan-Schreiber, eds, *De l'Arabie à l'Himalaya. Chemins croisés. En hommage à Marc Gaborieau* (2004), "Le confraternite sufi nella regione balcanica" in M. Stepanyants, ed., *Sufismo e confraternite nell'islam contemporanea. Il difficile equilibrio tra mistica e politica* (2003), and *The Revolt of African Slaves in Iraq in the 3rd/9th Century* (1998).

Stefan Reichmuth is a professor at the Faculty of Philology in Ruhr University of Bochum. His recent publications include "Murtada al-Zabidi (1732–1791) and the Africans: Islamic Discourse and Scholarly Networks in the Late Eighteenth Century" in S. S. Reese, ed., *The Transmission of Learning in Islamic Africa* (2004), "Beziehungen zur Vergangenheit: Murtada az-Zabidi (gest. 1791) und seine Archaologie islamischer Kultur" in *Asiatische Studien–Etudes Asiatiques* 56/2 (2002), and " 'Netzwerk' und 'Weltsystem': Konzepte zur neuzeitlichen 'Islamischen Welt' und Transformation" in *Saeculum* 51/2 (2000).

Part I

AL-MANĀR IN A CHANGING ISLAMIC WORLD

1

AL-MANĀR REVISITED

The "lighthouse" of the Islamic revival

Kosugi Yasushi

The intellectual map of the Islamic world has experienced a number of rather drastic changes during the twentieth century, continuing on from the turbulent years of the previous century. Various trends of thought and sociopolitical ideas stemming from the West, such as modernism, liberalism, nationalism, socialism, and communism, among others, appeared in Muslim societies, and all of these cast serious doubts on traditional Islamic thought and institutions. Especially modernism, often associated with Westernization, and nationalism, more often secular than not, were undermining traditional Islamic values, while profound socioeconomic transformation was undermining the basis upon which traditional Islamic societies, as well as their intellectual leaders, used to stand.

Against this backdrop, a new Islamic trend calling for a reform of Muslim societies appeared. As this trend voiced the aspiration to revive the Islamic world, or the Islamic *umma* (community), to use their own terms, we may call this trend Islamic revivalism. The journal of *al-Manār* (*Majalla al-Manār*),[1] the main subject of this article, was the major mouthpiece for this trend. It was published regularly between 1898 and 1935, and its intellectual heritage was maintained by later popular movements such as the Muslim Brotherhood in Egypt and the Association of Algerian 'Ulama' in Algeria. The trend, however, seemed to have lost its momentum by the early 1950s, when Arab nationalism and other secular trends started to overshadow the previous Islamic trends. Accordingly, the contributions of *al-Manār* appeared obsolete.

"*Manār*" in Arabic means a "lighthouse," or a "beacon." The journal tried to be a lighthouse in a turbulent ocean where all Islamic ships were suffering the awful storm of the modern world, metaphorically speaking. Many intellectuals in the Islamic world sought other solutions for their societies differing from that which Muhammad Rashid Rida (Muḥammad Rašīd Riḍā, 1865–1935), *al-Manār*'s founder and editor in chief, and his colleagues strove to formulate. For others, *al-Manār*'s orientation looked anachronistic, as it called for a return to the original purity of Islam. It was judged natural that it had failed by the 1950s.

After seeing the phenomena of Islamic revival in various parts of the world over the last three decades of the twentieth century, however, we can no longer subscribe to this view. This article offers an invitation to reevaluate *al-Manār* as a major platform of modern Islam, and to present an overview of its intellectual contributions.[2]

Re-evaluating Islam in the modern age

Scholarly inquiries into the nature of vitality of Islam in the political domains of the Middle Eastern countries started in 1978–1979, when specialists and observers of the region were surprised and perplexed to see an "Islamic revolution" in Iran. Since the revolutionary high times in the region had already passed with the decline of radical Arab nationalism,[3] a revolution alone, against what was considered the most mighty monarchy in the Gulf region, was a surprise. Furthermore, it was under an Islamic banner with many Islamic symbols, such as *jihad* (struggle) against *taghut* (illegitimate power) led by *faqih* (jurist) or *vali amr* (holder of authority), revolution by the oppressed who will become martyrs willingly, and the like.[4]

Although the present author had already noticed the beginning of an Islamic revival in Egypt in the latter half of the 1970s,[5] it was still on a lesser level, and the revolution in Iran came as a startling event, as was the case for other students of Middle East studies. Retrospectively, there were many signs of an Islamic revival in various parts of the region during the decade. For example, an Islamic bank was established in Dubai in 1975, starting a new initiative to reinstitute Islam in the economic domain, followed later by many other banks.[6] However, these signs were not well-noticed, and arguments over the Islamic revolution in Iran in academic circles, let alone the mass media, were mostly skeptical about its durability, and therefore tried to explain it in terms of its regional specifics and historical contingencies.

The events of the following years in the Middle East and elsewhere, however, proved that there was something more generally Islamic than regional or sectarian in these phenomena.[7] To cite just a few politically serious cases,[8] we had observed an armed revolt in Mecca, the most holy city of Islam, in November 1979, nine months after the revolution in Iran. This was the very first armed struggle against the Saudi kingdom since its establishment in 1932, and a popular revolt in the Eastern region of the kingdom followed the next month. Then, in the same month the Soviet invasion of Afghanistan occurred, sparkling Islamic resistance movements, or Afghan *mujahidin* guerrillas. In October 1981, President Sadat was assassinated in Egypt for his peace-treaty with Israel, as a part of a failed rebellion by Islamic radicals, while Bahrain, a conservative monarchy in the Gulf, experienced a failed coup by an Islamic liberation front in the same year. Revolutionary and opposition groups taking an Islamic color were becoming the rule, not the exception.[9]

The reasons why Islamic dimensions had been ignored or underestimated lay in the question of paradigms and analytical frameworks of our studies. Until that time, the predominant paradigms were modernization and nationalism. They were major paradigms for studies related to developing countries, not only in the Middle East but also in other regions of Asia and Africa, as well as in Latin America. This was occurring during the Cold War, and neither modernization studies nor nationalism studies were completely free from the reality of West–East bipolarity.[10] Both paradigms shared tendencies of secularism, and presupposed the tacit understanding that a modern society is a secular one, be it capitalist or socialist, where Islam continuously loses its sociopolitical significance.

Malcolm Kerr, the author of an authoritative book on the Islamic reformism of Muhammad 'Abduh (Muḥammad 'Abduh 1849–1905) and Rashid Rida,[11] wrote in 1960 that "Rashīd Riḍā and others of his school, whatever their intentions may have been, have facilitated the accomplishment of a great undertaking of secular reform in Islamic countries," thus concluding the failure of Rida and *al-Manār*.[12] Modernization and/or nationalism were well-rooted in the Middle East by then, or at least, seemed so to many, with their secularizing tendencies.

Once this premise came under serious doubt, studies in the field started to provide more accurate information on the Islamic revival. There were, and are today, grassroot activities which either produced Islamic revival or were produced themselves under Islamic revival. Islamic revival can be defined a reorientation of a Muslim society at mass level toward Islam (re-Islamization) after a significant degree of de-Islamization[13] has occurred, and that is accompanied by revitalization or reformulation of Islamic institutions, as well as Islamic discourses and symbols among Muslims in contemporary contexts.

This means that Islamic revival is far from anything "traditional." The term "traditional" indicates continuity from the past. The "revival" apparently presumes a discontinuity, as it is to revive something that ceased to be vital or functional. Hence, Muslims themselves sometimes refer to revival as an "awakening" from negligence or illness.[14]

To illustrate this point, let us take the example of zakat (*zakāt*), an obligatory charity for Muslims through payment of a prescribed portion of one's possessions. It is a part of the well-established Islamic tenets, and therefore the concept itself seems traditional. However, while collection of zakat was considered a duty of the state during premodern (Islamic) periods, it was suspended or left for private initiatives in the modern era, especially under national governments of the twentieth century. Revitalization of this institution is often called for as remedy for poverty, as a part of Islamic revival.[15] It involves reformulation of how and who should collect zakat, and how and for what it should be spent. Revived Zakat in a modern society is completely different from that of traditional society. Even though its religio-legal sanctions look identical because of the continuity of the legal codes related to it, the socioeconomic significance is quite different.

As collecting zakat cannot be done individually, and while modern states do not perform the duty of collection, an aspiration to activate zakat involves social organization. So, local "zakat committees" were organized in many places to fill the gap. The same can be said about building mosques. Mosques, or prayer halls, are crucially important for a Muslim district if one wants to perform his obligation of prayers. In new suburban districts or underdeveloped districts, there may not be a sufficient number of mosques, if any. Once its inhabitants aspire to have a mosque, they have to organize themselves for that purpose. When a mosque is built, its management or an organizational administration will be needed. Thus, activating Islamic teachings and institutions in a modern society necessitates collective social works, hence, what we may call "Islamic revival movements."[16]

Why should Islam, then, be revived? That was one of the most basic themes for *al-Manār* and its writers and associates, the Manarists.[17] For one, Abd al-Rahman al-Kawakibi ('Abd al-Raḥmān al-Kawākibī, 1854–1902), an Islamic thinker originally from Aleppo, argued the major causes of the decline of the Islamic *umma* in his *Umm al-Qurā* [The Mother of Cities, that is, Mecca] (*Meccan Conference*)[18] through the tongues of participants in a secret international conference in Mecca, supposedly held in 1316 AH [1898][19]

> The beginning of the 14th century A.H. is a time when defects and weakness cover all Muslims.... The Association [of Umm al-Qura][20] invited some scholars and political writers to investigate the reasons and to search for the best ways for the Islamic *nahḍa* (revival, or Renaissance), so that they will publish their opinions in Islamic papers of India, Egypt, Syria and of the Tatars.[21]

The participants included those from Aleppo, Damascus, Jerusalem, Alexandria, Cairo, Yemen, Basra, Nejd, Mecca, Medina, Tunis, and Fez in Arab regions, as well as of Kurdish, Iranian, Tatar, Kazan, Turkish, Afghan, Indian, Sind, and even Chinese and English origins. There was only one from Beirut, among the expected participants, who failed to arrive in time.[22]

They criticized the state of affairs of the Islamic world in general, and the Ottoman administrations in particular, and proposed social reform based on Islam properly understood. They urged the promotion of education among Muslims for the sake of the revival.

The theme of "revival" heard many echoes in later decades, especially in the latter half of the twentieth century. During the heydays of Arab nationalism, however, the Islamic dimension of al-Kawakibi was largely underestimated. As the conference ended by proposing an Arab caliphate, as a remedy to the shortcomings of the Ottoman empire, a Turkish-dominated dynasty, al-Kawakibi had been seen often as a pioneer of Arab nationalism.[23] This is apparently a point we need to reevaluate. He was an associate of *al-Manār*, and definitely Islamic in orientation.

In this sense, Dawish's following statement is plausible: "the shift in religious authority from the Turks to the Arabs was proposed for the sole purpose of Islamic regeneration, and the Arabic khilafa was projected to be not a revolutionary nationalist, but a symbol of Islamic unity."[24]

We certainly find emphasis of *'urūba* (Arabness, Arabism) in his and others' writings in *al-Manār*. Rida was also very prominent in this respect. As they called for a return to a pure Islam, that is to say, Islam of the first generations (the Salaf, literally, the predecessors), it coincides with the period when Muslims were basically Arab. Once a call is made to return to the Qur'an, the sacred scripture of Islam recorded in Arabic, the prominence of the Arabic and Arab culture must be emphasized.[25] However, as *al-Manār* in Arabic was read throughout the Islamic world, the Arabic language was considered universally Islamic in the minds of its readers. The Arabic has both national and transnational dimensions, and putting Arab Islamic thinkers along the line of Arab nationalism is precisely where one has to be very careful.

In evaluating al-Kawakibi's *Meccan Conference*, another important point is that this was a fictitious record of a conference that never occurred in reality. Beside what was said on the tongues of the participants, we must pay attention to why it was written as a record of an international conference. The message was that the Islamic *umma* should decide its affairs through a gathering of leaders, not depending on tyrannical, often not potent in the modern context, dynastic rulers.

This message seems to have recurred in Islamic conferences after the demise of the Ottoman empire. Among the early important meetings Rida was keen to record, there were the General Islamic Conference for the *khilafa* in Cairo in 1926[26] and the General Islamic Conference in Jerusalem in 1931.[27] Al-Kawakibi's aspiration was partially realized, one may observe, when the first Islamic Summit was convened in 1969, and an international body, the Organization of Islamic Conference (OIC) was set up to visualize the Islamic world in a contemporary form.[28]

Another answer to the question, why and how to revive, was given three decades later by Shakib Arslan (Šakīb Arslān, 1869–1946), who wrote *Limadhā ta'akhkhara al-Muslimūn wa taqaddama gharuhum?* [Why Are the Muslims Backward While Others Are Advanced?][29] Arslan saw a remedy in proper understanding of Islam and its application within contemporary realities.

The fact that his writing was meant to serve as an answer to a question sent by a Muslim in Borneo (present-day Indonesia) reveals the nature of *al-Manār*, as a journal for the entire Islamic world.[30] Shakib's work "is an enduring contribution; it went through three Arabic editions during his lifetime and was reissued in 1965 and again in 1981."[31]

Al-Manār contains quite a substantial amount of writings and information in its nearly thirty thousand pages from 1898 to 1935. After Rida's death, his immediate heirs published two issues. Then in 1939, the Association of Muslim Brotherhood, an heir in the call of Islamic reform in the form of popular organization, published the issues of the last volume until 1940. The government suppressed it, with the other journals of the Brotherhood in 1941.[32] *Al-Manār* is a treasure of historical sources for the Islamic areas of its days. Furthermore, when we read its writings in a broader perspective, and compare them with ideas in circulation in Islamic revival movements in recent decades, we see clear similarities as well as further developments. Some of the ideas, or lines of argument, are proved to have direct links, while others seem to have apparent echoes, though not proven in a definite manner. Many others still await scholarly investigation.

What is obvious for the present author is that *al-Manār* did not end its life by setting an Arab nationalism in a religious garment, nor giving an Islamic excuse for modernization of the Islamic world and resultant secularization. *Al-Manār* had its own aspirations and claims, and they were heard and followed, though they were overshadowed by other trends in decades preceding the current Islamic revival.

When the Islamic revival started to manifest itself, R. Stephan Humphreys clarified that Islam remained "a significant political force in the Arab lands after the Second World War,"

> due largely to the Muslim Brothers, who seemed to combine the militant activism of the Wahhābīya [of Arabian Peninsula], the Sanūsīya [of Libya], and the Mahdīya [of Sudan] with the reformist Quran-centered thought of the Salafīya and the anti-imperialism and mass politics of the secular nationalists.[33]

Salafiyya is a general term for a broad trend of Islamic thought, which claims and calls Muslims to found their understanding of Islam on that of the Salaf (the Pious First Generations).[34] Although the term is used in this article without the qualification of "modern," there was also premodern Salafiyya. Its greatest proponent was Ibn Taymiyya (1263–1328), and it was *al-Manār* that revived his teaching by printing his works and promoting his ideas in the journal.[35]

The central force of thought, the Salafi school, originated in the late Ottoman period. To borrow Lahoud's words, a "new intellectual movement in the Arab world," was "characterized by a renewal (*tajdīd*) of Islam, as a response to the emerging sociopolitical and technological changes. This *tajdīd* served as an intellectual platform for the *salafiyya*, and it developed primarily under the influence, in chronological order, of Jamal al-Din al-Afghani (d. 1897), Muhammad ʿAbduh (d. 1905), and Rashid Rida (d. 1935)."[36] In the last stage of this formative phase, the Salafi school of reformism was elaborated and disseminated by the journal *al-Manār*.

A brief description of *al-Manār*

The first journal calling for the revival of Islam, or that of the Islamic *umma* and its civilization, was *al-ʿUrwa al-Wuṯqā* (the Firm Bond)[37] published in Paris during an eight-month period in 1884. Though short-lived, it had an eminent impact on the Islamic countries. It gave a serious warning of the dangers of Western colonialism, and called for a reform of the *umma* and exercise of ijtihad (independent reasoning to find Islamic legal rules) to face the challenges of the time. Among the younger generation who received the message of this pioneering journal, was the young Muhammad Rashid Rida in Syria.

He was born in a village called Qalamūn, near the city of Tripoli on the eastern Mediterranean coast, in the year of 1865. The village belongs to Lebanon today, but in his days it was a part of *Sham* (historical Syria); Rida identified himself, and was identified by others, as a Syrian,[38] and was active in movements for the independent Syria.[39] He was educated under the reformist Shaykh Husayn Jisr of Tripoli (1845–1909),[40] and later obtained a qualification as an *'ālim* (independent scholar). When *al-'Urwa al-Wuṯqā* was published, he was still a young man, and was impressed by the journal. Rida recalled:

> I found a copy of *al-'Urwa al-Wuthqa* among my father's papers. When I read its articles on the call to pan-Islamism, the return of glory, power and prestige to Islam, the recovery of what it used to possess, and the liberation of its peoples from foreign domination, I was so impressed that I entered into a new phase of my life. And I became very fond of the methodology of these articles to make and prove its arguments on topics with verses from the Qur'an, and of its *tafsīr* (exegesis) which none of *mufassirs* (exegetes) have written. The most important points in which *al-'Urwa al-Wuthqa* distinguished itself were: (1) Allah's rules in His creation and the order of human society, and the reasons for the rise and fall of nations as well as their strength and weakness; (2) clarification that Islam is a religion of sovereignty and power, combining the happiness of this world and that of the hereafter, while implying that it is a religion both spiritual and social, civil and military, and that its military power is for the sake of protection of the just law, general guidance and prestige of the community, and not for the sake of imposition of the religion by force; and (3) for Muslims there are no nationalities except their religion, so they are brothers whose bloodline must not separate them, nor their languages nor their governments.[41]

Rida became so fascinated with their ideas that he was called "Adorer of al-Afghani" by others.[42] It was, however, only after more than ten years in 1897, when he learned the death of al-Afghani,[43] the founder of the journal of *al-'Urwa al-Wuṯqā*, in Istanbul, he decided to move to Cairo to join Muhammad 'Abduh, the editor in chief of the journal:

> When he [al-Afghani] passed away, my hope was hightened to get in touch with his viceroy Shaykh Muhammad 'Abduh to acquire his knowledge and opinions on Islamic reform. I waited until an opportunity appeared in the month of Rajab in 1315 [1897], and that was immediately after I completed my study in Tripoli, acquiring an *'ālim* status, permission to teach independently, from my mentors. Then I immigrated to Egypt, and established *al-Manār* for call to reform.[44]

While "everywhere the increased use of the printing press for publishing religious texts challenged the 'ulama's role as guardians and transmitters of knowledge," "[T]he reformers of Islamic law were aware of the opportunities that the print media opened up. They skillfully used periodicals and pamphlets to disseminate their opinions to a wide audience."[45] *Al-'Urwa al-Wuṯqā* and *al-Manār* were in their forefront.

Rida based himself in Cairo for more than three decades until his death, from where he made trips to Syria, Istanbul, India, Hejaz, and Europe.[46] *Al-Manār* was a "monthly magazine that researches the philosophy of religion and the affairs of society and civilization."[47] The title of the journal was taken from a *hadith*, "He [Prophet Muhammad] said that there were for Islam landmarks and a lighthouse, like a lighthouse of the path."[48]

> This is a voice calling in a clear Arabic tongue, and an appeal to the truth reaching the ear of a speaker of the *ḍād* letter [an Arab] and the ears of all Easterners, calling from a close place [Egypt, located between the West and the East] which both the Easterner and the Westerner can hear, and it spreads out so that the Turks and the Persians also receive it. It says, "Oh, the sleeping Easterner who enjoys sweet dreams, wake up, wake up! Your sleep has exceeded the limit of rest."[49]

The journal was published first as an eight-page weekly, then became a monthly journal from the second year.[50] He printed 1,500 copies for the first issues, and sent them to his acquaintances in Egypt and Syria. Soon the Ottoman authorities banned it in Syria and other provinces, Rida reduced the number of copies to 1,000. In a few years, however, the number of subscribers reached almost 3,000.[51] "By the twelfth year (1909), remaining copies of Volume I were selling for four times the original price; a second printing was therefore made, in the form which had been followed after the first year."[52]

His claim that it was addressed not only to Arabs but also to all Easterners proved to be true, as its "eventually gained a wide circulation from Morocco to Java."[53] Thus C. C. Berg wrote about the Indonesians: *Al-Manār*

> did not shine . . . for Egyptians alone. It illuminated the Arabs at home and abroad, the Moslems of the Malay Archipelago who studied at al-Azhar University or in Mecca, and the solitary Indonesian who had kept his old relations with the heart of the Moslem world after having returned to his border country of the Dār al-Islām. . . . And all these people now saw Islam in a new light . . . Those who had caught up and preserved the light of the *Manār* in Egypt, became lesser "manārs" for their environments, once back in Indonesia.[54]

It started as a modest journal and ascended to be a mouthpiece of the Islamic reform, as its reputation spread. One of the reasons was that, while others were complaining the miseries of the Islamic world, "*al-Manār* proposed the cures for the illnesses of the *umma* in a general form, then with details and proofs."[55]

A Western scholar, contemporary to Rida, wrote about him, "the leading pupil of Muḥammad 'Abduh during the latter's lifetime, and, since his death, his biographer, editor of his works, and the one who has principally carried on his tradition and interpreted his doctrines," and he was "the man who has been perpetuating 'Abduh's influence for the quarter of a century since his death,"[56] and "*Al-Manār* has been the organ through which his ['Abduh's] views have been given the largest publicity."[57]

While this function of *al-Manār* is confirmed, apparently Rida's role in formulating a revivalist version of Islamic teachings is not confined to his place as 'Abduh's pupil. This is very clear in the political domain. 'Abduh discouraged Rida from writing on political issues in *al-Manār*, and political writings increased only after 'Abduh's death, partly reflecting the deepening political crises of the Islamic world.[58]

When Rida passed away, the Grand Shaykh of al-Azhar at the time, Mustafa al-Maraghi (Muṣṭafā al-Marāghī, 1881–1945), a disciple of 'Abduh and a reformer of al-Azhar, attended a memorial gathering at his funeral,[59] and gave a speech with words of praise:

> Al-Sayyid Rashid[60] triumphed and his supporters and disciples became many, while there were once few supporters and disciples, and within academic circles there were found those who carry his principles and follow his path, and among the public those whose eyes were opened to light, and clouds of ignorance and falsehood were wiped out of their hearts.
>
> He didn't have any new principle in Islam, that could be justified as a school of his own, but his principle was the principle of the entire 'ulama' of the Salaf, that is, to return in judgment to God and His messenger by executing [the following Qur'anic order in the verse of] "and if you have a dispute concerning any matter, refer it to Allah and the Messenger" [Qur'an 4:59], and his principle was also that of the 'ulama' of the Salaf in choosing rules appropriate for the time and beneficial for nations in issues of ijtihad [where independent judgment should be exercised], and his principle was that of the 'ulama' of the Salaf in everything related to Divine attributes and the issues related to the last day, so he was a Salafi Sunni man who disliked *taqlid* (*taqlīd*, imitation, emulation) and propagated ijtihad, seeing it (ijtihad) an obligation upon himself and upon everyone capable.[61]

These words, even taking out the element of courtesy for the deceased, describe fairly Rida as the champion of Salafi school of thought, a reformist formulator of Islam. Associating him with these essential key terms, "Salafi," "Sunni," "ijtihad," and "anti-*taqlid* (antitraditional)," his major contribution was that he disseminated these ideas widely in the Islamic world through the most enduring and consistent medium in the modern era, the journal of *al-Manār*.

Contributions of *al-Manār* to modern Islam

The contributions *al-Manār* made toward modern Islam, or to put it more precisely, toward a reformulated understanding of Islam and its practices within the modern Islamic world, are multifaceted, and a careful examination is necessary to determine their extent. The difficulty stems partly from the scope and width of its circulations in geographical terms, and partly from the diverse nature of its topics. Some of its ideas were very innovative but it also promoted what was Islamic in a more general sense. Innovative arguments that had impacts on intellectuals are easier to discern and evaluate, while a more general contribution to the morale of Muslims in those days is subtle and difficult to determine. The reevaluation of *al-Manār* also involves the evaluation of the Islamic revival in later days, as this article calls for the reevaluation of *al-Manār* based on the evaluation of the recent revival. The evaluation of what has progressed over the last three decades or so, of course, may be even more controversial than the historical role *al-Manār* played.

The following remarks are, therefore, sketchy in nature, and offer only a limited outline, inviting to a further investigation.

Validity of Islam

The apparent, and most striking, feature of *al-Manār* is its endurance over a long span of time. Maintaining the publication of a highly intellectual nature for almost four decades, especially under the strong winds blowing against Islamic trends, both traditional and revivalist, was an achievement. Through this achievement, *al-Manār* contributed to the maintenance of the banner of credibility of the Islamic teachings in the modern context. *Al-Manār* insisted that Islam had been valid in the past, was valid in the present, and would be valid in the future.

In doing so, Rida depended upon al-Afghani and ʻAbduh to a great extent, especially at the beginning. This is partly because he had faith in their thought and believed that their cause was not only correct but also beneficial to all members of the Islamic world. Their authority and credibility were assets to him. Apparently, ʻAbduh's support and patronage during the first years of *al-Manār*, until his death in 1905, lent strength to the journal and its founder. *Al-Manār* advocated the ideas and thought of al-Afghani and ʻAbduh, and circulated them in four corners of the Islamic world. In his writing on the *khilāfa* (Caliphate), Rida commented that ʻAbduh was just short of becoming the paramount leader of the Islamic world.

> The *Ustādh-Imām* (mentor-imam) [ʻAbduh],[62] may God bestow mercy upon him, reached the leadership position in this *umma* and the level of those in authority in the religious and temporal affairs, and he came quite close to the leadership of the entire *umma*. But this potential was not realized, because the *umma* was not formulated in such a manner to make it possible to move on the line which he planned.[63]

One may get the impression that this was an overestimate for ʻAbduh. With this high esteem for his own mentor, Rida strongly advocated ʻAbduh's values through the pages of *al-Manār*. "If it were not for *al-Manār* most of ʻAbduh's thoughts and wisdom would have been lost, and his reforms and history unknown. And as a result of *al-Manār*'s influence, ʻAbduh had a party and followers in Tunis and Algiers."[64] Actually, they were numerous in the Maghrib: to name a few, Abd al-Aziz al-Thaalbi (ʻAbd al-ʻAzīz al-Tha ʻālibī, 1874–1944), Muḥammad al-Naḫīl and Ṭāhir b. ʻĀshūr in Tunisia, Ben Badis (ʻAbd al-Ḥamīd Ibn Bādīs, 1889–1940), and the Association of Algerian Scholars in Algeria, ʻAbdullāh Idrīs al-Sanūsī (d. 1931), Abū Shuʻayb al-Dukkālī (1878–1937), and Muḥammad b. al-ʻArabī al-ʻAlawī (1880–1964) in Morocco.[65] The list of beneficiaries, of course, is not just confined to the Maghrib countries, and should be longer.[66]

The journal was also read in South Asia, and Rida kept close ties with the leaders of the Khilafat movement, and *al-Manār* published many articles on and by these leaders. For example, the theory of Caliphate by Abu al-Kalam Azad was serialized in *al-Manār*.[67] Being a leader of the Khilafat movement supporting the Ottoman dynasty, Azad took the position of discarding the importance of a caliph being of Quraysh origin (of the tribe of Prophet Muhammad), a position in a sharp contrast to Rida's.[68] Azad was still a very close ally of *al-Manār* for the Islamic revival. To the east, the reformist Muhammadiyah established in 1912 in Central Java with a call for return to the Qurʼan and the Sunna,[69] which became the second largest Islamic organization in Indonesia today.[70]

Al-Manār's insistence on the validity of Islam in modern days generated strong support and encouragement for both ordinary and reform-minded Muslims in those days. In this sense, *al-Manār* should be placed in the category of Islamic journalism.[71] Rida was, therefore, not only an academic but also a journalist. This combination was essential in creating an Islamic journal of high quality. If such was one of the major objectives of *al-ʻUrwa al-Wuṯqā*, the first Islamic journal with a brief life, *al-Manār* as its successor was well managed over a sufficient span of time for its task, though it burdened Rida heavily with its time and energy requirements, as well as in financial terms.[72]

Other ideas of al-Afghani and ʻAbduh that *al-Manār* propagated included the Unity of the Islamic *umma*, solidarity of Muslims, harmony of Islam and modern civilization (revelation and reason), return to the pure and original message of Islam, exercise of ijtihad (independent reasoning) of the Islamic law and its applicability in the modern society, and new exegesis of the Qurʼan, appropriate for the modern time.

Of these, the central issue at the earlier stage was that of ijtihad (independent reasoning and judgment), because they had to establish the legitimacy of exercising ijtihad if they wanted to reform the Islamic law to meet the social needs of the day, and the Qurʼanic exegesis also requires ijtihad if new interpretations were to be made. Furthermore, in Rida's view, the unity of the *umma* could be achieved only if ijtihad was exercised correctly.

Ijtihad and reform of the Islamic law

For all reformers of the late nineteenth and early twentieth centuries, on both Islamic and pro-Western sides, the defects of traditional Islam seemed apparent, as its incapacity in dealing with the reality of the world under Western dominance proved. The tradition was deemed responsible for the decline of the Islamic world in their eyes.

Al-Afghani called for ijtihad to revive the *umma*, as he saw the inflexibility of the interpretations of the law a part of the decline. ʿAbduh tried hard to reform Islamic legal institutions and the jurists themselves, and once he was appointed the Grand Mufti of Egypt, the highest Islamic legal position in the state, he issued many *fatwa*s to express new interpretations. His *fatwa*s were recorded in Dār al-Iftāʾ (Mufti's Office) in two large files, each containing more than five hundred *fatwa*s.[73]

Rida had to move further, and elaborate the theme of ijtihad. The citadel of the traditional ʿulama,ʾ al-Azhar, was very conservative, and was keeping the tradition of *taqlīd* (imitation, emulation). Although ʿAbduh's pupils reformed al-Azhar,[74] it was only in later decades. In ʿAbduh's time, this was still what Rida had to struggle against. The traditional system of the jurists in those days was based on the dominance of the four Sunni schools of law, while each school attained a kind of independence, so that each could stay within its own tradition. The strong inclination toward *taqlīd* (imitation) of the preceding scholars was in the air.

There was also the serious question of the "closure of the gate of ijtihad." In the Western scholarship, this question has been debated as a historical question. Joseph Schacht stated that the gate was closed by the tenth century,[75] and the Schacht thesis was maintained until Wael B. Hallaq proved that this was not a historical fact and that ijtihad was exercised at least to the sixteenth century.[76]

On the other hand, it is also true that at the time of al-Afghani, Abduh, and Rida, there was a prevailing discourse of closure among the traditional scholars, especially those of the Hanafi school. The Hanbali school of law never acknowledged such a concept, as Rida relied on this position heavily. But, the Hanafi school was the official legal school of the Ottoman Empire, and the closure was presumed that against which Rida had to argue.

Rida wrote a dialogue in a serialized form in *al-Manār*, a dialogue between an aged traditionalist and a young reformer, apparently reflecting himself. The traditional shaykh seemed a typical conservative scholar of the time. What he said in the dialogue might be a little accentuated, as it was Rida's portrait of a traditionalist. Nevertheless, it must have reflected the reality of his time. What this conservative scholar was saying sounds today incredibly out of date, as the traditional and conservative ʿulamaʾ today are all generations after the reforms of al-Azhar, and they don't resemble those whose logic Rida had to struggle with.

Muḥāwarāt al-Muṣliḥ wa al-Muqallid (*The Dialogues between the Reformer and the Imitator/Traditionalist*) was published in *al-Manār* from Vol. 3, No. 28 (December 1900) to Vol.4, No. 22 (February 1902).[77] It contains a variety of topics, including definitions of man, early Islam, faith and disbelief, decline of the Islamic world and its causes, fatalism and reform, four schools of law, merits and faults of speculative theology, mysticism, saints, astrology, the Shiite and other factions, Judaism and Christianity, and interpretations of Islamic law.

The major issues that concern us here are the question of ijtihad, and the unity of *umma*. Lengthy arguments were exchanged between the two over the question of whether the obligation is ijtihad (reasoning) or *taqlīd* (imitation, emulation). The reformer strongly supports the necessity of ijtihad, and says:

> The basic fundamentals of Islam are proper creed, ethics, control of one's own soul, and worshipping Allah in an appropriate manner, and general principles for social relations such as protection of life, honor and property. All these principles were established in the time of the Prophet. . . . As for the details of social relations, after the foundations are laid such as justice of rulings, equality of rights, prohibition of transgression, deception, and treason, and *ḥadd* punishments for some crimes, and after the principle of *shūrā* (consultation) is established, the details are entrusted to those with authority among the scholars and rulers, who ought to be possessors of knowledge and justice, deciding what is best for the *umma* according to [conditions of] the time.[78]

This distinction between the essential principles and the non-essential details, which are subject of reasoning, was a very important contribution made by *al-Manār*. This distinction opens the latter space of flexible reasoning, without harming the concept of the eternal Shariʿa (Islamic law), since only the former is eternal and unchangeable. For many Muslims, this question had crucial importance, unless they were inclined toward a secular solution.

The reformer in the dialogue was also eloquent in quoting the words of the masterly predecessors of the traditionalists, forbidding the blind imitation of others. Since Rida's thinking was along the lines of the Hanbali school, which supports the continuity of ijtihad, he had an important segment of tradition as his resource. In the end, the reformer felt satisfied at the exhaustion of the arguments.

In Rida's opinion, *taqlīd* is not only wrong in itself but also in its creation of factionalism. If one insists on the obligation to follow a particular school, this in turn will create intolerance:

> What is harmful is fragmentation of Muslims into sects and parties, while each of them requires its members to follow a scholar whom they call an imam, and they follow him in every word and opinion, and assemble themselves against the followers of another scholar, leading finally to the negligence of the Book [Qurʾan] and the sunna (prophetic customs).[79]

To say that the ijtihad is possible is not sufficient. In order to put this principle in action, Rida published *fatwa*s (legal judgment in Islamic law) in *al-Manār*.

"Beginning in 1903, first under the title 'Question and Fatwa', and later in 'Fatwas of *al-Manār*', Rida responded to a wide variety of queries sent in by readers from all corners of the Muslim world." As they were collected and compiled, "the 2,592 fatwas first published in the pages of *al-Manār* constitute a remarkable record of the preoccupations and interests of early twentieth-century Muslims."[80]

Although *fatwa*s have been constantly issued throughout Islamic history, they were not considered as an exercise of ijtihad when the *taqlīd* tradition was strong. Rida opened, following 'Abduh, a new path of issuing *fatwa*s by his own judgment, that is, by ijtihad.

Reopening the gate of ijtihad had an impact that was gradually felt later. As Basheer M. Nafi says: "By liberating Islam from the monopoly of the traditional institutions, the reformists prepared the ground for the laymen, the modern Muslim intellectual and the Muslim professional, to speak on the behalf of Islam."[81] Rida, with other advocates of the ijtihad exercise, scored, therefore, a crucial point for later development of the Islamic revival movements.

Qur'anic exegesis

Al-Manār made a great contribution in the field of *tafsīr*, that is, "interpretation" or "exegesis" of the Qur'an. When it was serialized in *al-Manār* from 1901 (Vol. 4), it was simply called "Tafsīr al-Qur'ān al-Ḥakīm (Exegesis of the Wise Qur'an)," and was later published as a separate multi-volume title named *Tafsīr al-Manār* (Exegesis of al-Manar), or we may call it the Manarist interpretation of the Qur'an.

The Qur'an, being the primary source of legislation and the ultimate reference for human ideas in Islam, has seldom been disputed in Islamic history. Any idea of a thinker or any policy of a ruler that contradicts the Qur'an has faced the resistance of literati and the general population. However, the compatibility of an idea or of a policy, or the lack of it, be this in a theological, juristic, sociopolitical, or even scientific respect, with the Qur'an, also depends on how one can explain the relationship between the Qur'anic verses and this idea or that policy. This is why we find numerous references to Qur'anic verses in many kinds of Islamic writing.

In a sense, the history of Islamic thought is the history of how these justifications were made, or how authors tried to incorporate their ideas into the Qur'anic verses. And, each time a new idea succeeds in grounding itself on the Qur'an, the understanding of Qur'anic verses is also expanded.

However, the Qur'anic exegesis is an art or an Islamic science in itself. While it is not difficult to quote a few verses as a support of one's own argument, it is not at all easy to make interpretations of all verses related to the subject consistently in conformity with one's claim. If there is suspicion that it involves arbitrary interpretation or projection of wishful thinking into the verses, the claim can be discredited. Even if it gains temporary acceptance, it must bear its validity with the passing of time in the eyes of Muslim intellectuals and masses. Although there is no ecclesiastical authority to judge permissibility of a particular interpretation, it is not free for a Muslim intellectual to read arbitrarily ideas into the Qurʾan. Actually all existing *tafsīr*s in circulation have survived the test of time, and are accepted at one level or another.

Now, if we see the history of Islamic thought as a dynamic process of interpretation of Qurʾanic verses, *Tafsīr al-Manār* is nothing strange in itself. In form, it may even look conventional. When we open any page of *Tafsīr al-Manār*, it starts with some Qurʾanic verses, and the explanation of a particular word and its circumstances, how one should understand it within the context of the verses, and what kind of legal consequences one may draw from these verses. However, the uniqueness of *Tafsīr al-Manār* lies in its contents. The journal of *al-Manār* was meant to reaffirm the validity of Islam as a religion in the contemporary world, of Islam as a civilization in the modern context. In order to accomplish this, the editor and contributors of the journal had to introduce new ideas either as Islamic or as compatible with Islamic principles. *Tafsīr al-Manār* is an attempt to justify the reformulation of Islamic understanding of faith, society, life, and the world in modern days with its readings of the Qurʾanic passages. Dhahabi called this kind of modern *tafsīr* as "ethical (*adabī*) and social (*ijtimāʿī*) interpretation."[82] Another description is the "rational and social school of interpretation (*al-madrasa al-ʿaqliyya al-ijtimāʿiyya*)," given by al-Rūmī.[83] Both emphasize the social nature of interpretation. But the latter is critical of the rationalist element in it, while the first evaluates favorably its linguistic precision. Al-Muḥtasib named ʿAbduh's school of *tafsīr*, by emphasizing its reformist tendency, as "rational and revelational trend (*ittiğāh ʿaqlī tawfīqī*)" combining Islam and Western civilization.[84]

Tafsīr al-Manār is also innovative in that its success proved that the traditional form of *tafsīr* can still function as a vehicle for conveying new ideas through the interpretation of Qurʾanic verses.

We need a small note here on its authorship. *Tafsīr al-Manār* started, basing itself on the lectures about Qurʾanic verses given by Muhammad ʿAbduh and written by Rida. This sometimes gives the incorrect impression that Muhammad ʿAbduh was the real author and Rashid Rida only the record keeper, so that *Tafsīr al-Manār* is sometimes attributed to ʿAbduh rather than Rida. It is not accurate to say "Muhammad ʿAbduh presented his Qurʾanic exegesis in the form of lectures at al-Azhar University and within the scope of legal opinions (*fatāwā*, sig. *fatwā*) which were published separately as in the periodical, *al-Manār* ("The Lighthouse"), and later, with the author's approval, were compiled, revised from a literary viewpoint, and continued by Muḥammad ʿAbduh's pupil, Muḥammad Rashīd Riḍā."[85]

When we look actually into the pages of *Tafsīr al-Manār*, it is quite apparent that this is not a simple record of the lectures given by Muḥammad ʿAbduh. We find paragraphs beginning with *qāla al-ustādh al-imām* (the mentor-imam said): these refer to what Muhammad ʿAbduh said in his lectures. Sometimes, Rida gave summaries of the lectures, by saying "*qāla mā maʿnāhu*," or similar expressions. Then we find the word *aqūl*, "I say," writing Rida's own comments. This may be seen to resemble the traditional style, that is, instead of each author writing an independent *tafsīr*, one may add a *sharḥ* (explanation) to a preceding *tafsīr*. So it is possible to think that 'Abduh made the major interpretation, followed by Rida who added his notes. However, it is easy to find places where the passages of Rida are more abundant than the words of 'Abduh. For example, on the verse of "You are the best community that has been raised up for mankind," (chapter Āl 'Imrān, 110), Rida wrote:

> The essence of what the mentor-imam ['Abduh] said is: This description [of the best community] is true about those to whom it was first addressed. They were the Prophet, may Allah bestow blessings and peace upon him, and his companions who were with him, upon them be Divine satisfaction. They were once enemies, but God united their hearts so that, by Divine Grace, they became brothers. And they were those who tied each other by the Divine Rope [Islam] and were not disunited in religion to become partisans of particular sects, and they were those who were ordering the good and forbidding the evil.[86]

'Abduh continues to portray the companions with their praiseworthy natures and acts. Here we can see the very Salafi attitude of putting an emphasis on the model character of the first generation. Then, Rida adds his comment to accentuate the point:

> I say: This is the summary meaning of what the mentor-imam said, except the phrase "and his companions who were with him" [which needs an explanation]. This is from his words, but he intended these noble attributes and perfect characteristics for that perfect faith not for everyone for whom the *hadīth* scholars apply the term of a companion, such as a Bedouin who just embraced Islam and saw the Prophet only once . . .[87]

He clarifies that the loyal and enduring companions were the models to follow, not any companion. Then, he goes further, raising the question of later conflicts among these leading companions, and giving his answer to the question of internal divisions at length.

Sometimes Rida gave additional explanations, and on other occasions extended comments on his own line of arguments. He was always extremely polite when he raised an objection to 'Abduh's interpretation, obscuring the fact that he was raising a point against his mentor.[88]

'Abduh gave lectures on 5 out of the 30 volumes of the Qur'an, as it is conventionally divided. 'Abduh used to read what Rida wrote, mostly before the printing, and gave his approval.[89] 'Abduh passed away in 1905. Since then, Rida continued writing the *tafsīr* for another thirty years by himself, and it became progressively his own, though he was confident that if 'Abduh were to read his writings, he would have confirmed them.[90] He himself did not, however, complete *Tafsīr al-Manār*. He finished the 12th volume 4 months before his death.[91]

This work can be considered a collective work of ʿAbduh and Rida, or even of the Manarists,[92] as it is called *Tafsīr al-Manār*. This question of authorship is also related to the question of how we see the relationship among the "trio of Islamic Reform," namely, al-Afghani, ʿAbduh, and Rida. To use Badawi's words, "Al-Afghani was the inspirer of the Salafiyya school and ʿAbduh was its brains, but Rashid Ridha was its spokesman."[93] However, Rida's function was more than that of a spokesman. We may put them as follows: Al-Afghani lived the life of a busy revolutionary who wielded influence over young Muslims, but did not spend much time to write the details of what he advocated. ʿAbduh continued his mission, though on quite a different plane with a different mode, and founded theoretical principles on which the school of Islamic Reform and Salafiyya rests. Rida gave details to the principles, and tried to formulate them in more concrete manners in *al-Manār*. One might be tempted to say that Rida went down a particular line of argumentation too rigidly while ʿAbduh left certain difficult questions with ambiguous answers. Here is a secret concerning why other liberal disciples could be confident of their being ʿAbduh's followers while they distanced themselves from the Islamic line Rida pursued, despite Rida's monopolization of the position of the most favored disciple of ʿAbduh. Rida could not help but go into detail as the needs of the Islamic world at the time called for. He may be blamed for not having given perfect answers, but not for giving detailed answers. If we recognize this relationship between the three, the same is applicable to *Tafsīr al-Manār*. Al-Afghani initiated the task of reading the Qurʾan in the light of modern conditions of the Islamic world, and ʿAbduh later gave actual lectures on the Qurʾanic exegesis. Then, Rida recorded it, and expanded it with more details.

What are the methodological contributions of *Tafsīr al-Manār*? Although it looks basically conventional in its form, it is not void of new methodological contributions in the field. Here we refer to two of them. The first is the analytical summary of chapters. As a notable example, Rida cites, after giving a general description of topics in *Sūra al-Baqara* (Chapter of Cow), twenty-one legal points, or practical sanctions of the Islamic law, addressed to the Islamic community, putting numbers to these items, starting from (1) establishment of daily prayers and paying zakat, (2) prohibition of magic, (3) punishment for murders, kindness to parents and relatives, to (21) a prayer at the end of the chapter as a seal of practical sanctions. Then, he spelled out 33 "general legal principles and rules" in this chapter.[94] For anyone who is familiar with modern *tafsīr*s, this may not seem particularly impressive. Classical *tafsīr*s are, however, mostly written in a form called *tafsīr taḥlīlī*, that is, commentaries given to verses in their order in the Qurʾan.[95] As the sequential order of the Qurʾan does not follow the kind of order that a law book or a literary text book may follow, it is very difficult to grasp the general view of a chapter or to locate a particular issue in it. They neither give summaries of any chapter, nor a summary of what the exegete writes on that chapter.

So, *Tafsīr al-Manār* pioneers to give such descriptions of a chapter in order to facilitate its understanding by ordinary Muslims.

The second point: The earlier methodology was not just a convenient tool. It had a theoretical basis, which is the thematic integrity of each chapter. In earlier centuries, the concept that each chapter constitutes an integrated unit with central themes was not found. In Mustansir Mir's words, to see a "sura [chapter] as a unit," is a definite break with the traditional style of exegesis.[96] On this, we agree with Mir, but he omits 'Abduh and Rida from his list of most important exegetes in the twentieth century.[97] We would rather agree with 'Abdullāh Maḥmūd Shiḥāta that "'Abduh's contribution was in drawing the general idea of a chapter and the issues with which it deals and the principles and the realities it contains, and that it was carried on by Rida."[98] Shiḥāta cited the integrity of the chapter as the first of the nine foundations on which 'Abduh's methodology relied.

As we have seen earlier, *Tafsīr al-Manār* addressed the needs of Muslims at the beginning of the twentieth century. The journal was for those Muslims who aspired to revive the Islamic *umma*. Through its *tafsīr*, 'Abduh and Rida were able to justify reformist ideas with Qur'anic verses, and ground these ideas in sacred scripture. They also expanded understanding of the Qur'an by reading these ideas in its verses. As the Qur'an has been a living guide for Muslims throughout these centuries due to this dynamism of updating the understanding of the scripture according to the social and spiritual needs of each era, opening this function for the modern need was an extremely important role played by *Tafsīr al-Manār*.

Before the twentieth century, *Rūḥ al-Ma'ānī* by al-Alusi (1802–1854)[99] has been the last encyclopedic *tafsīr* of the classical brand. After this complicated and voluminous work in the middle of the nineteenth century, there was a gap of *tafsīr* writing until *Tafsīr al-Manār* appeared. Once *Tafsīr al-Manār* reestablished the art of exegesis to address the contemporary reader, modern *tafsīr*s began to flourish.[100]

A brief and selective list of works may include, from Egypt, *Al-Ǧawāhir fī Tafsīr al-Qur'ān al-Karīm* by Ṭantāwī Ǧawharī (d. 1940),[101] *Tafsīr al-Marāghī* by Aḥmad Muṣṭafā al-Marāghī (1881–1945),[102] and *Tafsīr al-Qur'ān al-Karīm* by Maḥmūd Shaltūt[103], from Tunisia, *Tafisīr al-Taḥrīr wa al-Tanwīr* by Muḥammad al-Ṭāhir b. 'Āšūr[104], and from Algeria, The *Tafsīr* of Ben Badis.[105] All of these are intellectually related to 'Abduh, Rida and *al-Manār*. An important work by the Syrian Salafi Reformer contemporary to Rida, Muḥammad Jamāl al-Dīn al-Qāsimī could be added to the list.[106] His *tafsīr* is commonly known as *Tafsīr al-Qāsimī*. In one of its editions, Rida's remarks of praise for al-Qāsimī are quoted as "the renewer of Islamic sciences" and "the reviver of the prophetic *sunna*" who is "one of the unifying links between the guidance of the Salaf and the civilizational ascent appropriate for the time."[107]

In the middle of the century, one of the most important works, probably one next to *Tafsīr al-Manār* in terms of its wide influence, appeared: *Fī Ẓilāl al-Qur'ān* by Sayyid Qutb (1906–1966).[108] Volumes of the work have been translated into English,[109] and it is widely read beyond the Arab countries. Its author was influenced by *al-Manār*, as "*Tafsīr al-Manār*... had a great impact on Sayyid Qutb, and he made it a major reference in writing his everlasting work, *In the Shade of the Qur'an*."[110]

The last two decades of the twentieth century also witnessed new *tafsīr*s, such as *Al-Asās fī al-Tafsīr* by Saʿīd Ḥawwā,[111] a leading ideologue of the Syrian Muslim Brotherhood, *al-Tafsīr al-Munīr* and *al-Tafsīr al-Wasīṭ* by a prolific Syrian scholar Wahba al-Zuḥaylī,[112] and *al-Tafsīr al-Wasīṭ* by the then Grand Mufti of Egypt and now Grand Shaykh of al-Azhar, Muḥammad Sayyid Ṭantāwī.[113] The continuity of the *tafsīr* literature as one of the most important avenue to express modern Islamic ideas in the form of Qur'anic exegesis seems firmly established by now, and it would not be an exaggeration to say that *Tafsīr al-Manār* had a major, if not the sole, role in opening this avenue.

Modern Islamic political theory

We should now turn to political theory. Rida and *al-Manār* lived in an era when the Islamic world was in one of the most serious periods of political turmoil. Most of the proponents of the Islamic revival took a defensive position against Western encroachment. Many of them were very critical of the shortcomings of the Ottoman dynasty but did not wish for it to be dismantled. One of the most serious calamities for the Islamic world was the demise of the Ottoman empire. When the new Turkish leadership abolished the Sultanate in 1922, thus ending the long reign of the dynasty over six centuries, and keeping a separate Caliphate as a symbolic institution, it created a terrible crisis in the planes of both political reality and political thought.

The Ottoman dynasty in its later days depended upon the dual institution of the Sultanate-Caliphate for its legitimacy.[114] For the larger part of the Islamic world, the Caliphate was the main concern, as this feature distinguished the Ottoman dynasty from all other polities and made it a representative of the Islamic world, at least for the majority Sunnis. After the republic was declared in 1923, the new Turkish government abolished the formal Caliphate in 1924. For Muslims of other lands, this was not a Turkish domestic issue.

Rida started to write his *al-Ḫilāfa, aw al-Imāma al-ʿUẓmā fī al-Islām* (*Caliphate, or the Supreme Leadership in Islam*)[115] immediately after the abolishment of the Sultanate, and ended its argument before the abolishment of the shadowy Caliphate. For Rida, by then it had become a nominal institution—that Caliphate was not worthy of the name—and he formulated a theory of Islamic *khilāfa* (Caliphate), which in his eyes was simultaneously realistic for the modern age.

Though lengthy and full of juristic arguments, his theory may be characterized, perhaps simplistically, by the following eight points[116]:

1 The *khilāfa* (Caliphate) is the sole legitimate Islamic polity for the *umma*;
2 It must be reinstituted in such a manner that it can function under contemporary conditions;

3 Government must be run by the Council of *Shūrā* (consultation), which is comprised of *Ahl al-ḥall wa al-ʿaqd* (people of authority). Currently, people of authority are not only Islamic scholars but also leaders of the political, military, economic, and other domains;
4 The *khalīfa* (Caliph) will represent the government, and he must be a qualified *mujtahid*, well-versed in Islamic knowledge and capable of exercising independent reasoning to guarantee rule by al-Shariʿa;
5 He must be of Quraysh origin (a descendant of the Quraysh, the tribe of Prophet Muhammad);
6 The Muslims must strive to realize Islamic government (or, governments, if necessary) under a *khalīfa*;
7 If circumstances do not permit a *khilāfa* with full conditions, even an imperfect *khilāfa* should be established;
8 While all Muslims are under this obligation, especially the Arabs and the Turks should cooperate together for its achievement.

It is not unfair to say that it is the masterpiece of the Sunni Caliphate theory in the twentieth century. It is so because of the power of its elaborate discussions, and it provided a sufficient ground for the supporters of the Caliphate as the sole legitimate polity. For others, especially for the generations after the 1940s, the topic lost relevance, and no serious rival theory was offered.[117]

If we look back at the history of Islamic political thought, we find in the premodern periods the classical theories of Caliphate by the famous al-Mawardi (975–1058),[118] and Abū Yaʿlā al-Farrāʾ (990–1065)[119] who was no less important, though less known, than al-Mawardi, and a concluding masterpiece of all classical theories by Šihāb al-Dīn Aḥmad al-Qalqašandī (1355–1418).[120] We may be tempted to say that Rida's comes after these in line as a modern masterpiece.[121]

Similarities between the classical theories and Rida's stem partly from the latter's numerous quotations from the former, to the degree that one may be tempted to claim that "Rida thinks the traditional system of government still the best."[122] Certainly Rida didn't hesitate to depend on great authorities in the past when appropriate for his own objectives. He was, however, far from being traditional. He mobilized all possible resources to make Islam viable under the contemporary conditions, and authentic according to the primary sources of Islam, that is, the Qurʾan and the Sunna. The combination itself is quite revivalist, and therefore modern, however classical it may look, departing from the traditional.

Kerr stated in his conclusion that

> [H]is revival of the classical theory of the Caliphate serves to remind us that the classical theory itself had not been a program for action but a hyperbolical, almost allegorical, rationalization . . . . Riḍā's constitutional theory, despite his intentions, does not represent a serious program but a statement of ideals.[123]

On the contrary, it seems to the author that Rida had a full intention to lay a theoretical ground of a modern Islamic state, but was not optimistic about the scheme he had. He proposed:

> [The proposal is]...to leave the issue of the *khilafa* (Caliphate) to the all Islamic peoples, and independent and semi-independent governments among them, and constitute a mixed independent committee or assembly with its headquarters in Istanbul, which will study all reports and proposals from the men of knowledge and judgment on the issue, and this will prepare an Islamic conference... [124]

If anything, Rida should be criticized for his lack of popular basis to translate his idea into an action plan, not for being unrealistic in his thinking itself. In fact, "he was increasingly marginal to the main events of the day. In a period when mass political organizations were being established, he remained without a formal organization to present his views."[125] *Al-Manār* being an intellectual journal, his ideas had to wait for a mass movement such as the Muslim Brotherhood for realization of any idea. Hasan al-Banna (1906–1949) established the organization in 1928, yet another reaction to the demise of the Ottoman Caliphate.

Kerr was content that Rida sanctioned modern, secular institutions through Islamic principles, and called it "assimilative function."[126] This judgment was quite understandable as it was the time "[s]ince the suppression of the Muslim Brethren in Egypt and the demise of the Islamic constitution of Pakistan, there has ceased to be any visible likelihood that Islamic legal and constitutional principles would be made to serve as the operative basis of a modern state in any Muslim country."[127] Now, after seeing many "visible" signs, such as the Islamic revolution in Iran and the *de facto* revival and expansion of the Muslim Brotherhood in Egypt,[128] as well as calls for Islamic constitutions, we may have a more positive, and probably fairer evaluation of Rida's theory.

Mahmoud Haddad criticizes the preceding works on political ideas of Rida as taking the theory on the *khilāfa* as an independent work, without contextualizing it in the development of Rida's political thought.[129] He came to the conclusion that "Riḍā, throughout his career, usually placed the political independence of Islam above all other concerns, including theoretical consistency."[130] His argument that Rida's seeming inconsistency in *al-Khilāfa* can be seen as the pragmatic attitudes seeking Islam's independence, is quite convincing. This also reminds us of his contribution to the legitimacy of an Islamic state as such in the twentieth century, when we see his theory from a distance, as a close look tends to draw us into its details as a Caliphate, a very specific form of the Islamic state.

We can now put his theory in the category of "governance by the jurist," together with Khomeini's "guardianship of the jurist (*wilāya al-faqīh*)" and Muhammad Baqir al-Sadr's political guidance of the "righteous authority (*al-marǧa'iyya al-ṣāliḥa*)."[131] Al-Sadr was very instrumental in the contents of the Islamic Constitution of Iran in 1979, no less than Khomeini's theory.[132] If we are to name Rida's theory in this respect, we may call it *khilāfa al-mujtahid* (Caliphate of the qualified jurist). Putting a jurist or a *mujtahid* on the top of the polity does not necessarily mean the government is run by Islamic scholars entirely. Actually, Rida conceived the *khilāfa* as governance by both secular and Islamic leaders,[133] as is the case of Iran after the revolution. He was apparently a pioneer in this category of ideas on the contemporary Islamic governance.

The third path in the middle

Rida named himself and his colleagues the "moderate party of Islamic reform (*ḥizb al-iṣlāḥ al-islāmī al-muʿtadil*)." Moderation (*iʿdāl*) means a balance between two extremes.

Al-Maraghi named three opponents of Rida at the time of his death, namely, "Disbelievers who do not believe in any religion," "non-Muslim opponents," and "Muslims who are stagnant." The first refers, if we take off its religious jargons, not to non-Muslims but to the Muslim secularists, the second, Christian opponents who were again mostly secular,[134] and the third the conservative traditionalists. Rida himself spoke of the *mutafarnij* ("Franconizer," that is, Westernizer, or "imitators of European laws and systems") and the imitators (conservative traditionalists), and himself between these two poles.[135] Hourani, in his work, which became a modern classic in the field, summarizes Rida's position: "[N]othing much could be hoped from the recognized religious institutions," but also "nothing could be expected of the 'westernizers' who had dominated public life for the last few generations." "Somewhere between the two extremes however stood a middle group, the 'Islamic progressive party': they had the independence of mind necessary to understand at the same time the laws of Islam and the essence of modern civilization."[136]

Apparently, what is in the middle between the two extremes changes its position from one period to another, as the social realities as well as the intellectual map change over time. Although Rida criticized the secularists seriously, and was criticized by them, what secularism meant had also changed greatly as secularization of each society was progressing.

In Egypt, before the death of ʿAbduh, the reform of the 'ulama' and al-Azhar seemed essential for legal and educational reforms, as the 'ulama' were the traditional bearers of these two domains. By the time Rida neared the end of his life, these two domains had mostly passed into the hands of secular institutions. The traditional was then much less a focus of the reformists, as it lost ground to the secularists. On the other hand, the trend of the Islamic revival started to have its leaders among the new generation educated in secular institutions, such as Hasan al-Banna and Sayyid Qutb of the Muslim Brotherhood.

What is certain at the macro level is, however, the general position of the Islamic reformers who tried to find a middle ground where they could combine Islam and modernity. The combination was that of two substances, contradicting each other, "Islam and modernity," "revelation and reason," "religion and modern civilization," "Islam and modern society," and the like, and therefore a way had to be found in between. By the middle of the twentieth century, their attempts were considered a failure, and functioned only to facilitate *de facto* secularization.[137] As discussed earlier in this chapter, the failure was not final, and could be considered a tentative setback, as far as the strength of reformism as a social idea is concerned. It continued to survive as an ideal to which many Muslims strove and are still striving, as they felt unable to abandon Islam or modernity.[138]

The reformers' capability to sustain the morale of the Muslims is not itself proof that this combination of seemingly contradictory natures can be successfully made. Basheer M. Nafi's restrained assessment, however, that "[W]hile no religious system could escape the impact of modernity unscathed, Islamic reformist thought paved the way for the assimilation of modernity with the least possible loss for Islam,"[139] is quite agreeable.

Yet, many cast doubts on the actual possibility of the combination proposed by the reformers. Many were, and are, openly skeptical.[140] Investigation of this issue continues to our day in a different garment. Popular topics among the students of the Islamic world today, such as "Islam and modernity," "Islam and modernization," and "Islam and democracy"[141] are but a few among them.

What has drastically changed the underlying assumptions and the tone of arguments came from a totally different direction in the latter half of the twentieth century, namely from East Asia. Japan's success in the postwar period, with its amazing economic growth from the 1950s to the early 1970s and subsequent rise as a leading economic power in the world in the 1980s, and the successes of the emerging economies in East and Southeast Asia following Japan's model, had changed the fundamental assumption that modernization can be done only through Westernization and therefore traditional cultures such as Islam and Confucianism were nothing but a hindrance to development.

A combination of the inherent culture and modernization can be done, as Japan did.[142] Can this also happen to Islam? In 1930, Rida stated in a lecture:

> We need an independent renewal like that of Japan to promote our economic, military, and political interests and develop our agricultural, industrial, and commercial wealth.[143]

Yet, for them, it was a distant dream. Can this actually happen now in the Islamic world? We don't yet have a definite answer. In the recent decades, Malaysia, a Muslim country, rose as a successful developing country. Mahathir Mohamad, Malaysia's prime minister from 1981 to 2003, was quite vocal in his country's "quest for the status of a fully developed nation by the year 2020,"[144] that is to become the first developed country in the Islamic world to prove that the combination of Islam and modernity is possible. This is certainly an interesting case.

What we have to consider now is whether the former assumption that the reformist project was by definition contradictory was right or not. The assumption should be judged, by now, premature, if not totally wrong.

There is another element in this discussion. It is the change of the nature of science and technology, or their bearers. In the days of Rida and *al-Manār*, we can see many of the reformers were from humanities backgrounds, including Islamic studies. In olden days, the "Easterners" had to acquire a "modern mind" which could work scientifically. Reformers actually advocated that the students in Islamic studies must learn modern sciences. Rida himself learned modern science under his enlightened mentor, Husayn Jisr, and advocated the importance of the combination. Lately, however, in the last three decades or so, we see that many leaders in Islamic movements are of natural sciences background. These medical doctors, scientists, and engineers do not seem to bother themselves with the profound question of how to acquire a "modern scientific mind," which many asked a century ago. It should be noted that Mahathir Mohamad is originally a medical doctor.

The medical doctors, scientists, engineers, and the like, are apparently the fruit of modernization in each country. Their turning to Islamic identity does not have a necessary correlation with the question of a "scientific mind," though we need a detailed survey on this question. One might be tempted to say, at least, that these professionals simply learned modern sciences in a modern way, and only when they acquired the sciences did they turn to Islam as their cultural identity.

If we look at what kind of Islam they turn to, however, we find one which ʻAbduh, Rida, and their colleagues founded, that is, a reformist understanding of Islam, based on the primary sources, the Qur'an and the Sunna, exercising ijtihad (independent reasoning) in the Islamic law, advocating that Islam and modern civilization can be merged together. It is not yet time to jump to the conclusion that the Manarists' formula of combining the two poles proved to be viable. We certainly need a re-evaluation of the issue, not only by examining the recent developments in the Islamic world but also by adding the latest debates on modernity and modernization in a truly global perspective.

Islamic revival in the later decades

After Rashid Rida passed away, Hasan al-Banna, the founder and the General Guide (Head) of the Society of Muslim Brotherhood, tried to continue the journal *al-Manār*. Though he did not succeed except to publish the issues of the last volume in five years, his movement carried out the mission of Islamic reform at a mass level. Al-Banna used to visit Rida, and inherited the ideas of *al-Manār* for Islamic reform and revival, in a much simplified and popularized version. We can say that, to the extent that he was a Salafi, he continued the mission of *al-Manār*, which established the modern Salafiyya.[145]

As noted earlier, while the trend of ideas *al-Manār* established continued to flow in the underground "water veins," metaphorically speaking, the momentum of the Islamic revival was lost in the 1950s to 1970s, when Arab nationalism and socialism swept across the Middle East scene. When the Islamic Revolution in

Iran shook the entire region, this was reversed, and the phenomena of the Islamic revival started to manifest itself not only in predominantly Shiite Iran, but also in Sunni countries. The Muslim Brotherhood re-emerged as a political force to be reckoned with in Egypt, Syria, Jordan, and Palestine, among other Arab countries. As *al-Manār* elaborated Sunni theories of the Islamic revival in the earlier decades, its ideas also started to surface.[146]

When Rida wrote his theory of "*khilāfa* of the *mujtahid*," or governance by the jurists, in the 1920s, it was seen as an obsolete nostalgia harkening to classical theory. When Ayatullah Khomeini's theory of "guardianship by the jurist" became the backbone of the new Islamic republic in Iran, few remembered the significance of Rida's theory. The political thesis that a qualified jurist should govern certainly reflects the contemporary plight of Muslims in the political domain, caught between the inability of the traditional Islamic elites and the non-Islamic nature of new ruling elites. As such, Rida was rather a forerunner, not an anachronistic observer in his time. Although the jurists' taking power is not particularly prospective currently in Sunni countries, their political roles have been strengthened to a great extent, after a long period of deterioration.

It seems that many of reform ideas Rida and the Manarists proposed were later accepted and incorporated by mainstream Islamic scholars. Rida and his colleagues probably called for too radical a reform at that time. As the "great majority of the reformist ulama, including 'Abduh, Rida, al-Qasimi and al-Jaza'iri, belonged to rural or small urban families, not to the entrenched ulama aristocracy of the urban notables,"[147] the establishment found their cause to be at odds with theirs. With the expansion of social space for the masses and the Islamic revival among them, however, their teachings began to reach more friendly ears. Today, what they advocated has become common sense. This subsequent success of the reformers obscures the innovativeness of their claims at their time. *Al-Manār* struggled hard to make ijtihad possible and to issue modern *fatwa*s. Exercise of ijtihad and innovative *fatwa*s have become more common today.

Of recent events of the Islamic revival, one conference attracts our attention. It was a founding conference of the World Union of Muslim Ulama, held in London in July 2004. It was a gathering of more than two hundred Islamic scholars from Muslim countries, many of them prominent in their own countries as well as transnationally in the larger Islamic world. The conference immediately reminds us of the Meccan conference of al-Kawakibi, or his proposal to convene an international conference to discuss the affairs of the Islamic *umma*.

The formation of the Union aimed to form a common platform where a viable body of men and women of knowledge could create a foundation for the unity of the Islamic *umma*, and prepare the Islamic law in a way suitable to the times.[148]

The conference invited not only Sunni scholars but also Shiite and Ibadi scholars. Among those who made the first addresses were Dr Ekmeleddin İhsanoğlu, the prospective secretary general of the OIC (as of January 1, 2005), Shaykh Aḥmad al-Khalilī, the Grand Mufti of Oman, the highest position in the Ibadi school, and Ayatullah Muḥammad 'Alī Tasḫīrī, a prominent Iranian Shiite jurist and the president of the World Forum for Proximity of Islamic Schools of Thought. The conference established the Union, and elected as its president, Shaykh Yusuf al-Qaradawi, three vice presidents, respectively from the Sunni, the Shiite, and the Ibadi.

Al-Qaradawi inherited, it seems to the present author, the reformist school of *al-Manār* in many ways. When he was young, he joined the Muslim Brotherhood, the organizational heir to the Manarists' thought, led by Hasan al-Banna. While al-Banna was an Islamic leader with a secular school education,[149] and the founder of a mass movement, al-Qaradawi is an Islamic scholar who always argues with the Qur'an and the Sunna, the way Rida used to do.

Rida called his group the "balanced (*mu'tadil*) Islamic reform party." Al-Qaradawi developed the concept of the "*wasaṭiyya* (middle way)."[150] He explains that Islam is of the *umma* of *'adl* (justice) and *i'tidāl* (balance).[151] The concept expresses itself as being in the middle of the path. While al-Qaradawi describes the *wasaṭiyya* as one of the main characteristics of Islam, it is his vision of Islam, as the reformers' vision of Islam for Rida and the Manarists was the truly authentic understanding of Islam.

More importantly, al-Qaradawi continues the mission of 'Abduh and Rida in issuing *fatwa*s to give answers to contemporary questions.[152] Al-Qaradawi says in his book on the question of *fatwa*:

> After that [the periods of traditional *fatwa*s], *fatwa*s of *al-'allāma al-mujaddid* [great renewer scholar] al-Sayyid Muhammad Rashid Rida had become famous, which were published in his noble Islamic journal, *al-Manār*, a journal which continued for thirty five years. Each issue always had one or more *fatwa*s, answering questions from the readers of the journal in the Islamic world. For this reason, the questions and answers did not represent any particular locality, but addressed problems the entire Islamic *umma* and Muslims in all corners of the earth were facing. . . .
>
> These *fatwa*s had many features. First, they treat modern issues and actual problems which peoples face and suffer and need to know the answers of Islamic law, or at least, contemporary Islamic ijtihad (judgment, reasoning) on them. Second, they are written with a spirit of intellectual independence, with freedom from bonds of sectarianism, imitation, and narrow-minded insistence on a particular view. He did not refer except to the Book [Qur'an], Sunna, and the foundations of the Islamic law. . . . Third, they carry the spirit of reform and the invitation to the balanced comprehensive Islam.[153]

Here we can see an apparent successor to the Manarists. The distance between the Manarists and this Union, however, can be seen in the question of *khilāfa* (Caliphate). Rida spoke in strong tones that the Islamic *umma* needed the true Caliphate as a necessary condition of its revival, and that the Muslims had an obligation to rebuild it. He spelled out in detail the conditions of the *khilāfa* in the contemporary context. In 2004, al-Qaradawi was very explicit that the Union does not seek to restore the *khilāfa*.

> Muslims used to have *khilāfa* that united them together, and embodied their unity. It is, according to the 'ulama's definition, deputyship of the Messenger [Muhammad] for the protection of Islam and administration of society, and it is religious and earthly leadership, both spiritual and temporal. The Muslims lived under this unifying banner for more than thirteen centuries, until the *khilāfa* was abolished in 1924, and with its end, Islamic *umma*'s assembly under the banner of Islamic faith was lost. . . . If *fatwa* changes according to the changes of time, place and situation, then our *fatwa* of today is: The 'ulama' are those who have to perform the roles of *khilāfa* (Caliphate) and *khalīfā*s (Caliphs).[154]

This does not necessarily mean that the Union departed from the point where Rida resided eighty years ago. Since Rida's theory emphasized essentially the necessity of an Islamic state and the leading function of the scholars in the affairs of the *umma*, both Rida's and the Union's positions can be seen as different formulations of the same school in different times. When Rida wrote *al-Khilāfa aw al-Imāma al-'Uẓmā*, the Caliphate was an important title just abolished, and therefore could be restored. After many decades without it, the title has become less significant than the substance of the polity itself. Yet, it took these many decades for Sunni scholars to declare what al-Qaradawi stated in a blunt manner.

Concluding remarks

Seen from the beginning of the twenty-first century, with the Islamic revival having become a reality, the groundwork which *al-Manār* and its contemporary counterparts had done could be judged as having great relevance for our understanding of the Islamic world in the modern era. By now, *al-Manār* seems quite successful in many ways, even as it was judged to the contrary four decades ago.

While we abstain from an oversimplification or overestimation of the roles of *al-Manār*, certainly a re-evaluation must be done in the context of studying Islamic thought in the contemporary world, from the late nineteenth century, throughout the twentieth century, and well into the twenty-first century.

Since the present author began to call for such a re-evaluation in the middle of the 1980s, simultaneous re-evaluations have been made in some quarters so that we see a better presentation of Rida and his school than before. The attempt has not, however, been satisfactory, and further investigations on the pages of *al-Manār* and their historical contexts should be made. It will enhance the understanding of not only the Islamic world but also international society at large, as the beam of the lighthouse was directed at both in those days.

Notes

1 A digitalized photographic edition of the complete set of the journal was published in 2003. Kosugi Yasushi (general editor), *Al-Manār 1898–1935 on CD-ROM* (Kyoto: COE-ASAFAS, Kyoto University, 2003), with *The Index of al-Manār*. The index was published originally in a book form in 1998. Yusuf H. Ibish, Kosugi Yasushi and Yusuf K. Khoury, *The Index of al-Manār* (Tokyo: Islamic Area Studies Project and Beirut: Turāth, 1998).

2 Studies on *al-Manār* after the 1970s in the West were not null, though few in number, such as Mahmud Osman Haddad, *Rashīd Riḍā and the Theory of the Caliphate: Medieval Themes and Modern Concerns* (New York: Columbia University, 1991, unpublished PhD dissertation); Emad Eldin Shahin, *Through Muslim Eyes: M. Rashīd Riḍā and the West* (Herndon: International Institute of Islamic Thought, 1993). Anthologies have not often made justice to *al-Manār*. Bias in an earlier collection as Anour Abdel-Malek, *Contemporary Arab Political Thought* (London: Zed Books, 1983) is quite understandable given the dominance of the nationalist paradigm (the original French edition was in 1970). The complete absence of Rida, though *al-Manār* is used as a source for ʻAbduh, in a recent work as Mansoor Moaddel and Kamran Talattof, eds, *Modernist and Fundamentalist Debates in Islam: A Reader* (New York: Palgrave Macmillan, 2002), for example, seems unfair. Charles Kurzman, ed., *Modernist Islam, 1840–1940: A Sourcebook* (Oxford: Oxford University Press, 2002) is well balanced and much fairer to Rida.

3 Many revolutions, including military coups with the names of revolutions, were made in the 1950s and 1960s in the Middle East, then with September Revolution in 1969 in Libya, a relatively calm decade followed. For the revolutionary decades, see Hisham B. Sharabi, *Nationalism and Revolution in the Arab World* (New York: Van Nostrand Reinhold, 1966).

4 See Rūḥ Allāh Khumaynī, *Islam and Revolution: Writings and Declarations of Imam Khomeini*, trans. Hamid Algar (Berkeley, CA: Mizan Press, 1981).

5 To cite a few, Islamic Groups (Ǧamāʻāt Islāmiyya) were active on university campuses; the Muslim Brotherhood was revived after dissolution for almost two decades, and its monthly organ, *al-Daʻwa* was widely read especially among the young generation with an Islamic inclination.

6 Fouad Al-Omar and Mohammed Abdel Haq, *Islamic Banking, Theory, Practice and Challenges* (London: Oxford University Press, 1996); Nicholas Dylan Ray, *Arab Islamic Banking and the Renewal of Islamic Law* (London: Graham & Trotman, 1995). Citing the case of Islamic banking as an example of Islamic revival may look unconventional, while arguments on the Islamic revival tend to focus on the political, as the entire issue is sometimes labeled under the title of "political Islam." See Nazih N. Ayubi, *Political Islam: Religion and Politics in the Arab World* (London and New York: Routledge, 1991). There was an apparent prominence of the return of Islam in the political domain after the revolution in Iran. However, the Islamic revival which *al-Manār* sought was much wider in scope, so is the later phenomenon of the Islamic revival.

7 For the Islamic "commonalities," see Kosugi Yasushi, "Restructuring Islamic Political Theories: Basic Concepts in a Contemporary Framework," in Kuroda Toshio and R. I. Lawless, eds, *Nature of the Islamic Community* (Tokyo: Keiso Shobo, 1991), 37–70. Twelve basic concepts are pointed as common between the Sunnis and the Shi'ite on pp. 53–59.

8 A substantial number of literature on these cases appeared, and the number increased sharply in the 1980s. See Asaf Hussain, *Islamic Movements in Egypt, Pakistan and Iran: An Annotated Bibliography* (London: Mansell, 1983); Yvonne Yazbeck Hadded *et al.*,

The Contemporary Islamic Revival: A Critical Survey and Bibliography (Westport, CT: Greenwood, 1991).

9 These events were described and analyzed in detail in Kosugi Yasushi, *The Islamic World* (Tokyo: Chikuma-shobo, 1998) [in Japanese].

10 Nationalism in those days was equated with anticolonialism, anti-imperialism, national liberation movements widely observed in the Third World, nonalignment, and Asian and African solidarity, and also often intermixed with socialism and backed by the Soviet Union and the Eastern Bloc, as well-illustrated in the cases of Arab nationalism.

11 Malcolm Kerr, *Islamic Reform: The Political and Legal Theories of Muḥammad ʿAbduh and Rashīd Riḍā* (Berkeley and Los Angeles, CA: University of California Press, 1966).

12 Malcolm Kerr, "Rashīd Riḍā and Islamic Legal Reform: An Ideological Analysis, Part II: Application," *The Muslim World* 50 (1960): 181.

13 The concept of "Islamization" used here is that an area or a region may be Islamized (spread of Islam as a religion among the population and accompanying cultural transformation of the society) while the new Muslims' understanding of Islam takes the form of local culture, as if Islam has become localized. Islamization is not therefore a one-direction movement toward Islam, but a complementary process of Islamization/localization-indigenization. By the same token, when de-Islamization occurs, exteriorization (to consider Islam as an element coming from the outside earlier) happens. When re-Islamization occurs, as observed in the recent Islamic revival, it is not re-localization or re-interiorization, but mostly modernization/contemporarization and globalization, that accompany it. See the argument in Kosugi Yasushi, "Reconsidering 'Unity and Diversity' in the Islamic World: A Methodological Inquiry," *Southeast Asian Studies* 37/2 (1999): 143–149 [in Japanese].

14 See, for example, ʿAndnān ʿAlī Riḍā al-Naḥwī, *Al-Ṣaḥwa al-Islāmiyya ilā ayna?* [Islamic Awakening, to Where?], Expanded 3rd ed. (Riyadh: Dār al-Naḥwī, 1993). "Awakening" can be *yaqẓa* in Arabic, as in Muḥammad ʿImāra, *Al-Ṭarīq ilā al-Yaqẓa al-Islāmiyya* (Cairo and Beirut: Dār al-Shurūq, 1990).

15 It is noted that one of the leading exponents of the Islamic revival today, Yūsuf al-Qaraḍāwī earned his *ʿālim* degree by a thesis on zakat. Yāsuf al-Qaraḍāwī, *Fiqh al-Zakāt*, 16th ed. [1st ed. in Egypt], 2 vols (Cairo: Maktaba Wahba, 1986) [The original edition appeared first in Lebanon in 1969].

16 This term was formally used first in Japan in 1985, as the title of the main symposium at the first annual conference of Japan Association of Middle East Studies. Since then, it has been in circulation and greatly appreciated academically, as an alternative to the controversial term "Islamic fundamentalism," which is too heavily colored by threat perceptions, and tends to focus on political and violent dimensions of the Islamic revival. How individual "awakening" can be translated into a social action is analyzed in Kosugi Yasushi, *The Contemporary Middle East and Islamic Politics* (Kyoto: Showado, 1994), 145–148 [in Japanese].

17 Charles C. Adams, *Islam and Modernism in Egypt: A Study of the Modern Reform Movement Inaugurated by Muḥammad ʿAbduh* (London: Oxford University Press, 1933), 205–247, uses the term the " 'Manar' Party" as ʿAbduh's followers. In this article, the Manarists are Rida and his associates/contributors to *al-Manār*, as liberals among ʿAbduh's disciples took a different path than Rida's.

18 Serialized posthumously in *al-Manār* 5 (1902–1903): 26–33, 65–71, 105–110, 141–146, 183–190, 223–228, 264–268, 304–308, 344–349, 381–385, 501–505, 668–678, 703–710, 771–778, 825–833, 859–864, 899–910. The page numbers from *al-Manār* given in this article are of the original. There is some incorrect numbering in the original, so certain numbers are printed twice in different places. The errata are clarified in the attached file in Kosugi, ed., *Al-Manār 1898–1935 on CD-ROM.*

19 Al-Kawākibī wrote the work in Aleppo, modified several times after he moved to Egypt in 1899. It was published as a book in 1900, then published in *al-Manār*. Samī al-Dahhān, *'Abd al-Raḥmān al-Kawākibī*, 4th print (Cairo: Dār al-Ma'ārif, 1980), 55. Al-Kawākibī's work as a book has been reprinted in Arab countries to this day. See the following edition, which also contains a detailed study by the editor on previous editions of the work: 'Abd al-Raḥmān Al-Kawākibī *Umm al-Qurā: Mu'tamar al-nahḍa al-Islāmiyya* ed. Muḥammad Jamāl Al-Ṭaḥḥān (Damascus: Dār al-Awā'il, 2002).

20 The name was given in its announcement in the previous number of the journal as "Siğill ğam'iyya Umm al-Qurā [The Record of Umm al-Qura Association]," *Al-Manār* 4 (1902): 956.

21 "Al-Kitāb al-maw'ūd bi-našrihi [The Work Promised of its Publication]," *Al-Manār* 5 (1902): 26.

22 Ibid., 27–28.

23 For example, Sylvia G. Haim, ed., *Arab Nationalism: An Anthology* (Berkeley, CA: University of California Press, 1962). A portion of Al-Kawakibi's work is titled as "The Excellences of the Arabs," and he was judged to be the "first true intellectual precursor of modern secular Pan-Arabism" in the editor's introduction (p. 27).

24 Adeed Dawisha, *Arab Nationalism in the Twentieth Century: From Triumph to Despair* (Princeton, NJ and Oxford: Princeton University Press, 2003), 24.

25 See, for example, 'Abd al-Ḥaqq al-A'ẓamī (an Iraqi author), "Al-'Arab wa al-'Arabiyya, bihimā ṣalāḥ al-umma al-Islāmiyya [The Arab and the Arabic, with Them There Will Be the Wellness of the Islamic *Umma*]," *al-Manār* 16 (1913): 753–771; "Lugha al-Islām wa al-lugha al-rasmiyya bayna al-mamālik al-Islamīyya [The Language of Islam and the Official Language among the Islamic Kingdoms]," *al-Manār* 24 (1923): 753–765; "Ahamm mā yajib 'alā muslimī al-a'ājim min al-lugha al-'Arabiyya [The Most Important Part of the Arabic Language Necessary for the Non-Arab Muslims (*fatwa*)]," *al-Manār* 29 (1929): 661–664.

26 Rida's reports on the conference in Cairo: *Al-Manār* 27 (1926): 208–232, 280–294, 370–377, 449–458.

27 Rida's reports on the conference in Jerusalem: *Al-Manār* 32 (1932): 113–132, 193–208, 284–292, 555–558. He was the chair of the committee of Islamic Call and Guidance (*al-da'wa wa al-iršād*) in the conference. The leading convener of the conference, Amin al-Husayni, had studied earlier with Rida in Cairo.

28 It goes without saying that the OIC is not Islamic in the traditional sense as it is an international organization of nation-states. This is, however, a proof of Islamic revival being modern, rather than traditional or archaic. For OIC, see Hasan Moinuddin, *The Charter of the Islamic Conference and Legal Framework of Economic Co-operation among its Member States* (Oxford: Clarendon, 1987); Saad S. Khan, *Reasserting International Islam: A Focus on the Organization of the Islamic Conference and Other Islamic Institutions* (Oxford: Oxford University Press, 2001).

29 Šakīb Arslān, "Jawāb al-Amīr Šakīb Arslān," *al-Manār* 31 (1930–1931): 355–370, 449–464, 529–553. For Arslan, see the chapter on him in the present volume.

30 The question sent by Muḥammad B. 'Umrān was (1) why the Muslims, especially "we, the Muslims of Java and Malaya," entered into a state of weakness and degeneration; (2) why Europeans, Americans, and Japanese made tremendous progress. *Al-Manār* 31 (1930): 355. Another example of an Indonesian question and Rida's answer is translated as Rashīd Ridā, "Patriotism, Nationalism, and Group Spirit in Islam," in John J. Donohue and John L. Esposito, eds, *Islam in Transition: Muslim Perspectives* (New York and Oxford: Oxford University Press, 1982), 57–59.

31 William L. Cleveland, *Islam against the West: Shakib Arslan and the Campaign for Islamic Nationalism* (Austin, TX: University of Texas Press, 1985), 115.

32 Richard P. Mitchell, *The Society of the Muslim Brothers*, new edition with a foreword by John O. Voll (New York and Oxford: Oxford University Press, 1993), 23. The last issue of *al-Manār* 35/10 was published in September 1940.
33 R. Stephan Humphreys "The Contemporary Resurgence in the Context of Modern Islam," in Ali E. Hillal Dessouki, ed., *Islamic Resurgence in the Arab World* (New York: Praeger, 1982), 77.
34 Respect for the Salaf itself is more generally observed, and not particular to Salafiyya, and as such, the term is used in an extremely varied ways by contemporary thinkers. See 'Abd al-Raḥmān b. Zayd al-Zanaydī, *Al-Salafiyya wa qaḍāyā al-'aṣr* (Rayadh: Dār Ašbīliyā, 1998), 31–49. In this article, the Manarist understanding of Salafiyya has been maintained.
35 As an example, a book review on Ibn Taymiyya's multi-volume *fatwa* collection, *al-Manār* 15 (1912): 555–556, praises the work, and says that it is available from the publisher or through Dār al-Manār.
36 Nelly Lahoud, *Political Thought in Islam: A Study in Intellectual Boundaries* (London: RoutledgeCurzon, 2005), 16.
37 Al-Sayyid Ǧamāl al-Dīn al-Afghānī, Šayḫ Muḥammad 'Abduh, *Al-'Urwa al-Wuṯqā*, ed. Sayyid Hādī Khūsrū Shāhī (Cairo: Maktaba al-Šurūq al-Duwaliyya, 2002).
38 See Thomas Philipp, *The Syrians in Egypt: 1725–1975* (Stuttgart: Steiner Verlaf Wiesbaden GmbH, 1985), 111–116.
39 On his political thought on *Sham* and actual involvement in Syrian politics, Suechika Kota has made a significant contribution. See his work based on his doctoral thesis, *Islam and Politics in Contemporary Syria: From Islamic Reformism to Muslim Brotherhood* (Kyoto: Nakanishiya, 2005) [in Japanese].
40 See a short tribute to him, *al-Manār*, 12 (1909): 560, and Rida's memoir on him, *al-Manār*, 21 (1919): 160–163. For other mentors of Rida, see Muḥammad Aḥmad Darnīqa, *Al-Sayyid Muḥammad Rašīd Riḍā: Islāḥātuhu al-ijtimā'iyya wa al-dīniyya* (Beirut: Mu'assasa al-Risāla and Tripoli: Dār al-Īmān, 1986), 23–35.
41 Riḍā, "Fātiḥa Tafsīr al-Qur'ān al-Ḥakīm," *Tafsīr al-Manār* 1 (Cairo: al-Hay'a al-Miṣriyya al-'Āmma li-l-Kitāb, 1972), 11. His first encounter with the journal, a similar account, is quoted from his biography of 'Abduh in Albert Hourani, *Arabic Thought in the Liberal Age 1798–1939* (London: Oxford University Press, 1967), 226.
42 'Abd al-Bāsiṭ Muḥammad Ḥasan, *Ǧamāl al-Dīn al-Afghānī wa atharuhu fī al-'ālam al-Islāmī al-ḥadīth* (Cairo: Maktaba Wahba, 1982), 229.
43 Al-Afghani is referred to in this article as "al-Afghānī (of the Afghan origin)." He was always described as "al-Afghānī" with the title of "al-Sayyid" (a descendant of Prophet Muhammad) in *al-Manār*. While his Iranian origin is basically accepted by Western and Iranian scholarship, this is not the case in Arab countries and Afghanistan. In the Arab and non-Arab Sunni countries, al-Afghani is called al-Afghani even to this day, a prolongation of the Manarists' position. In the latest, and probably best, collection of al-Afghani's works in Arabic and Persian, see a defense of al-Afghani by its Iranian editor: Sayyid Hādī Khūsrū Shāhī, "Ǧamāl al-Dīn al-Afghānī: Ḥayātuhu wa niḍāluhu," in al-Afghānī and 'Abduh, *Al-'Urwa al-Wuthqā*, 56–57.
44 Riḍā, "Fātiḥa Tafsīr al-Qur'ān al-Ḥakīm," 12.
45 Felicitas Opwis, "Changes in Modern Islamic Legal Theory: Reform or Reformation?" in Michaelle Browers and Charles Kurzman, eds, *An Islamic Reformation?* (Lanham: Lexington Books, 2004), 34–35.
46 Aḥmad al-Šarabāsī, *Rašīd Riḍā: Ṣāḥib al-Manār* (Cairo: Al-Majlis al-A'lā li-l-Šu'ūn al-Islāmiyya, 1970), 145–161. See his own reports of trips in *al-Manār*, as collected and edited in Yūsuf Ībish, ed., *Raḥlāṣt al-Imām Rašīd Riḍā* (Beirut: Bīsān, 2000).
47 *Al-Manār*, the front page of Vol. I, 2nd ed. (1327/1909).

48 *Al-Manār* 3 (1317/1900): 1 [The title page]. This is the first part of a longer *hadith*, not in any of the six canonical collections, but in minor collections.
49 "Preface of the First Volume of al-Manār [of the First Edition]," *al-Manār* 1, 2nd ed. [1909]: 9.
50 Ibid., 5. In the 2nd ed. which Rida put in circulation later, even the first volume was made in the new form, as he omitted news and telegrams with little enduring significance from the first issues.
51 Ibid., 3.
52 Adams, *Islam and Modernism in Egypt*, 180–181. The original of the journal available today for the first volume is from this second printing.
53 H. A. R. Gibb, *Mohammedanism: An Historical Survey*, 2nd ed. (London: Oxford University Press, 1964), 178.
54 C. C. Berg, "Indonesia," in H. A. R. Gibb, ed., *Whither Islam?: A Survey of Modern Movements in the Moslem World* (New York: AMS Press, 1973 [1932]), 268–269.
55 Muḥammad Rašīd Riḍā al-Ḥusaynī "Introduction to the Second Edition of the First Volume [written in 1327/1909]," *al-Manār* 1, 2nd ed., 8.
56 Adams, *Islam and Modernism in Egypt*, 177.
57 Ibid., 205.
58 Rida's writings on political issues were compiled in six volumes. Muḥammad Rašīd Riḍā, *Maqālāt al-Šayḫ Rašīd Ridā al-Siyāsiyya*, eds Yūsuf Ībish and Yūsuf Quzmā al-Khūrī (Beirut: Dār Ibn ʻArabī, 1994).
59 Commemorative gatherings were also held in Tunis, Baghdad, and Damascus. Al-Šarabāsī, *Rašīd Ridā*, 214–215.
60 As a descendant of Prophet Muhammad, he was called by the honorary title of "al-sayyid," indicating his lineage. After the republican revolution of 1952, the title became a word to mean "Mr" in Egypt, rather than a noble descent.
61 Šayḫ al-Ǧāmiʻ al-Azhar, "Ḫuṭba al-Ustādh al-Akbar," *al-Manār* 35 (1936): 187–188.
62 To call ʻAbduh by this title has become common in Egypt. It was Rida who started the title for ʻAbduh. Al-Amīr Šakīb Arslān, *Al-Sayyid Rašīd Ridā, aw ikhā' arbaʻīn sana* (Damscus: Maṭbaʻa Ibn Zaydūn, 1937), 7.
63 Rašīd Riḍā, "Ahl al-ḥall wa al-ʻaqd fī hādhā al-zamān" (a chapter in his treatise on the Caliphate), *al-Manār* 24 (1923): 59–60.
64 Anwar al-Jundī, *Tarājim al-aʻlām al-muʻāṣirīn fī al-ʻālam al-Islāmī* (Cairo: Maktaba al-Anglo al-Miṣriyya, 1970), 105, quoted in Assad Nimer Busool, "Shaykh Muḥammad Rashīd Riḍā's Relations with Jamāl al-Dīn al-Afghānī and Muḥammad ʻAbduh," *The Muslim World* 66 (1976): 281.
65 Emad Eldin Shahin, *Political Ascent: Contemporary Islamic Movements in North Africa* (Boulder, CO: Westview Press, 1997), 22–33; Emad Eldin Shahin, "Salafiyah," in John L. Esposito, ed., *The Oxford Encyclopedia of the Modern Islamic World*, III (New York & Oxford: Oxford University Press, 1995), 466–467.
66 For the echoes of *al-Manār* in Turkey, Central Asia, Southeast Asia, and China, please see the respective chapters in this volume.
67 Mawlānā Abū al-Kalām Muḥiy al-Dīn Āzād, "Kitāb al-khilāfa al-Islāmiyya," trans. ʻAbd al-Razzāq al-Mulīḥābādī, *al-Manār* 23 (1922): 45–56, 102–106, 193–201, 282–289, 361–372, 466–471, 509–512, 691–702, 753–757.
68 Ibid., 753–757. Azad subscribed himself to the equality of Muslims without ethnic distinction.
69 Nakamura, Mitsuo, *The Crescent Arises over the Banyan Tree: A Study of the Muhammadiyah Movement in a Central Javanese Town* (Yogyakarta: Gadjah Mada University Press, 1983).
70 Citing these cases is not to say that these were products of *al-Manār*'s influence. Such an "impact-response" approach would be too simplistic for all cases. For the reform trend in the Southeast Asia before *al-Manār*, see Azyumardi Azra, *The Origins of*

Islamic Reformism in Southeast Asia: Networks of Malay-Indonesian and Middle Eastern 'Ulamā' *in the Seventeenth and Eighteenth Centuries* (Crows Nest, Australia: Allen & Unwin and Honolulu: University of Hawai'i Press, 2004).

71 See the brief history of daily papers and journals with Islamic colors in Anwar al-Jundi's introduction in his *Tarīḫ al-ṣaḥāfa al-Islāmiyya I: Al-Manār* (Cairo: Dār al-Anṣār, n.d. [1983]). This book is probably the most concise introduction of the contents of *al-Manār*, volume by volume, with descriptions of the sociopolitical background. It divides *al-Manār* in four periods: From the beginning to the death of 'Abduh, to First World War, to the abolishment of the Caliphate, and to the death of Rida.

72 He owed two thousand pounds at his death, and his house was on mortgage. Al-Šarabāsī, *Rašīd Riḍā*, 169.

73 'Abd al-Ḥalīm al-Jundī, *Al-Imām Muḥammad 'Abduh* (Cairo: Dār al-Ma'ārif, 1979), 110.

74 See Kate Zebiri, *Maḥmūd Shaltūt and Islamic Modernism* (Oxford: Clarendon Press and New York: Oxford University Press, 1993).

75 Joseph Schacht, *An Introduction to Islamic Law* (Oxford: Clarendon Press, 1964), 70.

76 Wael B. Hallaq, "Was the Gate of Ijtihad Closed?", *International Journal of Middle East Studies* 16 (1984): 3–41.

77 Riḍā, "Muḥāwarāt al-Muṣliḥ wa al-Muqallid," *al-Manār* 3 (1900–1901): 635–640, 675–683, 715–725, 795–804; 4 (1901–1902): 51–60, 161–170, 205–217, 281–297, 361–371, 521–529, 567–573, 852–866.

78 Ibid., 4 (1901): 209–210.

79 Ibid., 362–363.

80 Muhammad Khalid Masud, Brinskley Messick, and David S. Powers, "Muftis, Fatwas, and Islamic Legal Interpretation," in Masud, Messick, and Powers, eds, *Islamic Legal Interpretation: Muftis and Their Fatwas* (Cambridge: Harvard University Press, 1996), 31. The compilation is: Ṣalāḥ al-Dīn al-Munajjid and Yūsuf Q. al-Khūrī, eds, *Fatāwā al-Imām Muḥammad Rašīd Riḍā*, 6 vols (Beirut: Dār al-Kitāb al-Jadīd, 1970–1971). When Muslim Brotherhood succeeded in publishing *al-Manār* for a brief period, Hasan al-Banna wrote his *fatwa*s. See the section in a collection of Banna's writings: Ḥasan al-Bannā, *Fiqh al-wāqi'* (Mansura: Dār al-Kalima, 1999), 43–75.

81 Basheer M. Nafi, "The Rise of Islamic Reformist Thought and its Challenge to Traditional Islam," in Suha Taji-Farouki and Basheer M. Nafi, eds, *Islamic Thought in the Twentieth Century* (London and New York: I. B. Tauris, 2004), 52–53.

82 Muḥammad Ḥusayn Ḏahabī, *Al-Tafsīr wa al-mufassirūn*, 2nd ed. (Cairo: Dār al-Kutub al-Ḥadītha, 1976), Vol. 2, 547–589.

83 Fahd b. 'Abd al-Raḥmān b. Sulaymān al-Rūmī, *Ittiğāhāt al-tafsīr fī al-qarn al-rābi' 'ashr*, 4th ed. (Riyadh: Maktaba al-Rušd, 2002), Vol. 2, 703–848.

84 'Abd al-Majīd 'Abd al-Salām al-Muḥtasib, *Ittiğāhāt al-tafsīr fī al-'aṣr al-rāhin* (Beirut: Dār al-Bayāriq, 1982), 101–125, 164–176.

85 Helmut Gätje, *The Qur'ān and its Exegesis: Selected Texts with Classical and Modern Muslim Interpretations*, trans. Alford T. Welch (London and Henley: Routledge and Kegan Paul, 1971), 42.

86 *Tafsīr al-Manār*, Vol. 4, 48.

87 Ibid.

88 'Abdullāh Maḥmūd Shiḥāta, *Manhağ al-Imām Muḥammad 'Abduh fī Tafsīr al-Qur'ān al-Karīm* (Cairo: Maṭba'a Ğāmi'a al-Qāhira, 1984), 204–205.

89 Riḍā, "Fātiḥa Tafsīr al-Qur'ān al-Ḥakīm," 15.

90 Ibid.

91 J. Jomier, "Al-Manār," EI^2, VI (1991), 361, states clearly that "[*Tafsīr al-Manār*] from the third year onward was the work of Rashīd Riḍā; it included lengthy extracts from

the commentary expounded by Muḥammad ʻAbduh in the evening lectures at al-Azhar, and the respective contributions of the two men were clearly distinguished."

92 Rida had worked on Verse 101 of the chapter of Yusuf (Joseph) at the end of his life (the chapter has 110 verses). Bahjat al-Bīṭār completed the exegesis of the chapter and published it as a booklet under Rida's name. Dhahabī, *Al-Tafsīr wa al-mufassirūn*, 567.

93 M. A. Zaki Badawi, *The Reformers of Egypt* (London: Croom Helm, 1978), 97. Badawi's overall judgment of the reformers' achievements is also negative.

94 *Tafsīr al-Manār*, Vol. 1, 91–102.

95 A typology of *tafsīr*s was proposed in Kosugi Yasushi, "Typological Inquiries into Exegesis of the Qurʼan: An Introduction to Tafsīr Studies," *The Toyo Gakuho* 76/1–2 (1994): 85–111 [in Japanese]. This was the first detailed study on the topic in Japanese.

96 Mustansir MIR, "The *Sūra* as a unity: A Twentieth Century Development in Qurʼan Exegesis," in G. R. Hawting and Abdul-Kader A. Shareef, eds, *Approaches to the Qurʼān* (London and New York: Routledge, 1993), 211–212.

97 Ibid., 212–217. Among the 6 *tafsīr*s listed, 3 were written in Arabic, namely, by Sayyid Quṭb, ʻIzzat Darwaza, both Egyptian, and Muḥammad Ḥusayn al-Ṭabāṭabāʼī, an Iranian.

98 Shiḥāta, *Manhaǧ al-Imām Muḥammad*, 36.

99 Shihāb al-Dīn al-Ālūsī, *Rūḥ al-mʻānī fī tafsīr al-Qurʼān al-ʻaẓīm wa al-sabʻ almathānī* (Beirut: Dār al-Fikr, 1978). See also Basheer M. Nafi, "Abu al-Thanaʼ al-Alusi: An Alim, Ottoman Mufti, and Exegete of the Qurʼan," *International Journal of Middle Eastern studies* 34 (2002): 482–486.

100 *Al-Manār* revived certain classical works. Rida's trust in and reliance on Ibn Kathīr among the classical *tafsīr*s (see, Shiḥāta, *Manhaǧ al-Imām Muḥammad*, 214–226) seems to be instructive in the popularity of Ibn Kathir's exegesis among today's Islamic activists with the Salafi inclination in the Arab countries.

101 Ṭantāwī Jawharī, *Al-Ǧawāhir fī Tafsīr al-Qurʼān al-Karīm* (Cairo: Muṣṭafā al-Ḥalabī, n.d.). This work was among the study materials for the Brotherhood members during al-Banna's time.

102 Aḥmad Muṣṭafā al-Marāghī, *Tafsīr al-Marāghī*, 5th ed. (Cairo: Muṣṭafā al-Ḥalabī, 1974).

103 Maḥmūd Shaltūt, *Tafsīr al-Qurʼān al-Karīm*, 7th ed. (Beirut and Cairo: Dār al-Shurūq, 1979).

104 Muḥammad al-Ṭāhir b. ʻĀšūr, *Tafsīr al-Taḥrīr wa al-Tanwīr* (Tunis: Al-Dār al-Tūnisiyya, 1984).

105 ʻAbd al-Ḥamīd b. Muḥammad b. Bādīs, *Tafsīr Ibn Bādīs fī al-Tadhkīr min Kalām al-Ḥakīm al-Ḫabīr* (Beirut: Dār al-Kutub al-ʻIlmiyya, 1995).

106 For al-Qāsimī, see David Dean Commins, *Islamic Reform: Politics and Social Change in Late Ottoman Syria* (New York and Oxford: Oxford University Press, 1990).

107 Muḥammad Ǧamāl al-Dīn al-Qāsimī, *Tafsīr al-Qāsimī al-musammā Maḥāsin al-Taʼwīl*, 2nd ed. (Beirut: Dār al-Fikr, 1978), vol. 10, 3. Originally in *al-Manār*, 17 (1914): 558.

108 Sayyid Quṭb, *Fī Ẓilāl al-Qurʼān* (Beirut: Dār al-Shurūq, 1973–1974).

109 Sayed Quṭb, *In the Shade of the Qurʼān*, vols 1–11 [out of the total 18 vols], trans. Adil Salahi and Ashur Shamis (Leicester: Islamic Foundation, 1999–2004). Vol. 30 of the work (exegesis of the thirtieth volume of the Qurʼan) was translated and published in English in 1979.

110 Aḥmad Rāʼif, "Tafsīr al-Manār" (the publisher's introduction), in Muḥammad Rašīd Riḍā, ed. *Tafsīr al-Manār*, No.1 (Cairo: Al-Zahrāʼ li-l-Iʻlām al-ʻArabī, 1991), 7–8.

111 Saʻīd Ḥawwā, *Al-Asās fī al-Tafsīr* (Cairo: Dār al-Salām, 1989) [The first ed.: 1985].

112 Wahba al-Zuḥaylī, *Al-Tafsīr al-Munīr fī al-'Aqīda wa al-Sharī'a wa al-Manhağ* (Beirut: Dār al-Fikr al-Mu'āṣir and Damascus: Dār al-Fikr, 1991); al- Zuḥaylī, *Al-Tafsīr al-Wasīṭ* (Damascus: Dār al-Fikr, 2001).

113 Muḥammad Sayyid Ṭanṭāwī, *Al-Tafsīr al-Wasīṭ li-l- Qur'ān al-Karīm* (Cairo: Dār al-Ma'ārif, 1992). Tantawi has been active in innovative interpretations on contemporary issues, though often controversial.

114 Hamid Enayat, *Modern Islamic Political Thought: The Response of the Shī'ī and Sunnī Muslims to the Twentieth Century* (Basingstoke and London: Macmillan, 1982), 52–53.

115 Muḥammad Rašīd Riḍā, "Al-Aḥkām al-šar'iyya al-muta'allaqa bi-l-ḫilāfa al-Islāmiyya," *al-Manār* 23 (1922): 729–752; 24 (1923): 33–67; "Al-Ḫilāfa al-Islāmiyya," *al-Manār* 23 (1922): 98–120, 185–200, 257–271, 345–373; "Fātiḥa kitāb al-ḫilāfa, aw al-imāma al-'uẓmā," *al-Manār* 23 (1922): 459–465. It was published as *al-Ḫilāfa, aw al-imāma al-'uẓmā* (Caliphate, or, the Supreme Leadership) by *al-Manār* Press in 1341 A.H. (1923). Printed on the title page, it was "presented to the courageous Turkish people and the reform party in Arab and Indian countries and the rest of Islamic peoples." It was translated in the West in French. *Le Califat dans la doctrine de Rašīd Riḍā: Traduction annotée d'al-Ḫilāfa au al-Imāma al-'uẓma (Le Califat ou l'Imamat suprême)*, trans. Henri Laoust (Beirut: Institut français de Damas, 1938). It has detailed notes (pp. 243–274), but omits the introduction that Rida wrote at the end of the serialization ("Fātiḥa kitāb al-ḫilāfa, aw al-imāma al-'uẓmā" earlier). An annotated Japanese translation, partially abridged, was published in 1987. Rashid Rida, *Modern Islamic Theory of Governance*, trans. Kosugi Yasushi (Niigata: Graduate School of International Relations, International University of Japan, 1987).

116 This is a summary from the author's study on Rida's work, Yasushi Kosugi, "Al-Manarists on the Islamic State," *Bulletin of the Graduate School of International Relations* 3 (1985): 35–53 [in Japanese]. See Enayat, *Modern Islamic Political Thought*, 70–83, for another version. This author sees Rida's work from a longer perspective, more positive than Enayat, as the summary here shows.

117 A notable exception is Ḥizb al-Taḥrīr (Liberation Party, or commonly known as Islamic Liberation Party), established in 1949 by a Palestinian, Taqī al-Dīn al-Nabhānī (d. 1977). It aims at establishing the *khilafa* (Caliphate) as an ideal Islamic polity. See Taqī al-Dīn al-Nabhānī, *Al-Ḫilāfa* (Ḥizb al-Taḥrīr, n.d.).

118 Abu'l-Hasan Al-Mawardi, *Al-Ahkam As-Sultaniyyah: The Laws of Islamic Governance*, trans. Asadullah Yate (London: Ta-Ha Publishers, 1996); Hamilton A.R. Gibb, "Al-Mawardi's Theory of the Caliphate," in Stanford J. Shaw and William R. Polk, eds, *Studies on the Civilization of Islam* (London: Routledge & Kegan Paul, 1962), 151–165.

119 Abū Ya'lā al-Farrā', *Al-Aḥkām al-Sulṭāniyya*, ed. Muḥammad Ḥāmid al-Faqī, 3rd ed. (Cairo: Muṣṭafā al-Ḥalabī, 1983); Yūsuf Ībish and Kosugi Yasushi, eds, *Qirā'āt fī al-fikr al-siyāsī al-Islāmī* (Beirut: Dār Amwāğ, 2000), 151–211.

120 Aḥmad b. 'Alī al-Qalqašandī, *Ma'āthir al-ināfa fī ma'ālim al-ḫilāfa*, ed. 'Abd al-Sattār Aḥmad Farrāğ (Kuwait: Wizāra al-Iršād wa al-Anbā', 1964); Ībish and Kosugi, eds, *Qirā'āt*, 315–342.

121 For the Sunni political theories of the classical periods, see Ībish and Kosugi, eds, *Qirā'āt*. For the entire spectrum of Islamic political thought from the eighth to the twentieth centuries, please consult a collection of primary sources in Yūsuf Ībish and Kosugi Yasushi, eds, *Turāth al-fikr al- siyāsī al- Islāmī* (Beirut: Turāth, 2005).

122 J. M. S. Baljon, *Modern Muslim Koran Interpretation* (1880–1960) (Leiden: E. J. Brill, 1961), 104. Baljon quoted from Rida's *al-Waḥy al-Muḥammadī*, whose small section on governance is based on *al-Ḫilāfa* and *Tafsīr al-Manār*. See Muḥammad Rašīd Riḍā, *al-Waḥy al-Muḥammadī*, 3rd ed. (Beirut: Mu'assasa 'Izz al-Dīn, 1406 AH [1985/6], 287–291 (The first edition: 1352 AH [1933/4]).

123 Kerr, *Islamic Reform*, 220.

124 Riḍā, "Al-Ḫilāfa al-Islāmiyya," *Al-Manār* 24 (1923): 372–373.
125 John O. Voll, "Fundamentalism in the Sunni Arab World: Egypt and the Sudan," in Martin E. Marty and R. Scott Appleby, eds, *Fundamentalisms Observed* (Chicago, IL and London: University of Chicago Press, 1991), 358.
126 Kerr, *Islamic Reform*, 221.
127 Ibid., 2.
128 For the revived Brotherhood and its activities, Yokota Takayuki made an important contribution based on field work in his PhD dissertation, *An Islamic Mass Movement in Contemporary Egypt: The Thought and Practice of the Muslim Brotherhood* (Graduate School of Asian and African Area Studies, Kyoto University, Japan, 2005) [in Japanese].
129 Mahmoud Haddad, "Arab Religious Nationalism in the Colonial Era: Reading Rashīd Riḍā's Ideas on the Caliphate," *Journal of the American Oriental Society* 117/2 (1997): 253–277. The main focus is on Henri Laoust, Malcolm Kerr, and Hamid Enayat.
130 Ibid., 277.
131 Muḥammad Bāqir al-Ṣadr, "Uṭrūḥa al-marğa'iyya al-mawḍū'iyya," in Muḥammad al-Ḥusaynī, ed., *Al-Imām al-šahīd al-sayyid Muḥammad Bāqir al-Ṣadr: Dirāsa fī sīratihi wa manhağihi* (Beirut: Dār al-Furāt, 1989), 383–390. An annotated Japanese translation of this short treatise was published with al-Sadr's other political treatises. Kosugi Yasushi, ed. and tr., *Revolution and State in Islam: Political Thought of the Contemporary Arab Shi'ites* (Niigata: The Institute of Middle Eastern Studies at International University of Japan, 1992). For al-Sadr, see Ḥusayn Baraka al-Shāmī *et al.*, *Muḥammad Bāqir al-Ṣadr: Dirāsa fī ḥayātihi wa fikrihi* (London: Dar al-Islam Foundation, 1996).
132 Chibli Mallat, *The Renewal of Islamic Law: Muhammad Baqer as-Sadr, Najaf and the Shi'i International* (Cambridge: Cambridge University Press, 1993), 59–78.
133 Haddad, "Arab Religious Nationalism in the Colonial Era," 274.
134 For Arab secularists in the nineteenth and early twentieth centuries, see Azzam Tamimi, "The Origins of Arab Secularism," in John L. Esposito and Azzam Tamimi, eds, *Islam and Secularism in the Middle East* (London: Hurst, 2000), 13–28.
135 Rīḍā, "Al-Aḥkām al-šar'iyya," *al-Manār* 24 (1923): 62–65.
136 Hourani, *Arabic Thought in the Liberal Age 1798–1939*, 242–243. Though a good summary, to translate the moderate Islamic reform party as "progressive" seems misleading. Basheer criticizes Hourani for his locating these positions as merely responses to the Western challenge (Nafi, "The Rise of Islamic Reformist Thought," 29–30). While Basheer's emphasis on the "inner impulses" is quite agreeable, we can still see Rida's own categorization as defining the positions in relation to Islam as he conceived.
137 See Kerr, *Islamic Reform*, 209–223.
138 It goes without saying that the very concept and contents of what modernity constitutes change. Here the author uses the term to mean both modern in the historical sense and modern as the "contemporary," thus including even what some would like to distinguish as "post-modern."
139 Nafi, "The Rise of Islamic Reformist Thought," 52.
140 See the debates in Nissim Rejwan "A Wild Goose Chase: To Cope, Must Islam 'westernize'?" in Michael J. Thompson, ed., *Islam and the West: Critical Perspective on Modernity* (Lanham: Rowman & Littlefield, 2003), 153–182.
141 See, for example, John Cooper, Ronald Nettler, and Muhammad Mahmoud, eds, *Islam and Modernity: Muslim Intellectuals Respond* (London: I. B. Tauris, 1998); Johan Meuleman, ed., *Islam in the Era of Globalization: Muslim Attitudes towards Modernity and Identity* (London: RoutledgeCurzon, 2002); Larry Diamond, Marc F. Plattner,

and Daniel Brumberg, eds, *Islam and Democracy in the Middle East* (Baltimore, MD and London: Johns Hopkins University Press, 2003); Akbar S. Ahmad, *Postmodernism and Islam: Predicament and Promise*, revised ed. (London and New York: Routledge, 2004).

142 On the Japanese model, or a non-Western path of modernity, the author is in debt to works by Murakami Yasusuke, Tsunoyama Sakae, and other pioneers in theoretical investigations on the Japanese paradigm. See Murakami Yasusuke, "Modernization in Terms of Integration: The Case of Japan," in S. N. Eisenstadt, ed., *Patterns of Modernity, II: Beyond the West* (New York: New York University Press, 1987), 65–88.; Murakami Y. and Kosai Yutaka, eds, *Japan in the Global Community: Its Role and Contribution on the Eve of the 21st Century* (Tokyo: Round Table Discussions on Japan in the Global Community, distributed by the University of Tokyo Press, 1986); Murakami Y., *An Anticlassical Political-Economic Analysis: A Vision for the Next Century*, trans. Yamaura Kozo (Stanford, CA: Stanford University Press, 1996). See also Kosugi Yasushi, "Tradition and Modernization: Reflections on Islam and Confucianism in Japan," in Osman Bakar and Cheng Gek Nai, eds, *Islam and Confucianism: A Civilizational Dialogue* (Kuala Lumpur: University of Malaya Press, 1997), 163–171.

143 Muhammad Rashid Rida, "Renewal, Renewing, and Renewers," trans. Emad Eldin Shahin in Kurzman, ed., *Modernist Islam*, 78.

144 Mahathir Mohamad, *Islam and the Muslim Ummah: Selected Speeches by Dr Mahathir Mohamad, Prime Minister of Malaysia*, ed. Hashim Makaruddin (Selengor Darul Ehsan, Malaysia: Pelanduk Publications, 1995), Vol. 1, 51.

145 On the Salafiyya in Syria, see an excellent work of Commins, *Islamic Reform*.

146 The other most important Sunni trend of Islamic revival, parallel to the Manarists and the Muslim Brotherhood, is the line of Iqbal, Mawdudi, and Jamaat-i Islami in South Asia, which despite its importance is out of scope of this article, and left untouched.

147 Nafi, *The Rise of Islamic Reformist Thought*, 40.

148 "Al-Bayān al-ta'sīsī li-l-Ittiḥād al-'Ālamī li-l-'Ulamā' al-Muslimīn," July 11, 2004, made available to the author by the secretariat.

149 Al-Banna's father was an Azhar scholar, and education at home was not secular.

150 Mawil Izzi Dien, *Islamic Law: From Historical Foundations to Contemporary Practice* (Edinburgh: Edinburgh University Press, 2004), 145.

151 Yūsuf Al-Qaraḍāwī, *Al-ṣaḥwa al-Islāmiyya bayna al-ǧuḥūd wa al-taṭarruf*, 2nd ed. (Cairo: Dār al-Shurūq, 1984), 28.

152 Yūsuf al-Qaraḍāwī, *Fatāwā Mu'āṣira*, 2 vols (Beirut, Damascus, and Amman: Al-Maktab al-Islāmī, 2000). He is also active in the European Council for Fatwa and Research as its president. See European Council for Fatwa and Research, *Fatwas of European Council for Fatwa and Research*, trans. Anas Osama Altikriti and Shakir Nasir Al-Utaydi (Cairo: Dār al-Ṭibā'a wa al-Nashr al-Islāmiyya, n.d.).

153 Yūsuf al-Qaraḍāwī, *Al-Fatwā bayna al-inḍibāt wa al-tasayyub*, 3rd ed. (Cairo: Dār al-Ṣaḥwa, 1992), 17–18.

154 Yūsuf al- Qaraḍāwī, "Kalima al-iftitāḥ," Mu'tamar al-Ittiḥād al-'Ālamī li-l-'Ulamā' al-Muslimīn, July 11, 2004, provided by the secretariat to the author.

2

AL-MANĀR AND POPULAR RELIGION IN SYRIA, 1898–1920

David D. Commins

On July 23, 1898 a Damascene subscriber to the Islamic modernist journal *al-Manār* wrote a letter to the editor complaining that the journal had ceased to appear for several weeks because the censor's office had confiscated copies of recent issues. In a comment on this letter, Rashid Rida, the journal's publisher, noted that the governors in Beirut and Damascus had banned the publication.[1] Years later, Rida reported that Ottoman authorities in Beirut and in Tripoli had banned the second issue published in 1898, on the orders of the sultan's religious advisor, Abu al-Huda al-Sayyadi, who knew that Rida was an admirer of the modernist figure Jamal al-Din al-Afghani (who had died in Istanbul the previous year).[2] Affirmation of Istanbul's alarm at Rida's enterprise comes from Russian and German diplomatic sources reporting in 1899 that Sultan Abdülhamid II was upset at Egyptian Khedive ʿAbbas Hilmi for allegedly sponsoring *al-Manār*'s publication.[3]

Why did the Ottoman authorities banish a religious reform periodical? Because under Sultan Abdülhamid (r. 1876–1909), religious issues were enmeshed with political controversy. *Al-Manār*'s mission of reforming Muslim beliefs and practices interfered with Ottoman efforts to establish an official version of Sunni Islam that would strengthen the sultan's authority. Part of these efforts included support for popular Sufism whereas Rida's journal called on Muslims to abandon such Sufism in the name of a return to Islam's original beliefs and practices. This oppositional stance was not coincidental. *Al-Manār* was part of a struggle over who had the authority to define proper religious practice, and that struggle naturally spilled over into Ottoman political battles. The present essay assesses the effectiveness of *al-Manār* in those struggles by examining the extent and limits of its influence in Syria. To properly situate the journal in its context, I first examine the place of popular religion as a pillar of Abdülhamid's power. I then consider *al-Manār's* opposition to the sultan and his religious policy, its function as a platform and arena for religious reformers, and measures of the journal's impact in Syria.

Politics and popular religion

M. Şükrü Hanioğlu's study of the Young Turks has demonstrated the breadth of opposition to Sultan Abdülhamid's regime throughout the Ottoman provinces during the 1890s, and that opposition's particular strength in Syria.[4] The Committee of Union and Progress established branches in several cities and towns between 1895 and 1897. Disgruntled military officers, civil officials, ulama, Sufis, and notables joined the underground movement, but its plan for a *coup d'état* launched from Syria was aborted when authorities uncovered it and ordered mass arrests. Such political threats from the activities and propaganda of constitutional forces had been worrying the sultan for a number of years, and it was, in part, to counter his critics that he embraced an Islamic policy to wrap his throne in the banner of religion. Perhaps the best known individual associated with that policy's implementation was the sultan's controversial Syrian adviser, Shaykh Abu al-Huda al-Sayyadi, whose prominence made him a target for religious reformers' attacks.

Controversy swirled around Sayyadi for two reasons: his power and his support for popular Sufism. He rose from humble circumstances in northern Syria to a position of tremendous influence in the sultan's court. His means to advancement appear to have included a charismatic personality, a knack for poetry, a fine singing voice, and a talent for ingratiating himself with the powerful. He took his first step in his climb to influence when he approached the mufti of Aleppo and asked to be appointed *naqīb al-ašrāf* (head of descendants of the Prophet) in the nearby Jisr al-Shaghur district.[5] Sayyadi was able to advance to other posts and ultimately made his way to Istanbul, where he made the right personal connections to gain an audience with the sultan. Abdülhamid's Islamic policy of fostering greater loyalty and support for the Ottoman sultanate depended on the allegiance of men such as al-Sayyadi, who published dozens of essays arguing for loyalty to the sultanate and adherence to religious practices and beliefs associated with popular Sufi orders.

Muhammad Salim al-Jundi, the Syrian historian of Mar'arrat al-Nu'man, Sayyadi's home district, offers a balanced assessment of this controversial figure that takes into account his influence-peddling and at the same time exonerates him from accusations of participating in the suppression of political dissent. On the former score, Sayyadi was reported to have determined that a railroad between Hama and Aleppo would not pass through Ma'arrat al-Nu'man, whose inhabitants desired its passage in order to revive local commerce, but through the village his brother resided in.[6] On another occasion, Sayyadi is supposed to have arranged the acquittal of a good friend who had committed a murder before a number of witnesses.[7] On the other hand, Jundi maintained that suspicions that he operated an extensive network of spies were unfounded. Jundi concluded that Sayyadi did not involve himself in the sultan's dealings with political opponents; rather, he sought to increase his following and to raise the status of the Rifa'iyya Sufi order above all others. He did use influence to get jobs for imams, muezzins, and other religious personnel; he forged a noble ancestry to get ahead; but he was loyal to the sultan and treated his followers well. In this view, Sayyadi's critics envied him and they had little legitimate ground for their complaints.[8] Envy there may well have been in abundance among men living in exile because, they believed, of Sultan Abdülhamid's repressive policies. But there was also the substantial issue of proper observance of religion, and on this point, Sayyadi stood for religious practices that had long been viewed with suspicion by ulama associated with the shari'a-minded Sufism that was present at the birth of religious reform in Syria.[9]

The first religious reformer to clash with Sayyadi was Jamal al-Din "al-Afghani" Asadabadi. Their initial encounter, however, was not at all contentious. In fact, it arose from Sultan Abdülhamid's effort to increase the prestige of his religious entourage by recruiting Afghani, and thereby buttress his campaign to be recognized as caliph.[10] Sayyadi played a part in the sultan's efforts to persuade Afghani to relocate from London to Istanbul in 1892. First, the sultan made an attempt through the Ottoman ambassador to London to convince the activist to take up residence in Istanbul, but to no effect. Abdülhamid then instructed Sayyadi to correspond with Afghani. It is not clear if two letters from the shaykh or other factors were the cause, but Afghani indeed decided to move to the Ottoman capital, perhaps from a hope that Sultan Abdülhamid might lead Muslim resistance to European encroachments. In Istanbul, Jamal al-Din initially got along quite well with the sultan and his Syrian advisor.[11] At some point in 1895, however, Sayyadi's opinion of Jamal al-Din became less sympathetic: he charged him with expressing heretical ideas, and he helped persuade the sultan that the activist was in fact dangerous.[12] Furthermore, Sayyadi is reported to have used his influence to thwart an effort by Afghani to release from prison some of his Iranian associates suspected of subverting the Qajar shah's regime.[13] Sayyadi also called into question Jamal al-Din's claim to be Afghan and indicated that he was in reality from Iran.[14]

Tensions between Sayyadi and Jamal al-Din appear to have fueled the enmity expressed by members of the religious reform camp toward Sayyadi. For instance, 'Abd al-Qadir al-Maghribi, a reformer and journalist from Lebanese Tripoli, apparently became a critic of the sultan's confidant as a result of Jamal al-Din's influence. Maghribi's background included attendance at the National School (*al-Madrasa al-Waṭaniyya*) founded by Shaykh Husayn al-Jisr, himself a precursor to the reform movement's attention to the need for Muslims to reconcile scientific advances with religious understanding of the natural world. At Jisr's school, Maghribi met another youth from Tripoli, Rashid Rida. Maghribi would frequently receive forbidden Egyptian newspapers through the consular mail and share them with Rida. Maghribi's first awareness of Afghani came from hearing the principal of Beirut's Sultaniyya School praise *The Firmest Bond*, published in 1884 (when Maghribi and Rida were 17 and 19 years old, respectively). The youth was so impressed by the reformist publication that he copied a number of articles by hand. In 1892, he traveled to Istanbul and met Jamal al-Din, who had himself just arrived there. On returning to Tripoli, he took to teaching the reformist opinions of Jamal al-Din and Muhammad ʿAbduh. He later became known as a critic of Sayyadi, supposedly because the sultan levied a special tax in Aleppo in order to pay for embellishing the tomb of Sayyadi's father,[15] but perhaps out of loyalty to Afghani.

Al-Manār's opposition to Sultan Abdülhamid and popular Sufism

Rida's early admiration for Afghani is well-known, as is his intention for *al-Manār* to serve as a pan-Islamic organ for the views of ʿAbduh.[16] In the journal's early years, the connection between opposition to the sultan and Sayyadi was evident when Rida published a full review in 1901 of ʿAbd al-Rahman al-Kawakibi's essay, *The Characteristics of Tyranny* (*Ṭabāyiʿ al-istibdād*), a scathing attack on the Hamidian regime.[17] The following year, Rida published the Aleppan author's next treatise for fundamental political and religious reform, *Mother of Cities* (*Umm al-qurā*), in serial form.[18] According to Albert Hourani, Kawakibi's attacks on the sultan and popular religion stemmed from personal animosity toward Sayyadi that arose from competition between his family and Sayyadi's for religious influence in Aleppo.[19] Rida reiterated support for Kawakibi's views in a laudatory obituary for him entitled, "Great Loss: On the Death of the Wise Scholar," where Rida described his delight at having become acquainted with him in Egypt during the previous two years, and he mentioned the essay on tyranny as a splendid work.[20]

Yet another Syrian associate of Rida's, ʿAbd al-Hamid al-Zahrawi, combined political opposition to the sultan with calls for religious reform. *Al-Manār*'s obituary on him summarizes this facet of his life.[21] Zahrawi's first effort was the underground publication of a journal in his hometown of Homs some time around 1895.[22] According to Rida, the journal was part of an effort by the Committee of Union and Progress (CUP) to save the Ottoman Empire from misrule by the sultan.[23] It addressed the question of Muslim leadership (*imāma*), the qualifications for leadership, the duty to depose an unjust leader (*imām*), and a call to fight tyranny. He distributed free issues by mail, but when the authorities heard about it, they issued orders to ban it.[24] In 1902, Zahrawi left the Ottoman lands for Egypt after a number of clashes with the authorities, including the tumult occasioned by his essay on law and Sufism.[25] In Egypt, he published an article in the newspaper *al-Muʾayyad* in response to the question of whether Sultan Abdülhamid was the rightful claimant to the caliphate. Zahrawi listed twenty-two reasons why the sultan was not fit to rule and called for his deposition.[26]

Explicit political opposition among Manarists was related to frequent criticism of popular Sufism. Rida's and Zahrawi's writings on Sufism reflected both a political stance of opposition to the Hamidian regime as well as their views on proper religious observance. In Rida's case, concern with this issue long preceded his familiarity with Afghani and the broader questions of political support for certain religious forms. In his later years, Rida wrote about an incident from his youth when he witnessed the Mawlawiyya order's blending of music and dance in its ceremony, and he recalled that he openly condemned the dervishes' exercises.[27] By the time he began publishing his journal, popular Sufism was not a purely religious question because Sultan Abdülhamid's policy of fostering loyalty to Ottoman sultanate included patronage for the Rifaʿiyya order. Moreover, favoring this particular order precipitated a reaction from adherents to the rival Qadiriyya order. Hanioğlu notes that Qadiri Sufis, particularly in Hama but also in general, tended to support the CUP's efforts in Syria between 1895 and 1897.[28] When Rida launched *al-Manār* in 1898, he addressed the rivalry between the Rifaʿiyya and Qadiriyya orders. The gist of one article was that the Rifaʿi Sufis incorporated forbidden innovations (*bidʿa*) into their ceremonies. Rida cited two of Sayyadi's publications that defended the customs of snake-eating, inserting needles in one's body, and walking on hot coals in Rifaʿi ceremonies because they effectively dispel the doubts of anyone who might deny the truth of religion. To support his criticism of the Rifaʿis, Rida quoted the Baghdad scholar Shihab al-Din al-Alusi's exegesis of the Qurʾan, where he observed that the practice of Rifaʿi Sufis walking on fire demonstrated their ignorance of religion.[29] Subsequent issues of the first volume discussed the controversy between Rifaʿis and Qadiris until a truce was reported.[30]

A second Manarist critic of popular religion, ʿAbd al-Hamid al-Zahrawi, published in 1901 a scathing attack on common views of Sufism and jurisprudence. The essay itself germinated from a correspondence between Zahrawi and Rida concerning the benefit and harm of traditional jurisprudence.[31] In the essay's section on Sufism, Zahrawi went much further than Rida's criticism of specific practices associated with the Rifaʿi order. He argued that Sufism is alien to Islam and was invented two centuries after Muhammad revealed the Qurʾan.[32] He considered it to be a concoction of philosophy and a few religious texts; and he regarded most Sufis as idlers who scheme to live on the gullibility of ordinary folk.[33] Such complete rejection of Sufism was not characteristic of the views of religious reformers during that period. The elder shaykh of Damascene Salafis, ʿAbd al-Razzaq al-Bitar, assessed the essay in his biographical dictionary entry on Zahrawi. In Bitar's view, the essay was correct in some respects, but contained excessively harsh criticisms of the ulama; to widely circulate the essay was not wise because it was certain to stir up trouble. He added that he found it curious that the essay had generated a strong response from prejudiced readers who concluded that its author was a heretic who deserved to be condemned to death.[34] Likewise, when Rida reviewed the essay, he noted that its author did not present a balanced view on law and Sufism, focusing only on the latter's negative aspects. He wrote that it should not have been published because it was one-sided, even though the author had good intentions.[35] Zahrawi's untempered assault on popular Sufism most likely stemmed from his political commitments, in particular what one biographer described as his desire to denigrate Abu al-Huda al-Sayyadi for backing the sultan; it should be noted, however, that Zahrawi does not mention either one in his essay.[36]

A more moderate reformist view on Sufism is found in the works of the leading Damascene reformer, Jamal al-Din al-Qasimi.[37] He had grown up in the milieu of shari'a-minded Sufism practiced by 'Abd al-Qadir al-Jaza'iri and local branches of the Naqshbandiyya order. He observed that the proper practice of Sufism deepened the believer's religious life by cultivating habits of worship and nurturing such praiseworthy personal traits as humility and sincerity. It was possible to hold Sufi ceremonies without straying from prescribed forms of worship. At the same time, Qasimi observed that many Sufis held views that could not be reconciled with the Qur'an and the Sunna. Further, eating fire and playing music at Sufi ceremonies gave an unfavorable impression of Islam to educated youth fascinated with European culture. Qasimi also condemned a common practice associated with popular Sufism: visiting tombs to seek the intercession of saints. It was permissible, however, to visit the tombs of deceased family members to honor their memories and to pray to God.

A more balanced approach also characterized Rashid Rida's review of Sayyadi's 1906 essay on the shari'a. Rida called it the best work seen by him because it took sensible positions on questions that would benefit ordinary Muslims. In particular, Rida commended the passage on the alms tax (*zakāt*) and urged Sayyadi to use his influence with Sultan Abdülhamid to collect the tax more regularly. On the other hand, Rida did criticize the shaykh for including passages about having visions of spirits, or jinn.[38] In another issue, Rida reviewed Sayyadi's essay on the five pillars of Islam that was intended for use in Ottoman state schools. Rida opposed its adoption as a text on the grounds that it used obscure Sufi terminology.[39] It seems that no matter how the reformers appraised Sayyadi's ubiquitous works, they could not ignore them.[40]

Two main points emerge from Manarists' writings on popular Sufism. First, politics and religion clearly overlap because criticism of popular Sufism was tied to opposition to Sultan Abdülhamid and his Sufi supporters like Sayyadi. Second, Manarists expressed a range of views on Sufism, from Zahrawi's unqualified attack to a more nuanced view expressed by Qasimi. More generally, Manarists viewed popular Sufism as a problem with different dimensions. It represented a deviation from true Islam; it also represented an obstacle to technical progress. This latter point is crucial because it indicates that an instrumental concept of religion was part of the Manarist outlook. The most immediate concern of early twentieth-century Ottoman Muslims in general was to increase the empire's economic, political, and military power. The reformers claimed that the Muslim world would remain vulnerable to European domination as long as Muslims did not revive true Islam, for only such a revival would make possible scientific and technical advances. Moreover, their outlook in both religious and secular realms emphasized the vanguard role of educated elites, ulama, and scientists, leading the ignorant masses. Given this emphasis on leadership, the reformers considered the political realm to hold the key to the interlocking issues of proper religious observance and technical progress: Sultan Abdülhamid was held responsible for blocking change in both areas.

The activities and writings of the Damascene author Rafiq al-'Azm illustrate the Manarist view on connections among politics, religion, and technical progress.[41] As a young man in the early 1890s, 'Azm became attached to a circle of reformist ulama that included Tahir al-Jaza'iri and Salim al-Bukhari. According to one source, 'Azm's home became the regular meeting place for this group every Friday after the congregational prayer.[42] The religious reformers associated with Ottoman officers and officials sympathetic to the movement for restoring the constitution. 'Azm himself joined the local branch of the CUP. When the authorities began a crackdown on constitutionalists in 1894, he moved to Egypt. Rida met 'Azm shortly after his own move to Cairo, and the two men developed a long and deep association on the basis of their common interest in social and political reform. They joined with Turks, Armenians, and Circassians residing in Egypt to found the Ottoman Consultation Society.[43] 'Azm served as the society's treasurer and Rida as head of the administrative council. When the society published a newspaper in 1907, 'Azm edited the Arabic portion. The society was disbanded following the 1908 constitutional revolution after 'Azm visited Istanbul and joined the CUP in order to unify the empire's constitutional forces.

One of the central ideas in 'Azm's writings is the primacy of knowledge as the basis of nations' power and wealth. This idea had become the widely accepted explanation for European domination over the Muslim world. 'Azm expressed the common modernist view that it was necessary for Muslims to catch up with Europeans in medicine, chemistry, mathematics, and engineering.[44] It is noteworthy that in *al-Manār*'s first volume, 'Azm published a short piece in which he argued that Sultan Abdülhamid's regime was to blame for the Ottoman Empire's backwardness in these fields because its censorship and suppression of scholarly societies perpetuated the empire's weakness and vulnerability.[45] A decade later, following the constitutional restoration in 1908, 'Azm saw an opportunity to remedy the recently deposed sultan's neglect of education, economic development, technical modernization, and efficiency.[46] The connection between 'Azm's modernist agenda and other writers' critique of popular religion may not be evident at first sight. But the two themes do share the intellectual elitism, one technical and potentially secular, the other scriptural and religious, that characterized the sultan's political opponents in the Committee of Union and Progress and in the Syrian religious reform camp.[47]

Al-Manār as a platform and arena for religious reform

Rida's journal served the cause of religious reform in three ways: by publishing the works of various authors; by reviewing reformers' books and essays; and by spreading the reputation of reformers in obituary notices. Among the most famous essays to appear in *al-Manār* were those by 'Abd al-Rahman al-Kawakibi. In a similar fashion, 'Abd al-Hamid al-Zahrawi's book on Muhammad's first wife, Khadija, appeared in *al-Manār* in serial form, and 'Azm put out portions of his own writings in his friend's periodical.[48] Reviews of reformers' works included

Tahir al-Jaza'iri's school primer on theology. The review served as an occasion to tout Jaza'iri to the journal's widespread audience as the most famous scholar and advocate of reform in Syria.[49] Rida also highlighted the writings of Jamal al-Din al-Qasimi with reviews of his works on topics not always directly related to religious reform, such as health (tea, coffee, tobacco).[50] A single review published in 1911 examined four of Qasimi's publications that give an idea of the range of concerns in the reform movement.[51] One essay represented the impulse to revive the classical heritage by publishing the eighth century hijri Shafi'i scholar al-Zirkishi's treatise on jurisprudence, philosophy, and logic. A second work introduced readers to religious duties; a third argued for using independent legal reasoning (*Iğtihād*) to support the use of the telegraph in declaring the beginning and end of Ramadan; the fourth essay under review was a summary of the history and nature of the fatwa. Other works by Qasimi that were reviewed included *Proofs of God's Unity* (theology),[52] *The Opinions of Arabs on Jinns* (literary history),[53] *The Balance of Judging Prophetic Traditions Sources* (legal theory),[54] *Wiping the Socks and the Soles* (ritual practice),[55] and *Sermons*.[56]

Besides publishing and reviewing reformers' works, Rida spread reformers' reputations through obituary notices. An issue in March 1905 announced the death of 'Abd al-Baqi al-Afghani, a Peshawar-born *'ālim* who had lived in India, Hijaz, and Syria.[57] Rida published extensive notices on Jamal al-Din al-Qasimi,[58] 'Abd al-Hamid al-Zahrawi,[59] 'Abd al-Razzaq al-Bitar,[60] Rafiq al-'Azm,[61] and Salim al-Bukhari.[62] A proper obituary for Tahir al-Jaza'iri did not appear, it would seem, because of some falling out between him and Rida. There is, however, a review of a biography of Jaza'iri written by one of his admirers, Muhammad Said al-Bani.[63] According to this review, Bani's biography inaccurately depicts Jaza'iri and inflates his importance. The review credits him with knowledge of numerous manuscripts and acknowledges his role in spreading government schools and founding public libraries in the 1870s and 1880s. At the same time, the review portrays him as stubborn, narrow-minded, and quarrelsome. He possessed neither great learning nor a talent for teaching. It seems, then, that Rida's journal could also convey splits within the reform camp and shifts from earlier estimations, recalling that years earlier Rida had called Jaza'iri a leading reformer and scholar.

Perhaps the most elusive facet of *al-Manār*'s role in Islamic reform in Syria is the ways that readers responded to and used the journal.[64] Jamal al-Din al-Qasimi's library in Damascus contains evidence of how he used the journal in developing and forming his ideas.[65] A copy of his *Proofs of God's Unity* contains his handwritten notes citing an opinion of Muhammad 'Abduh's, published by *al-Manār*, to support ideas in his own essay.[66] In this instance, Qasimi finds new evidence in Rida's journal to bolster a work that he had already published and that Rida had reviewed.[67] The review explains to readers that Qasimi referred to 'Abduh in the work without referring to him by name but by describing him as "a recent sage" (*ḥakīm min al-muta'aḫḫirīn*) and that he drew on Rida's journal when he cited "certain men." Rida also noted that Qasimi did not mention Rida's or 'Abduh's name because he composed the work when Sultan Abdülhamid was still in power, when their mention could incur persecution.[68]

Al-Manār was also embedded in a web of exchanges on the Shiʿi practice of cursing Muʿawiya. The exchanges appear to have begun with Rida's fatwa against the practice. A Singapore reformer of Hadramawt origins, Muhammad ibn ʿAqil, wrote to Rida and informed him that he intended to collect and publish in an essay the opinions of traditionists and historians who found fault with Muʿawiya for opposing ʿAli and who argued that Muʿawiya could not be regarded as a trustworthy source of Prophetic traditions.[69] Rida advised against this, and he urged Ibn ʿAqil not to exaggerate differences of opinion on an issue that is not a fundamental aspect of religion.[70] The Singapore reformer went ahead with his project anyway. We learn how Qasimi became involved in this issue from notes he recorded in the margin on his copy of the title page of his own essay on the subject. Ibn ʿAqil sent Qasimi a copy of his essay, perhaps in draft form. Qasimi then wrote to a Meccan scholar, ʿAbd-Allah al-Zawawi, inquiring about Ibn ʿAqil, and his Meccan friend replied that the man was a studious scholar-merchant who had composed an essay on Muʿawiya that differed from Rida's view. Qasimi wrote some observations on the essay, probably criticisms, because Ibn ʿAqil then wrote again. In this letter, he asked for the reformer's indulgence for his mistakes because he was very occupied with his trade and there were very few books in his part of the world.[71] In addition to the notes that Qasimi made on his essay, his published biography reproduces a number of letters in which he mentioned this issue. He wrote to a friend in Jeddah, Muhammad Nasif, describing Ibn ʿAqil's essay as one written in a fine style and with sound reasoning. Qasimi stated, however, that he did not wish to revive the feud between ʿAli and Muʿawiya because it opened the door for degrading ancestors who related Hadiths from Muʿawiya and his companions. So he told his correspondent that he wrote to Ibn ʿAqil and stated that he would rather promote moderation, evidently to avoid aggravating tensions between Sunni and Shiʿi Muslims.[72]

A more public form of reaction came out when Ibn ʿAqil's essay was published. Rida issued a notice, but not a review, about it, in which he observed that the essay had created a controversy among Muslims in Singapore and Java, and that readers were soliciting Rida's opinion of the essay. He commented that he opposed the practice of cursing Muʿawiya, but preferred not to discuss the essay and advised Muslims excited over the issue not to go overboard in attacking each others' opinions.[73] The matter did not end there, however. Qasimi then composed and published an essay pointing out what he considered to be mistakes in Ibn ʿAqil's essay. The reformer wrote that he intended his essay to set out an alternative point of view, but not to discredit Ibn ʿAqil, whose work he credited for displaying the author's broad knowledge and independent use of reason (*iǧtihād*, but not in the technical legal sense).[74]

Rida described Qasimi's essay in the context of a piece on the entire controversy. He noted that a certain Sayyid Hasan ibn Shihab had written an essay refuting Ibn ʿAqil. Rida suggested that Ibn Shihab envied Ibn ʿAqil's scholarly status among fellow Hadramis in Singapore and nearby parts, so he composed his refutation to gain the support of ulama in a contest with Ibn ʻAqil. There followed a rebuttal of this work by a certain Shaykh Abu Bakr ibn Shihab, a teacher in Hyderabad, whom Rida termed the most famous living Hadrami scholar. For readers seeking an exemplary way to respond to Ibn ʻAqil's points, Rida recommended Qasimi's essay for its balanced critique and the moderate tone it adopted in expressing disagreement with Ibn ʻAqil. It was particularly noteworthy that Qasimi recognized certain merits in the essay. Rida concluded that if all controversial issues were addressed in such a style and tone, then Muslims would not suffer from such deep divisions.[75] That Qasimi and his friend Muhammad Nasif remained concerned with the issue is reflected in their correspondence. Qasimi wrote to Nasif in January 1911 reporting that a new essay had come out in Singapore rebutting Ibn ʻAqil.[76] The following month, Qasimi informed Nasif that he had recently seen a reference to a speech by ʻAli forbidding anyone to curse Muʻawiya. The reformer then wrote that he wished he had seen that particular reference before so he could have included it in his essay.[77] Three years later, Qasimi received a letter from a Kuwaiti scholar announcing the completion of yet another rebuttal to Ibn ʻAqil's essay, one that incorporated some of Qasimi's observations.[78]

The entire episode illustrates two aspects of *al-Manār*'s influence. First, it served as a platform for debating issues of concern to men versed in Islamic history and religious sources. By coming out at regular intervals in printed form, the journal represented a new kind of more widely disseminated expression of venerable conversations among Muslims on a range of religious matters: ritual, law, theology, history, heresiography, exegesis, and so forth. Second, the journal's articles were part of public and private conversations carried on through book publishing, private correspondence, and notations in personal copies of essays. A clue to the limits of the journal's influence is embedded in the requisite literacy and interest in these kinds of issues as well as to its disdain for expressions of popular religion.

Gauging *al-Manār*'s influence

That Rida's journal made only limited headway in winning Muslims of Syria to its point of view may be inferred from a singular incident and from the association between Manarist views and Amir Faysal in the immediate postwar years. The singular incident occurred when Rashid Rida visited Damascus in October 1908, three months after the constitutional restoration that he had long favored and striven for.[79] During his visit, opponents to the new constitutional regime incited a disturbance by rousing a mob against Rida and the Damascene reformers he associated with (Jamal al-Din al-Qasimi and ʻAbd al-Razzaq al-Bitar). Rida delivered a public lecture at the city's main congregational mosque on the subject of educational reform. In the course of his talk, he was asked to address a completely different issue touching on popular religious observance, namely, praying to saints at their tombs for intercession with God, which he was known to oppose.

His attempt to skirt the issue, the bold challenge to his opinion on the matter, and his quick exit from the mosque all indicate his awareness that in the court of public sentiment, the reformist position was out of favor. In fact, he was advised to leave the city at first opportunity for his own safety and for the sake of public order. It appears that a decade of publishing the reformist line had not made much of an impression in Damascus.

Yet another decade later, popular nationalism swelled in Damascus and other Syrian towns during the brief rule of Amir Faysal.[80] Historian James Gelvin paints a convincing portrait of two distinct nationalist subcultures, one popular and another elitist. The late Ottoman reformers' interest in the sciences, technology, schools, libraries, and leadership by intellectuals characterized the views of Faysal's supporters.[81] These men perpetuated the Manarists' idea of society's need for a vanguard of educated men to lead society as well as their conviction that their own educational attainments entitled them to leadership.[82] Gelvin's account shows that these themes did not strike a responsive chord beyond a small segment of educated opinion whereas the proponents of popular nationalism were able to mobilize in a brief span a significant portion of the country's urban population. One small detail reflects the continuation of disagreements between reformist and conservative ulama factions from before the First World War into the Faysali era and the alignment of these factions with elitist and popular nationalist camps, respectively. In 1911, members of the reformist faction had attended a play on a historical theme. The conservative faction's journal *al-Ḥaqā'iq* published a number of articles and readers' letters condemning theatrical performance as an innovation forbidden by Islam.[83] Eight years later, men surrounding Amir Faysal staged plays to rally patriotic feeling to his cause. Members of the popular nationalist committees, however, included in their ranks individuals opposed to theatre since the earlier controversy.[84]

Conclusion

The Manarists' failure to reshape popular religious attitudes in Syria in the journal's first twenty years cannot be blamed on censorship. Sultan Abdülhamid certainly did his utmost to minimize any impact. On the other hand, he was deposed in 1909; Syria then had nearly ten years of constitutional government and a brief period under Amir Faysal, himself surrounded by men of modernist outlook. In order to fully understand the limits on *al-Manār*'s influence, it is not sufficient to focus on its publisher, its contributors, and its sympathizers. More attention should be paid as well to the defenders of more conservative religious views, and in particular to their resonance with the values and outlook of popular urban culture. Then we would know better why Rida's message had not much altered many Muslims' notions of proper religious observance and why the sultan and the shaykh did not need to censor the journal after all.

Notes

1 *Al-Manār* 1/24 (1898): 380–382.
2 *Al-Manār* 12/1 (1909): 3. In yet another issue, Rida included *al-Manār* in a list of newspapers and books that had been banned under Sultan Abdülhamid: *al-Manār* 15 (1912): 796.
3 L. Hirszowicz, "The Sultan and the Khedive, 1892–1908," *Middle Eastern Studies* 8 (1972): 299, 309 n. 122.
4 M. Şükrü Hanioğlu, *The Young Turks in Opposition* (New York: Oxford University Press, 1995), 105–107.
5 Muḥammad Salīm al-Ǧundī, *Tārīḫ Maʿarrāt al-Nuʿmān*, 3 vols (Damascus: Ministry of Culture, Tourism, and Nationalist Guidance, 1963–1967), 2: 218. The post did not even exist at the time because the population was mostly ʿAlawi—a heterodox sect that does not concern itself with descent from the Prophet. It may be that the Ottoman authorities agreed for political reasons. Selim Deringil documents efforts under Sultan Abdülhamid II to convert heterodox sects to Sunni Islam. Sayyadi's appointment to this post preceded Abdülhamid's reign, so perhaps it had nothing to do with such a policy, or such measures were already applied. Selim Deringil, *The Well-Protected Domains: Ideology and the Legitimation of Power in the Ottoman Empire, 1876–1909* (London: I. B. Tauris, 1998), 68–84. Details on Abu al-Huda's career appear in Butrus Abu-Manneh, "Sultan Abdulhamid II and Shaikh Abulhuda al-Sayyadi," *Middle Eastern Studies* 15 (1979): 131–153.
6 Al-Ǧundī, *Tārīḫ Maʿarrāt al-Nuʿmān*, 1: 214–215.
7 Ibid., 1: 257–258.
8 Ibid., 2: 222–229; a similar view is echoed by ʿAbd al-Ḥafīẓ al-Fāṣī, *Riyāḍ al-ǧanna aw al-mudhiš al-muṭrib*, 2 vols. (Rabat: Wataniyya Press, 1932), 2: 149. Fasi wrote that Sayyadi's enemies included frustrated seekers after treasure, who were neglected by the sultan and more sincere critics of the sultan unhappy with Sayyadi's support for him.
9 On the sources of religious reform in Syria, see David Commins, *Islamic Reform: Politics and Social Change in Late Ottoman Syria* (New York: Oxford University Press, 1990), 21–48.
10 Nikki R. Keddie, *Sayyid Jamāl ad-Dīn "al-Afghānī:" A Political Biography* (Berkeley, CA: University of California Press, 1972), 380.
11 Sayyadi's letters to Afghani are paraphrased in Keddie, *Sayyid Jamāl ad-Dīn* 370; on Afghani's early relations with Sayyadi, see 372.
12 Ibid., 383.
13 Ibid., 382.
14 Albert Hourani, *Arabic Thought in the Liberal Age, 1798–1939* (London: Oxford University Press, 1970), 108, 112.
15 Sāmī Dahhān, *Qudamāʾ wa muʿāṣirūn* (Cairo: Dār al-maʿārif, 1961), 273–276; Keddie also describes Maghribi's acquaintance with Afghani, 379.
16 Hourani, *Arabic Thought in the Liberal Age*, 226–228.
17 *Al-Manār* 4/3 (1901): 105–106.
18 *Al-Manār* 5 (1902).
19 Hourani, *Arabic Thought in the Liberal Age*, 271.
20 "Asab ʿaẓīm bi wafā ʿālim ḥakīm," *al-Manār* 5/6 (1902): 237–240.
21 "Al-Sayyid ʿAbd al-Ḥamīd al-Ẓahrāwī," *al-Manār* 19/3 (1916): 169–178.
22 The title of the journal is given as *al-Minbar* by Adham al-Ǧundī in *Aʿlām al-adab wa al-fann*, 2 vols. (Damascus: Voice of Syria Press, 1954), 1: 11. Qadrī Qalʾāǧī gives the same name and writes that Zahrawi was 25 years old when he issued the journal; *al-Sābiqūn* (Beirut: Knowledge for the Millions Press, 1954), 31–32. A biographical notice by Aḥmad Nabhān al-Ḥumṣī gives the journal title as *al-Munīr*. "Tarǧama

al-Sayyid ʿAbd al-Ḥamīd ibn al-Sayyid Muḥammad Šākir ibn al-Sayyid Ibrāhīm al-Ẓahrāwī," *al-Manār* 21/3 (1919): 151. Rida's obituary notice cited earlier gives the same title.

23 "Al-Sayyid ʿAbd al-Ḥamīd al-Ẓahrāwī," 169.

24 Qalʾāǧī, *al-Sābiqūn*, 31–32; al-Ḥumṣī, "Tarǧama al-Sayyid ʿAbd al-Ḥamīd ibn al-Sayyid Muḥammad Šākir ibn al-Sayyid Ibrāḫīm al-Ẓahrāwī," *al-Manār* 21 (1919): 151.

25 On his departure to Egypt, see al-Ǧundī, *Tārīḫ Maʿarrāt al-Nuʿmān*, 1: 11; on the controversy over Zahrawi's essay, see Commins, *Islamic Reform*, 55–59.

26 Adham al-Ǧundī, *Šuhadāʾ al-ḥarb al-ʿālamiyya al-kubrā* (Damascus: Arab Press, 1970), 97.

27 Hourani, *Arabic Thought in the Liberal Age*, 225, citing Rashid Rida's *al-Manār wa al-Azhar*.

28 Hanioğlu, *The Young Turks in Opposition*, 55–56, 106–107.

29 "Al-Ḥikma al-šarʿiyya fī muḥākama al-qādiriyya wa al-rifāʿiyya," *al-Manār* 1/31 (1898): 598–601.

30 "Ǧarāʾid sūriyya al-mutaʿbada," *al-Manār* 1/32 (1898): 665–667; "al-Inṣāf min mazāyā al-ašrāf," *al-Manār* 1/33 (1898): 639–647.

31 ʿAbd al-Ḥamīd al-Zahrāwī, *al-Fiqh wa al-taṣawwuf* (Cairo: Al-Umumiyya Press, 1901): 2–11.

32 Ibid., 41–43.

33 Ibid., 61.

34 ʿAbd al-Razzāq al-Bīṭār, *Ḥilya al-bašar fī taʾrīḫ al-qarn al-ṯāliṯ ʿašar*, 3 vols. (Damascus: Arabic Language Academy, 1961–1963), 2: 792.

35 "Al-Fiqh wa al-taṣawwuf," *al-Manār* 4/21 (1902): 838–839.

36 Anwar al-Ǧundī, *Tarāǧim al-aʿlām al-muʿāṣirīn fī al-ʿālam al-islāmī* (Cairo: Anglo-Egyptian Bookshop, 1970), 215.

37 For Qasimi's views on Sufism, see Commins, *Islamic Reform*, 80–82, and the sources cited therein.

38 Review of *al-Ḥaqīqa al-bāhira fī asrār al-šarīʿa al-ṭāhira*; cited in *al-Manār* 9/4 (1906): 309–311.

39 Review of *Firqān al-qulūb*; cited in *al-Manār* 9/7 (1906): 550–552.

40 The index of Jamal al-Din al-Qasimi's personal library includes five works by Sayyadi.

41 "Rafīq al-ʿAẓm: Wafātuhu wa tarǧamatuhu," *al-Manār* 26 (1925): 288–299; additional biographical information is found in the journal of another Syrian religious reformer, Muḥibb al-Dīn al-Ḫaṭīb, "Rafīq al-ʿAẓm," *al-Zahrāʾ* 2/3–4 (1925): 224–234.

42 Al-Ḫaṭīb, "Rafīq al-ʿAẓm," 226.

43 In addition to the ʿAzm obituaries listed in n. 42, see Hasan Kayalı, *Arabs and Young Turks: Ottomanism, Arabism, and Islamism in the Ottoman Empire, 1908–1918* (Berkeley, CA: University of California Press, 1997), 46.

44 Rafīq al-ʿAẓm, *Tanbīh al-afhām ilā maṭālib al-ḥayā al-iǧtimāʿiyya wa al-islām* (Cairo: al-Mawsuʿa Press, 1900), 66–67; ʿAzm also develops this theme in *al-Durūs al-ḥikmiyya li'l-nāšiʾa al-islāmiyya* (Cairo: Al-Muʾayyad Press, 1899).

45 Rafīq al-ʿAẓm, "Man al-masʾūl (al-ḥukūma am al-šaʿb)," *al-Manār* 1/45 (1898): 866–869.

46 Rafīq al-ʿAẓm, "al-Inqilāb al-maymūn," *al-Manār* 12/5 (1909): 340–349.

47 On the intellectual elitism of the Syrian reformers, see Commins, *Islamic Reform*, 78, 87–88, 102, 143. On intellectual elitism in the Committee of Union and Progress, see Hanioğlu, *The Young Turks in Opposition*, 205–208.

48 Zahrawi's work came out in volumes 11 and 13; ʿAzm's in volume 10. Rida's journal, however, was not the only platform for publishing reformers' works, especially after the 1908 constitutional restoration. For example, the Damascene reformer Jamal al-Din al-Qasimi had a work on the traditionist al-Bukhari issued in a Sidon journal (*al-ʿIrfān* 4/1 (1912): 28–35; 4/2: 65–72; 4/3: 99–107; 4/4: 165–171), and his essay on the jurist's

opinion (fatwa) appeared in a Damascus review (*al-Muqtabas* 6/2 (1911): 89–116; 6/3: 177–197; 6/4: 275–298).

49 Review of *al-Ǧawāhir al-kalāmiyya fī al-'aqā'id al-islāmiyya, al-Manār* 5/23 (1903): 914–915. The journal also reviewed Jaza'iri's *Tawǧīh al-naẓar ilā uṣūl al-āṯār* on the Hadith sciences in *al-Manār* 15/2 (1912): 160, and called it an indispensable work.

50 Review of *Risāla fī al-šāy wa al-qahwa wa al-duḫḫān* in *al-Manār* 7/8 (1904): 313.

51 "Maṭbū'āt al-Šayḫ Muḥammad Ǧamāl al-Dīn al-Qāsimī," *al-Manār* 14/11 (1911): 870–872. The works were *Šarḥ luqṭāt al-'aǧlān, Tanbīh al-ṭālib ilā ma'rifa al-farḍ wa al-wāǧib, Iršād al-ḫalq ilā al-'amal bi ḫabar al-barq*, and *al-Fatwā fī al-Islām*.

52 *Al-Manār* 12/5 (1909): 387–388.

53 *Al-Manār* 14/3 (1911): 230, *Maḏāhib al-a'rāb*.

54 *Al-Manār* 16/1 (1913): 69, *Mīzān al-ǧarḥ wa al-ta'dīl*.

55 *Al-Manār* 18/4 (1915): 317, *al-Masḥ 'alā al-ǧawrabayn wa al-na'layn*.

56 *Al-Manār* 18/7 (1915): 556–560; 18/8: 61–634; 18/9: 692–695, *Maǧmū' ḫuṭab*.

57 *Al-Manār* 8/2 (1905): 79–80.

58 *Al-Manār* 17/7 (1914): 558–560; 17/8 (1914): 628–636.

59 "Maṣābunā bi'l-Zahrāwī wa Kaylānī," *al-Manār* 19/2 (1916): 124; 19/3 (1916): 169–178; Ḥumṣī, "Tarǧamāt al-Sayyid 'Abd al-Ḥamīd," *al-Manār* 21/3 (1919): 150–152; 21/4 (1919): 207–211.

60 Muḥammad Bahǧa al-Bīṭār, "Tarǧjama al-Šayḫ 'Abd al-Razzāq al-Bīṭār," *al-Manār* 21/6 (1919): 317–324.

61 "Rafīq al-'Aẓm: Wafātuhu wa tarǧamatuhu," *al-Manār* 26/4 (1925): 288–299.

62 "Wafā al-'allāma al-ǧalīl al-Šayḫ Salīm al-Buḫārī," *al-Manār* 29/8 (1928): 633–634.

63 Sayyid Ṣāliḥ Muḫliṣ Riḍā, *al-Manār* 22/8 (1921): 635–640.

64 Information on subscriptions would also be welcome. In a 1909 letter to a correspondent in Jeddah, Qasimi mentioned that Rida was sending him issues of the journal. Ẓāfir al-Qāsimī, *Ǧamāl al-Dīn al-Qāsimī wa 'aṣruhu* (Damascus: al-Hashimiyya Press, 1965), 591.

65 The Qasimi Library is described in Commins, *Islamic Reform*, 179.

66 Qasimi indicated that the piece by 'Abduh appeared in volume 11, number 12.

67 The point for which Qasimi found support is on page 56 in his text. Rida reviewed *Dalā'il al-tawḥīd* in *al-Manār* 12/5 (1909): 387–388. The review praised Qasimi's use of classical and recent scholars to present a compendium on theological reasoning.

68 Qasimi also kept a copy of *al-Manār's* review of his essay, *Pleasing Responses* (*al-Aǧwiba al-murḍiyya*), which deals with a matter of jurisprudence. The copy in the Qasimi library of this work contains new footnotes that he wrote.

69 Muhammad ibn 'Aqil helped manage a Malay reformist journal, *al-Imām*. I owe this information to Azyumardi Azra's chapter in this volume, which mentions Ibn 'Aqil. Prof. Azra noted that Ibn 'Aqil's "Shi'i" bent is the subject of an article by Werner Ende, "Schiitische Tendenzen bei sunnitischen Sayyids aus Hadhramaut: Muhammad b. 'Aqil al-'Alawi," *Der Islam* 50/1 (1973).

70 "Al-Naṣā'iḥ al-kāfiyya li man yatawallā Mu'āwiya," *al-Manār* 13/2 (1910): 152; "Kitāb al-naṣā'iḥ al-kāfiyya wa al-rudūd 'alayhi wa al-intiṣār lahu," *al-Manār* 14/4 (1911): 314–316; Ǧamāl al-Dīn al-Qāsimī, *Naqd al-naṣā'iḥ al-kāfiyya li man yatawallā Mu'āwiya* (Damascus: al-Fayha' Press, 1910), 2.

71 Muḥammad ibn 'Aqīl, *Al-Naṣā'iḥ al-kāfiyya li man yatawallā Mu'āwiya*, copy in Qasimi library, Jamal al-Din al-Qasimi's handwritten notes on title page. Qasimi gave the date of the letter from Ibn 'Aqil as July 1908.

72 Letter to Muhammad Nasif, July 30, 1909, in Ẓāfir al-Qāsimī, *Ǧamāl al-Dīn al-Qāsimī wa 'aṣruhu*, 602–603. On the margin of page 221 in his copy of Ibn 'Aqil's essay, Qasimi wrote that he read it in the course of the last ten days during the evening. He dated his note July 22, 1909, so he wrote to Nasif eight days later.

73 "Kitāb al-naṣā'iḥ al-kāfiyya," *al-Manār* 14 (1911): 314–316.
74 Ǧamāl al-Dīn al-Qāsimī, *Naqd al-naṣā'iḥ*, 2–3.
75 "Kitāb al-naṣā'iḥ al-kāfiyya," *al-Manār*.
76 al-Qāsimī, *Ǧamāl al-Dīn al-Qāsimī wa 'aṣruhu*, 617.
77 Ibid., 618.
78 Letter from 'Abd al-'Azīz ibn Aḥmad al-Rašīd al-Baddāh, March 1914; Al-Qāsimī,Ǧamāl al-Dīn al-Qāsimīwa'aṣruhu, 551–554.
79 The incident is described in detail and sources are given in Commins, *Islamic Reform*, 128–132.
80 For details of popular nationalism in the Faysali period, see James Gelvin, *Divided Loyalties: Nationalism and Mass Politics in Syria at the Close of Empire* (Berkeley, CA: University of California Press, 1998).
81 Gelvin cites officially sanctioned sermons that urged Muslims to strive for technical progress; Gelvin, *Divided Loyalties*, 190.
82 Ibid., 194–195, 203–204.
83 Commins, *Islamic Reform*, 122.
84 Gelvin, *Divided Loyalties*, 258–259.

3

THE MANARISTS AND MODERNISM

An attempt to fuse society and religion

Mahmoud Haddad

The first generation of American independence witnessed an energetic, almost a convulsive, effort to "create" an American culture. There was to be an American language, and Noah Webster set himself resolutely to champion American speech and prove its superiority to British speech. There was to be an American literature . . . an American education . . . an American science . . . and even an American arithmetic, for as Nicholas Pike wrote: "As we are now an independent nation it was deemed proper that we should have an independent arithmetic."[1]

In Europe it was also felt necessary to hide the more offensive aspects of utilitarian industrial modernism under the cloak of an earlier age. One historian wrote:

> In London even the railway stations struck archaic poses: Euston Station sought in its façade escape to ancient Greece, St. Pancras to the Middle Ages, Paddington to the Renaissance. This Victorian historicism expressed the incapacity of city dwellers either to accept the present or to conceive the future except as a resurrection of the past.[2]

Although not everyone who wrote in *al-Manār* can be considered a Manarist, it is commonplace for *al-Manār* to be associated with the Salafi movement. In the words of W. Ende:

> The origin and early development of the *Salafiyya* in [Egypt and Syria] is above all connected with the names of al-Afghani [1839–1897], ʻAbduh [1849–1905], al-Kawakibi [1854–1902], and Rashid Rida [1865–1935] . . . . With *al-Manār*, the last mentioned created in Cairo in 1898 the most influential organ of the *Salafiyya*. From 1926 onwards, *al-Manār* was joined by *al-Fatḥ* (Cairo), a periodical of similar tendency which, after the death of Rashid Rida and the cessation of *al-Manār* in 1935, was considered until 1948 the most important (although not the only) journalistic forum of the *Salafiyya* in Egypt . . . . Its editor and main

> author, Muhibb al-Din al-Khatib...had founded, together with his Syrian compatriot ʻAbd al-Fattah Katlan [d. 1931], the *Maṭbaʻa Salafiyya* (including a bookshop), a printing press whose production reflects all the essential desiderata of the movement.[3]

It is necessary to point out from the outset, that the Salafiyya or the Manarists/Salafis were not a homogenous group, nor even a group, and even when taken as individuals they are not devoid of contradictions and inconsistencies in their various expositions. It should be made equally clear that the Manarists' thinking was not completely rigid and underwent changes over time. The most glaring example of such developments and differences of opinion is Rashid Rida's transformation in the last phase of his life into a spokesman for the Wahhabi movement in the Arabian Peninsula, and its comparison with Muhammad ʻAbduh's earlier description of the same movement. In 1902, ʻAbduh lauded the Wahhabiyya for brushing away the dust of tradition and removing the layers that stood between men and a true study of the Qurʼan and the Hadith, so as to allow them to derive God's teachings from the source.[4] For ʻAbduh, however, the Wahhabiyya could be more narrow-minded than the traditionalists. He was bold enough to say:

> Though its members may denounce many innovations and corruptions that have been added to the faith unjustly over the years, they advocate a strict interpretation of the literal text, with no regard for the principles on which Islam was built and for which the Prophet called. These are no scholars, and no friends of civilization.[5]

The main thesis of the *Salafiyya* was the need for Islamic renewal or reform (*tağdīd*) in order to modernize and update the religious law (shariʻa), even if that entailed partial Western influence. It proposed to do so by marrying two trends: an Islamic trend that called for going back to the early sources of Islam (i.e. the Qurʼan and the Hadith) shunning harmful innovations (*bidʻa*) that came later, and a second trend, the modern Western trend of thought. Thus, it considered itself a modernist movement that accepted Western ideas, but within the general Islamic cultural framework. This approach made the *Salafiyya* face a double challenge from opposite directions: one from the old Islamic school of imitation (*taqlīd*) that adhered to interpretations of older ulama, and the second from the newer trend of secularization and uncritical westernization represented by the new emerging elite in the Arab and Muslim worlds. Additionally, the Salafi reformists perceived a need to work harder to inject Muslim moral values into Islamic society before Western style secularism or irreligion had a chance to seep in, or to reverse what they perceived to be not just secularism but de-Islamization. The need to preserve an Islamic identity was extremely relevant in this regard.

Explicitly or implicitly the Manarists/Salafis acquiesced in or rather called for the separation of religion and politics, and in this they were very different from the contemporary Islamic movements that call for their fusion.[6] The former were, probably without knowing it, in agreement not with ideological, but with historical Islam which organized Islamic society and the Islamic state according to separate norms. As Gibb and Bowen once noted, in the days before the 1979 Iranian revolution, religion and state in Islam were united "only in the realms of theory."[7] What the Manarists/Salafis were after was a fusion or unity of religion and society rather than of religion and state.

This may be confirmed by the writings of a number of Manarists/Salafi thinkers. Shaykh Muhammad 'Abduh, in his interpretation of the Sura *al-'Imrān*, wrote:

> The worst thing that can bedevil the faith and lead to a loss of the true Book [the Qur'an] is to put the livelihood of religious scholars and their ranking in the hands of princes and rulers. Religious scholars must be totally independent of rulers, particularly the oppressive ones. I cannot comprehend the purpose of putting scholarly ranks and wages in the hands of kings and princes, except to render these golden chains into bonds around their necks, with which they can be led to where the unjust rulers wish to deceive the public in the name of religion and hold them servile. If the public were to realize this they would not put much stock in the pronouncements of any official scholar bound by these chains. In the Ottoman Empire, religious ranks were bestowed not only on ignorant men but even upon children. There is a long poem mocking this sad state of the State written by a scholar from Tripoli (Syria). Yet, later on and from among those same scholars adorned with fancy outfits and shining medals, and who daily praised their benefactor the sultan, emerged some who declared their desire for the state to reform. This position was a ruse to mislead the public about their true allegiances. Is it possible then to trust a scholar close to the oppressive rulers?[8]

'Abduh went on to say:

> Scholars of the early generations (*salaf*) used to avoid the embrace of unjust rulers more stridently than they would avoid snakes and scorpions. There are many sayings and accounts about this, including the Prophet's hadith: "There will come after me princes [one rendition is: lying and unjust princes], and whomsoever befriends them and believes their lies and helps them in their oppression is not of me, nor I of him, and will not join me in heaven." (Relayed and authenticated by Tirmidhi, Nasa'i, al-Hakim, and Bayhaqi). Another hadith mentioned, "You shall have imams who control your livelihood, tell you lies and misrule among you. They will not be satisfied until you approve of their evil and believe their lies. You must stay true to the Right as long as they will tolerate it, and if they cross that boundary then whoever among you dies in opposition will die a martyr." (Relayed by al-Tabrani, with variations. We chose it because it includes the phrase "they will control your livelihood."[9])

The contemporary state of Islamic society was the subject of ʿAbduh's response to Renan, the French philosopher, who asked where exactly lay the general atrophy in Islam that was leading others to argue that religion is an obstacle in the path of Muslims, preventing their success and progress. Would it be correct to assume that this rigidity is in the nature of the faith?[10] ʿAbduh answered that this rigidity has to do with the relation that developed between religion and politics and not with Islam *per se*.[11] He said that we hear about political authorities arresting those who revive the arguments of the Salafi scholars calling for renewal, but these measures are not an expression of adherence to the faith. The traditional scholars afflicted with rigidity (*ğumūd*) who instigate such steps are motivated by envy and not by concern for the welfare of the religion. The arrests are a political necessity, out of fear that if one scholar was allowed to escape from the bonds of tradition, the practice might spread and others might follow. Then perhaps the practice would spread to other matters outside religion, leading to freedom of thought, which the conservatives abhor.[12] ʿAbduh concluded on a light, but revealing note:

> If you wish to argue that politics involve the oppression of thought, religion and science, then I agree. May God protect us from politics, from the word "politics," from the meaning of politics, from each letter in this word, from each image of it that comes to my mind, from each person that speaks or thinks of politics, and from each form of the verb "politics."[13]

Equally important, Rafiq al-ʿAzm (1867–1925) wrote in *al-Manār* in 1904 about the reasons for the decline of Islamic nations, asking:

> Is it not saddening and heartbreaking that there is not a single Muslim nation that can match the smallest Christian emirate in progress and advancement? Consider states like Bulgaria, Serbia, and Romania, which only recently seceded from the great [Ottoman] Islamic nation, how they have outstripped the Muslim nation and have become its most stubborn opponents. What, I wonder, is the cause of such devastating and pervasive inertia that has enslaved the Muslims, interrupted their system, and made them lag behind other nations? Christians and Buddhists have outdistanced the Muslims in progress, their opponents have subjugated them over authority, and their rivals have defeated them in all aspects of life in all areas of the world.[14]

After considering many answers based on religion, ethnicity, or character, and dismissing them all, he came to a rather novel conclusion for a Muslim:

> As a divine religion, Islam is only meant for the happiness and good of mankind. And no rational human being can claim that Islam prohibits its

> followers from attaining the happiness that God intended for His people through religion. It is only different minds throughout different ages and nations that differ in their comprehension of the meaning of religion. As is well known, the first nation to receive Islam was the Arab nation, which was steeped in aberrance and Bedouinism, and which had no social laws or an advanced or civilized system of government. When Islam came down to the Arabs with its rules, exhortations, commands, and prohibitions, they found in it an accessible goal, a momentous event, and eloquent wisdom. Thus, they embraced Islam and considered it the only and ultimate thing in their lives. They went to such extremes in their belief that it blinded them from the fact that excessiveness in religion, to the extent of associating it with all worldly matters, especially the political life of the nation, is a departure from the true intent of religion. It is a strong distortion of the Prophet's legislation: "If what troubles you is a religious matter, then come to me with it. But if it is a worldly matter, then you are more cognizant of it than I."[15]

Such was the result of the Arabs' total devotion to religion, in their Bedouin days, and their failure to place politics separately so that it may develop and grow in line with the developing state of affairs of the Muslims themselves. An indication of their error in that matter is the fact that the Bedouin governments that did not embrace aspects of civilization and did not keep pace with the changing times and with the advanced countries and their forms of government are still to this day considered by many the least developed among Muslim states. The people of such "Bedouin" states as those of the Maghreb and of the Arabian Peninsula are seen in the Middle East as most ignorant of social life, and their deteriorating state of affairs is perceived as a proof of this overall situation.

This is identified by many authors as the cause of the disasters that have afflicted Muslims and the source of their social misery to the present day. According to these authors, a nation that has placed itself in such a position of shunning worldly affairs and of attaching all matters of civil progress to religion and of succumbing to its despotic rulers for hundreds of years cannot strive for an advanced state or learn the lessons of the past without long toil and great hardships. The Muslims could have learnt from "non-religious" [*sic*] Japan which collectively rose and embraced the means of progress and advancement, reached in thirty years the level of European nations, and challenged the greatest "Christian" nations—while Muslim rule was being wrested away and the states of the Muslims were threatened with extinction, and developed nations dominated them and their governments. There is not a single Muslim state that would have willingly undertaken the formation of an advanced government that could have matched the smallest European nation; that would have repelled the raids of civilized peoples who fought the Muslims for survival with the power of knowledge and the weapons of civilization, or that would have purged governments of their elements of deadly corruption. The Europeans had enslaved three quarters of the

Muslims, and before the lapse of a quarter of a century, they might have taken control of the remaining quarter of them. That quarter might have lost their countries to the Europeans had they remained steeped in error and ignorance, and if they did not manage their own affairs and stop relying on their tyrannical governments, the kind of tyranny that consumed kingdoms, toppled towers of glory, and drained the strength of nations while they lie unaware.[16]

One of the characteristics of the Manarist/Salafi trend is that it opted for selective modernism—that is if we think of modernism as an approximation of the stage that the West had reached in thought or behavior at that time. It therefore did not see a problem in accepting modern thinking and found it compatible with Islam in certain areas. In others, it refused modern, or more precisely Western, thinking or behavior as incompatible with Islam. The yardstick one may generally use to differentiate among its varying stances is to evaluate whether a certain stance was in contradiction with basic Islamic teachings or if it posed a problem to Islamic identity according to their definition of it or to historical circumstances. For the Manarist/Salafi movement, modernism was to be respectful of Islam, of the Arabs, and of their past. In that sense, it was necessary to weave the national with the religious. Otherwise, modernism would remain alien and devoid of any acceptable identity (see Appendix). From this perspective, modernism advanced the cause of an Arab nationalism intertwined with Islam. An article entitled, "Love of the Arabs is a True Pillar of Islam,"[17] published in *al-Fatḥ* in 1947 is a case in point. More importantly, and much earlier, Muhammad ʻAbduh considered that modernism implicitly entailed Arab cultural nationalism and revival in the form of modernizing the Arabic language by going back to study its sources and enabling it to express new genres of literature.[18]

As an example of a modernism that is compatible with Islam, a series of articles by Rashid Rida in 1907 is most revealing.[19] The series, entitled "The Benefits and Harms of Europeans in the East," lists clearly what benefits the Muslims got from the Europeans. Rida cited, as the first benefit, "independent thought" and said that newspapers write plenty about the independence of nations, but rarely about the independence of the individual, which is the foundation for the independence of the larger group called the nation. He went on to say that "civilization is a form of human perfection of individuals. Its opposite is tyranny, which prevents the perfection of individuals that is required in civilization. Tyranny manipulates individual independence, and controls the learning behavior of individuals."[20] Rida proceeded to explain that in countries where tyranny is predominant, the educational system is built on imitation and rote learning, following the nature of government. Thus, since the East is more rooted in imitation than the West, it is also more rooted in tyranny. Although Europe suffered from tyranny more in the Middle Ages than the East, in modern times the tables were turned. Consequently, science and business thrived in Europe to unprecedented levels while the East remained backward. This allowed Europe to penetrate into the East, colonizing the land, spreading the call for its own religion, and seeking profits. People of the two areas mixed together and created mutual ties, when

Europeans established schools in the East, and took over many positions and functions. Rida interestingly concluded:

> This is a major benefit we have derived from Europeans. We should be grateful to them for the education, and learning they possess. A Muslim should not deny that, or fail to use the argument that, the noble Qur'an itself has taught us to dismantle imitation, and that it is founded on the principle of independent logic. Though this is true... it was not a factor in this age of awakening of the East in general and the Muslims in particular. Our proof is that today our men of religion remain the staunchest enemies of independence [of thought], and the most beholden to imitation. We should be fair, and express our gratefulness to those who have awakened us to our self-interest.[21]

The second benefit we acquired from the Europeans, according to Rida, was "the emergence from tyranny."[22] He surveyed Islamic and Eastern history in a very open and liberal way and concluded that tyranny was the norm in these lands even before European colonization started. For him, "the greatest benefit that the East has derived from the Europeans is knowledge of what a government should be. That deep conviction leads to an attempt to replace absolute authority in the hands of individuals with a government subject to the rule of consultation (*šūrā*) and religious law (shar'ia). Some, like Japan, have reached that goal. Others, like Iran, have proceeded along that path. Still others, like Egypt and Turkey, continue to struggle toward that end, with speech and printed word."[23] Again, Rida's conclusion is not based on any Islamic premise:

> A Muslim should not say that this form of government is a foundation of our faith, and that we derive it from our own clear Book (the Qur'an), and from the conduct of the early caliphs, not from contacts with Europeans and understanding of Western affairs. Without such contacts, Muslims would not have realized that this is a true aspect of Islam. Otherwise, the first to declare the need for fulfilling this command of the faith would have been religious scholars in Constantinople, Egypt, and Morocco. In fact, however, most of them remain staunch supporters and tools of tyrannical governments ruled by individuals. Most of those who demand the rule of consultation, which is subjected to laws, are those who have become familiar with Europe and European ways.[24]

The third and last benefit which Rida thought the East had received from Europe was "communal societies or communal organizations." Rida writes that social scientists believe that the primary factor in furthering the advancement of nations is voluntary communal organizations that are obviously independent of the state. For him, such organizations or societies have led the way to the development of science and art, to the increase in glory and power, and to the accumulation of wealth. They also helped spread Europe's religion throughout the world and guaranteed European domination of East and West.[25] He added that the East had preceded the West in all forms of civil and social progress, but civilization in the East remained lacking and was not established on firm foundations which, according to him, caused it to collapse. The reason was that these foundations were the creation of individual effort and not based on work through communal societies. "Without these societies, modern Western civilization would not have been as strong and as deserving of stability and longevity."[26] Rida then made the point that,

> Today, we see the East beginning to learn from the West how to create communal societies and corporations. The Japanese have been very successful in this field and have reached a level of maturity. The Ottomans and Egyptians remain in a state of childhood in this life of collective effort. Yet, without this effort, it is impossible for a nation to reach maturity . . . .
>
> [Voluntary] societies and corporations are the measure of a nation's progress and its life. This is indisputable. You should not be deceived by the brilliant achievement of one individual, or several, in some science or enterprise. If they do not find in their nations societies that appreciate their value and assist them into bringing to life the fruits of their brilliance, the efforts of these individuals will be wasted and their abilities squandered.[27]

It is noteworthy that in the series of articles entitled, "The Benefits and Harms of Europeans in the East," Rida's impressions were exclusively about benefits with no mention of any harmful effects.

This attitude is drastically reversed on the eve of the First World War. The threat of European colonization, its realization in the core Arab-Muslim areas, and the rise of extreme or militant secular movements calling for near complete Westernization similar to that in Atatürk's Turkey, had drastically changed the political and cultural picture. From that point on there would be no escape from political issues. These were connected with national and religious integrity and identity. More importantly, they were not simply concerned with the issue of religion and state as expressed by the wisdoms received from a revealed religion, but came to encroach on the relation between religion and society. With the spread of European colonization on the eve of the First World War, Rida perceptively commented:

> It is not Islam that shuns the Europeans, but the Europeans who force Islam to give them a wide berth. Harmony between them is not an impossibility, but the way to reach it requires the exercise of a large mind.[28]

Nothing can better describe the new type of conflict that developed between the Manarist/Salafi defenders of Islamic identity and the "new modernists" or

Westernizers than the controversy about the wearing of a hat or a turban. This episode exemplifies the clash between Islamic society and religion on the one hand and the state on the other. In an article entitled "The Turban and the Tarbush [fez]," *al-Fatḥ*, edited by Muhibb al-Din al-Khatib,[29] reprinted a commentary that had previously appeared in the pro-British Egyptian newspaper *al-Muqattam*. The latter had published a piece by an unknown writer accusing Muhibb al-Din al-Khatib, who was himself a wearer of the fez, of becoming an advocate of wearing turbans. The writer claimed that the subject had nothing to do with religion and that Islam had no specific costume or required appearance. This was a matter best left to social customs and personal taste. Islam never introduced any such requirements. Anyone who claimed that religion required a certain outfit was making a false allegation at the expense of the faith and misrepresenting Islam. Indeed, the turban worn today as a symbol for religious scholars was not the same one worn by the good ancestors. Neither did our worthy ancestors wear a *qūftān*, *ğūbba* (overcoat), or belt as is common today. All these were recent introductions.

Al-Khatib replied the next day ridiculing some of the minor points made by his adversary. However, he made a lengthy defense of wearing the turban for reasons having to do with both Islamic identity and economic independence:

> The turbans are the crowns of the Arabs. They were the symbol of the Arabs and the Muslims when they were masters. They were also the ornament of their heads and the pride of their manhood. When Muslims became enslaved, some of their nation stooped low enough to follow the ways of other nations, a stage which was the subject of a pioneering psychological analysis by Judge Wali al-Din Abu Zayd ʻAbd al-Rahman ibn Khaldun.[30]

The author then makes a point about the "economics of wearing Islamic dress" that is rarely found elsewhere:

> Before some Muslims moved away from the turban to the fez, they used to wear textiles produced in their own lands. National industry used to have teeming markets, and the trade of the East was in the hands of the Easterners. This provided the livelihood for hundreds of thousands of workers, many of who have since turned into thieves or beggars. Ever since the Ottoman Sultan Mahmud [II] adopted the Frankish costume, the East has paid to the west hundreds of millions of pounds as the price for foreign textiles. Households in the West prospered with this income, while their equivalent in the East went bankrupt. Every pound that left the pocket of the Easterners to the coffers of the West in payment for their clothes was a nail in the structure of the Western domination of the East. One wishes that the turban had remained our symbol. Then we would have preserved our beauty and dignity. The textile industry in the East would have progressed, and we would have preserved our economic

> independence to assist us in protecting our national independence, or at least in restoring it.[31]

The shock of the abolishment of the caliphate in Turkey in 1924 and the pursuit of a policy undermining the shari'a in both state and society had two effects in the Muslim World. For one, it empowered similar trends in other Muslim countries; for the other it put the modernist Manarist/Salafi forces in those countries on the defensive, pushing them to abandon their middle ground and lash out against the Westernizing elements. Such was the shock that the *Nation Arabe* published by Shakib Arslan in Geneva wrote in March 1930 that

> the Turkey of Angora or Ankara, as it now wants to be called, prides itself of being in the process of complete modernization in a European sense. Hat, dance, Roman alphabet, Swiss civil code, Italian penal code, etc., they have gone as far as possible in breaking with the past. It is said that they no longer even tolerate oriental music, and at a given moment they spoke of changing even Turkish cuisine in the strictest sense into a purely Occidental cuisine.[32]

Even more theatrical projects were proposed, such as that of replacing Turkish first names, almost all of Arabic origin, with Latin or Germanic first names. Instead of Ali Rıza, Ismail Haqqı, Hüsseyin Kâzım, etc., one would thenceforth be named Jean, Jules, Marcel, Xavier, William, Max, etc. That was to say that Kemalist Turkey was no longer content with Western teachings in the sciences, arts, law, and regulations, but wanted to become completely European in a social sense. In order to better break with the past, they even thought of no longer teaching Turkish history. Some wanted Turkish history to begin with Mustafa Kemal, and no longer wanted to speak of the events which linked Turkey to Asia. The difficulty with this attempt, however, was, according to our authors, that it went around the issues by playing with historical and geographical truths and claiming that Turkey had always been a European power and had never received anything from Asia. It is thus that Tevfik Raşid Bey, the Turkish Minister of Foreign Affairs, declared at the disarmament Conference in Geneva something which, moreover, had no relation to the purpose of the Conference, that is, that all of Turkish history proved that it had always been an essentially European country. "The Kemalist Turks, not content therefore to be Europeans in the future, want to have been Europeans in the past. They do not intend to modernize in the manner of Japan, for example, and seek to be taught European knowledge by adapting themselves to modern technology, while remaining essentially Japanese. No, the Kemalist Turks were determined to focus on a radical revolution which left little trace of their past." Such attitudes in the name of "progress" made Shakib Arslan disapprovingly write that the Turkish method of "modernization is merely an attempt to extinguish the Muslim spirit."[33]

Earlier, in June 1929, Rashid Rida had written a preface for the thirtieth volume of *al-Manār*.[34] One of the topics that he discussed was "The Renewal of Our Atheists and the Renewal of the Westerners (Franks)."[35] Rida started his attack early by comparing the developments that were taking place in Europe with the opposite kind of developments taking place in the Arab and Muslim worlds:

> The destruction of the Islamic aspects of government by renegade Turks and what appear to be initial indications that the Afghan and Iranian governments are emulating them, as well as the events in Egypt (and the contagion is spreading to every province) have tempted colonialists and Christian missionaries in Europe to deliver the *coup de grâce* to Islam, sweep away all vestiges of Islamic rule, and to revive Christianity and consolidate it in the West and the East.[36]

Rida presented the following list that included, according to his evaluation, some of the efforts by Europeans to renew their religion, most of which he regarded as pretexts to transgress against the Islamic religion:

1 British and other Protestant missionaries had convened one conference after another in Jerusalem, the cradle of Christianity, to consult about increasing the effort to Christianize Muslims. One of their organizations in London had published a statement claiming that the only territory where Islam had truly deep roots was in the Arabian Peninsula. Moreover, it alleged that only 100 dedicated missionaries were needed to destroy it in its first cradle and last redoubt.
2 The French government returned to Catholic organizations all of the money and endowments that it confiscated from them in order to encourage them to spread Christianity in the French colonies in North Africa and Syria.
3 New books were being published in French and other languages reviling Islam and urging the Christianization of Muslims, by force if necessary. Rida had published some excerpts from their books in this and in previous volumes and promised to publish more in the future.
4 The Italian government had reconciled with the Vatican, restoring to the Pope political sovereignty in his domain and hundreds of millions of his (frozen) assets, thus reinvigorating the Catholic Church and commencing a new era in the revival of Christianity, in both the East and West. This did not harm Muslims *per se* unless the Church transgressed against them, and it remained less injurious than secularism and atheism.
5 The organizations calling for the unification of all Christian churches and sects had shown a greater activism in the East and West. In fact, they had made some progress in that direction.
6 The religious revivalist movement in England was only second to that of Italy. By now the controversy surrounding the suggestion to amend the official Book of Prayers, and the parliament's repeated rejection of it, had

become well known. Other organizations had been formed to look into Christian doctrines and the traditions of the Church, with a view to reconciling them with science and the modern age.

7 Italian and British publications were competing to spread the message urging women to return to (religious) decency in dress and public conduct, and especially to resist the latest excesses in display of feminine charms and dissoluteness, which leads to moral depravity. Some of these writings by well-known British writers had been published in Egyptian newspapers. Moreover, the Italian prime minister, who was a great reformer, had banned excesses in dress, dancing, and swimming, hoping by reviving religion and morality to renew the strength and greatness of his nation. Furthermore, every virtuous man found this praiseworthy.[37]

As for the lessons to be derived from "Europe's renewal and the renewal of our atheists,"[38] as he put it, Rida held that the renewal of "our country's atheists" and advocates of disbelief and licentiousness entailed the destruction of religious bonds and the elements of honor and dignity, namely everything that tied the nation together, gave it strength, unified its word, and preserved it morals. They called disbelief and debauchery originality in renewal and progress and advancement in civilization. They referred to religious consciousness and chastity as old and worn-out notions.[39]

Indeed, for Rida, their mockery and corruption were spreading and the threat that they posed was growing with the growth of magazines and newspapers through which they squirted their poison. This was so despite their low prestige and bad reputation; none of them had superior skill in a useful science or a good deed. Rather, their influence came through the attractiveness of their expression, which they employed to sanction the desires of old trespassers and young juveniles. Knowledgeable people asserted that much of the extent of uncertainty of belief, corrupted honor, and debauched women could be attributed to the corrupting influence of magazines and newspapers.[40]

Rida then shifted to another more sensitive topic, showing not the moderate modernist face, but the conservative side of the Manarists/Salafis, when it came to the issue of women. Writing under the subtitle, "The Danger of Liberating Women,"[41] he wrote that the question of female anarchy, called women's liberation (which was shamelessness exemplified by the preference of removing the veil over the chastity exemplified by the veil), had brought Egypt and other Europeanized Eastern peoples to an abyss that threatened their dignity, family unit, health, and wealth, even though the depraved advocates of licentiousness and cuckolding may have called this danger a civilizing renewal.[42]

Rida makes the point that nowadays, women, housewives, mothers, and educated maidens roam the streets day and night with men, their arms around each others' waists. They frequent promenades and nightclubs in different states of dress and nudity, holding hands with men and more. Some of them swim at sea, in front of men or even with men. Some frequent mixed dance halls where they dance with men in a state much worse than their foreign counterparts, in terms of nakedness, impudence, wantonness, buffoonery, and silliness. Some of them visit the salons where they have their hair cut and their backs and bosoms beautified. There they meet their lovers; ask not what they speak openly and what they promise secretly. Do not mention the multiplicity of secret brothels, let alone the prevalence of the open ones and the personal trysts. Naturally, the many newspapers and magazines instigate to this temptation. Thus, one of the most serious consequences of this corruption is a decrease in the number of marriages. This threatens the nation by stopping its demographic growth, leading to its diminution and potential extinction.[43] But one should not derive the conclusion that Rida's stance on the issue at hand was novel at that time. In 1908 Qasim Amin (1863–1908), the Egyptian writer in the circle of Muhammad ʿAbduh's friends, had died. Rida was very reserved in his eulogy. He described Amin who had called for shunning the veil and was well-known as the "liberator of the [Muslim] woman," which was the title of his first book on the subject, as having been more theoretical than practical and that his writings were in contradiction to the general opinion of the majority of people.[44] Rida was also critical of Amin, though more mildly, when Muhammad ʿAbduh was still alive and when Amin published his second book entitled *al-Marʾa al-ǧadīda* ("The New Woman") in 1901.[45]

Rida went on sounding a pessimistic note when he stated:

> The enemies of Islam lie in wait and are happy for the ignominy that Muslims brought on their faith. They are paving the way for enslaving Muslims and colonizing their countries. They carefully monitor every faint whisper for reform that issues from the mouth of any Muslim ruler and every movement for renewal that might arise among them. Then they set out to caution their governments and to urge the neutralization of its salutary effects. They work to defame the advocates of such movements so that unaware Muslims may turn away from them. This is demonstrated in the article "What is Said about Islam in Europe," printed in this volume and based on the writings of Jules Sicard,[46] a French military man, Father Lammens, a Jesuit priest, and Dr Snouk [Hurgonje], a Dutch statesman. Consider what these Europeans have to say about the Imam [Muhammad ʿAbduh] and the owner of *al-Manār* and their call for reform, *al-Manār* and its analysis, the *Epistle of Unicity* [*Risālat al-tawḥīd* by Muhammad ʿAbduh] and its implementation, and their views regarding the modern Europeanization movement. It should be noted that our authors (the owner of *al-Manār* and the Imam [Muhammad ʿAbduh]) lament the fact that this movement has begun to erode the fundamentals of religion. They also lament the fact that the ideas of Shaykh Muhammad ʿAbduh, which struck root among thinkers and had wide appeal among Muslim youth, now are most vehemently rejected by the ossified and ultraconservative turban wearers. As the Europeans above put it, "for this reason, one finds that the followers of ʿAbduh are diminishing and are unable to publicize

their ideas because they are few in number and face strong resistance from the conservatives."[47]

Yet, Rida does not despair and, in a twist, he perceives "good omen for reform." First, he takes heart that his old enemies at al-Azhar have received a higher budget, that the book *The Epistle of Unicity* (*Risālat al-tawḥīd*) by Shaykh Muhammad ʿAbduh started to be taught at that institution, and, better still, that the books of the medieval Islamic scholar Ibn Taymiyya have become standard authoritative texts for basing fatwas. Some of the latter's works, according to Rida, have been used to reform personal statutes in canonical courts. Moreover, the Mufti of Jerusalem is considered one of his disciples, as is the head of the Islamic Council recently established in Beirut.[48] Ibn Taymiyya (661–728/1263–1328) was, of course, not known for works that would give later credence to what the Manarists/Salafis would strive for, that is, separating Islamic state and society, but rather the opposite. He had written the *Siyāsa šarʿiyya*, a model for a profoundly Islamic state in accordance with the shariʿa.[49] He was a great Muslim scholar engaged in defending Islamic cultural and religious identity at a time when the threat of Mongol invasion was casting a long shadow upon the Arab Muslim world.[50]

Second, and in another expression of optimism, Rida cited the formation of the Organization of Muslim Youths (*Ǧamʿiyyat al-šubbān al-muslimūn*) and its opening of numerous chapters in Arab countries. He proceeded to say that *al-Manār's* message included, among other things, arguments to counter bad innovations and myths, arguments to refute the suspicious theses of atheists and unbelievers, and arguments to expose the calumnies of imitators of the Europeans. It further included warnings against the deception of missionaries, the errors of materialists, and the dangers of colonialism.[51] The predominant emphasis on these objectives, together with the revival of the tradition of Ibn Taymiyya, put in question whether the Manarists/Salafis were still "the reform party which occupies the middle ground between the party of uncritical imitation and ossification and the party of modernism identified with renewal."[52] But there is a possible rationalization: the state increasingly interfered in the affairs of Islamic society through extreme Westernization, thus making it very difficult for the Manarist/Salafi trend to chart a middle course and preserve the independence of society and religion from the state. In actuality the Manarist/Salafi trend lost its *raison d'être* and, having paved the way for other groups advocating extreme Islamization, found nowhere to go.

Appendix

From Muhibb al-Din al-Khatib's *The Campaign for Renewal and Reform: Does it have Wise Leaders, and Have They Drawn for it Wise Plans?*[53]

Renewal and reform are not mere desires; they are necessities of the first order to preserve the last breath of national life and to protect the last vestige of national greatness. Otherwise, we would be as good as finished.

We have exchanged the art of transcription for the art of printing. And whereas we used to cross the sea in sailboats for purposes of trade or pilgrimage, we now do so on steamers. Furthermore, our Islamic governments stripped their soldiers of bows and catapults and equipped them instead with automatic rifles, hand grenades, and amazingly heavy artillery.

My ancestors used to read and write using oil lamps for light, whereas I dispensed with the lamp willingly and happily to enjoy electric lights, which make the night brighter than day. I write this section and in front of me is a letter from a friend in Baghdad; my answer will be sent by airplane to be delivered in a couple of days instead of a month as in past days.

All this is renewal; all this is well and necessary. But it entails extraneous elements that shame me when I remember them. It is part and parcel of renewal and reform not to deceive my people or myself by concealing them.

For renewal in printing to be genuine [for example], and for me to feel pride in it, the printing press, its materials and parts, and the paper used should all be manufactured in my homeland using native labor. This way, its cost as well as the wages of its labor remain inside the homeland, enabling it to expand its sources of power and might.

For renewal in sea transport to be genuine, the steamer should be one that flies the flag of my nation and whose parts are made in my homeland.

For renewal in armament to be genuine, Islamic governments must not be dependent on others to obtain the gun or the hand grenade or the cannon. Rather, they ought to put themselves on a path such that after 1 year or 10 or 30 years they would manufacture weapons in their own factories using their own laborers and engineers.

Therefore, renewal is necessary and inevitable if we are to carry out what we have been enjoined to do when facing enemies, namely "to organize all of the power we are able to muster." And reform is inescapable if we intend to shed the cloak of obsequiousness.

There is in the East today—I mean the Arab East, which encompasses West Asia and North Africa—a thing called a renewal movement. To me it is axiomatic that renewal of both the Arab East and the Islamic East is the way to survival. I am expressing this sincerely and candidly, because if I arrive at the truth of something and believe in it, nothing will prevent me from broadcasting it for all to hear. I have made it plain in what I have said that the campaign for renewal cannot be considered a jihad, or a holy struggle in the way of God and the homeland unless it is based on clear principles and strives for specific goals, and follows correct plans. Moreover, its leaders should work for it sincerely, voluntarily, and with enthusiasm. In other words, they should be free of spies and planted intriguers.

The true colors of the leaders of the renewal movement will remain unknown until the movement's principles, goals, and plans are specified. Thereafter, those who work sincerely and with conviction for the realization of the stated goals and commit themselves not to lead the nation astray will be true leaders of renewal in the way of God and the homeland. Those who have other ways and other goals are moles in our ranks working for the benefit of our enemy. This is true whether they serve the enemy wittingly or whether they are mere tools who do the job unconsciously.

There is then genuine renewal, and there is a tainted one, the distinguishing criteria being the specific principles, goals, and plans and the extent of adherence to them. Moreover, one cannot distinguish a traitorous reformer until his message is tested and found to aim at leading the nation away from the correct path.

What then are the principles, goals, and plans of the true renewal movement that the Arab East needs?

- We want to be intrinsically powerful and respected by powerful nations. This is an important goal.
- We must preserve our national, patriotic, and religious existence. We ought to sever the hand that would cut our connection with this principle.
- The plan that would reconcile this principle with that goal requires us to borrow from any source the means of power that we need. Of course, we ought to preserve all elements of our national, patriotic, and religious existence that cannot be regarded as factors of meekness and impotence. The more numerous and significant the elements we find appropriate to keep, the greater the proof of our worth, of good fortune, and of God's blessings. By the same token, the fewer elements and the lesser in importance we find necessary to borrow from others, the more reason we have not to change our character and to melt into another. The upshot of this is: we ought to keep all parts of our national character except what is harmful; and we ought not to borrow anything from others unless it is necessary.

Our national and religious existence is akin to the body of a man. Would a man accept to cut his ears, even if they are not graceful, or to scrape off his skin, even if it is afflicted with smallpox? Or would he sever his fingers, even if they were thick? He who would accept this would not be in his right mind. None of us would accept to sever his sick hand, especially if a medicinal cure is available. We ought to defend our character with all of our might, even unto death. We should sacrifice of it only the excess hair and nails, and remove from it only the dirt that a bath would remove. And he who calls on me to cut muscle or bone or nerve from my body is an enemy or a messenger of the enemy. What I can legitimately borrow from others should be confined to things that would help me to organize times of work and leisure, procure the means of work and production, and secure the requirements of health, well being, and all other factors that contribute health and strength to the body.

We want a renewal that will teach us to organize our lives and to manage our places and offices of business. We favor a renewal that will help us replace the manufactured goods of others with goods that we manufacture ourselves in our homeland.

We want a renewal that would make us aware that we were once the mightiest and most knowledgeable of nations and that would stir us to strive to become in the near future one of the mightiest and most knowledgeable of nations.

We want a renewal that would make us aware that our forefathers were able, after eliminating the Byzantine and Persian empires, to foster the most advanced industries in the world, and that would spur us to become one of the most advanced manufacturing nations.

But a renewal that exploits our present relative insignificance to convince us that we never amounted to anything and that we lack the germ to achieve high rank; or a renewal that exploits our present relative ignorance to convince us that we never had knowledge and that we lack the germ to become knowledgeable; or a renewal that exploits our state of dissolution and anarchy to convince us that our history is inferior and that our only life is through merging with Europeans body and soul; suffice it to say that a renewal of this sort would undoubtedly be a plot conceived by enemies and carried out in the East by enemies in friends' clothing.

I do not hesitate to state firmly and clearly that ignorance is better than a renewal with which foreigners intend to "colonize" our hearts so as to spare them the toil of colonizing our lands. That is because when we become theirs, the slave and his belongings belong to his master. Would the youth of the glorious Arab East accept this sort of renewal?

Jesus, peace be upon him, says: "Ye shall know them by their fruits" ["Do men gather grapes of thorns, or figs of thistles?" (Mathew 7:16)]. The test of those who call for renewal and reform is to look at their message: do they encourage to earn power through virtue and knowledge; do they manifest the signs of good counsel to their nation, the respect for its ideals, and the revivification of its feats? If so, then they are true messengers of reform. But if they fill the newspapers with ravings that have no relation to development, or have no purpose except to deceive innocent youth about their history with allegations that they descend from a nation without a virtuous past or an accomplished civilization, then they are without doubt conspirators in our midst. Perhaps an enemy who declares his enmity is less harmful than the bearer of such a rotten fruit to a nation seeking goodness and good standing.

Notes

1 Allan Nevins and Henry Steele Commager, *A Pocket History of the United States* (New York: Pocket Books, 1976), 147.

2 Carl E. Schorske, *Thinking with History: Explorations in the Passage to Modernism* (Princeton, NJ: Princeton University Press, 1998), quoted by Gordon A. Craig, "The Good, the Bad, and the Bourgeois," *New York Review of Books* (August 13, 1998), 8.

3 W. Ende, "Salafiyya," *EI*[2], s.v.

4 Muḥammad ʿAbduh, *al-Islām wa al-naṣrāniyya maʿa al-ʿilm wa al-madaniyya*, 2nd ed. (Cairo: Dār al-manār, 1323 [1905]), 116. This work is a compilation, first published in 1905, of articles published in *al-Manār* in 1902.

5 Ibid., 116–117.

6 Johannes J. G. Jansen, *The Dual Nature of Islamic Fundamentalism* (New York: Cornell University Press, 1997), 12–13.
7 H. A. R. Gibb and Harold Bowen, *Islamic Society and the West: A Study of the Impact of Western Civilization on Modern Culture in the Near East* (London: Oxford University Press, 1957), 1: 1; 2: 79. See also Ira Lapidus, "The Separation of State and Religion in the Development of Early Islamic Society," *International Journal of Middle Eastern Studies* (October 1975): 363–385.
8 Muḥammad ʻAbduh, *Tafsīr al-Qurʾān al-ḥakīm* (Cairo: s.l., n.d.): 4: 283–284.
9 Ibid., 384.
10 ʻAbduh, *al-Islām wa al-naṣrāniyya*, 119–120.
11 Ibid., 122.
12 Ibid., 120–121.
13 Ibid., 121.
14 Rafīq al-ʻAẓm, "Hādhā awān al-ʻibar," *al-Manār* 7/8 (June 30, 1904): 307.
15 As related by Ahmad, Muslim, and Ibn Baja, cited in al-ʻAẓm, "Hādhā awān al-ʻibar," 308–309.
16 Al-ʻAẓm, "Hādhā awān al-ʻibar," 311–312.
17 "Maḥabba al-ʻArab aṣl min uṣūl al-islām," *al-Fatḥ* (Dūʼl-Qaʻda 1367 [1947]): 257–258.
18 ʻAbduh, *al-Islām wa al-naṣrāniyya*, 120–121.
19 Rašīd Riḍā, "Manāfiʻ al-ūrubbīyīn wa maḍāruhum fī al-šarq," parts 1–3, *al-Manār* 10/3 (May 12, 1907): 192–199; 10/4 (June 11, 1907): 279–284; 10/5 (July 11, 1907): 340–344.
20 Riḍā, "Manāfiʻ al-ūrubbīyīn wa maḍāruhum fī al-šarq," part 1, *al-Manār* 10/3 (May 12, 1907): 197.
21 Ibid., 199.
22 Riḍā, "Manāfiʻ al-ūrubbīyīn wa maḍāruhum fī al-šarq," part 2, *al-Manār* 10/4 (June 11, 1907): 279.
23 Ibid., 282.
24 Ibid., 283.
25 Riḍā, "Manāfiʻ al-ūrubbīyīn wa maḍāruhum fī al-šarq," part 3, *al-Manār* 10/5 (July 11, 1907): 340.
26 Ibid., 341.
27 Ibid., 343–344.
28 In "Russian and French Moslem Subjects," *The Near East and the Anglo-Egyptian Mail* (July 19, 1911), 250.
29 "Al-ʻimāma wa al-tarbūš," *al-Fatḥ* (Rabīʻ al-Ṯānī 14, 1353 [1934]), 8–9.
30 Ibid.
31 Ibid.
32 Shakib Arslan, "Le modernisme turc et la civilisation arabe: Une mise au point," *La Nation Arabe* (March 1930): 39.
33 Šakīb Arslān, in *al-Fatḥ* (Dūʼl-Qaʻda 29, 1352 [January 1934]), 1–5, 16–17.
34 Rašīd Riḍā, "Fātiḥa al-muğallad al-ṯalāṯīn," *al-Manār* 30/1 (June 7, 1929): 1–16.
35 Ibid., 10.
36 Ibid.
37 Ibid., 10–11.
38 Ibid., 11.
39 Ibid., 11–12.
40 Ibid., 12.
41 Ibid.
42 Ibid., 12–13.
43 Ibid.
44 Rašīd Riḍā, "Muṣāb Miṣr bi-Qāsim Amīn," *al-Manār* 11/3 (May 1, 1908): 226–229.

45 Rašīd Riḍā, "Ra'y al-nās fī al-kitāb wa ra'yunā fīhi," *al-Manār* 4/1 (February 20, 1901): 30–34.
46 Author of *Le Monde musulman dans les possessions françaises* (Paris: Librairie Coloniale et Orientaliste Émile Larose, 1928).
47 Riḍā, "Fātiḥa al-muğallad al-ṯalāṯīn," 13–14.
48 Ibid., 14–15.
49 Ibn Ṭaymiyya, *al-Siyāsa al-šar'iyya fī iṣlāḥ al-rā'ī wa al-rā'iyya* (Beirut: Dār al-kutub al-'arabiyya, 1966).
50 H. Laoust, "Ibn Ṭaymiyya," *EI*[2], s.v.
51 Riḍā, "Fātiḥa al-muğallad al-ṯalāṯīn," 13–14.
52 Ibid., 16.
53 Muḥibb al-Dīn al-Ḫaṭīb, "Ḥamla al-tağdīd wa al-iṣlāḥ wa ḥal lahā qāda ḥukamā' wa hal rasama lahā al-ḫiṭaṭ al-ḥakīma?," *al-Hadīqa*, 5 (Cairo: al-Maṭba'a al-salafiyya, 1349 [1930–1931]): 190–206. Khatib wrote this piece at a time when, according to him, Cairo's intellectual and cultural atmosphere was too influenced by Western culture with all its positive and negative attributes. Most of the intellectuals used to look at any Islamic inclination as representative of reaction and rigidity. See Muḥibḇ al-Dīn al-Ḫaṭīb, *Muḥibb al-Dīn al-Ḫaṭīb: Ḥayātuhu bi-qalamihi* (Damascus: Ğam'iyya al-tamaddun al-islāmī, 1979): 78.

4

THE INFLUENCE OF *AL-MANĀR* ON ISLAMISM IN TURKEY

The case of Mehmed Âkif

Kasuya Gen

In the years from 1908 to 1918, starting with the 1908 revolution that opened the floodgates for publication up till the Ottoman defeat in the First World War, intellectual circles in the Ottoman Empire eagerly took up the discussion of the place and role of Islam in Ottoman society. The so-called "Islamic modernism" or "Islamic reformism," often used interchangeably with movements calling for *ıslah* (reform), *ihya* (revival), and *tecdid* (renewal), was one of the most influential current within the Empire.

It is sometimes mentioned that the ideas of the three major modern Salafi thinkers in the Arab world, Jamal al-Din al-Afghani (1838–1897), Muhammad ʻAbduh (1849–1905), and Rashid Rida (1865–1935), were the ideological roots of Islamism (*İslamcılık* in Turkish) in the Ottoman Empire during this period. Their ideas of Islamic reform permeated the articles in *al-ʻUrwa al-Wuṯqā* ("The Indissoluble Bond") published by Afghani and ʻAbduh in Paris in 1884, and Rida's periodical *al-Manār* ("The Lighthouse," 1898–1935), whose impact was felt on Islamic currents throughout the Muslim world.

This article is meant to be a reexamination of the impact of *al-Manār* and the "Manarists" on the development of Islamism in Turkey from 1908 to 1918.

Islamism (*İslamcılık*) in Ottoman thought after 1908

Before engaging in a discussion of the impact of *al-Manār* and of the Manarists on Islamism (*İslamcılık*) in Turkey, we will begin by categorizing Islamism as it appears within Ottoman intellectual currents after 1908. According to Niyazi Berkes, Ottoman intellectual circles at that time can be divided into three schools of thought: Westernists, Islamists, and Turkists.[1]

The Westernists came out of the 1908 revolution as the most vigorous group, despite their lacking the sectlike cohesion of the Islamists and Turkists, except for the followers of the late Ottoman political theorist "*Prens*" Sabahaddin

(1877–1948). The Westernist school had two prominent figures, the poet Tevfik Fikret (1870–1915) and Dr Abdullah Cevdet (1869–1932), one of the founders of the *İttihad ve Terakki Cemiyeti* (Committee of Union and Progress), which was the primary ruling power in the Ottoman Empire in the period 1908–1918. Without attacking religion itself, the former attacked the doctrines of the Islamic state in his famous poem *Tarih-i kadim* ("Ancient History"), written in 1905 but which remained unpublished during Abdülhamit II's reign. The latter, known for his atheism, published the review *İctihad* (1904–1932), first in Geneva then in Cairo, which became the chief organ of Westernist ideas. *İctihad* was published until Cevdet's death in 1932 and provided much of the inspiration for Mustafa Kemal (later Atatürk)'s reforms during the early years of the Republic. In all cases, the Westernists appeared as the opponents of the Islamists, and the clash of the two helped to develop the Turkist position as an alternative.[2]

With regard to the Islamists, it should be noted that they did not constitute a single block, and that at least three broad subdivisions can be observed among them. The first is that of the traditionalists: many prominent Turkish-speaking Ottoman ulama opposed the modernist current in the Muslim world during the late nineteenth and early twentieth centuries. The opponents to a modernist Islam voiced their ideas in the periodical *Beyânülhak* ("Presentation of the Truth," 1908–1912), the organ of the *Cemiyyet-i İlmiyye-i İslâmiyye* (Association of Islamic Scholars), and were led by Mustafa Sabri Efendi (1869–1954), who was to become *Şeyhülislâm* in the years 1919–1922, and to go into exile after the Republic was proclaimed in 1923. The motto of *Beyânülhak*, "*amr bi'l-ma'rūf wa nahī'an il-munkar* (Command that which is approved and prohibit that which is rejected),"[3] symbolically expressed how particularly disturbed its contributors were by the proposal to reopen "the gate of *iğtihād* (independent judgment)" in Islam, bypassing the precedents established by the classical commentators of Islam. They criticized such proposals as the notion of *mezhepsizlik* (the refusal of submitting oneself to a theological school), since it meant undermining the traditional legal apparatus (the Islamic schools of law).[4] This accusation can still be heard in contemporary Turkey.

The second subdivision is a group gathered around the *İttihâd-ı Muhammedî Cemiyeti* (the Mohammedan Union), and the newspaper *Volkan* ("The Vulcano," 1908–1909) led by the Naqshbandi *şeyh* Derviş Vahdetî (1870–1909). The latter instigated the counterrevolution of April 1909, better known in Turkish history as the "*31 Mart Vak'ası* (March 31 Incident)," and was hanged together with other figures of the group. One of the survivors of this incident was Bediüzzaman Said Nursî (1876/77–1960), who later became the founder of the Nurcu movement, probably the largest Islamic *cemaat* in twentieth-century Turkey. The *Volkan* pledged itself to fight against the Committee of Union and Progress (CUP) régime. According to this newspaper, the new régime after the revolution of 1908 was not Islamic, but made up of *dehrîs* (secularists), and its promoters did not apply the shari'a under the pretexts of the presence of non-Muslim nations within the Empire, and of pressures from European great powers.

The third and most influential circle of Islamists gathered around the journal *Sırât-ı müstakîm* ("The Straight Path"), founded by Mardinîzâde Ebul'ulâ and Eşref Edib [Fergan] (1882–1971) in 1908; from 1912 onwards, it was entitled *Sebîlürreşâd*, which has a meaning similar to that of *Sırât-ı müstakîm*. The editor of the journal was Mehmed Âkif [Ersoy] (1873–1936). Among the *yazı kadrolari* (core writers) appearing in the list of the *Sırât-ı müstakîm* were intellectuals such as Manastırlı İsmail Hakkı (1846–1912), Bereketzâde İsmail Hakkı (1851–1918), Babanzâde Ahmed Naim, a member of *Meclis-i Maarif*, Abdürreşid İbrahim (1857–1944), Bursalı Mehmed Tâhir (1861–1925), Salih Eş-Şerif-et Tunusî, Ferid Bey, Ahmed Agayef (1869–1939, later to become Ahmed Ağaoğlu), Yusuf Akçura (1878–1935), Halim Sabit [Şibay] (1883–1946), Ali Şeyh-i el-Garib Efendi, Tahir-el Mevlevî, Midhat Cemal [Kuntay] (1885–1956), İbrahim Alaeddin [Gövsa] (1889–1949), Halil Halid, Edhem Nejat, Alim-Can el-Derisî, Hasan Basri, Gıyaseddin Hüsnü, and Ragıb Bey.[5] Other leading contributors to the *Sırât-ı müstakîm* and the *Sebîlürreşâd* were such as Aksekili Ahmed Hamdi, Mehmed Fahreddin, *Şeyhülislâm* Mûsâ Kâzım (1858–1921), Eşref Edib, Hasan Hikmet, Ömer Rıza, S. M.Tevfik, and Mehmed Şemseddin [Günaltay] (1883–1961).

The *Sırât-ı müstakîm* published many translations of articles by well-known modernist authors like Muhammad 'Abduh, Muhammad Farid Wadjdi (1875–1954) and Azmizâde Refik (Rafik Bek al-'Azm?). This gave the journal modernist tendencies. The *Sırât-ı müstakîm* and its successor *Sebîlürreşâd* became the organ of Islamic modernism and pan-Islamism in the Ottoman Empire, and had a wide circulation among not only Ottomans, but also Turkic peoples outside of the Ottoman lands, especially in the Russian Empire.[6]

For the other categorizations, one may cite Hilmi Ziya Ülken, who classified Turkish Islamists into four groups: (1) traditionalists like Babanzâde Ahmed Naim, (2) modernists like İzmirli İsmail Hakkı (1868–1946) and Mehmed Şemseddin [Günaltay], (3) those espousing a moderate stance between traditionalists and modernists like the *Şeyhülislâm* Mûsâ Kâzım Efendi, and (4) anti-modernists like Mustafa Sabri Efendi.[7]

Both traditionalist and modernist Ottomans seem to have shared the conviction that Anatolian Islam as it appeared in the Sufi lodges or *tekke*s, and in the madrasas, was suffused with superstition, to which they proposed various solutions. Young Turk Islamic reforms essentially consisted of reorganizing the judicial and educational systems along the lines of the "modernizing" tendencies of the Young Turks. But "modernizing" did not necessarily mean "secularizing." In 1916, the *Şeyhülislâm* was removed from the cabinet, and during the next year his jurisdiction was limited in various ways. In 1917, the shari'a courts were brought under the control of the Ministry of Justice, the madrasas were brought under the Ministry of Education, and a new Ministry of Religious Foundations was created to administer the *waqf*s. At the same time the curriculum of the higher madrasas was reorganized, and the study of European languages was made compulsory. In essence, the Young Turks seemed to regard these reforms as having revitalized Islam and strengthened the Islamic society.[8]

The Turkists[9] appeared later than the other two groups. They can be divided into two groups according to their place of origin. One group consisted of *Osmanlılar* (Ottomans) such as Ziya Gökalp (1876–1924), the theoretician *par excellence* of Turkish nationalism. The other consisted of Turkic exiles, mostly from Russia, such as Yusuf Akçura (1878–1935), author of the pan-Turkist manifesto *Üç Tarz-ı Siyaset* ("Three Types of Policy") in 1904, as well as Ahmed Agayef (1869–1939) and Halim Sabit [Şibay] (1883–1946). The Turkists published reviews in their organs such as the *Genç kalemler* ("Young Pens," 1911–1912), *Türk yurdu* ("Homeland of the Turk," 1911–1914), and *İslâm mecmuası* ("Islamic Review," 1913–1918).

But the ideological relationship between the three schools of thought under the headings of "Westernists," "Islamists," and "Turkists" was complex, and the categories themselves mutually overlapped. Their organs were supported by different intellectual circles owing to changing conditions, and they sometimes made ideological alliances for political purposes. The authors who sided with the Westernists on one issue sometimes appeared to be Islamists on another. For example, as Niyazi Berkes notes, the *İctihad*, known as a Westernist organ, showed frequent interest in Islamic reforms and allotted pages to Muhammad ʻAbduh long before the Islamists said anything about him.[10] Similarly, while the *İslâm mecmuası* is known to have been published by Turkists, it displayed a wide range of contributors. These included ulama such as *Şeyhülislâm* Mûsâ Kâzım Efendi, İzmirli İsmail Hakkı, and Şerafeddin [Yaltıkaya] (1879–1947), who introduced the pioneer Salafi thinker Ibn Taymiyya (d. 1328) in the *İslâm mecmuası*. It also included Islamic modernists such as Mûsâ Cârullah Bigi (1875–1949), Mehmed Şemseddin [Günaltay], Halim Sabit [Şibay], Turkists such as Ziya Gökalp, Ahmed Agayef, Kâzım Nami [Duru] (1876–1967), and Köprülüzâde Mehmed Fuad (1890–1966), a founder of Turkology in Turkey. What the *İslâm mecmuası* eagerly contended was the need for an Islamic reform of Ottoman society. The motto "*Dinli bir hayat, hayatlı bir din* (A Religious Life, an Existential Religion)," was printed on the front cover of every issue. It therefore seems improper to classify the journal only within the current of Turkism.[11] Yusuf Akçura, known as a Turkist, and Bereketzâde İsmail Hakkı, known as an Islamist, were involved with both the *İslâm Mecmuası* and the *Sırât-ı müstakîm*. Though the majority of the contributors to the *Sırât-ı müstakîm* were Islamists, ranging from traditionalists to modernists, there were many authors who were not, or who later took different political courses. Examples include Ahmed Agayef, Ahmed Midhat Efendi (1844–1912), Yusuf Akçura, Bursalı Mehmed Tâhir, Cami [Baykurt] (1869–1949), Edhem Nejad, Emrullah Efendi (1858–1914), Feyzullah Sacid (Ülkü), Halil Halid, İbrahim Alaeddin [Gövsa], İsmail Gasprinski (1851–1914), Ispartalı Hakkı, Kazanlı Ayaz [İshakî] (1878–1954), and Midhat Cemal [Kuntay]. It can be seen that these three categories are neither universal nor diachronic.

Furthermore, within the category of "Islamists," the framework of "traditionalist" versus "modernist" is itself debatable. Interestingly enough, in spite of the Salafi tendency of the *Sırât-ı müstakîm*, the *Sebîlürreşâd*, and the *İslâm mecmuası*, some contributors had links with Sufi orders. Unlike in the Arab world, where the doctrine of anti-Sufism were spreading, little radical opposition to the role of the Sufi orders can be observed in Ottoman Islamist circles. Sufi groups published periodicals such as the *Cerîde-i sûfiyye* ("Sufi Journal," 1909–1919), *Tasavvuf* (1911), *Muhibbân* ("Men of Love," 1909–1919), *Hikmet* ("Wisdom," 1910–1911), and *Mihrab* (1923–1925) and founded their associations *Cemiyyet-i Sûfiyye-i İttihadıye* and *Cemiyyet-i Sûfiyye*. They represented a wide political spectrum, including both members of the *İttihad ve Terakki Cemiyeti* and members of the opposition party, the *Hürriyet ve İtilâf Fırkası* (Freedom and Association Party). The president of the *Cemiyyet-i Sûfiyye* was *Şeyhülislâm* Mûsâ Kâzım Efendi, who belonged to the Naqshbandi order as well as to the *İttihad ve Terakki Cemiyeti*.[12] Articles on Ibn Taymiyya were published in the pages of the *Mihrab*.[13] Babanzâde Ahmed Naim was a member of the Khalwati order.[14] Bediüzzaman Said Nursî's collective writing, entitled the *Risale-i Nur* ("Epistle of Light,") clearly shows the influence of Naqshbandi-Khalidi teachings. Simply labelling Sufi orders as "traditionalist" brings the risk of obstructing the understanding of Ottoman Islamic currents.

Furthermore it should also be added that, with the exception of the émigrés, who could think of the nation as a notion crossing over the Ottoman borders, all three schools of thought were inseparable from Ottomanism until the end of the Ottoman state. Regardless of whether they were Islamists or not, the question of how to save the Ottoman state was most fundamental.

The influence of *al-Manār* on Mehmed Âkif's Islamism

In order to avoid categorical generalizations, we will focus on a Turkish nationalist-Islamist poet, an outstanding figure among Islamists in the Young Turk era, Mehmed Âkif [Ersoy] (1873–1936). Since Âkif continued to wield a profound influence on the later development of Islamism in Turkey, this will constitute a case study of the influence of *al-Manār* and "Manarism" on Islamic intellectual currents in Turkey.

Âkif was born in Istanbul. His father Mehmed Tahir was a migrant from Ipek in Albania (the modern Peć in Serbia and Montenegro), his mother of Bukharan origin. After receiving his early education in a traditional school and learning Arabic from his father,[15] Âkif attended the Fatih *Rüşdiye* or secondary school.[16] Graduating from the *Rüşdiye* school, he continued his higher education at the *Mekteb-i Mülkiye* (School of Political Science) in Istanbul and then at the *Mülkiye Baytar Mektebi* (Civilian Veterinary School). He served as a veterinary surgeon from 1893 onwards for twenty years. After the 1908 revolution, he actively began to publish poems and articles, while at the same time lecturing on literature at the *Dârülfünun* (later Istanbul University), and still at the same time gained fame as a preacher committed to Islamic reform and national integration of the Ottoman State or pan-Islamic unity. After leaving his job in 1913, he taught at various schools and preached at mosques in Istanbul.

Âkif continued to show a strong interest in pan-Islamism through the period of the *İkinci Meşrutiyet* (Second Constitution). During the Balkan wars of

1912–1913 and the First World War he worked for the *Teşkilât-ı Mahsusa* ("Special Organization," the Intelligence Service) of the CUP and tried to disseminate pan-Islamic propaganda in Egypt, Hijaz, Najd, Lebanon, and Germany. Furthermore he was appointed as the first *başkâtip* (secretary-general) of the *Dârü'l-Hikmeti'i-İslâmiyye* (Academy of Higher Islamic Studies) attached to the *Şeyhülislâm*'s office in 1917, but after the First World War lost his post when he joined the newly formed Anatolian resistance movement against the Greek forces which had entered Anatolia in 1919. Âkif became a deputy of the first Grand National Assembly in 1920 and the author of the new national anthem, the *İstiklâl marşı* ("Independence March") showing a religious enthusiasm in 1921. He traveled from town to town and propagated the idea that the "Independence War" would be the last struggle for the existence of Islam. However he became increasingly anxious about the course of events beginning with the abolition of the Caliphate in March 1924, a consequence of the Independence War. Unlike other ideologists of his time, such as Ziya Gökalp, Âkif was unable to adjust his ideas to the secular nationalist ideals of the Republic and left Turkey voluntarily for Egypt in 1926 to stay with an old friend, Abbas Halim Paşa (1866–1934), a member of the Khedival family of Egypt. Until 1936 he lectured on Turkish literature at Cairo University. Âkif also engaged in translating the Qur'an into Turkish at the request of the *Diyânet İşleri Riyâseti* (Directorate of Religious Affairs) of Turkey, although he did so unwillingly, for he had a firm belief in the impossibility of translating the Qur'an. He eventually retracted what he had written, fearing that his work might be used as Atatürk's secular Turkicisation plans. The eventual fate of his translation remains to this day a controversial and mysterious episode of his life. He died shortly after his return to Turkey in 1936.

Already as a student, Âkif devoured the Islamic classics, especially the poetry of Ibn al-Farid (1181–1235) and Sa'di Shirazi, as well as French romantic and naturalist authors such as Victor Hugo and Émile Zola.[17] He published Turkish translations of the Persian classics Sa'di and Hafiz in the *Servet-i fünûn* in 1898,[18] and his own poetry in the *Resimli gazete* ("Illustrated Gazette") from 1897 to 1898, and then he wrote poetry on social themes, although he was unable to publish these under the Hamidian censorship. After the 1908 revolution opened the floodgates for publication, Âkif and his friend Eşref Edib started publishing the *Sırât-ı müstakîm*. After 1908 Âkif published all of his poetry, articles and translations in the *Sırât-ı müstakîm* and the *Sebîlürreşâd*. From 1911 onwards he began publishing collections of all of his poetry under the title "*Safahat* (Phases)," with a total of 109 poems in seven volumes: *Safahat* (1911), *Süleymaniye kürsüsünde* ("At the Süleymaniye's Pulpit," 1912), *Hakkın sesleri* ("Voices of the Truth," 1913), *Fatih kürsüsünde* ("At the Fatih's Pulpit," 1914), *Hatıralar* (Memoirs, 1917), *Asım* ("Hanging," 1924), and *Gölgeler* ("Shadows"), which was published in Egypt in 1933 and contains his works written during the years 1918–1933.[19]

As to the ideological roots of Mehmed Âkif's Islamism, it is often stressed that the modern Salafiyya, represented by Jamal al-Din al-Afghani, Muhammad 'Abduh, whose works were banned during the Hamidian era, and Rashid Rida, made a deep impact on him. Âkif obviously did take sides with 'Abduh's school. Âkif's many translations of 'Abduh and of his Egyptian disciple Muhammad Farid Wadjdi (1875–1954), famous for his encyclopaedia and commentary of the Qur'an, show the influence of 'Abduh's teachings.[20]

On the other hand, Âkif described various Muslim personalities in the *Sırât-ı müstakîm* and the *Sebîlürreşâd*. As to his editorials and columns which are not contained in the *Safahat*, my research yielded thirteen referring to Namık Kemal (1840–1888), the writer, poet, and one of the prominent leaders of the *Yeni Osmanlılar* (Young Ottomans), four referring with respect to 'Abduh, two praising and defending Afghani, attacked by the *Şeyhülislâm* at his first stay in Istanbul and slandered as a "*Vehhabî* (Wahhabi),"[21] and only one reference to Rida.[22] As to the Young Ottomans other than Namık Kemal, three mention Ziya Paşa (1825–1880), a writer and poet who served as third secretary to the Sultan Abdülmecit II, three refer to Yusuf Halis Efendi (1805–1882),[23] one refers to Ahmed Midhat Paşa (1822–1884), known as the architect of the Ottoman constitution and parliament, one refers to Ahmed Midhat Efendi (1844–1912), the father of Turkish popular journalism, one mentions İbrahim Şinasi (1824–1871), and one Şemseddin Sami (1850–1904). In the *Safahat*, which contains all his published verses, one refers to Afghani and 'Abduh in long verse *Asım*.[24] As for Rida, no verse makes mention of his name.[25]

These figures seem to prove that Mehmed Âkif was under the strong influence of the Young Ottomans as well as that of Afghani, 'Abduh and Wadjdi, while he had few intellectual links with Rashid Rida, the publisher and editor of *al-Manār*.[26] Mehmed Âkif supported the idea of Namık Kemal and Ziya Paşa as he has stated himself.[27]

It would be possible to argue that the Young Ottomans projected the earliest systematic expression of Islamic modernism comparable to Rifa'a Rafi' al-Tahtawi (1801–1873)'s in Egypt and Khayr al-Din (1810–1889)'s in Tunisia. The Young Ottomans reinterpreted and popularized the concepts of *şura* (Ar. *šūrā*, counsel), *bi'at* (Ar. *bay'a*, oath of allegiance) and *icma* (Ar. *iğmā'*, consensus of the learned) to mean an elected parliament and constitutionalism. Mardin suggests that nineteenth-century Islamic modernist currents were able to find a meeting point with Young Ottoman thinkers.[28] The Young Ottomans considered the superficial adoption of parts of European culture as immoral. They opposed the trend of legal secularization that had started with the *Tanzimat*. Namik Kemal rejected a Europeanization "which consists of letting women walk around with 'naked arms.' "[29] It was also the Young Ottomans who invented the concept of pan-Islamism (*İttihad-ı islam*, or Islamic unity), even if as a kind of national integration ideology of a multiethnic empire (*İttihad-ı anasır*, or National [Ottoman] unity). As early as the late 1860s, the newspaper *Hürriyet* ("Freedom"), published by the Young Ottomans in London between 1868–1870, had argued about pan-Islamism.[30] In the 1870s, the newspaper *Basiret* ("Insightfulness," or "Watchfulness"), published by the Young Ottomans in Istanbul for a decade between 1869 and 1879 and the most widely read popular newspaper of its time, had made further progress toward pan-Islamism.[31]

Âkif is known to have read the works of Namık Kemal and Ziya Paşa in his youth, along with the Islamic classics and French romantic and naturalist literature. Âkif, like the Young Ottomans, maintained an anti-despotic and constitutionalist stance in his works. Bereketzade İsmail Hakkı, whose articles appeared in Kemal's newspaper *İbret* ("Warning," 1870–1873), maintained close connections with him.[32] This proves the existence of a link between the Young Ottomans, who were the first intellectual group to espouse Islamist ideas in Ottoman history, and the Young Turk Islamists. The Ottoman Islamists (Islamic modernists) of the Young Turk era such as Mehmed Âkif were able to build upon the intellectual legacy of the Young Ottomans.

Interestingly enough, Âkif seemed to see ʻAbduh as one of the "regional [in this case Egyptian] *ʻālims*" in the world of Islam.[33] His editorial includes the following passages:

> *Manastırlı kim idi? Müteahhirîn-i ulemânın en büyüklerinden idi. Şu son zamanlarda Şeyh Muhammed Abduh diyâr-ı Mısır'ın; Mevlâna Hüseyin Cisr Suriye'nin; Şeyh Emin Kürdistan'ın en büyük hakîmi, en meşhûr ulemâsı olduğu gibi Manastırlı da bu diyarın en mütebahhir bir âlim-i nihrîri idi* (Who was Manastırlı? He was one of the greatest ulama of the recent years. As Shaykh Muhammad ʻAbduh of the Egyptian land, Shaykh Amin of Kurdistan and Mawlana Husayn Jisr of Syria are the wisest and most famous *ʻālim*s [in their regions], so was Manastırlı [İsmail Hakkı] the most perfumed and the wisest *ʻālim* in this region [i.e., in Manastır]).[34]

We can here see the world from Âkif's eyes, from Istanbul as the seat of the Caliphate, which for the Ottomans is nothing less than the center of the world of Islam.

Conclusion

As Şükrü Hanioğlu has pointed out, in contrast to Egypt, Ottoman statesmen believed that their destiny lay in Europe. Moreover, the Turkish ulama, due to their proximity to the establishment, were uneasy about producing ideologies that challenged the westernization movement, leaving fervent popular feeling against westernization without a strong guiding ideology. On the other hand, the Islamic movements led by reformers such as al-Afghani, ʻAbduh, and Rida, namely the Salafi or Manarist movement which emerged in Egypt and Syria, had little influence on the Turkish intelligentsia of the Empire until 1908.

Even the Islamic reformism movement after 1908, represented by the *Sırât-ı müstakîm* and subsequently by the *Sebîlürreşâd*, was relatively weak in comparison to parallel movements in the Arab provinces. Contrary to these Arab lands resisting against colonial encroachment, in the Ottoman state the Islamic state was somehow in existence. It cannot be taken for granted that Manarist thought was adopted in the same context in Istanbul.[35]

Furthermore, in the 1920s–1930s, at the time of Mustafa Kemal Atatürk, a Kemalist form of secularism (*laiklik*) gradually replaced Islami. The *Sebîlürreşâd*, which published articles against the secularist policies of the newly established Republic, was characterized as "reactionary" and banned in 1925 by the *Takrir-i Sükûn Kanunu* (Law on the Maintenance Order). The voice of *al-Manār* could no longer easily reach Turkey.

Notes

1 Niyazi Berkes, *The Development of Secularism in Turkey* (Montreal: McGill University Press, 1964), 337.

2 Ibid., 337–338. Mehmed Âkif's antipathy and criticism toward Fikret's *Tarih-i kadim* provides an example of this lasting antagonism.

3 Quoted by Berkes, *The Development of Secularism in Turkey*, 340.

4 Şerif Mardin, *Religion and Social Change in Modern Turkey: The Case of Bediüzzaman Said Nursi* (Albany, NY: State University of New York Press, 1989), 143–144. As for Mustafa Sabri Efendi's thought, see Mustafa Sabri, *Dinî Müceddidler* (Istanbul: Sebil Yayınevi, 1969).

5 *Sırât-ı müstakîm* 6/131 (Şubat 1326[1911]).

6 On the *Sırât-ı müstakîm* and *Sebîlürreşâd*, see Akshin Somel, "Sırat-ı Müstakim: Islamic Modernism in the Ottoman Empire, 1908–1912," *The Journal of the Middle East Studies Society at Columbia University* 1/1 (1987): 55–80; Esther Debus, *Sebilürreşâd: Eine vergleichende Untersuchung zur islamischen Opposition der vor- und nachkemalistischen Ära* (Frankfurt am Main: Peter Lang, 1991); "Sırat-ı Müstakim," *Türk Dili ve Edebiyatı Ansiklopedisi* (Istanbul: Dergah Yayınları), 8 (1998): 6–9; Abdullah Ceyhan, *Sırat-ı Müstakîm ve Sebîlürreşad Mecmuaları Fihristi* (Ankara: Diyanet İşleri Başkanlığı, 1991), a table of contents of the *Sırât-ı müstakîm* and the *Sebîlürreşâd*.

7 Hilmi Ziya Ülken, *Türkiyede Çağdaş Düşünce Tarihi*, 2 (Konya: Selçuk Yayınları, 1966), 443.

8 Arai Masami, *Turkish Nationalism in the Young Turk Era* (Leiden: E. J. Brill, 1992), 93–95. Şükrü Hanioğlu insists that the heavy Islamic rhetoric and references used by the Young Turks in their writings should be deciphered, and that even the titles of Young Turk organs such as *Ezan, Hak* ("Right"), *İctihad*, or *Meşveret* ("Consultation") had been selected for their appeal to a Muslim readership: M. Şükrü Hanioğlu, *The Young Turks in Opposition* (New York: Oxford University Press, 1995), 200.

9 Since the term "Turkism" is often confused with pan-Turkism, and even (pan-) Turanism, we must bear in mind their differences while remembering that these terms overlap at certain points.

10 Hanioğlu, *The Young Turks in Opposition*, 340. For example, see Abdullah Djevdet, "Des morts qui ne meurent pas: Cheikh Mohamed Abdou," *Idjtihad* 9 (October 1905); Abdullah Cevdet, "Şeyh Muhammed Abduh," *İctihad* 11 (April 1906). The *İctihad* also had interviews with ʻAbduh, such as Abdullah Cevdet, "Şâhzâde Şeyh-ül Reis Hazretleriyle mülâkat," *İctihad* 126 (January 1914).

11 On the *İslâm Mecmuası*, see Arai, 83–95, 141–154; Tuba Çavdar, "İslam Mecmuası," *Türkiye Diyanet Vakfi İslam Ansiklopedisi* (Istanbul: Türkiye Diyanet Vakfı), 23 (2001): 53–54.

12 Mustafa Kara, *Din, Hayat, Sanat Açısından Tekkeler ve Zaviyeler* (Istanbul: Dergâh Yayınları, 1980, second ed.), 275–297; "Cem'iyyet-i Sûfiyye," *Türkiye Diyanet Vakfi İslam Ansiklopedisi*, 7 (1993): 335.

13 Kara, *Din, Hayat, Sanat Açısından Tekkeler ve Zaviyeler*, 283.

14 Somel, "Sırat-ı Müstakim: Islamic Modernism in the Ottoman Empire," 78.

15 Mehmed Tahir was a *müderris* (madrasa teacher) and *mürid* of the Naqshbandi order. Eşref Edib, *Mehmed Akif: Hayatı, Eserleri ve 70 Muharririn Yazıları* (s.l.: Asârı İlmiye Kütüphansesi Neşriyatı, 1938), 517–518.

16 Âkif learned at this school Turkish, Arabic, Persian, and French. His favorite teacher was Hoca Kadri Efendi, who exiled himself in Egypt during Abdülhamid's reign, and published there the newspaper *Kanun-i esasi* ("Constitution"); he then went to Paris and stayed there until the First World War. Âkif himself states that Hoca Kadri Efendi had a great influence on him. Cf. Edib, *Mehmed Akif: Hayatı, Eserleri ve 70 Muharririn Yazıları*, 517–518.

17 Mithat Cemal, *Mehmet Akif* (Istanbul: Semih Lûtfi Kitabevi, 1939), passim.

18 "Bedayiü'l-Acem," *Servet-i fünûn*, 16/399 (1314 [1898]): 401, 403.

19 On Âkif's life and ideas, see Edib, *Mehmed Akif: Hayatı, Eserleri ve 70 Muharririn Yazıları*; Cemal, *Mehmet Akif*; Fevziye Abdullah Tansel, *Mehmed Akif: Hayatı ve Eserleri* (Istanbul: Kanaat Kitabevi, 1945); İsmail Kara, *Türkiye'de İslâmcılık Düşüncesi*, 1 (Istanbul: Risâle Yayınları, 1986), 309–406; Fahir İz, "Meḥmed 'Ākif", *EI*[2]; Zeki Sarıkan, *Mehmet Akif* (Istanbul: Kaynak Yayınları, 1996); İsmail Kara, "İslâm modernizmi ve Akif'e dair birkaç not," *Vefatının 60. Yılında Mehmed Âkif Sempozyumu Bildirleri: 30 Aralık 1996* (Istanbul: İslâm Tarih, Sanat ve Kültürünü Araştırma Vakfı, 1997): 43–54.

20 Âkif's translations from 'Abduh in the *Sırât-ı müstakîm* are: "Müslümanlıkta esaslar," 1/10, 24 (Teşrinievvel-Kanûnusani 1324[1908–1909]); "Bugünkü müslümanlar, yahud müslümanlığa müslümanlarla ihticâc," 1/25 (Kanûnusani 1324 [1909]); "Ataletin intac ettiği fenalıklar," 1/26–27 (Şubat 1324 [1909]); "Atalet ve mekatib-i resmiye talebesi," 2/28 (Şubat 1324 [1909]); "Atalet geçici bir hastalıktır," 2/29 (Şubat 1324 [1909]); "Arapların fünûnu ve keşfiyatı," 2/32 (Mart 1325 [1909]); "Kaza ve kader," 2/35–36 (Nisan 1325 [1909]); "Din ne kadar müsaid imiş?," 2/37 (Mayıs 1325 [1909]); "Garb medeniyeti nasıl bulmuş?," 2/38 (Mayıs 1325 [1909]); "Müslümanların esbab-i inhitâd ve meskeneti," 2/39 (Mayıs 1325 [1909]); "Milletler üzerinde câri olan Kavânin-i İlâhiye," 2/40 (Mayıs 1325 [1909]); "Fezâil ve rezâil," 2/44 (Haziran 1325 [1909]); "Emel ve talebe-i mecd," 2/46 (Temmuz 1325 [1909]); "Şeref," 2/47 (Temmuz 1325 [1909]); "Zikr-i cemil," 2/48 (Temmuz 1325 [1909]); "Mülkü muhafaza esbabı," 2/9 (Temmuz 1325 [1909]); "Milletin mâzisi, hâli ve hastalıklarının çaresi," 2/50 (Ağustos 1325 [1909]); "Hıristiyanlık ve müslümanlık," 2/51 (Ağustos 1325 [1909]); "Vahdet-i islâmiye," 2/52 (Ağustos 1325 [1909]), "Vahdet ve hakimiyet," 3/53 (Ağustos 1325 [1909]); "Cinsiyyet ve diyaneti-i islâmiye," 3/54 (Eylül 1325 [1909]); "Taassub," 3/55 (Eylül 1325 [1909]); "Merhum Şeyh Muhammed Abduh'un Mösyö Hanotaux'a cevabı," 3/61–63 (Teşrinievvel -Teşrinisani 1325[1909]); "Hanûtû ve islâm," 3/64, 68, 71 (Teşrinisani-Kanûnuevvel 1325 [1909–1910]); "İslâm ve Hanotaux," 3/69–70 (Kanûnuevvel 1325[1909–1910]); "Laf ne kadar çok da, iş ne kadar az," 3/72 (Kanûnusani 1325 [1910]); "Asr Sure-i Celilesinin tefsiri," 3/73–77 (Kanûnusani-Şubat 1325[1910]). One article of 'Abduh was translated by Âkif in the *Sebîlürreşâd*: "Fezâil ve rezâil," 24/612 (Eylül 1340 [1924]). The earlier 'Abduh's articles (no. 61–71) replying to Gabriel Hanotaux (1853–1944), a French historian and statesman, were published in book form: Mehmed Âkif, *Hanûtû (Hanotaux)'nun Hücumuna karşı Şeyh Muhammed Abduh'un İslâmi Müdafaası* (İstanbul: Tevsi-i Tibaat Matbaası, 1331[1914]). Âkif introduced this famous controversy between 'Abduh and Hanotaux before translating these articles: "Hanûtû (Hanotaux) ile Şeyh Muhammed Abduh'un münakaşası—Hanûtû'nun makalesi," *Sırât-ı müstakîm* 3/57–60 (Eylül—Teşrinievvel 1325[1909]).

Muhammad Farid Wadjdi (Muhammed Ferid Vecdi)'s refutation of Qasim Amin's *Taḥrīr-al mar'a* was translated by Âkif under the title "Müslüman kadını," *Sırât-ı müstakîm* 1/3–19 (Ağustos-Kanûnuevvel 1324 [1908–1909]) and then published in book form as Muhammed Ferid Vecdi, Mehmed Âkif (tr.), *Müslüman Kadını* (Istanbul: Ahmed Saki Bey Matbaası, 1325[1909–1910]). Âkif's short preface shows clearly his sympathy to Wajdi. The other works of Wadjdi translated by Âkif are: "Hadikay-ı fikriye," *Sırât-ı müstakîm* 2/27–41, 43–48 (Şubat 1324-Temmuz 1325 [1908–1909]); "Bütün alem-i islâm'a açık mektup," *Sırât-ı müstakîm* 2/43 (Haziran 1325 [1909]); "Müslümanlıkla medeniyet," *Sırât-ı müstakîm* 5–7/126–132, 134–138, 141–144, 146, 149–156, 158–159, 161–163 (Kanûnusani 1326-Teşrinievvel 1327 [1911]); "Felsefe: maddiyyun meslek felsefesinin edyana hucûmu," *Sebîlürreşâd* 12/298 (Mayıs 1330 [1914]). Wadjdi was the editor-in-chief of the official journal of the Azhar University from 1933 to 1952: J. J. G. Jansen, "Muḥammad Farīd Wadjdī", *EI*[2].

Âkif also translated Azmizâde Refik's article from *al-Manār*: "Müslümanlıkta ferdin hakimiyeti ile cemaatın hâkimiyeti," *Sırât-ı müstakîm* 4/82–84 (Mart-Nisan 1326 [1910]).

21 Mehmed Âkif, "Cemâleddin Efgâni," *Sırât-ı müstakîm* 4/90 (Mayıs 1326 [1910]); "Hasbıhal," *Sırât-ı müstakîm* 4/91 (Mayıs 1326 [1910]).

22 Mehmed Âkif, "Medeniyet-i islamıye tarihinin hataları," *Sebîlürreşâd* 1:8/187 (Mart 1328 [1912]). There exists, however, a series of translations of Rida's "Akaid-i islamiye" by A. Hamdi Aksekili in the *Sebîlürreşâd* 10–11/237–245, 247–250, 268, 270–273 (Mart-Teşrinisani 1329 [1913]).

23 On Halis Efendi, one of the first Turkish authors of a French-Turkish grammar: *Miftah-ı lisan* (1849–1850), see Şerif Mardin, *The Genesis of Young Ottoman Thought: A Study in the Modernization of Turkish Political Ideas* (Princeton, NJ: Princeton University Press, 1962), 210–211.

24 The following refers to Afghani and 'Abduh in *Asım*: "Mısr'ın en muhteşem üstâdı Muhammad 'Abdu, Konuşurken neye dâirse Cemâleddin'le; Der ki tilmîzine Afgan'lı [The greatest Master in Egypt, Muhammed 'Abduh. He always relates his talks with Jamal al-Din and says to be an Afghani's disciple.]". Mehmed Âkif Ersoy, *Safahat*, comp. M. Düzdağ (Istanbul: İz Yayıncılık, 2nd ed., 1995), 429. Translation mine.

25 It must be remembered that Rida harbored feelings against the Young Turks. During his stay in Istanbul from 1909 to 1910, he was disappointed with the Turkish nationalist policy of the CUP. After his return to Egypt, he began to publicly criticize the centralization policy of the CUP, made under the cloak of pan-Islamism, and to advocate the decentralization of the Ottoman Empire. On Rida's decentralization or federalist idea, see Kobayashi Seiichi, "Rashid Rida's View on the Decentralization of the Ottoman Empire" (in Japanese), *Seinan Ajia Kenkyū* [The Bulletin of the Society for Western and Southern Asiatic Studies, Kyoto University] 40 (1994): 39–54. During the First World War, Rida supported the "Arab revolt" in Hijaz.

26 Kara, "İslâm modernizmi ve Akif'e dair birkaç not," 49.

27 *Servet-i fünûn* 54/1429 (Teşrinievvel 1335[1919]).

28 Mardin, *The Genesis of Young Ottoman Thought*, 82.

29 On Kemal's Islamist ideas, Mardin, *The Genesis of Young Ottoman Thought*, 280–319.

30 Jacob M. Landau, *The Politics of Pan-Islam: Ideology and Organization* (Oxford: Oxford University Press, 1994), 2–3.

31 It must be remembered that Afghani stayed in Istanbul from 1869 to 1871. On *Basiret*'s pan-Islamism or Islamism, see İlhan Yerlikaya, *XIX. Yüzyıl Osmanlı Siyasi Hayatında Basiret Gazetesi ve Pancermenizm, Panislamizm, Panslavizm, Osmanlıcılık Fikirleri* (Van: Yüzüncü Yıl Üniversitesi Fen-Edebiyat Fakültesi Yayınları, 1994), 113–120; Kemal H. Karpat, *The Politicization of Islam: Reconstructing Identity, State, Faith, and Community in the Late Ottoman State* (New York: Oxford University Press, 2001), 121–124.

32 Somel, "Sırat-ı Müstakim: Islamic Modernism in the Ottoman Empire" 67–68.

33 Kara, "İslâm modernizmi ve Akif'e dair birkaç not," 50.

34 Mehmed Âkif, "Ya hasreten ba'de hasretin ale'l-mü'minîn," *Sebîlürreşâd* 9/225 (Kanûnuevvel 1328 [1912–1913]). Translation mine.

35 Hanioğlu, *The Young Turks in Opposition*, 10. The Turkish Islamist Sezai Karakoç also stated that Islamic modernist thought in the Ottoman Empire was weak in relation to its counterparts in Egypt and India. Sezai Karakoç, *Mehmet Âkif: Hayatı, Aksiyonu, Düşünceleri ve Şiiri* (İstanbul: Yağmur Yayınevi, 1968), 22–24.

5

ECHOES TO *AL-MANĀR* AMONG THE MUSLIMS OF THE RUSSIAN EMPIRE

A preliminary research note on Riza al-Din b. Fakhr al-Din and the *Šūrā* (1908–1918)

Stéphane A. Dudoignon[1]

The question treated in this chapter will be the diffusion of *al-Manār*, not outside of Egypt, nor even simply outside the Arab world, but according to some authors outside the *dār al-islām* itself, that is, among the Sunni Muslim communities of the Russian Empire, with special mention of the Turkic-speaking Muslim communities of the Middle Volga and the Western Urals. The Muslims of the Middle Volga had been submitted to Russian authority since the mid-sixteenth century. They had then faced successive Christianization campaigns, especially during the eighteenth century, in the immediate aftermath of Peter the Great's reforms. At the turn of the twentieth century, after new statuses for the Russian peasantry were implemented between 1861 and 1907, it was the turn of the Muslim populations of the Eastern Urals and Siberia to be confronted with the massive migration of Slavic peasants coming from Russia's heartland.

In the particular social context of the late nineteenth and early twentieth centuries, characterized by an overall confrontation of the Christian and Muslim faiths, newspapers and journals from the central part of the Islamic world began to be distributed extensively in these regions, albeit irregularly and to varying degrees from one location to another. Among these periodicals, *al-Manār* enjoyed a special status. During the short period of relative political liberalization, which lasted from the revolution of 1905 to the beginning of the civil war in the winter of 1917, it was the journal from the distant Islamic world that was probably most often quoted, translated and commented in the press of the Sunni Muslim communities of the Russian Empire.[2]

Some Muslim intellectual circles of European Russia even considered *al-Manār* as a model to be followed, if not imitated. This perception gave rise to the creation of a Turkic copy or emulation of it: the journal *Šūrā* (Council), edited in an ottomanized Tatar language in the southern Uralian city of Orenburg by the outstanding *'ālim* and popularizer Riza al-Din b. Fakhr al-Din (1859–1936).

Šūrā was to become one of the most significant editorial enterprises of the entire Muslim press of Russia, from its creation in January 1908 up to its suppression by the Bolsheviks exactly ten years later in January 1918.

***

As a matter of fact, Muhammad 'Abduh's death in 1905 was globally synchronic with the first revolution of Russia, in the immediate aftermath of which a highly politicized Muslim press could make its appearance throughout the Russian Empire. In spite of censorship, this press could enjoy a relatively high degree of autonomy during the years 1905–1911, and again during the revolutionary year from March 1917 to the very first months of 1918. It is during this last period that 'Abduh's influence could be expressed fully, albeit posthumously, in the public life of the Muslim communities of the Russian Empire.

We may remember that Egypt, and in particular Cairo's religious institutions, exerted during those years a sort of fascination on the Sunni Muslims of the Russian Empire. The prestige of Egyptian Islamic culture appears, for example, in the debates that arose in the 1900s about the style of the Great Mosque which was to be built in Saint Petersburg during the years preceding the First World War. In 1908 the architectural commission, which included prominent members of the local and imperial Muslim community, attributed the first place to a project called "Arabesque," a concrete-made imitation of the Mamluk architecture of Baybars' time.[3] In 1908 also, during the World Islamic Congress which was convened that year in Cairo, the Tatar polygraph from Crimea Ismail Gaspralï (Gasprinskij, 1869–1914) locally published three issues of his journal *al-Nahḍa* ("Revival") in Arabic language, with the aim of promoting the idea of the unity of the Muslim world.[4]

However, newspapers and journals created in Russia after 1905 remained under the strict control of the imperial censorship. This situation obliged Muslim journalists and columnists to restrain from making explicit references to the outside Islamic world, for fear of being accused of "Pan-Islamism" or "Pan-Turkism" (two grievances commonly formulated against nonconformist Muslim authors of the Russian Empire in the years preceding the First World War). For this reason, among others, intellectual borrowings made by the new Muslim press of Russia from *al-Manār*, and from other periodicals of the external Islamic world, took place during a relatively short period, and were restricted to questions which would not arouse the concern of censors. This sometimes makes difficult the identification of influences from the outside, most particularly that of *al-Manār* and the Manarists.

***

Nevertheless, the way for cultural borrowings from Cairo had been paved during the previous decades by numerous travels of pilgrims and *ṭalabat al-'ilm* from Russia, the Caucasus and Central Asia, to Egypt, and sometimes from Egypt on to Mecca. Muhammad 'Abduh and *al-Manār*'s influences were thus far from being limited to the press. They were also present in a new network of reformed and modernized madrasas, which had been created in the Middle Volga and the Urals since the late 1880s.

Up to the closure of these madrasas by the Bolsheviks in 1918–1919, young Tatar or Bashkir theologians and Arabists, who had received their intellectual education at al-Azhar, popularized in Russia ideas partly inspired by Muhammad ʻAbduh's teaching. (Recent documental discoveries even suggest that despite the eventual emigration of many of these young ulama, after 1920, from Russia to Turkey, the Arabic peninsula, Xinjiang, Manchuria, or Japan, their reformist teachings continued to be perpetuated in some of the learned circles of European Russia, of the Caucasus and of Central Asia, at least until the great purges of 1937—largely due to the vitality of traditional discussion circles in the Muslim communities of the young USSR.)[5]

In the early twentieth century the Sunni Muslim communities of the Russian Empire were particularly well prepared to receive and to take profit from ʻAbduh's teachings and Rida's writings, thanks to their social and cultural evolution since the end of the eighteenth century. In the 1900s and 1910s, an authoritative quotation of ʻAbduh, or the translation of a paper from the prestigious *al-Manār* were sometimes intended not to introduce a new idea, but to reinforce or to confirm a position already adopted by particular Muslim clerics of Russia. In such cases, a quotation is not to be interpreted by modern historians as the sign of an unequivocal transfer or borrowing from Egypt to Russia, from the Arab to the non-Arab world, or from a giver to a receiver—in short, from a center to a periphery of the world of Islam. "Ideas such as those of ʻAbduh were 'in the air' in the last quarter of the nineteenth century,"[6] and the most self-evident appearances of servile imitation may sometimes be misleading.

A well-prepared substratum

The questions that arise here are: what was *relevant* in ʻAbduh's teachings and in *al-Manār's* editorials for the Muslims of Russia? Through which canals and to which extent could the influence of *al-Manār* be propagated among the Muslim communities of the Russian Empire? Who were the interpreters, popularizers, or contradictors of ʻAbduh and Rida's ideas in Russia? As we shall try to suggest in this paper, the political context of the Russian Empire in the aftermath of the 1905 revolution, and the discussions about the confessional character of the Russian state presented a very favorable substratum for the diffusion of *al-Manār*, notably through permanent disputes about the place of Islam in the process of modernization.

In fact, the entrance of the Muslim communities of the Russian Empire into the twentieth century was not characterized by a general movement toward secularization, as was the case for Ottoman Turkey during the same period (although the dominant Eurocentric and state-centered view of Turkey's modern history may perhaps have led to an overevaluation of the secularization of Turkish society during the nineteenth and twentieth centuries).

As for the Muslims of Russia, we should rather speak of a growing political instrumentalization of religion in the framework of a still confessional Christian Orthodox state. Most of the quotations and readings of ʻAbduh and *al-Manār* must be resituated in this peculiar context, which naturally led to the valuation of Islam as a source of civilization and as a guide to social reform.

By the first years of the twentieth century, the Middle Volga had been submitted to Russian power for three centuries and a half (from the time of the conquest of the khanate of Kazan by Ivan the Terrible in 1551). Only at the end of the eighteenth century did the Russian state put an end to its policy of conversion, encouraged or forced, of the Muslim populations of the Volga and the Urals to Orthodox Christianity. Russian authority had been successfully challenged in the Urals by endemic *ġazawāt*s from the 1730s to the 1770s (i.e. predating Muhammad bin ʻAbd al-Wahhab's movement in the Arabian Peninsula).[7] The Edict of Religious Tolerance signed by Catherine II in June 1773 forbade the Orthodox clergy from intervening in the affairs of the other confessions of the Empire. The aim of this political step was to bring peace among the Muslim populations of the Volga and the Urals. It was also supposed to win over those of the Qazaqs who had been recently integrated into the Empire, as well as the subjects of the khan of Crimea, which was to be annexed to Russia in 1783.

At the same time, the Czarina's government was creating the nucleus of an official Muslim "clergy," following the model of structures instituted earlier in the century by Peter the Great for a better state control of the Orthodox Church. A *muftiyyat* was created in Ufa in 1782, and a Spiritual Assembly of the Muslim Law in 1788 (first in Ufa, then in Orenburg after 1796).[8] In addition to controlling the religious hierarchy, this system was intended to turn the Hanafi Sunni Muslims of European Russia, as well as those of the more recently annexed territories of the northern Qazaq steppe and Crimea, away from the authority of the Ottoman sultan-caliph.

Nevertheless, the weak financial means of the *muftiyyat* and of the Spiritual Assembly, and the discussed religious legitimacy of both bodies, aroused a debate among the Muslim subjects of the Czar that lasted until the end of the imperial period: could the Russian Empire be considered a *dār al-islām* if the shariʻa was restricted to those acts otherwise executed by notaries, while the Orthodox clergy enjoyed official support for its conversion campaigns? Should the faithful obey fatwas elaborated under the supervision of the Russian Ministry of the Interior by a religious bureaucracy devoid of great spiritual authority? These discussions undermined all of the theological and judicial polemics of the nineteenth and early twentieth centuries.

Between the reign of Catherine II and the 1880s Islam, as promoted by the "Tatar"[9] mullahs under the formal leadership of the mufti, was seen by the Russian authorities as an instrument for pushing Russian influence toward the Black Sea, the Qazaq steppe, and southern Central Asia along the caravan roads. However, after Central Asia was conquered in the 1870s and camels were replaced by trains in the 1880s, the "Tatar" commercial intermediaries lost a great part of their initial function. The steppe populations, which had been previously subjected to a new wave of Islamic proselytism, came to be considered a new target for Orthodox Christian missions. After the Islamic renewal of the late eighteenth and early nineteenth century, this late nineteenth-century revival of Orthodox Christian missionary activity in several regions of the empire with a predominantly, if not exclusive Muslim population (like the Urals or the Qazaq steppe),[10] contributed to make confessional considerations the focus of public debates in the late nineteenth and early twentieth centuries.

The colonizer was used to viewing the pastoral Turkic-speaking populations of the Urals and the Steppe territory as former pagans less attached to the Muslim faith than the sedentary agrarian and urban communities of the Middle Volga and of the southern Central Asian oases. In addition to making efforts to convert them to Orthodoxy, the Bashkirs and Qazaqs were submitted to a new policy of school instruction given in vernacular languages. Literacy was taught in the "national" Cyrillic alphabets, which had been elaborated in the early 1870s under the direction of Nikolai Il'minskii (1822–1871), the director of the Kazan seminar for Orthodox missionaries.[11]

Under influence from the Ottoman Empire and the Southern Caucasus, Muslim *literati* of the Middle Volga attempted to face this new challenge through the elaboration of a "new method" (*uṣūl-i ğadīd*) for teaching the Arabic alphabet in Turkic languages, using a phonetical principle which was to replace the old syllabic one. The *uṣūl-i ğadīd* was first experimented in an elementary school (*maktab*) which was opened in Crimea in 1881 by the Sorbonne-educated polygraph Ismail Gasprali̇ (the future editor of the short-lived *al-Nahḍa* in 1908). It was then spread throughout the Russian Empire by means of the journal *Tarğumān* ["The Interpreter"] which was created by the same Gasprali̇ two years later, and was to remain the main platform for the central *ğadīdiyya* tendency until the beginning of the First World War.

Such an innovation introduced a radical change in the practices of reading, which had until then been based on manuscripts of sacred texts written in the classical Arabic language.[12] The establishment of a fixed teaching program, which would be common to all pupils belonging to the same level, and the distribution of pupils into different classes, entailed rupturing the strong personal relationship that had previously existed between masters and their disciples. This transformation gave a new impetus to the anti-brotherhood discourse, which from the late eighteenth century onwards had developed in Inner Eurasia in connection with new readings and interpretations of Ahmad Sirhindi's works. It led to the harsh criticism by increasing numbers of young reformist *mutakallim*s, such as Musa Jar-Allah Bigi (1875–1949), a former pupil of Muhammad 'Abduh at al-Azhar, against the traditional mode of transmission of learning and spiritual authority among the Sufi *ṭuruq*.[13] (We must note, however, that the adoption of the *uṣūl-i ğadīd* did not necessarily mean a revolution in the master–pupil relationship. Sometimes the choice of the *uṣūl-i ğadīd* could even go with a powerful renewal of the cult of the *muršid*, and a reinforcement of the spiritual link between the former and his disciples. Such was, for example, the case of the well-known Shaykh Zayn-Allah Rasuliyeff (1833–1917), the founder and *mudarris* of the Rasuliyya madrasa of Troitsk in the Eastern Urals, whose personal prestige and authority went far in Western Siberia and in the Qazaq steppe, up to the years following the 1917 revolution.[14] As we can observe in this case, the *ǧadīd* reform was implemented with a great variety of applications, which can hardly be summarized under the common denomination of "Jadidism," as has been done by modern historians.)

However, the fact remains that after 1905, direct access to an autonomous press allowed a young generation of *literati* with an intermediate status in the ranks of the *muftiyyat*, like the *qārī*s or the teachers (*mu'allim*s) of the *ǧadīd* schools, both of whom had not finished the full cycle of the classical madrasa, to supersede the influence of the ulama, and to turn upside down the traditional hierarchy of the *minbar*s. The diffusion of the *uṣūl-i ǧadīd* and the propagation throughout European Russia of the print press in Arabic characters rapidly undermined the position of religious representatives as dominant transmitters of the learned culture. At the same time, the first modernized madrasas begun to appear in the Middle Volga and the Urals. From the prestigious Muhammadiyya which was reformed in Kazan starting in 1891 by the Bukhara-educated *'ālim* 'Alimjan Barudi (1857–1921), who had met with Jamal al-Din al-Afghani (1838/9–1897) and Muhammad 'Abduh in Cairo on his way to Mecca in 1887,[15] to the no less famous 'Āliyya which was created in Ufa in 1906 by Ziya Kamali (1873–1942), a former pupil of 'Abduh—like the previously mentioned Musa Bigi, a fellow student of Kamali at al-Azhar, and the latter's hajj companion from Cairo to Mecca during their study years.[16]

The economic and social positions of the ulama were further shaken by the fact that both modernized *maktab*s (schools) and madrasas were financed not through the traditional *awqāf* and *zakāt* which had previously been administered by the *muftiyyat* and the Spiritual Assembly, but by direct patronage of benevolent societies (*ḫayriyya ǧam'iyyatlarī*).[17] The latter were to be created in increasing number after 1905, on the initiative of wealthy individuals, or of the local Muslim communities. They had two very different, although not contradictory, models: the Christian Orthodox charitable organizations that had multiplied throughout the Empire since the 1890s, and the benevolent associations that were promoted by 'Abduh in Cairo in the last decade of the nineteenth century.

In both the reformed *maktab*s and madrasas, accent was put on the renewal of Islamic ethical education, notably through the translation or adaptation in Tatar of the classical ethics (*aḫlāq*) literature from Arabic, Persian, and Chaghatay Turkic. (Hence, in the years preceding the First World War, one could regularly read in the Muslim press of Russia Tatar translations of al-Jahiz, side by side with apparently anachronistic controversies on the adaptation of Sa'di's works for Turkic audiences.)

We can find several reasons for this general insistence on moral education. The first was doubtlessly the need to differentiate the Muslim communities from the dominant Christian communities. This need was sharply felt in the Urals, in Siberia and in the northern Qazaq steppe, three regions under intensive Slavic colonization and exposed to subsequent social violence. Such a need for differentiation can explain the interest shown by Muslim *literati* of European Russia of the nineteenth and early twentieth centuries, in the rigorist ideas developed much earlier by the Indian Muslim reformist thinker Shah Wali-Allah of Delhi (1703–1762), and which spread toward Inner Eurasia through the continental Sufi networks of the Naqshbandiyya-Mujaddidiyya.[18]

A second motive for this ethical renewal was a general need for public respectability. This new sentiment was directly linked with the rapid progression of capitalism among Muslim communities of the Russian Empire, and with the appearance of new Muslim wealth with a strong need for honorability.[19] We may notice in this respect that the general movement toward Islamic moral rigorism (with *new* arguments about alcoholism, or the wearing of the veil by women and young girls) echoed similar tendencies in the Orthodox Christian communities of the Russian Empire. As to capitalism itself, although it was sharply criticized by renowned reformist ulama for its fragmenting effects among Muslim communities of the Russian Empire, its specific attributes and devices, in particular the principles of interest loan and the modern credit banks, were generally praised in the modernist Tatar press as the only means for the Muslims of the Empire to face the encroachments of the Russian business community.[20]

A madrasa-centered modernization movement

The result of these concordant evolutions was an overall renewal and reinforcement of Muslim communal consciousness and institutions. This began with the madrasas, which played a key role in the modernization process of European Russia until the very first years of the Soviet period. At the same time, as we have suggested in the preceding paragraphs, this general process occurred during a period of strong challenge to the traditional authority of the ulama. How can we explain this paradoxical success of a madrasa-centered model of modernization in European Russia at a time when the region was exposed to fierce controversies on the status and legitimacy of the Muslim clergy?[21]

The most tempting explanation is to be found in the double pressure exerted by the Russian state and by the Orthodox church, in particular during the periods of intensive missionary activity, that is, from the 1710s to the 1760s, and again in the last decades of the nineteenth century. How did the Muslim inhabitants of European Russia face the previously unseen demographic, economic, social, and cultural pressure of the Russian state and society? In touch with the contemporary intellectual currents that circulated inside Russian society itself, modern education and family values were soon identified as the key tools for the preservation of the Islamic community under Christian domination.

Nevertheless, up to the end of the Czarist regime Russian legislation forbade the creation of higher educational institutions in languages other than Russian.

The only tolerated schools in vernacular languages were the "confessional" (*konfesional'nye*) ones, whose teaching program was restricted to religious matters. For implementing their own educational renewal the Muslims of Russia enjoyed a limited choice of three possibilities: (1) entering Russian schools, technical institutes, and universities, all placed under the more or less formal supervision of the Christian Orthodox clergy; (2) attending the so-called "Russo-Tatar" (*russko-tatarskie*) or "Russo-indigenous" schools (*russko-tuzemnye školy*) which had been created since the 1870s, but which were perceived by many Muslim subjects of the Czar as an instrument of Russification and Christianization; (3) reforming their own "confessional" *maktabs* and madrasas (or *dīnī* madrasas—"religious schools"—as they were called in official practice since the 1780s).

The *dīnī* madrasas offered limited possibilities for developing disciplines outside the classical *'ulūm-i 'arabiyya*, such as modern history, geography, mathematics, or the European languages. However, the modernized madrasas of European Russia, which appeared in the late 1880s, included these disciplines in their curriculum and contributed greatly to disseminating them among the Muslim communities of the Empire. Moreover, the religious teaching given by the reformed madrasas of Crimea, the Volga region, and the Urals was deeply influenced by Salafi and reformist ideas imported from the outside Islamic world.

These trends permitted a deep renewal in the perceptions of the nature and in the social function of Islam in the context of Imperial Russia. The origins of this renewal must be sought in both the intellectual movements which developed in Inner Eurasia since the end of the eighteenth century, and in the direct influence of 'Abduh on the Turkic students from the Russian Empire who attended al-Azhar or used to read *al-Manār*.

After Catherine II's Edict of Religious Tolerance, and the creation of the *muftiyyat*, the *ṭalaba*s of the Volga, the Urals, and Siberia had been once again permitted to attend the greatest of the Hanafi madrasas in Bukhara, Samarqand, and Kabul. Students from European Russia arrived there en masse at a time when a strong reformist movement was spreading from India to Russia via Afghanistan and Central Asia, through the previously mentioned networks of the Mujaddidiyya. In the spirit of the pre-Mongol Hanafi tradition, the renewal of *kalām* raised new questions about the choice between *taqlīd* and *iğtihād* in the theological and judicial problems that were not addressed in the Qur'an or the Sunna.

The influx of the *ṭalaba*s from Russia contributed to an unprecedented renewal of theological studies in the old Bukharan madrasas. In the first decade of the nineteenth century, a young nonconformist scholar from the village of Korsa on the Middle Volga, 'Abd al-Nasir Abu'l-Nasr al-Qursawi (1776–1812), aroused an acute controversy about the night prayer (*'išā'*) in sub-boreal regions.[22] These arguments, and the subsequent debates among Inner Eurasian Hanafis about the reopening of the *iğtihād* found their way to the Middle-Volga region, thanks to Shihab al-Din al-Marjani (1818–1889), an *'ālim* from Kazan.[23] Although Marjani spread throughout European Russia the idea of a cultural decay of the Central

Asian oases, his teachings, and publications were deeply influenced by his early years in the madrasas and libraries of Bukhara and Samarqand. (Even the idea of an overall "decadence"—*inqirāż*—of Central Asia may have been inspired to him by mid-nineteenth-century reform-minded Bukharan ulama, only to be later reinforced by his reading of contemporary Russian orientalist literature.)[24]

In his historiographical works Marjani praised the first centuries of Islam among the Volga Bulghars, and the practice of the shari'a in the Hanafi *madhhab* before the Mongol invasion.[25] In so doing, the Kazan *'ālim* was stressing the central place occupied by Islam in the collective memory of the Volga Muslims. At the turn of the century, the role of Islam as a structuring element for the community life of Muslims of European Russia was being reinforced by colonization movements linked with the great migrations of Slavic peasants toward the Urals, Siberia, the northern Qazaq steppe, and the Caucasus.

After the Crimean War of 1854–1855 (which was largely perceived among the Muslims of Russia as an Ottoman victory over the Russian Empire), and during the period of political reforms under the Czar Alexander II (r. 1855–1881), the local Muslim communities which had been forcibly converted to Orthodoxy during the eighteenth century asked permission to return openly to the practice of Islam—something that they would only be allowed to do only after the second Edict of Religious Tolerance of 17 (30) April 1905.[26] Forced migration, departure for the Ottoman Empire, and the memory of conversion were closely associated in the collective mind of the Muslim communities of European Russia on the eve of the twentieth century.[27]

In this general context characterized less by secularization than by an overall re-Islamization process, and by a growing political instrumentalization of religion in the framework of a still confessional state, the presence of a powerful group of Bukhara-educated ulama favorable to the new ideas, and the rich private patronage of an emerging Muslim bourgeoisie, also contributed to orient the cultural renewal toward a reform of the *maktab*s and madrasas. Except for the specificities of the *uṣūl-i ğadīd* and the debates on the translation of sacred texts and moralist literature, one can only be surprised by the parallels between the reform of the madrasas of Russia and the events observed slightly earlier in Cairo, in spite of very different social and political substratums.

As in the case of al-Azhar, the program of reforms implemented in the first modernized madrasas and *maktab*s of European Russia from the late 1880s onwards was essentially practical. Like their colleagues in Cairo, the reformist *mudarris*es (madrasa teachers) of Kazan, Orenburg, and Ufa were mainly preoccupied with enriching the curriculum with new subjects, namely modern and secular ones. The reformers of the Islamic educational system advocated the creation of fixed course schedules, the distribution of pupils among different levels instead of in haphazard classes organized around individual teachers. Annual examinations were to be organized for all courses of the new teaching programs so as to guarantee academic standards comparable to those of the Russian *gimnazii*, technical institutes, and universities.[28]

As to the content of teaching, instead of secondhand commentaries and explanations by late medieval authors, preference was given to the use of great texts by the classical scholars of Islam, as was also done in al-Azhar. The content of the program was deeply marked by the heritage of both Jamal al-Din al-Afgani and Muhammad ʿAbduh. The overall practice of Qurʾanic justification of the most recent scientific discoveries followed a form of casuistry initiated by al-Afghani during his years of teaching at al-Azhar. At the same time, one could observe a general focusing of *kalām* on the central pillars of the religion so as to arouse a more vital faith in the fundamental beliefs of Islam, in the spirit of ʿAbduh's *Tawḥīd*.[29]

As for the infrastructures to be created, in Russia, like in Cairo, many authors expressed concern about the need for public libraries to take the place of private collections of books, which some of the more authoritative ulama often gathered in their own residences. In the absence of initiatives from the Russian state authorities, some of the leading figures of the *ğadīd* circles, like ʿAlimjan Barudi in Kazan, and later Riza al-Din b. Fakhr al-Din in Orenburg, would gather huge personal collections of books accessible to the students. (Some of these libraries were to be offered by their owners to the Soviet authorities in the aftermath of the October 1917 revolution, which allowed them to escape destruction or dispersion.) Simultaneously, an editorial system was rapidly developed for the impression of didactical literature, which multiplied throughout the Empire from the mid-1880s.[30] Similar insistence was put on the improvement of sanitary conditions in mosques, *maktab*s, and madrasas: the quality of architecture was one of the key criteria for the various assessments made by the early twentieth-century Muslim press of Russia of this or that modernized educational institution.

Like al-Azhar, the reformed madrasas of European Russia were accused by the most conservative ulama of being mere schools of philosophy and literature, if not instruments of cultural Europeanization. Moreover, at the turn of the twentieth century, these madrasas had to face fierce criticism from their own students: the *ṭalaba* revolts of the years 1905–1914 in the Middle Volga and the Urals gave way to the *iṣlāḥī* (reformist) movement in Tatar press and literature. Young writers who had received their education in the first *ğadīd* schools of the late nineteenth century, like the novelist Muhammad ʿAyyaz Ishaqi (1878–1954) and the poet ʿAbd-Allah Tuqay (1886–1913), sharply criticized the madrasa-centered strategy of modernization of the Muslim communities of Russia, in a spirit close to that of the revolted *ṭalaba* of al-Azhar in the same years.[31]

In the same way as al-Azhar in the early 1910s, the most advanced madrasas of Russia would have to change several times their curricula in order to adapt it to the demand of students, and in order to face challenges from the competition. In a first phase they diversified their programs in accordance with the unattractive prospects of the clerical path, in a country where the *muftiyyat* and the Muslim Spiritual Assembly had very limited needs for qualified staff. In the mid-1910s, however, the reformed madrasas compensated the creation of special courses for future *muʿallim*s by reassessing the religious sciences in the special curriculum.

At the same time, voices began to request the opening of a teacher training college in Ufa, the seat of the *muftiyyat*. Some former Azharians even ventured to demand the creation of a national university. Only after the 1917 revolution could some attempts be made in this matter, although not in European Russia itself, where the Bolsheviks were too prompt to establish exclusive power, but in the Republic of Azerbaijan, and in the former Russian protectorates of Central Asia (in particular in the Soviet Popular Republic of Bukhara, which escaped from Moscow's complete control until 1923).[32]

Such characteristics correspond more or less to the innovations that were progressively introduced in al-Azhar starting in 1872. Our question, however, is whether we can speak of unequivocal cultural borrowings from Cairo? In fact, although scarcely documented before the Russian revolution of 1905, al-Azhar's direct influence is without doubt. It can be detected in the content of the teaching of the reformed madrasas of European Russia, as well as in the manner in which organizational matters inside these madrasas were dealt with. The intermediaries for this influence between Egypt and Russia can also be easily identified. They were the Tatar and Bashkir ulama and *literati* who had established occasional contacts with al-Afghani and/or ʿAbduh, whether in Egypt or during the former's short visit to Saint Petersburg in 1888; or the leading Tatar or Bashkir students of the *Riwāq al-Turk* at al-Azhar at the turn of the century.

Among the former, we can see very different figures of the Muslim clergy of Russia, such as ʿAtaʾ-Allah Bayazitoff (1847–1911), the Muslim chaplain (*āḫūnd*) of the Imperial Guard of Saint Petersburg and editor of the journal *Nūr* ("The Light"), published in Tatar in the capital of the Russian Empire between 1904 and 1914.[33] His role as intermediary between the Muslim community of Russia and the Russian authorities allowed Bayazitoff to obtain permission to build the Great Mosque of Saint Petersburg (he was a member of the architectural commission that elected the "Mamluk" project), and to organize throughout the Empire a collection of funds for its construction.[34] Although a cleric with a conservative reputation who practiced a form of political quietism, Bayazitoff was the author of popular booklets in which he echoed and discussed al-Afghani's writings on the Islamic legitimity of modern sciences.[35] An outsider with a strategy opposite to that of Bayazitoff, the pan-islamist activist ʿAbd al-Rashid Ibrahimoff (1857–1944) is much better known to modern historians.[36]

Another more central figure of the Muslim communities of the Russian Empire is the Bukhara-educated *ʿālim* ʿAlimjan ʿAliyeff, *alias* al-Barudi (1857–1921). Al-Barudi met with al-Afghani and ʿAbduh in Cairo during his pilgrimage to Mecca in 1887 before he undertook, in 1891, a fundamental reform of the Muhammadiyya madrasa, which had been founded in Kazan by his father Muhammadjan.[37] The founder and editor of the journal *al-Dīn waʾl-Adab* ("Religion and Good Manners," 1906–1908 and 1913–1917),[38] al-Barudi used the press to popularize his own form of madrasa teaching focused on the key subjects of the *ʿilm al-tafsīr* and the *uṣūl al-fiqh*. His lectures were inspired by the renewed Hanafi tradition as practiced in the Bukharan reformist circles in the mid-nineteenth century, and based upon a rational approach of the fundamental texts of Islam, the Qur'an, and the Sunna. Emerging as a respected shaykh of the Naqshbandiyya after his return from a short Syrian exile in 1908–1910, al-Barudi was to be elected as the new mufti of the Muslims of Inner Russia in the aftermath of the February revolution in May 1917. During the tragic years of his short term as mufti, between 1917 and his death in 1921, he tried to promote the reformist ideas and principles that he had taught as *mudarris* of the Muhammadiyya and shaykh of the local Naqshbandiyya. (One of his most notable innovations was the admission of the first female qadi in the *muftiyyat*.)

Al-Barudi's successor as mufti of Inner Rusia in 1922, Riza al-Din b. Fakhr al-Din, who had studied in a provincial Russian madrasa and knew about al-Afghani through the reading of *al-ʿUrwa al-wuṯqā*, met with Jamal al-Din in Saint Petersburg in 1888, only one year after al-Barudi. As we can see through these illustrative examples, the direct contact with al-Afghani and ʿAbduh, whether problematic as in the case of Bayazitoff, or more productive as the cases of Ibrahimoff, al-Barudi, and Fakhr al-Din, crossed the whole spectrum of the reformist conglomeration inside the Muslim clergy of Russia, at the very beginning of the reform of the madrasas between the 1880s and 1890s.

Ten years later, at the turn of the twentieth century, travel to Cairo and Istanbul had become a common feature in the biography of Russian Muslim intellectual figures. From the 1890s onwards, a combination of administrative measures and travel facilities contributed to ease the pilgrimage to Mecca for the Muslims of Russia. These new conditions allowed a growing number of learned people and students from the Russian Empire with various social backgrounds to undertake long stays in Istanbul, and on occasion in Cairo, under pretext of the hajj or otherwise. We must insist on the extreme significance that the pilgrimage to Mecca at the turn of the twentieth century had upon the appearance of modern Muslim intelligentsias in the Russian Empire, whether in Kazan or in Bukhara. Modern historians, who are generally more interested in secularization processes or in modern nation building, have largely underestimated this phenomenon. An elementary statistical survey, which remains to be done, would reveal that a surprisingly high percentage of the leading figures of the various *ǧadīd* tendencies, whether from European Russia or from Turkestan, took part in the hajj at an early adult age, although in the present official circles of Russia and of Central Asia these same figures are nowadays considered to have been at the vanguard of secularization and Europeanization.

One of the consequences of the relative liberalization of personal circulation in the 1890s was the great number of Muslim students from the Russian Empire who attended al-Azhar. Their presence there is revealed to us by the functioning of the *Riwāq al-Turk* at the turn of the century, and by the creation of a "Fraternity of the Tatar students in Cairo" (*Qāhirada tātār ṭalabasī ǧamʿiyyatī*) in 1906,[39] which was to play a significant role in the diffusion of innovations from al-Azhar.[40] The return to Russia of the young Azharian theologians and Arabists after the revolution of 1905 created a strong generational cleavage inside of the Muslim "clergy," between official mullahs and ulama, most of whom had been educated in the traditional madrasas of Russia,[41] and a handful of young theologians with the legitimacy of al-Azhar and a strong taste for radical discourse.

There is not sufficient space here to offer the reader a complete presentation of these young theologians. Let us simply say a few words on three of them who left a deep imprint on the history of the reformed madrasas and the Muslim press of Russia in the 1910s.[42] We have already mentioned the two outstanding theologians Ziya Kamali (1873–1942) and Musa Jar-Allah Bigi (1875–1949).[43] Both studied in the same years at al-Azhar and accomplished the hajj together from Cairo to Mecca. They were followed in Egypt by the Arabist Dhakir al-Qadiri (1878–1954), who would later popularize the writings of leading Egyptian intellectuals on the status of women in the Muslim society of Russia.[44] After their return, all became prominent sources of intellectual inspiration for the political party *Ittifāq al-muslimīn* (Union of the Muslims), which was created in 1905 to promote the interests of the Muslim communities of the Russian Empire; they taught in the most famous reformed madrasas of Russia, and wrote regularly in the *Šūrā*. All left Russia between the revolution and the time of collectivization, and eventually died in exile (Bigi in Cairo, Kamali and Qadiri in Turkey). Their work would be popularized in Turkey and in the Near-East by a younger fellow student of al-Azhar, ʻAbd-Allah Battal (1882–1969), the author of comments on ʻAbduh's *Tawḥīd* and of papers on female education.[45]

The Azharians, however, also had to face the secularist trend of the first Muslim students educated in Russian and European universities and technical institutes. Last but not least, inside the *ğadīd* tendencies, they would have to mingle with reformist ulama and *udabā* of an older generation, with a Bukharan or "Russian" background, who dominated the cultural life in European Russia up to the Bolshevik take over. Differences would soon appear between these various tendencies of the *ğadīd* loose conglomeration. These variations can be compared with those existing between ʻAbduh and his Syrian disciple Rashid Rida. Curiously enough, the audacious and sometimes radical Tatar and Bashkir Azharian theologians of the 1905 generation were generally keen to claim that they were followers of ʻAbduh, while the more well-established figures of the *ğadīd* press and publishing system, like Riza al-Din b. Fakhr al-Din, the editor of the *Šūrā* in Orenburg, were getting closer to Rida and the *Manār*.

Despite all of these elements of proximity, differences are clearly evident between the reforms at al-Azhar and the changes that were implemented in the madrasas of European Russia from the late 1880s onwards. In the Russian Empire, the lack of direct state control and the weakness of the *muftiyyat* prevented any centralization of the reform movement. The renewal of the madrasas responded to a multiplicity of private initiatives, to which the most conservative ulama and mullahs could hardly oppose a united front. For this reason, among others, the transformation of the modernized madrasas of Kazan, Ufa, and Orenburg seems to have advanced more quickly than at al-Azhar, despite the fact that their first significant initiatives came later than in Cairo.[46]

Budgetary questions, and the thorny problem of teachers' salary were perceived in very similar terms in both Egypt and Russia. However, if compared with the rest of the Islamic world, the Russian Muslim community was in a special situation, under the longest-lasting Christian domination ever seen by the umma, and with only limited financial means in the hands of the *muftiyyat*. This peculiar state of things forced each madrasa to look to private patronage for financial support, and to modify its own curriculum according to the demands of the public. This determining role of private financing and public demand explains the very big qualitative and quantitative inequalities which existed in the first years of the twentieth century between a few well-equipped urban institutions of the Middle Volga and the Urals (like the previously mentioned Muhammadiyya of Kazan, ʻĀliyya of Ufa, and Husayniyya of Orenburg),[47] and those which depended on the mobilization of more modest local communities in rural and remote areas.

At the same time, an important if not a key role was played by modernized madrasas in rural or semi-rural zones, such as the Bubi madrasa in Izh-Bobino (in the district of Sarapul in the western Urals, now in Bashkortostan). It is there that from 1895 onwards ʻUbayd-Allah Niʻmatullin, known as Bubi (1866–1936), a former pupil of the Bubi madrasa in Istanbul, and his younger brother ʻAbd-Allah (1871–1922), a prolific theologian and translator of Muhammad ʻAbduh, undertook the modernization of their local madrasa. Confronted with the fierce opposition of the most conservative Muslim clergy, their adversaries denounced them to the Russian police as notorious "Pan-Islamists" and they were prosecuted. When the brothers were imprisoned in 1911 the madrasa was closed. In spite of its short history, the case of the Bubi madrasa is interesting as it contributed to the propagation of reformist ideas—notably through literal translations from ʻAbduh's works—in rural zones situated far from the main cultural crossroads of European Russia.[48] In this sense, the Bubi madrasa appears as a perfect instrument for the diffusion of Azharian intellectual fashions to a remote northern periphery of the umma. At the same time, the geographical location of the Bubi madrasa, its dimensions, and its history, make it a very different institution from its far-away Egyptian model, if not the latter's exact opposite.

Riza al-Din bin Fakhr al-Din and the *Šūrā*

Like Rashid Rida, the Bubi brothers and many Muslim reformist thinkers of Russia were born in rural areas. Such was the case of the Tatar-Bashkir theologian and polygraph Riza al-Din b. Fakhr al-Din b. Sayf al-Din (in Russian Rizaetdin Fakhretdinov, 1859–1936), who was born in the village of Kuchuchat in the governorate of Samara on the Middle Volga.[49] The son of a local mullah, he received his primary education in his father's *maktab* before attending the *ḥuğra* of the *mudarris* ʻAbd al-Fattah bin ʻAbd al-Qayyum in Nizhnye Chelchely, a village only 15 km from Kuchuchat. During his last years of study in the countryside of the Middle Volga, Riza al-Din was initiated to the works of such reformist thinkers of his time as the Tatars Qursawi and Marjani, as well as Jamal al-Din al-Afghani and Muhammad ʿAbduh (he went to Saint Petersburg in 1888 to meet personally with the former, who left a deep impression on him).[50] Riza al-Din simultaneously begun a prominent and abundant literary career with four manuals on the Arabic language, *fiqh*, and ethics, which were published in Kazan in 1887–1888 and brought immediate public attention to their author.

After serving as the imam of the village of Ilʾbak from 1889 to 1891, Riza al-Din was nominated to the Spiritual Assembly of the Muslim Law and moved to Ufa, where he was able to complete his intellectual education as an autodidact. Recognized by Shihab al-Din al-Marjani as one of the most promising authors of the young generation,[51] Riza al-Din was able to continue his biographical work by publishing between 1900 and 1909, the first thirteen fascicules of his unfinished *Āṯār* ("Monumentae"), a biographical dictionary of the great intellectual figures of the Russian Muslimhood, with critical theological considerations on their works. In the same spirit, he published in Orenburg in 1906 a series of critical biographies on great classical authors of Islam, *Mašhūr ērlar* (Great Men): Ibn Rushd, Abuʾl-ʿAla al-Maʿarri, al-Ghazali, and Ibn Taymiyya. This penultimate work bears the deep imprint of the Central Asian renewal of *kalām* studies as it had been transmittted to the Volga-Urals region by Marjani (al-Ghazali was one of the most often revisited authors in mid-nineteenth century Bukharan madrasas); it also reveals the influence of al-Afghani's casuistry on the Qurʾanic justification of modern sciences. As to Riza al-Din's monograph on Ibn Taymiyya, it suggests the influence of ʿAbduh and Rida's rehabilitation of the great thirteenth-century Hanbali theologian.[52] Like Rashid Rida, although personally hostile to the heterodox practices of Sufi brotherhoods (like the Naqshbandi shaykh al-Barudi), he remained close to modernized forms of Sufism, as can be seen in the biography of Zayn-Allah Rasuliyeff of Troitsk that Riza al-Din published during the revolutionary year.[53]

He had earlier devoted a book to famous women of the Islamic world, from both the remote and more recent past, which was dominated by ethical preoccupations.[54] Similarly, the didactical novels that he published in the first years of the twentieth century were centered on female characters confronted with the moral decay of the Muslim community. Allegedly inspired by nineteenth-century Russian literature (especially Dostoevskii and Tolstoi), his works reinterpreted its themes in a militant *ǧadīd* spirit. Although these works are devoid of great literary originality if compared with the average Tatar *ǧadīd* literature of that time, they nevertheless brought their contribution to the ethical response of the Muslim community of Russia, and tell much about the epoch in which they were written.[55]

Riza al-Din's theoretical works of the same period are concerned with refuting the theory of miracles by saints, and the insistence on *karāma* as an exclusive attribute of the Prophet Muhammad. Through this abundant literary production, in which he constantly advocated the purification of Islam and the focusing of religious teaching on the Qurʾan and the Sunna, Riza al-Din b. Fakhr al-Din acquired as early as the first decade of the 1900s, the status of one of the most outstanding spokesmen for the reformist trend in the Muslim communities of

European Russia. Ethical problems, notably through the "women question," continued to occupy a central place in his work up to his final years and well after the 1917 revolution.[56] In this matter Riza al-Din advocated not perfect equality between women and men (an anachronism often formulated by apologetic modern critics), but the better integration of women in the public life of the Muslim community. In a country where the Muslim population did not enjoy the same electoral rights as the Orthodox community, Riza al-Din's preoccupations, like those of 'Ata'-Allah Bayazitoff in Saint Petersburg before him, continued to be less political than ethical until the 1917 revolution. His appeals focused on the reform of the family-based and school-based Islamic educational system.

In the aftermath of the first revolution of Russia, in 1906 Riza al-Din gave up his charge as qadi of the Spiritual Assembly and moved to Orenburg in the Southern Urals to act as vice chief redactor of the newspaper *Waqt* ("Time"). The latter had been created that same year by the Ramiyeff brothers, Muhammad Shakir (1857–1912) and Muhammad Dhakir (1859–1921), two wealthy Muslim entrepreneurs active in gold extraction. The *Waqt*'s chief redactor and copublisher was the pamphleteer and traveler Muhammad Fatih Karimi (1870–1937), an early representative of the Tatar didactical *ǧadīd* literature.[57] On the initiative of the Ramiyeffs, Riza al-Din participated in the foundation of a new biweekly journal, *Šūrā* ("The Council"), a supplement to the *Waqt*. As its chief redactor, Riza al-Din would steer the new journal from its inception in January 1908 to its banning by the Bolsheviks in January 1918.

The *Šūrā* was generously patronized by the Ramiyeffs, and in the 1910s Karimi and Riza al-Din's salaries each amounted to about 70–80 roubles a month, twice that of the *mudarris* of a well-established madrasa in the same period.[58] Riza al-Din was thus able to fully dedicate himself to his new task, devoting much time and means to the accumulation of a large library and documental collection. His exceptionally prolific editorial and literary work during the decade 1908–1918 offers one of the very first, and still a very rare, example of professional intellectual activity outside of the madrasa system of the Muslim communities of the Russian Empire. At the same, however, Riza al-Din b. Fakhr al-Din accepted to serve as *mudarris* and to teach the Hadith, one of his favorite subjects, at the Husayniyya madrasa of Orenburg. The three Husaynoff brothers, prominent figures of the new industrial Muslim bourgeoisie of the southern Urals, had created this madrasa in 1889. It seems that Riza al-Din developed closer relations with one of them, Ahmad Bay Husaynoff (1837–1906), who is presented in a biography by Riza al-Din as a model benefactor of the Muslim community, and the incarnation of the potential for an Islamic ethics of capitalism.[59]

Interestingly enough, in order to better compete with the most prestigious madrasas of Kazan and Ufa, in the early 1910s Riza al-Din and the Husaynoffs promoted a rearrangement of the curriculum (which, since 1889, had been dominated by secular sciences) in favor of the religious disciplines. They also prolonged the curriculum of the *'ulūm-i šar'iyya* from a total of 12 years to 14 years, which was more in accordance with the classical tradition of the madrasas than with the overall practice of the *ǧadīd* educational institutions after the late 1880s. Among its more temporary teaching staff, the Husayniyya brought, from time to time, such brilliant Azharians as the theologian Musa Jar-Allah Bigi and the Arabist Zakir al-Qadiri, who both exerted some influence upon the editorial content and overall orientation of the programs of the *Šūrā*.

Accused several times of Pan-Islamism by the Russian authorities, Riza al-Din had his most problematical works censored during the years preceding the First World War, especially those dealing with the demands of the Muslim community, or protesting against governmental measures concerning Muslim communal institutions.[60] The same thing happened to his biography of the Ottoman Turkish reformer and popularizer Ahmed Midhat, a book that Riza al-Din submitted to the censorship during the Second Balkans War.[61] Things did not go better after the Bolshevik takeover in November 1917. Deprived of his resources after the closure of the *Šūrā* by the new Russian government, Riza al-Din was invited by the new mufti ʿAlimjan Barudi, one of the leading figures of the former *ǧadīd* circles, to recover his position as a qadi of the Muslim Spiritual Assembly. Riza al-Din thus returned from Orenburg to Ufa.

After Barudi's sudden death in 1921, Riza al-Din fulfilled the latter's functions before being officially elected in 1923 chairman (mufti) of a newly created "Central Spiritual Board of the Muslims of Inner Russia and Siberia," which was to replace the old Spiritual Assembly. As the mufti of Russia, Riza al-Din led the 1926 Soviet delegation to the first World Islamic Congress in Mecca. Although his official functions and the new political climate prevented him from openly expressing his views, this period of his life seems to have been marked by a growing pessimism about Western civilization and sympathy for the neo-Hanbali movements which were gaining impetus throughout the Muslim world. Riza al-Din's ideological turn was marked by a tendency toward a general over-evaluation of the role of Islam in the history of mankind, an idealization of the Islamic Orient in opposition to the Christian West, and a growing reluctance for inter-confessional dialogue.

However the history of the *Šūrā* came to an end even before this change. Thus, at least from this perspective, the evolution of the *Šūrā* is not comparable to that of *al-Manār*. The two journals shared nevertheless many common characteristics, up to and including Rashid Rida's pro-Wahhabi tendencies. Moreover, *al-Manār* clearly appears not only as the implicit model of the *Šūrā*, but also as the most oft quoted periodical publication from the outside Islamic world, especially in the years 1908–1909 and again in 1917.

The *Šūrā* was a "literary, scientific and political" ("*adabī, fannī wa siyāsī*") supplement to the newspaper *Waqt*, also sponsored by the Ramiyeffs. Like *al-Manār* it was created in close association with the printing house of the *Waqt* (*Waqt maṭbaʿasī*), which published most of Riza al-Din's works until its closure in 1917. Like *al-Manār*, the *Šūrā* was, from beginning to end, the work of one man. As such, it had an intimate relation with Riza al-Din's teaching at the Husayniyya madrasa. At the same time, the journal enjoyed the contribution of many authors from the Muslim reformist movement. Riza al-Din's fellow companion, Muhammad Fatih Karimi, signed a considerable number of papers and columns on educational questions. The teachers of the Husayniyya, like Musa Jar-Allah Bigi and Zakir al-Qadiri offered a more or less regular collaboration and had their works extensively commented before the latter's departure to Ufa in 1909. The journal received the regular collaboration of many independent and famous columnists such as the Kazan Tatar nationalist thinker Yusuf Aqchura, the female writer Mahbub-Jamal Aqchurina, the lawyer and politician from Ufa Salim Giray Janturin, the polygraph and memorialist Jamal al-Din Walidoff, the previously mentioned former Azharian student and specialist of questions on education ʿAbd-Allah Battal, *et al.* The Bashkir traveler Nushirwan Yaʾusheff (d. 1917)[62] used to send numerous and regular correspondences from the various areas that he was visiting throughout Inner Eurasia. In a spirit which had been that of the Tatar *ǧadīd* and *iṣlāḥī* literature since the end of the nineteenth century, Yaʾusheff's columns were centered on problems such as the decadence of Islam, the progress of colonization, or the history and current situation of the Turks of Western and Eastern Turkestan. Such a thematical orientation permitted him to exert the deepest impact upon the Turkestanian readership of the *Šūrā*, especially during the revolutionary year 1917.[63]

The sending of open letters by readers from the whole Sunni Muslim Inner Eurasia made the *Šūrā* a kind of platform for proponents of Islamic reform throughout the Russian Empire.[64] In terms of the geographical expanse and quality of its audience, the *Šūrā* can be compared only with the more conservative journal *Dīn wa maʿīšat* ("Religion and Life"), which was published in Orenburg in the years 1906–1917 as a tribune for Muslim clerics of the Russian Empire. The letters to the editor published in the *Šūrā* reveal that it also functioned, like the *Dīn wa maʿīšat*, as a forum for questions touching upon the dogmas and rituals of Islam.[65] Its audience explains for a large part the exceptional duration of the *Šūrā*, a rare phenomenon in the history of the Muslim press of Russia, even if the constant financial support by Muhammad Zakir Ramiyeff proved salutary in various circumstances.

In spite of a long list of collaborators, a big part of the literary production in the *Šūrā* was written by Riza al-Din himself (under his name, his initials, or various pseudonyms, if not anonymously).[66] His encyclopedic expertise, his extensive personal coverage of the mainly Russian academic literature of his time, especially in history, oriented the *Šūrā* toward a highly cultured minority readership very similar to the readership of the *Manār*. Through his activity as popularizer of European and Russian science for a Muslim audience, Riza al-Din can also be compared with the Ottoman Ahmed Midhat, to whom he devoted a very laudative biography in which Midhat himself is compared to both Suyuti and Tolstoi.[67]

The publication by Riza al-Din of a set of comments on the Hadith gave him a high reputation in the Muslim religious establishment of the Russian Empire.[68] It permitted the *Šūrā* to enjoy a much larger audience than most of the other journals of the Russian Muslim communities. These were generally aimed at more targeted audiences, and revealed the segmentation of the Muslim communities of Inner Eurasia into multiple factions and ideological trends. Riza al-Din tried to maintain the link between these different factions, at least until the year 1917, when the *Šūrā* took on a more political complexion, although it was eclipsed by more radical publications and movements. On the major contemporary questions relevant to the umma, the *Šūrā*'s leading articles, like those in the *Manār*, conveyed progressive but still orthodox views based on detailed arguments and formulated with great moderation.

At the same time, the *Šūrā* provided extensive news from throughout the whole worlds of Islam, with special attention to the Ottoman Empire, by means of innumerable quotations and translations from Arabic, Ottoman, and North Indian newspapers and journals. The relatively free treatment of the events from a region such as Xinjiang allowed the journal and its partner, the *Waqt*, to receive correspondences by prominent figures of the East Turkestanian Muslim communities, and to also enjoy some credit in that region.[69] After the end of real Muslim participation in the debates of the State Duma in 1907, news from the Muslim communities of the Russian Empire, through excerpts of the Tatar press such as the *Waqt*, were focused on the reform of education and on Muslim teachers' congresses of the 1910s. In addition, the journal offered innumerable editorials about the activity of Orthodox missionaries; papers on the relations between Muslims and Christians; studies on the greatness and decadence of nations; and reviews of books from the whole Muslim world. This very wide scope, which remained without equivalent in the Muslim press of Russia before the October revolution, made the *Šūrā* an irreplaceable link between dozens of regular authors and occasional correspondents writing from throughout Sunni Muslim Inner Eurasia. In that respect, although Russian censorship imposed strong limitations on the free circulation of information, the *Šūrā* reproduced in Inner Eurasian dimensions the world-scale project of the *Manār*.

Without being affiliated to any particular school of thought, Riza al-Din's journal had adopted the overall reformist line of the Salafi tendencies. There was, however, a very important difference with Egypt and the other regions of the Islamic world, and that was the *Šūrā*'s strategy of accommodating with Russian authorities, who supported a more conservative Islam consisting of brotherhoods, sanctuaries, and popular "non-political" piety. The *Šūrā* nevertheless shared with the *Manār* a general will for restoring Islam to its past vigor, and for reestablishing the trust of the faithful in traditional values. This was to be done by means of a biweekly magazine with the fittings of a contemporary journal, redesigned in the 1910s according to the aesthetical innovations of Art Nouveau and Jugen Stijl.

Riza al-Din's constant interest in history was always oriented toward comparison and confrontation between Islam and non-Islam. His evocations of the Volga Bulghars and of the Golden Horde are indeed based on nineteenth-century Russian historiography (Karamzin and Rychkov are often quoted and commented with regard to the Golden Horde and the Khanate of Kazan, as well as Bartol'd about Central Asia). However, like Marjani before him, Riza al-Din persistently insisted on the history of conversion to Islam, and on the practice of the shari'a in the Hanafi *madhhab* in the pre-Mongol era.[70] His general nostalgia for the Volga Bulghars was nuanced by the first controversies, once again influenced by contemporary Russian historiography, about the arrival of the Tatars in the early thirteenth century and their influence upon the progress or regress of Islamic civilization in the Volga-Urals region.[71]

The first translation from Muhammad 'Abduh appeared as early as the Autumn of 1908,[72] and was followed by many others. Those from al-Afghani appear slightly later,[73] but the mention of their author seems to have been globally avoided until the end of the Imperial period (one must remember Riza al-Din's problems with the Russian authorities for his alleged "Pan-Islamism" during the years preceding the First World War). The first extensive papers devoted by the *Šūrā* to the biography of Shaykh Jamal al-Din appeared after the edition of excerpts of the Ottoman and Arabic press;[74] they were published by Riza al-Din in the confused period after the October revolution, and just before the final closure of the journal.[75] In addition to these two key figures, the *Šūrā* published in its section on "Famous Men and Great Events" numerous biographical notices on the great figures of Christian civilization, like the philosophers Descartes and Spinoza, undertaking an implicit reflection upon the causes of the decadence of Islam and the need for the rehabilitation of reason. In a spirit which is also very close to that of *al-Manār*, the series also devoted numerous biographical essays to the rulers and learned peoples of the Islamic world, from both the classical and modern periods.[76]

Among the common themes developed in parallel by both the *Šūrā* and the *Manār*, we find the same insistence on key subjects such as the education of women and their place in the Muslim community,[77] the place and role of the ulama in society (through endless debates about the collection of the *zakāt*, for instance),[78] or the response of the Muslim communities to Christian missionary activity. The highly politicized subject of the conciliar movement, which occupied a central place in the *Manār*, is treated with many rhetorical precautions in the *Šūrā*, which prefers to devote more attention to the congresses of Muslim teachers of Russia. Concerned with the unity of the community, the *Šūrā* made constant appeals for Muslims to transcend inner divisions. However, like Rashid Rida, Riza al-Din and the Ramiyeffs' great project was to teach about the compatibility of Islam with reason and science, in the best interest of mankind (*maṣlaḥa*).

Beyond this typological comparison—which could equally well have stressed such common features as the general aspect of both journals, the distribution of their various sections, their volume numbering and pagination, the presence of annual indexes in both of them, etc.—, more can be learned about the reception of its message by the Muslim readership of Russia through the translations, quotations, and comments on *al-Manār*. At first glance, *al-Manār* appears in the *Šūrā* beside many other journals and newspapers from Egypt and the Arab Near-East (like *al-Mu'ayyad* and *al-Hilāl*), especially when covering contemporary political and cultural events. The *Manār* was not even the unique vehicle for the popularization of 'Abduh's thought in Russia, since the old *al-'Urwa al-wuṯqā* continued to enjoy a high reputation at the turn of the 1910s, and to be read and commented in Russia well after its disappearance.[79] In addition to the press, Egyptian books rapidly began to be diffused even in the most remote regions of the Russian Empire, thanks to the development of mail-order sales through catalogues dispatched by Arab and even some Tatar bookstores in Cairo, or by Muslim booksellers in Russia.[80]

For the Muslim readership of Russia, however, the *Manār* remained the main canal for the penetration of al-Afghani and 'Abduh's teachings in the early twentieth century. The Qur'anic justification of science was in a good position,[81] followed by multiple echoes to 'Abduh's *tafsīr*,[82] and comments on his *Tawḥīd*.[83] For key texts concerning general aspects of Islam in the modern world, *al-Manār* clearly appeared as the most authoritative source and its articles were translated, quoted and commented.[84] The translation of the *Manār* itself, in addition to the translation of the sacred and classical texts of Islam, responded to a fundamental need expressed by both the contributors and the readership of the *Šūrā*. Voices rose in the 1910s demanding the construction of a Turkic national community by allowing all of its member to freely access and read its texts, that is, texts written in the vernacular Turkic languages of Inner Eurasia, and freed from the "Arabisms" and "Persianisms" that had previously made it impossible for common people to read written literature. The Arabic sources of the Islamic renewal were not to be forgotten or eliminated: they were to be properly translated.[85] Modernization, as it was conceived within this logical framework, presupposed the existence of a corporation of good specialists of the Arabic language and literature. The *Šūrā* gave extensive publicity to former Azharian students, who constantly advocated improving the teaching of Arabic in the madrasas of European Russia as a key means for social transformation. At the same time, Riza al-Din and Muhammad Zakir Ramiyeff's journal never ignored the strong currents for Turkification and for transition from an umma to a nation, which were expressed with growing impetus in the Muslim press and political life of Russia during the decade preceding the 1917 revolution.[86]

Conclusion

What we have tried to suggest in this preliminary study is that al-Afghani, 'Abduh, and Rashid Rida's works were largely discussed in the 1900s–1910s among the Muslim communities of the Russian Empire, notably by means of translation from and comment on the *Manār*. This was notably so by the protagonists of the whole reformist spectrum, to whom the *Šūrā* offered a unique platform during the last decade of the Imperial period. Ideological relations between the different schools of thought were as complex in Russia or Central Asia as they were in Egypt or the Ottoman Empire during that transitional period, and such categories as modernism and traditionalism ("Jadidism" and "Qadimism" in the case of Russia) were often overlapping. Significantly, the *Manār* was even more often quoted, translated, and commented in the reputedly conservative (if not reactionary) journal *Dīn wa ma'īšat* of Orenburg, than in any other journal of the Muslim press of the Russian Empire including the *Šūrā*. Further studies should focus on the various echoes to *al-Manār* in the Muslim communities of Russia, which could shed new light upon the varieties of modernization strategies.

These studies should further stress the clear disequilibria between an apparent giver and an apparent receiver. Allusions to *al-Manār* in the Muslim press of Russia are indeed much more numerous than references to the Muslims of the Russian Empire in *al-Manār*. If we take into account the rich intellectual substratum of the Russian Muslimhood at the end of the nineteenth century, the strength of its re-Islamization processes, and the openness and dynamism of the Muslim press in the years 1905–1917, such dissymmetrical relations between the *Šūrā* and its model the *Manār* do not necessarily speak in favor of the latter. What about the effective influences from Cairo? Paradoxically, that of al-Azhar seems to be more easily traceable after 'Abduh's death, which coincided with the revolution of 1905 and with the beginning of the politicization of the *ǧadīdiyya* movement through the Muslim press and Russian Muslim congresses, and through the creation of the party *Ittifāq al-Muslimīn*. 'Abduh's influence seems to have grown with the young Azharian intelligentsia, which rapidly politicized after 1905, while that of the *Manār* gained in the clerical milieus organized around the main reformist madrasas and around the community's press. We can only imagine what would have been the evolution of the *Šūrā* after 1917: this could be the subject of further research on the personal evolution of Riza al-Din b. Fakhr al-Din during the early decades of the Soviet period.

For the moment, our first reading of the *Šūrā* as an echo to *al-Manār* has suggested to us that, for early twentieth-century Muslim spiritual leaders of European Russia, modernization, and even the transition from umma to nation, did not necessarily go with or through secularization. It could even mean the contrary, a modernization *through* Islamization (or re-Islamization), to the extent that the laws and regulations of the Russian Empire offered no real satisfactory alternative. Although the role of the colonial powers should not be overestimated in the history of Islam in the nineteenth and twentieth centuries, the case of the *Šūrā* and of its understanding of *al-Manār* shows us in which way and in which measure the long-lasting domination of a Christian state with a policy of confessional discrimination could orient the development strategy of an Islamic minority. This should encourage researchers to attempt to re-place the *Šūrā* in the history of sensibility, and to deal with this exceptional document as a source for religious perception, ethics, and inter-confessional relations in the context of a colonial state, in a period of spectacular expansion of capitalism.

Such an approach would also permit external observers to understand why leaders of current Islamic movements throughout European Russia read now the early twentieth-century *Šūrā* with renewed curiosity. Although reinterpreted by the post-Soviet authorities of the Volga-Urals region in a purely secular fashion, and within the logical framework of the old ideology of "peoples' friendship," Riza al-Din b. Fakhr al-Din's work must be replaced in its original context of an overall confrontation between Islam and Christianity. This may help explain why "Jadidism" is so often appropriated by contemporary proponents of social and political Islamization in the former USSR.

Notes

1 The author would like to express his gratitude to Prof. Hisao Komatsu for his friendly help in the last stage of the redaction of this paper, and for having given him the possibility to consult his personal reproductions of the *Šūrā* as well as those kept on microfilm at both the Tōyō Bunkō and the Faculty of Letters of the University of Tokyo.

2 For a general overview of this press, see the classic and still irreplaceable work by Alexandre Bennigsen and Chantal Lemercier-Quelquejay, *La presse et le mouvement national chez les musulmans de l'Empire russe avant 1920* (Paris—Den Haag: Mouton, 1964). See also Dilara M. Usmanova, "Die tatarische Presse 1905–1918: Quellen, Entwicklungsetappen und quantitative Analyse," in Michael Kemper, Anke von Kügelgen, Dmitriy Yermakov, eds, *Muslim Culture in Russia and Central Asia from the 18th to the Early 20th Centuries*, 1 (Berlin: Klaus Schwarz Verlag, 1996), 239–278.

3 See the anonymous paper: "Pitirburġ ǧāmi'ning rasmī" [The Draft for the Great Mosque in Saint Petersburg], *Šūrā* (Orenburg) 1/16 (1 *ša'bān* 1326 [15 [28] August 1908]): 516–517 (the two dates in square brackets are respectively those of the Christian Julian—the official one in the Russian Empire—and Gregorian calendars). The project was disapproved by the Russian authorities for its "Pan-Islamic" character and was replaced by another of a more colonial design, with its main body in Caucasian style and a cupola seeking to imitate that of Tamerlane's funeral complex in Samarqand (both Caucasus and Central Asia were included among the territories of the Russian Empire).

4 Cf. notably Thomas Kuttner, "Russian *Jadidism* and the Islamic World. Ismail Gasprinski in Cairo—1908," *Cahiers du monde russe et soviétique* 16/3–4 (1975): 383–424.

5 For more details on this aspect, see my paper: "Islam et nationalisme en Asie Centrale, au début de la période soviétique (1924–1937). L'exemple de l'Ouzbékistan, à travers quelques sources littéraires," *Revue des mondes musulmans et de la Méditerranée* 95–98 (2002): 43–73.

6 Albert Hourani, *Arabic Thought in the Liberal Age, 1798–1939* (Oxford: Oxford University Press, 1962; reed. Cambridge: Cambridge University Press, 1995), 222.

7 On Bātiršā's uprising in 1755, see: Iskander Giliyazov, "Die Islampolitik von Staat und Kirche im Wolga-Ural-Gebiet und der Batïrša Aufstand von 1755," in Kemper *et al.*, ed., *Muslim Culture in Russia and Central Asia* [quoted in note 2]: 69–90; by the same author, "Mulla Batyrša i ego pis'mo imperatrice Elizavete Petrovne [Mullā Bātiršā and His Address to the Empress Elizabeth]," in Damir Ishakov, ed., *Iz istorii Al'met'evskogo regiona* (Elements of History of the Region of Almetevsk) (Almetevsk: Izdatel'stvo Tatpoligraf, 2000), 129–140.

On Muslim participation in the so-called Pugačev revolt, see notably: I. M. Gvozdikova, *Baškortostan nakanune i v gody krest'janskoj vojny pod predvoditel'stvom E. I. Pugačeva* [Bashkortostan at the Eve of and during the Peasant War under the Leadership of Emeljan Pugačev] (Ufa: Kitap, 1999), 346–360 ff.; Salavat Tajmasov, *Vosstanie 1773–1774 gg. v Baškortostane* (The 1773–1774 Uprising in Bashkortostan) (Ufa: Kitap, 2000), 184–257.

For a general approach of Russian legislation on the Muslims of Russia, and of the successive reactions of the Muslim communities to it, see Aydar Nogmanov, "L'évolution de la législation sur les musulmans de Russie, de la conquête de Qazan à la guerre de Crimée," in Stéphane A. Dudoignon, Dämir Is'haqov, and Räfyq Möhämmätshin, eds, *L'islam de Russie. Conscience communautaire et autonomie politique chez les Tatars de la Volga et de l'Oural, depuis le* XVIII*e siècle* (Paris: Maisonneuve et Larose, 1997): 115–130.

8 Danil' Azamatov, *Orenburgskoe magometanskoe duhovnoe sobranie v obŝestvennoj i duhovnoj žizni musul'manskogo naselenija Južnogo Urala v konce* XVIII–XIX *vv.* [The Muslim Spiritual Assembly of Orenburg in the Social and Spiritual Life of the Muslim Populations of the Southern Urals, Late 18th–19th Centuries] (masters thesis, Rossijskaja akademija nauk, Ufimskij naučnyj centr, Institut istorii, jazyka i literatury, 1994), 51–85 ff.; Danil' Azamatov, "Russian Administration and Islam in Bashkiria (18th–19th Centuries)," in Kemper *et al.*, ed., *Muslim Culture in Russia and Central Asia*, 91–112; still by the same author, "The Muftis of the Orenburg Spiritual Assembly in the 18th and 19th Centuries: The Struggle for Power in Russia's Muslim Institution," in Anke von Kügelgen, Michael Kemper, Allen J. Frank, eds, *Muslim Culture in Russia and Central Asia from the 18th to the Late 20th Centuries, 2. Inter-Regional and Inter-National Relations* (Berlin: Klaus Schwarz Verlag, 1998): 355–384.

9 Up to the 1870s the ethnonym "Tatar" (in Russian *tatar, tatarskij*) was commonly used by the Russian administration as a superordinate to designate the Turkic-speaking Muslim population of the Empire: cf. Donald Ostrowski, *Muscovy and the Mongols. Cross-Cultural Influences on the Steppe Frontier, 1304–1589* (Cambridge: Cambridge University Press, 1998), XIII. This term retained something of its inclusive characteristics in Muslim sources of the early twentieth century. However the Russian practice evolved during the nineteenth century, especially after the conquest of Central Asia in the 1860–1880s. At this time, the imperial administration tried to establish a distinction between the Crimean, Volgian, and Siberian "Tatars," and the other Muslim populations of European Russia, the Caucasus, and Central Asia, so as to fight against the threats of the day, that is, "panislamism" and "panturkism." From that time on, the term Tatar was to become restricted to the Tatar-speaking Muslim populations of Crimea, the Middle and Lower Volga, and Western Siberia. On these questions, see A. J. Frank, *Islamic Historiography and "Bulghar" Identity among the Tatars and Bashkirs of Russia* (Leiden: E. J. Brill, 1998), 5–6, 42–43.

10 Paul Werth, *Subjects for Empire: Orthodox Missions and Imperial Governance in the Volga-Kama Region, 1825–1881* (PhD diss., University of Michigan, 1996); Robert Geraci, "Russian Orientalism in an Impasse: Tsarist Education Policy and the 1910 Conference on Islam," in Daniel R. Brower and Edward J. Lazzerini, eds, *Russia's Orient. Imperial Borderlands and Peoples, 1700–1917* (Bloomington, IN: Indiana University Press, 1997), 138–161.

11 Ingeborg Baldauf, *Schriftreform und Schriftwechsel bei den Muslimischen Russland— und Sowjettürken (1850–1937)* (Budapest: Akadémiai Kiadó, 1993), 3–52.

12 On this key aspect of Muslim reformism see: Adeed Khalid, *The Politics of Muslim Cultural Reform. Jadidism in Central Asia* (Berkeley, CA, Los Angeles, CA, and London: The University of California Press, 1998), 114–154.

13 See for example Thierry Zarcone, "Un aspect de la polémique autour du soufisme dans le monde tatar, au déut du XX*e* siècle: mysticisme et confrérisme chez Mûsâ Djârallâh Bîgî," in Dudoignon *et al.*, eds, *L'Islam de Russie*, 227–247; Ilšat Gyjmadiev, "Musa Bigiev sufičylyk hakynda [Mūsā Bīgīyeff about Sufism]," in Rašat Ämirxanov and Väliulla Jag'kub, eds, *Idel buenda sufičylyk: tarixy häm üzenčälekläre* [Sufism in the Volga Region: Its history and Specificities] (Kazan: Iman näšrijaty, 2000), 49–54.

14 See Hamid Algar, "Shaykh Zaynullah Rasulev: The Last Great Naqshbandi Shaykh of the Volga-Urals Region," in Jo-Ann Gross, ed., *Muslims in Central Asia. Expressions*

of Identity and Change (Durham, NC and London: Duke University Press, 1992), 112–133; see also Marsil' Farhšatov, "Rasulev, Zajnulla, and Rasulija," in S. M. Prozorov, ed., *Islam na territorii byvšej Rossijskoj imperii. Enciklopedičeskij slovar'* (Islam on the Territory of the Late Russian Empire. An Encyclopaedic Dictionary), 1. (Moscow: Izdatel'skaja firma "Vostočnaja literatura" R[ossijskoj] A[kademii] N[auk], 1998): 85–86, further references.

15 Marsil' Farhšatov, "al-Barudi," in *Islam na territorii byvšej Rossijskoj imperii*, 2: 14–15; R. Ämirxan, "Möhämmädija Mädräsäse [The Muhammadiyya Madrasa]," in Röstam Mähdiev, ed., *Mädräsälärdä kitap kištäse. Mäšhür mäg'rifat üzäkläre tarixynnan* [The Bookshelves in the Madrasas. Elements of History of Famous Educational Institutions] (Kazan: Tatarstan kitap näšrijaty, 1992), 12–32.

16 Tavkil' Kamalov, *Zija Kamali: mysliteľ, prosvetiteľ, religioznyj dejateľ* [Ẓiyā Kamālī: Thinker, Educator, Religious Figure] (Kazan: Izdatel'stvo Iman, 1997), 8–9; see also Marsil' Farhšatov, "Kamali, Zija," in *Islam na territorii byvšej Rossijskoj imperi*, 1: 41–42.

17 Stéphane A. Dudoignon, "Qu'est-ce que la *qadîmîya*? Eléments pour une sociologie du traditionalisme musulman, en Islam de Russie et en Transoxiane (au tournant des XIXe et XXe siècles)," in Dudoignon *et al.*, eds, *L'Islam de Russie*: 207–226; by the same author, "Status, Strategy and Discourse of a Muslim 'Clergy' under a Christian Law: Polemics about the Collection of the *Zakāt* in Late Imperial Russia," in Stéphane A. Dudoignon and Hisao Komatsu, eds, *Islam in Politics in Russia and Central Asia, Early 18th—Late 20th Century* (London—New York: Kegan Paul International, 2001): 43–73.

18 On the mutual articulation between India and Central Eurasia through the Naqshbandiyya-Mujaddidiyya during the nineteenth century, see the exploratory study by Anke von Kügelgen, "Die Entfaltung der Naqšbandīya Muǧaddidīya im mittleren Transoxianien vom 18. bis zum Beginn des 19. Jahrhunderts: ein Stück Detektivarbeit," in *Muslim Culture in Russia and Central Asia*, 2: 101–152; see also Baxtiyor Babadžanov, "On the History of the Naqšbandīya Muǧaddidīya in Central Asia in the Late 18th and Early 19th Centuries," in *Muslim Culture in Russia and Central Asia*, 1: 385–413.

19 Cf. M. Kemper, "Musul'manskaja elita i duh kapitalizma [The Muslim Elite and the Spirit of Capitalism]," *Tatarstan* 1997/8: 75–81.

20 See G. N. Hismätova, "XX gasyr bašynda tatar ǧämgyjatynda 'riba' mäs'äläse [The Question of Interest Loan in the Early 20th-Century Tatar Society], in J. G. Abdullin, R. M. Amirhanov, and F. M. Sultanov, eds, *Islam v istorii i kul'ture tatarskogo naroda* [Islam in the History and Culture of the Tatar People] (Kazan: RIC Škola, 2000), 155–162.

21 For comparison with contemporary developments in other regions of the Russian Empire, such as the Southern Caucasus and Siberia, where madrasas played a more limited role in the social life and modernization strategies of the Muslim communities, see: François Georgon, "Une note sur le modernisme en Azerbaïdjan au tournant du siècle," *Cahiers du monde russe* 37/1–2 (1996): 97–106; Stéphane A. Dudoignon, "Un islam périphérique? Quelques réflexions sur la presse musulmane de Sibérie à la veille de la Première Guerre mondiale," *Cahiers du monde russe* 41/2–3 (2000): 297–340.

22 Michael Kemper, "Entre Boukhara et la Moyenne-Volga: 'Abd an-Naṣîr al-Qûrṣâwî en conflit avec les oulémas traditionalistes," *Cahiers du monde russe* 37/1–2 (1996), 41–52; by the same author, *Sufis und Gelehrte in Tatarien und Baschkirien, 1789–1889. Der islamische Diskurs unter russischer Herrschaft* (Berlin: Klaus Schwarz Verlag, 1998), 278–286; G. G. Idijatullina, "Problema idžtihada i Abu Nasr Kursavi [The Question of *iǧtihād* and Abū'l-Naṣr Qūrṣāwī]," in D. G. Tumaševa *et al.*, eds, *Katanovskie čtenija* [Katanov Conferences] (Kazan: Izdatel'stvo Master Lajn, 1998), 128–135.

23 Thierry Zarcone, "Philosophie et théologie chez les djadids. La question du raisonnement indépendant (*iǧtihâd*)," *Cahiers du monde russe* 37/1–2 (1996), 59–60.

24 Stéphane A. Dudoignon, "La question scolaire à Boukhara et au Turkestan russe, du 'premier renouveau' à la soviétisation (fin du XVIIIe siècle-1937)," *Cahiers du monde russe* 37/1–2 (1996), 134–146. The stereotypes about the decadence of Central Asia, which were common in the late nineteenth and early twentieth-centuries Tatar literature and press—including the *Šūrā*—were vehemently discussed by Turkestanian intellectuals during the 1900s and 1910s. See for instance the critique of a travel account published by the Tatar writer Muḥammad Ẓāhir Bīgī: "Māwarā al-Nahrga sayāḥat [A Journey to Transoxiana]," *Šūrā* 1/5 (*ṣafar* 11, 1326 (March 1 [14], 1908)): 148–149. For an example of Tatar representations and Turkestanian answers to them, see 'Abd al-Karīm Sa'īd's classical reformist view of the "decadence" of Islam in Central Asia, in particular in the khanate of Khiva: "Rūḥsiz 'ālam [A Soulless World]," *Šūrā* 2/18 (*ramażān* 13 1327 [September 15 [28], 1909]): 549–551; and in the same "reformist" spirit, a protestation of the representation given by 'Abd al-Karīm Sa'īd of a decadent and moribund Khwarezm: Qārī Muḥammad Raḥīm, untitled correspondence from Bukhara, *Šūrā* 2/20 (*šawwāl* 13, 1327 [October 15 [28], 1909]), 632–633.

25 Frank, *Islamic Historiography and "Bulghar" Identity among the Tatars and Bashkirs of Russia*, 149–157; N. G. Garaeva, "Materialy 'Vafjjat al-Aslaf' Š. Mardžani po istorii Povol'žja [The Materials of Š. Marğānī's *Wafīyāt al-aṣlāf* for the History of the Volga Region]," in R. M. Amirhanov *et al.*, eds, *Mardžani: nasledie i sovremennost'* [Marğānī: His Heritage and Actuality] (Kazan: Izdatel'stvo Master Lajn, 1998), 51–60.

26 For a rare demographic analysis of this "apostasy" movement, see D. M. Ishakov, *Istoričeskaja demografija tatarskogo naroda (XVIII-načalo XX vv.)* [Historical Demography of the Tatar People (18th–Early 20th Centuries)] (Naberezhnye Chelny: Pečatnyj Dvor, 1993), 97–99.

27 See the documents published by I. N. Morozov and N. N. Semenova, eds, *Agrarnyj vopros i krest'janskoe dviženie v Tatarii XIX veka* [The Agrarian Question and Peasant Movement in 19th-century Tataria] (Moscow—Leningrad: Izdatel'stvo Akademii nauk SSSR, 1936), 156–164; see also Kemal H. Karpat, "The *Hijra* from Russia and the Balkans: The Process of Self-Definition in the Late Ottoman State," in Dale F. Eickelman and James Piscatori, eds, *Muslim Travellers. Pilgrimage, Migration, and the Religious Imagination* (London: Routledge, 1990): 131–152; Christian Noack, *Muslimischer Nationalismus im Russischen Reich. Nationsbildung und Nationsbewegung bei Tataren und Baschkiren, 1861–1917* (Stuttgart: Franz Steiner Verlag, 2000), 45–49.

28 See notably M. N. Farhšatov, *Narodnoe obrazovanie v Baškirii v poreformennyj period, 60–90^e gody XIX v.* [Popular Instruction in Bashkiria during the Reform Era (from the 1860s to the 1890s)] (Moscow: Nauka, 1994), 77–95.

29 See notably R. Ämirxan, "Möhämmädija Mädräsäse," 26–30; Söläjman Rähimov, " 'Galija' Mädräsäse [The 'Āliyya Madrasa]," in *Mädräsälärdä kitap kištäse*, 118–119.

30 See Abrar Karimullin, *Tatarskaja kniga poreformennoj Rossii* [The Tatar Book in Russia during the Reform Era] (Kazan: Tatarskoe knižnoe izdatel'stvo, 1984), 37–98.

31 See Ä. H. Safina, "G. Ishaqyj häm Tuqay iğatlarynda šäkert'lär mäs'äläsene čagylyšy [The *Ṭalaba* Question in the Works of Isḥāqī and Tuqāy]," in F. K. Bäširov, ed., *Tuqaj häm XX gasyr mädänijate. Šagyjrdneŋ 110 ellygynda bagyšlangan xalyqara konferencija materiallary* (Kazan: IJaLI im. G. Ibragimova ANT, 1997), 158–160; Michael Friederich, *Ghabdulla Tuqaj (1886–1913). Ein hochgelobter Poet im Dienst von tatarischer Nation und sowjetischem Sozialismus* (Wiesbaden: Harrassowitz Verlag, 1998), 93–108.

32 See Komatsu Hisao, *Kakumei no Chūō Ajia. Aru jadīdo no shōzō* [Revolutionary Central Asia. A Portrait of Äbduräuf Fiträt] (Tokyo: Tōkyō Daigaku Shuppansha, 1996), 191–219.

33 Bennigsen and Lemercier-Quelquejay, *La presse et le mouvement national*, 44–45; R. Muhametshin, "G. Bajazitov," in R. Muhametshin, ed., *Istoričeskie portrety. Duhovnaja kul'tura i tatarskaja intelligencija* (Kazan: Izdatels'tvo Magarif, 2000): 42–46.

34 On Bāyazītoff and his role among the Muslim community of Russia, see the assessment written in 1920 by the *muftī* [ʿĀlimğān Ḥazrat Bārūdī], *Pamjatnaja knižka (Xäter däftäre)* [Book of Memories], trans. from Tatar to Russian by E. Nigmatullin (Kazan: Izdatelʼstvo Iman, 2000), 63–64. See also Anas B. Khalidov, "The History of Islam in St-Petersburg," *Religion, State and Society* 22/2 (1994): 245–249.

35 See [Ataulla Bajazitov], *Vozraženie na reč' Ernesta Renana "Islam i nauka" Sankt-Peterburgskogo muhamedanskogo ahuna imam džamija hatyb mudarrisa Ataully Bajazitova* [Reply to Ernest Renan's Lecture on "Islam and Science" by the Muslim Āḫūnd ʿAṭā'-Allàh Bāyazītoff, *Ḫaṭīb, Mudarris* and *Imām-Ǧāmiʿ* of Saint Petersburg] (Saint Petersburg: Tipografija A. S. Suvorina, 1883); by the same author, *Islam i progress* [Islam and Progress] (Saint Petersburg: Tipografija A. S. Suvorina, 1898); by the same author, *Otnošenie islama k nauke i k inovercam* [The Attitude of Islam Towards Science and Non-Believers] (Saint Petersburg: Tipografija Nur, 1906).

36 On Ibrahimoff's relations with al-Afghani in particular, see Ismail Türkoğlu, *Sibiriyalı Meşhur Seyyah Abdürreşid Ibrahim* [ʿAbd al-Rašīd Ibrāhīm, a Famous Siberian Traveller] (Ankara: Türkie Diyanet Yayınları, 1997). See also the paper by Hisao Komatsu in the present volume.

37 See Farhšatov, "al-Barudi," 14–15, bibliography.

38 Bennigsen and Lemercier-Quelquejay, *La presse et le mouvement national*, 59–60.

39 See Zavdat Z. Minullin, "Zemljačestva i blagotvoritelʼnye obŝestva tatarskih učaŝihsja v musulʼmanskih stranah (načalo XX v.)," *Mir islama* (Kazan) 1 (1999): 135–144; English translation available as "Fraternal and Benevolent Associations of Tatar Students in Muslim Countries at the Beginning of the 20th Century," in Anke von Kügelgen, Michael Kemper and Allen J. Frank, eds, *Muslim Culture in Russia and Central Asia* (Berlin: Schwarz, 1998), 271–280.

40 See for example Qāhirada Tātār Ṭalabasī Ǧamʿiyyatī, "Miṣr al-Qāhirada: al-Azhar (Miṣrdan) [In Cairo: al-Azhar (A Correspondence from Egypt)]," *Šūrā* 1/4 (*muḥarram* 26, 1326 [February 15 [28], 1908]), 114–116; 1/6 (*ṣafar* 25, 1326 [March 15 [28], 1908]), 168–171; 1/7 (*rabīʿ al-awwal* 13, 1326 [April 1 [14], 1908]), 200–202. About the Fraternity of the Muslim Students from Russia in Mecca, and its relations with the Fraternity in Cairo, see the anonymous column: "Makka-yi Mukarramada Rūsiya islām ṭalabasīniŋ ğamʿiyyat-i ʿilmiyyasī [The Learned Society of Students from the Russian Muslimhood in Mecca]," *Šūrā* 3/6 (*rabīʿ al-awwal* 17, 1327 [March 15 [28], 1910]), 191–192.

41 Azamatov, *Orenburgskoe magometanskoe duhovnoe sobranie*, 355–384.

42 See Madina Rahimkulova, *Medrese "Husainija" v Orenburge. 2oe dopolnennoe jubilejnoe izdanie, posvjaŝennoe 160-letiju Ahmet baja Husajnova* [The Ḥusayniyya Madrasa in Orenburg. 2nd Edition, Completed in the Honor of the 160th Birthday of Aḥmad Bāy Ḥusaynoff] (Orenburg: Jana Vakyt, 1997), 56–60; about the teaching staff of the Madrasa-yi ʿĀliyya in Ufa, see Rähimov, " 'Galija' mädräsäse," 115.

43 See the anonymous paper "Taʾrīḫ-i adiyān darslarī [Lectures in the History of Religions]," *Šūrā* 2/22 (*ẕūʾl- qaʿda* 15, 1327 [November 15 [28], 1909], 679–682. This is the presentation to a course prepared by Musa Bigi for the Ḥusayniyya starting in 1906, and dealing with the diversity of religions, a key issue in ʿAbduh's teachings and work.

44 About al-Qādirī, see Bennigsen and Lemercier-Quelquejay, *La presse et le mouvement national*, 81–82; Dudoignon, "Un islam périphérique?," 302–304, 322–328.

45 Abdullah Battal-Taymas, *Rizaeddin Fahreddinoğlu* (Istanbul: M. Siralar Matbaası, 1958); by the same author, *Musa Carullah Bigi* (Istanbul: M. Siralar Matbaası, 1958); by the same author, *Âlimcan Barudî* (Istanbul: M. Siralar Matbaası, 1958). Also see by the same author, "Türk dünyasında Usulü Cedit hareketi [The Movement of the *Uṣūl-i Ǧadīd* in the Turkic World]," *Türk Kültürü* 2/18 (1964), 119–125.

46 See notably Bayart Dodge, *Al-Azhar. A Millenium of Muslim Learning* (Washington, DC: The Middle East Institute, 1974), 132.

47 See M. Rähimkulova and A. Hamidullin, " 'Hösäjnija' mädräsäse [The Ḥusayniyya Madrasa]," in Mähdiev, ed., *Mädräsälärdä kitap kištäse*, 74–114; Rahimkulova, *Medrese "Husajnija" v Orenburge*, 4–15.

48 Abdallah Bubi, *Bubi madrasasining qisqa ta'rixi* [An Abridged History of the Bubi Madrasa] (Bubi-Sarapul and Ghulja: *s.n.*, 1913–1918; reprinted in cyrillic alphabet by Raif Märdanov and Söläjman Rähimov, Kazan: *s.n.*, 1991). For other analogous examples from the eastern Volga-Kama region, see: I. R. Gabdullin and R. R. Ibragimova, "Mektebe i medrese Bugul'minskogo i Menzelinskogo uezdov v konce XIX—načale XX vekov [The *Maktab*s and Madrasas of the Districts of Bugul'ma and Menzelinsk in the Late 19th and Early 20th Centuries)," in Ishakov, ed., *Iz istorii Al'met'evskogo regiona*, 174–179.

49 Although the recent bibliography on Rižā al-Dīn b. Faḫr al-Dīn remains very problematic due to the tendency of most authors to ignore the religious aspects of his work and to promote secularist interpretations of it, we may mention the following contributions: in addition to the previously mentioned monograph by Battal-Taymas, *Rizaeddin Fahreddinoğlu*, see Mahmud Tahir, "Risaeddin Fahreddin," *Central Asian Survey*, 8/1 (1989): 111–115; F. N. Bajšev, *Občestvenno-političeskie i nravstvenno-etičeskie vzgljady Rizy Fahretdinova* [The Socio-Political and Ethical Conceptions of Rižā Faḫr al-Dīnoff] (Ufa: Kitap, 1996); Ġaisa Hösäjnov, *Rizaitdin bin Fäxretdin* (Ufa: Kitap, 1997); Mädinä Rähimkulova, ed., *Rizaetdin bin Fäxretdingä 140 jaš tulu mönäsäbäte belän (1859–1936)* [On the Occasion of Rižā al-Dīn b. Faḫr al-Dīn's 140th Anniversary (1859–1936)] (Orenburg: Agenstvo Pressa, 1998); Raif Märdanov, Zavdat Miŋullin, and Söläjman Rähimov, eds, *Rizaetdin Fexretdin. Fänni-biografik Ğyentyk / Rizaetdin Faxretdinov. Naučno-biografičeskij sbornik* [Rižā al-Dīn b. Faḫr al-Dīn. Collected Studies and Elements of Bibliography] (Kazan: Ruxijat näšrijaty, 1999); M. Farhšatov, "Fahretdinov, Rizaetdin," in *Islam na territorii byvšej Rossijskoj imperii*, 1, 94–95; Ismail Türkoğlu, *Rusya Türkleri arasındaki yenileşme hareketinin öncülerinden Rizaeddin Fahreddin* [Rižā al-Dīn b. Faḫr al-Dīn, the Vanguard of the Renewal Movement among the Turks of Russia] (Istanbul: Ötüken neşriyatı, 2000).

50 Rizaetdin Fahretdinov, "Moja avtobiografija (My Autogiography)," trans. from Tatar to Russian by R. Märdanov, in Märdanov, Miŋnullin, and Rähimov, eds, *Rizaetdin Fexretdin. Fänni-biografik Ğyentyk/Rizaetdin Faxretdinov. Naučno-biografičeskij sbornik*, 100.

51 Riza al-Din published the manuscript of Marğānī's hajj account with a short biography of the great Kazan *'ālim*: Riẓā al-Dīn b. Faḫr al-Dīn, *Riḥlat al-Marğānī* (Kazan: Tipo-Litografija naslednikov M. Čirkovoj, 1897). On this work, see my paper: "Us et usages du voyage et de sa narration, par les lettrés et savants de Russie au tournant du XXe siècle. La *Riḥlat al-Marğānī* (1880)," presentation at the round table *L'Univers en partage*. 3: *La relation de voyage et ses usages*, dir. Alain Roussillon (Rabat: Université Mohamed V, January 26, 2001).

52 Riẓā al-Dīn b. Faḫr al-Dīn, *Ibn Ṭaymiyya* (Orenburg: Waqt maṭba'asī, 1913), passim (Mašhūr ērlar mağmū'asindan 5-nğī ğuz' [Series on Great Men, 5]).

53 Riẓā al-Dīn b. Faḫr al-Dīn, *Šayḫ Zayn-Allàh Ḥaẓrat tarğuma-yi ḥālī* [A Biography of Šayḫ Zayn-Allàh] (Orenburg: Waqt maṭba'asī, 1917); for a short analysis of Riza al-Din's writings on Rasuliyeff, see Mäsgud Gäjnetdinov, "Taškyn kočagynda bir majak [A Lighthouse in the Tempest]," *Gasyrlar avazy* (Kazan) 1/2 (1997): 136–141.

54 Rižā al-Dīn b. Faḫr al-Dīn, *Mašhūr ḫātūnlar* (Famous Ladies), 2nd ed. (Orenburg: Muḥammad Fātiḥ b. Ġilmān Karīmoff Maṭba'asī, 1904); on this work see Türkoglu, *Rusya Türkleri arasındaki yenileşme hareketinin öncülerinden Rizaeddin Fahreddin*, 312–314.

55 After a long period of censorship under the Soviet regime, Riza al-Din' s fiction works *Salīma, yāki 'iffat* [Salīma, or Virtue] (Kazan: *s.n.*, 1899) and *'Isma, yāki 'amal wa ğazā'* ['Isma, or Crime and Punishment, 1903] (Orenburg: *s.n.*, 1903) were read again in the decade preceding Perestroika in Tatarstan, and curiously reinterpreted in a purely

secular sense: see for instance Möhämmät Gajnullin, *Tatar ädipläre* [Tatar *Literati*] (Kazan: Tatarstan kitap näšrijaty, 1978), 79–98.

56 See my paper "Women at Stake, and Protagonists in the Intellectual Life of the Muslim Communities of European Russia, Siberia and the Qazaq Steppe (Early 20th Century)," communication to the colloquium *Intellectuals in Islam in the 20th Century: Situations, Discourses, Strategies*, Tokyo: Islamic Area Studies Project, October 13–15, 2000.

57 On Karimi, see a short biographical sketch with a rich bibliography in Türkoğlu, *Rusya Türkleri arasındaki yenileşme hareketinin öncülerinden Rizaeddin Fahreddin*, 350–353; B. Sultanbekov, "F. Karimi," in *Istoričeskie portrety*: 111–117.

58 Raif Märdanov, " 'Šura' žurnaly [The Journal *Šūrā*]," *Gasyrlar avazy* (1999/1–2): 227–243 and especially 232.

59 Rižā al-Dīn b. Faḫr al-Dīn, *Aḥmad Bāy Afandī* (Orenburg: Waqt maṭba'asī, 1911), especially 22–24 (chapter on "Diyānatī wa aḫlāqī [His Religiosity and Ethics]"), 24–28 (chapter on "Umīd wa fikrlarī [His Hopes and Thoughts]"), and 51–52 (chapter on "Ḥağğ ga yubārmak [Sending to the Pilgrimage]," a eulogy of the financial support given by Aḥmad Bāy Ḥusaynoff to the organization of the Pilgrimage to Mecca).

60 See for example Rižā al-Dīn b. Faḫr al-Dīn, *Rūsiya musulmānlarīniŋ iḥtiyāğlarī wa ānlar ḥaqinda intiqād* [The Needs of the Muslims of Russia and the Critiques about Them], ed. Imām Ḫayr-Allàh al-'Uṯmānī (Orenburg: Muḥammad Fātiḥ b. Ġilmān Karīmoff Maṭba'asī, n.d.), *passim*.

61 Riẓā al-Dīn b. Faḫr al-Dīn, *Aḥmad Midḥat* (Orenburg: Waqt maṭba'asī, 1913).

62 See his obituary by Mīr Muḥsin Šīr Muḥammad (from Tashkent), "Sayyāḥ Nūšīrwān Afandī Yā'ūšeff [The Traveller Nūšīrwān Afandī Yā'ūšeff]," *Šūrā* 10/18 (*ẕū'l-ḥiğğa* 11, 1335 [September 15 [24], 1917]), 419–420.

63 Cf. Shin'ichiro Ōishi, "Nushiruvan Yaushefu no Torukisutan shūyū ni tsuite [About Nūšīrwān Yā'ūšeff's Journeys to Turkestan]," *Kōbe Daigaku Shigaku Nenpū* 13 (1998), 20–36; reviewed by Hisao Komatsu in *Abstracta Iranica* 22 (2001): 130.

64 See, for example, a letter from the Turkestanian *adīb* and playwriter Hajji Mu'in b. Shukr-Allah Katta-Qurghani asking for more attention on the problems of teaching Arabic language and literature: Ḥāğğī Mu'īn b. Šukr-Allàh, untitled correspondence from Samarqand, *Šūrā* 8/24 (*ṣafar* 21, 1334 [December 15 [28], 1915]), 759. The author complains about the lack of attention of the *Šūrā* to Arabic classical literature and to biographies of great Arab scholars and scientists of the past. Significantly, Ḥāğğī Mu'īn also asks for the publication of more biographies on the great figures of Central Asian history (such as Amīr Tēmūr, Ulūġ Bēg, or Bābur), and of those of modern Ottoman culture (such as Namık Kemal or Şemseddin Sami). On Ḥāğğī Mu'īn's theatrical works, and the Tatar influence on it, see Šuhrat Rizaev, *Ğadid dramasi* [The *Ğadīd* Drama] (Tashkent: Šarq, 1997), 86–87, samples of his work on 245–316.

65 See, for example, Muḥammadğān Muḥammad Sāliḥ Ūğlī Ḫūğandī, untitled correspondence from Qarghali [Orenburg], *Šūrā* 1/18 (*ramaẓān* 3, 1326 [September 15 [28], 1908]): 573–576. In it the author, a Muslim traveller from the city of Khujand in Russian Turkestan, questions the Editor on the ritual of the *namāz-ğum'a*, making references to both Abu Hanifa and al-Marjani. Having asked in vain for a fatwa from the ulama of Tashkent and Bukhara, Muḥammadğān decided to submit his question to the *Šūrā*.

66 Statistics in Märdanov, " 'Šura' žurnaly," *passim*.

67 Riẓā al-Dīn, *Aḥmad Midḥat*, 42–46.

68 Riẓā al-Dīn b. Faḫr al-Dīn, *Ğāmi' al-kalīm šarḥī* (Orenburg: Waqt Maṭba'asī, 1916); on this work, see a short summary by Türkoğlu, *Rusya Türkleri arasındaki yenileşme hareketinin öncülerinden Rizaeddin Fahreddin*, 296–298.

69 Cf. Shin'ichiro Ōishi, " 'Wakuto' shijō no Buruhan Shahido no kiji ni tsuite [Burhān Šahīd's Articles in the *Waqt*], *Seinan Ajia Kenkyū* 49 (1998): 68–84; reviewed by Hisao Komatsu in *Abstracta Iranica* 22 (2001): 130.

70 In the series "Mašhūr ādamlar wa buyūk ḥādiṯalar [Famous Peoples and Great Events]," which was sometimes published anonymously by Riza al-Din himself: [Rižā al-Dīn b. Faḫr al-Dīn], "Ǧa'far bin 'Abd-Allàh (Ālmās bin Sāskī)," *Šūrā* 1/1 (20 *ẕū'l-ḥiǧǧa* 20, 1325 [January 10 [23], 1908]), 4–7. This is about the king of the Bulghars who is credited by tradition for the conversion of his people to Islam in the early tenth century CE. Significantly, the paper was published in the very first issue of the *Šūrā*; by the same author, "Bērkē Ḫān," parts 1 and 2, *Šūrā* I/2 (*muḥarram* 1 1326 [January 21 [February 4], 1908]): 34–38; I/3 (*muḥarram* 16, 1326 [February 5 [18], 1908]), 65–76. This is the first of a long series of papers about the Golden Horde, from its conversion to Islam up until the Russian conquest of the khanate of Kazan in 1551.

71 Cf. for example Darwīš (a pseudonym frequently employed by Rižā al-Dīn b. Faḫr al-Dīn), "Ūzimizga 'ā'id [About Us]," *Šūrā* 1/4 (*muḥarram* 26, 1326 [February 15 [28], 1908]), 107–110.

72 'Abduh made his first appearance as an author in the seventeenth issue of the journal: [Muḥammad 'Abduh], "Musulmānlarda salaflar aṯarlarī yūq ('Allāma-yi mašāhīr Muḥammad 'Abduh niŋ 'al-Islām wa al-nusrāniyya' nām risālasindan tarǧuma) [There is no Trace of the Companions among the Muslims (A Translation of the Treaty on 'Islam and Christianity' by the Most Famous *'Ālim* Muḥammad 'Abduh)]," translated from Arabic to Tatar by Badr al-Dīn 'Umrānī, *Šūrā* 1/17 (*ša'bān* 18, 1326 [September 1 [14], 1908]), 527–528.

73 [Ǧamāl al-Dīn al-Afġānī], "Islām dīnī (Šayḫ Ǧamāl al-Dīn al-Afġānī ḥaẓratlarīning *Radd al-dahrīyīn* nām aṯarindan iqtibāsan tarǧuma īdilmišdir) [The Islamic Religion (A Partial Translation of the *Refutation of the Materialists* by Šayḫ Ǧamāl al-Dīn al-Afġānī)]," translated from the Arabic to the Tatar by Muḥammad Hādī b. 'Īnān Sa'dī, *Šūrā* 1/22 (*ẕū'l-qa'da* 5, 1326 [November, 15 [28], 1908]), 701–704. See also 'A[bd-Allàh] Baṭṭāl, "Ġarb ma'īšatindan [About Life in the West]," *Šūrā* 3/13 (*rağab* 7, 1328 [July 1 [14], 1910]), 401–402. In this paper, which is the answer to an article from the Russian journal *Musul'manin* ("The Muslim") of Paris with a flattering evocation of the "*vie parisienne*," the author makes critical considerations about a world in which everyday life is not administered by religious laws.

74 See, for example, Meḥmed 'Ākif [Ersoy], "Šayḫ Ǧamāl al-Dīn wa Muḥammad 'Abduh (*Ṣīrāṭ al-mustaqīm* maǧallasindan ālindī) [Šayḫ Ǧamāl al-Dīn and Muḥammad 'Abduh (taken from the journal *Ṣīrāṭ al-mustaqīm*)]," *Šūrā* 3/12 (*ǧumādī al-āḫir* 20, 1328 [June 15 [28], 1910]), 370–372.

75 RF [Rižā al-Dīn b. Faḫr al-Dīn], "Mašhūr ādamlar wa ulūġ ḥādiṯalar: Šayḫ Ǧamāl al-Dīn [Famous Peoples and Great Events: Šayḫ Ǧamāl al-Dīn]," parts 1–9, *Šūrā* 10/14 (*šawwāl* 8, 1335 [July 15 [28], 1917]): 313–316; 10/15 (*šawwāl* 25, 1335 [August 1 [14], 1917]): 338–341; 10/16 (*ẕū'l-qa'da* 10, 1335 [August 15 [28], 1917]): 361–365; 10/17 (*ẕū'l-qa'da* 27, 1335 [September 1 [14], 1917]): 386–388 (with a photograph of al-Afghani on the front page); 10/18 (*ẕū'l-ḥiǧǧa* 11, 1335 [September 15 [28], 1917]): 409–413; 10/19 (*ṣafar* 7, 1336 [November 9 [22], 1917]): 433–436; 10/20 (*ṣafar* [*sic*], 1336 [November [*sic*], 1917]): 457–461; 10/21 (*ṣafar* 12, 1336 [December 13 [18], 1917]): 481–485; 10/22 (*ṣafar* 14, 1336 [December 15 [28], 1917]): 497–499; 10/23–24 (*rabī'al-awwal* 30, 1336 [December 30, 1917 [January 12, 1918]]): 513–517.

76 See for instance RF [Rižā al-Dīn b. Faḫr al-Dīn], "Mašhūr ādamlar wa ulūġ ḥādiṯalar: 'Abd al-Qādir Ǧazā'irī [Famous Peoples and Great Events: 'Abd al-Qādir the Algerian]," parts 1 and 2, *Šūrā* 8/22 (*muḥarram* 21 [*sic*], 1333 [November 15 [28], 1915]; the *hiǧrī* date is erroneous): 673–676; 8/23 (*ṣafar* 7, 1334 [December 1 [14], 1915]), 706–707.

77 'A[bd-Allàh] Baṭṭāl, "Ḫātūnlar wa taraqqī [Women and Progress]," 3/5 (*rabī' al-awwal* 3, 1328 [March 1 [14], 1910]): 136–139; anonymous paper, "Ḫātūnlarnī ta'līm (*al-Hilāldan*) [The Education of Women (from *al-Hilāl*)]," *Šūrā* 3/8 (*rabī' al-āḫir* 18,

1328 [April 15 [28], 1910]): 250, a paper about the al-Jami'a school, an educational institution for young girls in Cairo and other topics.

78 See Riżā al-Dīn b. Faḫr al-Dīn, *Maktab wa zakāt, ḫazīna wa zēmstwā yārdimī* [The School and Its Financing through the *Zakāt*, the Treasury, and the *Zemstvos*] (Orenburg: Karīmoff, Ḥusaynoff wa širkāsī [*sic*], *n.d.*), *passim*.

79 M. Hādī (from Cheliabinsk), "Qadr Mas'alasī (Čīlābī šahrinda rūs mu'allimī; ustāẕ wa imām Muḥammad 'Abduh Ḥażratlarīniŋ 'al-'Urwa al-wuṯqā' da yāzilmiš maqālasī) [The Question of Destiny (A Russian Teacher in the City of Cheliabinsk; a Paper written by the Master and Imam Muḥammad 'Abduh in *al-'Urwa al-wuṯqā*)]," *Šūrā* 2/6 (*rabī' al-awwal* 6, 1327 [March 15 [28], 1909]): 166–169. See also the anonymous paper "Ġazīta wa žūrnāllār. 3. 'Arabī tīlinda (Newspapers and Journals. 3. In the Arabic Language)," *Šūrā* 2/11 (*ğumādī al-awwal* 21, 1327 [June 1 [14], 1909]): 322–325.

80 Anonymous notice, "Dār al-kutub al-'arabiyya [The Palace of the Arab Books]," *Šūrā* 2/9 (*rabī' al-āḫir* 23, 1327 [May 1 [14], 1909]): 279. This is an account of the activities of a bookshop with the same name in Cairo, followed by an advertisement for its free catalogue. Another anonymous advertisement for a bookstore which proposed Turkish translations of Arabic books on the history of Islam can be found in another issue, with the address in French (the language of the International Postal Union): "Egypte, Azhar, M. Ahmed Ourmantchieff," *Šūrā* 1/12 (*ğumādī al-awwal* 29, 1326 [June 15 [28], 1908]): 393. In 1901 the bookstore Šarq Kutubḫānasī (Orient Library), owned by Aḥmad Isḥāqoff in the remote city of Orsk on the fringe of the eastern Urals and northern part of the Qazaq steppe (i.e. very far from the Mediterranean), was selling books, notably madrasa textbooks from Egypt, Beirut, Istanbul, and India at "reasonable prices." Isḥāqoff was proposing to the readers to send his catalogue, entitled *Asāmī al-kutub* (Book Titles). Found in the classified advertisements of the *Šūrā* 3/2 (*muḥarram* 17, 1328 [January 15 [28], 1910]): III.

81 See Muḥammad Tawfīq Afandī Ṣidqī, "Qur'ān wa 'ilm. Luġat, ta'rīḫ, ğuġrāfiyā, ṭibb wa ġayrlarga dā'ir darslar (Mu'tabar 'al-Manār' mağallasindan Muḥammad Tawfīq Afandī Ṣidqī yāzilmiš maqālalardan iḫtiṣār īla tarğuma īdilmišdir) (The Qur'an and Science. Lectures on Lexicography, History, Geography, Medicine, etc. [Abridged Translation from a Paper Written by Muḥammad Tawfīq Afandī Ṣidqī in the Famous Journal *al-Manār*])," *Šūrā* 3/5 (*rabī' al-awwal* 3, 1328 [March 1 [14], 1910]), 131–132.

82 Miyān 'Abd al-Awwal al-Ġaffārī, "Dīnlīlar wa dīnsizlar (Šayḫ Muḥammad 'Abduh Ḥaẓratlarīniŋ Tafsīrindan bir qadr taṣarruf īla muqtabas)," parts 1 and 2, *Šūrā* 3/9 (*ğumādī al-awwal* 5, 1328 [May 1 [14], 1910]): 265–267; 3/10 (*ğumādī al-awwal* 19, 1328 [May 15 [28], 1910]), 299–301.

83 Imām wa Mudarris Sarwar al-Dīn [b. Miftāḥ al-Dīn] "Tawḥīd, ḥayāt, islām (Divine Unity, Life, Islam)," parts 1–10, *Šūrā* 1/11 (*ğumādī al-awwal* 15, 1326 [June 1 [14], 1908]), 349–352; 1/12 (*ğumādī al-awwal* 29, 1326 [June 15 [28], 1908]), 382–384; 1/14 (*ğumādī al-āḫir* 29, 1326 [July 15 [28], 1908]), 431–433; 1/15 (*rağab* 17, 1326 [August 1 [14], 1908]), 482–484; 1/18 (*ramażān* 3, 1326 [September 15 [28], 1908]), 567–569; 1/21 (*šawwāl* 20, 1326 [November 1 [14], 1908]), 671–672; 1/23 (*ẕū'l-qa'da* 21, 1326 [December 1 [14], 1908]), 716–717; 2/2 (*muḥarram* 5, 1327 [January 15 [28], 1909]), 37–39; 2/4 (*ṣafar* 7, 1327 [February 15 [28], 1909]), 101–102; 2/5 (*ṣafar* 21, 1327 [March 1 [14], 1909]), 134–136; 'Abd-Allàh Baṭṭāl, "Risāla at-tawḥīd (Šayḫ Muḥammad 'Abduh ta'līfī) (The *Risāla al-tawḥīd*, a Work by Šayḫ Muḥammad 'Abduh)," *Šūrā* 2/19 (*šawwāl* 28, 1327 [October 1 [14], 1909]), 588–591.

84 See the anonymous paper "'Umūmī islām nadwasī (Miṣrda čiqmāqda ūlān dīnī 'al-Manār' muqtabas) [The Debate on Islam (Summarized from the Religious [Journal] *al-Manār* published in Egypt)]," *Šūrā* 1/3 (*muḥarram* 16, 1326 [February 5 [18], 1908]), 74–77.

85 Hādī, "Bāy ham yārlī dīllar, tūrkča yūġālġān sūzlar [Rich and Poor Languages; Words Absent in Turkic]," *Šūrā* 3/7 (*rabī' al-āḫir* 4, 1328 [April 1 [14], 1910]), 206–208.

On the Urdu translation of 'Abduh's works, see the anonymous chronicle "Muḥammad 'Abduh," *Šūrā* 3/11 (*ğumādī al-āḫir* 6, 1328 [June 1 [14], 1910]), 348.

86 'Ārif Šakūrī (Qāhirada rūsiyalī turk ṭalabasī ğam'iyyatī īčūn ra'īs [The Chairman of the Fraternity of the Turkic Students from Russia in Cairo]), "Dīnī madrasalarimizda 'Arab lisānīniŋ ahammiyatī wa 'Arab lisāninda dars kitāblarī [The Significance of the Arabic Language in our Religious Schools and the Textbooks of Arabic Language]," *Šūrā* 3/12 (*ğumādī al-āḫir* 20, 1328 [June 15 [28], 1910]), 357–361; for a discussion on this matter, see for example Mullā Šihāb al-Dīn (from Chistopol), "'Arab tilī bizga kīrak būlāmī? [Do We Need the Arabic Language?]," *Šūrā* 10/14 (*šawwāl* 8, 1335 [July 15 [28], 1917]), 325–325.

6

RATIONALIZING PATRIOTISM AMONG MUSLIM CHINESE

The impact of the Middle East on the *Yuehua* journal

Matsumoto Masumi

China has a Muslim population of about 18 million. They are divided into ten national minorities or nationalities. According to official records, they are an important component of the 56 nationalities in China. Sometimes translated into English as "Muslim Chinese," Sino-Muslims or Hui (*Huizu*s 回族 are referred to as "Hui" in this chapter), they are the third most populous nationality in China with a population of 9.8 million according to the 2003 census.

Contrarily to such minorities as the Uyghurs, who are also Muslims, and the Tibetans, who are alleged to have separatist tendencies, the Hui as a whole have tried to remain loyal to the Chinese State and its rulers. Except for a few insubordinate groups, many Hui literati, military leaders, and religious leaders called *ahong*s (originally *āḫūnd* in Persian) supported the Nationalist Party (Guomindang, abbreviated as GMD) in the Republican Era (1912–1949). Some of them migrated to Taiwan with the GMD. On the other hand, some started to support the Chinese Communist Party (abbreviated as CCP) in the middle of the 1930s. Since 1949 they have supported the People's Republic. Particularly since the initiation of the Reform and Open Policy, some of them have been promoted to the top cadres of the state. They have worked as decision-makers in the People's Republic, particularly in the field of policy-making with regards to ethnic minorities. In addition to advocating freedom of religion and the preservation of a plurality of ethnic characters, they have called for increased national sentiment, not only from the Hui but from all people in China, especially from those who are ethnic minorities.

In retrospect, the GMD's ideology was the Three People's Principle, which stressed Chinese nationalism rather than the endorsement of various religious and ethnic differences. On the other hand, the CCP, as the follower of Karl Marx, seemed to believe in the evils of religion. Rather than pursuing their own political entity separate from China, why did the Hui choose to support these two parties and political systems whose ideologies seemed to be in contradiction to their belief in Islam?

Patriotism and nationalism are the answers to this question. For these modern ideologies to penetrate into Hui society, advanced *ahong*s and literati initiated the Chinese Islamic revival movement (sometimes referred as the "Chinese Islamic reform movement" or "Chinese Islamic new cultural movement") since the late Qing period. The keyword of the movement was *aiguo aijiao* 愛國愛教 ("love the fatherland and love Islam"), which identified patriotism as faith toward the religion. Because of this logic, patriotism became one of the most touted virtues for the Hui.

This catchword was broadly accepted in Chinese Hui society during the war against Japan. In order to spread the slogan, methods such as preaching by *ahong*s and Islamic periodicals were utilized. For example, the *Yuehua* 月華 journal was published from 1929 until 1948. Issuing more than 4,000 copies at its peak, it was the most influential and longest lasting periodical of Hui society in the period before the founding of the People's Republic in 1949.

This chapter examines how the Hui strove to be patriotic and nationalistic in modern terms, and based on their traditional Islamic understanding as well as their reinterpretation of the Qur'an and the Hadith. In addition we shall try to argue how the Islamic revival and Islamic reformism in the Middle East influenced Hui society in China, and what the role of *Yuehua* journal took within this context.

The Hui in the twentieth century

The Hui are a true minority, with only 0.7% of China's population of 1.2 billion. Dispersed in every province, every autonomous region, and every prefecture, county and city, there is no region without Hui inhabitants. They are in charge of agriculture and transportation services as well as commercial activities. Some have been successful in gaining high positions as cadres in the CCP. Taking advantage of Muslim networks in China as well as in foreign countries, some have found lucrative jobs after the initiation of the Reform and Open policy.

The Hui's history in twentieth-century China was, however, affected by the hardships of turbulent times. Like other ordinary Chinese people, Muslims in China faced the collapse of the Qing dynasty, the establishment of the Chinese Republic in 1912, the political, economic, and social confusion caused by the interference of Western powers, and the opposition of the GMD and the CCP. Moreover, they were involved in the turmoil of the Sino-Japanese war, the civil war, and the establishment of the People's Republic in 1949. Religious suppression during the Cultural Revolution brought the destruction of mosques and the prohibition of religious activities. In other words, as an explicitly minority group, the Hui have had to survive in China and, if necessary, have had to fight to surmount obstacles facing them. In order to adjust the Hui as a group to the new and changing circumstances, *ahong*s, literati, and local elites strove to reform religion and install both national and ethnic identity in the minds of Muslims. In this chapter we will call these *ahong*s, literati, and local elite the "Islamic reformers" or the "Islamic revivalists" of China.

We shall first attempt to divide the Hui's twentieth-century history from the perspective of Islamic reformers:

1 A period of awakening in the late Qing, 1907–1911
2 Adaptation to Republican China, 1912–1937
3 Participation in the Anti-Japanese War, 1937–1945
4 Civil war between the GMD and the CCP, 1946–1949
5 Adaptation to the People's Republic and the social reforms, 1949–1958
6 Calamity during the anti-rightist campaign and the Cultural Revolution, 1958–1976
7 The new Islamic revival, 1979–until now.

The first three periods listed here can be considered as the rise and flourishing of the Islamic revival in the Chinese context. The seventh period can be seen as a resumption of another flourishing period for the Islamic revival, due to the promotion of religion and religious culture by the government, and recognition of the Hui's right to political participation as a nationality. Moreover, in terms of developing improved diplomatic relationship between China and other Islamic countries, one can attest to the importance of domestic Islamic matters in the last twenty years.

Due to space limitations, we will only examine and discuss the former three periods covering four decades. We can assess, however, that the endeavors made by Islamic reformers in these four decades brought a legacy of relatively high prestige for the "Hui nationality" in the People's Republic.

The concept of "unity of being" as basis of patriotism—a philosophy for the maintenance of a peaceful society

Concepts of patriotism and nationalism did not exist in pre-modern China. The Hui, however, kept a basic logical concept that was capable of developing into patriotism in the modern period. This concept is the "unity of being." Muslims emigrating from Central Asia to China during the Mongol period brought this interpretation of Islam from their homeland, where the philosophy of the "unity of being" (*waḥdat al-wuğūd* in Arabic) had prevailed since the eleventh century. The Chinese Muslims called *laojiao* (老教 the Old Sect or *Gedimu* 格迪目, *qadīm* in Arabic) inherited this philosophy.[1]

The structure of the unity of being is as follows. All existence and phenomena in this world are outflows from the only ultimate and supreme existence, Allah. Human beings, as the outflow of Allah, have their virtuous deeds allocated to them by Allah. After the completion of virtues, a human being can become a perfect man/woman and return to the origin of the existence, Allah.

Several outstanding philosophers developed a unique understanding of Islam at the end of the Ming and the beginning of the Qing era. Among them, Wang Daiyu 王岱輿, Ma Zhu 馬注, and Liu Zhi 劉智 were the most famous. They attempted to explain the unity of being with Confucian terminology, and with Zhuzi's terminology in particular, since their spoken language had already become Hanyu after their long residence in China.

We can characterize their philosophy as the appreciation of co-existence in Chinese society under the rule of the Mandate of Heaven. Consequently the philosophy called for a duplicate faith toward Allah and toward the Mandate of Heaven, who was the real ruler of this world. This was called "the theory of double faith." These philosophers recognized non-Muslim masters, including the Mandate of Heaven, as the outflows of Allah, and considered them to be entrusted as the ruling power of Allah. Completing the philosophy of Islam in China, Liu Zhi stated that if each obeys to the rules of the Mandate of the Heaven, then the preconditions for the mental practice of human completion would exist and social peace would be maintained. Sincere attitudes toward one's life would lead to the peace of both family and homeland in this world. From there, a person could attain complete human perfection.

According to this logic, Muslims should implement virtues similar to those of Confucians, who were governed by the Mandate of the Heaven. The Hui, as a minority group in Chinese society, were allowed to live in the Chinese Empire because of this doctrine. However, since *laojiao* was interpreted in Hanyu and according to Confucian terminology, Muslims in Xinjiang whose language was Turkic did not accept *laojiao* Islam.

Nevertheless, because of Hui uprisings in Yunnan and Shanxi in the nineteenth century and after their subjugation by Qing troops, the Hui were labeled as "insurrectionists." However, despite suppression of these uprisings by the Qing, they had no other homeland than China. Surviving Hui had to reconstruct their communities and overcome the Han prejudice against them.

China's Islamic revival and the Chinese state

The period of awakening, 1907–1911

We have argued that *laojiao* belief theorized the concordance of Islam and Confucianism. Adhering to *laojiao* Islam, *ahong*s and literati tried to find new methods to accommodate Islamic belief with new and modern trends of thoughts in the late Qing.

Both constitutionalists and revolutionaries argued about the method of introducing modernity in China after the Russo-Japanese War. By then, people in China had been permitted to go abroad if conditions allowed them, and some privileged Hui had the opportunity. Some paid a visit to Mecca and absorbed the new Middle Eastern Islamic interpretation of revivalism. Some visited Japan as students and absorbed the essence of Western modernism. Adhering to the traditional Islamic philosophy harmonious with Confucianism, and influenced by modernizing trends and by the worldwide Islamic revival, "advanced" *ahong*s and literati in China also initiated an Islamic revival movement in Chinese characters.

What is the role of *ahong*s and literati in Hui societies? *Ahong*s are to be responsible for pointing the essence of human life and world order to Muslims in the community. In concrete terms, they teach Muslims how to implement virtuous deeds in this world. Therefore, *ahong*s receive enormous respect from Muslims in the community. As for their economic aspects, *ahong*s of *laojiao* do not possess property. But their living costs, their activities in mosques, as well as their management of *jingtang*s,[2] Qur'anic schools attached to mosques, are sustained by *tianke* 天課 (*zakāt*) and *sadaqah* by Muslims in the community. Ordinary Hui children are sent to the *jingtang* to learn how to live a moral life based on the teachings of the Qur'an and other writings. Muslims allocate fees for *tianke* and *sadaqah* according to their income. Therefore, even in the past, Hui literati and local power holders, who in many cases were landlords or entrepreneurs, were generous contributors of *tianke* and *sadaqah* to support the religious activities of the community.

The social and economic status of these literati and local power holders was highly interdependent on Han society, since most of their commercial clients were Han. Items that they dealt with differed in accordance to regional characteristics. For example, they monopolized wool dealing in Tianjin, they were very successful entrepreneurs in jewelry and antique industries in Shanghai,[3] and dealings in fur and items for Chinese medicine was handled by Hui horse traders in Yunnan, who enjoyed a continued and regular relationships with Muslims in Burma and Thailand.[4]

The Islamic revival movement initiated by these *ahong*s and local elites can thus be seen supporting the fusion of the Han and the Hui. This is due to the Islamic reformists' belief that neither faith toward Islam nor Hui communities in China could exist without cooperation and concord with the Han majority.

The Islamic revival initiated by literati

Hui literati in Japan initiated the first concrete movement for Islamic revival. Enthusiasm for studying in Japan grew because of the eradication of the appointment examination for bureaucrats in 1905. Ostensibly more than 10,000 Qing students were studying in Japan at that time. Most of them were sons of local powers and gentry. Among them, thirty-six Hui students organized the *Liutong Qingzhen Jiaoyuhui* 留東清眞教育會 or "Association for Islamic Education in Tokyo" in 1907. Most of them also had membership in the *Zhongguo Tongmenghui* 中国同盟會 or Chinese Revolutionary Association. Accordingly, as revolutionaries, these Hui students were convincing supporters of a modern republican state system instead of the old imperial system. With enough Confucian knowledge to be involved in the examination system, and with the *Islamic* philosophy that they had learned at *jingtang*, they felt a responsibility for improving their society.

They asserted their need to pursue three directions, that is, the development of nationalism, the reform and promotion of Islam, and the acceptance of modernism, particularly in modern education. These three elements would, they argued, be indispensable to creating favorable conditions essential for the future of not only the Hui ethnic group but for all of China. The reform of Islam, however, was the most important, since "religions have the power to transform society."[5] In the coming era of the nation-state, these Hui students believed that it was necessary to reform the Islamic doctrine (*laojiao*) that had until then been understood according to the traditional imperial system. They believed that faith toward the emperor should be replaced by faith toward the new state, and also assured that this could be done if the Qur'an and Hadith, as well as the writings of *Wang Daiyu, Ma Zhu and Liu Zhi*, were more carefully and enthusiastically examined.

The Arabic words for "Islam" or "Muslim" had been almost forgotten during the Qing's long isolation. First identifying themselves as Chinese "Hui" as well as "Muslims," they also began to perceive themselves as "Chinese" when they studied abroad. Encounters with several Muslims from the Middle East in Tokyo also inspired such ideas. That is to say, they began to set up both a national identity and an ethnic identity. National identity was necessary to build a nation-state. Ethnic identity was, they believed, also necessary to represent ethnic rights within the framework of a nation-state. Furthermore, as successors to the philosophy of the unity of being, they believed that doing three "correct" and "virtuous" acts, such as the step-by-step construction of a strong and wealthy nation-state, the promotion of modernism, and the reformation of Islam within the modern framework of nation-state, was the fulfillment of Allah's will.

As revolutionaries, Hui students participated in the Revolution of 1911. The three goals that they pursued in the Republican period were consistent with those of the Islamic reformers.

Islamic revival by **ahongs***: a period of adaptation to Republican China, 1912–1949*

*Ahong*s were expected to be responsible for the lives of Muslims and the future of the community. Listening to the *ahong*s' preaching, people understood the meaning of human life and the truth of Islamic belief. Therefore, in an era of drastic transformation of thoughts, *ahong*s were expected to adjust the doctrine of Islam to make it compatible with the new era.

Some reputable *ahong*s who were widely known in Chinese Hui society initiated a new trend of the Islamic revival in China. One of the most prominent and respected *ahong*s was Wang Kuan (Haorang) 王寬 (浩然) *Ahong* (1848–1919) in Beijing. Witnessing the reality of Islamic revivalist movements in regions of Turkey, Egypt, and Arabia when he visited Mecca and the Middle East in 1906, he decided to reform Islam in China. Upon coming back to China, the Revolution of 1911 had occurred, and Wang Kuan met Sun Yatsen in September 1912, expressing support for the newborn Republican state.

At the very beginning of the Republican era, Wang Kuan was the most influential *laojiao ahong* in China, and he determined that faith toward the Mandate of the Heaven of the imperial period should be replaced by faith toward the state.

He believed that patriotism should be reinterpreted as virtuous behavior that would resolve social contradictions and bring pacification to society.

Wang Kuan and other *ahong*s at the beginning of the Republican period consistently interpreted patriotism within the traditional framework of the unity of being. They failed, however, to discover a concrete basis for patriotism in the Qur'an and the Hadith. Muslims generally regarded the contents of the Qur'an as guidance for daily life. The speeches of the *ahong*s were strictly based on the Qur'an and the Hadith. If a basis for the *ahong*'s command was not found in the Qur'an or Hadith, Hui people in the community would not follow him, or might even lose their trust in Islam. The lack of basis for patriotism was a weak point in mobilizing the Hui people to participate in nationalist activities.

In the 1920s, several Hui students and *ahong*s began to be sent to al-Azhar in Egypt, largely due to the efforts of literati and *ahong*s as well as to the development of transportation. Wang Jingzhai 王静齋 (1879–1949), an *ahong* from Tianjin, studied there for half a year in 1921. After coming back to China in 1923, he translated the Qur'an into Hanyu for the first time. Adhering to traditional *laojiao*, but also influenced by modern trends of thought in the reform of the society, he also supported the new republican state and obtained membership in the GMD. Quite in accordance with the literati, he also pursued the reform of Islam in China in light of nationalism and modernism, especially in the field of education.[6]

The Islamic revival movement in China was to be the "glue" of Chinese national integration. This also meant that all Muslims within the legitimate territory of China were to obey the orders of the Chinese central government. As subcontractors of the central government, the Islamic reformers were to assist them. That is to say, the Islamic revival movement aimed at creating a unified Islamic understanding of Hui ethnicity and of the political position of the "Hui" nationality. According to this logic, the "disobedient" Muslims who did not "improve" their religious way of life, theological curriculum, or political stance would be put under the tutelary guidance of the Islamic reformers, otherwise not only their lives but the whole Chinese nation-state would be overcome by the ambitions of outside aggressors.

Terms such as "progressive," "advanced," or "reforming" were keywords to characterize Islamic reformers in China. In a social atmosphere that appreciated "progress and evolution" in view of nation-building, they apparently recognized themselves as *xianzhi xianjuezhe* 先知先覚者, or those qualified to enlighten the "backward" peoples of the tutelage period, in accordance with Sun Yatsen's theory of the three steps of social evolution. The Islamic reformers were determined to play a role as teachers and leaders to instruct "ignorant" Muslims and make them adhere to the Chinese nation.

The role of the *Yuehua* journal

We have seen the outline of the roles of Islamic reformers in the development of the Islamic revival movement in China. The movement took place simultaneously in many regions of China. It is interesting to see that there was no substantial center for the movement. Many *ahong*s and literati in major cities such as Beijing, Tianjin, Jinan, Nanjing, Shanghai, Kunming, Guangzhou, Xi'an, Chengdu, Xining, and Ningxia were mobilized and followed the movement, founding branches of the Chinese Islamic Association for Progress in each city. That is to say that, under the network of the association, Islamic reformers shared the same tendency to have a double identity as a nation and as Hui, and tried to educate themselves to the idea that there were other Muslims in China. Some of them were in charge of publishing periodicals and books on Islam, while some ran modern schools instead of *jingtang*. Here, we will examine the Chengda Normal School and its bulletin, the *Yuehua*.

The Chengda Normal School

In April 1925, "advanced" *ahong*s, local power holders, and the elite founded a normal school named Chengda Normal School 成達師範學校 exclusively for Hui youth in Jinan, Shandong. Aiming at the reform of traditional *jingtang* education, Chengda later developed into the most famous and influential normal school in Hui society.

Combining modern and Islamic education, its curriculum was unique, with an even combination of "teaching-fostering" courses and religious courses. The "teaching-fostering" courses included subjects such as Hanyu, mathematics, history, English, science, music, physical education, and psychology. The religious course, on the other hand, included subjects such as Arabic, Qur'anic studies, Hadith studies, *tawḥīd*, and the history of Islam.

When the Jinan incident occurred in 1928, a part of the school was destroyed. It moved to Beiping (at that time the formal name of Beijing) under the financial assistance of Ma Fuxiang 馬福祥, a prominent and wealthy Hui warlord of the Northwest. The concrete educational purpose of the school was as follows. First, rapprochement of the Hui and the Han was to be furthered while the Hui's national and ethnic identity was to be fostered. Second, the quality of the *ahong*s should be improved to adapt to the methods of inquiry required by the times. Third, the training of good teachers at modern schools was to be implemented in order to recover the Hui ethnic character. Fourth, the Hui as an ethnic group were to be effective and active in the service of the Chinese State. Finally, mosques under the strong control of *ahong*s, and with the authority to interpret the doctrine of Islam, were to be put under the command of a public organization enjoying a consensus.[7] That is to say, even though the school was a private school, it worked to foster students that would be effective in nation-building and promote religion.

The **Yuehua***—an introduction to international Islamic affairs and to the promotion of nationalism: the first stage, 1929–1930*

The *Yuehua* 月華 began to be published in October 1929 in Beiping, every ten days, as a bulletin of the Chengda Normal School. The proposal to publish it was made by progressive literati of the Huabei region, such as Tang Hesan 唐柯三, the principal of the school, Sun Shengwu 孫繩武, Sun Youming 孫幼銘, and Zhao Zhenwu 趙振武. Zhao Zhenwu became the chief editor. When literati discussed the importance of issuing periodicals, Ma Fuxiang agreed to support the plan financially. Claiming that publication was important to promoting Islam in China, Ma continued to donate 100 yuans every month until June 1932, when he was near death. We now ask the question of why he contributed to the development of the Chengda and the *Yuehua*?

Subordinate to Jiang Jieshi, Ma Fuxiang was a powerful warlord of the Northwest. Believing in *laojiao* Islam, he was also a pious follower of the unity of being. As personnel responsible for the security of the region, he worried about the frequent turmoil among the Hui, particularly among the *menhuan* (saintly lineages of the Sufi tradition). Some of them called for rebellion against the Chinese State and rejected the Han's interference. The Islamic reformers were convinced that the turmoil was caused by the ignorance of *menhuan* Muslims, who only seemed to interpret the doctrine of Islam as jihad against non-Muslims. Most ordinary Muslims in China, and the *menhuan* in particular, were exceedingly poor and illiterate. Ma recognized that they followed blindly the commands of the *ahong* of the community, and that the lack of modern knowledge and a correct understanding of Islam was the cause of the prevailing poverty of the Hui and of their backwardness and ignorance. That is why he decided to contribute financially to the *Yuehua*, expecting to make the journal a confirmed guide for Muslims in difficulty.[8]

The purposes of the journal are drafted in the first edition, and are almost the same as those of the Chengda Normal School:

1 Promotion of Islam in China in accordance with modern trends
2 Introduction of Muslims from the whole world
3 Development of the Huis' knowledge and promotion of their position in China
4 Resolution of the misunderstanding between the Old Sect and the New Sect
5 Development of a national identity among the Hui
6 Promotion of Hui education and improvement of their livelihood.[9]

Almost all the articles in the journal were written in Hanyu and contributed by *ahong*s, literati, and students of Chengda and other normal schools. The journal's goal was consistent until the suspension of its publication in 1948, although there were minor changes in the contents.

In the first two years, the contents of the *Yuehua* were limited to relatively narrow fields, reflecting the moderate trends of the Islamic revival in China until 1931. With regard to point 1 in the list, there were few accurate translations or interpretations of the Qur'an and the Hadith. With regard to point 2, contributors translated English books on Islamic affairs written by Westerners, but there were few direct translations from Arabic. Exceptions included Wang Jingzhai *Ahong*'s translation from Arabic and the presentation of Wang Cengshan 王曾善, who had studied in Istanbul University and witnessed the reality of modernism in Turkey. Information about domestic Hui affairs, on the other hand, was limited to the Hui communities around Beiping.

Although there were few articles based on actual experience, these writers understood the importance of worldwide movements, especially that of the Muslim Brotherhood initiated by Hasan al-Banna in 1928.[10] Articles based on actual experiences were written and translated by Wang Jingzhai *Ahong*. When Wang studied in Egypt, the Middle East was experiencing the surge of the Islamic revival movement. The three directions of the movement were Islamic revival, modernism, and nationalism.[11] Leaders of the movement had tried to discover foundations for these three vectors in the Qur'an and the Hadith. In particular, a phrase from the Qur'an—"Why cannot we fight along with the way of Allah? Weren't we driven out from our home and separated from our children?"[12]—was familiar to scholars of Islamic jurisprudence in Egypt. Wang quoted the interpretation of the given phrase by his professor at al-Azhar as follows:

> We all have the responsibility to protect our parents' country. Once one's estate is stolen and one is separated from his wife and children, he ought to fight bravely against the rapacious enemy. Without this intention, any prayer has no meaning. One might not feel ashamed to see his homeland perish and his family pass away unless he recognized the importance of this matter.[13]

In addition to the Qur'anic verse cited here, a phrase from an alleged hadith "*ḥubb al-waṭan min al-īmān* (love of the *waṭan* [*patrie*, fatherland, homeland] is an article of faith)" was first introduced to China by Wang Jingzhai.

Modern scholars of Islam have pointed out that none of these phrases exist in the real Hadith. The term *waṭan* cannot be found in the Qur'an. This might mean that the term *waṭan* had not existed in Arabic at the time of the Prophet Muhammad. However, this doubtful sentence was thought to appear somewhere in the Hadith and was widely known to Muslims in the Middle East early in the nineteenth century.[14] Apparently Wang himself heard the word *waṭan* for the first time in Egypt. Annoyed about how to interpret this popular word from the Middle East, he cites a prominent Egyptian religious leader:

> *Waṭan* in Arabic means the place where you live. Modern scholars of Islamic jurisprudence call *waṭan* the land where people's rights, duties, lives and fortunes are entrusted. That is to say, there is no contradiction between people's freedom and statehood. In other words, a state cannot do without freedom. The French scholar Molière claimed "there is no state in an era of despotism." *Waṭan* is the place where people possess political rights, like in the ancient Latin term.[15]

The original text, he noted, was found in the journal of the Wafd Party of Egypt. According to the Qur'anic phrase, and to the popular phrase of the alleged hadith, Wang concluded that loving one's fatherland or state was one of the virtues that Muslims should strive for.

We can assess the period from 1912 to 1930 as an era focused on promoting rather than moderating nationalism, as well as an Islamic reform movement based on both the theory of the unity of being and the Islamic revival in the Middle East. Even though Japan tried to establish military hegemony in the Northeast, this country did not yet seem to have any intention of becoming aggressive against the whole of China. Therefore, in spite of Wang Jingzhai's introduction to the foundations of patriotism from the Hadith, the Islamic reformers in China had not yet emphasized the anti-imperialist tendency that characterized the Islamic revival in the Middle East.

Direct contact with Egypt and the anti-Japanese movement, 1931–1936

The *Yuehua* ostensibly changed its character after the printing of its third volume in 1931.[16] Not only did its format change from a newspaper style to a magazine style, but so did its contents. More information directly pertaining to Egypt began to appear as Islamic reformers reinforced their orientation and opinions with regards to discussions taking place in Egypt.

The year 1931 was epoch-making for the Islamic revival movement in China. Four students, including Ma Jian 馬堅 (1906–1978), who was later to translate the Qur'an into Hanyu, were for the first time officially sent from the Shanghai Islamic School to the al-Azhar University in Egypt, from where they began to send articles for the *Yuehua*. This meant that these students came to play the role of correspondents, notifying people in China of Islamic affairs in the Middle East, as well as of circumstances in the world outside of China. Furthermore, twenty-two overseas periodicals on Islam in various languages, such as English, German, Arabic, Malay, and Turkish, began to be exchanged. Furthermore, the World Islamic Meeting held in Palestine invited Muslim delegates from China (although a variety of reasons prevented them from attending). In other words, compared to the previous two years, information on the whole Islamic world became more tangible and accurate from 1931 onwards.

Moreover, a crisis in the domestic environment allowed the application of this new input on Islamic theory. This was Japan's occupation of the Northeast. In order to meet the demand of readers who wished to acquire new knowledge in order to overcome the new difficulties, more than four thousand copies of the *Yuehua* were issued, spreading throughout Hui communities all over China. The following is an outline of the contents of *Yuehua* since 1931:

1 Commentary of the Qur'an and the Hadith, *tafsīr*.
2 Translation of Arabic and English books and criticism.

3 Critiques of religious questions in China, of Hui education, Hui organization, economy, current issues, etc.
4 Reevaluation of Hui history in China and discussions of its intermingling with Chinese culture.
5 Research on various mosques and Hui communities in Anhui, Guangxi, Chahar, Suiyuan, Jiangxi, Shandong, Henan, Jiangsu, Shanxi, and Gansu.
6 Introduction of Muslim personalities from the whole world. This entailed an introduction to Islamic revivalist trends and current issues in Egypt, Afghanistan, Turkey, Syria, Algeria, India, Yugoslavia, and Iran.
7 Literature.

These contents are very similar to those of *al-Manār* ("The Lighthouse") edited by Rashid Rida in Egypt. There is no evidence that contributors of the *Yuehua* subscribed to this journal, which was well known to the whole Islamic world. Yet it is likely that they understood the popular editorial styles of Islamic revivalist journals and tried to follow their trends.[17]

The most important changes in volume three (1931) was the presentation of the Qur'anic annotations based on their translation from Arabic. Known as one of the most "advanced" *ahong*s to support the Chengda Normal School and the *Yuehua*, Ma Songting *Ahong*, the leading *ahong* of Chengda,[18] discussed the reason why the journal had started to publish translations and commentaries of the Qur'an (*tafsīr*).

> The Qur'an is the source of all the beliefs and doctrines of Islam. Scholars have always extracted the code of the times and the regions from its source and abided to its authority. We have been in China for more than a thousand years. The language and habits have been assimilated. Along with the times, we had to draw adequate activity and codes from the source. Therefore, we wish to reveal the real doctrine of Islam, make ourselves adapt to the current environment and understand the Qur'an better.... Even though there are several schools and orders of Islam in China, we must not be tangled by prejudice. If we comprehend the true meaning of the Qur'an, then we will be free from mistakes."[19]

Some articles began to be translated from Arabic journals published in Egypt. These were *Mağmū' al-rasā'il* ("Anthology of Theses"), *Iršād* ("Guidance"), and *al-Fatḥ* ("The Victory") of Cairo, which were traded or sent to China by mail. Articles concerning Egyptian social reforms, particularly in *al-Fatḥ*, were often translated into Hanyu in volume three (1931) and four (1932) of *Yuehua*—for example, an article entitled "Why Don't You Try?," written by the Egyptian writer Muhibb al-Din al-Khatib and translated from *al-Fatḥ*. The content was an appeal to Muslims in Egypt to stop smoking, since smoking was only beneficial to foreign powers, which were imperialistic exploiters of the people in Egypt.

The publication of this article in the *Yuehua* of January 1932 was ostensibly a contribution to the rise of the anti-Japanese movement, which included strikes and demonstrations in the coastal regions of China in the wake of the Mukden Incident of September 18, 1931. The article was intended to offer a methodology of concrete action for confronting the imperialists.

As discussed earlier, the Islamic reformers in China upheld traditional *laojiao* Islam based on the philosophy of the unity of being. In addition to this psychological structure, the modern era brought with it powerful new influences from the Middle East, and especially from Egypt.

The Qur'anic interpretation by Muhammad 'Abduh was the basis of the Egyptian reform movement aimed at expelling Western imperialists. 'Abduh regarded Islam's early years as its most glorious and ideal era. The delay of scientific progress in the Islamic world, and the subsequent suppression by Western powers was attributed to the oblivion of the pure virtues of the original Islam. Therefore, if each Muslim retrieved these original Islamic virtues, the conditions of their livelihood could improve sufficiently to become equal to those in the Western world and the glorious status of Muslims could be restored.

With the acceptance of outside information, especially from Egypt, the Islamic reformers in China must have been surprised and excited at the concurrence of the goals of their twenty-year movement with the goals pursued by reformers in Egypt. Reformers in China confirmed that the interpretation of Islamic texts in Egypt, made by respected scholars of Islamic jurisprudence whose mother tongue was Arabic, was more orthodox and proper than the old interpretations in China, which had long been isolated from the center of the Islamic world. That is why they were eager to absorb Egyptian thought.

The most important incident that spurred this tendency was the Mukden Incident. Just after this, the *Yuehua* appealed to the Hui to save the country, declaring that the Hui's spirit against the aggressors was a part of the Chinese nation's spirit and of its appreciation of justice.[20] The Islamic reformers also perceived that anti-aggression struggles should be shared among all Muslims who were suppressed by imperial powers, in complete accordance with the Egyptian reformers.

The Islamic reformers in China also persisted in their efforts to fulfill their responsibility to protect their own *waṭan* against aggressors. The alleged Hadith, "The love of *waṭan* is an article of faith" became the foundation of the struggle.[21] Proclaiming the Hui an inalienable part of the Chinese nation, the *Yuehua* became the leading journal of the anti-Japanese movement among the Hui. Needless to say, it regarded Japanese penetration into China as a threat to the whole Chinese nation. Therefore, even if Japan proposed favorable conditions for the Hui to build a *Huihuiguo* nation-state guaranteeing "the right of national self-determination," they would reject the proposal. They used to declare: "We are Muslims in China, not Muslims in Turkey nor Muslims in Persia. We are not Muslims from Muslim states. We have to demand a status of nationality as an integral part of the Chinese nation."[22]

The influence of Nūr al-Islām

Because of the strengthened bond with the al-Azhar University, articles in the bulletin of al-Azhar *Nūr al-Islām* ("Light of Islam") began to be frequently translated into Hanyu and published in the *Yuehua* starting with volume four (1932). Since most of the articles in *Nūr al-Islām* were written by professors of al-Azhar, Islamic reformers believed that its Islamic interpretations were a guiding light or authority in resolving various contradictions and antagonisms among Islamic believers in China.

For example, applauding *Nūr al-Islām*, Yang Sishi 仰思室 wrote that he had already found in the bulletin effective solutions for the conflicts among the schools and Sufi orders in Chinese Islam. The three big problems of Islam in China at that time were whether vocalizing the Qur'an was permissible, whether *ḫuṭub* (words of worship in Arabic) could be translated into other languages, and whether the Qur'an itself could be translated into foreign languages. *Nūr al-Islām* proclaimed that vocalizing the Qur'an was not permitted because its prohibition was evident in Muhammad's words, that *ḫuṭub* could be spoken in languages other than Arabic, and that translation of the Qur'an was also not a problem.[23] In order to show the appropriateness of *Nūr al-Islām*'s Islamic interpretation, Yang Sishi translated an article by its chief editor advocating translation of the Qur'an.[24]

First published in 1929, *Nūr al-Islām* was a bulletin of the al-Azhar University, then considered the most prestigious academy for Muslims in the world. In 1932 another five students were dispatched to al-Azhar from the Chengda Normal School, eventually forming a group together with the five who preceded them. In accordance with the decision of the Chinese students in al-Azhar, contributors of the *Yuehua* had no choice but to give particular esteem to *Nūr al-Islām*. This meant that not only *Yuehua* but almost all Islamic reformers in China were put under the strong theoretical influence of al-Azhar.

The specific impact of the Risālat al-tawḥīd

Similarly, the *Yuehua* seemed to inherit the spirit of *al-Manār*. Clear evidence of this was that a picture of a lighthouse began to decorate the front page of the *Yuehua* starting with Volume 5 (1933). This alteration of design was ostensibly inspired by *al-Manār*. Furthermore, the tendency to put emphasis on annotation was accelerated in 1933 when 'Abduh's *Risālat al-tawḥīd, Renzhuxue Dagang* 認主學大綱 (this title was later changed to *Huijiao Zhexue* 回教哲學 when it was published as a book in 1934) began to be translated into Hanyu by Ma Jian and serialized in the *Yuehua*. Ma Jian explains why he decided to translate this book as follows:

> According to the appraisal by Rashid Rida, who is the chief editor of *al-Manār* and the best disciple of Muhammad 'Abduh, this book concisely summarizes the points of *tawḥīd* and is the most helpful for

> beginners. When I first saw Professor Shaykh Ibrahim al-Jibali of the Institute for Islamic Philosophy at al-Azhar, I asked him whether or not there was a new book on *tawḥīd*. He immediately introduced this book and recommended me to study it by myself. During my free time, I always read it, caught the meaning and made questions and notes to ask Professor al-Jibali once a week.... Because of the Professor's deep knowledge and modesty, I never gave up studying and also benefited in many ways. Taking advantage of summer vacation this year, I translated the book into Hanyu in order to make it useful to people in China.[25]

The serialization of *Renzhuxue Dagang* continued until Volume 6, Number 34–36 of December 30, 1934. It was expected to help Muslims in China to gain accurate knowledge of *tawḥīd* and to confirm their belief in Islam.[26] In addition to Ma Jian's translation of the *Risālat al-tawḥīd*, Pang Shifian 龐士謙 translated the *History of Islam* or *Yisilan Zongjiaoshi* 伊斯蘭宗教史 by Professor Muhammad Khuzuli of the University of Egypt, originally published in 1920, and which he began to serialize in 1933. The translation of these important books, as well as the arrival of two professors from al-Azhar to the Chengda Normal School, doubtlessly stimulated the Islamic revival in China.

For example, Zhou Zhongren translated from *Nūr al-Islām* the Qur'anic annotation by Shaykh Ibrahim al-Jibali, who was the very person who had recommended Ma Jian at al-Azhar to translate Muhammad 'Abduh's *Risālat al-tawḥīd*.[27] This meant that not only Chengda but the whole Islamic revival movement in China was strongly affected by al-Azhar in terms of the interpretation of doctrine, the methodology of education, and the curriculum. At al-Azhar, the contents of education had come to be "pressed more firmly into a Western inspired mold" under the direction of president al-Maraghi after 1933.[28]

Recognized as "messiahs" for reforming Islam in China, there were high expectations for the two professors Sayyid Muhammad Dali and Muhammad Ibrahim Filfila, who came to China after arrangements were made by both King Fu'ad of Egypt and the president of al-Azhar. King Fu'ad expected them to be a cultural bridge between Egypt and China. They taught Arabic, Islamic philosophy, and theology to students at the Chengda Normal School.[29] Doubtlessly, they were expected to strengthen not only the bond between al-Azhar and Chengda, but also diplomatic and trade relations between Egypt and China.

Systematization of patriotism and belief in Islam

In relation to the accelerated progress of Islamic reforms under Egyptian assistance, the slogan "Love fatherland and love Islam (*aiguo aijiao* 愛國愛教)" was also rearranged. It began to reutilize and advertise the alleged hadith: "The love of *waṭan* is an article of faith." Under the instruction of two professors from al-Azhar, the *ahong*s, faculty members, and students of Chengda were ostensibly inspired by this hadith, which had already occupied the most important position among Islamic revivalists in Egypt in their promotion of political, economic, social, and religious reforms against Western imperialists. Aiming at scientific and industrial progress, as well as at the promotion of Hui ethnicity as an element for forming a nation, the phrase became a substantial basis for the national progress of China.

At a conference held at the YMCA Beiping in 1933, Ma Songting *Ahong*, the most important religious leader of Chengda, made the following address:

> The Prophet Muhammad said, "*ḥubb al-waṭan min al-īmān*" or "the love of fatherland is an article of faith." In other words, if there is no love of the fatherland, then people will lose faith. Muslims appreciate faith the most. Because of this morality, there is no Muslim who does not accomplish his duties for the state, nation, religion, birthplace and family.... Recently, Muslim countries such as Persia, Afghanistan and Arabia achieved independence and Turkey has recovered its strength and wealth. Moreover, Muslims in Egypt and India have succeeded in their Islamic revival. In China, Muslims have achieved patriotic activities since the Ming and the Qing periods. If you research into historical books, you can understand this fact easily. Recently we have encouraged the harmony between the Hui (Muslims) and the Han for the common benefit of the whole country. What represents the distinctive spirits of Muslims is that, if someone oppresses or slanders us, everybody, even retailers or trainees, will offer resistance. This means that Muslims in China accept love of association and the doctrine of Islam. If each one can show the virtue of loving their own fatherland and religion, then other countries and religions will give up invading China."[30]

Ma Songting identified the Hui as a part of Muslims outside of China. Encouraged to know the reality of the Islamic revival in the world, he was appealing to Christian youths in Beiping, saying that historically patriotic Chinese Muslims had already begun to contribute toward the construction of a strong Chinese state. There was thus the possibility of fostering nationalism and patriotism among the followers of foreign religions, and Ma Songting wanted to emphasize that there was no contradiction between pious belief in religion and patriotic feeling.

The Islamic reformers in China recognized Chinese Muslims neither as a national nor as a territorial entity. Rather, they understood themselves as sharing common boundaries, territorial integrity, and national identity with other ethnic groups or religious groups such as the Han, the Mongols, the Tibetans, and Christians. In this sense, co-existence and mutual understanding with peoples of various backgrounds were indispensable conditions for the nation-building of China.

There was a distinct difference between Egyptian Islamic reformers and Chinese Islamic reformers concerning the concept of *waṭan*. The former recognized *waṭan* as their state in which the Muslim majority took leadership. Reformers in Egypt even requested that the King expel or contain Christian missions, even though Christians occupied 20% of the whole population.[31] The multiethnic and multi-religious character in their exclusive *waṭan* was not so desirable.

The Islamic reformers in China, on the other hand, reinterpreted *waṭan* as a Chinese State where the majority was non-Muslim. Identifying themselves as an indispensable and integral part of the Chinese nation, and also identifying Islamic culture as an important element of a multifaceted Chinese culture, the patriotic phrase of the given hadith became widespread among Hui in all of China. The Hadith was recognized as the true words of the Prophet Muhammad and was expected to contribute in persuading some "disobedient" Hui to stop conflicts against the Han. At the same time, it was expected to inform the Han that their Hui counterparts were not enemies but supporters of China. Therefore, extracting a convenient and helpful discourse from Egyptian reformers and mingling it with their original discussions, Islamic reformers in China constructed their own theory on nationalism.[32]

Students dispatched from Chengda to al-Azhar were supposed to be trained in bringing orthodox Islamic interpretation to China. Because Ma Songting *Ahong* succeeded in drawing scholarships for Chinese students from King Faruq, the successor of King Fu'ad, another sixteen students were sent from China in 1937. However, when these Chinese students gathered in Egypt, the hot tide of Islamic reform, including *al-Manār*'s influence, had already dispersed into the whole of the Islamic world and changed its characters according to regional features. In other words, Chinese students were latecomers to the center of the Islamic revival movement, which had reached its peak in the 1920s.

Though there was no direct influence of *al-Manār* in China because of the time lag, progressive Hui elites and *ahong*s appreciated and absorbed many aspects of Islamic reform which Muhammad 'Abduh and Rashid Rida had initiated and promoted. In other words, the Islamic revival movement in China can be evaluated as another fruit of the work by reformers in Egypt. It has been broadly acknowledged that 'Abduh and Rida's works exerted a great influence upon Muslims in from the Western Sahara to the Dutch East Indies. These tides also reached the Far East in the 1930s, where the seeds of nationalism and anti-imperialism were sown.

In memory of the late King Fu'ad, the Fude Library 福德圖書館 was founded at Chengda in September 1936 and collected Arabic books, mostly donated by King Fu'ad to Ma Songting *Ahong*. The aim of the library was to make people in China acknowledge the close relationship between the Arabic and Chinese civilizations. They believed that understanding Islamic affairs was a key to protecting China, because Muslims mostly inhabited the frontier regions. Thus, Islam was not only a religious matter but also a highly political one that was intimately related to the fate of the whole Chinese nation.[33] The Islamic reformers reconfirmed that the Chinese nation needed to be an entity that consisted of various ethnicities and histories.

The Yuehua *after Japan's invasion of China, 1937–1944*

The outbreak of the Sino-Japanese War in July 1937 had a great impact on the whole Chinese population. Thriving anti-Japanese feeling among Chinese helped to transform the Islamic reform movement into a more patriotic one. This also meant that it needed more concrete foundations if it were to inspire Muslims in China to participate in anti-Japanese activities. We will now discuss the reaction of the contributors to *Yuehua* and the changes in its publishing environment.

The publication was suspended for almost ten months from June 1937 until April 1938 because of the confusion caused by Japanese invasion. In order to avoid occupation by the Japanese Army, the publishing house of *Yuehua* and the Chengda Normal School evacuated to Guilin, homeland of General Bai Chongxi 白崇禧. With a background in *laojiao* Islam, Bai Chongxi was an influential General of the Nanjing Government. From April of 1938 onwards, from its new headquarters in Guilin on the southern frontier of Guangxi, the *Yuehua* continued to send the same messages to Muslims in China. This meant that the Nanjing Government approved and assisted the printing and dissemination of new issues of *Yuehua*. This also meant that the direction thus far pursued by the Islamic reformers corresponded with that of the Nanjing Government under the anti-Japanese National United Front. Subsidies given by the government to Chengda in Guilin, however, were minimal.[34]

The *Yuehua*'s anti-imperialist campaign stemmed from an accurate analysis of the status quo. In accordance with the severe war conditions, the *Yuehua* began to praise with increasing frequency the Chinese nation's glorious past and multicultural character, the unity of the nation, and to call for the establishment of a strong state after the victory over Japan. In order to defeat Japan, they also stressed the promotion of antiwar education as well as a strong defense against Japan's intrigues aimed at destroying the unity of the Chinese nation by applying the method of "divide and rule."

The Islamic reformers in China already understood that Japan was pursuing aggression with excuses when it claimed "Mongolians and Muslims have the right to self-determination and the right to establish their own nation-states," and they set out to reject these arguments.[35] Not only the *Yuehua* but also other journals such as *Huijiao Dazhong* in Zhongqing, *Qingzhen Zhongbao* in Kunming or *Tujue* in Nanjing were sending almost the same messages. As the most prestigious journal under the Nationalist Government's authorization and surveillance, the *Yuehua* took the leadership of the literary anti-Japanese campaign in Hui society.

The *Yuehua* continued to publish and quote from the Qur'an and the Hadith in order to explain the Muslims' concrete justification for participation in a defensive war, and also in order to explain the need to submit to a single national leader, Jiang Jieshi. Translations of articles from the *Mağallat al-Azhar* (previously *Nūr al-Islām*) reinforced this tendency.[36] Egypt was also engulfed in the events of the Second World War, and the Qur'an, the Hadith, and transcriptions of historical wars began to be reinterpreted in accordance with the state of the conflict. Since

Muslims both in China and Egypt struggled for the same goal, Islamic theories imported from Egypt were also applicable to the Chinese situation. A "national emergency" was directing Muslims in China to translate the Qur'an. This was regarded not only as a religious activity, and as one meant to establish an ethnic identity, but also as a national activity.

In addition, the most distinct difference between prewar and postwar days was the appearance of the discourse on martyrdom. The *Yuehua* began to call for glorious death in the name of the state and against the enemy. The anti-Japanese war began to be regarded by Muslims as a sacred and just war, jihad.[37] Xue Wenbo 薛文波, a leading teacher of Chengda, wrote a verse entitled "Song of the Hui with an anti-Japanese determination":

> The enemies have made their horses drink water from the Yellow River
> The sacred war for national protection has begun
> Muslims have a real spirit, feel ashamed to indulge in living
> But we feel proud to participate in the battle
>
> Mosques have been burned down to ruins
> Innocent women and children are shedding blood
> Alas, in China we fifty million Muslims
> Are in disgrace
>
> Religion shows us the way of martyrdom
> Do we feel reluctant to bleed for justice?
> At the defeat of Japan, we yell out and rejoice
> Then Muslim men will undress their military uniform.[38]

Martyrdom had until then not been considered to be a glorious act, since ethnic identity as a "Hui" was originally based on the thoughts of *Huiru*s, to which this notion was not familiar. However, the Islamic reformers in China had no choice but to modify this principle in the face of the unprecedented invasion by a foreign power. Since patriotism had begun to occupy the highest position among human virtues, "glorious death for our own state" came to be judged as an act of religious martyrdom in reference to the Qur'an and the Hadith.[39]

This important transformation from the mere furthering of patriotism to that of national salvation, for which any sacrifice could be made, was brought forth by the political change. The Nationalist government called for a national salvation movement and for spiritual mobilization after 1939. At the same time, the slogan of "love homeland and love Islam" was converted into "save homeland and save Islam" *qiuguo qiujiao* 救國救教.[40]

The hadith concept of "love of the fatherland is an article of faith" was stressed over and over again. In order to encourage the Hui to fight against Japanese invaders, this concept was spread to Hui societies throughout China by means of journals, speeches, and radio broadcasts by *ahong*s and the elite, as well as by travels of the Hui elite to frontier regions for promotional purposes.

"A message to all Muslims in China from the Chinese Islamic Association for National Salvation" was issued in Ramadan, 1940. It clearly spelled out the duties of Muslims in such difficult conditions. After an explanation of the Islamic revival and Muslim nation-building efforts throughout the world, it declared that Muslims in China should not emphasize their own ethnic self-determination but should focus on national self-determination together with other ethnicities in China. It continued:

> We have to implement the teaching "the love of the fatherland is an article of faith" by the Prophet Muhammad and to inherit the Hui's glorious history in China. In addition, let us reinforce our unity and participate in the twice more difficult task of supporting a defensive war and promoting religion.... We hope that *ahong*s and the elite will initiate a movement of prayer during Ramadan and implement group prayer to support our intimate feeling toward Islam. A sincere unity of Muslims should be developed to contribute power towards the expulsion of Japan.[41]

During the anti-Japanese war, *ahong*s were not only at the front of the cultural resistance, but also were enthusiastically supporting the resistance movement in the battlefield. Taking advantage of their prestigious status over ordinary Muslims in the community, the *ahong*s spoke to the people of the necessity to participate in the war, and if need be of the glories of becoming a *šahīd*. Prominent and influential *ahong*s such as Xin Zongzhen 辛宗眞 in Hebei and Hu Songshan 虎嵩山 of the Ikhwani school in Ningxia, mobilized Muslims in the Hui communities. In the end, the difficult and painful war against Japan brought the formation of a double identity as Hui and as member of the Chinese nation.

The CCP's policy toward the Hui: a legacy of Islamic reform

In the wake of the historical coalition between the GMD and the CCP in 1937 in the Shan-Gan-Ning Anti-Japanese Base Area, the CCP implemented its own policy toward ethnic minorities, the Hui, and the Mongols in particular. In view of the formation of the Anti-Japanese National United Front, Mao Zedong presented the new line of the CCP in his *On the New Phase* in 1938 and *On New Democracy* in 1940. He stated that the CCP should recognize the Hui and other ethnic minorities as integral parts of the Chinese nation, and that China should thus be a unitary state. Until the coalition, however, the CCP advocated introducing a federal system in China, and Mao's new line was quite contrary to the CCP platform.

Newly recognizing themselves as the only legitimate successors of Sun Yatsen's nationalism, the CCP declared that the Hui had equal political and economic rights with the Han. At the same time the party guaranteed them freedom of religion, the preservation of their ethnic culture and customs, and support for ethnic and cultural development. Regional autonomy, which for sixty years had been the pillar of the CCP's policy toward ethnic minorities, was composed of a combination of the nationalist discourse of Sun Yatsen, Marxism–Leninism, and the wishes of ethnic minorities, the Hui in particular. The Hui had a population of about 1,500 in the base area.

Concerning the wishes of the Hui, we have acknowledged the fact that the ideology of "Hui ethnicity as a part of the Chinese nation" and their claim to equal political rights with the Han were advocated and spread by the Islamic reformers. However the concurrence of the CCP's minority policy and the Islamic reform movement did not happen by chance. Li Weihan was a top-ranking Han cadre of the CCP and was responsible for drafting the new policy toward ethnic minorities after 1938. While writing the booklet *Huihui Minzu Wenti* ("The Hui Question"), he immersed himself for more than two years in books on Islam and journals by the Islamic reformers published in the end of the 1930s. These were *Yuehua*, *Huijiao Dazhong*, *Huijiao Qingnian Yuebao*, and *Tujue*.

Li asserted that the Hui, as a *minzu* (nationality) had political rights, educational rights, and other rights equal to those of the Han, while he simultaneously emphasized that the party should eliminate poverty and forced assimilation, as well as fight racial discrimination. He also claimed that the CCP's minority policy should grant the Hui all of their wishes and follow the "correct" directions of the Islamic revivalist movement.[42] That is to say, the CCP praised and supported the Islamic reformers' efforts and orientation up to then. In particular, the Islamic reformers' enthusiastic encouragement of all Muslims in China to participate in the anti-Japanese War as well as their promotion of anti-Japanese education, were applauded. The orientation of the Islamic reformers helped create the blueprint that would help the CCP in formulating its policy for a unified nation-state that would include multiple ethnicities.

The favored status of the Hui as a "nationality" in the People's Republic can be understood as a reward for their inclusive patriotic attitude toward the Chinese State. The Islamic reformers also considered the CCP's policy as ideal for their moral existence. A close relationship was thus built between the CCP and the Hui nationality.

However, the CCP and the Islamic reformers intentionally disregarded the possibility that other ethnic groups in China might wish to have their own nation-state disassociated from China. Both the CCP and the Islamic reformers failed to ponder the more dangerous potentialities of national disintegration. The remedy for any such insurgency was military suppression or conciliation. When the CCP recognized that ethnic problems were equivalent to "Hui problems" and that these could be resolved by use of the methodology propounded by the Islamic reformers, it was clear that new ethnic problems would emerge after the victory over Japan and the GMD. It is needless to say that the separatist movements of the Tibetans and the Uyghurs characterized these problems. As long as the CCP and its followers upheld a unitary state system, appeased "disobedient nationalities" by pointing to the example of "obedient nationalities," and continued to implement national integration through the Islamic reformers' policies from the republican era, these difficult problems could not be resolved.

Conclusion

At the beginning of the nation-state era, Islamic reformers consisting of *ahong*s, literati, and local elites rediscovered and reevaluated the philosophy of the "unity of being" as the core of a new Hui identity. They regarded this new ethnic identity as indispensable for China's nation-building and implemented the Islamic revival movement in order to coexist with the other ethnicities. They also took responsibility for the new political and social situation, since all of these phenomena were outflows of the one and only absolute existence, Allah. Absorbing and digesting "newer and better" Islamic interpretations from the outside, *ahong*s were expected to always be responsible for the protection of the material and spiritual lives of Muslims, not only in their own communities but also in the broader Hui community of China. The Hui local elite and power holders, with their Confucian and Islamic backgrounds, also felt the burden of saving, enlightening, and leading "backward" people out of poverty, ignorance, and a situation in which their political rights were not assured. In order to adjust the reality of the world to the doctrine of Islam, they needed to be accountable to the community to which they belonged. The founders of the Chengda Normal School and the publishers of *Yuehua* were some of the most progressive elements of these Islamic reformers.

Essentially, both *ahong*s and the local elite displayed a double faith toward Allah and the ruler of this world. Therefore, at the beginning of the nation-state era, it was rather easy for them to produce a new national identity instead of the simple faith toward the Mandate of Heaven. Their nationalistic tendency throughout the twentieth century can be explained by their psychological structure.

They were pioneers in declaring that Chinese culture had a multiple but unified character. They also asserted that ethnic identity and national identity should coexist within one's mind. This concept is still active in the CCP's policy toward ethnic minorities, in which the CCP attempts to educate and persuade ethnic minorities in China to have both an ethnic and a national identity. This assertion has common points with Fei Xiaotong's famous statement which is, at the same time, the People's Republic's official definition of the Chinese nation, namely that "the Chinese nation has a multiple and unified structure."

In order to support and promote the concept of patriotism and nationalism in the 1930s, the Hui appreciated the discussions of Islamic reform movements in Egypt that were taking place at the time. In fact, these discussions had considerable impact on the foundation and development of the Islamic revival movement in China. The Egyptian reformers' works were applied in order to promote nationalism, modernism, and Islamic reform in China. These concepts "imported" from Egypt contributed to making the Islamic reformers in

China an established and distinguished mainstream force, not only among Muslims in China but also in terms of the People's Republic's policy toward ethnic minorities.

However, it is very important to point out that the Chinese reformers only extracted some of the essence of the Egyptian reformers' discussions, which they rearranged in a form more suitable to the Chinese situation. In other words, the style of their activities and their moral basis could not be completely free from their traditional philosophy of the unity of being. The concrete basis of patriotism, however, was supplemented by the alleged Hadith identifying faith toward Allah with faith toward *waṭan* (fatherland). "Love fatherland and love Islam" was regarded as the most effective moral code for Muslims in China. Its slogans were hung on the wall of mosques, just as the slogan of "hurrah for the emperor" used to be seen in mosques in the Qing era. The slogan was taught in schools for Hui children and preached by *ahong*s in mosques every Friday. Under the tutelage of the educational system initiated by the Islamic reformers, the Hui's obedience to authority became a religious theory.

We have discussed the policy of regional autonomy adopted by the People's Republic at the request of the Islamic reformers. In addition, we may point out that the discussion of the Islamic reformers with regard to the Chinese nation is very similar to the more recent official discourse about the Chinese nation with a multiple and unified structure. The three directions advocated by the Islamic reformers, nationalism, modernism, and the promotion of Islam have been again carefully upheld since the initiation of the Reform and Open Policy in 1978.

As long as they advocated patriotism as the highest political and moral code, the Hui's political status in the state was guaranteed. If we set aside the Tibetans and Uyghurs, ethnic problems have apparently been minimal during the last two decades, at least in China's provincial districts. It seems that in China ethnic consciousness does not always seem to lead to the ethnic nationalism that brought the tragedies of Yugoslavia or Chechnia. This means that the ethnic identity of various national groups in China, for the most part fuses with the central government's purpose of national integration. There may be objections that such ethnic identity in China is a "pseudo identity" that is manipulated by the government. However, as we sought to prove in this paper, the Islamic reformers' efforts for national integration, at least, cannot be underestimated.

Notes

1 Matsumoto Akiro 松本耿郎, "Ba Rengen cho 'Tenpō Seiri Abunchūkai' no kenkyū 馬聯元著「天方性理阿文注解」の研究," *Tōyōshi kenkyū* 58/1 (1999).

2 Ma Shouqian 馬壽千, "Huizu Yisilanjiao de Jingtang Jiaoyu 回族伊斯蘭教的經堂教育 [Jingtang Islamic Education of the Hui]," in *Xibei Huizu yu Yisilanjiao* 西北回族與伊斯蘭教 [Northwestern Hui Nationality and Their Islam] (Yinchuan: Ningxia Renmin Chubanshe, 1994), 239–242. Also see several papers on *Jingtang* in Xi'an

Yisilan Wenhua Yanjiuhui 西安伊斯蘭文化研究會, ed., *Yisilan Wenhua Yanjiu* 伊斯蘭文化研究 [Islamic Cultural Studies] (Yinchuan: Ningxia Renmin Chubanshe, 1998).

3 Chu Ketong 朱克同, "Guwan shichang he zhubao yishi—Shanghai Huizu Musilin de Chuantong Hingye 古玩市場和珠寶集市—上海回族穆斯林的傳統行業 [Antique Markets and the Traditional Occupation of Jewerly]," in Zhongguo Isilanjiao Yanjiu Wenji Bianxuezu, ed., *Zhongguo Isilanjiao Yanjiu Wenji* 中國伊斯蘭教研究文集 (Yinchuan: Ningxia Renmin Chubanshe, 1988), 465–474.

4 Yang Zhaojun 馬超群 Ma Chaogun 馬超群, and Ma Weiliang 馬維良 (eds), *Yunnan Huizu shi* 馬維良 [History of the Hui of Yunnan] (Kunming: Yunnan Minzu Chubanshe, 1989), 201–204.

5 Cai Dayu 蔡大愚, "Liutong Qingzhen Jiaoyuhui xu「留東清真教育會序」[Introduction to the Islamic Educational Association in Tokyo]," in Liudong Qinzhen Jiaoyuhui 留東清真教育会, ed., *Xing Hui Pian* 醒回篇 (Reprint, Yinchuan: Ningxia Renmin Chubanshe, 1992), 85.

6 Wang Jingzhai, "Wushi nian qiuxue zishu 五十年求學自述 [Memoir of My Fifty-Year Study]," in Li Xinghua and Feng Jingyuan, eds, *Zhongguo Isilan Jiaoshi Cankao Ziliao Xuanbian (1911–1949)* 中國伊斯蘭教史參考資料選編 (Yinchuan: 1985), 622–623.

7 Ma Songting, "Zhongguo Huijiao yu Chengda Shifan Xuexiao 中國回教與成達師範學校 [Islam in China and the Chengda Normal School]," *Yugong* 5/11 (1936).

8 Jing Jidang 金吉堂 "Gu Ma Fuxiang xiansheng xingbang jiaoyu shilüe 故馬福祥先生興辦教育史略 [The Late Ma Fuxiang's Promotion of Education]," *Yuehua* 7/25, 26, 27 (September 30, 1936).

9 *Yuehua* 1/1 (November 5, 1929).

10 Li Tingbi 李廷弼, "Yisilan shisi shiji shidai zhi qingnian 伊思蘭十四世紀時代之青年 [The Muslim Youth in the Fourteenth Islamic Century]," *Yuehua* 2/6 (February 25, 1930).

11 Kosugi Yasushi, *Gendai Chūtō to Isurāmu seiji* 現代中東とイスラーム政治 [The Modern Middle East and Islamic Politics] (Tokyo: Shōwadō, 1994), 10–12.

12 Al-Qur'an (surah 2: 246).

13 Wang Jingzhai, trans. and interpretation, "Jinshou Huijiao yu Aihu Guojia「謹守回教與愛護國家」[Protection of Islam and Love of the Fatherland]," *Yuehua* 2/3 (January 25, 1930).

14 C. Ernest Dawn, "Ideological Influences in the Arab Revolt," *The World of Islam: Studies in Honor of Philip K. Hitti* (New York: Macmillan, 1959).

15 Wang, "Jinshou Huijiao yu Aihu Guojia."

16 Ma Songting 馬松亭, "Wunian yilai zhi *Yuehua* bao「五年以来之月華報」[The *Yuehua* Journal in These Five Years]," *Yuehua* 6/28, 29, 30.

17 The following is a list of journals or papers traded in exchange for the *Yuehua* from 1931 until the mid-1930s: *al-Fattāḥ* (Cairo) seemed to be the earliest journal acquired by the editors of the *Yuehua*; *al-Saṭḥ* (Cairo), *al-Islām* 5, 6 (Tunis), *Moslemische Revue* (Berlin), *al-Šabān al-salamīn, Sırat-ı müstakim* 1 (Istanbul), *The Islamic Review* (London), *Pembela Islam* (Java), *The Mirror of Truth and Guide to Happiness, Mohammad and Christ, The Call of Islam, Back to Qur'an, The Ahamadiyya Movement, al-Hudā* (Singapore). (From several issues of the fifth volume of *Yuehua*).

18 Concerning the bibliography of Ma Songting, see Sai Shengbao, "Aiguo zhuyizhe, Yisilan jingxue jiaoyujia Ma Songting Daahong 愛國主義者、伊斯蘭經學教育家馬松亭大阿衡," *Huizu Yanjiu* 2 (1992).

19 Ma Songting, "Wunian yilai zhi *Yuehua* bao."

20 Ma Yugui 馬毓貴, "Guonan fangyin! Jiaobao suqi! 國難方殷！教胞速起！ [National Difficulties Will Come Soon! Muslims, Wake Up Soon!]," *Yuehua* 3/27 (September 25, 1931).

21 Yisilan Xueyouhui, "Yisilan Xueyouhui kangri xuanyan 伊斯蘭學友會抗日宣言 [Anti-Japanese Declaration by the Muslim Students Association]," *Yuehua* 3/35 (December 15, 1931).

22 Xue Wenbo 薛文波, "Zhongguo Huizu de diwei he bensheng yingyou de renshi 中國回族的地位和本身應有的認識 [The Status of the Hui Nationality and the Required Consciousness]," *Yuehua* 4/10, 11, 12 (April 5, 1932).
23 Yang Sishi 仰思室, "Duiyu Aiji huiguang yuekan de pingyu 対於埃及回光月刊的評語 [Assessment of *Nūr al-Islām*]," *Yuehua* 4/33 (November 25, 1932).
24 Muhammad Hazar Hoseini, "Zhuanshu Gulan zhi yiyi wei waiguowen 轉述古蘭之意義爲外國文 [Transfering the Right Meaning of the Translation of the Qur'an into Foreign Languages]," trans. Yang Sishi, *Yuehua* 5/1, 2, 3, 4, 5 (1993).
25 Ma Jian, "Renzhuxue dagang," *Yuehua* 5/27 (September 25, 1933).
26 "Bianjishi Tanhua 編輯室談話," *Yuehua* 5/30 (October 25, 1933). In addition to the *Risālat al-tawḥīd*, Ma Jian translated Husayn al-Jisr's *Sağāyiġ dīn al-Islām* into Chinese and entitled it *Huijiao Zhenxiang* 回教眞相 [The Reality of Islam], under the recommendation of professor Jibali of al-Azhar. The translation was finished in 1937 and published in Zhongqing. Ma Jian also translated a book to solve the question of contradictions between science and religion. Husayn al-Jisr came from Tunisia and was a disciple of Muhammad 'Abduh.
27 Zhou Zhongren 周仲仁 "Gulanjing yijie 古蘭經譯解 [Commentary of the Qur'an]," *Yuehua* 6/34, 35, 36 (December 30, 1934).
28 J. Jomier, "Al-Azhar," *EI*^{2}.
29 "Felifeile Boshi zai Zhongshan Gongyuan Huanying dahui xishang zhi jiangyan ci 福力腓樂博士在中山公園歡迎大會席上之講演詞 [Dr Filfila's Speech at the Welcome Conference at the Zhongshan Park]" *Yuehua* 5/25 (September 5, 1933).
30 Ma Songting, "Huijiao yu rensheng 回教與人生 [Islam and Life]," *Yuehua* 5/35 (December 15, 1933).
31 Ma Zishi 馬子實 (馮堅), "Aiji Huijiaotu hujiao yundong 埃及回教徒護教運動 [The Egyptian Muslim Movement for the Protection of Islam]," *Yuehua* 5/26 (September 15, 1933).
32 To some extent, Islamic reformers in China were inclined to support Muhammad Iqbal of India who insisted on the formation of one Indian nation upon the fusion of both Hindu and Muslims. Information on Iqbal, a prominent leader of the Islamic reform movement in India, was partly transmitted by another of *Yuehua*'s correspondents Hai Weiliang 海維諒, who studied at the Lucknow Islamic Institute in India. See Hai Weiliang "Indu zhuming Huijiao shiren Ikeba boshi zhi lunzheng 印度著名回教詩人依克巴博士之論政 [The Famous Indian Poet Iqbal's Political Discussions]," *Yuehua* 5/29 (October 25, 1933).
33 Ai Yizai 艾宜栽 "Bannian lai de Beiping Chengda Shifan Xuexiao 半年来的北平成達師範學校 [The Chengda Normal School in the Last Six Months]," *Yugong* 7/4 (1936).
34 Liu Tongsheng 劉東聲, "Chengda Shifan Xuexiao xiaoshi shuyao 成達師範學校校史述要," *Huizu Yanjiu* 11 (1993): 72.
35 Mu Fu 牧夫 "Cong Beijing Huijiaohui dao Zhongguo Huijiao Zonglianhehui 「從北京回教會到中國回教總聯合會」," in Wenshi Ziliao Yanjiuhui, ed., *Wenshi Ziliao Xuanbian* 文史資料選編 32 (Beijing: Beijing Chubanshe, 1987).
36 (*Mağallat al-Azhar* 6/9) *Yuehua* 11/28–30 (1939); (*Mağallat al-Azhar* 11/7) *Yuehua* 13/1–3 (1941); (*Mağallat al-Azhar* 11/7) *Yuehua* 13/4–9 (1941); (*Mağallat al-Azhar* special edition 1939) *Yuehua* 13/10–12 (1941); (*Mağallat al-Azhar* 11/4) *Yuehua* 13/28–30 (1941); (*Mağallat al-Azhar* 6/9) *Yuehua* 13/28–30 (1941); (*Mağallat al-Azhar* 6/9) *Yuehua* 13/28–30 (1941).
37 Anonymous, "Yuehua Luntan 月華論壇" *Yuehua* 10/14, 15, 16 (September 5, 1938).
38 Xue Wenbo, "Zhongguo Huizu kangzhenge 中國回族抗戰歌," *Yuehua* 11/18 (September 25, 1939).
39 Zheng Daoming 鄭道明, "Cong Huijiao zhi zhanzheng quanyi shuodao women de shensheng kangzhan 從回教之戰争詮釋說到我們的神聖抗戰 [Interpretation of Our Holy War from the Perspective of Islamic War]," *Yuehua* 11/4, 5, 6 (February 25, 1939).

40 "Guilin Tongxiang daxu Huimin Juxing shendan Jinian shengkuang 桂林東鄉大墟回民舉行聖誕紀念盛況," *Yuehua* 11/10–15 (May 25, 1939).
41 "Zhongguo Huijiao Qiuguoxiehui gao quanguo Huibao shu 中國回教救國協會告全國回胞書 [Message from the Chinese Islamic Association for National Salvation to all Muslims in China]," *Yuehua* 12/28, 29, 30 (October 25, 1940).
42 Minzu Wenti Yanjiuhui 民族問題研究會, ed., *Huihui Minzu Wenti* 回回民族問題 (Reprint, Beijing: Minzu Chubanshe, 1981), 129.

7

THE TRANSMISSION OF *AL-MANĀR*'S REFORMISM TO THE MALAY-INDONESIAN WORLD

The case of *al-Imām* and *al-Munīr*

Azyumardi Azra

The spread and influence of modern Islamic reformism to the Malay-Indonesian world since the early twentieth century have been recognized by many scholars of Malay-Indonesian Islam. In a general way, scholars have delineated the influence of such reformist scholars or activists as Jamal al-Din al-Afghani, Muhammad 'Abduh, Rashid Rida, and others in reformist or modernist organizations such as the Sarekat Islam, Muhammadiyah, Persatuan Islam, or Jong Islamieten Bond. Little attention, however, has been paid to the channels of transmission of modernist or reformist ideas from the Middle East, especially Cairo and Mecca, to the Malay-Indonesian world.

There is no doubt that the printed word was the instrumental means responsible for the transmission of modernist or reformist ideas to the Malay-Indonesian world. It is within this context that we can appropriately place the reformist journal *al-Manār*, which significantly influenced the course of Islamic reformism in the region. The journal not only directly influenced the spread of Islamic reformism through its own articles, but was most influential in stimulating the publication of similar journals within the Malay-Indonesian world. This chapter is an early attempt to delineate and comprehensively discuss the transmission of Islamic reformism to the Malay-Indonesian world by means of journals, namely by the two indigenous journals *al-Imām* and *al-Munīr*.

Regarding the journal *al-Manār* itself, a brief note should be made. It is well known that the backbone of *al-Manār* was the reformist scholar Muhammad Rashid Rida. Deeply influenced by Afghani and especially by 'Abduh, his main mentor, Rida published his own magazine, *al-Manār* ("The Lighthouse"), which first appeared in 1898 in Cairo as a weekly, and subsequently as a monthly, until his death in 1935. The objectives of *al-Manār* were to articulate and disseminate the ideas of reform and preserve the unity of the Muslim umma. It was Rida himself who edited most of the articles that appeared in *al-Manār*. Therefore, one can argue that *al-Manār* was the personal work of Rida.[1]

Al-Manār and the Malay-Indonesian world

In her fascinating study of Indonesian students in Cairo, Abaza has correctly argued that, during colonial times, Cairo played an important role as a center for the publication and circulation of journals and magazines. There were a number of magazines and journals published in Cairo that were circulated in the Malay-Indonesian world. In addition to *al-Manār*, which is under discussion here, it is also known that the journal *al-'Urwa al-Wuṯqā*, a predecessor of *al-Manār*, was in circulation in the Malay-Indonesian world.

It is important, however, to point out that Cairo also received a number of magazines and journals published in the Malay-Indonesian world. It seems possible to find in the collection of the Cairo National Library, Dār al-Kutub, Malay-Indonesian magazines and journals such as *al-Iqbāl* (Java), *al-Hudā* (Singapore), *al-Mir'a al-muḥammadiyya* (Yogyakarta), *al-Taḫīra al-islāmiyya*, and *al-Iršād* (Pekalongan). Considering this, Cairo is seen playing an undeniably crucial role in the mutual transmission of ideas from one region to another. In fact, Cairo was not only the center for the publication of Arabic literature, but also a center for Malay literature as well.[2]

The influence of *al-Manār* on the Malay-Indonesian world can hardly be overestimated. Despite Dutch efforts to ban it from entering the Archipelago, it was regularly read in various parts of the region. In fact, it has been suggested that *al-Manār* was reasonably well circulated within the Malay-Indonesian world by several means.

The first is smuggling. It appears very likely that *al-Manār* was mostly smuggled into Indonesia through certain ports where Dutch supervision was lax. Mukti 'Ali points out that *al-Manār* was smuggled into Indonesia, or more precisely into Java, for instance, via the port of Tuban in East Java, where there was no customs supervision. According to Pijper Bluhm-Warn, the adviser to the Dutch Government for Native and Arab affairs, who was also responsible for supervising the spread of Islamic literature in Indonesia, the Dutch did not censor the shipment of *al-Manār* to Ahmad Surkati, founder of the Irshad movement in the archipelago.[3]

The second means by which *al-Manār* was brought into Indonesia was by way of certain hajjis who returned after their pilgrimage to Mecca and Medina, where the journal was in wide circulation. It is well known that from the early history of Islam in the archipelago, especially from the sixteenth century onwards, the pilgrimage had been an effective means of the transmission of not only Islamic ideas, but also of a large amount of literature from the Middle East to the region. It is therefore not difficult to understand why Snouck Hurgronje, the leading adviser to the Dutch colonial government on Islamic affairs, suggested that the Dutch pay special attention to supervising returning hajjis.[4]

The third means of transmission of *al-Manār* was returning students either from Cairo or Mecca and Medina. As Roff shows, the number of Malay-Indonesian students in these places grew significantly in the early 1920s.[5] This increase allowed them to establish organizations and publish their own journals, the most prominent of which was the *Seruan Azhar*.[6] The *Seruan Azhar* itself, as we will see later, played an important role in the continued Islamic intellectual discourse in the Malay-Indonesian archipelago.

The fourth means was through certain "appointed" agents. This is clear in the case of Sayyid Muhammad ibn 'Aqil ibn Yahya, one of *al-Imām*'s leading associates in Singapore. In an obituary to the Sayyid, Rashid Rida mentions that he took the trouble to circulate *al-Manār* in Singapore, Java, and the entire Indonesian archipelago.[7]

The spread of *al-Manār* was not confined to the Dutch East Indies and the Straits. *Al-Manār*, and *al-Imām*, also circulated in the Kota Bharu area of Kelantan. As Nik Hassan makes clear, together with other reformist journals such as *Pengasuh* (first printed in Kota Bharu in 1918), *al-Iḫwān* (first printed in Pulau Pinang in 1926), and *Saudara* (first printed in Pulau Pinang in 1928), it played a crucial role in the spread of Kaum Muda ideas in the Kelantan region. All of these journals were among the most important sources of reformist ideas among such ulama as Haji Muhammad Yussof bin Muhammad, popularly known as Tok Kenali (1868–1933), Haji Wan Musa bin Haji Abdul Samad (1874–1939), and Haji Ahmad Manam (1834–1938).[8]

It is clear that the influence of *al-Manār* went beyond journals, magazines, and reformist organizations. *Al-Manār* even inspired certain writers to write novels containing the reformist ideas that it preached. Shaykh al-Hadi, mentioned earlier, for instance, wrote a novel entitled *Farīda Ḫānum* that is set in Cairo in late 1894. Despite the fact that the work is fiction, he wished to give some sense of realism and credibility through references to "real people, places, and events." Thus, for instance, he mentions the names of Cairo streets; he also described the Egyptian ruler, Muhammad 'Abduh, the journal *al-Manār*, and even several Egyptian feminists. As Hooker points out, the specific reference to Muhammad 'Abduh and the reformist journal *al-Manār* in the closing pages of the novel, locate the narrative firmly in the context of reformist Islam.[9]

Another such novel is *Hikayat Percintaan Kasih Kemudaan* written by Ahmad Kotot (b. 1894), a native Malay. This novel also included the theme of Islamic reformism preached by *al-Manār*. Although the novel was written in a Malay setting, it is distinguished by its Islamic reformist underpinnings.

Al-Imām: mouthpiece of reform (1906–1908)

It is doubtless that *al-Imām* ("The Leader") was one of the most important channels of the transmission of *al-Manār*'s ideas to the Malay-Indonesian world. In his classic study, Roff concludes that, in the first place, *al-Imām* was a radical departure from standard journals in the field of Malay publications. It was distinguished from its predecessors both by its intellectual stature and intensity of purpose, and by its attempt to formulate a coherent philosophy of action for a society faced with the need for rapid social and economic change. Second, Roff argues that the range and orthodoxy of *al-Imām* was representative of the incipient movements, which could be seen growing in almost every aspect of Malay life.[10]

The fact that *al-Imām* was inspired by and modeled on *al-Manār* has been agreed upon by many scholars including Roff. It was from the Egyptian reformist movement that the writers and sponsors of *al-Imām* derived, almost in totality, their reformist ideas. Therefore, like the *al-Imām* circle in the Minangkabau area, the reformist group in Malaya that was responsible for the publication of *al-Imām* was known as "*kaum al-Manār*", or the "*al-Manār* faction." An examination of the contents of *al-Manār*, as detailed by Adams,[11] makes clear the extent to which *al-Imām* was modeled upon it; and the Malay journal contains abundant references to and excerpts from *al-Manār*.[12]

Thus, it is clear that *al-Imām* was one of the most important intellectual loci of reformist Muslims in the Malay-Indonesian world. In addition to being known as "*kaum al-Manār*," as has been pointed out earlier, this reformist group was also popularly known as the "*kaum muda*," the young reformist group, as opposed to the "*kaum tua*," the old traditionalist group. The "*kaum muda*," as one might expect, was inspired and influenced by such reformist Middle Eastern figures as Afghani, ʿAbduh, Rida, and the like, and proposed the renewal of Islam. On the other hand, the "*kaum tua*" was the proponent of the established and traditional Islam. The reformist tendency represented by the *al-Imām* group can be seen in the biography of its editors and publishers. These were Shaykh Muhammad Tahir bin Jalaluddin al-Minangkabawi al-Azhari, the first editor, Sayyid Shaykh bin Ahmad al-Hadi, a Melaka-born Malay-Arab who was a frequent and colorful contributor; Haji Abbas bin Muhammad Thaha, a Singapore-born Minangkabau, the second editor, and Shaykh Muhammad Salim al-Kalali, an Acehnese merchant who was director of *al-Imām* during its first two years.[13]

The most notable figure, not only among the editors of *al-Imām*, but also among the "*kaum muda*" was Shaykh Muhammad Tahir bin Jalaluddin al-Minangkabawi al-Azhari, who was born in Kototuo, Bukittinggi in West Sumatra in 1869. His father, Shaikh Muhammad, also called Shaykh Tahir, was a well-known ulama in his area, a son of Shaykh Ahmad Jalaluddin or Tuanku Sami, a judge of the Paderi in the Padri Movement in Central Sumatra in the late eighteenth and early nineteenth centuries.[14] His father died when he was 2 years old, followed by his mother when he was 8. When he was 12 years old (*c.*1881), he was sent to Mecca where he stayed with his well-known cousin, Shaykh Ahmad Khatib al-Minangkabawi. Ahmad Khatib was known not only as a teacher of many Jawi students in the Holy City, but was known as the grand *imām* of the Shafiʿi madhhab in the Haram.[15]

After studying in Mecca for about fourteen years he went to Cairo to study *ʿilm al-falak* (astronomy) at al-Azhar. It was during his four-year sojourn in Cairo that he was introduced to the teachings of the celebrated reformist Muhammad

'Abduh. It is also reported that he formed a close relationship with the most brilliant of 'Abduh's students, Muhammad Rashid Rida. It is said that later, in 1898, when Rida founded *al-Manār*, Muhammad Tahir contributed articles to its columns. If this is true, then he sent his writings to *al-Manār* from Mecca, where he lived and taught from 1897 to 1899. Whatever the case, it is clear that he was profoundly influenced by the reformist ideas voiced in the circle of *al-Manār*.

In 1899 Muhammad Tahir returned from Mecca to his homeland in West Sumatra. However, he chose Malaya instead of Sumatra as his home, and on 28 September of that year settled in Kuala Kangsar in the State of Perak, where he married a Malay girl. A year later, he was appointed religious officer by the Sultan of Perak, Idris Murshidil Mu'azzam Shah, and in August 1904 he was commissioned as a member of the council of the chiefs and religious elders of the State of Perak. Although he chose to settle in Perak, Muhammad Tahir frequently traveled to Riau-Lingga and Sumatra.

In 1903 he was invited, together with his close friend Sayyid Shaykh bin Ahmad al-Hadi, to accompany a "mission" to Mecca and Cairo, which included the sons of the Sultan and Raja Muda of Riau. Two years later, in 1905, he went to Singapore, where he initially joined his friends to help organize the pilgrim brokerage on the island, a business in which he had been involved since his latest sojourn in Mecca. It was during his stay in Singapore that he met a number of ulama, wealthy people, and personalities who were knowledgeable, able, and willing to work collectively to publish a journal to be known as *al-Imām*, beginning in July 1906.[16]

It is important to point out that while serving as the editor in chief of *al-Imām*, Muhammad Tahir was involved in various other activities. Before and after the First World War he taught in various institutions, the most prominent of which was Madrasa al-Mansur in Penang, which was established by his friend Sayyid Shaykh bin Ahmad al-Hadi. In 1928 he visited his homeland in Sumatra and was immediately arrested by the Dutch authorities for six months on suspicion of being a leftist with Communist leanings in his religious teaching.[17] After a thorough investigation, the Dutch found no evidence supporting their suspicion against him and he was freed. He then returned to Malaysia and settled in Johor until his death in 1957. Muhammad Tahir wrote several books in Arabic and Malay, dealing with religious matters in general and astronomy in particular.

As Roff argues, Muhammad Tahir seems to have combined both the reformist spirit evident among a section of the Jawi community in Mecca in the 1880s and 1890s, and something of the more sophisticated modernism of contemporary religious thought in Cairo. It is also clear that he was profoundly influenced by the Pan-Islamism of Afghani and by the reformist ideas of 'Abduh, ideas that were current in the *al-Manār* circle. Therefore, it is not surprising for him and his friends to fashion *al-Imām* in the image of *al-Manār*.[18]

The second intellectual figure that was closely connected with *al-Imām* was Haji 'Abbas bin Mohammad Taha, who succeeded Muhammad Tahir as editor of *al-Imām* and officially reorganized it in March 1908. Though he was born in

Tanjung Pagar, Singapore in 1885, his parents were from the Minangkabau area in West Sumatra. When he was a small boy, he was sent by his parents to Mecca to acquire religious knowledge. On returning to Singapore in 1905 he worked mainly as a teacher. In 1906 he published a book on education and its philosophy entitled *Kitab Sempurnaan Pelajaran* (the Book of Perfection in Education). When *al-Imām* ceased its publication in December 1908, he was appointed qadi of the Tanjung Pagar district, where he remained active in the reformist cause, founding and editing the weekly newspaper *Neracha* ("The Scales") in 1911, followed by its companion monthly journal *Tunas Melayu* ("The Malay Seeds") in 1913. As Roff points out, these two reformist intellectuals were dedicated to the goals elaborated by *al-Imām* in 1906. Concerned about the religious conflict that erupted between "Kaum Muda" and "Kaum Tua," Haji ʻAbbas urged the formation of a special association of religious leaders. For that purpose, in 1936 he made an appeal to found the Persekutuan Ulama Kaum Semenanjung ("the pan-Malayan Association of Ulama"). In the same year he was appointed chief qadi of Singapore. He was also in close association with Burhanuddin al-Helmi, a politically orientated young reformist activist, who was also of Minangkabau origin. Together they were involved in the debate against "Kaum Tua," which inspired Haji ʻAbbas to write a booklet entitled "Risalah Penting pada Masalah Jilatan Anjing di atas Empat Mazhab" ("An Important Booklet on the Case of Being Licked by a Dog According to the Four Madhhabs of the Sunni").[19]

The next pillar of *al-Imām* was Sayyid Shaykh bin Ahmad al-Hadi (1862–1934). Born in Malacca, his father Ahmad al-Hadi was of Hadhrami descent, and his mother was Malay. As a boy he attended for some years a well-known madrasa in Kuala Trengganu. When he was 14 years old, his father took him to Pulau Penyengat, Riau, where his father had connections with the royal house. There he was adopted by Raja Ali Kelana bin Raja Ahmad, half brother of the Sultan and also Raja Muda (then heir apparent to the Sultan), and brought up with the royal children.[20]

As a young man, Sayyid Shaykh was put in charge of the *rumah wakaf*, the hostel in which travelers were accommodated while visiting the court. Here he had the opportunity to be on familiar term with many noteworthy ulama and to further his own religious knowledge and interests through discussions and debates. In the early 1890s he assisted in the formation of the Persekutuan Rushdiyyah, a study club similar to those set up in Singapore at about the same time, and took an active interest in its activities.[21]

His close association with the court circle can be seen from the fact that on more than one occasion he accompanied the sons of the Sultan and Raja Muda on the pilgrimage to Mecca and to Egypt and the Levant, traveling in 1903 with Muhammad Tahir, with whom he had forged a close friendship. It is perhaps because of these visits that he was reported to have studied in Mecca. But, as Roff points out, it is unlikely that Sayyid Shaykh received much formal religious education during these visits. There is no doubt, however, that he became familiar, probably through the influence of Muhammad Tahir, with the ideas current in the Middle Eastern metropolitan centers of Islam at this time.

During this period Sayyid Shaykh had already been living in Singapore; since 1901 to be precise, for that is when he was appointed by his adoptive father, Raja Ali Kelana, initially as agent and then as manager of his brickworks company. In 1906 he took a leading role in the establishment of *al-Imām*, increasingly becoming a prominent figure in the Malay-Muslim community. Even though he was not an *'ālim* of the calibre of Muhammad Tahir, he was very sharp and eminently suited to the polemicist and propagandist role in which he cast himself. In the course of his long and varied career he was known as a shari'a lawyer, educator, merchant, and publisher; however, he is today mostly remembered in journalism and literature.

It is important to note in passing that Sayyid Shaykh's connection with the Riau court and its intellectual circles contributed to *al-Imām*'s special importance in the Riau region, as argued by Andaya.[22] According to this author, the fidelity with which *al-Imām* relayed Arabic opinion on a variety of issues assured it a high standing in the Riau court, where it was read by the Sultan himself. The interest of the Penyengat princes in *al-Imām* was also stimulated because a number of them, notably Raja Hitam and Raja Ali, were active contributors, while they personally knew the editors. In addition to Sayyid Shaykh's special position mentioned earlier, Muhammad Tahir Jalaluddin traveled several times to the area, giving advice and religious instruction. Thus, Andaya concludes, the relationship between the founders of *al-Imām* and the Riau court meant that, as Snouck Hurgonje remarked, the journal was a "suitable place for [Raja Ali and his advisers] to publish their desires and grievances." *Al-Imām*, which subscribed to pan-Islamism, responded accordingly to their grievances, as will be discussed later.

The next pillar of *al-Imām* was Shaykh Muhammad Salim al-Kalali, who was its first managing director. Though only very little information is available about him, it is known that he was an Acehnese of Hadhrami descent, and that he was a generous merchant residing in Singapore. Despite his epithet of "shaykh," and although several major articles such as "*al-Ummah wa al-watan*" are attributed to him,[23] Roff believes that his importance to *al-Imām* was less as a scholar or writer than as a businessman.[24]

The last figure associated closely with *al-Imām* was Shaykh Sayyid Muhammad bin 'Aqil. When the management of *al-Imām* was commercially reorganized in March 1908, resulting in the establishment of the *al-Imām* Printing Company Ltd., Sayyid Muhammad 'Aqil was chosen and appointed as the Company Director ("*mudir*"). Little is known about him, although he acquired a certain public fame beyond the Malay-Muslim community when he was put on trial with two others in 1908 for the murder of Sayyid 'Abd al-Qadir al-Sagoff, another leading Singaporean Hadrami. Though the trial ended inconclusively, Sayyid Muhammad bin 'Aqil was subsequently cleared of all blame when it was discovered that a principal witness for the prosecution had committed systematic perjury. Later, an important study found that he had a strong tendency toward Shi'ism.[25]

What was the content of *al-Imām*? For the purposes of this paper it is worthy to cite Roff, who has delineated the realm of concern of *al-Imām*.[26] *Al-Imām*'s first concern was with religion and not directly with social, even less with political change. At the same time, such a tripartite division would have in some measure been foreign to the editors and writers of the journal, who shared the traditional Islamic concept of the undifferentiated umma in which spiritual, social, and political well-being is subsumed under another criteria—the good and profitable life lived according to Divine Law.

With this in mind, it is not surprising to find that the attention of the editors and writers was to turn, in the first place, to the state of Malay society. According to Roff, almost all of the thirty-one issues of the journal contain at least one article, and often more, analyzing the ills of the community. In self criticism and condemnation, *al-Imām* reveals the backwardness of the Malays, their domination by alien peoples, their laziness, their complacency, their bickering among themselves, and their inability to cooperate for the common good.

In *al-Imām*'s analysis the root cause of the decline of the Muslim peoples from their past glory is that they have ceased, in their ignorance, to follow the commands of God as expressed through the mouth and the life of His Prophet Muhammad. As an instrument for discovering and understanding the Divine Law, man has been gifted with *'akal* (reason), an intelligence it is incumbent upon him to use and to develop. Islam is not, writes *al-Imām,* as its detractors allege, hostile to knowledge and progress as exemplified by the West. On the contrary, a proper understanding of and submission to the law and spirit of Islam is "our only means of competing successfully with those who now rule and lead us."[27]

Proceeding with its diagnosis, *al-Imām* goes on to exhort certain groups of people to take the necessary action. It urges the rulers and traditional leaders to form associations to foster education, economic development, and self-awareness. It also urges the ulama to cleanse an Islam that had been adulterated by impurities of customs and belief derived from *'adat* and from other religions. The ulama that transmit the impure Islam should be brought to a sense of their errors and obligations. For this purpose, *al-Imām* put strong emphasis on the need to return to the Qur'an and Hadith, and to practice *ijtihad* (independent reasoning and judgment) rather than *taklid buta* (blind acceptance of intermediary authority) for their understanding.

Al-Imām pays attention not only to socio-religious matters, but also to political issues. One of the pet issues taken up by *al-Imām* relates to pan-Islamism. This is of course not surprising, since its intellectual genealogy is *al-Manār* and *al-'Urwa al-Wuṯqā*, both of which are closely related to Jamal al-Din al-Afghani, one of the most important pioneers of pan-Islamism.

Thus, when the issue of the "Caliphate" was brought forward by the Turkish Sultan Abdülhamid, *al-Imām* also took it up enthusiastically. Right from the very beginning of its existence, *al-Imām* printed news on Turkey at the same time as news on Japan. Under the heading "Turkey and Japan," *al-Imām* discusses the proposed Congress of Religion to be held in Tokyo. It is reported that Sultan Abdülhamid had sent telegrams to the Emperor of Japan and dispatched three special envoys to Japan in order to attend the Congress.[28]

To further the Caliphate cause, *al-Imām* listed some achievements of Sultan Abdülhamid. According to the journal it is important to inform anxious readers of the latest news on Turkey. *Al-Imām* gave detailed accounts of the capability of a Turkish warship complete with its capacity, arms, and speed "for those who would like to read it."[29]

Despite this seemingly powerful Turkish army, however, *al-Imām* reminds the Ottomans to continue their effort to improve their military strength, for the Empire is surrounded by mighty enemies. *Al-Imām* was convinced that only with the modernization of its army could the Ottoman Empire be on par with other European powers. Again, *al-Imām* expects that the readers are satisfied with its news and accounts of Ottoman military development.[30]

Al-Imām's attachment to the Caliphate question appears to have led it to lavishly praise Sultan Abdülhamid. In its reports *al-Imām* describes the Sultan as a caring ruler whose main concern was rebuilding the Empire's infrastructure by building schools, railways, and other means of communication. According to *al-Imām*, the noble efforts of the Sultan were challenged by the formidable West. In facing this challenge, the journal hoped that the Turks would be more resilient and prayed that they would be protected until the end.[31]

It may seem strange that the editors of *al-Imām* were not aware that the Sultan was the subject of strong criticism in Turkey and the Middle East. *Al-Imām*, in an innocent way, believed that Sultan Abdülhamid was sincere in his efforts to revitalize the old Ottoman Empire. It asserts that there was no other existing Islamic government than that of the Ottoman Empire. *Al-Imām* thus deplored unfavorable reports about the Empire by the Western press, which, it believed, were part of the conspiracy to undermine it.[32] According to Othman, however, when Sultan Abdülhamid was deposed from the throne by the Young Turks in 1908, *al-Imām* changed its attitude and now shifts its admiration in support of the Young Turks, which it viewed as the patrons of Islam.[33]

As indicated earlier, in connection with the biography of Sayyid Shaykh, *al-Imām* paid special attention to the destiny of the Riau court suffering under the encroachment of the Dutch. In an editorial published in September 1906, *al-Imām* pondered the fate of those countries that had lost their independence and preserved nothing else than "a collection of texts and stories."[34] Furthermore, as Andaya argues, a number of *al-Imām*'s articles clearly reflected the resentment felt by Riau toward the changes in court protocol introduced by the colonial government, and above all toward the abolition of the Yamtua Muda post.

In 1906 Tengku Osman, the Sultan's eldest son and Raja Ali's son-in-law and protégé who had been at school in Cairo during the crisis over the 1905 Treaty, returned. In its November issue, *al-Imām* published verbatim his speech to the Rushdiyyah Club: "I think, sirs," he said, "You must all be very worried and sad to see what has recently occurred in our beloved homeland."[35] *Al-Imām* also published an article by Sayyid Shaykh, which accused foreigners of placing Eastern peoples under slavery, of showing duplicity and disrespect to Eastern rulers, and of closing the doors to knowledge.[36]

How large was the extent of *al-Imām*'s influence? To answer this question, one may first look at its circulation. Roff admits that, although its subscribers may have been few in number, *al-Imām* also came into the hands of religious teachers, particularly those in the new style madrasas (modern religious schools). For them *al-Imām* was an invaluable source in dealing with such diverse and controversial questions such as the validity of certain hadiths, payment for burial prayers, certain practices associated with *tarekat* such as the Naqshbandiyya, the wearing of European clothing, and interest on loans from savings bank. Roff concludes that though there is no clear evidence of the size and nature of its audience, there is little doubt that a majority of its readers came from the intellectually and socially more sophisticated elements of the towns, and from those who were religiously educated and had received some introduction to Muslim polemics from their pilgrimage to Mecca.[37]

It is important to note that *al-Imām* also had representatives (*wakil*) in many Malay states, and that some of its most cogent contributions came from Malay correspondents in Johor, Perak, and Pahang. Though perhaps the bulk of its readership was within British Malaya, there is no doubt that *al-Imām* was also in circulation in other parts of the Malay-Indonesian archipelago. In fact, a high proportion of its correspondence came from the Dutch East Indies, particularly Sumatra. It is well known that Shaykh Muhammad Tahir Jalaluddin, the founder of the journal, sent copies to his friends and pupils in Minangkabau. As a result, as Hamka testifies, *al-Imām* exercised considerable influence on reformist thought and led directly to the establishment of a similar journal in 1911, *al-Munīr*.[38]

As Daya points out, *al-Imām* was a source of pride for the Minangkabau Muslims; it was established by one of their best-known ulama, and an intense correspondence linked certain Minangkabau ulama with Shaykh Tahir Jalaluddin. Furthermore the travels of Minangkabau *perantau* (migrants) who brought *al-Imām* with them, Daya argues, practically made *al-Imām* a possession of Minangkabau Malays. There was a good number of agents, subscribers, and correspondents of *al-Imām* in this area; and a number of articles written by Minangkabau ulama were also published in *al-Imām*. All of those related with *al-Imām* in one way or another were collectively called "*kaum al-Manār*" (the *al-Manār* group). It is therefore not surprising if, when *al-Imām* ceased its publication, it was lamented by Minangkabau reformist ulama; and this led to the increasing need for publication of their own journal, *al-Munīr*.[39]

It is clear that the impact of *al-Imām* was not confined to giving rise to new similar journals in the Malay-Indonesian world. As Roff points out, it is in its impact on the new type of education, embodied by its encouragement of the more ambitious and elaborate new kind of madrasa (religious schools), that the immediate impact of the reformist group may be most clearly seen. *Al-Imām* also encouraged the formulation of a system of education that, ideally, was to take account of the need not only for a purified Islam but for modern secular knowledge as well.[40] Thus, what *al-Imām* basically proposed was a reformed system of religious education in which, upon a sound basis of doctrinal instruction, Arabic, English, and modern educational subjects would be taught.

Al-Imām not only paid much attention to matters regarding education, it also seems to have had specific educational aims. There were at least five of them promoted by *al-Imām:* first, to convince the Muslim community that knowledge is the first thing enjoined by God in the Holy Qur'an, and that the Qur'an contains all knowledge that is necessary for human progress;[41] second, to introduce a new system of education based on the Qur'anic doctrine;[42] third, to establish educational institutions with a sound curriculum and syllabus;[43] fourth, to encourage and assist Muslim youths in advancing their studies abroad;[44] fifth, to urge the rulers, traditional chieftains, and knowledgeable ulama, to take immediate action to enhance the system of Islamic education in the country.[45]

There are also *al-Imām*'s other numerous exhortations on education, ranging from reiteration of the benefits of education, explanations of the different types of education, warning of the danger of ignorance, to suggestions to parents not to allow their children to sleep during daytime. The concern of *al-Imām* was indeed wide-ranging. Furthermore, *al-Imām* was interested not only in ideas, but also in the establishment of institutions that would support the spread and maintenance of these ideas. The most important of the institution that *al-Imām* helped to establish was the Madrasa al-Iqbal al-Islamiyya founded in Singapore in 1908. Run by an Egyptian, 'Uthman Effendi Raffat, this madrasa borrowed much from modernism in Egypt and the West. It was undoubtedly the forerunner of many others organized in similar lines throughout the Malay Peninsula and other parts of the Malay-Indonesian archipelago during the next few years.

Al-Munīr (1911–1916): the Kaum Muda type of reformism

When *al-Imām* ceased to publish, the Kaum Muda, especially those in Sumatra, must have felt that they had lost an important mouthpiece. They soon sought to publish a new journal that could succeed it. Prominent leaders of Kaum Muda in West Sumatra, who founded the journal *al-Munīr* ("The Illumination"), finally took the initiative. As Adams correctly points out, if one takes into account its intellectual genealogy, it was only natural that *al-Munīr* should take over the role of *al-Imām* in spreading Kaum Muda teachings and opposing all enemies of Islam.[46]

According to Yunus, *al-Munīr* was the first Islamic journal published in Padang in 1 Rabi' II 1329/April 1911. *Al-Munīr*, however, did not last long; it ceased its publication in 1916 because, according to Yunus, its printing press was burned down.[47]

The founder of *al-Munīr* was Haji 'Abdullah Ahmad, one of the most important scions of Islamic reformism in the Minangkabau area in the early twentieth century. Before providing his brief biography, it is important to point out that 'Abdullah Ahmad's idea to publish a journal similar to *al-Imām* came to his mind during his visit to Singapore in 1908. It was on this occasion that he learned about questions related to the journal's publication, management, and editorship. In addition, he also took the opportunity to gain insights from *al-Imām*'s experience in establishing the Madrasa Iqbal al-Islamiyya.[48] As soon as he returned, he established his well-known school, "Sekolah Diniyyah al-Islamiyyah."[49] In the case of *al-Munīr*, however, it was only three years later that he was able to establish the journal.

Most scholars agree that 'Abdullah Ahmad was the sole pioneer of *al-Munīr*. Though their statements are different, Hamka, Alfian, and Djaja agree that it was 'Abdullah Ahmad who took the initiative to publish *al-Munīr*.[50] Benda, however, asserts that in addition to 'Abdullah Ahmad, 'Abdul Karim Amrullah was also an initiator of *al-Munīr*, although this does not seem to be supported by any sources.[51] In its first issue, 'Abdul Karim Amrullah is referred to as a contributor from Maninjau. Furthermore, there is not a single writing of his in this first issue; most of the writings were by 'Abdullah Ahmad.[52] In addition, Hamka, the son of 'Abdul Karim Amrullah, points out that "his father moved from Maninjau to Padang in early 1912 to help Abdullah Ahmad in his school, since the latter was already very busy with it."[53]

Born in Padang Panjang in 1878, he came from an ulama family; his father Haji Ahmad was an ulama and a textile trader. After finishing his elementary education, he traveled to Mecca in 1899 where he studied with Shaykh Ahmad Khatib al-Minangkabawi, a leading Jawi ulama in the Holy City at the time. He returned to Indonesia in 1905 and devoted himself to teaching and *dakwah* activities in Padang Panjang. Here he began to establish himself as an ardent reformist by opposing *bid'a* (unwarranted innovation) and *khurafat* (delusion). Around 1906 he moved to Padang, the capital city of West Sumatra, to succeed his uncle as a teacher. Later he established the Jama'ah Adabiyah, the seed of a school that he would later found. With the financial support of Muslim traders he founded the Adabiyah Diniyyah School in 1909.[54]

'Abdullah Ahmad made use of the Adabiyah institution as the organization that was responsible for the publication of *al-Munīr*. As for the Jama'ah Adabiyah itself, it consisted mostly of traders who were the backbone of Adabiyah activities, including the publication of *al-Munīr*.[55] *Al-Munīr* was published fortnightly, using the Malay language with Arabic characters. Most of the issues consisted of sixteen pages. From its very first edition, *al-Munīr* proclaimed itself as "a journal of Islamic religion, knowledge, and information" (*Majalah Islam, Pengetahuan dan Perkhabaran*).

What was the mission of *al-Munīr*? In the first issue, the editors explain the meaning of *al-Munīr* itself. In the first place, "*al-Munīr*" means "candle," or other things that illuminate their environment. Within the context of this meaning, *al-Munīr* wished to be the candle and light of the Muslim umma in the Dutch East Indies, which were suppressed by the Dutch. In a more detailed manner, the editors of *al-Munīr* explain the goals of the journal. First, to lead and bring the Muslim umma to progress based on Islamic injunctions; second, to nurture peace among nations and human beings; third, to light the Muslim umma with knowledge and wisdom.[56]

It is important to note that in its explanation of the function of an Islamic journal, *al-Munīr* highlights that an Islamic journal is like a teacher who gives to its readers guidance in the right path, reminds them of their wrongdoings in the past, consoles those in grief, helps those suffering from misery, awakens them to virtues, and sharpens their reason. As Ali writes, this explanation is reminiscent of *al-Imām*'s ideas, and is a further indication that *al-Munīr* was eager to continue *al-Imām*'s mission.[57]

The publication of *al-Munīr* was warmly welcomed by many readers, as shown by the number of letters of congratulation from its readers. For example, a letter from Sayyid Hasyim bin Thahir was sent from Palembang. The letter, in addition to congratulating the editors for their noble efforts, expected them to manage the journal in a wise manner, and to continually provide their readers with balanced information from all segments of Muslim society.[58] However, *al-Munīr* received not only favorable responses, but also negative reactions when it made mention of an unidentified "trouble maker" (*tukang kacau*). It is likely that the "trouble maker" was among the Kaum Tua who opposed Kaum Muda as represented by *al-Munīr*, although the root cause may run deeper. Tamar Djaja argues that there was also criticism of *al-Munīr*, because some critics believed that preaching by means of a journal was a Western innovation, and adopting the Western way was *bid*ʿ*a* (unwarranted innovation).[59]

Al-Munīr's spirit of reform can be clearly seen in its insistence on the importance of organization as a vehicle to further the Muslim umma. According to *al-Munīr*, organization is a means for channeling the spirit of reform, encouraging enterprising, vigor, and enhancing the nobility of knowledge (*kemuliaan ilmu*). It is a way of cultivating brotherhood of mankind and nations.[60]

Like *al-Manār* and *al-Imām, al-Munīr* was radical in its religious orientation. It published articles on subjects that had hitherto been considered taboo by the Kaum Tua. For instance, the wearing of neckties and hats, and the taking of photographs, which had been considered *haram* (unlawful, forbidden) by the Kaum Tua, were openly discussed in *al-Munīr*, which informs its readers that such things had never been forbidden by the Qurʾan and Hadith. *Al-Munīr* also taught that the Friday *khutba* (sermon before prayers) could be delivered in a language that the congregation could understand. Furthermore, according to *al-Munīr*, Muslims should not blindly follow (*taklid*) a specific Islamic legal school, and it insists that the Shafiʿi school of law, which is adhered to by most Indonesian Muslims, is not the only valid interpretation of Islamic legal precepts. Even, the Shafiʿi madhhab can draw upon the three other Sunni legal tradition, that of the Hanafi, Maliki, and Hanbali schools of Islamic legal thought.[61]

Conclusion

It is hard to be certain which came earlier, reformist magazines and journals or Salafi-oriented organizations. It seems that in the case of Indonesia, the appearance of these reformist journals and magazines took place at almost the same time as the rise of Salafi organizations, such as the Muhammadiyah, Persatuan Islam, and others. The publication of magazines and journals only stimulated the further expansion of Salafi organizations in Indonesia. As a result,

Salafi-oriented organizations had strong ideological support, which contributed to their ever-increasing influence in Indonesian Muslim society.

In the case of the Malay Peninsula, on the other hand, the spread of reformist journals and magazines seems to have had only a limited impact on the expansion of Salafi ideas. Even though the publication of *al-Imām* preceded that of *al-Munīr*, reformist organizations never struck deep roots in Malay society in general. Islamic reformism was still a long way from gaining momentum in Malay society. This is due to both the domination of states in Islamic institutions and the interpretation of Islam by Malaysian Muslims, who still hold fast to what in Indonesia is called "Islamic traditionalism." Only in the late 1970s did Islamic reformism begin to get a firmer hold in Malaysia.

Notes

1 Emad Eldin Shahin, "Rashid Rida, Muhammad," in John L. Esposito, ed., *The Oxford Encyclopedia of the Modern Islamic World* 3 (Oxford: Oxford University, 1995), 412; J. Jomier, *EI*[2], s. v. "Al-Manār."

2 It initially seems that a certain number of works by early Malay-Indonesian scholars such as al-Raniri, al-Sinkili, al-Makassari, Muhammad Arsyad al-Banjari, and al-Palimbani were printed in Istanbul. Subsequently, however, their works were also printed in Cairo, Mecca, and Medina.

3 See Jutta Bluhm-Warn, "*Al-Manar* and Ahmad Soorkattie. Links in the Chain of Transmission of Muhammad 'Abduh's Ideas to the Malay-Speaking World," in Peter G. Riddell and Tony Street, eds, *Islam: Essays on Scripture, Thought and Society* (Leiden: Brill, 1997), 296–297.

4 Azyumardi Azra, *The Transmission of Islamic Reformism to Indonesia: Networks of Middle Eastern and Malay-Indonesian Ulama in the Seventeenth and Eighteenth Centuries* (PhD dissertation, Columbia University, 1992).

5 William Roff, "Indonesian and Malay Students in Cairo in the 1920's," *Indonesia* 9: (1970).

6 See Mohammad Redzuan Othman, "Call of the Azhar: The Malay Students' Sojourn in Cairo before World War II," *Sejarah* 3 (1994–1995): 95–110.

7 Bluhm-Warn, "*Al-Manar* and Ahmad Soorkattie," 297.

8 Nik Hassan, "Nik Abdul Aziz bin Haji," in *Islam di Kelantan* (Kuala Lumpur: Persatuan Sejarah Malaysia, 1983), 16–17, 27.

9 Virginia Matheson Hooker, "Transmission through Practical Example: Women and Islam in 1920s Malay Fiction," *JMBRAS* 67 (2): 96–97; cf. William Roff, *The Origins of Malay Nationalism*, 2nd ed. (Kuala Lumpur: Oxford University Press, 1967), 82–83.

10 Roff, *The Origins of Malay Nationalism*.

11 Charles C. Adams, *Islam and Modernism in Egypt* (London: Oxford University Press, 1933).

12 Roff, *The Origins of Malay Nationalism*, 59.

13 In the case of the Malay Peninsula, Roff has discussed debates and conflicts that took place among the "*kaum muda*" and "*kaum tua*." See Roff, *The Origins of Malay Nationalism*, 56–90. As for Indonesia's case, see, among others, Deliar Noer, *The Modernist Muslim Movement in Indonesia 1900–1942* (Kuala Lumpur: Oxford University Press, 1973); Taufik Abdullah, *Schools and Politics: The Kaum Muda Movement in Indonesia (1927–1933)* (Ithaca, IL: Cornell University, 1971); and Burhanuddin Daya, *Gerakan Pembaharuan Pemikiran Islam: Kasus Sumatera Thawalib* (Yogyakarta: Tiara Wacana, 1995).

14 For further accounts of the Padri Movement see, among others, Christine Dobbin, *Islamic Revivalism in Changing Peasant Economy: Central Sumatra 1784–1847* (London: Curzon Press, 1983).

15 Roff, *The Origins of Malay Nationalism*, 60–63; Abu Bakar Hamzah, *Al-Imam: Its Role in Malay Society 1906–1908* (Kent: University of Kent at Canterbury, 1981; Kuala Lumpur: Pustaka Antara, 1991).

16 Hamzah, *Al-Imam*, 124–127; Roff, *The Origins of Malay Nationalism*, 60–61.

17 At this time West Sumatra was experiencing a rise in Communist unrest.

18 Roff, *The Origins of Malay Nationalism*, 61; Hamzah, *Al-Imam*, 127.

19 Roff, *The Origins of Malay Nationalism*, 63–64; Hamzah, *Al-Imam*, 132–137.

20 Pulau Penyengat already had a reputation as a center of Malay learning, largely due to the literary works of Raja Ali Haji, born Raja Ahmad, and to other members of his family. It was by this time a frequent stop on the itinerary of traveling religious scholars. For further details see Roff, *The Origins of Malay Nationalism*, 44–46; Winstedt, "A History of Malay Literature," *JMBRAS* 31 (1958); and S. H. Tan, *The Life and Times of Sayyid Shaykh al-Hadi* (thesis, History Department, University of Singapore, 1961).

21 Roff, *The Origins of Malay Nationalism*, 63–64; Hamzah, *Al-Imam*, 137–142. It is important to note that most of the Bugi princes in the area joined this Rushdiyyah Club, and among its prominent leaders was Raja Ali Haji's own son, Raja Khalid Hassan, better known as Raja Hitam, who militantly opposed the presence of the Dutch in Riau. For further information, see Barbara W. Andaya, "From Rome to Tokyo: The Search for Anti-Colonial Allies by the Rulers of Riau, 1899–1904," *Indonesia* 24 (1977): 123–156.

22 Andaya, "From Rome to Tokyo," 139–140.

23 This article was in fact written by a certain Muhammad Murtaji.

24 Roff, *The Origins of Malay Nationalism*, 64; Hamzah, *Al-Imam*, 120–121.

25 Roff, *The Origins of Malay Nationalism*, 64; Hamzah, *Al-Imam*, 123–124; Werner Ende, "Schiitische Tendenzen bei sunnitischen Sayyids aus Hadhramaut: Muhammad bin 'Aqil al-Alawi," *Der Islam* 50 (1973): 1. For a further account of the case of Sayyid Muhammad bin 'Aqil, see William Roff, "Murder as an Aid to Social History: The Arabs in Singapore in the Early Twentieth Century," paper delivered at the *International Workshop on Arabs in South-East Asia (1870–c.1990)*, Royal Institute of Linguistics, and Anthropology (KITLV): Leiden, 1997.

26 Roff, *The Origins of Malay Nationalism*, 56–57.

27 Cited in Roff, *The Origins of Malay Nationalism*, 56.

28 *Al-Imām* 1/1 (July 23, 1906); Mohammad Redzuan Othman, "The Malay Perspective and the Ottoman Response," *Sejarah* 4 (1996): 97–108. The Caliphate question was of course a big issue in Indonesia. For a further discussion see Martin Van Bruinessen, "Muslims of the Dutch East Indies and the Caliphate Question," *Studia Islamika: Indonesian Journal for Islamic Studies* 2/3 (1995): 15–40.

29 *Al-Imām* 1/2 (August 21, 1906): 63; Othman, "The Malay Perspective," 102.

30 *Al-Imām* 1/7 (January 16, 1907): 211; Othman, "The Malay Perspective."

31 *Al-Imām* 1/9 (March 16, 1907): 281–284; Othman, "The Malay Perspective."

32 *Al-Imām* 2/5, 7 (November 1907): 101–102; Othman, "The Malay Perspective."

33 Othman, "The Malay Perspective," 103.

34 *Al-Imām* 1/3, 19 (September 1906): 77; cf. Andaya, "From Rome to Tokyo," 140.

35 *Al-Imām* 1/5, 17 (November 1906): 77.

36 *Al-Imām* 1/6, 18 (December 1906): 170–172.

37 Roff, *The Origins of Malay Nationalism*, 64, 66.

38 Roff, *The Origins of Malay Nationalism*, 66–67; Ajahku Hamka, *Riwajat Hidup Dr. Abd. Karim Amrullah dan Perdjuangan Kaum Agama di Sumatera* (Djakarta: Widjaja, 1958), 48.

39 Daya, *Gerakan Pembaharuan Pemikiran Islam*, 118–119.

40 Roff, *The Origins of Malay Nationalism*, 66.
41 *al-Imām* 2/12 (June 4, 1908): 279; 2/3 (September 9, 1907): 84–89; 1/1 (July 23, 1906): 1–6.
42 *al-Imām*, 2/11 (May 3, 1908): 338.
43 *al-Imām*, 3/3 (August 29, 1908): 104.
44 *al-Imām*, 2/10 (April 3, 1908): 356.
45 *al-Imām*, 2/3 (September 9, 1907): 84–89; cf. Hamzah, *Al-Imam*, 57.
46 Adams, *Islam and Modernism in Egypt* [*supra* n. 11], 140.
47 Mahmud Yunus, *Sejarah Pendidikan Islam di Indonesia* (Jakarta: Hidakarya Agung, 1996), 79; Mahmud Yunus, *Sejarah Islam di Minangkabau* (Jakarta: al-Hidayah, 1971), 48.
48 Noer, *The Modernist Muslim Movement in Indonesia 1900–1942*, 39.
49 *Al-Munīr* 5 (1915): 68; cf. Amir Syahruddin, *Pemikiran dan Usaha-usaha Abdullah Ahmad terhadap Pembaharuan Pendidikan Islam* (Masters thesis, Post-Graduate Programme, IAIN Syarif Hidayatullah, Jakarta).
50 Hamka, *Riwajat Hidup Dr. Abd. Karim Amrullah dan Perdjuangan Kaum*; Alfian, *Muhammadiyah: The Political Behavior of a Muslim Modernist Organization under Dutch Colonialism* (Yogyakarta: UGM Press, 1989), 108; Tamar Djaja, *Pusaka Indonesia: Riwayat Hidup Orang-orang Besar Tanahair*, 2 (Jakarta: Bulan Bintang, 1966), 700.
51 H. J. Benda, "South-East Asian Islam in the Twentieth Century," in P. M. Holt, A. K. S. Lambton, and B. Lewis eds, *The Cambridge History of Islam*, 2A (Cambridge: Cambridge University Press, 1984),189.
52 Syamsuri Ali, *Al-Munir dan Wacana Pembaharuan Pemikiran Islam 1911–1915* (Master thesis, Post-Graduate Program, IAIN Imam Bonjol, Padang, 1997), 26.
53 Hamka, *Kenang-kenangan Hidup* I (Jakarta: Bulan Bintang, 1974), 14.
54 Noer, *The Modernist Muslim Movement in Indonesia 1900–1942*, 38–39; Sanusi Latief ed., *Riwayat Hidup dan Perjuangan 20 Ulama Besar Sumatera Barat* (Padang: Islamic Centre Sumatera Barat, 1981), 107–111.
55 *Al-Munīr* 1/1 (1911): 1; Noer, *The Modernist Muslim Movement in Indonesia.*
56 *Al-Munīr*, 1/1 (1911).
57 Ali, *Al-Munir dan Wacana Pembaharuan Pemikiran Islam 1911–1915*, 53.
58 *Al-Munīr* 1/2 (1911): advertisement page.
59 Djaja, *Pusaka Indonesia: Riwayat Hidup Orang-orang Besar Tanahair* 2: 701.
60 *Al-Munīr* 2/1 (May, 1912).
61 Yunus, *Sejarah Islam di Minangkabau*, 47; Adam, *Islam and Modernist in Egypt*, 140.

Part II

INTELLECTUALS IN CHALLENGE

Situations, discourses, strategies

8

THE ARABO-ISLAMIC CONSTITUTIONAL THOUGHT AT 1907

'Abd al-Karim Murad (d. 1926) and his draft constitution for Morocco

Stefan Reichmuth

The period between 1870 and the First World War is generally regarded as the culmination of European imperial hegemony. At the same time it brought about a remarkable chain of constitutional movements and revolutions in distant parts of the world. This included Europe itself where constitutional order underwent dramatic changes, leading in some cases such as Italy and Germany to the establishment of entirely new national states and constitutional monarchies. Even the Russian Empire became a constitutional state in 1905. At the same time substantial steps towards constitutional and representative government were taken in countries as different as Egypt, the Ottoman Empire, Iran, British India, and also Japan and China.[1] Despite an abundance of publications about each country and, even more about the philosophical and legal aspects of constitutionalism, the comparative study of the European and non-European constitutional movements and doctrines of this time does not seem to have found much attention until now.

Whether there are indigenous roots of the constitutional theories and charters that were put forward in the Middle East and North Africa during the course of the nineteenth century is still open to debate. Elie Kedourie, who saw the history of the ruling institution in these regions mainly in terms of Wittfogel's "oriental despotism," did not see much substance or grounding of a constitutional process that coincided with a period of imperial weakness. In his opinion, the "grant" of the constitution by the sovereign ruler to his subjects (such as happened in Tunis, Egypt, and the Ottoman Empire) did not indicate a compromise between state and society.; it was "a parody rather than the analogue of what was obtained in Western Europe."[2] According to Kedourie, constitutionalism under these conditions became "a mere device used by different factions within the official classes to pursue their rivalries."[3]

Autocratic rule, however, has not been the only concept offered for a historical interpretation of Islamic political institutions. In W. Montgomery Watt's analysis of the religio-political struggle of the early ʿAbbasid period between the emerging Shiʿa and Sunna groupings, the Shiites are indeed described as the "autocratic block" which supported the unlimited religious and political authority of the caliph, and which had its roots mainly among the bureaucrats of the empire, many of whom were of Persian extraction. The *ahl al-sunna*, on the other hand, drew their support largely from what Montgomery Watt has called the "general religious movement" and the emerging "religious institution." With their demand that the life of the empire should be based on the revealed law, the *ahl al-sunna* are seen by him as a "constitutional block" which finally came to gain the recognition and support of even the caliphs themselves. For this political antagonism, which found expression in different historical and theological disputes, a parallel to European political thought and controversy is explicitly drawn by this author.[4]

Later periods also saw the emergence of a peculiar type of the Islamic city state in different regions, which was governed by a federation of local communal Muslim groups and headed by an elected qadi or a qadi family holding this office for several generations. This type is represented most aptly by ports or merchant cities like Mogadishu (Maqdishu) in the Somali coast in the fourth/tenth century, or Timbuktu, which flourished since the ninth/fifteenth century at the southern fringe of the Sahara in present-day Mali.[5] Timbuktu in particular is significant for the concept of a semi-corporate community (*ǧamāʿa*) of scholars headed by a qadi, which can be recognized behind the ruling patriciate of this city which managed to absorb other emerging powerful urban groups well until the nineteenth century.

A closer look at Ottoman political institutions in the classical period also suggests a good deal of consultative and representative mechanisms, some of which were even formally recognized by the sultans. This holds for the Imperial Council (*divân-i hümâyun*) which included leading administrators, bureaucrats, military commanders and religious scholars under the chairmanship of the Grand Vizier,[6] and even more so for the so-called "Council-on-Foot" (*ayak divânı*), a special assembly convened by or even forced upon the sultan for the discussion of urgent matters and complaints. Cases of such councils are documented for the sixteenth and seventeenth centuries by Uzunçarşılı.[7] In one of his examples, appeal is made to the caliphal function of the ruler. A well-established and legal pattern of consultation also comes out at the provincial level where local scholars, notables or military groups were sometimes the most powerful elements within the provincial divans.[8] Consultation and representation of local and regional interests were thus restricted to later times of imperial decline but were part and parcel of the established pattern of administration. Two Muslim intellectuals of the later nineteenth century who attempted to justify the constitutional limitation of the power of the ruler, the Tunisian historian Ibn Abi Diyaf (d. 1874) and the Ottoman writer and poet Namık Kemal (d. 1888), even referred to the precedence of the political role of the Janissaries who were said to have given explicit permission by Süleyman the Magnificent to dethrone a trespassing sultan and who thus, as "people in arms," had for a long time provided an effective constitutional check to the Ottoman executive.[9]

The challenge of European political institutions can be first noticed among Ottoman bureaucrats in the early eighteenth century. Dadić, a Dalmatian who visited Istanbul at that period, mentions the strong interest of the Ottoman Effendis in the form of government prevailing in Venice, and their idea to convert the imperial divan into a parliamentary council of the Venetian type.[10] Perhaps related to this kind of discussion was an outline of the three systems of government existing in human society—monarchy, aristocracy, democracy—which was presented by the famous Hungarian convert İbrahim Müteferrika (d. 1745), himself a high-ranking Ottoman bureaucrat,[11] in his treatise *Usûlü'l-hikem fî nizâmi'l-ümem*, where he also made far-reaching proposals for military reforms along European lines.[12]

There can be no doubt that the challenge of European hegemony and of European political institutions was crucial for the constitutional and revolutionary movements which emerged outside Europe in the latter part of the nineteenth century. But the interplay of internal and external factors produced quite different results for each of them. As mentioned earlier, constitutions in the Middle East and North Africa in the nineteenth century were formally granted by the ruler—something that had also happened in several European monarchies at different points of time after 1815. Constitutional initiatives like those in Tunisia and Egypt had been initiated by the monarchs who were hoping to enhance both internal support and international recognition for their government by introducing a constitution and some elected consultative or legislative bodies. When increased pressure from the European powers exposed the failure of the local monarchies and, at the same time, made them more and more autocratic, constitutional demands quite often became the rallying point for all those who stood in opposition to the existing order.

Constitutionalists in different countries of North Africa and Asia belonged to those groups of the administrative and urban elite which had been exposed to European forms of education and had very often spent considerable time in Europe itself. Models of French, British, and also Italian political thought and organization can be seen at work in many of their writings and activities.[13] At the same time, most of the constitutional movements rose in states and among social groups with age-old traditions of scribal and scholarly training. Despite their quite different educational outlook, constitutionalists were still connected in many ways to the older educational and scribal institutions. Sometimes they belonged themselves to old scholar or scribe families and still shared some of their interests. Commercial groups had strong connections to both older and younger educational elites. No wonder, then, that the constitutional ideas of the younger generation of intellectuals were shaped for the most part by an unmistakable blend of European and indigenous ideas and patterns of thought. With external pressure and internal opposition rising around 1900, larger segments of the scholarly elite and their students were drawn into the constitutional movements.

Within the Islamic context, the blend of European ideas of constitutional government and nationalism with basic ethical and political concepts derived from Islamic thought can be demonstrated in an exemplary way for the group of the Young Ottoman intellectuals and their successors, the Young Turks.[14] The political and constitutional aims of the latter movement which brought together many different groups in opposition to Sultan Abdülhamid II were strongly supported by Islamic reformists in Syria and Egypt, with Rashid Rida being perhaps the most prominent,[15] and some of the concepts of Islamic thought which had been first developed by the Young Ottomans and were then further transmitted and discussed among their successors have remained highly relevant for political Islam until the present. This is true in particular for the discussion about the sovereignty (Ar. *ḥākimiyya*, Ottoman *hakimiyyet*) of God and that of the People, still central to Islamic political discourse even today. The alliance of intellectuals and Islamic scholars and activists of different ethnic background in opposition to the Ottoman Emperor finally contributed to the restoration of the Ottoman Constitution in 1908.

The most spectacular success of an Islamic constitutional movement, however, can be seen in the Constitutional Revolution in Iran, where the support of large parts of the Islamic scholarly elite was crucial for the establishment of both Majlis and the Constitution in 1906.[16] From the First to the Fifth Majlis, elected members with higher Islamic education made up for a solid proportion of the deputies, at times even providing a clear majority.[17] In Iran as well as in the Ottoman Empire and in Egypt, Islamic scholars and reformists of this period tried to develop an Islamic framework for a constitutional system and to defend it against their opponents who regarded their activities as directed against Islam and who supported the prerogatives of their rulers. At the same period, even the Muslim members in the First and Second Russian Dumas (1906, 1907) included a good number of mullahs and deputies with madrasa education.[18]

***

The constitutional draft which was written in Morocco at the same period and which shall be discussed here also shows the strong interest of Islamic reformist scholars in local movements of opposition and constitutional reform, which had increased in response to European imperial encroachment. It was a period when Islamic scholars and more Europeanized intellectuals were still political allies in opposition to their governments and remained closely engaged in intellectual debate. This made for specific blends of political expression which can be easily criticized for their inconsistencies and which have, therefore, not been found worthy of much attention. Later periods and crises frequently led to political parting of ways and required much more clear-cut ideological decisions.[19] The earlier blend of concepts nevertheless shows the importance of the Islamic discourse for the national movements of their time, and it is this heritage rather than older patterns of Islamic thought which provided the base for political Islamism in the later part of the twentieth century.

In the case of Morocco, constitutional proposals came up in a period of growing interference of France and Spain into the affairs of the country and of a political and economic crisis that accompanied this. At the international conference held in Algeçiras in 1906 different plans of reform under European control had been set up for Morocco. These plans, while officially recognizing the sovereignty of the sultan and the integrity of the country, for all practical purposes amounted to joint French and Spanish control of its police force, economic resources and financial institutions.[20] In an earlier stage of the crisis, when France had already presented similar proposals, the Moroccan sultan 'Abd al-'Aziz had convened an "Assembly of Notables" (*Mağlis al-a'yān*, 1904–1905),[21] mainly, as it seems, in order to muster public support against the imminent French interference. Although without much success in the negotiations, the assembly had encouraged some leading scholars in their resistance against both foreign encroachment and against the failing policies of the sultan. Most prominent among them at that time was Muhammad b. 'Abd al-Kabir al-Kattani, the powerful leader of the Zawiya of the Kattaniyya brotherhood in Fez. The years after 1905 were marked not only by open intervention of foreign powers but also by growing opposition of the religious scholars against the sultan, who was finally deposed and replaced by his brother 'Abd al-Hafiz. The latter received the *bay'a* of the scholars of Fez in 1908 and was one year later recognized also by the French, after 'Abd al-'Aziz had abdicated himself in July 1908.[22]

There are three extant constitutional proposals for Morocco from this critical period of modern Moroccan history.[23] The first, which was written already in 1324/1906, goes back to a Moroccan from Salé, 'Ali b. Ahmad Znibar.[24] A second one was published in four editions of the Arabic journal *Lisān al-'arab* in Tangier between 11 October and 1 November 1908.[25] This journal had been founded by the Nammur brothers, two Lebanese emigrants living in Tangier. The circumstances which led to the third draft had been unknown for a long time. The text which directly refers to the Act of Algerçiras (issued on 7 April 1906) was not published until much later, and then without a clear indication of its author.[26] It was only in the early 1980s, when the Moroccan historian Muhammad al-Mannuni obtained another manuscript of this text from a bookseller in Fez, that the text could be ascribed with fair certainty to 'Abd al-Karim Murad, a visiting scholar and traveler from Tripoli (Lebanon) who refers to himself as the author in a note at the end of the manuscript.[27]

Up to the present day 'Abd al-Karim Murad (also called in some sources al-Muradi) has remained a hardly known figure in the transnational Islamic networks of the early twentieth century.[28] Information about his life and activities which covered Morocco and the French and British colonies and protectorates of West Africa can be drawn from some of his Moroccan contemporaries,[29] French colonial intelligence for the Afrique Occidentale Française,[30] and some writings of Islamic scholars in Nigeria where Murad settled and finally died.[31] Al-Mannuni calls him "the Envoy of the East to the West" (*mab'ūṯ al-šarq ila'l-ġarb)*,[32] which would seem to refer, however, to intellectual mediatorship rather than to any clear-cut political task.

'Abd al-Karim b. Sayyid 'Umar b. Mustafa b. Shaykh Murad belonged to a prominent Sayyid family from Tripoli. He was born around 1860. His early education still remains obscure. His strong interest in both Islamic disciplines and "modern" subjects (*al-ʿulūm al-dīniyya waʾl-waqṭiyya*, as he called them) which comes out later in his own educational activities would suggest an influence of the most famous scholar of Tripoli of the late nineteenth century, Husayn al-Jisr (1845–1909) and his school experiment, *al-Madrasa al-Waṭaniyya* (1879–1882).[33] This would link him further to his contemporary Rashid Rida (1865–1935) who also came from the Tripoli area and had been a student of this school.

ʿAbd al-Karim Murad spent some time as teacher in Medina before he went to West and North Africa (the *nisba al-Madanī* which appears at the end of the draft would seem to be related to this stay in Medina). He apparently spent several years as itinerant trader of Arabic books and as Islamic teacher in different parts of West Africa like Sierra Leone, Ivory Coast and southern Nigeria. Already at this early stage he is said to have assisted local Islamic communities in the foundation of Arabic schools and Islamic societies. Coming to Fez in 1324/1906,[34] he stayed in Fez in the Zawiya of the Kattaniyya, writing as a correspondent for the Cairo newspaper *al-Muʾayyad* which was well known for its Islamic orientation. He dedicated a grammatical commentary to the Moroccan Sultan ʿAbd al-ʿAziz, propagating—without success—the establishment of a modernized school for Moroccan children which was to be called *al-Maqāṣid al-ʿAzīziyya*. This name easily evokes the model of the famous *Ğamʿiyyat al-Maqāṣid al-Ḫayriyya* and its schools in Beirut.[35] His own teaching activities are said to have included Qurʾanic recitation (*tağwīd*), but also geography, astronomy, arithmetic and even history and politics. His circle became an important place for conversation, political discussion and lectures. Two prominent scholars for whom constitutional inclinations are also mentioned elsewhere, the qadis ʿAbd al-Hafiz al-Fasi and al-Mahdi al-Fasi (d. both 1383/1963–1964), had been among his students.[36] Among his writings mentioned by Brockelmann[37] for the Qarawiyyin Library in Fez is another treatise called *al-Siyāsa*, which further illustrates his political interests.

Murad left Morocco in 1908 and traveled back to West Africa where his presence is attested, in French intelligence reports from December 1908–1911, in French West Africa (Senegal, Ivory Coast, Dahomey), with contacts to prominent Sufi leaders like Ahmadu Bamba and Malik Sy in Senegal, being engaged in the trade of Arabic books and negotiating the publication of Arabic texts written by local West African scholars[38]. The French authorities remained suspicious of him and expelled him to Morocco in 1912. He was not to stay in the new French Protectorate, either. From 1913–1914 onwards he could be found again in British West Africa, teaching in Sierra Leone and Lagos, finally settling in Kano where he died in 1926 or, according to another source, in 1928.[39] In Kano again, one of the key figures of the expanding Tijaniyya brotherhood, Muhammad Salga (d. 1939), was among his students.[40] In 1922 Murad had gone to Europe and visited the Amir Shakib Arslan in Lausanne, providing him with information about Islam and the Muslims in Nigeria.[41] He thus can be seen in touch with prominent figures of Middle Eastern and Islamic politics until the end of his life.

By his educational background and activities, 'Abd al-Karim Murad strongly resembles other Salafi scholars of Syro-Lebanese origin like Rashid Rida who had clear constitutional inclinations and in this respect felt strongly encouraged by the spectacular Japanese victory over Russia and by the Iranian constitutional revolution. The text of the draft constitution fully fits into this outlook. As it explicitly mentions the new Iranian monarch Muhammad 'Ali Shah whose accession to the throne was on 8 January 1907, it was probably written not long after that, because there is no hint to the tension between the Shah and the parliament which intensified from May 1907 onwards.[42] Equally, any impact of the troubles in Morocco which led to the French occupation of Wujda on 29 March 1907[43] and of Casablanca and its surroundings in May, is absent from the text. On the other hand, an anonymous report about the Moroccan crisis of 1905, published in Rida's journal *al-Manār*,[44] might perhaps already be considered as originating from Murad's pen, as it shows the same interest in educational reforms and in the establishment of modernized schools with Arabic as the language of instruction, which is otherwise known for our author. This would mean that he was in Morocco already in that year.

***

The introduction of the draft[45] praises the people of the Maghrib for their outstanding virtues in the fields of ethnic unity (*ittiḥād al-ğins*), religious steadfastness (*al-tamassuk bi'l-dīn*) and love for the Sultan (*ḥubb al-sulṭān*). These virtues are regarded by the author as a firm base for future progress and sovereignty, as shown by the Japanese and Iranian examples. The ruler is nevertheless reminded that he has nowadays to give priority to the interest of the common people (*al-'āmma*) if he wants to keep dignity and respect for himself and his country. His own greatness depends on them. He has to enlighten his subjects, to educate and to encourage their industrial production and their inventions. Training in all those crafts which are necessary for human welfare is in itself a collective duty (*farḍ kifāya*) in Islam. The appeal to commercial interests aiming at a strong and autonomous national economy is typical also for other constitutional movements in the Islamic countries of that time, as for example in Iran where the Majlis was determined to prevent foreign loans and to regain control of the customs which had been in foreign hands.[46]

Both the Japanese and the Iranian rulers have transformed their absolute monarchy into constitutional rule and have overcome their decadence. The Japanese soon became famous for their schools, and their army even defeated China and Russia. Iran used its parliament to enhance just and fair administration by deriving a general law code from the divine Shari'a. For Morocco there is an urgent need for similar reforms after the Algeçiras Conference and the growing interference of foreign powers in the country which is being met with increasing rejection and fear by the people. All the subjects of the sultan desire reforms to be introduced by legal means under control of the Moroccan government. They agree to keep the treaties with the foreigners and to carry out the decisions of the conference, but in such a way as they will be equally acceptable to the people and to the foreign powers, and in accordance with the Shari'a. It would seem that to achieve this would have been quite an uphill task.

The first proposed plan of the author[47] is the introduction of a parliamentary system. In order to retain independence and autonomy *vis-à-vis* the foreign powers, a parliament (called by him sometimes *Mağlis al-milla*, sometimes *Mağlis al-umma*) should be established, which is to deliberate all matters "in such a way as to find God's pleasure and the acceptance of the foreigners." It will increase legitimacy in their eyes, as they regard a parliament as sacrosanct in its decisions and respect the laws issued by it. In European countries laws are based on reason and experience, in their own case, however, they have to be derived from the principles of the Shari'a, as is done in Iran. This gives the ruler a much better position in his negotiations with the foreign powers. The author thus refers to the earlier strategy of Muslim rulers like those of Tunisia and Egypt who had hoped to gain both internal support and external recognition by constitutional changes. Needless to say, their experiences had not been too encouraging, as they had not been able to stop their financial crises and to prevent the occupation of their countries. At this stage, however, the pressure of popular opposition at home had become a far more powerful argument. Reference to the Divine Law quite conceivably could serve to make legislation sacrosanct and inviolable.

The literary background of the author's thought comes out in his version of the famous "Circle of Equity," a classical concept of Arabo-Islamic as well as Ottoman political thought which he adapted from two versions of this cycle in Ibn Khaldun's *Muqaddima*.[48] The starting point of Murad's cycle is the dignity of the subject (*'izz al-mamlūk*) which is achieved only through the Shari'a, which again is only safeguarded by power (*mulk*). The power of men is based on wealth (*māl*), achieved only by cultivation (*'imāra*).[49] Cultivation, however, depends on justice, only to be attained by a reform of the officials (*bi-iṣlāḥ al-'ummal*), which needs upright viziers (*istiqāmat al-wuzarā'*) and, on top of all, a king who himself cares for the well-being of his subjects (*tafaqqud al-malik aḥwāl al-ra'iyya bi-nafsihi*). Some telling deviations from Ibn Khaldun's text can be noted here: Ibn Khaldun's starting point is royal dignity, *'izz al-mulk*, linked to the Shari'a, which is replaced here by the dignity of the subject, *'izz al-mamlūk*. Equally, a sentence at the end which stresses the necessary power (*iqtidār*) of the ruler to discipline[50] his people—so that he may rule them, not they him—has been simply cut off by our author. Both changes clearly shift the focus away from the king and provide a direct link between the Shari'a and the people. Murad's cycle starts with the king's subjects and ends with them, referring to the Shari'a as a source of their personal and public standing. The indicated role of the king is to look after his subjects rather than to master them.

Both military and financial institutions have to be strengthened if foreign intervention is to be brought to an end. The second plan[51] calls for the establishment of a standing army (*'askar ğarrār*) which would be self-supporting, to consist of armed citizens who were to undergo daily military training—a particularly bold proposal in the context of Moroccan politics, given the delicate balance of power between the Makhzan and the regional tribal groups which was more or less falling into pieces in the period in question. A third plan[52] was intended to generate a solid stock of internal public income (*māl dāḫilī*). It included an elaborate outline of a basic reform of the pious foundations in order to generate the necessary funds for education, welfare and public investment. It concentrated supervision of the foundations and of the institutions of education, health and public welfare in the hands of a Council of the five leading ulama officials on top of a highly hierarchic body of administration. This would have left the religious institution with a degree of power and influence far beyond even that of the Ottoman *şeyhülislam* and his centralized hierarchy in the last period of the Empire.[53]

By referring to the recommendation of consultation (*šūrā*) in the Qur'an (3: 159 *wa-šawirhum fī'l-amri*; Q. 42: 38 *wa-amruhum šūrā baynahum*), ʿAbd al-Karim Murad uses the common-stock argument for consultative government in an Islamic state.[54] Rashid Rida, too, had a lot to say about *šūrā* in his *al-Manār* during these eventful years.[55] Murad proposes the establishment of two Chambers of Parliament: a "National Assembly" (*Mağlis al-umma/Mağlis al-milla*) whose member are to be elected for five years by each tribe and each town, and an "Upper House" (*al-Mağlis al-aʿlà*) with members appointed from the royal family, the administration and the National Assembly. The deputies should not only be literate but also versed in the most common commentary of Malikite *fiqh*, Khalil's *al-Muḫtaṣar*. This shows the framework of religious and legal scholarship which the author had in mind for the political elite of the country and which also comes out in other points.

Majority decisions in parliament are to be based on each deputy's understanding of the Qur'an, the Sunna and the interest of the country (*maṣlaḥat al-bilād*). *Maṣlaḥa*, too, was an important issue for Islamic reformism of the time: Rashid Rida even regarded it as the most important criterion in the worldly affairs of the Islamic community.[56]

Affairs to be decided by the Majlis include the following[57]: international treaties, control and budgets of ministers and governors, introduction and collection of taxes. All taxes which are in contradiction to the Divine Law are to be abolished. Decisions are further to be made about government expenditures, about military training of the citizens, supervision of the government officials and appeals and complaints of the citizens to the parliament. Regular reports on all government activities would be demanded and discussed. This would have given the parliament full control over both administration and judiciary.

The proposed codification of Law and the compilation of a Law Code[58] explicitly refers to the model of the Ottoman *Mağallat al-aḥkām al-ʿadliyya* (*Mecelle*, issued 1869–1878).[59] Based on the regulations of the Maliki madhhab, it should be compiled by a committee of eight ulama. They should write it in simple language, easy to understand for everybody. Like all other matters of concern it should be discussed by both Houses and after decision issued by royal decree. International treaties approved by the parliament should equally be added as appendix to the

Law Code. All jurisdiction would have to follow this Code which would be open only to amendment by the Majlis itself. This approach to legislation is in remarkable contrast to the pattern of Islamic jurisdiction still prevailing in Morocco at that period. It would have restricted the qadis to those legal opinions which happened to have been fixed by the Law Code! This was actually to happen later in the legislation of most Islamic countries.

Of particular interest is the suggestion of a new Police Law which is to be issued in accordance with the Shariʿa and with the interest of the country, after thorough study of those of the Ottoman Empire, Egypt, Tunisia and Iran.[60] A Police School is to be established for the training of a qualified police corps whose members are knowledgeable enough to interact successfully with the French and Spanish officers acting under the Algeçiras Act. Appeal against police action is also to the Majlis. This reform was clearly designed to counter the French and Spanish control over the Moroccan police force which had just been established.

As the author saw it, the ruler would derive an increase of his glory and of God's pleasure with him if he introduced constitutional rule. It would further add significantly to the dignity and accountability of his administration. Growing wealth and prosperity would result for his country, and he would gain further recognition of neighbouring Islamic states, which was hoped to strengthen their support in times of need. It was even promised that the loyalty of those tribes outside of the control of the Makhzan would be strengthened, due to good governance and to the general respect for the Shariʿa which no Muslim could deny. This was to be the cornerstone of the new constitutional régime.

It is very easy to criticize this draft for its political naivety and its limited familiarity with Moroccan institutions, points which have already been raised by Abdallah Laroui.[61] The powers and responsibilities of the ruler himself, and the question of his liability to parliamentary control are not even mentioned. The problem of the regional balance of power in the country was hardly given attention. A general obedience to Islamic Law was simply taken for granted, once a central representative body was established. This Islamic design of a constitutional system for Morocco somehow gives the impression of a utopian experiment to be applied in an archaic and retarded country.[62]

The author's confidence in the Shariʿa as a source of dignity and a firm baseline for public consensus and political institution-building nevertheless reflects an important strand of Islamic political thought of the later nineteenth and early twentieth centuries, which perhaps could most aptly be described as "Shariʿa patriotism."[63] This attitude comes out already in the political thought of the Young Ottomans, especially with Namık Kemal who had even identified the Shariʿa with the concept of Natural Law which he had found in Rousseau and which he had tried to adapt for his purposes.[64] Recourse to the Shariʿa as a major source of legitimacy, for both ruler and state, had dominated official life in the days of the caliph-sultan Abdülhamid II.[65] It also loomed large in the heated discussions of the newly established Ottoman parliament since 1908, with Westernists and

Islamists in fierce contest, and Turkist nationalism gradually emerging in between.[66] After all, this was a period when Islamic scholars had entered the political arena on a large scale, in Iran as elsewhere. For all its deficiencies the text shows the opening of the scholars' discourse towards the current affairs of the Muslims, even of those far beyond their own communities. As this draft constitution was published later by the prominent Moroccan politician ʿAllal al-Fasi, it provided an important link between the older reformism which was rooted in the Middle Eastern Salafiyya, and the Islamic strand of Moroccan nationalism which developed in Morocco since the 1930s.[67]

Acknowledgments

This article greatly profited from discussion following the presentation of the paper at the conference. I am particularly grateful to Yann Richard for his suggestions concerning the dating of the constitutional draft presented here.

Notes

1 See for a useful, though somewhat outdated bibliography concerning constitutional developments in Europe and elsewhere in the nineteenth and early twentieth centuries, Abdul-Hadi Hairi, *Shiʿism and Constitutionalism in Iran: A Study of the Role Played by the Persian Residents in Iraq in Iranian Politics* (Leiden: E. J. Brill, 1977), 249ff.; see further Klaus Fröhlich, *The Emergence of Russian Constitutionalism: 1900–1904. The Relationship between Social Mobilization and Political Group Formation in Pre-Revolutionary Russia* (The Hague: Nijhoff, 1981); Andrew James Nathan, *Peking Politics, 1918–1923: Factionalism and the Failure of Constitutionalism* (Berkeley, CA, Los Angeles, London: University of California, 1976); Theodore McNelly, *The Origins of Japan's Democratic Constitution* (Lanham, MD: University Press of America, 2000). For a short overview of the constitutional developments and revolutions in the Middle East and North Africa in the nineteenth and twentieth centuries, see B. Lewis and A. K. S. Lambton, "Dustūr", *EI²*, 2: 638–657; J. Landau, "Madjlis", *EI²*, 5: 1033–1043; C. Findley, "Madjlis al-Shūrā", *EI²*, 5: 1082–1086.

2 Elie Kedourie, "The Fate of Constitutionalism in the Middle East", in *Arabic Political Memoirs and Other Studies* (London: Frank Cass, 1974): 1–27, here 1ff.

3 Ibid., 26. He only excepts Lebanon, where various social interests found representation in the political setup, from this assessment.

4 For the whole issue, William Montgomery Watt, *Islamic Political Thought: The Basic Concepts* (Edinburgh: University Press, 1987 [1st publication 1968]), 82–89, 140 n. 11 with further reference. See also his "The Significance of the Early Stages of Immamite Shiʿism," in *Early Islam: Collected Articles* (Edinburgh: University Press, 1990), 166.

5 See E. Cerulli and G. S. P. Freeman-Grenville, "Maḳdishu", *EI²*, 6: 128ff.; Elias N. Saad, *Social History of Timbuktu. The Role of Muslim Scholars and Notables, 1400–1900* (Cambridge: Cambridge University Press, 1983), 120 ff. *et passim*.

6 See for example, Stanford J. Shaw, *History of the Ottoman Empire and Modern Turkey*, 1. *Empire of the Gazis: The Rise and Decline of the Ottoman Empire* (Cambridge: Cambridge University Press, 1991 [1st publication 1976]), 118 ff.; Robert Mantran, ed., *Histoire de l'Empire ottoman* (Paris: Fayard, 1989), 184–189.

7 İsmail Hakkı Uzunçarşılı, *Osmanlı Devletinin Saray Teşkilâtı* (Ankara: Türk Tarih Kurumu Basımevi, 1988 [1st publication 1945]), 225–229.

8 For example, Mantran, ed., *Histoire*, 350; for Egypt, Ibrahim El-Mouelhy, *Etude documentaire: Organisation et fonctionnement des institutions ottomanes en Egypte (1517–1917)* (s.l.: Imprimerie de la Société turque d'histoire), 8 ff.

9 H. Talloen, "La structure du pouvoir souverain selon l'historien tunisien Ibn 'Abi Diyaf (1802–1874)," in *Mélanges d'islamologie dédiés à la mémoire de A. Abel par ses collègues, ses élèves et ses amis* (Brussels: Publications du Centre pour l'étude des problèmes du monde musulman contemporain, 1974), 2: 391–399; Şerif Mardin, *The Genesis of Young Ottoman Thought: A Study in the Modernization of Turkish Political Ideals* (Princeton, NJ: Princeton University Press, 1962), 310. See also Godfrey Goodwin, *The Janissaries* (London: Saqi Books, 1997), 232, for the rather peculiar and hot-heated form of "Janissary democracy" which bequeathed "a curious tradition of popular leadership" to Middle-Eastern societies.

10 Nicolae Jorga, *Geschichte des Osmanisches Reiches* (Darmstadt: Wissenschaftliche Buchgesellschaft, 1990 [1st publication Gotha, 1908–1913]), 4: 370 ff.

11 See on him esp. Niyazi Berkes, *The Development of Secularism in Turkey* (London: Hurst, 1998 [1st publication: McGill University Press, 1964]), 36–46; Niyazi Berkes, "Ibrāhīm Müteferriḳa," *EI*², 3: 996 ff.; Stefan Reichmuth, "Islamic Reformist Discourse in the Tulip Period (1718–1730): Ibrahim Müteferriqa and His Arguments on Printing," in Ekmeleddin İhsanoğlu, ed., *International Congress on Learning and Education in the Ottoman World, Istanbul, 12–15 April 1999. Proceedings* (Istanbul, 2001): 149–161.

12 İbrahim Müteferrika, *Usûlü'l-Hikem fî Nizâmi'l-Ümem*, ed. Adil Şen (Ankara: Türkiye Diyanet Vakfı, 1995), 130 ff.

13 For the influence of Italian poets, political writers and activists like Alfieri, Pellico and Garibaldi on Young Ottoman and Arab intellectuals, see Mardin, *Young Ottoman Thought*, 20 ff.; Albert Hourani, *Arabic Thought in the Liberal Age, 1798–1939* (Cambridge: Cambridge University Press, 1987 [1st publication: 1962]), 271. As Italian nationalists also had to put up with a particularly strong religious heritage with universal implications, their aims and strategies were of great interest to the Arab and Ottoman intellectuals of that period.

14 For the Young Ottomans and their ideology, mainly Mardin, *Young Ottoman Thought, passim*; Mümtazer Türköne, *Siyasî İdeoloji Olarak İslamcılığın Doğuşu* (Istanbul: İletişim Yayıncılık, 1991); Hüseyin Çelik, *Ali Suavî ve Dönemi* (Istanbul: İletişim Yayıncılık, 1994). For the Young Turks and their alliance with the Syrian Salafiyya, see especially Hasan Kayalı, *Arabs and Young Turks: Ottomanism, Arabism and Islamism in the Ottoman Empire, 1908–1918* (Berkeley, CA, Los Angeles, London: University of California Press, 1997).

15 For Rashid Rida, his cooperation with the Young Turks and his interest in and support for the constitutional developments in Iran and Istanbul, see the different articles and reports in the volumes of *al-Manār* 9–12 (1324/1906–1327/1909–1910); also Kayalı, *Arabs and Young Turks*, 46. For his justification of constitutionalism by referring to the obligatory *al-amr bi'l-ma'rūf wa'l-nahī 'an al-munkar*, see Michael Cook, *Commanding Right and Forbidding Wrong in Islamic Thought* (Cambridge: Cambridge University Press, 2000), 510 f.

16 For the Iranian Constitutional Revolution of 1906–1907, see Edward G. Browne, *The Persian Revolution, 1905–1909* (London: Frank Cass, 1966 [1st publication: Cambridge, 1910]); Hairi, *Shi'ism and Constitutionalism*; Ervand Abrahamian, *Iran between Two Revolutions* (Princeton, NJ: Princeton University Press, 1982).

17 David Menashri, *Education and the Making of Modern Iran* (Ithaca, NY, London: Cornell University Press, 1992), 274 ff., table 22.

18 First Duma: 6/25; Second Duma: 6/36; see the table in Dilyara Usmanova, 'The Activity of the Muslim Fraction of the State Duma and Its Significance for the

Formation of a Political Culture among the Muslim Peoples of Russia (1906–1917)', in Anke von Kügelgen, Michael Kemper, and Allen J. Frank, eds, *Muslim Culture in Russia and Central Asia from the 18th to the Early 20th Centuries*, 2: *Inter-Regional and Inter-Ethnic Relations* (Berlin: Klaus Schwarz Verlag, 1998): 417–455, here 441–449.

19 This process has been described in detail for the Ottoman Empire before, during, and after the First World War by Berkes, *Secularism*, chapters 11–17.

20 For a comprehensive overview of the events and developments between 1904 and 1921, see for example, Roger Le Tourneau, *Histoire du Maroc moderne* (Aix-en-Provence: Publications de l'Université de Provence, 1992), 110–142; Abdallah Laroui, *Les origines sociales et culturelles du nationalisme marocain* (1830–1912) (Paris: Maspero, 1977), 371–414.

21 Le Tourneau, *Histoire*, 118 ff.; Laroui, *Origines*, 374 ff.; Ralf Elger, *Zentralismus und Autonomie: Gelehrte und Staat in Morokko, 1900–1931* (Berlin: Klaus Schwarz Verlag, 1994), 74 ff.

22 See for these events: Le Tourneau, *Histoire*, 121–125; Elger, *Zentralismus*, 79–90, 101 ff.

23 See Jacques Cagne, *Nation et nationalisme au Maroc: Aux racines de la nation marocaine* (Rabat: Dar Nachr al Maarifa, 1988), 471–495, 501–543; Laroui, *Origines*, 374–382, 403–405; Elger, *Zentralismus*, 88 ff.; Franz Kogelmann, *Islamische fromme Stiftungen und Staat: Der Wandel in den Beziehungen zwischen einer religiösen Institution und dem marokkanischen Staat seit dem 19. Jahrhundert bis 1937* (Würzburg: Ergon Verlag, 2000), 121 ff.

24 Arabic text in Muḥammad al-Mannūnī, *Maḏāhir yaqzat al-Maġrib al-ḥadīṯ* (al-Dār al-Bayḍā [Casablanca]: al-Ǧam'iyya al-maġribiyya li'l-ta'līf wa'l-našr, 1405/1988), 2: 407–421, facsimile of the first page 407. French abstract and translation in Cagne, *Nation et nationalisme*, 471–479, 501–510.

25 See for this: Laroui, *Origines*, 403 ff.; Cagne, *Nation et nationalisme*, 485–495; Le Tourneau, *Histoire*, 124 f.

26 First published by the famous Moroccan politician Muḥammad 'Allāl al-Fāsī in his book *Hufriyyat 'an al-ḥaraka al-dustūriyya fī al-Maġrib qabla'l-ḥimāya* (Rabat: Maṭba'a al-Risāla); French summary and partial translation in Cagne, *Nation et nationalisme*, 479–484, 511–522.

27 Al-Mannūnī, *Maḏāhir*, 2: 405 ff. (about the author and his activities in Morocco), full text of the draft pp. 422–445, facsimile of the last page of the manuscript containing the end of the text (in Maghribi handwriting) and a final gloss (in Oriental handwriting, presumably by the author himself): *qalahu'l-'abd al-faqīr... 'Abd al-Karīm Murād al-Tarābulūsī al-Madanī....* A vague hint to that author by 'Allāl al-Fāsī himself in *Hufriyyat*, 8, is mentioned already by Cagne, *Nation et nationalisme*, 479 n. 206.

28 A first attempt at a reconstruction of his career has been undertaken by Stefan Reichmuth and J. O. Hunwick, "Traces of a Forgotten Lebanese. Notes and Inquiries about 'Abd al-Karim Murad/al-Muradi (d. 1926/8) and His Activities in North and West Africa," *Sudanic Africa*, forthcoming.

29 Gathered by al-Mannūnī, *Maḏāhir*, 2: 311 ff.

30 Ms. Fonds ancien AOF, Aix-en-Provence.

31 Especially two books by Ādam 'Abd-Allàh al-Ilūrī (d. 1992): *al-Islām fī Nayǧariyya* (1st ed., Cairo: 'Abd al-Ḥamīd al-Ḥanafī, 1369/1949–1950), 43 ff. (with photograph); *Nasīm al-sabā fī aḫbār al-islām wa 'ulamā bilād Yūrūbā* (2nd ed., Cairo: Maktabat al-adab, 1987), 175, 178 ff., 191, 195 ff.

32 al-Mannūnī, *Maḏāhir*, 2: 311 ff.

33 On Husayn al-Jisr, his writings and activities, Johannes Ebert, *Religion und Reform in der arabischen Provinz. Husain al-Jisr at-Tarabulusi (1845–1909): Ein islamischer Gelehrter zwischen Tradition und Reform* (Frankfurt/M. Bern, New York, Paris: Peter Lang, 1991).

34 Year given by his contemporary, Muḥammad ʿAbd al-Ḥayy al-Kattānī, cf. al-Mannūnī, *Maḏāhir*, 2: 311.
35 Cf. Albert Hourani, "Djamʿiyya," *Encyclopaedia of Islam*, 2nd ed., 2: 429.
36 Cf. Elger, *Zentralismus und Autonomie*, 88. ʿAbd al-Hafiz was the uncle of the prominent Moroccan politician ʿAllal al-Fasi, see Laroui, *Origines*, 378; he might thus be considered as a possible source for the transmission of the draft to his nephew. For the collaboration of his circle with the Nammur brothers in Tangier mentioned earlier, see 380, n. 29.
37 Carl Brockelmann, *Geschichte der Arabischen Literatur* (Leiden: E. J. Brill, 1937–1949), *Supplement* 2: 1017.
38 See note 31.
39 1926: Ādam al-Īlūrī, *al-Islām fī Nayğiriyya wa'l-šayḫ ʿUṯmān b. Fūdiyū al-Fūlānī* (3rd ed., *s.l.*, 1398/1978), 152. 1347/1928: al-Mannūnī, *Maḏāhir*, 2: 312.
40 John O. Hunwick, ed., *Arabic Literature of Africa*, 2: *The Writings of Central Sudanic Africa* (Leiden, New York, Köln: E. J. Brill, 1995), 261.
41 Šākib Arslān, *Ḥāḍir al-ʿālam al-islāmī* (Cairo: al-Maṭbaʿa al-salafiyya wa-maktabatuha, 1343/1924–1925), 322.
42 Both Muzaffar al-Din Shah who had signed the Constitution on 30 December 1906, shortly before his death, and his successor Muhammad ʿAli Shah are mentioned in the text, al-Mannūnī, *Maḏāhir*, 2: 425. For the dates, see for example, "Dustūr," *EI*², 2: 651 ff.
43 Le Tourneau, *Histoire*, 119 ff.
44 *Al-Manār* 8 (1323/1905), 158 ff.
45 al-Mannūnī, *Maḏāhir*, 2: 422–426.
46 See for example, "Dustūr," *EI*², 2: 652.
47 al-Mannūnī, *Maḏāhir*, 2: 426–431.
48 Ibid., 427. An abbreviated fusion of the first part of the first version (the Mobedan's speech to the Sassanian emperor Bahram) with the end of the second version (a speech of Khusraw Anushirwan), both quoted from al-Masʿudi in Ibn Ḫaldūn, *Kitāb al-ʿibār wa-dīwān al-mubtadā' wa'l-ḫabar* (Beirut: Dār al-kitāb al-lubnānī, Maktabat al-madrasa, 1983), 1: 64 ff.; Ibn Khaldun, *The Muqaddimah. An Introduction to History*, trans. Franz Rosenthal (New York: Pantheon Books, 1958), 1: 80. For the "Circle of Equity" and its use by Ottoman writers see Lewis V. Thomas, *A Study of Naima* (New York: New York University Press, 1972), 78; Norman Izkowitz, "Men and Ideas in the Eighteenth Century Ottoman Empire," in Thomas Naff and Roger Owen, eds, *Studies in Eighteenth Century Islamic History* (Carbondale, IL, Edwardsville: Southern Illinois University Press—London, Amsterdam: Feffer & Simons, 1977), 23 ff.
49 For *ʿimāra*, a notion practically identical with *ʿumrān*, the central term in Ibn Khaldun's theory of civilization, see F. Rosenthal in Ibn Khaldun, *Muqaddimah* 1: lxxvi ff., 80 n. 80. *ʿUmrān* is often translated as "civilization," a connotation which might come in here also for *ʿimāra*.
50 The Arabic word used by Ibn Khaldun (1: 65) here is *ta'dīb*.
51 al-Mannūnī, *Maḏāhir*, 2: 432 ff.
52 Ibid., 435–443.
53 For the aspirations of the Sheykhü'l-Islamate after 1908 to reform the madrasa system and to regain control of the Ottoman educational and legal institution, see Berkes, *Secularism*, 413 ff.
54 For *šūrā* in the context of contemporary Islamic political thought see especially Roswitha Badry, *Die zeitgenössische Diskussion um den islamischen Beratungsgedanken (shura) unter dem besonderen Aspekt ideengeschichtlicher Kontinuitäten und Diskontinuitäten* (Stuttgart: Steiner, 1998); Gudrun Krämer, *Gottes Staat als Republik: Reflexionen zeitgenössischer Muslime zu Islam, Menschenrechten und Demokratie* (Baden-Baden: Nomosn, 1999).

55 See for example, *al-Manār* 9 (1324/1906), 553 ff.; 10 (1325/1907), 68, 281 ff.; 12 (1327/1909–1910), 606–611.
56 For example, *al-Manār* 12 (1327/1909–1910), 606–611.
57 al-Mannūnī, *Maḏāhir*, 2: 428 ff.
58 Ibid.
59 See C. V. Findley, "Medjelle," *EI²*, 6: 971 ff., with further literature.
60 al-Mannūnī, *Maḏāhir*, 2: 429.
61 Laroui, *Origines*, 378 ff.; see also Kogelmann, *Islamische fromme Stiftungen*, 98 ff.
62 Quite harsh views of Morocco were expressed by Rashid Rida himself, *al-Manār* 1 (1315–1316/1897–1898), 272 ff.; further 9 (1324/1906), 156 ff., and especially 10 (1325/1907), 554–557, where he qualifies the European supremacy in Morocco as a necessary victory of Order against Chaos. In comparison with the Moroccans, the Christians as bearers of a higher civilization even have to be regarded as righteous (*ṣāliḥūn*). For Rida, this victory of Knowledge and Order over Ignorance and Corruption follows Divine Providence as expressed in the Qur'an. Long-standing Middle Eastern prejudices against Maghrib seem to come out in full here.
63 In adaptation of the German term *Verfassungspatriotismus* (constitutional patriotism) which was coined by Jürgen Habermas and which had a considerable impact on the constitutional debate in Germany after reunification.
64 See Mardin, *Young Ottoman Thought*, 292 ff.
65 See for this Berkes, *Secularism*, 253–270; Selim Deringil, *The Well-Protected Domains: Ideology and the Legitimation of Power in the Ottoman Empire, 1876–1909* (London, New York: I. B. Tauris, 1999), 44–67.
66 See the exemplary account of this development given by Berkes, *Secularism*, 337–366.
67 For this so-called "Neo-Salafiyya," of which 'Allal al-Fasi was a leading figure, see E. J. Rosenthal, *Islam in the Modern National State* (Cambridge: Cambridge University Press, 1965), 154, 158, 325; 'Allal al-Fasi, *The Independence Movements in Arab North Africa* (New York, 1970), 113 ff.; 'Allal al-Fasi, *Ḥadīṯ al-Maġrib fī'l-Mašriq* (Cairo: al-Maṭba'a al-'ālamiyya, 1956), 23; 'Abd al-Razzāq al-Dawwāy, "Allāl al-Fāsī ka-namūdhağ li'l-fikr al-salafī al-ğadīd fī'l-Maġrib', in *Fī'l-intalliğānsiya fī'l-Maġrib al-'arabi* (Beirut, 1984), 105–118. I owe these references to Thomas Kerkloh MA, Dortmund.

9

CONSTRUCTING TRANSNATIONAL ISLAM

The East–West network of Shakib Arslan

Raja Adal

The interwar period saw the division of the greater part of the world into a colonized East and a colonizing West, and within the East into partly overlapping Arab and Islamic worlds. The East, the West, the Arab world, the Islamic world, each had its human networks. At the same time, the very concepts of an Arab world and of an Islamic world competed with local nationalisms, with Westernization, and with each other. As a literary figure belonging to the cultural milieus of Beirut, Cairo, and Damascus, and as the Arab *amīr al bayān*, "the prince of eloquence," Shakib Arslan was strongly connected to the Arab world. As a former student of Muhammad 'Abduh, a close friend of Rashid Rida, and an important contributor to the journal *al-Manār*, he was a spokesman for the Islamic revival. As a resident of Switzerland, the publisher of the journal *La Nation Arabe*, and a perpetual anticolonial activist, he was a regular figure at anticolonial congresses and in Paris, Berlin, and Rome.

During the entire interwar period, Shakib Arslan's position at the crossroad of various regions and worldviews gave him influence throughout an extensive region that stretched from the Arabian Gulf states and the Arab East, through Western and Eastern Europe, and to the Maghreb. At the same time, Arslan was "arguably the most widely read Arab writer of the interwar period,"[1] and the Egyptian press diffused his lifetime production of more than 2,000 articles and 20 volumes throughout the Arab and Islamic world. In French, his journal *La Nation Arabe* allowed him to reach Arab students with a Western education, non-Arab Muslims who did not know Arabic, Western policy makers, and anti-colonial activists, introducing concepts of the Arab world and the Islamic revival to new audiences.

This chapter traces the members of Arslan's transnational network, looks into the manner that it was constructed, and ultimately asks for its *raisons d'être*, for the reasons that drove it into being. It does so through a systematic analysis of the thousands of proper names that appear throughout the 2,437 pages and 38 volumes of *La Nation Arabe*. This approach made it possible to unearth pertinent passages scattered throughout the text and overlooked by previous studies of Shakib Arslan, which have only made cursory use of the journal.[2] More importantly, systematic indexing allowed the text itself to provide the key figures which were the pillars of Arslan's transnational network, and upon which the framework of this article is based.[3]

Its structure is based upon a spatial division of Shakib Arslan's network into regions. After a brief introduction on Arslan himself, it begins with his connections to the highest echelons of the Ottoman state at the time of the dissolution of the Empire, and with the networks and plans of the exiled community in the first few years of the interwar period. The second section returns to the links geographically closest to Arslan's birthplace in the mountains of Lebanon, to the land that lay between those mountains and Istanbul, namely to the intellectual milieu of Damascus and Beirut. From the last days of the First World War and until 1937 Shakib Arslan was an exiled nationalist leader, and it is testimony to the intellectual influence that he exercised from afar if after a twenty-year absence he received a hero's welcome in Beirut and Damascus. The third part is about Europe, where Arslan published *La Nation Arabe*, collaborated with the leadership of European anticolonial movements, organized the European Muslim Congress, and strove to maintain ties between Eastern Europe and the other centers of the Islamic world.

A fourth section describes how, to the largely independent Arab and Muslim states of Ibn Saud in the Hijaz and Nejd, of Imam Yahya in Yemen, and of Faisal in Iraq, Arslan offered his services for council and, when necessary, mediation, engaging in the difficult task of drawing the three monarchs toward greater Arab unity. While the situation in the Arab East was complex and highly politicized, fraught with the rivalry of the Husaynis and Nashashibis in Palestine, with that of the independent kingdoms of the Hijaz-Nejd, Yemen, and Iraq, and with the aggressive factionalism of the Syrian independence movement, the Maghreb provided a welcome respite. A fifth section deals with how Arslan came to be known as the protector, strategist, and mastermind of the Maghreb's independence movements, mobilizing the Islamic world for such causes as the repeal of the Berber Dahir. This, in turn, gave the leaders of North African independence movements studying in Paris a new sense of pan-Arab and pan-Islamic consciousness. The sixth section concerns Arslan's close links with the intellectual world of Cairo, which printed Arslan's works and diffused them throughout the Arab world. Yet it so happens that, as the country where ʻAbduh and Rida lived, Arslan's Egyptian network becomes most relevant when studied in the context of the Islamic revival and irrespective of geographic location, and so the last section will be about "the Manarists."

***

Shakib Arslan was born to one of two families that have traditionally assumed the leadership of Mount Lebanon's Druze community, a heterodox sect of Isma'ili

Islam. It is unknown when and how he entered the mainstream of Sunni Islam, later to become one of its chief publicizers, but at the age of 16 he was strongly influenced by classes taught at the Madrasat al-Sultaniyya by Muhammad ʿAbduh, who was exiled in Beirut. For his whole life, he remained a follower of ʿAbduh's Islamic reformist movement and a member of ʿAbduh's political and literary circles.

Druze on his father's side and by inheritance, Arslan's mother, as well as his wife, were Circassian, a Muslim minority group from the Caucasus. It is revealing of Arslan's Ottoman background that, although an emblematic figure of interwar pan-Arabism and pan-Islam, he was originally born a member of a heretic sect not considered Islamic by the majority of Sunnis, was ethnically half non-Arab, and eventually married a foreign immigrant of non-Arab origin. Although his wife Salima had lived in the region of Salt in north Jordan since her childhood, she testifies to only knowing Turkish at the time of their marriage.[4]

Arslan received a modern education, first at an American protestant school, then at the Maronite Christian Madrasat al-Hikma (also known by its French appellation *La Sagesse*), and finally at the Ottoman Madrasat al-Sultaniyya. In the course of his education he learned French, Ottoman Turkish, some English, and quickly distinguished himself as a singularly gifted writer of Arabic. For the rest of his life, and to this day, the Arab world knows him as "*amīr al-bayān*," the "prince of eloquence." This title is significant in two ways. When the two words are taken separately the second refers to his literary genius, while the first makes reference to his title of Amir, a responsibility he first came to assume at the age of 17, when his father died and he became governor of the Shuf Mountains in south central Lebanon. Although Arslan would eventually leave the confines of Lebanese Mountain politics, throughout his life he would remain a prodigious writer and a natural political leader.

While Arslan published extensively in Arabic, the one journal that he edited himself was in French. Printed in the vicinity of Geneva and mostly edited with his colleague Ihsan al-Jabiri, *La Nation Arabe* appeared from 1930 to 1938 in thirty-eight volumes.[5] It is interesting to compare *La Nation Arabe* and *al-Manār*, in that Arslan and Rida shared an exceptionally close friendship and were proponents of very similar visions of the Islamic revival movement, both belonging to the school of Muhammad ʿAbduh. Many of the articles that Arslan wrote for *La Nation Arabe* he rewrote in Arabic and addressed them to *al-Manār*'s readers after making slight changes to accommodate the different readership. Although published in French and Arabic respectively, and addressed to different, although overlapping, audiences, the two journals can often be seen sharing the same source. *Al-Manār* operated in the context of Islam as a contemporary religion while *La Nation Arabe* was a "political, literary, economic, and social journal" operating in the contemporary world approached from an Islamic perspective. In other respects, Arslan differed from Rashid Rida. Their difference is illustrated by the one time the two friends were at odds. It was in

1915, at a time when Arab nationalists, including Rida, were earnestly beginning to oppose the Ottoman state. Arslan, as a member of the Ottoman parliament, and more importantly as one raised in the context of its multi-ethnic, multi-lingual cosmopolitanism, could not imagine Arabs separated from Turks embarking alone upon their political destiny. Deceivingly entitled *La Nation Arabe*, Arslan's journal dealt as much with the Arab world as with the non-Arab regions of the Islamic world.

The Ottoman world, its loss, and the endeavor to restore it

Born in nineteenth-century Mount Lebanon and schooled in an Ottoman civil service school, Shakib Arslan's adoption of the reformist Islamic themes taught by Muhammad 'Abduh in Beirut only strengthened his attachment to a multi-ethnic Ottoman Empire, seat of the Caliphate and barrier against foreign encroachment. His enthusiasm for the empire is perhaps most clearly expressed by the Ottoman campaign of 1911–1912 to preserve Cyrenaica against Italian conquest. Arslan, a Druze Amir and former *mutaṣarrif* (provincial governor) of Mount Lebanon rushed to the front, spending eight months fighting with the regular Ottoman troops. The battle was lost and the empire continued shrinking, but it was there that Arslan met the young Turkish officers from the Committee of Union and Progress (CUP), who would come to seize power in 1913 and draw Arslan into the innermost circles of Ottoman rule.

Among them was Enver Paşa, who along with Talat Paşa and Cemal Paşa was member of the triumvirate that held power in Istanbul from 1913 until the end of the First World War.[6] The friendship that bound Arslan, an Arab Ottoman Amir and writer, to Enver Paşa, a Turkish Ottoman general of lower class origins, deserves closer examination. On the ideological plane, the CUP is seen by revisionist historians such as Hasan Kayali not as the logical precursor of Turkish nationalism, but only as an advocate of secular Ottoman nationalism, which the party adopted in 1908 only to abandon at the end of the Balkan wars in 1913. With the Balkan possessions lost, and the Ottoman Empire reduced to predominantly Muslim subjects, there occurred what Kayali describes as an "Islamist reinterpretation of Ottomanism." As a result "the Unionists came to rely on religion in their quest for centralization and social harmony much as their nemesis Abdulhamid had."[7]

The friendship and partnership between Enver Paşa and Shakib Arslan, however, begun in 1911 and continued until the former's death eleven years later, transcending the CUP "conversion" to Islamist politics, and the exile of both Enver and Arslan. It would be an easy answer to say that both Enver and Arslan had a vested interest in the Ottoman state and thus fought for its preservation, and subsequently for its restoration. In terms of military ventures, both can be seen engaging in lost causes, which, if not outright romantic, had very little chances of success. The conditions of Enver Paşa's death in the mountains of Eastern

Bukhara are described by Arslan in *La Nation Arabe*:

> Enver Paşa, to whom I had explained all of the [hidden] intentions of Bolsheviks when they invited him to settle in Moscow by promising him wonders, soon realized that the Bolsheviks were using him to threaten the English and that, in reality, they detested him no less than they detested the English. It is then that he secretly went, disguised as a peasant, to Bukhara and chased the Russians out of this kingdom which they had subjugated and ruined. Since the fight was not equal, Enver could not hold more than one year, and died as a martyr in a battle in which, with 300 fighters he held his own against 12,000 Russian soldiers.[8]

On the political stage, Arslan and Enver Paşa would closely cooperate in the years of exile after 1917. In the meantime, after his election to the Ottoman parliament in 1913, Arslan had the much less enviable position of being one of the leading Arab Ottoman figures in Damascus during Cemal Paşa's reign of terror. Later accused of collaboration during Cemal's suppression of Arab nationalist movements, Arslan insisted that in his position as representative to the Ottoman parliament, it was his responsibility to struggle to alleviate the deportations, executions, and food shortages by negotiating with Cemal Paşa. He claims to have done this in frequent meetings with the latter, and to have had recourse to the other two members of the Ottoman triumvirate, Talat Paşa and Enver Paşa, to attempt to alleviate the famine that hit Syria and Lebanon.[9]

As for Kemal Paşa, the future Atatürk, whom Arslan first met when he was chief of staff of Enver's army, they met again at the Café Maskot in Berlin in the late summer of 1917, on the day that British troops were entering Jerusalem. Expressing his anguish at the fate of Jerusalem and Palestine, Arslan confessed to his companion his fears about the tragic situation of Islam. Kemal Paşa, who would one day become the father of the secularist Turkish nation-state, is said to have told Arslan:

> We shall take it [Jerusalem] back, we shall take it back... *inshaallah* [God willing], we shall take it back; and if I say "*inshaallah*" it is as a good Muslim that I say it, because I am Muslim before all else; but it is certain that we shall take it back.[10]

Before becoming a secularist Turkish nationalist, and in the presence of Arslan, Kemal Paşa spoke very much like his fellow Ottoman companions, although perhaps with a more consciously expressed profession of faith.

In the immediate aftermath of the war and with the Ottoman Empire occupied, Arslan exiled himself in Berlin, along with the CUP leadership, which included Enver and Talat. In those immediate postwar years, as Allied ambitions in the former Ottoman lands became clearer, with the Balfour declaration that promised a Jewish homeland in Palestine, with the violent end brought by the French to

Faisal's independent kingdom in Syria, and before the commercial agreements of March 1921 between the Soviets and Britain had been signed, a coalition of Arabs and Turks under the banner of Islam and allied to the Soviet Union did not appear to be a completely improbable scenario. It is in this context that Enver Paşa founded the Islamic International (or Islamintern) as an extension of the CUP. Based in Moscow, Enver envisaged a decentralized organization consisting of regional cells spanning the entire Islamic world, each with its own strategy but operating within a general framework and with an overarching goal: the freedom and self-government of Islamic lands.[11]

The long cold voyage to Moscow was not easy for the Arab and Turkish exiles who accepted the invitation. Arslan had previously been in contact with the Soviet Politburo member Zinovev in Saint Moritz in order to communicate a message from King Faisal, and met him again, along with Trotsky, in Moscow during the third general conference of the Komintern.[12] The commemorative photograph of the Islamic International Conference members shows an out of place and depressed group of Arabs and Turks, for demoralization must have been all the more complete after Talat's assassination earlier that year in Berlin. Shakib Arslan wrote Enver that the loss of Talat represented "not only a loss for the CUP, not only a loss for the Turkish people, but a loss for the whole Islamic world."[13] Enver's death a year later marked the end of Arslan's hopes for a restoration of the empire.

While the CUP's political position changed with circumstances, adapting the ideologies of Ottomanism, Islamism, and Turkish nationalism to the various conditions existing during their rise to power and subsequent downfall, a common underlying cultural background can be seen in the personal relationship between Arslan and Enver Paşa. As Kayali points out, "the Ottoman state—'sick man' though it may have been—actually had more resilience in its last decade than historians generally credit it with."[14] Not only the state, but what may be called an "Ottoman culture" seems to also have embodied the ideals of men such as Shakib Arslan and Enver Paşa, and its resilience may very well have survived the demise of the empire and, as shall later be seen, its legacy found heirs in future generations.

Syria

Shakib Arslan's relationship with Syria during the interwar period, from 1917 to 1937, was that of an exile. Yet to former Ottomans like Arslan, Syria meant greater Syria and included not only the French mandates of Syria and Lebanon but also the British mandate of Palestine. It was accepted, however, that the political conditions created by the colonial powers were unavoidable, at least in the short term. The "Syrian Congress," which met in 1921 in Geneva to petition the League of Nations Permanent Mandates Commission, changed its name to "Syrian-Palestinian Congress" upon the request of the Palestinian delegates who contended that, their region being under British mandate, their agenda might also have to differ.[15] Shakib Arslan himself quickly realized that bargaining included compromise, and in his discussions with de Jouvenel accepted the idea of a plebiscite to determine whether Tripoli and the other regions added to Lebanon in 1920 would join a Syrian or a Lebanese independent state.[16]

Shakib Arslan's official position was that of head of the three member permanent delegation of the Syrian-Palestinian Congress to the League of Nations in Geneva. Although the Congress's first meeting in 1921 was unsuccessful in obtaining the League of Nations' interference in British and French mandatory policy, the idea of a permanent delegation to represent the Syrian issue to the League gained renewed urgency in the summer of 1925, when the Syrian revolt broke out. The revolt, and its violent suppression, coincided with 'Abd al-Karim's revolt in the Rif Mountains of Morocco, and for an instant it seemed as if France's colonial empire had been fragilized. It is in this context that Arslan moved to Switzerland to express the aspirations of the Syrian and Palestinian independentists to the League of Nations Permanent Mandates Commission and to the European world.

The delegation had three members. In addition to Shakib Arslan, there was Ihsan al-Jabiri, Arslan's partner from 1925 until his return to Syria in 1937 to become governor of the district of Latakia. Jabiri was an Arab Ottoman from a prominent family of Aleppo, who had once served as municipal leader. Educated in Istanbul and with a higher law degree from Paris, Jabiri was an aristocratic member of his world, who held several positions in the high Ottoman bureaucracy before becoming Chamberlain of King Faisal during the latter's short reign. He was, in Arslan's words, "our colleague and companion of arms in the patriotic struggle that we have together pursued in Europe, since the Syrian-Palestinian Congress held in Geneva in 1921, and until the completion of the Franco-Syrian treaty in 1937."[17]

The third member of the delegation was Sulayman Kin'an, a Maronite from Mount Lebanon who had been a representative in the twelve member Lebanese Administrative Council, which from 1861 to 1919 was the governing body of Mount Lebanon. In 1920 it declared the independence of Lebanon in opposition to the French Mandate, and in 1921 Kin'an was a delegate to the Syrian-Palestinian Congress, submitting a request to the League of Nations for Lebanese independence within its pre-1920 frontiers.[18] In later years, Kin'an was replaced by Riyad al-Sulh, whose father Riza al-Sulh was interior minister in Faisal's cabinet at the time of the imposition of the French mandate in 1920.[19] A member of Beirut's Sunni merchant bourgeoisie, Riyad al-Sulh was to become the independent Lebanese Republic's first prime minister in 1943.

Beyond the immediate associates of Shakib Arslan in Geneva, there were of course the great alliances and rivalries that characterized the fractious Syrian independence movement. Within this landscape, Arslan can be clearly positioned as the close friend, ally, and advisor of three major actors, Rashid Rida, Hajj Amin al-Husayni, and his younger brother 'Adil Arslan; and as the antagonist of two others, Michel Lutfallah and especially 'Abd al-Rahman Shahbandar.

Although vice-president of the Syrian-Palestinian Congress, one of its active participants, and a lifelong ally of Arslan, the Syrian nationalist aspect of Rashid Rida has often found itself overshadowed by his position in the Islamic revivalist movement. Yet Rida's writings in *al-Manār* bear the stamp of his ideas on Syrian unity, and of the Islamic content of his Arab and Syrian nationalism. Unlike Arslan, Rida was involved in the Arab Nationalist movement before and during the First World War, and this was the only time when the two friends were at odds. Yet with the war ended, Arslan lost the Ottoman state, which he had defended to the very end, and Rida realized that the Arab revolt had resulted not in independence but in European colonization. During Arslan's difficult period of transition from Ottomanism to Arabism, it was Rida who, in Cleveland's words, "played the major role in reintegrating Arslan with the Arab leaders who had been alienated by his wartime policies [in support of the Ottoman empire]."[20] Thus was Arslan elected Secretary of the Syrian-Palestinian congress, later to become its prime animator.

On the whole, Khoury is justified in stating that Palestinian delegates to the congress were wary of Syrian elements who adopted an increasingly narrow territorial form of nationalism focusing on a smaller Syria, compromising on the issue of Zionism, and attached to the Hashemites, who were suspect in Palestinian eyes.[21] However, while this view was applicable to the Lutfallah and Shahbandar faction within the congress, the situation was different in the case of Arslan and Rida. Indeed, Khoury notes that although both Jabiri and Arslan were exiled, they were looked upon admiringly by the younger group of ultra-nationalist Istiqlalists as leaders of exemplary integrity, who were not reluctant to confront the controversy over Palestine.[22] *La Nation Arabe*, the delegation's journal published by Arslan, dealt extensively with the Palestinian issue, regularly reproducing the numerous resolutions sent by the Syrian-Palestinian Congress, which by the 1930s was dominated by Arslan and his allies, to the League of Nations. As the years advance it propeled the issue to the forefront of all others, attributing to it crisis proportions. In its 8 years of publication, the journal devoted 11% of its articles including one special issue to the Palestinian question, and regularly published reports of Zionist congresses in Europe and lists of European politicians and publications with their stance upon the issue, while calling for Arabs and Muslims to unite.

In that section of the Arab world referred to as Palestine, Arslan was closely allied to Hajj Amin al-Husayni, Mufti of Jerusalem, and President of the Supreme Muslim Council of Palestine. The Mufti of Jerusalem held a traditional role in a traditional Arab-Muslim world, that suddenly found itself faced with powerful international pressures. The rapid succession of events beginning with the First World War and the Arab revolt, the end of the Ottoman Empire and the coming of the British, the sudden separation from other parts of Syria and the alarming increase in Jewish immigration, entailed a drastically new brand of political action. For assistance in such matters, from the 1920s until the end of the Second World War, the Mufti turned to Arslan. By 1935, Arslan had written to the Mufti more than 100 letters, and in the next 10 years it is probable that Arslan's stream of letters and advice increased.[23] In 1936, when David Ben Gurion, one of the leaders of the Zionist Executive and the future first Prime Minister of Israel, sought to make an agreement with Arab leaders, it was Shakib Arslan and Ihsan al-Jabiri whom he visited in the former's home in Geneva. Ben Gurion had been in contact with an Arab interlocutor, Musa 'Alami, who told him that the main leader with decisive power in Palestine was the Mufti, and that the Mufti paid attention to the views of the Istiqlalist leaders outside of "Palestine," and especially to those of Arslan and Jabiri: "It was Musa Alami's opinion that I [Ben Gurion] should first of all meet Jabri and Arslan. He would write to them about his talk with the Mufti. The Mufti attached much weight to their opinion, and they to his."[24]

Arslan and the Mufti both vigorously opposed British and French colonization in the Arab and Islamic world. In an attempt to gain leverage against the British and French, they set about finding European allies willing to oppose British and French hegemony, and in Europe the counterweights to Britain and France were Italy and Germany. In Palestine, the Husayni faction was the political adversary of the Nashashibi faction, which was allied with the British administration. In 1935, Syrian journals close to the Nashashibis published a letter from Arslan to the Mufti meant to discredit the latter. The letter outlined a plan by Arslan for making Italian propaganda in the Arab world, and although it was eventually widely accepted to be a fake, it created a storm of controversy and involved Arslan in the fierce atmosphere of Jerusalem politics. The ideological positions and practical alliance between Arslan and the Mufti were common knowledge, and compromising either of them had repercussions on the other. During the Second World War, both Arslan and the Mufti found themselves on the side of Germany and Italy, the Mufti spending several years in Berlin and Arslan advising him on what policies to pursue.[25]

The third significant relationship of Shakib Arslan was, not surprisingly, his brother 'Adil. One of the leading young Istiqlalists, 'Adil Arslan was close both ideologically and politically to his older brother Shakib. His presence further cemented the alliance within the Syrian-Palestinian Congress between the young pan-Arab Istiqlalists and Shakib Arslan. In fact, 'Adil Arslan and the Istiqlalists, Shakib Arslan, Rashid Rida, and Hajj Amin al-Husayni formed a closely-knit block within the Syrian-Palestinian Congress. During the Syrian revolt, toward the end of 1925, young Istiqlalists created with Hajj Amin al-Husayni a special finance committee in Jerusalem. Istiqlalist leaders such as Shukri al-Quwwatli, who opposed the Hashemites, were amenable to receive aid from Ibn Saud, and they also began to channel other funds toward the Jerusalem Committee rather than to the Cairo Executive of the Syrian-Palestinian congress. This was a challenge to Michel Lutfallah, President of the Syrian-Palestinian Congress, who owed his position to his funding of congress activities. The situation reached a crisis when in October 1927 Shakib Arslan resigned from the Executive of the Syrian-Palestinian Congress, pushing Rashid Rida and the Istiqlalist wing of the executive in Cairo and Jerusalem to take the leadership by ousting Lutfallah. The latter formed his own executive committee, and by December there were two antagonistic Syrian-Palestinian Congress committees. Opposing what has at times been called the "Istiqlalist faction," the "Rida-Istiqlalist faction," or the "Rida-Arslan faction," was Michel Lutfallah's ally 'Abd al-Rahman Shahbandar, an Arab nationalist from before the First World War who became one of the rebel chiefs during the Syrian revolt and an exiled independentist afterwards.[26] The rift between Shahbandar and Shakib Arslan mirrored the one dividing many of the Syrian nationalists, and it would never heal.

The reasons for the schism within the Syrian-Palestinian Congress may appear surprising when one considers that its members were all fighting a difficult battle against the French and British for Syrian-Palestinian independence. Yet the similarity stops there, and deep ideological rifts separated each party's vision of the society, of the future, and of the best way to achieve it. In a perceptive passage, Khoury elaborates:

> The Arslan-Istiqlali branch of the movement was avowedly pan-Arabist, anti-Hashemite, and opposed to cooperating with the British. It stood for the complete liberation of all Arab peoples and territories from foreign rule and the establishment of a unitary Arab state.... Shahbandar's People's Party and the dominant faction on the Syrian-Palestine Congress Executive [until 1927] were close to the Hashemites and willing to cooperate with the British to accomplish their more limited goal, the establishment of an independent Syrian state. On the question of Lebanon, the Lutfallah-Shahbandar faction, under the influence of Michel Lutfallah, appeared willing to accept a Greater Lebanon.[27]

In the 1921 meeting of the Syrian-Palestinian Congress, the lines separating these two parties were already drawn, and in later years ideological rifts would combine with personal antagonisms to usher a split of the congress.

During the Syrian revolt of 1925–1926, the competition between the two factions was fierce, but still left a certain amount of cooperation for their common cause. For a moment there appeared the possibility that a treaty could grant Syria a limited independence while securing France's strategic and economic interests.[28] The unpopular French commissioner Maurice Sarrail was replaced by the relatively liberal de Jouvenel. The new commissioner telegraphed Shakib Arslan in Geneva, inviting him for talks in Paris. In a first meeting in November 1925, Arslan's moderation impressed de Jouvenel. Khoury writes that some members of the Syrian-Palestinian Congress headquartered in Cairo, namely Lutfallah and Shahbandar, were irritated by Arslan's success in securing access to a high-ranking French official. Upon their meeting de Jouvenel in Cairo, they took a hard line of no compromise which alienated the High Commissioner, who buried the accords. This was not, however, the end of the story, for Arslan's journal *La Nation Arabe* reveals that there was a subsequent meeting with de Jouvenel the following July in Paris, in which Arslan, his associate Jabiri, as well as Lutfallah participated in three working sessions, "during which several conditions [of the agreement] were defined."[29] Arslan believes that it was the influence exercised by the Maronite Lebanese Shukri Ghanem on the head of the Poincaré government, and French officials rather than factionalism within the Syrian-Palestinian congress, that made the accord fail. According to Arslan, de Jouvenel reported to Poincaré that "we thought it possible to speak with the Syrian nationalists to see if there was the possibility of an agreement," to which Poincaré is said to have answered, "[to speak] with the enemies of France."[30] Shortly afterwards, de Jouvenel was replaced by Ponsot as High Commissioner of Syria.[31]

Ten years later, in 1936, when the Syrian delegation led by Hashem al-Atasi, leader of the National Bloc and soon to be president of the Syrian Republic, went to Paris to sign the treaty with France, al-Atasi, Sa'dallah al-Jabiri, and Riyad al-Sulh made several trips to Geneva to consult with Arslan. The French were also careful to gain his consent to the treaty, and the French vice-minister of foreign affairs, Viénot, met Arslan for lunch in Geneva. Afterwards, Viénot wrote to the French High Commissioner in Syria Martel that Arslan's influence, both inside of Syria, where he constituted a counterweight to Shahbandar's opposition to the treaty, and in the Arab world, made him a "factor which we cannot ignore."[32] Cleveland further notes that "Arslan's support could not guarantee the treaty's passage in the Syrian chamber but his opposition could sabotage it."[33] On the contrary Shahbandar's opposition to the treaty did not prove fatal, and it is a testimony to Arslan's network inside and outside Syria that, as an exile who had not personally participated in Syrian politics for two decades, he still represented an inescapable linchpin in any agreement between France and Syria.

It is argued by Cleveland that Arslan used his position as representative of the congress in Geneva to air his personal views, using *La Nation Arabe* as his "personal mouthpiece."[34] Yet once the schism in the congress was finalized in 1927, one can observe an uninterrupted stream of correspondence and perpetual consultations between Shakib Arslan, Rashid Rida, Hajj Amin al-Husayni, and 'Adil Arslan. After the pro-Hachemite and secularist wing was separated from the Syrian-Palestinian Congress, the Arslan-Rida-Husayni alliance within the congress was united in both its goals and ideology. Whether the Lutfallah-Shahbandar branch of the Syrian-Palestinian Congress exhibited a similar unity would require a separate study, yet in light of the remarkable homogeneity shown by the Arslan-Rida-Husayni alliance within the congress we may need to revise our image of a fractionalized Syrian exile community, divided along not only ideological but also regional and personal interests.

Europe

If Arslan's literary and political career flourished under the Ottoman Empire, it is for the second career that he began at the age of 56 in Europe that he is most often remembered. Arslan most probably owes his encyclopedia definition, "perhaps the most prominent activist for Muslim political causes between the world wars," to his 20 years as an anticolonial, pan-Arab, and Islamic activist in interwar Europe.[35] Kramer also sees Arslan as one of the two principal spokesmen of the Arabs in the West, along with George Antonius, writing that "between them, these two prolific polemicists repackaged the Arab argument in terms intelligible to foreign audiences, and some of their texts resonate to this day."[36]

Arslan enjoyed a complex relationship with Europe. It was the seat of the imperial powers which he fought, yet with his first forays into diplomacy he began his lifelong quest to find a European power that could help Arabs and Muslims achieve freedom and modernization. When Arslan first went to Europe in 1889, Tunis had already been occupied by France in 1881 and Egyptian independence thwarted by British troops in 1882. The initial enthusiasm of such writers such as Tahtawi and Khayr al-Din toward a benevolent and friendly Europe had long passed.[37] For Arslan, writes Cleveland, "Europe represented an imperial threat, not an admirable culture."[38] While it is clear that, since Arslan's earliest days, Europe already embodied the colonizer, scattered evidence exists of his affection for a Europe other than the one which he daily confronted in his anticolonial struggle. In the guest book of the Goethe Museum in Berlin is scribbled a forgotten poem, written in honor of Goethe during Arslan's first visit to Germany on October 10, 1917:

> I bowed the head of my muse before his gate
> Before his doorstep how many have lay prostrate
> Although he is not of my community nor my kin
> The community of man in literature is one
> (For if a common genealogy we do not share
> Between us literature holds the place of the father)[39]

In his anticolonial campaign waged in Europe, Arslan was a natural ally of European anticolonial movements, and essentially of the French left. If the support of a part of the British left wing for Zionism might have caused an obstacle to a rapprochement with British socialists, it was with the French socialists and radical socialists that Arslan had the most affinity. In the course of defending causes in the Arab East and North Africa, Arslan attended socialist and anti-imperialist congresses in Berne in 1919, Genoa in 1922, and Brussels in 1927, and, despite his vocal aversion to Communism, the tenth Anniversary of the Bolshevik Revolution in Moscow in 1927. Demonstrating his sympathetic but skeptical stance *vis-à-vis* socialism, he would tell the French socialist leader Marcel Cachin in 1919: "we have doubts, even about you; statesmen of the left, once in power, become dreadfully imperialist." Yet in the case of Cachin, nineteen years later Arslan could still express his continued esteem and sympathy.[40] Most prominent among the French friends of Arslan is Jean Longuet, grandson of Karl Marx and vice-president of the foreign affairs commission in the French chamber of deputies. In Longuet's obituary Arslan would reiterate the same theme of truthfulness in the fight against imperialism: "Jean Longuet did not joke about socialist principles ... he advocated a truthful socialism without seeking personal profit, but also without exaltation and without subversive activities." At the news of both the deaths of Longuet and Pierre Renaudel, another French socialist, Arslan writes of feeling a "true emptiness" at the loss of "real friends."[41]

Arslan's relationship with Germany was entirely different. He developed links not with the left, but with the Foreign Service officers and academics whose careers could be traced back to Wilhelmian Germany, and to Kaiser Wilhelm II himself. One of the earlier contacts of Arslan with Germany was in 1898, when the Kaiser declared in Damascus that Germany was the protector of 300 million Muslims throughout the world. Standing by his side was Arslan, who had been appointed by Sultan Abdülhamid II as the Kaiser's escort in the city.[42] In 1934, Arslan went to see the deposed Kaiser in Doorn,[43] and in the March–April 1935 issue of *La Nation Arabe* he would engage in a thirteen page defense of the former Kaiser against charges of having initiated the First World War, at the end of which Arslan asks the same question as his reader: "Why have we taken the trouble, we who are not Germans, of defending the ex-emperor of Germany against these ignominious lies?" To this question, Arslan gives a double reply. First, it is in the name of truth and of resistance against the hegemony of the Allies, who wish to throw the responsibility of the war on Germany and its emperor. The Ottoman Empire's alliance with Germany and subsequent partition at the hands of the allies make Arslan understandably sympathetic toward such resistance. Second is the Kaiser's approach toward Islam:

> This man has, for his whole career, shown an unshakable impartiality with regard to Muslims. He was the only sovereign of Christian Europe—despite his attachment to his religion and despite being himself head of the Lutheran Church—who could see Islam as a good religion that could inspire consideration and respect.[44]

Arslan goes even further, attributing half of the popularity of Germany in the Islamic world to the political policies of Wilhelm II, the other half being attributed to the simple fact that Germany, having no colonies, attracted less complaints from Muslims.

As a member of the Ottoman parliament's Foreign Affairs Committee, Arslan had opportunities to interact with the empire's wartime ally, Germany. He was, for example, the intermediary between the Grand Vizier of the Ottoman Empire Said Halim and the German ambassador to Istanbul Wangenheim when relations between both were strained.[45] He had barely returned to Istanbul from his first visit to Germany in 1917 when Enver Paşa sent him back to Berlin to negotiate certain problems between the Empire and Germany regarding the Caucasus and the Russian fleet in the Black Sea.[46] With the war ended, Arslan was again in Germany, as president of the Oriental Club, and his relationship with its intelligentsia and leadership continued throughout the interwar period. In an article on the Arab language, Arslan recounts the long evening he spent in 1930 at the home of Hindenburg, President of Germany's

Weimar Republic, discussing such questions as the abundance of words in Arabic that mean "sadness," and the scarcity of those that mean "happiness."[47]

The German governing elite and German orientalists of the interwar period continued to treat Arslan not only as a notable politician who commanded respect for his knowledge of and influence upon the Arab world, but as a living literary prodigy. The journal of the German Society for Islamic Studies carried at least nine book reviews, collections of open letters, translations of articles, or news briefs about Shakib Arslan between 1915 and 1938. This included a 93-page article, 1 part of a 3 part series on contemporary Arabic literature, containing a 13-page biography based on a personal interview of Arslan and 80 pages of translation of some of his works.[48] The editor of the journal and chairman of the German Society of Islamic Studies was Professor Georg Kampffmeyer, who lectured on Arslan's literary works in his seminars on oriental languages in Berlin and regarded him as a living example of the renaissance of Arabic literature.[49] In a review of Arslan's extensive commentary on the Arabic translation of Lothrop Stoddard's *The New World of Islam*, Kampffmeyer describes it as a "source of highest importance in the study of the contemporary history of the Orient...from the pen of such an admirable Oriental as the Emir Shakib Arslan." The work itself illustrates:

> The attitude which the Emir, and doubtlessly a significant portion of the contemporary Arab Orient, is taking towards the contemporary world, [an attitude] which is decisive in determining their approach to the present and the future of Islam, in other words for the self-perception of Islam and for its religious and nationalist attitudes, especially that of the Arab Orient with regards to the European incursion.[50]

In this short passage, Kampffmeyer seems to be pointing to the growing Salafi movement and the influence which it would exert upon the Islamic world.

Among Arslan's European associates and friends one figure stands out, that of "the famed orientalist and friend of the Orient, our friend for forty years, the German baron Max von Oppenheim."[51] It is characteristic for Arslan to use the traditional figure forty when referring to his closest friends. In many ways, the intellectual pursuits and political involvement of Shakib Arslan and Max Freiherr von Oppenheim ran parallel. A German foreign service officer at the turn of the century, von Oppenheim resigned in 1910 to pursue an interest in archeology and the excavation of the Hittite city of Tell Halal that he had discovered. A world authority on the Hittites, von Oppenheim also seems to have had a deep knowledge of and wide connections in the Arab world, and in times of crisis was called upon to return to the Foreign Ministry. Melka writes that it is von Oppenheim who, as a young Foreign Office official under Kaiser Wilhelm II, inspired the previously mentioned Damascus speech of 1898, in which the Kaiser styled himself as the protector of Muslims. It is unknown when and how Arslan and von Oppenheim first met, but it must have been during those last years of the nineteenth century, when both were young high-ranking representatives of their respective governments, each with his talent, Arslan in literature and von Oppenheim in archeology. Until their death in 1946 they remained in frequent correspondence, and it seems that while von Oppenheim was Arslan's primary link to the official policy-making circles of the German Foreign Office, Arslan was von Oppenheim's primary Arab advisor on Middle Eastern and Islamic affairs.[52]

Von Oppenheim exhibited a lifelong interest in allying Germany to the Islamic world, and like Arslan, his model was the Ottoman-Wilhelmian alliance before the First World War. Also similar to Arslan, von Oppenheim drew grand plans for expelling the French and British from the Middle East and for building an alliance with Ibn Saud. It is interesting that the proposals made to the German Foreign Office in the fall of 1940 by the Mufti Hajj Amin al-Husayni and the Prime Minister of Iraq 'Ali al-Gaylani were similar to those made by von Oppenheim. Melka writes that "the similarity may have been accidental, but even in the absence of correspondence with Arslan for this period the writer is inclined to believe that he, and possibly also von Hentig and Grobba, in some way inspired the major lines of von Oppenheim's memorandum."[53] Melka's conclusions are all the more plausible when seen from the perspective of Arslan, for at this time he is said to have written Husayni a constant stream of letters advising him on what course to take, and in September and October 1939 went to Berlin, where he met von Oppenheim.[54] While it is understandable to see Arslan bent on pushing Germany into a declaration of intentions *vis-à-vis* the Muslim world and an active support of anticolonialism, von Oppenheim's reasons for favoring such an alliance are less clear. They may have stemmed from an academic interest in the Arab world and the memory of the Ottoman-Wilhelmian alliance. Von Oppenheim, Arslan, and Husayni were, however, unable to tip Germany into an Islamic alliance. For one, von Oppenheim's influence seemed to show signs of decline. His well-known Jewish ancestry, although apparently overlooked by the Nazi leadership in view of his services to the state, was coupled with an aristocratic background.[55] Similar to Arslan, his career and vision was rooted in the Ottoman-Wilhelmian politico-cultural alliance and this did not fit well with the new ultra-nationalist racial ideologies.

If Arslan's relations with the French state were strained and antagonistic, and if his relations with the German state rested on relations with the Foreign Office and its career bureaucrats, those with Italy were almost solely based on the one person who held power in the state. Arslan probably knew Benito Mussolini since 1922, when the latter was still editor of *Popolo d'Italia*, and wrote fiery articles defending the Arab cause. Their first meeting must have been during the congress of the League of Oppressed Nations held in Genoa in 1921. At that time, Arslan, who was president of the Oriental Club in Berlin and secretary of the Genoa congress expressed the gratitude of the delegates for the liberal manner in which they had been allowed to conduct their activities in Italy.[56] Thereafter Arslan would always refer to "our friend Mussolini" or "our old friend Mussolini," even when engaging in the fiercest attacks against the Duce's policy in Libya.

Arslan was close to Ahmad al-Sharif al-Sanusi, head of the Sanusiyya tariqa, which was at the heart of the resistance movement in Libya, and his attacks against Italy were virulent. Yet criticizing Mussolini's policies, Arslan adopts the tone of an advisor: "We can assure our old friend Mister Mussolini that all of this will serve him in nothing . . ."[57] At other times, he would chide: " . . . but our friend Mussolini needs conquests, and the gods are thirsty."[58] For his campaign against the Italians, Arslan would even receive a thankful note from 'Umar al-Mukhtar, the military leader of the Libyan resistance, whom he knew since 1911 when they had fought with the Ottoman troops in an attempt to defend Tripolitania. A few months before his capture and execution by the Italians, Mukhtar wrote to Arslan:

> They are excusable, those who cannot believe all of what is said and written about the Italian atrocities, because it is actually difficult to believe that in the world there are men who behave in this unbelievable manner, but it is unfortunately only too real.[59]

From 1930 to 1933 at least twelve virulent criticisms of Italian policies appeared in *La Nation Arabe*, similar to the ones aimed against France and later Great Britain. They were in line with Arslan's uncompromising anticolonial stance. During the year 1933, the articles in *La Nation Arabe* were critical of Italy, but began pointing toward specific policies which it could take to improve the situation of Arabs in its colonies. The Arab press reported that Mussolini wished to meet Arslan, but that the latter refused until the inhabitants of the Green Mountain in Libya had been repatriated. This condition was fulfilled, and in January 1934 *La Nation Arabe* printed the first positive article about Italy. This was followed by Arslan's trip to Rome during which he met Mussolini twice, as well as the Marquis Theodoli, president of the Permanent Mandates Commission of the League of Nations. At the 1935 Muslim Congress of Europe, the Italian orientalist Laura Vagliera was the only non-Muslim allowed to attend and present a paper in Arabic on "What Europe thinks of Islam." Arslan himself read a letter from a Libyan correspondent who wrote that great strides had been taken, although much remained to be done in Italian administered Libya.[60]

Arslan explains the process which brought him to negotiate with Italy in the following manner:

> When we cried out in condemnation against the unbelievable acts which General Graziani had committed, Mussolini sought to have a conversation with us and sent us an envoy to find out what should be done to repair these wrongs. We answered that before anything else, the Arabs should be reintegrated into their homes. He did it and saved them from a certain death . . . also upon our request, three to four hundred Arabs condemned to twenty to thirty years of prison term were amnestied. On our request also, the properties which are called "*waqf*" . . . were restituted to the Muslims. . . . Muslim education . . . was restored in all state schools. . . . We asked for the prohibition of all Christian religious propaganda among Muslims. . . . Mussolini himself told us that it was absolutely forbidden and that he would never tolerate such propaganda . . . .[61]

Although criticized for reaching a settlement with Italy, Arslan knew that he needed allies in Europe, and of the three colonial powers, France, Britain, and Italy, Mussolini was most sensitive to the good and bad press that appeared about Italy in the Muslim world, making him susceptible to negotiations. On the Syrian question, his attitude always seemed "correct and even well-meaning" to Arslan.[62] Mussolini's Italy gave an independentist leader like Arslan a rare occasion to influence the official policy of a colonial power, and if Arslan's grander political schemes of a general Italian-German alliance with the Arab world against the British and French did not materialize before the outbreak of the European war, he in the meantime caused a flurry of secret service reports and considerable worry to French authorities.

Not one to equate the Islamic world with the Arab world, Arslan's Islamic network stretched within Europe. Although there seems little evidence that the nationals of European states who were Muslim engaged in widespread anticolonial campaigns, *La Nation Arabe* mentions several of both immigrant and European background. Much more numerous were the Muslim communities from Eastern Europe. They had been subjects of the Ottoman Empire, and during the first Balkan War of 1912 Arslan had coordinated the activities of the Red Crescent, an Egyptian benevolent society, to assist Muslim refugees in the Balkans. In the Ottoman parliament, Arslan had not only been an intermediary with Germany, but had also been on the committee responsible for managing the strained relations with Russia.[63] Finally, a more personal detail is that Arslan's mother and his wife Salima were from the Caucasus. It may thus not be so surprising if Arslan, in his new role as pan-Islamic activist in Geneva, came to devote time to the Eastern European Islamic world.

La Nation Arabe carried regular articles, and even polemics, regarding Eastern European Islam. Between 1932 and 1936, eight articles about Islam in Bulgaria, Rumania, Poland, Yugoslavia, and Hungary appeared under the pen of Smail Džemalović, including one well-known polemic between him and André Girard, law professor at the University of Paris, about the condition of Muslims in Bulgaria.[64] What is interesting is not only that such articles had an academic value, but that they brought to Europe controversies that raged in the Bulgarian, Turkish, and Arabic press, thus contesting the monopoly that European academics and Christian missionaries exercised on the representation of these regions.[65]

Although the information that we have about Arslan's trip to Eastern Europe is disparate and incomplete, in the vastly unexplored field of Eastern European Islam we can locate flashes of Arslan's passage in the region. In 1931 Arslan would make a quick visit to Yugoslavia, and a longer one in December 1933 and January 1934, "to spend Ramadan with my Yugoslavian friends." He would then continue to Belgrade, then Budapest, where he was a guest of the former Hungarian Minister of Justice Stefan Barscy and members of the Association of Gül Baba, a group dedicated to the construction of a mosque near the tomb of a fifteenth-century dervish saint in Budapest. Throughout the interwar period Arslan seems to have had regular contact with Hungarian Muslims and with

Huszein Hilmi Durics, who came to be recognized as their Mufti in 1934–1936. In the 1930s he would continue writing letters and making occasional visits, encouraging Hungarian Muslims to continue their attempts to build a mosque at Gül Baba and assuring them that they enjoyed the support of the Muslim world, with which he appears to have been their primary link.[66]

The small Muslim community in Budapest consisted of no more than a few hundred Bosnian immigrant workers of humble origins. It had remained unknown in the Muslim world and was largely isolated, writes Popovic, until the early 1930s when Arslan was almost single handedly responsible for the publicity it began receiving in the Arab and Muslim press:

> The situation changed suddenly in 1932, and from that date on we can find a series of notices concerning Hungarian Islam. It must be stressed, however, that on the ground nothing had changed, and that it was nothing other than a campaign begun by the Emir Shakib Arslan, who, while preparing the European Muslim Congress of Geneva (in 1933?) [*sic*], had sought to strengthen the position of this isolated Muslim community of Central Europe.[67]

In this way, Arslan was developing the links of Eastern European Muslims with the Arab East and the greater Muslim world. One of the central events in the development of this trans-regional Islamic consciousness would be the European Congress of Muslims, which Arslan presided in Geneva in September 1935.

The congress was strictly European, in that it brought together about 60 to 70 delegates, all of whom were residents of Europe. If we look at the Permanent Committee that was established after the congress, it consisted of Geneva's prominent Muslims, with Arslan and Jabiri from Syria, Ali al-Ghayati, ʻAbd al-Baqi al-ʻUmari, Zaki ʻAli, and Mahmud Salim al-ʻArafati from Egypt, and a former Iranian prime minister Tabataba'i. The council of delegates, on the contrary, included the leaders of Muslim communities from all of Europe, with Iqbal ʻAli Shah from England, Omar Stewart Rankin from Scotland, Messali Hadj from France, H. v. M. Aly Mohri-Eddine from Switzerland, Mohammad-Aly van Beetem from Holland, Ghassam Zade from Austria, Bernard Barbiellini Amidei from Italy, Huszein Hilmi Durics from Hungary, Jakub Szynkiewicz from Poland, and Dervis Korkut from Yugoslavia. These delegates included an approximately even number of European nationals and of immigrants from Muslim countries. The language of this multinational grouping was officially Arabic, the language of Islam, although delegates also expressed themselves in Turkish, English, German, and French, the latter being most commonly used.[68]

A European Muslim Congress being a unique occurrence, it is not surprising if most speeches concerned local issues. Popular topics included the construction of mosques, the education of children, the rights of Muslims in European countries, and the way in which Muslim communities, most of them religious minorities within their respective states, were treated by their governments. Yet these local issues were Islamic issues, and as such acquired universal relevance. The congress thus asked for contributions from the whole Muslim world to help build a mosque in Warsaw, while individual members expressed the hope of eventually building mosques in Budapest, Amsterdam, and Geneva. Telegrams and press releases in the name of the congress acknowledged the Yugoslav and Polish governments for the favorable treatment of their Muslim populations. The Palestinian question and the holy city of Jerusalem were similarly considered not as political but as religious issues concerning all Muslims, and the congress sent telegrams to all concerned parties. For Western Europe and its nascent Islamic community, the gathering was an early and still limited show of solidarity. For Eastern Europe, the congress was part of ongoing efforts by Arslan, Hajj Amin al-Husayni, and others, to maintain and revive its links with the wider Muslim world in the aftermath of the end of the Ottoman Empire.

Several prominent figures from Eastern Europe were in attendance at the congress. One of the most respected was Jakub Szynkewicz, a Pole of Tatar origin, who had earned a doctoral degree with a dissertation on "Rabghuzi's Syntax" in Berlin and was in close relationship with Georg Kampffmeyer, chairman of the German Society for Islamic Studies, which Szynkewicz had helped found. He was highly regarded by members of German academia, and the society's journal *Die Welt des Islams* described the qualities most appreciated by his German hosts:

> Without doubt, Dr. Jakub Szynkiewicz is one of the most capable Muslims in Europe, highly gifted in organization, of great capabilities, a man, who with his powerful and pure Islamic strength of character combines reason and an extraordinary spiritual culture.[69]

In 1925 Szynkewicz was elected by the Pan-Polish Muslim Congress Mufti of Poland, a position which he used to create links between Poland's Muslim community and the rest of the Islamic world.[70] He was, for example, active in the society of Muslim youths in Cairo, and later succeeded in obtaining a grant of land from the Polish government to construct a mosque in Warsaw. Szynkewicz was a member of the Oriental Club in Berlin when Arslan was its president, and later visited Arslan in the winter of 1934–1935.[71] Having attended the Muslim Congress in Cairo in 1926, he headed a Polish delegation to the European Muslim Congress.

The largest delegation at the congress was the 7-member Yugoslav delegation, with its members giving 5 of the 19 speeches. Derviš Korkut, museum curator and editor of a journal in Belgrade, presented the history of Yugoslav Muslims, Vejsil Alisan, president of the Council of Ulama of Uskub, spoke of religious educational organization in Southern Yugoslavia, Džemaludin Čaušević, former president of the Council of Ulama and a statistician, gave details, and Abdul Hamid Huramović, president of the Muslim Association and member of the Oriental Institute of Warsaw, did not speak about Yugoslavia but about Islam in Poland. The Yugoslav delegation was thus not only large but also vocal. Its head was the widely acknowledged leader of the Balkan Muslim world, Salim Muftić,

Mufti of Sarajevo since 1914, president of the Council of Ulama and head of the Bosnian delegation to the Jerusalem congress four years earlier. He was the one to make the first address after Arslan's introduction and a minute of silence in remembrance of Rashid Rida. In an obituary Arslan would describe him as "one of the most eminent notables not only of the Balkans, but of the whole Islamic world."[72]

Outstanding questions about the congress remain. One is tempted to ask why it was a *European* Muslim congress, while all previous congresses were universal in that they were open to all Muslims irrespective of geographic origin. Whatever its reason, this appellation may highlight that Europe was a region possessing its own internal logic. Arslan was conversant in its language, but also had deep and unquestionable roots in Arab culture and in the Islamic revivalist movement. To those in Europe he represented the link to that wider Islamic world in the Arab East. To those in the Arab East, his role was to provide a link in the other direction.

The independent Arab states

While most of the Arab world lay under the dominion of foreign mandatory powers, the kingdoms of the Arab East provided an arena where an Arab and Islamic culture was relatively free to develop. Had Arslan accepted Ibn Saud's offer to bring his family to the Saudi capital and become a high official in his administration,[73] or had he been present and active in local politics in Syria, Lebanon, Iraq, or elsewhere, his perspective on specific social, economic, or cultural policies might have developed. As an international activist based in Geneva, his strategy was to transcend dynastic divisions and apply the ideal of an Arab and Islamic community to the relations between Faisal's kingdom in Iraq, Ibn Saud's kingdom in the Hijaz and Nejd, and Imam Yahya's kingdom in the Yemen. Other regions of the Arab, it was believed, would join this community as their independence progressed.

Although Arslan had supported the Ottoman Empire in the face of Sharif Husayn of Mecca until 1918, he supported Husayn's son, Faisal, in his efforts to unite Iraq and Syria under his throne. Before becoming king of Iraq, Faisal had, for a few short years, enjoyed the position of king of Syria before the French mandate was imposed in 1920. These few years, however, remained in the imagination of nationalists and Istiqlalists such as 'Adil Arslan, Shakib's brother, and Ihsan al-Jabiri, his associate in Geneva, as a golden time when Syria had been ruled by an Arab monarch with its nationalist intelligentsia charting the future. Although he became king of Iraq, the memory of Faisal remained in the mind of many Syrian nationalists, and the prime obstacle to his claim for the throne of Syria seemed to be the French mandate.

Much more immediately achievable were Arslan's plans to build a united Arab state. These were outlined in a series of articles, and lobbied for in the course of several trips and negotiations that sought to create "an alliance of the three independent Arab states" as a first step to Arab unity.[74] The central point of contention was the personal rivalry between Ibn Saud, King of the Hijaz and Nejd, and Faisal of Iraq, whose father the Sharif Husayn of Mecca, had been expelled from the Hijaz by Ibn Saud. In 1929, Arslan made a highly publicized pilgrimage to Mecca, where he spent the summer as the personal guest of Ibn Saud in the latter's summer residence in Taef. From there he worked on improving relations between Ibn Saud and his neighbors to the North and South. Although little is known about the specific discussions of that summer, the most pressing need seems to have been the creation of trust between the two foes. Arslan takes credit for conceiving the project with King Faisal at Antibes in Southern France in early 1930,[75] which resulted in the signing of a treaty of friendship on February 22, 1930.

More than a loose treaty, however, Arslan had hoped for a true alliance, military and otherwise, between the two Arab states. On the morning of Faisal's death, September 7, 1933, Arslan had a one-and-one-half hour meeting with the Iraqi monarch, most of which was spent discussing plans for strengthening the pan-Arab alliance with Ibn Saud. According to Arslan, Faisal seems to have been so enthused by the idea that he is said to have told him: "I may be the personal adversary of Ibn Saud, but for the good of the Arabs I must be his brother. Actually, without Ibn Saud the center of the Arabic peninsula would have fallen in anarchy. Had Ibn Saud not been there, we would have had to create him." Two years after Faisal's death, the project of a more thorough alliance was realized between the successor to the throne of Iraq, Ghazi, and Ibn Saud, later to be joined by Imam Yahya of Yemen. Arslan calculated that the alliance of these 3 nations created a bloc of 18 million subjects, which would rise to 40 million once Syria-Palestine and Egypt participated.[76]

If the ambitions of Ibn Saud had been successfully accommodated with those of Faisal and his successor, the relations between Ibn Saud's and his Southern neighbor, Imam Yahya of the much smaller state of the Yemen, only became more belligerent. Already in 1929, during his pilgrimage to Mecca, Arslan had discussed the contentious issue of the province of Asir, on which both monarchs laid claims. The matter came to a confrontation in 1934, when armies of about fifty thousand men from each side clashed. The war between two of a handful of independent Arab or Islamic monarchs was understandably a grave threat to pan-Arab and pan-Islamic solidarity.

Shortly after the beginning of the conflict, the permanent bureau of the Islamic Congress in Jerusalem under the leadership of Hajj Amin al-Husayni named a four-man delegation to arbitrate between both sovereigns. The committee consisted of Amin al-Husayni himself, Muhammad 'Ali, a former minister in the Egyptian government, Hashim al-Atasi, the acknowledged leader of Syria's independence movement, and Shakib Arslan. The arbiters were eventually successful in tempering Ibn Saud's military ardor, but for Arslan, even in the midst of the fiercest fighting, Arabs could be seen engaging in nothing other than a family feud, "for the Arab nation is the Arab Nation, always forming a single bloc, sharing the same feelings and traditions. This unity of customs and of feelings surpasses all other considerations for the Arabs."[77] It is in the light of such words and actions that Arslan's postwar reputation as a hero of Arab nationalism can be understood.

In 1929, most probably in a rhetorical flourish, Ibn Saud nominated Arslan as his "ambassador in Europe."[78] Arslan acted, however, less like an ambassador than like a senior counselor. As previously mentioned, his personal loyalty was to the Arab and Islamic cause, and he entertained brotherly relations with each monarch as long as they served that cause. Yet to his last days, he not only arbitrated between the monarchs of the Arab Peninsula, but advised these formerly Bedouin tribal leaders, ignorant as they were of modern European politics and of how to maneuver in the international arena. In Arslan's last days, during the Second World War, he sent information bulletins with detailed information about the international situation and the progress of the war to Ibn Saud and in Imam Yahya.[79] With his Saudi passport, and enjoying a high statute with Ibn Saud, at least until the mid-1930s, Arslan could have gone to live with his family in the Hijaz as the monarch's advisor and honorary guest. Yet something must have kept him in Switzerland where he was under the eye of the secret service of half a dozen nations, homesick, and perpetually in debt. It may have been the appreciation that distance allowed the Arab "prince of eloquence" to look at the branches of the Arab and Islamic world from aloof, granting him a unique role at the forefront of what he saw as the road to its reunification.

The Maghreb

Most often understood as a pan-Arab leader coming from the Eastern centers of the Arab world, Arslan's appearances in the history of the Maghreb are limited to a few scattered paragraphs describing the unique attraction that he exerted upon nationalist movements of the region. The most complete account of his influence upon the Maghreb remains Cleveland's general chapter on his mentorship of the young North African nationalists. Yet specific studies, such as Merad's analysis of the Algerian Islamic reformist journal *al-Šihāb*, or Halstead's interviews with Moroccan nationalists in the late 1950s and early 1960s, give an important insight into Arslan's role, and into how he was perceived by the Moroccan nationalist elite. The analysis of *La Nation Arabe*, combined with a knowledge of Arslan's networks in the Muslim, Arab, and European world, reveal a surprising role for Arslan. Throughout the interwar era, he shaped the doctrines and strategies of nationalist students in Paris, of the ulama from each region, and of Islamic revivalist thinkers in the Maghreb.[80]

Morocco's nascent nationalist movement consisted of highly educated young men, often from prestigious families, who were marginalized by the overwhelming influence of the French protectorate and the general apathy of the Moroccan public. The catalyst that allowed them to ignite Moroccan nationalism was the promulgation of the Berber Dahir on May 16, 1931.[81] The Berber Dahir is significant in that Berbers, who had been Islamized in the early days of Islam, and were thus placed under the jurisdiction of Islamic law and liable to Islamic courts, were now placed under the jurisdiction of French courts and Berber tribunals that applied a revived traditional Berber law antecedent to Islam. To Muslims throughout the world, it seemed that France was seeking to de-Islamize the Berbers as a first step to their Christianization. These fears were fanned by the increased presence of French missionaries in rural areas of Morocco, and by the prohibition for Moroccans from the "Arab regions" of going to the "Berber regions" without a special permit, which prevented Muslim clerics in the cities from maintaining contact with the Berbers. While some saw in this a policy of de-Islamization, others saw it as another application of the colonial policy of "divide and rule."

The Berber Dahir had three consequences. The first is the *yā laṭīf* ("O God!") incantations, usually recited in mosques at times of great calamity. Previously reserved for such disasters as plagues of locusts, the *yā laṭīf* was for the first time harnessed by the nationalists for political action. Beginning in the great mosque of Rabat on a Friday after the communal prayer, the *yā laṭīf* incantations spread throughout Morocco, a powerful means for the nationalist elite to impart to the masses its sense of crisis at the breaking of the union uniting Berbers and Arabs under the banner of Islam. Second, as a result of the widespread *yā laṭīf* incantations and the protests that accompanied them, the young Moroccan Sultan agreed to receive a delegation to discuss the grievances of the population. The future Muhammad V of Morocco was young, educated completely under the protectorate, and did not yet have the will or the power to oppose the French administration. This first meeting with the nationalists, however, was a first step to what years later become an alliance crucial to both the independence movement and the Moroccan monarchy.

Yet the slow rise in the political consciousness of the Moroccan masses and of the Sultan would only bear fruit in later years. The immediate pressure exerted on the French came from the third measure, the international campaign. A storm of protest from the Arab and Islamic world caused committees in defense of Moroccan Muslims to spring up from Java to Berlin, an economic boycott to be enacted against French goods in India, and a petition by the ulama of al-Azhar asking the Egyptian King Fuad to personally intervene before the French government.[82] International organisms found themselves submerged by telegrams of protests and, in the words of Julien, Shakib Arslan "integrated Muslim Morocco into Islamic ritual by making all of the faithful participate in the trials of their Maghrebi brothers."[83]

Arslan denounced the Dahir in a dozen articles in *La Nation Arabe* and wrote in the Arabic press, mostly in the Egyptian journal *al-Fatḥ*. In successive analyses of French policy in Morocco, Arslan compared the Ottoman Empire's religious policy, which allowed each religious minority to be ruled by its own laws, with the attempt by republican France to separate the Berbers from the Arabs under the pretext that they had different ethnic customs.[84] Arslan was not only active in publicizing the issue in the press, but was central in drawing the resolution sent by the Islamic Congress held in Jerusalem in 1931 to the League of Nations. Arslan provided the link between the congress members, and namely its president Hajj Amin al-Husayni, and Makki Nasiri, the young Moroccan nationalist who drew up the resolution with Arslan and Jabiri in Geneva. Approved by the Congress, the resolution was signed by its president and forwarded to the League of Nations.[85] In the end the protest about the Berber Dahir attained much more dramatic proportions outside of Morocco than inside, where French authorities maintained a relative calm. The prime reason, writes Le Tourneau, was Arslan:

> This incomparable conductor sparked throughout the entire Muslim world a concert of protests against French politics in Morocco, a frenzy that was in marked contrast with the calm that was reigning inside of the country. Because of Shakib Arslan, Morocco was at the forefront of Islamic events.[86]

The results had both immediate and more long-term repercussions. In immediate terms, the international protests contributed to placing the Islamic world and the anticlerical European left squarely against the Berber Dahir, leading to its replacement in 1934.[87] Indirectly, however, the Berber Dahir awakened a new consciousness among Moroccan and North African nationalists. A few years later, on October 4, 1937, Arslan was second vice-president of the Bludan Congress against Zionist immigration to Palestine, when throughout Morocco's cities protests were organized to mark Morocco's solidarity with the Palestinian cause.[88] Before 1930, such a mass demonstration of Arab and Islamic unity between inhabitants of the Northwest tip of Africa and those around Damascus and Jerusalem would have been almost unimaginable. No one more than Arslan could claim credit for sowing the seeds of a transnational consciousness, manifested as it was in the protest against the Berber Dahir.

Arslan's active involvement in Moroccan politics can be dated to 1930. At that time, the pages of *La Nation Arabe* announced that Arslan would make an academic visit to the Iberian peninsula to prepare a work on the history of Muslim Spain.[89] In addition to its scholarly purposes, however, the trip constituted an occasion to travel to Morocco and meet some of its most prominent young nationalists, future leaders of the independence period and the postcolonial era. Arslan first stopped in Paris, where he was met at the train station by ʻAllal al-Fasi and Balafrej, described by Halstead as the two highest ranking members of the Moroccan nationalist movement.[90] Although both were students in Paris at this time, Fasi came from a prominent family of Fez and had received a traditional education at the Qarawiyin University, while Ahmad Balafrej was from Rabat and had received a completely Western education at French elite schools. Both young students, who were to lead Morocco to independence in 1956, are known to have visited Arslan in Geneva. Yet Balafrej, the future founder of the Moroccan Istiqlal Party, stands out as one of the dearest "spiritual sons" of the Amir. Halstead remarks that despite having been so thoroughly gallicized in French schools, Balafrej is said to have been "more profoundly affected politically by Arslan than by his formal education."[91] Arslan did not limit his relationships to politics or even to the intellectual life of his young followers. In response to an interrogation from the Swiss police, and asked why he sent Balafrej

500 Swiss Francs whenever he could afford it, Arslan answered that "I came to his aid because I consider him a little like my son."[92] Of Arslan's "spiritual sons," many came from the Maghreb.

Arslan could only stay for a few days in Paris, and soon left for Madrid and Southern Spain. After completing their examinations, Fasi and Balafrej joined him there, and all three of them visited the convent at Escorial to examine Arabic documents relating to the period of Islamic rule in Spain.[93] From there Arslan proceeded to Tangier, where he was quickly notified of a decree expelling him from the French zone, and pursued his journey to Tetouan, a neighboring city under Spanish control. In Tetouan he spent four days at the house of 'Abd al-Salam Bennuna, an acknowledged leader, former Minister of the Makhzen, and founder and director of an indigenous electrical company and free school.[94] Arslan had been in contact with Bennuna long before meeting him, for both must have been members of the same Islamic reformist networks in the Arab world. After 1931 and before his death in 1935, Bennuna went to see Arslan once, stopping in Geneva on his return from Berlin.[95] During his stay in Tetouan, receptions welcomed Arslan as a prominent literary figure from the Arab East whose reputation and writings had long preceded his arrival. His presence not only flattered the Moroccans, but helped bridge the gaps separating the heterogeneous independence movements in Tetouan, Rabat, Fez, and throughout Morocco.

Both in Geneva and when he went to Paris, Arslan entertained numerous North African visitors and students, keeping the French secret service busy. Arslan even took one of the Moroccan nationalist leaders, Mohamed al-Ouezzani, as his private secretary in Geneva from September 1932 until the summer of 1933.[96] In 1936, the Spanish civil war between General Franco's insurgents and the Republican loyalists provided a splendid opportunity to play off one faction against another. Arslan traveled to Madrid where he was joined by Ouezzani and 'Umar 'Abd al-Jalil to offer help against Franco in return for the independence of Northern Morocco.[97]

While the campaign against the Berber Dahir found expression in the pages of *La Nation Arabe*, *al-Fatḥ* of Cairo and other journals, by the 1930s Arslan was highly experienced in political activism on the European scene, had extensive networks in Europe, the Arab world, and the Islamic world, and was probably the most prolific Arab writer of his age, with a regular stream of articles appearing in the Arab press. All of this brought undeniable benefit to young Moroccans seeking an Arab-Islamic identity and an anticolonial strategy. When Ouezzani engaged in a conflict with Fassi and Balafrej, Arslan admonished his "spiritual sons" to exhibit moderation and unity, and when circumstances required it, Arslan became a father figure, financially assisting his protégés, despite his own precarious financial position.

In addition to the Islamic reformists, Arslan seems to have enjoyed the respect of some in the younger and largely secular generation. With the French socialists in power and the Franco-Syrian Treaty placing Syria on the road to independence in 1937, Arslan traveled to a hero's welcome in Paris. A special banquet was given in his honor by the Moroccan nationalist movement, and on this occasion the secular leader of Tunisia's independence movement, the future President of Tunisia Habib Bourguiba, devoted an entire issue of his nationalist journal *L'Action tunisienne* to Arslan.[98]

However, the most spectacular and oft-cited example of Arslan's influence over the young nationalists is the "conversion" of Messali al-Hajj during his stay in Geneva. The young and radical leader of Algerian workers in France was the founder of the Étoile Nord-Africaine, which was a close and faithful ally of the French Communist party. The French court having condemned him to yet another term in prison, Messali al-Hajj found refuge before Arslan in Geneva, where he stayed for half a year in 1936. It is difficult to know what privately occurred during those few months, but when Messali al-Hajj reappeared in Paris, he had traded his militant Communist stance advocating Algerian independence for an equally adamant Arab nationalist and Islamic approach to the problem. In 1933, Messali's party the Étoile Nord-Africaine published in its French language journal *El Ouma* a new political program declaring its "fraternity in the unity of Islam," but without abandoning its adamant nationalist and proletarian stand.[99] Messali's Islamic allegiance had superseded his Communist allegiance, resulting in mutual accusations and a break with the Communist party.[100] Joining himself to the Algerian ulama, to Tunisia's New Destour Party, and to the Action Marocaine party of the Moroccan reformers, writes Julien, Messali "rallied to the solid, prudent and skillful program defended by the leaders of the Maghreb parties with spiritual allegiance to Shakib Arslan. The revolutionary had given way to the Muslim."[101]

Throughout the Maghreb, Arslan is known to have been in contact with leading Islamic reformers. In Libya Arslan entertained an intimate friendship with Sidi Ahmad al-Sharif al-Sanusi, leader of the Sanusiyya tariqa and of the resistance against Italian colonization: "For 20 years, our correspondence did not cease for more than two months at most, not to mention the time that we lived together in Mersin [Southern Turkey]." Arslan was, however, more than a counselor to independence movements, for in studying the contents of the Algerian reformist journal *al-Šihāb*, Ali Merad engages in an unprecedented appraisal of Arslan's influence within the circle of Ibn Badis' Algerian Islamic reformist movement:

> The Emir Shakib Arslan exercised such intellectual seduction and moral and political influence on the [editorial] team of *Šihāb* that it is impossible to analyze the cultural doctrine of the Algerian reformists without taking into account the thought of the Emir. Since he settled down in Switzerland (Geneva-Lausanne), in the aftermath of the First World War, and especially since he began to publish *La Nation Arabe*, Shakib Arslan became not only a master, but a true oracle to the Algerian elite of Arab culture. Mentor for some, director of conscience for others, counselor whose advice was received with humble gratitude, orator whose language made sensitive souls fall into ecstasy, writer whose fluid and pure prose was a delectation for all lovers of the beauty of the classical tongue, Shakib Arslan was all of this at the same time, and even more.[102]

Perhaps more so than most other figures of his time, Shakib Arslan's Arab, Ottoman, and European culture allowed him to exercise a varied and multifaceted influence upon those who knew him.

La Nations Arabe was not only read in Paris, but despite its proscription in all French mandates and colonies, it continued to be smuggled into Morocco, where it was known to a relatively wide audience of nationalists.[103] Yet with regard to the Maghreb, it is difficult to characterize Arslan as a pan-Arab, for he was ideologically much less so than many others.[104] He advocated an Eastern Arab nation that included Egypt, and encouraged the countries of the Maghreb to cooperate and establish as many links as possible, both among themselves and with the rest of the Arab and Islamic world. Yet for tactical reasons, and partly because he feared that in his time it might lead to a new form of intra-Arab colonialism, Arslan did not favor an Arab nation that would extend from the Gulf to Morocco. For such a moderate stance, Arslan was the subject of virulent attacks by such pan-Arabs as Sulayman Baruni.[105] Although outside of the concern of this paper, it may be said that Arslan's identity lay more in a cultural form of Arabism than with pan-Arabism, and most of all in the Islamic revivalist movement. To young students from the Maghreb, he offered a modern and Islamic doctrine capable of adapting their complex relationship with modern West, which they both absorbed and rejected, and their awakening Arab and Islamic identity.

The Manarists

Although this chapter has thus far adopted a regional division of Arslan's network, this section will refer not to a region but to a school of thought. While the Islamic reformer Rashid Rida certainly had a role in Syrian nationalism, his main role was neither in Syria nor in Egypt but within the world of *al-Manār* and of the ideas that it propagated in the Islamic world. Similarly, while Muhammad ʻAbduh, Muhammad ʻAli Taher, and Ahmad Shawqi were all Egyptians, they addressed themselves to the whole Islamic world and to all Arabic readers. Most restless of all was Afghani, and it is to him that Arslan is most often compared.

The process which would bring Arslan out of Lebanese mountain society began when he was sixteen and met Muhammad ʻAbduh, who in 1886 was lecturing in Beirut. Rashid Rida met Arslan in ʻAbduh's classes and, in the words of Arslan, "the links of friendship that have united us for forty years were caused by our having the same leader."[106] A few years later, in 1890, Arslan was introduced to ʻAbduh's circle in Cairo, to Saʻd Zaghlul, ʻAli Yusuf, and the literary and political elite of Egyptian society. For Arslan, who was known as a close associate of Rida and a frequent contributor to *al-Manār*, it is more than probable that after ʻAbduh's death, the network of *al-Manār* continued to provide Arslan with links throughout the Islamic world.

On his way back from a trip to Paris in 1889, Arslan stopped in Istanbul and met Afghani.[107] Upon Afghani and ʻAbduh's teachings, and in association with Rida, he was to strike the ideological roots that anchored his fluid and geographically diffuse network. Contemporary observers agree that it is Arslan's perpetual adherence to a cause that provided him with the unflinching continuity that ran through his painfully long exile, his strategic alliances with European powers that often bordered on intrigue, and his network that included rulers of the Ottoman Empire and Arab nationalists, antagonistic Arab kings, and links with Communist, Fascist and capitalist states.[108]

Except at one time in their life, during Rida's days in the Ottoman Decentralization Committee which competed with the Ottoman state, evidence shows Rida and Arslan in frequent consultation regarding both political philosophy and strategy. Before leaving his country to engage on his expatriate existence in Egypt, next to ʿAbduh and as editor of the journal *al-Manār*, Arslan was one of two people that Rida turned to for advice.[109] Yet once both were exiled, Arslan was more often than not barred from spending time in Egypt and their chances to meet were rare. They occasionally did, such as during the meeting of the Syrian–Palestinian delegation in Geneva in 1921, and the short time Arslan was able to spend in Rida's house during his one-day special permission to land in Egypt in 1929, but such chances were fleeting and often took place under conditions of tight security surrounding Arslan.[110] After Rida's death in 1935, Arslan promised a commemorative work based on their close collaboration, most of it by correspondence:

> Having had the same master, having been bonded together for 40 years, having had a continuous correspondence without any secrets left untold, we have promised, in our memorial writings on our very dear and illustrious friend, a special work on him, which will be entitled *The Sayyid Rashid Rida or a Fraternity of Forty Years*. The Arab press has already noted this promise, which we will strive to carry out as faithfully as we have carried out our promise concerning our other friend Ahmad Shawqi, the greatest contemporary Arab poet.[111]

Arslan's commemorative work for Ahmad Shawqi was written in 1932 and entitled *Shawqi, or a Friendship of Forty Year*s. Shawqi and Arslan first met as young poets in the student district of Paris in 1889. Arslan had already engaged in a political career that would lead him to abandon literature, and Shawqi was at the beginning of a literary career that would make him one of the most famed Arab poets of the century.[112] Arslan's relationship with Shawqi was literary, and it highlights Arslan not as a politically involved activist, but as *amīr al-bayān*, a literary phenomenon of his age, who was much read and appreciated:

> Shawqi is a living dead whose body alone is absent from us but whose soul and spirit, in communion with millions upon millions of souls, will remain eternally as long as there will remain on this planet something called "the Arab language."[113]

Arslan claims to have chosen the title of Shawqi's first diwan of poetry, "We have parted physically but remain united in mind and heart," which makes for an accurate description of Arslan's exiled existence and his relationship with his closest friends.[114]

Conclusion

In eschewing a geographical division of Arslan's network when describing the "Manarists" there lies the possibility for an alternative approach. Arslan's network can be seen as operating on three ideological planes, linking the intellectual currents of Arabism, Islamism, and anticolonialism. The anticolonial network brought together those colonized who were unhappy with their fate, anticolonial activists in colonial countries, and non-colonial countries. Within its framework can be placed all independentist movements, Arslan's links with the anticolonial left in colonial countries, and the state institution in non-colonial or semi-colonial countries. This included Mussolini in Italy, which had few colonies in the Arab and Muslim world, and Germany, which had none. Although French socialists might have cringed at the thought of being lumped with the Fascist regimes, from the perspective of Arslan, they all served the anticolonial cause.

The second network can be referred to as that of Arabism. It regrouped all Arabic speakers, yet did not call for their political union. Arslan's foreseeable goal was to unite the three independent states of Ibn Saud in the Hijaz and Nejd, Imam Yahya in the Yemen, and King Faisal in Iraq. This initial union was later to be joined by the states in geographic Syria and by Egypt, creating a larger Eastern Arab state. There is no evidence to show that union with the Maghreb was thought to be feasible or even desirable. Often using the term "the Arab nation," namely as the title of his French language journal, Arslan has frequently been labeled an Arab nationalist. Yet Arslan's Arab nation drew from Arslan's multifaceted and complex existence, blending into his anticolonial network for strategic reasons, and striking its deepest roots in the Islamic network.

The network of Islamic revivalism clearly concerned all Muslims, but was centered upon the Islamic revivalist movements of each region. Arslan's response was not specifically directed toward the redefinition of Islam or the adaptation of Islamic legal codes to contemporary conditions. This was left to those with a more traditional Islamic education. Arslan, the product of a French, American, and Ottoman civil education, had a different role to play. Muslim students and professionals in Europe, and the newly educated elites inside the Muslim world, were yearning for a worldview that did not see the Islamic religion as flowing counter to the modern world. Europe was important in that for all Muslim students or workers who went there, it provided a stage where the Islamic worldview and Western modernity came in contact. Arslan's network helped Islamic reformists who had little knowledge of Europe to deal with the complexities of European politics, while reassuring nationalist leaders such as Balafrej or Messali al-Hajj that Islam could be a contemporary force in both the personal and public sphere.

It thus contributed to creating links to outside worlds, outside of geographic regions but also outside of the cognitive categories of East and West, Islam and Christianity, and tradition and modernity. It opened its members unto the new opportunities of a wider, interrelated, and contemporary world.

Arslan's network served multiple purposes with regards to the Islamic and non-Islamic world, the Arab and non-Arab world, and the struggle against colonialism. It was there, and it was used to link people belonging to different networks together. It impressed upon many a new form of Arab and Islamic consciousness, it had an impact on the history of the region, and it proclaimed the principles of the Islamic revival and the political existence of Arabs. Yet we must consider the possibility that Arslan's network did not fulfill a solely instrumentalist function. The address made by Salim Muftić at the European Muslim Congress points in a different direction. Muftić states that Bosnian Muslims "remain in a perfect communion of thought and feeling with all of their coreligionists in the Orient as well as the Occident, and in good fortune as well as in plight."[115] This points to the possibility that the creation of a global umma was in itself a goal of Shakib Arslan, independently from any good that may be derived from it. The construction of Shakib Arslan's network, to the extent that it was principally an Islamic network, was not only justified by its impact upon the Islamic world, but by its very existence.

Notes

1 William L. Cleveland, *Islam Against the West: Shakib Arslan and the Campaign for Islamic Nationalism* (Austin, TX: University of Texas, 1985), xxi.

2 These include Juliette Bessis, "Chékib Arslan et les mouvements nationalistes au Maghreb," *Revue historique* 526 (1978): 467–489; Cleveland, *Islam Against the West, passim*; Axel Havemann, "Between Ottoman Loyalty and Arab 'Independence': Muhammad Kurd 'Alī, Ğirği Zaydān, and Šakīb Arslān," *Quaderni di Studi Arabi* 5–6 (1987–1988): 347–356; Martin Kramer, *Arab Awakening and Islamic Revival: The Politics of Ideas in the Middle East* (New Brunswick, NJ: Transaction, 1996); and Marie-Renée Mouton, "Le congrès syrio-palestinien de Genève (1921)," *Relations internationales* 19 (Fall 1979): 313–328.

3 For the index of proper names and journal titles in *La Nation Arabe*, see Raja Adal, *La Nation Arabe: Contents and Index* (Tokyo: Islamic Area Studies, 2002).

4 From Sharabasi's interview with Salima Arslan in 1954. Aḥmad Šarabāṣī, *Amīr al-bayān Šakīb Arslān* (Cairo: Dār al-kitāb al-'arabi, 1963), 125–126.

5 Reprint, *La Nation Arabe* (England: Archive Editions, 1988).

6 Chekib Arslan, "A propos de l'Éthiopie: La situation des Musulmans de ce pays. Document écrasant," *La Nation Arabe* 6/12–13 (September–November 1936): 691–692.

7 Hasan Kayali, *Arabs and Young Turks: Ottomanism, Arabism, and Islamism in the Ottoman Empire, 1908–1918* (Berkeley, CA: University of California Press, 1997), 116–143, 211.

8 Chekib Arslan, "Sur le Bolchevisme: L'Éternelle légende de l'influence bolcheviste sur le réveil national du monde musulman," *La Nation Arabe* 3/10–12 (October–December 1932): 29–30. Translation mine.

9 Chekib Arslan, "La mort du Patriarche maronite," *La Nation Arabe* 2/10–11 (November–December): 53–54.

10 Chekib Arslan, "La mort de Kémal Ataturk," *La Nation Arabe* 8/20–21 (September–December 1938): 1081. Translation mine.

11 Yamauchi Masayuki, *Nattoku shinakatta otoko: Enveru Pasha, Chū Tō kara Chūō Ajia he* [Enver Pasha, the Unsatisfied Man: from the Middle East to Central Asia] (Tokyo: Iwanami Shōten, 1999), 69, 284–288.

12 Ibid., 69, 292.

13 Letter from Shakib Arslan to Enver Paşa, March 11, 1921, cited in Yamauchi, *Nattoku shinakatta otoko* 326.

14 Kayali, *Arabs and Young Turks*, 3.

15 Mouton, "Le congrès syro-palestinien de Genève (1921)," 321, 322.

16 Philip S. Khoury, *Syria and the French Mandate: The Politics of Arab Nationalism, 1920–1945* (London: I. B. Tauris, 1987), 231.

17 Chekib Arslan, "La « Nation Arabe » privée pour le moment de la collaboration de notre cher collègue M. Djabri," *La Nation Arabe* 8/16–17 (January–April 1938): 910.

18 Mouton, "Le congrès syrio-palestinien de Genève (1921)," 315 n. 7.

19 Ihsan el-Djabri, "La Syrie du 8 mars au 26 juillet 1920," *La Nation Arabe* 1 [2] (April 1930): 82 n. 1. It was not Riyad al-Sulh himself, as writes Mouton, but his father Riza who was minister of the Interior in Faisal's cabinet.

20 Cleveland, *Islam Against the West*, 49.

21 Khoury, *Syria and the French Mandate*, 222.

22 Ibid., 222, 227.

23 Chekib Arslan, "L'Armée Rouge: instrument de la Révolution Mondiale. Le monde civilisé en danger," *La Nation Arabe* 5/4 (March–April 1935): 281.

24 David Ben Gurion, *My Talks with Arab Leaders*, ed. Misha Louvish, trans. Aryeh Rubinstein and Misha Louvish (New York: The Third Press, 1973 [1967]), 28, 33. The meeting is described by al-Jabiri in Ihsan el-Djabri, *La Nation Arabe* (November–December, 1934): 144–146; and by Ben Gurion in his *My Talks with Arab Leaders*, 35–40.

25 Kramer, *Arab Awakening and Islamic Revival*, 109.

26 Khoury, *Syria and the French Mandate*, 227–240.

27 Ibid., 240.

28 Arslan writes that the 1925–1926 treaty draft differed almost in nothing other than details from the Franco-Syrian treaty signed in October 1936. Chekib Arslan, "Le traité franco-syrien," *La Nation Arabe* 6/12–13 (September–November 1936): 642.

29 Ibid., 642–643.

30 Chekib Arslan, "Il y a, paraît-il, un comité franco-musulman.: Toujours l'Afrique du Nord," *La Nation Arabe* 5/2 (November–December 1934): 133–134.

31 In "Factionalism among Syrian nationalists during the French mandate," Khoury depends on an unpublished manuscript by Edmond Rabbath, a student in Paris at the time of the Arslan-de Jouvenel meeting. This document describes the November 1925 meeting, during which Arslan's moderation successfully impressed the French High Commissioner de Jouvenel, who asked for more time to work out an accord. Although Khoury does not mention the second meeting in 1926, *La Nation Arabe* sheds light on its three working sessions, and on Arslan's conclusion as to why the talks failed. Chekib Arslan, "Le traité franco-syrien," 641–648; and by the same author, "Le départ de M. Ponsot," *La Nation Arabe* 4/7–9 (July–September 1933): 37–38. Arslan's version of events is partly confirmed by the French socialist Robert-Jean Longuet's article in *Clarté* of March 1938, reproduced in Robert-Jean Longuet, "A propos de la Syrie," *La Nation Arabe* 8/16–17 (January–April 1938): 891–897; by E. Lévi-Provençal, "L'Émir Shakib Arslan," *Cahiers de l'Orient contemporain* 9–10 (1st and 2nd trimesters, 1947), 5–19; and by Meir Zamir in his *The Formation of Modern Lebanon* (Ithaca, IL: Cornell University Press, 1985), 198.

32 Bureau politique, Etat-major, theatre d'operations de l'Afrique du Nord, *Contribution à l'étude de l'activité politique de l'émir Chekib Arslan*, 29H35 (Aix-en-Provence, 1940), 28–29. Despite his conciliatory tone regarding the treaty, Arslan seems to have had serious reservations, both about drawing the frontiers of Greater Lebanon without a plebiscite and about abandoning Iskanderun to Turkey. See Chekib Arslan, "Le traité franco-syrien," 645; and by the same author, "L'ennemi de la France que je suis?" *La Nation Arabe* 8/16–17 (January–April, 1938): 801–802.
33 Cleveland, *Islam Against the West*, 86.
34 Ibid., 69.
35 "Arslan, Shakib," in Reeva S. Simon, Philip Mattar, and Richard W. Bulliet, eds, *Encyclopedia of the Modern Middle East* (New York: Macmillan, 1996), 37–39. The same definition appears in David Commins, *Historical Dictionary of Syria* (Lanham, MD: Scarecrow, 1996), 37–39.
36 Kramer, *Arab Awakening and Islamic Revival*, 7.
37 Albert Hourani, *Arabic Thought in the Liberal Age: 1798–1939* (Cambridge: Cambridge University Press, 1983): 67–95.
38 Cleveland, *Islam Against the West*, 11.
39 Translation from Arabic is mine.
40 Chekib Arslan, "L'ennemi de la France que je suis?:" 809.
41 Chekib Arslan, "La mort de l'orientaliste italien Nalino," *La Nation Arabe* 8/20–21 (September–December 1938): 1192–1193.
42 R. L. Melka, "Max Freiherr von Oppenheim: Sixty Years of Scholarsip and Political Intrigue in the Middle East," *Middle Eastern Studies* 1973/1: 81.
43 Ministère Public Fédéral Suisse, "Procès-verbal d'audition," Doc. C10.7 E 4320 (B) 1984/29 vol. 13 (Geneva, October 6, 1938), 3.
44 Chekib Arslan, "Qu'est-ce que vous voulez qu'un homme d'Etat français dise de Guillaume II ?," *La Nation Arabe* 5/4 (March–April 1935): 249. Translation mine.
45 Ibid., 254.
46 Widmer, "Emir Shakib Arslan," *Die Welt des Islams* 19 (1937): 7.
47 Chekib Arslan, "La grammaire arabe est la grammaire la plus classique et la plus parfaite," *La Nation Arabe* 5/3 (January–February 1935): 194.
48 Widmer, "Emir Shakib Arslan." For Arslan's reaction to Widmer's article see Chekib Arslan, "Notre dette de reconnaissance à l'honorable Pasteur M. Widmer, de Berne," *La Nation Arabe* 8/16–17 (January–April 1938): 898.
49 Widmer, "Emir Shakib Arslan," 3–4.
50 Georg Kampffmeyer, review of *Ḥāḍir al-ʿālam al-islāmī*, by Lothrop Stoddard and annotated by Shakib Arslan, *Die Welt des Islams* 15 (1933): 117–119. Translation mine.
51 Chekib Arslan, "Les Hittites ne sont pas turcs et les Turcs ne sont pas hittites," *La Nation Arabe* 7/14–15 (January–April 1937): 780.
52 Melka, "Max Freiherr von Oppenheim," 81–93.
53 Ibid., 86.
54 Bureau Politique, "Contribution à l'étude de l'activité politique de l'émir Chekib Arslan," 47.
55 Melka, "Max Freiherr von Oppenheim."
56 British Foreign Office, "Letter from R. Graham of the British Embassy in Rome to the Earl of Balfour," June 5, 1922, in A. L. P. Burdett, ed., *Arab Dissident Movements, volume 2: 1905–1920* (England: Archive Editions, 1996), 101.
57 Chekib Arslan, "Les atrocités italiennes fascistes en Tripolitaine," *La Nation Arabe* 2/10–11 (November–December 1931): 47.
58 Chekib Arslan, "Pour supprimer le nomadisme, il n'est pas nécessaire de déposséder la population," *La Nation Arabe* 3/3–4 (March–April 1932): 50.

59 Chekib Arslan, "Omar Moukhtar," *La Nation Arabe* 2/8–9 (September–October 1931): 5–6. Translation mine.
60 "Urkunden: Der Muslimische Kongreß von Europa," *Die Welt des Islams* 17/3–4 (1935): 101.
61 Chekib Arslan, "Le problème éthopien," *La Nation Arabe* 6/8–9 (January–April 1936): 514–515. Translation mine.
62 Chekib Arslan, "Le conflit italo-éthiopien et les arabes [*sic*]: Les musulmans d'Abysinie," *La Nation Arabe* 5/5 (May–June 1935): 309–310.
63 Chekib Arslan, "Qu'est-ce que vous voulez qu'un homme d'Etat français dise de Guillaume II ?," *La Nation Arabe* 5/4 (March–April 1935): 253.
64 The polemic begins with a short introduction by Arslan in Chekib Arslan, "La vérité sur la situation des Musulmans en Bulgarie," *La Nation Arabe* 3/10–12 (October–December 1932): 10–12; this is followed by the argument of Džemalović in Smail Aga Djemalovitch, "Les Musulmans en Bulgarie," *La Nation Arabe* 3/10–12 (October–December 1932): 12–20; the answer by Girard can be found in André Girard, "La situation des Musulmans en Bulgarie," *La Nation Arabe* 4/1–3 (January–March 1933): 39–46; finally comes a counter-reply by Džemalović in Smail Aga Dchemalovitch, "Les musulmans en Bulgarie," *La Nation Arabe* 4/4–6 (April–June 1933): 38–44.
65 Among European journals, other than *La Nation Arabe*, and the reports of Christian missionaries, Popovic mentions *Oriente Moderno*, which tracked information appearing in the Turkish and Arab press. For further information on the controversy between Džemalović and Girard, see Alexandre Popovic, *L'Islam balkanique: Les musulmans du sud-est européen dans la période post-ottomane* (Wiesbaden: Harrassowitz, 1986), 82–85.
66 Bureau Politique, "Contribution à l'étude de l'activité politique de l'émir Chekib Arslan," 18. György Lederer, "Sur l'islam à Budapest," in Stéphane A. Dudoignon and Catherine Servan-Schreiber, eds, *La transmission du savoir dans le monde musulman péripherique* (Istanbul: Isis, forthcoming), 469.
67 Popovic, *L'Islam balkanique*, 191.
68 Chekib Arslan, "Le Congrès Musulman d'Europe," *La Nation Arabe* 6/10–11 (October–November 1935): 417–424.
69 "Urkunden: Der Muslimische Kongreß von Europa," 104. Translation mine.
70 I. Takacs, "Szynkiewicz, Jakub," in Marc Gaborieau, Nicole Grandin, Pierre Labrousse, and Alexandre Popovic, eds, *Dictionnaire biographique des savants et grandes figures du monde musulman périphérique, du XIXe siècle a nos jours*, 1 (Paris: CNRS -EHESS, 1992): 55.
71 Chekib Arslan, "Une mosquée à Varsovie," *La Nation Arabe* 5/5 (May–June 1935): 334.
72 Chekib Arslan, "Pertes très douloureuses," *La Nation Arabe* 8/18–19 (May–August 1938): 1028; by the same author, "Le Congrès Musulman d'Europe," *La Nation Arabe* 5/7 (October–November 1935): 418–424. Alexandre Popovic, "Muftić, Salim," in Marc Gaborieau *et al.*, eds, *Dictionnaire biographique*, 2: 67.
73 "Adā' al-amīr shakīb li-farīḍat al-ḥağğ," *Al-Manār* 30/2 (July 8, 1929): 160.
74 Chekib Arslan, "L'Alliance des trois pays arabes indépendants: L'Etat Seoudite, le Yemen et l'Irak," *La Nation Arabe* 6/8–9 (January–April 1936): 469.
75 Ibid.
76 Ibid., 470–471.
77 Chekib Arslan, "La paix fraternelle entre les deux souverains arabes," *La Nation Arabe* 5/1 (September–October 1934): 40–47.
78 "Adā' al-amīr shakīb li-farīḍat al-ḥağğ," 159.
79 These bulletins were intercepted by the British services, who transferred them on to the French. Bureau Politique, "Contribution à l'étude de l'activité politique de l'émir Chekib Arslan," 51.

80 See John P. Halstead, *Rebirth of a Nation: The Origins and Rise of Moroccan Nationalism, 1912–1944* (Cambridge, MA: Harvard University, 1967); Ali Merad, *Le réformisme musulman en Algérie de 1925 à 1940. Essai d'histoire religieuse et sociale* (Paris: Mouton & Co, 1967).
81 A copy of the Dahir may be found in Halstead, 276–277.
82 Ibid., 184–186.
83 Charles-André Julien, *L'Afrique du Nord en marche: Nationalismes musulmans et souveraineté française* (Paris: René Julliard, 1972), 133.
84 See the first article by Arslan on the Berber Dahir published in two parts as "Tribunaux Berbères," *La Nation Arabe* 1/6–7 (August–September 1930): 22–28 and *La Nation Arabe* 1/8 (October 1930): 5–7.
85 For the nationalist response to the Berber Dahir see Halstead, *Rebirth of a Nation*, 181–186. For a translation of the text of the resolution, see Chekib Arslan, "Résolution concernant la désislamisation des Berbères," *La Nation Arabe* 3/5–6 (May–June 1932): 33–34.
86 Roger Le Tourneau, *Evolution politique de l'Afrique du Nord musulmane, 1920–1961* (Paris: Armand Colin, 1962), 185. Translation mine.
87 For Arslan's comments on the new Dahir, see Chekib Arslan, "Et le fameux Dahir berbère?" *La Nation Arabe* 5/4 (September–October 1934): 63–66.
88 Julien, *L'Afrique du Nord en marche*, 151.
89 For two articles on the history of Arabs in Spain and Southern France, see Chekib Arslan, "A la recherche des vestiges de la civilisation arabe en Espagne," *La Nation Arabe* 1/5 (July 1930): 193–200; and "A la recherche des vestiges arabes en Espagne et dans le Midi de la France," *La Nation Arabe* 2/3 (Mars 1931): 19–31.
90 Halstead, *Rebirth of a Nation*, 165.
91 Ibid., 129. From Halstead's interviews with 'Umar 'Abd al-Jalil, Mahdi Bennuna, and Muhammad al-Fasi in 1959.
92 Ministere Public Federal Suisse, "Procès-verbal d'audition," Doc. C10.7 E 4320 (B) 1984/29 vol. 13 (Geneva, October 14, 1938), 2.
93 Bureau Politique, "Contribution à l'étude de l'activité politique de l'émir Chekib Arslan," 13.
94 Chekib Arslan, "Une Campagne de mensonge," *La Nation Arabe* 2/ 8–9 (September–October 1931): 36.
95 Chekib Arslan, "Une perte très douloureuse: la mort de Hadje Abdessalam Bennouna," *La Nation Arabe* 5/3 (January–February 1935): 209–210.
96 Halstead, *Rebirth of a Nation*, 129. From Halstead's interview with Mohamed Hassan al-Ouezzani in 1959.
97 Ibid., 238. From Halstead's interview with Ahmed Mekouar in 1963.
98 Ibid., 486; for the special issue devoted to Arslan, see Habib Bourguiba, "Un vétéran de la lutte anti-coloniale: l'Emir Chekib Arslan," *L'Action tunisienne*, June 3, 1937.
99 Julien, *L'Afrique du Nord en marche*, 108.
100 Le Tourneau, *Évolution politique*, 327.
101 Julien, 109; for Arslan's opinion on Messali al-Haj, see Chekib Arslan, *La Nation Arabe* (January–April, 1937): 782–784.
102 Merad, *Le réformisme musulman en Algérie*, 365. Translation mine.
103 Halstead, *Rebirth of a Nation*, 127. Halstead's conclusion comes from personal interviews with Messaoud Chiguer, Ibrahim al-Kattani, Mohammed Lyazidi, and Mohamed Hassan al-Ouezzani in 1959.
104 Cleveland's work is the first to portray Arslan as an Islamic revivalist as much as an Arab nationalist. Le Tourneau characterizes Arslan as an "apostle of nationalism," and Halstead writes of Arslan as a " 'secular' Arab nationalist." Le Tourneau, *Evolution Politique*, 71; Halstead, *Rebirth of a Nation*, 127.

105 For the controversy between Arslan and Baruni, see Merad, *Le réformisme musulman en Algérie*, 370. Arslan also advocated a more limited form of Arab union in the pages of *La Nation Arabe*. For example, see Chekib Arslan, "Ils prennent leurs désirs pour des réalités: dissertation d'un Général français sur le Panislamisme et le Panarabisme," *La Nation Arabe* 8/18–19 (May–August 1938): 925–946.

106 Chekib Arslan, "La disparition d'une des plus grandes figures de l'Islam Rachid Ridha," *La Nation Arabe* 5/7 (October–November 1935): 448.

107 Lūṯrūb Studard, *Ḥāḍir al- 'ālam al-islāmī*, trans. 'Ağāğ Nuwayhīḍ, comp. Shakīb Arslān, 4 vols. (Beirut: Dār al-fikr 1971), 1–2: 298. This is the Arabic translation of Lothrop Stoddard's *The New World of Islam* (New York: Charles Scribner's Sons, 1922). It is so extensively annotated by Shakib Arslan that it became several times the size of the English original, and one of Arslan's major works.

108 See Cleveland, *Islam Against the West*; Kramer, *Arab Awakening and Islamic Revival.*

109 Chekib Arslan, "La disparition d'une des plus grandes figures de l'Islam Rachid Ridha," *La Nation Arabe* 5/7 (October–November 1935): 448. The other was 'Abd al-Qadir Kabbani, a notable from Beirut.

110 Arslan's permission to stop in Egypt was only obtained after a special intervention before Hafiz Afifi, the Egyptian foreign minister and friend of Arslan from before his move to Europe. "Adā' al-amīr Šakīb li-farīḍat al-ḥağğ," 157. On Arslan's exclusion from Egypt, Cleveland explains that "King Fu'ad was not anxious to ease the passage of a notorious associate of 'Abbas Hilmi to the state of Ibn Saud." Cleveland, *Islam Against the West*, 73.

111 Chekib Arslan, "La disparition d'une des plus grandes figures de l'Islam Rachid Ridha," 450. Translation mine.

112 Chekib Arslan, "Le plus grand deuil des lettres arabes contemporaines," *La Nation Arabe* 3/7–9 (July–September 1932): 51–52.

113 Ibid., 52. Translation mine.

114 Ibid.

115 Chekib Arslan, "Le Congrès Musulman d'Europe," *La Nation Arabe* 5/7 (October–November 1935): 418.

10

MUSLIM INTELLECTUALS IN BOSNIA-HERZEGOVINA IN THE TWENTIETH CENTURY

Continuities and changes

Alexandre Popovic

To speak about the general situation of Muslim intellectuals in the Balkans and in the whole South Eastern European area, we must start, at the beginning, with some very global considerations, like the following four points, but, of course this list can be easily developed.

1 We can observe in these regions many groups of Muslims, as far as their "ethnicity" and their spoken language are concerned: there are Muslims of Albanian origin, Turkish origin, Greek origin, and also various groups of Muslims of Slavic origin (Bulgarians, Serbs, Macedonians, Croatians, those of Bosnia-Herzegovina (B.-H.) etc.), and finally some smaller groups, composed of Muslims of Gypsy origin, Wallachian origin, Circassian origin, etc.
2 However, the personal trajectories and the intellectual development of these various peoples were, to a large extent, influenced at the same time by the possibilities (or by the lack of possibilities) offered by the country where they lived (Albania, Bulgaria, Greece, Hungary, Romania, and former Yugoslavia), according to the local attitudes and to the local atmosphere toward the different groups of the Muslim communities existing in each of these countries, and toward Islam in general.
3 This situation must be observed also in relation with various periods, because the behavior was not the same throughout the twentieth century, and was depending, of course, on numerous internal and external factors, political or of another nature.
4 Finally, the last—and the most important point—is evidently the personal degree of religiosity of the members composing this community, where it is possible to observe, globally, on one side—the more or less secularized groups of people, who are considering themselves only as being "of Muslim

origin," but not "Muslims" at all, and even, some times, totally atheistic groups; and on the other side—more or less religious Muslim groups, who are composed of two main subgroups: the religious people in their private way of life; and the religious people "in a professional way" (let us say, active, or very active members of the Muslim religious community).

Let us see now, after this preliminary remarks, and very quickly, what we can say, about one of these particular "ethnic" groups, more precisely about the Muslims of B.-H., during three successive periods of the twentieth century (1878–1945; 1945–1990; and since 1990).

First period: 1878–1945

We can observe in B.-H. at the end of the Ottoman period (1878), like in many other parts of the worlds of Islam, the presence of two main groups of Muslim intellectuals: on one side—the *qadîm*-s (or "qadîmists," which are "Conservatives," or "Traditionalists"), claiming the necessity of a return to the "purely Islamic sources," that is, those of the very first times of Islam; and, on the other side—the *jadîd*-s (or "jadîdists," which are "Modernists," or even better "Renovators"), claiming the necessity of some reforms (according to the development of the modern world).[1]

However, very soon after the end of the Ottoman era, and for different reasons, the situation became more and more difficult. The main problem was, of course, the indispensable necessity for the Muslims of B.-H. to create their own "nationality"—*vis-à-vis* the two other populations of the "new homeland": the Serbs of B.-H. (who were Christian Orthodox), and the Croatians of the B.-H. (who were Christian Catholics); and, for the first time, after 1878—within the "Austro-Hungarian Empire"; for the second time, after 1918—in the framework of the "State of the Serbs, Croats and Slovenians" (a new State which became in 1929 "the State of the Southern Slavs," that is "Yugoslavia"); and for the third time, after 1941, during the Second World War—within the fascist "Independent Croatian State."

The second problem was the necessity to articulate this new "nationality" of the Muslims of B.-H. with the world of Islamic umma in general (which meant on one hand with the worlds of Islam, and on the other hand—and much more precisely—with the Ottoman world). In the case of the Ottoman world, the problem was not only the question of the relationship of this identity with the Ottoman Empire, but also when they had to live together in the past, with a special attention (of course) to the past of B.-H. and its particularities, during the very long centuries of Ottoman power (1463–1878).

It was, in reality, a very hard task, which split in the next decades the "qadîmist" and the "jadîdist" groups in some new fractions (thanks also to the irruption of some new possibilities in the domain of the "Western," or more exactly the European modern education); and that, especially after the end of the

First World War, and the creation of the "South-Slav Kingdom" (December 1918)—which introduced some additional complexities. In particular, in this new State some other groups of Muslim populations existed (Turks, Albanians, and some other, much smaller groups), having their proper vision of the Ottoman past and heritage, which may have not been corresponding (and some times were not corresponding at all) with those of the Muslims of B.-H.

In this way, it is clearly possible to observe during this period, in each of the two mentioned groups of Muslim intellectuals of B.-H.—at least—two main fractions, and sometimes three, or more:

In the "qadîmist" group, there was on one side the fraction of the "Pures and Hards" (who were called by their adversaries "the Obtuses," or "the Dumbs," or "the Hopelessly narrow-minded")[2]; and on the other side, some "Semi-reformists," who had studied, generally for some years, in Istanbul or in Cairo (at al-Azhar, indeed) as, for example, the two very important figures of the Bosnian Muslim Community at that time, the *Reis ul-ulema* Džemaludin Čaušević (1870–1938),[3] and the famous theologian Mehmed Handžić (1906–1944).[4]

In the "jadîdist" group, it was also possible to observe two main subgroups:

First—the fraction of the, let us say "a little bit more moderate religious Muslim intellectuals," who had sometimes studied (most of them just for some years) in Vienna, in Budapest, or in Zagreb, as had done the renowned poet, politician, historian as well as historian of local Ottoman literature, Savfet-beg Bašagić (1870–1934),[5] the Arabist (specialist of the Qur'an and *tafsīr*) Šukrija Alagić (1881–1936),[6] and the very prolific writer on Islamic topics (but, for different reasons, hated by the ulama of B.-H.) Osman Nuri Hadžić (1869–1939).[7]

Second—the fraction of completely secularized "Yugoslav intellectuals of Bosnian-Herzegovinian Muslim origin," without any ties with the local Muslim religious community, like the most important Yugoslav orientalist of that time, professor at the University of Belgrade, and founder in 1926 of the first chair of Oriental studies in Yugoslavia, Fehim Bajraktarević (1889–1970);[8] the specialist of Islamic law and professor at the Belgrade Faculty of Law, Mehmed Begović (1904–1990);[9] and the Director of the famous "State Medrese King Alexander" of Skopje, Ahmed Mehmedbašić (1877–1942).[10] To this same fraction also belonged a very great number of many other Yugoslav intellectuals (doctors, engineers, teachers, professors, politicians, artists, sportsmen, etc.), which considered themselves only "of Bosnian (or of Herzegovinian) Muslim origin," and having little to do (or absolutely nothing to do) with this religious origin, to such a point that it would be really a nonsense to try to include them here, into the different categories of "Muslim intellectuals." It would be better to put them in the category of something like: "Bosnian (or Herzegovinian) intellectuals," but within this case one other difficulty exists, because all the Serbian and Croatian non-Muslim intellectuals of Bosnia-Herzegovina are, of course, also "Bosnian (or Herzegovinian) intellectuals."

Finally, between these two extreme fractions of the "new jadîdists," it is necessary to make a room for some well-known Muslim personalities, who are in reality somewhere in the middle, between these two last groups, as for example: the very important member of the High Direction of the Muslim Community, Hasan Rebac (1890–1953);[11] the politician and Minister in the Royal Government, Mehmed Spaho (1883–1939);[12] the famous scholar (belonging to one of the most important Naqshbandi families of Bosnia), specialist of Persian language and literature, and professor at the University of Sarajevo, Šaćir Sikirić (1893–1966);[13] and a well known self-taught historian, Hamdija Kreševljaković (1888–1959).[14]

But, what is particularly necessary to understand is the importance of the political situation of the B.-H. Muslim community, in the intricate general political game existing during these first three post-Ottoman period (and afterwards also, of course, as we shall see in the next pages): the Austro-Hungarian period (1878–1918),[15] the Period of the Yugoslavian Kingdom (1918–1941),[16] and that of the Croatian Fascist regime during the Second World War (1941–1944/45).[17] The authorities of these different regimes, the leaders of some groups opposing these regimes, or the leaders of opponent political parties tried to attract the Muslim population of B.-H. to their own camps. From these actions resulted the creation of some new groups of Muslim intellectuals in B.-H., like some pro-Serbian, or pro-Croatian, or pro-Ottoman (or, after the fall of the Ottoman Empire, pro-Turkish) groups and subgroups, about which we have a very rich historical material, thanks to some archives, to the different Muslim newspapers of that time, and even to some extremely important books and articles (where it is possible to find the names of the principal personalities, with some details of their biographies).

A similar process occurred in the case of three modern ideologies, in the development of which a certain number of Muslim intellectuals of B.-H. were—more or less—implicated, according to their personal engagement. Here, on the one hand I would like to speak about "two general ideologies," which were common to the Muslim and to the non-Muslim populations: that is Communism and Fascism. Both had their own groups and groupings (in which it is possible to follow the individual, or the collective trajectories of some Muslim intellectuals of B.-H., thanks especially to the newspapers and the periodical press, but also to some archive documents, and to a large number of publications, concerning particularly Communist groups). On the other hand, one very specific group of Muslim intellectuals appeared in B.-H.: the famous Pan-Islamistic group called "*Mladi muslimani*" (Young Muslims) founded in Sarajevo, Mostar, and Zagreb in March 1941, about which there are several important publications by Xavier Bougarel.[18] (In the next part of this chapter, will be quoted some important names of B.-H. Muslim intellectuals, belonging to each of these last three groups.)

Second period: 1945–1990

The general situation of each of these groups and their fractions became much more difficult when the Communist Party of Yugoslavia took power in the country, at the end of the Second World War in 1944–1945, and kept it during forty-five years, establishing the "Socialist Republic of Yugoslavia" under the highly dictatorial regime of Josip Broz-Tito, and his different and successive camarillas.[19]

It was, of course, one of the numerous variants of the "Eastern Socialist Republics," but with some particularities, owing to some special conditions. Two main factors, one internal, the other external, must be kept in mind if we want to understand the general situation of each of the different groups of B.-H. Muslim intellectuals at that time. First: the very special status of the Muslim population of B.-H., which until 1968 had no proper "nationality," within the extremely intricate puzzle of different "nations" and "nationalities" in Yugoslavia. Second: the fantastic opportunity for the Muslims of B.-H. given by Tito's decision at the Bandoeng Conference of the "Non-Engaged" bloc of countries in 1955 (a movement that became some time later the "Non-Aligned" bloc, with a clear dominance of Islamic countries), to try and play the leading roles in this bloc (with Nasser and Nehru), by using the card of the Muslim Community of Yugoslavia, especially with the most educated part of this community, that is that of B.-H.[20]

From this moment onwards, a new era began for all groups and subgroups of Muslim intellectuals of B.-H., for about forty years. A large spectrum of political, social, and religious possibilities was created, which was absolutely unimaginable before, but, of course, under some specific conditions. These conditions were, above all, the obligation to insist very strongly on the importance of the social aspects in Islam (much more than on the religious one), and, on the other hand, the necessity to insist on the great importance of one of the extremely popular phantasms of that time, which was "Arab Socialism."

In the complex game played by the principal actors of that time, two main groups of Muslim intellectuals of B.-H. can be observed: the religious one, and the secular one, but it is necessary to divide each of them in several subgroups:

Within the religious group—the first subgroup was that of the "domesticated high official leaders" of the "Muslim Religious Community," who were chosen after lengthy deliberations and verifications in secret meetings, by the Yugoslav Communist authorities. The principal task of these men was to claim officially their (false) attachment to the Socialist Republic of Yugoslavia and to its ideology, to serve the interest of the State and the different populations of Yugoslavia, as well as that of the Muslim Religious Community, etc. At the top of this group stood the Head of this Religious Community, the *Reis ul-ulema*, Sulejman Kemura (1908–1975), who is called today "the Red Reis";[21] after him came his closest collaborators ("the religious and cultural 'referents' "—who were kinds of religious and political *commissars* of the Muslim Community during the Communist regime)—as were, for example, Husein Djozo (1912–1982),[22] Abdurahman Hukić (1921–1990),[23] Ahmed Smajlović (1938–1988),[24] and some others.

Behind this first subgroup, and more or less linked to it (but at some distance), a much larger subgroup existed: that of the "domesticated Muslim religious actors," composed of the small fry: senior executive members of the Muslim

Religious Community, directors of the Muslim newspapers and publications, journalists, etc. Generally speaking, these men used to share in common three main particularities: (a) they were of humble rural origin; (b) after finishing their first studies in the Gazi Husrev-beg Medrese in Sarajevo, and thanks to different kinds of grants and scholarships offered by some Arabic countries, they had studied some years Islamic theology and "Islamic sciences" in various places (in Egypt, Libya, Iraq, or in some of the Arab States of the Gulf area); and (c) they were affiliated, at one time or another, to certain important personalities of the first subgroup, or to certain (religious or/and political) Muslim pressure groups in B.-H. Their number was relatively high, but only very few of them (as the above mentioned Ahmed Smajlović, for example), had had the opportunity to become "first-class leaders" of the Muslim Religious Community of B.-H., or of the Socialist Republic of Yugoslavia.

The third subgroup of religious Muslim intellectuals of B.-H., during this period, was composed of personalities who had been (or had been considered) clearly in opposition to the Communist regime. A lot of names should be mentioned in this category of people, as that of the learned Qadiri shaykh Fejzulah Hadžibajrić (1913–1990);[25] those of the well-known Muslim religious writers and historians of the Bosnian-Herzegovinian Islamic community: Muhamed Hadžijahić (1918–1986);[26] Mahmud Traljić (b. 1918);[27] Kasim Hadžić (1917–1990);[28] Hivzija Hasandedić (b. 1915);[29] Alija Nametak (1906–1987),[30] etc.; or that of the specialist of Oriental manuscripts Kasim Dobrača (1910–1979);[31] without forgetting the most famous personality of all this category of Muslim religious opponents, the former President of B.-H., Alija Izetbegovič (1925–2003).[32] Nevertheless, let us remember that some of the Muslim opponents to the Communist regime have been, at the time of the Second World War, active members of the above mentioned Pan-Islamistic group of the "Young Muslims" or collaborated more or less actively with the Croatian Fascist authorities, and spent therefore after 1945 some years in prison, while others were condemned to death and executed.

As far as the group of secular Muslim intellectuals of B.-H. (which was composed of the politicians, scholars, engineers, doctors, professors, teachers, artists, etc.) is concerned, during this period one can observe some similarities with the situation of the different religious subgroups mentioned earlier, but we need to distinguish—at least—four subgroups, if we want to understand the extreme complexities of their position.

The first subgroup was formed by the principal Muslim Communist political leaders, like Džemal Bijedić (1917–1977),[33] and Hamdija Pozderac (1924–1989).[34] Their main preoccupation was, of course, the most important political problem of the Muslim population of these two regions at that time, that is, the eventuality of the creation, and of the official recognition by the authorities of the Yugoslav State (and by the Central Committee of the Yugoslav Communist Party) of a very bizarre "Muslim nation" within the Federal Republic of B.-H., which had been effectively proclaimed in 1967.[35]

The second subgroup of secular Muslim intellectuals was composed of some "official Muslim Marxists," close to (and working for) the Yugoslav Communist authorities, but with very tight links with a Muslim Religious Community of B.-H. Among them we can mention here the "First-class secular Muslim politician" (and principal representative of the ideology of "ethnic Muslims of B.-H.") Atif Purivatra (b. 1928);[36] the Marxist philosopher and *enfant terrible* of the secular Muslim intelligentsia, Muhamed Filipović (b. 1929),[37] who was excluded several times from (and re-integrated into) the Yugoslav Communist Party, but played (and is playing still today) multiple roles in the various (and often opposite) political, religious, and nationalist Muslim groups and coteries. We can also mention in this subgroup another very well-known "Marxist philosopher of the Sarajevo circle," Fuad Muhić (1941–1991),[38] *et al.*

The third subgroup of secular Muslim intellectuals in B.-H. between 1945 and 1990 was composed of the numerous Communist (or at least leftist, and sometimes allegedly leftist) scholars such as the historians: Hamdija Kapidžić (1904–1974),[39] Enver Redžić (b. 1915),[40] Avdo Sućeska (b. 1927),[41] and Hasan Sušić (1937–1991);[42] the historians of literature Muhsin Rizvić (b. 1930),[43] and Alija Isaković (1932–1997);[44] the sociologist of religious problems Esad Ćimić (b. 1931),[45] and many others.

Finally, the fourth subgroup of secular Muslim intellectuals during this period was that of the many opponents to the Yugoslav Communist regime who pretended not to be one of them, such as the historians of the Ottoman period Hamid Hadžibegić (1898–1988),[46] Alija Bejtić (1920–1981),[47] Hazim Šabanović (1916–1971),[48] Adem Handžić (1916–1998);[49] the epigraphist Mehmed Mujezinović (1913–1981),[50] and many others.

Third period: 1990–2000

The end of the "Communist era" was followed by the civil war of 1992–1995 in B.-H. (the Muslims speak generally of "genocide"). These events introduced several new complexities in the relationship between the different groups and coteries of Muslim intellectuals which existed before. They unified, or divided and subdivided along new schemes and diagrams. New alliances and new schisms appeared with new religious, nationalistic, and ideological mixtures. This obliged the Muslims, once again, to re-interpret the recent and remote past of B.-H., as well as the role played in this past by different local personalities (whose biographies were remodelled, according to the needs of the time).

Moreover, this difficult *aggiornamento* was extremely complicated by the strong implications of some external Muslim or non-Muslim "Great Powers," from the East and the West (such as Iran, or the different Arabic and other Muslim states, organizations and ideological groups), on one side, and by the multiple pressures and actions coming from the "Western" side, that is, from the USA, NATO, EU, etc.).

Of course, we cannot examine here, even very quickly, the intricacies of this extremely unsteady new situation. Let us describe summarily its principal contours. There are now four main groups of "Muslim intellectuals": two religious, and two secular.

First, there is a "religious-political group," with well-known personalities such as the former President of B.-H. Alija Izetbegović, his sometimes "First Minister," sometimes "First Opponent" Haris Silajdžić (b. 1945)[51], and behind them several other personalities with very precarious careers.

Second, the "religious-theological group of scholars" in which at least three "first-class personalities" can be mentioned: the new *Reis ul-ulema* Mustafa Cerić (b. 1952);[52] the specialist of Qur'ranic studies Enes Karić (b. 1958);[53] and one of the best specialists of Islamic law, Fikret Karčić (b. 1955).[54]

As for the two secular groups: we have on one side, the very numerous group of "secular Muslim politicians," such as the "eternal chameleon" Muhamed Filipović and many others; and on the other side, the group of the "old-style/new-look scholars," such as the historian Mustafa Imamović (b. 1941);[55] Amir Ljubović (b. 1945),[56] a specialist of the Ottoman Muslim literature of B.-H. written in Arabic, Persian, and Turkish languages, and some others.

Let us add to the enumeration of all these groups and subgroups, one very special group: that of the Muslim intellectuals who left the country and lived in the early twentieth century, or are living today, outside their homeland, such as the learned *mufti* of Mostar and teacher at the University of Istanbul, Ali Fehmi Džabić (1853–1918);[57] the well-known historian and professor of Ankara University, Muhamed Tayyib Okić (1902–1977);[58] the librarian and prolific historian of the Bosnian cultural life, living in Austria, Smail Balić (b. 1920);[59] the founder of the "Boshnakian Institute" in Zurich and politician Adil Zulfikarpašić (b. 1921);[60] the specialist of medieval Arabic philosophy, living in Paris, Tarik Haverić (b. 1955); the Ottomanist living in the USA Nenad Filipović (b. 1962), and many others.

Some concluding remarks

This is a very long period and an extremely intricate set of individual and collective trajectories. Therefore, let us say just some words in connection with some of the main themes of our conference: *situations*, *discourses*, *strategies*, *continuities*, *changes*.

The complexity of the *situations* is clearly the result of several constraints. The nature of these constraints may be of different orders: religious, nationalist, economic, social, political, ideological, and so on, but more often it is, in fact, a sort of mixture of all of them.

Moreover, all the *discourses* of the Muslim intellectuals of B.-H., in each of these different periods of the long twentieth century (even those of the completely secularized groups) were obviously (and still are) strongly influenced by unavoidable requirements, and at first by the "general line" imposed by the political authorities of the state, in connection with the inextricable game of relationship between the neighbouring non-Muslim groups of population (each of them having, of course, its own vision of the past, and its own hopes for the future, which are evidently in complete opposition with those of Muslim groups).

As far as the *strategies* used by the Muslim intellectuals are concerned, they were extremely changing (as we have seen in the preceding pages). Nevertheless, it is clear that, during each period and according to new circumstances (speaking only about the groups of the religious Muslim intellectuals of B.-H.), there were always two main trends: *continuity* on the one side, and *change* on the other side. Both should serve the principal goal of the "Muslim population" of the two regions, that is to say the absolute necessity to make of this "religious community" (which is, however, composed to a large extent of more or less secularized people) a "nation." This "nation" should have a specific name and should be guided by a kind of "Islamic" ideology. Nevertheless, it should assemble together, at the same time and under the same banner, the religious (and the very religious), as well as the secular (and the very secular) part of the population of B.-H. And, as it is often the case with minority groups, we can observe the same process going on: it consists in grabbing all the possible advantages offered by the political situation of the time, and when new authorities arrive, to dissociate the Muslim community from the previous ideology, position and the activities of their former official leaders, presenting them as (more or less horrible) traitors of the Muslim community. This, in order to fit into a new deal, thanks to some subterfuges coming from the stock of the "eternal Islamic values."

In the field of *change*, we must examine very carefully some particularly "neuralgic" points, such as: the new theories and the new interpretations concerning the phenomenon of Islamization (or the "conversion to Islam," or the "expansion of Islam"); the image of the "Turks," and of all the Ottoman past, either rejected or rehabilitated; the reassessment of the ancient and present relations with the neighboring non-Muslim populations, as well as the relations with other Muslim communities of the Balkans, and the rest of the Islamic umma; and in a word, what we could call the "invention of the past."

***

In this short essay, the names of around fifty—among the most representative Muslim intellectuals of B.-H. in the twentieth century—have been mentioned. They represent a sample of about 5–10% of the names which ought to appear in a serious study on the subject. The aim of this chapter was not to elaborate a kind of "Who's who?," but to describe the main trends which appeared within this society in the course of a long and eventful period. Those who have written and still write about it are generally of two kinds. On one side, those who write the "holy story" of one or another group, without criticizing the data given by their informants. On the other side, those who select some names in only one group, according to their own point of view or ideology, in order to give a picture, which is supposed to be a general one. (In this way, some authors are describing the "European Islam" in B.-H.!) Except a few cases, even in former Yugoslavia, the problem has always been that the non-Muslims (and the Muslims themselves) have never had a precise idea on the subject. The main reason is that the biographical data, in encyclopedias or elsewhere, have always been "arranged."

To conclude, I must draw very strongly the reader's attention to one crucial point: if one wish to study seriously this subject, it is absolutely essential to examine in detail the very rich local Muslim press (newspapers and periodicals) which exists since the last third of the nineteenth century—since these questions are there less often altered or falsified (or at less "taboo-ized") than in a great number of books and articles.

Notes

1 We know more than thirty authors and activists belonging to these two groups. For each we would have to present their biographies and their points of view about these topics. But this cannot be done here, of course.

2 It would not be appropriate of course to mention here the names of persons belonging to this category, or to be too harsh on them. These men had their ideas and have done what they believed they had to do.

3 For the biography of Džemaludin Čaušević (1870–1938) and his works, see: Anonymous, *Ko je ko u Jugoslaviji* (Beograd-Zagreb, 1928): 25; O. Hadžić, *Narodna Enciklopedija* (Zagreb, 1929), s. v. (4: 937, of the Cyrillic edition); M. Handžić, *Novi Behar* (Sarajevo) 11/20 (1937–1938): 309–312; Š. Sikirić, *Novi Behar* (Sarajevo) 11/20 (1937–1938): 314–316; A. Balagija, *Les musulmans yougoslaves* (Algiers, 1940): 116–119; M. Hadžijahić, *Hrvatska Enciklopedija* (Zagreb, 1944), 4: 207–208; H. Šabanović, *Enciklopedija Jugoslavije* (Zagreb, 1956), 2: 546; Anonymous, *Glasnik Vrhovnog Islamskog Starješinstva* (Sarajevo, henceforth: *GVIS*), 27 (1964): 470–475; M. Traljić, *Takvim 1971* (Sarajevo, 1970): 92–97; A. Purivatra, *Jugoslavenska Muslimanska Organizacija u političkom životu Kraljevine Srba Hrvata i Slovenaca* (henceforth: *JMO*) (Sarajevo, 1974): see Index, 639; Anonyme, *GVIS* (Sarajevo) 1983/1–2: 371; A. Nametak, *Sarajevski nekrologij* (Zürich: Bošnjački Institut, 1994), see: Index, 298; M. Djilas and N. Gaće, *Bošnjak Adil Zulfikarpašić* (Zürich, Bošnjački Institut, 1994): 38, 40; Š. Filandra, *Bošnjačka politika u xx. stoljeću* (Sarajevo, 1998): 59 (and *passim*, see: Index, 402).

4 For the biography of Mehmed Handžić (1906–1944) and his publications, see: H. Kreševljaković, *Kalendar Narodna Uzdanica za 1945 godinu* (Sarajevo, 1944), 24–31; *El-Hidaje*, 8 (Sarajevo), 1944–1945 (see all the whole issue); R. Y. Ebied and M. J. L. Young, *EI*^{2}, Supplément 5–6 (Leiden, 1982), s. v., 354 (of the French Edition); Anonymous, *GVIS* 1983/1–2: 374; A. Popovic, "Handžić Mehmed" in M. Gaborieau, N. Grandin, P. Labrousse, and A. Popovic, eds, *Dictionnaire biographique des savants et grandes figures du monde musulman périphérique, du XIXe siècle à nos jours* (Paris: CNRS-EHESS, 1992), 1: 52 (henceforth: *Dict. Biogr.*); A. Nametak, *Sarajevski nekrologij* (see: Index, 300); Filandra, *Bošnjačka*: 161 (and *passim*, see: Index, 404).

5 For the details of the life, political activities, and principal writings of Savfet-beg Bašagić (1870–1934), see: H. Kreševljaković, *Znameniti i zaslužni Hrvati* (Zagreb, 1925): 20; O. Hadžić, *Narodna Enciklopedija* (Zagreb, 1926), 1, s. v. (p. 136 of the Cyrillic edition); E. Mulabdić, *Novi Behar* (Sarajevo) 19–21 (1933–1934), see the whole issue; I. A. Milićević, *Glasnik Zemaljskog Muzeja* (Sarajevo, henceforth: *GZM*), 46 (1934): 5–9; F. Bajraktarević, *Prilozi za orijentalnu filologiju* (Sarajevo, henceforth: *POF*), 2 (1951 [1952]): 315; N. Filipović, in "Odžakluk timar…," *POF*, 5. (1954–1955): 252–253; Š. Sikirić, ibid.: 321–322 (note 1); H. Šabanović, *Enciklopedija Jugoslavije*, s. v. (Zagreb, 1955), 1.: 384; Anonymous, *GVIS* 27

(1964): 152–155; M. Traljić, *Takvim 1971* (Sarajevo, 1970): 88–92; M. Rizvić, *Život* 20/1–2 (January–February 1971): 6–17; M. K., *Preporod* 2/14 (1.4.1971): 7; A. Purivatra, *JMO*: Index, 638; A. Kadribegović, *GVIS* 1984/4: 473–495; Nametak, *Sarajevski nekrologij*, Index: 29; Djilas and Gaće, *Bošnjak A. Z.*, Index: 233; Filandra, *Bošnjačka politika*, 22 (and *passim*, see: Index, 401).

6 For the biography and writings of Šukrija Alagić (1881–1936), see: A. Nametak, *Hrvatska Enciklopedija*, s. v. (Zagreb, 1941), 1: 168–169; Anonymous, *Preporod* 2/10 (1.2.1971): 7; Anonymous, *GVIS* (1983/1–2): 369; Popovic, *Dict. biogr.*, 1: 51 (with some additional references).

7 For the biography and writings of Osman Nuri Hadžić (1869–1939), see: M. Krasović, in *Znameniti i zaslužni Hrvati* (Zagreb, 1925): 102; D. Pantić, *Narodna Enciklopedija*, s. v. (Zagreb, 1929), 3: 782–783 (Cyrillic edition); I. Kecmanović, *Enciklopedija Jugoslavije*, s. v. (Zagreb, 1958), 3: 650; Nametak, *Sarajevski nekrologij*, see Index, 300; Filandra, *Bošnjačka politika*: 22, 271, 302.

8 For the biography and works of Fehim Bajraktarević (1889–1970), see: H. Kreševljaković, *Hrvatska Enciklopedija*, s. v. (Zagreb, 1941), 2.: 105; H. Šabanović, *Enciklopedija Jugoslavije*, s. v. (Zagreb, 1955), 1: 286–287; M. Djukanović, *Anali Filološkog Fakulteta* (Belgrade) 10 (1970): 1–7; K. Ašković, *Anali Filološkog Fakulteta* (Belgrade) 10 (1970): 9–28; M. Hadžijahić, *Anali Gazi Husrev-begove biblioteke* (Sarajevo, henceforth: *AGHBB*) 1 (1972): 132–134; A. Popovic, *Journal Asiatique* 260/1–2 (1972): 178–185; I. Eren, *Güney-Doğu Avrupa Araştırmaları Dergisi* (Istanbul) 2–3: 181–216.

9 For the biography and publications of Mehmed Begović (1904–1990), see: B. Nikolajević, *Enciklopedija Jugoslavije*, s. v. (Zagreb, 1955), 1: 409; J. Šamić, *Turcica* 16 (1984): 216–217; I. Džananović, *Glasnik Rijaseta Islamskog Starješinstva* (Sarajevo, henceforh: *GRIS*), 1990/5: 167–171.

10 For the biography and work of Ahmed Mehmedbašić (1877–1942), see: M. Memić, *Velika Medresa i njeni učenici u revolucionarnom pokretu* (Skopje: Fonografika, 1984), see Index, 290.

11 For the biography and publications of Hasan Rebac (1890–1953), see: Anonymous, *Ko je ko u Jugoslaviji* (Belgrade-Zagreb, 1928): 128; F. Slipičević, *Preporod* 3 [130] and 4 [131] (1.2.1976): 13, (15.2.1976): 13 (series of articles, interrupted—without any explanation—after the second issue, but published before in: *Sloboda* (Mostar) 32–38 (11.8.1975–22.9.1975); M. Memić, *Velika Medresa i njeni učenici u revolucionarnom pokretu* (see Index: 291); Djilas and Gaće, *Bošnjak A. Z.*, 132; Filandra, *Bošnjačka politika*: 200.

12 For the biography and publications of Mehmed Spaho (1883–1939), see: Anonymous, *Ko je ko u Jugoslaviji* (Belgrade-Zagreb, 1928), 136–137; O. Hadžić, *Narodna Enciklopedija* (Zagreb, 1929), 4.: 286–287 (Cyr. ed.); Anonymous, *Glasnik Islamske Vjerske Zajednice* (Sarajevo, henceforth: *GIVZ*) 7/8 (1939): 305–311; Balagija, *Les musulmans yougoslaves*: 134–135; A. Purivatra, *Enciklopedija Jugoslavije* (Zagreb, 1968), 7.: 498; Purivatra, *JMO*, *passim*; Nametak, *Sarajevski nekrologij*: 306; Djilas and Gaće, *Bošnjak A. Z.*, Index: 237; Filandra, *Bošnjačka politika*: 79 (and *passim*, see: Index, 410).

13 For the biography and publications of Šaćir Sikirić (1893–1966), see: Anonymous, *GVIS* 29 (1966): 604–606; S. Grozdanić, *Radovi Filozofskog Fakulteta u Sarajevu*, 4, Sarajevo, 1966–1967: 413–415; Anonymous, *GVIS* 1967/11–12: 545–548; Anonymous, *Preporod* 2/25 (15.9.1971): 14; M. Traljić, *Takvim 1977* (Sarajevo, 1976): 222–227; I. Morina, *Tan* (Priština) 539 (1980): 8; Anonymous, *GVIS* 1983/1–2: 377–378; Nametak, *Sarajevski nekrologij*, Index, 305.

14 For the biography and publications of Hamdija Kreššvljaković (1888–1959), see: B. Vodnik, *Narodna Enciklopedija* (Zagreb, 1927), 2: 449 (Cyr. ed.); M. Traljić *et al.*, *Novi Behar* (Sarajevo) 13/1–6 (15.9.1939): several articles; E. Rossi, *Oriente Moderno*

23 (1943): 125–129; H. Kapidžić, *Godišnjak Društva Istoričara Bosne i Hercegovine* (Sarajevo), 10 (1959): 419–424; Nametak, *GVIS* (1959/10–12): 497–503; A. Babić, *Enciklopedija Jugoslavije* (Zagreb, 1962), 5.: 393; M. Traljić, *Takvim 1970* (Sarajevo, 1969): 128–133; Anonymous, *Preporod* 2/22 (1.8.1971): 6; Anonymous, *Takvim 1979* (Sarajevo, 1978): 349–353; Nametak, *Sarajevski nekrologij*, Index, 302; Djilas and Gaće, *Bošnjak A. Z.*, 14; Filandra, *Bošnjaćka politika*: 167, 170, 302, 377.

15 See R. J. Donia, *Islam under the Double Eagle: the Muslims of Bosnia and Hercegovina, 1878–1914* (Boulder, CO: Columbia University Press, 1981); F. Hauptmann, *Die Österreichisch-Ungarische Herrschaft in Bosnien und der Hercegovina 1878–1918, Wirtschaftspolitik und Wirtschaftsentwicklung* (Graz: Institut für Geschichte, 1983); A. Popovic, *L'Islam balkanique. Les musulmans du sud-est européen dans la période post-ottomane* (Berlin: Wiesbaden, 1986): 269–291; A. Babuna, *Die nationale Entwicklung der bosnischen Muslime. Mit besonderer Berücksichtigung der österreichisch-ungarischen Periode* (Frankfurt a. Main: Europäischer Verlag der Wissenschaften, 1996); Filandra, *Bošnjaćka politika*: 9–54.

16 See Popovic, *L'Islam balkanique*: 311–336; Filandra, *Bošnjaćka politika*: 55–152.

17 Popovic, *L'Islam balkanique*: 336–342; E. Redzic, *Muslimansko automaštvo i 13 SS divizija* (Sarajevo, 1987); A. Popovic, "La presse des musulmans des Balkans au cours de la Seconde Guerre mondiale (1941–1944/45)," *Etudes balkaniques. Cahiers Pierre Belon* 4 (1997): 199–211 (in part. 211–221); Filandra, *Bošnjaćka politika*: 155–195.

18 Z. Ključanin, *Mladi Muslimani* (Sarajevo, 1991); S. Trhulj, *Mladi Muslimani* (Zagreb, 1992); X. Bougarel, "Un courant panislamiste en Bosnie-Herzégovine," in G. Kepel, ed., *Exils et royaumes. Les appartenances au monde arabo-musulman aujourd'hui* (Paris, 1994): 275–299; X. Bougarel, "From Young Muslims to the Party of Democratic Action: the Emergence of a Pan-Islamist Trend in Bosnia-Herzegovina," *Islamic Studies* 36/2–3 (1997): 533–549; and his doctoral thesis *Islam et politique en Bosnie Herzégovine: le Parti de l'Action Démocratique* (Paris: Institut d'Etudes Politiques, 1999), 2 vols.

19 A. Popovic, "La politique titiste envers les religions et ses conséquences," in M. Bozdemir, ed., *Islam et laïcité. Approches globales et régionales* (Paris, 1996): 97–103; Filandra, *Bošnjaćka politika*: 197–344.

20 A. Popovic, *Les musulmans yougoslaves (1945–1989). Médiateurs et métaphores* (Lausanne, 1990).

21 For the biography of Sulejman Kemura (1908–1975), see the very numerous obituaries published in the Yugoslav Muslim press in 1975 and after this date; Anonymous, *GVIS* (1983/1–2): 375; Nametak, *Sarajevski nekrologij*, several passages, see Index, 302, and 283–288; Djilas and Gaće, *Bošnjak A. Z.*, 83.

22 For the biography and publications of Husein Djozo (1912–1982), see: Anonymous, *Preporod* 11 [283] (1.6.1982): 9–11; Anonymous, *GVIS* (1983/1–2): 372–373; Filandra, *Bošnjaćka politika*: 349 (and *passim*, see Index, 403); and very numerous articles in the Yugoslav Muslim press, especially in the period 1958–1979.

23 For the biography of Abdurahman Hukić (1921–1990), see: Anonymous, *GVIS* (1983/1–2): 375; A. Kadribegović, *Preporod* 13 [476] (1.7.1990): 16; A. Kadribegović *GRIS* (1990/3): 113–115; Nametak, *Sarajevski nekrologij*: Index, 301.

24 For the biography and publications of Ahmed Smajlović (1938–1988), see: Anonymous, *GVIS* (1983/1–2): 378; Anonymous, *Preporod*, 17 [433] (1.9.1988): 14; Anonymous, *GVIS* (1988/4): 468–469; Filandra, *Bošnjaćka politika*: Index, 410.

25 For the biography and publications of Fejzulah Hadžibajrić (1913–1990), see: Anonymous, *GVIS* (1982/1): 60–62; Anonymous, *GVIS* (1983/1–2): 373; Šamić, *Turcica* 16 (1984): 234–235; Anonymous, *Šebi Arus 1985* (Sarajevo, 1985): 67–74; D. Tanasković, *Politika* (23.1.1990); Z. Fajić, *Preporod* 10 [474] (15.5.1990): 17; Anonymous, *Islamska Misao* (Sarajevo), 137 (May 1990): 49–51; E. Durmišević, *GRIS* (1990/3): 116–118; A. Gaši, *Šebi Arus 1990*, Sarajevo, 1990: 39–45; M. Traljić, *AGHBB* (Sarajevo), 15–16 (1990): 287–291.

26 For the biography and publications of Muhamed Hadžijahić (1918–1986), see: A. Purivatra, *JMO*, Index, 642; Šamić, *Turcica* 16 (1984): 237–238; M. Traljić, *AGHBB* 13–14 (1987): 251–256; Filandra, *Bošnjaćka politika*: 206 (and *passim*, see: Index, 404).

27 For the biography and publications of Mahmud Traljić (b. 1918), see: Šamić, *Turcica* 16 (1984): 270; Nametak, *Sarajevski nekrologij*: 307; Filandra, *Bošnjaćka politika*: Index, 411; Anonymous, in *Ko je ko u Bošnjaka* (Sarajevo, 2000): 402.

28 For the biography and publications of Kasim Hadžić (1917–1990), see: M. Mahmutović, *Preporod* 15 [239] (1.8.1980): 14–15; Anonymous, *GVIS* (1983/1–2): 373; M. Mahmutović, *Preporod* 24 [487] (15.12.1990): 15; M. Omerdić, *GRIS* 1990/6: 109–112 (biography), and 1991/1: 108–132 (bibliography).

29 For the biography and publications of Hivzija Hasandedić (b. 1915), see: Anonymous, *Preporod* 15 [190] (1–15.8.1978): 10–11; Anonymous, *GVIS* (1983/1–2): 374; Šamić, *Turcica* 16 (1984): 246–250; Anonymous, in *Ko je ko u Bošnjaka*: 182.

30 For the biography and publications of Alija Nametak (1906–1987), see: Anonymous, *GVIS* (1983/1–2): 377; Šamić, *Turcica* 16 (1984): 256; M. Traljić, *AGHBB* 15–16 (1990): 293–299; Nametak, *Sarajevski nekrologij*, Introduction, 7–10; Filandra, *Bošnjaćka politika*: 160, 299, 302.

31 For the biography and some of the publications of Kasim Dobrača (1910–1979), see: V. Monteil, ed., *Annuaire du monde musulman*, 4th ed. (Paris, 1954): 410; Anonymous, *GVIS* (1983/1–2): 372; Nametak, *Sarajevski nekrologij*: Index, 299; Filandra, *Bošnjać ka politika*: Index, 403.

32 For the biography and publications of Alija Izetbegović (1925–2003), see: Djilas and Gaće, *Bošnjak A. Z.*, Index, 235; Filandra, *Bošnjaćka politika*: 375 (see also Index, 405); Bougarel, *Islam et politique*, *passim*; Anonymous, in *Ko je ko u Bošnjaka*: 210.

33 For some details on the biography of Džemal Bijedić (1917–1977), see: T. Vujasinović, *Enciklopedija Jugoslavije* (Zagreb, 1955), 1: 558; Nametak, *Sarajevski nekrologij*: 279; Filandra, *Bošnjaćka politika*: Index, 401.

34 For some details on the biography of Hamdija Pozderac (1924–1989) and some of his publications, see: *Zbornik radova 1961–1976* (Sarajevo: Univerzitet u Sarajevu, Fakultet Političkih Nauka, 1976): 365; Djilas and Gaće, *Bošnjak A. Z.*: 219; Filandra, *Bošnjaćka politika*: 309 (see also Index, 409).

35 See some details in Popovic, *L'Islam balkanique*: 344–346.

36 For the biography and publications of Atif Purivatra (b. 1928), see: *Zbornik radova 1961–1976*: 366–367; Djilas and Gaće, *Bošnjak A. Z.*: 116; Filandra, *Bošnjaćka politika*: 323 (see also Index, 409); Anonymous, in *Ko je ko u Bošnjaka*: 331–332.

37 For the biography and publications of Muhamed Filipović (b. 1929), see: Djilas and Gaće, *Bošnjak A. Z.*: Index, 234; M. Sokolija, *Tunjo. Velik turban pod njim hodže nema* (London, 1995); Filandra, *Bošnjaćka politika*: 258 (see also Index, 404).

38 For the biography and publications of Fuad Muhić (1941–1991), see: Filandra, *Bošnjać ka politika*: 269, 282, 302, 356.

39 For the biography and publications of Hamdija Kapidžić (1904–1974), see: I. Kecmanović, *Enciklopedija Jugoslavije* (Zagreb, 1962), 5: 190; Anonymous, *Radovi Filozofskog Fakulteta u Sarajevu* (Sarajevo) 4 (1966–1967): 405–409; M. Ekmečić, *Univerzitet danas* (Belgrade) 1–2 (1974): 53–54; S. Balić, *Südost-Forschungen* (München) 33 (1974): 321–323; Purivatra, *JMO*, Index, 644; Nametak, *Sarajevski nekrologij*, Index, 301.

40 For the biography and publications of Enver Redžić (b. 1915), see: Purivatra, *JMO*: Index, 650; Filandra, *Bošnjaćka politika*: Index, 409; E. Redžić, *Bosna i Hercegovina u drugom svjetskom ratu* (Sarajevo, 1998): 481; Anonymous, in *Ko je ko u Bošnjaka*: 338.

41 For the biography and publications of Avdo Sućeska (b. 1927), see: Purivatra, *JMO*: Index, 651; Šamić, *Turcica* 16 (1984): 263–267; E. Stanek, *POF* (Sarajevo) 46 (1996 [1997]): 175–185; Filandra, *Bošnjaćka politika*: 235 (see also Index, 410);

Anonymous, in *Ko je ko u Bošnjaka*: 370; A. Ljubović and L. Gazić, eds, *Orijentalni Institut u Sarajevu 1950–2000* (Sarajevo: Orijentalni Institut, 2000): 125–126.

42 For the biography and publications of Hasan Sušić (1937–1991), see: Anonymous, *Zbornik Radova 1961–1976*: 382–383; M. Rizvić, *GRIS* (1991/5): 651–653; Filandra, *Bošnjaćka politika*: 236, 266, 378.

43 For the biography and publications of Muhsin Rizvić (b. 1930), see: Šamić, *Turcica* 16 (1984): 260; Filandra, *Bošnjaćka politika*: 297 (see also Index, 409).

44 For the biography and publications of Alija Isaković (1932–1997), see: Djilas and Gaće, *Bošnjak A. Z.*: 116; Filandra, *Bošnjaćka politika*: 271 (see also Index, 405); *Književnik i mislilac Alija Isaković*, Sarajevo, 1998.

45 For the biography and publications of Esad Ćimić (b. 1931), see: Djilas and Gaće, *Bošnjak A. Z.*: 218–219; Filandra, *Bošnjaćka politika*: Index, 402; Anonymous, in *Ko je ko u Bošnjaka*: 100.

46 For the biography and publications of Hamid Hadžibegić (1898–1988), see: Anonymous, *GVIS* (1983/1–2): 373; Šamić, *Turcica* 16 (1984): 235–236; K. Hadžić, *Preporod* 8 [424] (15.4.1988): 14; Ljubović and Gazić, *Orijentalni Institut u Sarajevu*: 99–100.

47 For the biography and publications of Alija Bejtić (1920–1981), see: Anonymous, *POF* 31 (1981): 7–9; Nametak, *Sarajevski nekrologij*: 259–260; Ljubović and Gazić, *Orijentalni Institut u Sarajevu*: 117–118.

48 For the biography and publications of Hazim Šabanović (1916–1971), see: A. Sućeska, *POF* 18–19 (1968–1969 [1973]): 5–7; Z. Bostandžić, *Politika* (26.3.1971); Fil., *Preporod* 2/14 (1.4.1971): 7; S. Balić, *Südost Forschungen*, 30 (1971): 300–304; M. Hadžijahić, *AGHBB* 1 (1972): 136–138; S. A. Alić, *POF* 22–23 (1972–1973 [1976]): 7–10; B. Nurudinović, *POF*: 11–32; Anonymous, *GVIS* (1983/1–2): 378; Nametak, *Sarajevski nekrologij*: Index, 306; Filandra, *Bošnjaćka politika*: Index, 410; Ljubović and Gazić, *Orijentalni Institut u Sarajevu*: 110–113.

49 For the biography and publications of Adem Handžić (1916–1998), see: Šamić, *Turcica* 16 (1984): 244–246; A. Aličić, *POF* 47–48 (1997–1998): 9–15; M. Bavčić, *POF*: 191–199; Ljubović and Gazić, *Orijentalni Institut u Sarajevu*: 113–115.

50 For the biography and publications of Mehmed Mujezinović (1913–1981), see: Anonymous, *Preporod* 14–15 [165–166] (15.7.–15.8.1977): 10–11; K. Hadžić, *Preporod* 11 [259] (1.6.1981): 26; M. Traljić, *Šebi Arus 1981* (Sarajevo, 1981): 34–38; Anonymous, *GVIS* 1983/1–2: 376–377; Anonymous, *AGHBB* 9–10 (1983): 327–333; Anonymous, *Šebi Arus 1990* (Sarajevo, 1990): 6; Nametak, *Sarajevski nekrologij*: 254–255.

51 For the biography and publications of Haris Silajdžić (b. 1945), see: Filandra, *Bošnjaćka politika*: 384–385; Anonymous, in *Ko je ko u Bošnjaka*: 357.

52 For the biography of Mustafa Cerić (b. 1952), see: Anonymous, *Preporod* 388 (15.10.1986): 2; Djilas and Gaće, *Bošnjak A. Z.*: 146; Anonymous, in *Ko je ko u Bošnjaka*: 83–84.

53 For the biography and publications of Enes Karić (b. 1958), see: Anonymous, *GVIS* 1983/1–2: 375; N. Čančar, *Preporod* 447 (1.4.1989): 2; Anonymous, in *Ko je ko u Bošnjaka*: 229–230; X. Bougarel, "Trois définitions de l'islam en Bosnie-Herzégovine," in M. Gaborieau and A. Popovic, eds, *Islam et politique dans le monde (ex-) communiste* (*Archives de Sciences Sociales des Religions*, 46e année, n° 115, juillet–septembre, Paris, 2001): 183–201.

54 For the biography and publications of Fikret Karčić (b. 1955), see: Anonymous, *GVIS* 1983/1–2: 375; Anonymous, *Preporod* 14 [454] (15.7.1989): 12; Bougarel, "La diversité de l'islam bosniaque," *passim*.

55 For the biography and publications of Mustafa Imamović (b. 1941), see: M. Imamović, *Historija Bošnjaka* (Sarajevo, 1998): 2; Filandra, *Bošnjaćka politika*: 264 (see also Index, 405); Anonymous, in *Ko je ko u Bošnjaka*: 207.

56 For the biography and bibliography of Amir Ljubović (b. 1945), see: Šamić, *Turcica* 16 (1984): 252–253; Anonymous, in *Ko je ko u Bošnjaka*: 263; Ljubović and Gazić, *Orijentalni Institut u Sarajevu*: 143–144.

57 For the biography and publications of Ali Fehmi Džabić (1853–1918), see: I. H. Mehinagić, *GVIS* 7/1–3 (1956): 22–30; B. Djurdjev, *EI*², s. v. (Leiden, 1965), 2: 698–699 (of the French edition); I. H. Mehinagić, *AGHBB* 2–3 (1974): 81–96; S. Balić, *Biographisches Lexikon zur Geschichte Südosteuropas* (München, 1974), 1: 451–453; A. Nametak, *AGHBB* 4 (1976): 187–199; Donia, *Islam under the Double Eagle*, Index, 234; Popovic, *Dict. biogr.*, 1: 51; Djilas and Gaće, *Bošnjak A. Z.*: 36.

58 For the biography and publications of Muhamed Tayyib Okić (1902–1977), see: A. Ljubović, *POF* 25 (1975 [1977]): 9–11; H. M-d., *Preporod* 8 [159] (15–30.4.1977): 5; K. Hadžić, *GVIS* (1977/3): 365–370; S. Balić, *Südost Forschungen* 36 (1977): 235–239; *Prof. M. Tayyib Okiç Armağanı* (Ankara, 1978); S. Balić, *Islam Tetkikleri Enstitüsü Dergisi* 7/1–2: 330–336; I. Morina, *Tan*, 548 (12.4.1980): 6; M. Traljić, *AGHBB* 7–8 (1982): 275–277; Nametak, *Sar. nekr.*: 70–72.

59 For the biography and publications of Smail Balić (b. 1920), see: F. H. Eterovich, ed., *Croatia. Land, People, Culture*, 2 vols. (Toronto: University of Toronto Press, 1964–1970), 2: 512–513; Anonymous, *Der Donau Raum* (Wien) 20/1–2 (1975): 128; H. Hajdarević, *Preporod* 24 [487] (15.12.1990): 10–11; Djilas and Gaće, *Bošnjak A. Z.*: 130–131; Filandra, *Bošnjačka politika*: 361, 365, 370; Anonymous, in *Ko je ko u Bošnjaka*: 54.

60 For the biography of Adil Zulfikarpašić (b. 1921), see: Djilas and Gaće, *Bošnjak, Adil Zulfikarpašić* (Zürich: Bošnjački Institut, 1994). Filandra, *Bošnjačka politika*: 361 (see also Index, 412); Anonymous, in *Ko je ko u Bošnjaka*: 421.

11

FROM SOCIAL DEVELOPMENT TO RELIGIOUS KNOWLEDGE

Transformation of the Isma'ilis in Northern Pakistan

Nejima Susumu

For the Isma'ilis, the twentieth century will be regarded as a time of social and religious revival. After a long period of time since the fall of Alamut in 1256, Isma'ilis have come back to the center stage of the worlds of Islam. This time, it is through NGO activities in the field of social and cultural development, not through armed political struggle. Various self-help programs to build schools, manage health care service, and preserve architecture of the past under the Aga Khan Development Network (AKDN) have been demonstrating the Isma'ilis' abilities to tackle social problems. It shall be made clear that the AKDN is non-denominational, involving thousands of non-Isma'ilis in its activities. Still, Aga Khan is the honorific title of the Isma'ili Imam, and the AKDN is, as its name suggests, under the general control of the Imamat (office of Imam). Most of the AKDN activities are found in areas where Isma'ilis are predominant. In the Isma'ili communities the NGO activities exist as an integral part of community life along with the religious organizations (for a detailed description of Isma'ili community life, see Nejima 2002).

The AKDN is following and promoting this trend, and this Muslim minority community with a living and hereditary Imam actually has become predominant in the field of social development. As a consequence, the Imamat has acquired more religious authority, and the *Jama'at* (Isma'ili community) has become a better defined and more autonomous community. This is particularly true in Northern Pakistan (the Northern Areas and Chitral District). In this mountainous region, the AKDN has successfully undertaken many "model cases." The Aga Khan Rural Support Programme (AKRSP) has innovated a model for participation of the rural poor (Khan and Khan 1992), and organized more than 70,000 members, or over 70% of rural households, in the first decade (AKRSP 1993). Later on, the Government of Pakistan officially acknowledged the model and adopted it in all the provinces of the country. In 1997 the Aga Khan Education Service (AKES) operates 177 schools (usually known as Diamond Jubilee (DJ) schools) with 850 teachers. The number of students, girls and boys, exceeds 20,000. The Aga Khan Health Service (AKHS) provides service, especially for mother and child health care, with 38 medical units. It has trained more than 700 volunteers as community health workers and trained birth attendants. The renovation of the Baltit Fort (Hunza Valley) by the Aga Khan Trust for Culture has been praised by President Leghari as "an excellent role model for the restoration of many historical structures in Pakistan" (*The Ismaili Pakistan* 1997/42).[1] In the 1990s the concept of social development—the local community's active participation in their own health care, primary education, sanitation, and other basic human needs in collaboration with NGOs—has become important. It has become mainstream practice.

With anthropological data from villages in Northern Pakistan, we would like to delineate the features of the contemporary Isma'ili community. The AKDN provides permanent occupations for hundreds of educated youth that otherwise may find no place in the rural economy. They come back to villages as DJ school teachers, AKHS local officers, or Lady Health Visitors. While they get income from the NGOs, they take the initiative to participate in other volunteer activities at the same time. For example, a DJ teacher may record the accounts for the Village Organization, a vehicle for rural development initiated by the AKRSP. Or he may reconcile disputes in the Arbitrary Panel, and collect *zakāt* (tithe) as a member of Local Council (LC). Besides, the Isma'ilis have now started studying their own religious texts, namely those of Nasir Khusraw. Having professional religious scholars in their own community is a step toward joining mainstream Islam, and it also enables them to contribute to the reconstruction of Islamic civilization through NGO activities. Therefore we believe that the locale clearly demonstrates the transformation taking place among the Isma'ilis as a whole.

The Isma'ilis in the early twentieth century

Northern and Southern Pakistan

The followers of Aga Khan, the Isma'ilis are distributed across the Indian Subcontinent, the Middle East, Central Asia, and East Africa. They live in North American cities and in Europe as well. The Imamat has its center in Eiglemont, near Paris. Today, Pakistan is the largest homeland for the Isma'ilis: about half a million of them live in this country, whence in the 1980s they were estimated around 400,000 (Kreutzmann 1989: 149). The Pakistani Isma'ilis are categorized into two groups, ethnically and linguistically quite different. One is that of the Khoja, known as a Karachi-based business community. The Khojas lead a reputed business network and have been a driving force in the modernization of the *Jama'at* (Isma'ili community), and their history is well-documented (cf. Bocock 1971; Clark 1976, 1978; Masselos 1978; Nanji 1974, 1978, 1983; Papanek 1962; Rattansi 1987; Walji 1974).

In 1845, Aga Khan I arrived in India from Persia, namely to the Khoja community. It was the starting point of the new history of the community. Here, as Gellner points out, the Isma'ili Imam was given the financial and social means for doing something quite different (Gellner 1981: 108). It was Aga Khan III who started "something quite different" on a full-scale. During his long reign (1885–1957), while cultivating friendship with Western elites, the Imam promoted the modernization of the Khoja community. Profound changes took place in the Khoja community. The *jama'at-khana*, a center of prayer and assembly now features many kinds of organizations. A council system has been established for administration and arbitration. The Isma'ilia Association deals with religious affairs. Cooperative banks channel loans to the individual merchants. The Education Board provides schools, and so on. Offices have been filled with eager volunteers (the Imam officially nominates them). Aga Khan III was issuing *farman*s (royal decrees) and exercising general control over all the organizations. Thus a modern Jamaat was formed with the volunteer works motivated not only by economic profit, but also by spiritual fulfillment.

The other group, much less studied as the Isma'ilis, is located in the northern corner of Pakistan. This is a border region between Central Asia and South Asia within the high mountains of the Karakorum-Hindukush. They are distributed throughout the numerous valleys, speaking various languages: Khowar, Shina, Burushaski, Wakhi, and so on. Life is mainly based on an agro-pastoral economy, with ever-increasing emphasis on off-farm income (on the rapid socio-economic changes in Northern Pakistan, see Stellrecht 1998; Stellrecht and Bohle 1998; Stellrecht and Winiger 1997).

Mountain farmers

Historically speaking, there were many principalities ruled by local rulers (called *mir, mehtar*, or *raja*) in the North until the 1970s. Besides the local political system, there was a religious hierarchy in the Isma'ili community (*pir, khalifa*, and *murid*). *Pir*s (elders, masters) used to have a deep influence among the Isma'ilis, which is expressed through a ritual of personal obedience (Holzwarth 1994: 39–40). A British administrator, John Biddulph, residing in Gilgit in the 1870s, wrote as follows (in the text, "Maulai" means "Ismaili," "Kunjoot" refers to "Hunza"):

> The countries inhabited by the Maulais are roughly divided among a number of *Pir*s, who are treated by their disciples with extraordinary respect. The office is hereditary, and Maulai families transfer their spiritual obedience from father to son. For instance, Shah Abdul Rahim of Zebak, who is honoured and respected as being next in rank to Aga Khan himself, has disciples in Sirikol, Kunjoot, Zebak, Yassin, and Badakhshan, but other *Pir*s have also disciples in those places. The respect paid to the *Pir*s by their disciples is unbounded; if they ask for a

> son or a daughter of any house, no refusal is dreamed of. One of them once said to me: "If I ordered a father to kill his own son, he dare not refuse." Whenever they move about, they maintained out of their superfluities, and they live entirely on the offerings of their disciples. Presents of horses, cattle, clothes, fruits, wheat, etc., are continually being made, and the best of everything a Maulai possesses is given to his *Pir*. A portion of these offerings is converted into coin and sent yearly to Aga Khan, and agents travel yearly from those remote parts to Bombay solely for the purpose of conveying these contributions to him.
>
> (Biddulph 1880: 119)

At the turn of the twentieth century, Aga Khan III had consolidated his authority in Bombay. Still, the *pir*s in this remote area maintained autonomous religious authority. *Pir*s might not have sent all the offerings to the Imam, and kept some portion for themselves or redistributed it within the local community. Disposal of the offerings was left to the *pir*s' discretion (Holzwarth 1994: 41; see also Keshavjee 1981 and Shahrani 1979 for similar situations in Iran and Afghanistan respectively).

Reforms from the center

Reforms among the Khojas were not easily emulated among the Ismaʿilis of the hinterlands such as Northern Pakistan. As mountain farmers with a subsistence economy, they did not have the capital of which the Khojas could dispose. But the region was also changing in its own way. Toward the turn of the century, the British tightened their control on the principalities of Chitral, Hunza, Ghizr, etc. It was the time of the Great Game between the Russian and the British Empires. This situation eventually had crucial impacts on the Ismaʿilis. As the newly created international borders came under increasing tension, *pir*s in the Pamirs faced difficulties in communicating with followers in British territory. At the same time, thanks to the British administration, which improved the transportation system from Srinagar to Gilgit, the Imam obtained a way to convey his message—and extend his control—more directly and efficiently to his followers in this mountain region. From that time onwards, most *pir*s disappear from the stage of local religious history (see Hunzaʿi 1991). Instead, the *mir* of Hunza, the sole Ismaʿili ruler in the region, came to the fore as the agent of the Imam. Mir Muhammad Nazim Khan was granted an audience with the Imam in 1903 in Delhi (Müller-Stellrecht 1979: 56–57). One of his sons went as far as Zanzibar to do homage to Aga Khan III (Müller-Stellrecht 1979: 375). Beforehand, *pir*s had monopolized the communication with the Imam.

Aga Khan III introduced reforms to the mountainous region under the "Pax Britanica." In 1922 and 1923, the Imam sent delegations to the various Ismaʿili communities. Important steps taken at that time were the construction of *jamaʿat-khana*s and the introduction of money orders for sending tithes (Müller-Stellrecht

1979: 218–220). The Imam nominated mukhi and kamria to be in charge of the management of each *jama'at-khana* (Kreutzmann 1989: 154–165, follows the development in Hunza from that time onwards). In 1946 Aga Khan III instructed the followers to build the first DJ schools (Felmy 1997: ch. 5; Hunzai 1991: 56–60). Since the British had established one or two primary schools in each principality, a few literate youths were available. They were to be appointed as the first DJ teachers.

The *Pir* as a modernizer

In the following sections we would like to investigate the changes taking place among the Isma'ilis using anthropological approaches. Our fieldwork was done between 1993 and 1995 in the villages of the upper Ghizr. First, we examined the early stage of school education in Ghizr through the life history of a *pir* family. The informant's life exemplifies the transformation of the Isma'ilis at that time.[2]

Our *pir*, hereafter mentioned as Pir Sahib as called in his locality, was born in 1929 in Yarkand (Xinjiang). Pir Sahib claims that his family is originally from Badakhshan, and that an Imam has nominated his ancestor as a *pir* and gave him the title of *khwaja*. King Taj Moghol was also from the Khwaja, says Pir Sahib (Taj Moghol is a legendary king of Badakhshan, who is said to have conquered the Chitral and Gilgit in the fourteenth century CE: see Dani 1989: ch.6).

Pir Sahib's grandfather lived in Wakhan[3] and used to visit Aga Khan in Bombay every year to deliver *zakāt* and to get religious instructions. In June, when the snow of the Baroghil Pass melted, he used to cross the pass between the Wakhan and Ghizr. Then he used to join another *pir* in Mastuj and to visit Bombay in the latter's company. The family moved to Yarkand in *c.* 1908. Pir Sahib says that *pir*s at that time used to move as they liked. Wakhan is a narrow valley similar to that of Ghizr, so his father was happy to settle in the town, Pir Sahib suggests. They lived among the Isma'ilis and spoke Persian. After twenty-five years, Yarkand was drawn into harsh conflicts and, in 1933, the family had to leave the land. Pir Sahib remembers the forty days' journey through the mountain path, spent on the back of a donkey. They moved to Mastuj, relying on another *pir* family there. In 1946, they came to the upper Ghizr and finally settled there. They were received with the respect of the Isma'ilis. The raja also exempted them from tax and corvée out of respect. Pir Sahib says that his father visited neighboring villages. However, there were not so many *pir*s active in the area, and their activities were not institutionalized. Religious education was limited among the *pir* families, and to some extent in those of *khalifa*s. At the age of 17, in 1946, Pir Sahib began to study at the Gupis Primary School, an educative institution established by the British. He recollects:

> There was a school in Gupis, Yasin, Gulapur and in another village respectively. Admission was easily available since people were not eager to study. The population was small and people were busy with cultivation.

> They had many livestock as well. About 30 students were studying in the school. Many of them were teenage boys like me. At that time, people did not appreciate that girls go to school, so that there was no single girl in the class. At school we used to learn Urdu and Persian languages, the geography of the Gilgit region, and mathematics. There was no class of Islam.
>
> (Dani 1989: 413)

This was a turning point in Pir Sahib's life. He became a DJ teacher after studying only three years in the primary school. Pir Sahib remembers the first days of the DJ school:

> We started the classes in a small room attached to the *jama'at-khana*. There was just one blackboard in it. About thirty five boys were coming from the surrounding villages. Sunni boys joined from the beginning. The course was for six years and there was no tuition fee. There were classes of Urdu language, mathematics, social science, and Islam. At that time, the only middle school was in Gilgit. Very few students could reach that place. We had English class after the 5th grade, at least until 1992. In the present DJ school, English language is taught from the beginning. Since I had never studied English at school, I learnt it by myself. I picked up words with dictionary, one by one. But then it was Urdu that we needed: we were eager to write letters, fill application forms, or talk to officers from Pakistan. Through the 1950s English was not that much required. The DJ school was originally intended only for boys.[4] It became mixt in the course of time, but parents did not agree to send their daughters to school. If a girl came, she seldom attended the classes until graduation.[5]

While coming from a traditional family, Pir Sahib became one of the forerunners of modernization. The role he played was quite important and decisive for the transformation of an illiterate farmers' society.

A new collective leadership

In 1960 Aga Khan IV visited Northern Pakistan for the first time in Isma'ili history (Hunzai 1991: 70–74; Kreutzmann 1989: 157). The Harvard-graduate Imam was impressed with his followers' dedication. Since then, much attention has been paid to Northern Pakistan. The abolition of the principalities and the opening of the Karakorum Highway in the 1970s brought about further crucial changes in Northern Pakistan. The Isma'ili community had produced many young literates by the 1980s and the collective leadership of the younger generation has emerged. The appearance of *wa'iz*s (lecturers) clearly demonstrates this tendency, since *wa'iz* progressively took the place of the *pir*s in the field of religious instruction.

The wa'iz

Our *wa'iz* was born in 1962 in a village in upper Ghizr, two years after the first visit of Aga Khan IV. He is from an ordinary farmer's family. He has studied at DJ primary and middle school, and at the Government highschool. In 1980, he has advanced to the Government College in Gilgit. The same year, the Gilgit branch of the Shi'a Imami Isma'ili Tariqa and the Religious Education Board for Pakistan (hereafter ITREB) started a training project for *wa'iz*s. He applied for it, and then studied hard for four years. From 9:00 to 13:00, he was at College and studied Islamic history, Islamic studies, the history of Pakistan, Persian and English languages. The medium for education was Urdu, except for English class. From 14:30 to 17:30, he was being trained in the ITREB. The subjects were Arabic and Persian languages, Islamic history, Islamic philosophy, Islamic literature, Hadith, Greek philosophy, and logic. Arabic and Persian languages were being taught in these respective languages. In addition, there was an English class. Two PhD holders were lecturing systematically to the trainees. In 1984 he finished the training course and college. Since then he works as a *wa'iz*.

Riding on his motorbike, the *wa'iz* goes from village to village. The *wa'iz* is a local channel of the religious information from the higher rank and the Imam's English *farman*. To perform his duty, he has to use several languages. In the ITREB, the flow of information and reporting is communicated through English as well as through Urdu language. In the villages, the *wa'iz* uses local languages such as Khowar and Shina: he must explain and comment on the words of the Imam in local languages, so that every follower can understand them. The *wa'iz* also holds religious classes called YAR in *jama'at-khana*s.[6] In the classes the *wa'iz* gives a plain explanation of the Imamat, the Qur'an, Islamic history, and the principles of Isma'ilism.

On the one hand, the *wa'iz* upholds the religious tradition of Badakhshani Isma'ilis. He learns Persian in the training and esteems Nasir Khusraw very highly. However, this does not mean that the *wa'iz* follows the *pir*'s old style directly: his learning and teaching style come as a consequence of the systematization of the religious knowledge within Isma'ili organizations.

The children of Aga Khan

Moreover, the *wa'iz* is not alone. He is among those young leaders working in the Isma'ili Council system, Arbitration Panel, Tariqa Board, and others. (These religious organizations are not NGOs open to everyone, but basically only for the socio-religious affairs within the Isma'ili community.) The young leaders have much in common. They are born in dispensaries of the AKHS, study at DJ school, and proceed to College with scholarships from the AKES. In Gilgit, they may stay in the Shah Karim al-Husayni Hostel named after the present Imam. They come back to villages as DJ teachers, AKHS local officers, or Lady Health Visitors. The tendency is widespread in the upper Ghizr, Hunza and elsewhere. In other words, they are products of the AKDN in social development. Now they are men of influence in their own villages. We now examine their socio-religious activities.[7]

The Local Council

The most important organization at the local level is the Council system. Twenty-five LC and five Regional Councils (RC), under the Federal Council (FC) in Karachi, stretch over all the Isma‘ili villages in the Northern Areas. In the villages, every *jama‘at-khana* is under a certain LC. In Ghizr, there are 4 LCs: Gupis, Pingal, Phandar, and Gologh Muli. In the Yasin Valley, there are also 4 LCs. These 8 LCs are under Gupis Regional Council. The members of the RC is made of experienced volunteers. The RC gives instructions to the less experienced members of LC, or deals with issues that cannot be handled at the LC level. The RC members are so qualified that they can theoretically discuss the regional problems with the Imam. The FC is located in Karachi and its members are mainly composed of the Khojas. Keeping communication with the Imam, the FC decides the direction of the Pakistani Isma‘ilis.

The Imam's instructions come to the villagers through the Council system. The Council also collects the *zakāt* and delivers it to the Imam. In principle the *zakāt* is made of 10% of the income, paid in cash, but due to the less stable economic situation, it is set slightly lower compared to the Khojas. The Isma‘ilis emphasize that the *zakāt* is meaningfully used for the development of villages. The problems in the villages are moved out through the Council system, and the Imam decides how to tackle them. Until then, the collected *zakāt* is kept in a bank in Karachi. Eventually it comes back to the villages for various expenditure. People claim that the *zakāt* has never been squandered on the whims of the Imam.

The Panel

"His Highness the Prince Agha Khan Shi‘a Imami Isma‘ili Masalti-o-Salisi Panel" is a spin-off organization out of the Council system. It is specialized in conducting mediation and arbitration. Its trademark is a crown that symbolizes the Imamat. The Panel is basically an arbitration body for solving troubles and disputes within the Isma‘ili community. The Government of Pakistan officially acknowledges it. Therefore, the Panel can deal with injury and murder as well as marriage and business troubles. To obtain essential knowledge of the Pakistani laws, members are trained in Gilgit. There are upper Panels in Gilgit and Karachi, and the latter has among its members professionals with a judicial background. With problems concerning land and water, local Sunnis can be concerned since they live together in most villages in Ghizr. If they agree, the Panel offers a table for negotiation. Sometimes a civil judge in Gupis sends cases to the Panel, but the reverse does not happen. It is claimed that the advantages of the Panel are that it is "free, fast and just." In the Panel, one does not have to submit any particular paper. He or she can discuss the matter fully in his/her mother tongue. On the contrary, the government judicial system has a very poor reputation. People have to attend trials repeatedly. Since it may take years until judgment, the cost of attending these formalities in remote places is regarded as too expensive. There are always rumors of bribery in and around Government offices.

Regardless of one's tenet, people call it *jirga* and are ready to accept its proposal when one is concerned. The *jirga* is a judicial system that used to be based on the authority of the raja (and later, of the British Political Agent). "The raja's rule was tyranny, but we could solve the matter very quickly at that time." "We used to solve the case at once." "We did not take bribes." The elders who once were *jirga* members unanimously claim this to be true. These claims also imply criticism of the present Government. Here, there is a base for wider acceptance of the Panel or new *jirga*, which is under the authority of the Imamat.

The Ismaili Tariqa and the Religious Education Board

The ITREB deals with religious education and publications. Tariqa (Ar. *ṭarīqa*) originally means "path" of an ascetic practice. It also refers to such or such specific mystic order. Through this word, it is the Isma'ili attitude of putting significance on the inner (*bāṭin*) meaning of the Qur'an that is understood. The organization is called the "Isma'ilia Association," as well. Its headquarters are again in Karachi and take charge of religious education and information as a whole. The ITREB publishes various journals and books, mainly for the Isma'ili audience. At the local level, the main task of the Board is religious education of children. Boys and girls of more than 5 years old attend 2-hour classes to learn the recitation of the Qur'an. Children also study the history of the Imams. As already mentioned, the *wa'iz* holds YAR classes for adults.

Nasir Khusraw as an intellectual root

In the previous sections, we have seen how the leadership within the Isma'ili community has been transformed in Northern Pakistan. These new leaders are produced and supported by various NGO activities. Though the AKDN is nondenominational, in the Isma'ili life NGOs and religious organizations complement each other. Then, what are the implications for religious studies? This question is not easy to answer, since most Isma'ilis hesitate to talk about religion with non-Isma'ilis. Nonetheless, some important steps have been taken, and it is possible for outsiders to make some observations. Therefore in this section we will try to deal with this issue despite our still much limited information sources.[8]

Within religious studies, the focus is put on the Fatimid Isma'ili philosopher and missionary Nasir Khusraw (1004–after 1072 CE). Of course, Nasir Khusraw has been known for more than a century in the West, where first attempts of study and translation of his work have been made as early as *c.*1880 (Schimmel 1993: 1). Here it is important to emphasize that the tradition of the well-known Fatimid philosopher is deeply rooted in Northern Pakistan.

Nasir Khusraw was born in Balkh (in the North of modern Afghanistan) and is famous for his journey to Mecca and Cairo. Later, he resided in Yumgan, a remote mountainous region of Badakhshan. Yumgan is not far from Chitral and the Isma'ilis in Northern Pakistan revere Nasir Khusraw as their first missionary from Badakhshan. The "*Isma'ili Mission in the Northern Areas: A Historical Review*" begins with a mention of Nasir Khusraw as the first to have propagated the Isma'ili doctrine to the region (Hunza'i 1991), where many local folk tales narrate Nasir Khusraw's miracles (cf. Schomberg 1938). Another piece of evidence to demonstrate Nasir Khusraw's significance in the North is a ritual called *chiragh-i rawshan*, a lamp-lighting ceremony attributed to Nasir Khusraw and performed on the third day after a death. The *chiragh-i rawshan* is performed to console and give a message about the dead's life in the other world; it invites the living ones to focus on the mystical presence of the Imam, who is identified with a spiritual lamp. Thus, through folk tales and traditional ritual, Nasir Khusraw has long been known and familiar among the Isma'ilis as a great saint.

His writings can be divided into three categories: a prose memoir of his travels, poetry, and philosophical books (Hunsberger 2000: 114). Yet works of his such as the *Safar-nāma, Dīwān, Wağh-i dīn* and others have not been widely accessible to the faithful until very recently, and in the past only a small number of people used to be familiar with his philosophy. This is not strange when considering that the community was largely based on agro-pastoralism and had only very scanty means for reproducing the scholarly class from generation to generation. Now, thanks to widespread education, many young persons with scientific and technical MAs and BAs are eager to acquire by themselves a higher religious knowledge. When they turn to religious studies, Nasir Khusraw is always a focal point.

Nasir Khusraw studies have been developed mainly in the Hunza Valley, where social development is most advanced among Northern Isma'ilis. It is 'Allama Nasir Hunza'i ('Allāma Nāṣir al-Dīn Nāṣir Hunza'ī) who started serious study on Nasir Khusraw. Nasir Hunza'i was born in 1917 in Hunza. Being a member of a *khalifa* family, he must have been closer to religious learning, although in general, circumstances in Hunza were then far from ideal for education. He was able to attend school for only one year, and acquired knowledge mainly by himself. Later, when he was in Xinjiang to propagate Isma'ilism, he was arrested. While in prison, he experienced a spiritual awakening. So far, the prolific thinker has published more than 150 books and pamphlets, which made him be known under the title of 'Allama, or greater scholar.

Beside translating the *Wağh-i dīn* and other works of Nasir Khusraw into Urdu, Nasir Hunza'i has written several articles about this great figure. One of these articles, "Pir Nasir Khusraw, A Universe of Knowledge," has been published in the *Tazkira-yi Sayyidnā Pīr Nāṣir Ḫusraw* (Iqbal *et al.* 1992). This is the record of two Ismaili conferences on Nasir Khusraw held in Chitral (October 1989) and Gilgit (November 1990). Beside Nasir Hunza'i's, it includes more than twenty articles. Topics are extremely broad and cover various aspects of Nasir Khusraw's life, works, and influence in Central Asia. The book is epoch-making, since the articles were mainly written by the educated young generation for their fellow readers. Another important work of Nasir Hunza'i is his *Chirāgh-i Rawshan* (1993), the first written interpretation (*ta'wīl*) of the ritual, exploring its various esoteric significations.

'Allama Nasir Hunza'i has established several private institutions and taught many students. Originally installed in 1961 in Hunza, the Danishgah-i Khanah-i Hikmat has been relocated in Karachi since 1977, and become a locus of religious studies. The 'Allamah Research Institute Foundation, or Idara-i ARIF, has been established by his students in Canada. Nasir Hunza'i's works include as well poetry in Burushaski, the vernacular tongue of Hunza. The BRA, or Burushaski Research Academy, specializes in the study of the language, and Nasir Hunzai is also known locally as Baba-e Burushaski (Father of Burushaski). There are thousands of young Isma'ilis from the North studying and working in Karachi. Nasir Hunza'i's circle attracts students from this population (there are students from Afghanistan too). Among his students, colleagues, and ex-colleagues, one can mention the following figures.

Ghulam 'Abbas Hunza'i has written his Master thesis (McGill University) on the concept of pleasure in the philosophy of Nasir Khusraw. He has worked with the ITREB, and is presently working with the AKHS. Shahnaz Hunza'i has had a unique career: she is one of the Khoja women married to Hunza, and masters the local Burushaski language. She is the author of a thesis on the concept of *qiyāmat* (resurrection of the Last Day) in Nasir Khusraw's thought at the Institute of Isma'ili Studies (IIS, London), in which she has translated a few chapters of the *Ḫwān al-iḫwān* into English. 'Azizullah Najeeb, one of the editors of the *Taẕkira*, has completed his Doctoral Degree on Nasir Khusraw from Hamdard University in Karachi. He was working as a *wa'iz* when the Gilgit branch of the Isma'ilia Association was first established. Fida 'Ali Isar Hunza'i is the author of *Isma'Ili Mission in the Northern Areas*; he has also translated selected poems of the *Dīwān* in Urdu, and it is published from ITREB (Hunza'i 1998–1999).

But these intellectual movements are not limited to Northern Pakistan or Karachi, and are in fact resonating with the center. We can see it through the example of another student of Nasir Hunza'i's—Faqir Muhammad Hunzai (*sic*), a Research Associate at the IIS. He has been translating the 'Allama's works from Urdu into English in collaboration with his wife, who is from the East African Khoja community. He undertook his post-graduate studies at Karachi University, where he was studying philosophy, Arabic, and Persian language and literature. The holder of a PhD from McGill University (Islamic Studies), he is active at the IIS and his works include *The Shimmering Light. An Anthology of Isma'ili Poetry* (1996), which collects nineteen poems from the *Dīwān*, and *Nasir Khusraw: Knowledge and Liberation* (1998), a new edition and English translation of the *Gušāyiš wa rahāyiš*.

Thus the local intellectual movement originating from the Northern Pakistan appears closely linked with the center or the IIS. The Institute of Isma'ili Studies has been established in 1977 with the object of promoting Islamic scholarship and learning in general, and Isma'ilism in particular. The IIS offers a graduate program in Islamic Studies and Humanities, which attracts students from Isma'ili communities around the world. Since the mid-1990s, the Institute has vigorously published academic books and research papers on Isma'ilism, especially that of the Fatimid period. In one of the IIS publications, Heinz Halm writes: "under the Fatimids and through their efforts, Cairo became one of the centres of Islamic culture and art, and a focus of a scholarship and science" (Halm 1997: xiv). For the Isma'ilis who have achieved social, cultural, and economic uplift through NGO activities, the Fatimid golden age is associated with their own efforts to reconstruct Islamic civilization under the Imamat. It is quite understandable that, in such an overall framework, Nasir Khusraw is highly esteemed in the center as well as in the North.

Conclusion

The change in authority transmission

In the Isma'ili community in Northern Pakistan, the forms and features of leadership have changed considerably. Within a century, especially in the last fifty years, they have gradually established a collective leadership. "Now we don't have much to do" says Pir Sahib, relaxing in his porch, listening to a Persian program on the radio. "The institutes do it." Religious tradition is revived by the activities of the ITREB. Furthermore, researchers in the IIS in London are eager to edit the classical texts. Local *wa'iz*s may follow this academic trend.

Religious organizations as well as NGOs offer leadership to the educated youth regardless of their origin. They can go up the hierarchy of the religious organizations, from Local to Regional offices. Beside the Imam's encouragement, respect and prestige within the community are the rewards for one's volunteer work. The young generation shares the following features as local leaders under the present Imamat.

1. They personify the equality of the followers.
2. With higher education, they are fluent in reading and writing English, as well as Urdu.
3. They are in charge of managing organizations based on their merits, not by holy ancestry.
4. Reflecting their own transformation, they have started to produce religious knowledge directly related to the Great Tradition, or the texts of Nasir Khusraw, who was formerly known only through miracles and rituals.

The new leaders make a good combination with the Imam. As the supreme leader of the AKDN, Aga Khan IV is well known in the development circles: he makes speeches in UN conferences, or holds international conferences in partnership with the World Bank. For this Imam, those who talk about high hopes for the AKRSP's grassroots program are the best counterpart. Local *pir*s with traditional ritual and holy ancestry are not able to follow in the Imam's footsteps.

The change of leaders at the local level reflects not only the internal changes of Northern Pakistan. The way these changes were institutionalized demonstrates but also the direction of self-reform in the Isma'ili community as a whole. The holy ancestry except that of the Imam has been denied, and collective leadership has become an organizational principle. Thanks to religious and NGO activities, the northern *Jama'at* of the mountain farmers and the southern *Jama'at* of the Khojas have become one with regard to institutionalization.

An emerging civil society and identity

The change in the modes of acquisition and transmission of literacy has been intermingling and strengthening the tendency of self-help among the Isma'ilis. It has made the Isma'ili community more egalitarian and autonomous. If it does not oppose the state, in Pakistan as well as in Tajikistan, it does virtually replace the local administration in various fields. Among the Isma'ili religious organizations, persistence in voluntarism is a most visible feature. At the same time, volunteers are being nominated to their offices by the Imam himself. This appointment is a source of honor and prestige that excites the Isma'ilis' efforts. Through the volunteer works, the Isma'ilis nurture their personal relationship with the Imam. Thus institutionalized voluntarism has an aspect of large-scale expression of spiritual dedication to the Imam. The consequence is the construction of an autonomous space, which can be termed "civil society" in the contemporary world. It is interesting enough that the century-old office of Imamat is the founding stone of the new civil society.

Being a minority in Pakistan, the Isma'ili version of the revival movement has its own subtlety too. The AKDN's nondenominational attitude, inviting non-Isma'ilis as well as Isma'ilis for development has created an image of openness to both the Imamat and the Jamaat. "Participation for development" has, at the same time, produced a particular meaning within the Isma'ili community. Since the NGOs' activities are well coordinated with the religious organizations in the community, they have contributed to the creation of a new identity among Isma'ilis. It also means the creation of a boundary between Isma'ilis and non-Isma'ilis. This boundary strengthens their identity, often by tacitly contrasting themselves with the others. This factor can be exclusionary and may cause negative social results. Higher religious studies, though still embryonic, are interesting in this regard. Through studying Nasir Khusraw and the Fatimid Golden Age, the Northern Isma'ilis will be able to widen and deepen their religio-cultural identity. In other words, Nasir Khusraw can be a passport to the Great Tradition for Northern Isma'ilis. By invigorating religious studies, the latter will be able to identify themselves in their own community in the North, in the Pakistani Isma'ili community, and in the world of Islam in general.

Notes

1 The data mentioned here was kindly given from the offices of AKES and AKHS.
2 The narratives given here are paraphrased to be compact by the author.
3 There are "Khuja families" in Wakhan. See Shahrani 1979: 56.
4 Nowadays AKES's main task is education for girls.
5 Interview conducted by the author in May 5, 1995.
6 YAR stands for Youth and Elder Religious Course. Yar means "friend" in Urdu.
7 The Isma'ilis are not eager to offer the information about their socio-religious activities. From time to time, however, some of them kindly gave me some information.
8 I highly owe 'Allama Nasir Hunza'i and Shahnaz Hunza'i for the information. I would like to express special acknowledgment to them.

References

Aga Khan Rural Support Programme [AKRSP], 1993, *Tenth Annual Review* (Gilgit: Aga Khan Rural Support Programme).

Biddulph, J., 1880, *Tribes of the Hindoo Koosh* [reprint, Graz: Akademische Druck-u. Verlagsanstalt, 1977].

Bocock, R. J., 1971, "The Ismailis in Tanzania: A Weberian Analysis," *British Journal of Sociology* 22/4: 365–380.

Clark, P. B., 1976, "The Ismailis: A Study of Community," *British Journal of Sociology* 27/4: 484–494.

—— 1978, "The Ismaili: sect in London: Religious Institutions and Social Change," *Religion*, 8: 68–84.

Dani, A. H., 1989, *History of Northern Areas of Pakistan* (Islamabad: National Institute of Historical and Cultural Research).

Felmy, S., 1997, *The Voice of the Nightingale: A Personal Account of the Wakhi Culture in Hunza* (Karachi: Oxford University Press).

Gellner, E., 1981, *Muslim Society* (Cambridge: Cambridge University Press).

Halm, H., 1997, *The Fatimids and Their Traditions of Learning* (London: I. B. Tauris) [IIS].

Holzworth, W., 1994, *Die Ismailiten in Nordpakistan: Zur Entwicklung einer Religiosen Minderheit im Kontext Neuer au enbeziehungen* (Berlin: Das Arabische Buch).

Hunsberger, A. C., 2000, *Nasir Khusraw, The Ruby of Badakhshan: A Portrait of the Persian Poet, Traveller and Philosopher* (London: I. B.Tauris) [IIS].

Hunzai, F. M., 1996, *The Shimmering Light. An Anthology of Ismaili Poetry* (London: I. B. Tauris) [IIS].

—— 1998, *Nasir Khusraw: Knowledge and Liberation* (London: I. B. Tauris) [IIS].

Hunza'ī, A. N. H., 1993, *Chirāgh-i Rawshan*, trans. by Faqir Muhammad Hunzai and Rasida Noormohamed-Hunzai (Karachi: Khanāh-i Hikmat Idarāh-i 'Arif).

Hunza'ī, F. A. I., 1991, *Šumālī 'Ilāqaǧāt men Ismā'īlī Da'wat: Ek Ta'rīḫī Ǧā'za* (Karachi: Shia Imami Ismaili Tariqa and Religious Education Board barā'e Pakistan (in Urdu)).

—— 1998–1999, *Kalām-i Pīr Nāṣir Ḫusraw* (7 vols) (Karachi: Shia Imami Ismaili Tariqa and Religious Education Board barā'e Pakistan (in Urdu)).

Iqbāl, S. M., Naǧīb, 'A., Ḫān, M. B., and Ḫākī, Ǧ. A., 1992, *Taẕkira-yi Sayyidnā Pīr Nāṣir Ḫusraw* (Karachi: Shia Imami Ismaili Tariqa and Religious Education Board barae Pakistan (in Urdu)).

The Ismaili Pakistan 1997/1.

Keshavjee, R. H., 1981, *The Quest for Gnosis and the Call of History: Modernization among the Ismailis of Iran* (PhD thesis, Harvard University).

Khan, M. S., and Khan, S. S., 1992, *Rural Change in the Third World: Pakistan and the Aga Khan Rural Support Program* (New York: Greenwood Press).

Kreutzmann, H., 1989, *Hunza: Ländliche Entwicklung im Karakorum* (Berlin: Dietrich Reimer Verlag).

Masselos, J. C., 1978, "The Khojas of Bombay: The Defining of Formal Membership Criteria during the Nineteenth Century," in I. Ahmad, ed., *Caste and Social Stratification among the Muslims in India* (New Delhi: Manohar): 97–116.

Müller-Stellrecht, I., 1979, *Materialen zur Ethnographie von Dardistan (Pakistan). Aus den Nachgelassenen Aufzeichnungen von D. L. R. Lorimer. Teil I. Hunza* (Graz: Akademische Druck-u. Verlagsanstalt).

Nanji, A., 1974, "Modernization and Change in the Nizari Ismaili Community in East Africa: A Perspective," *Journal of Religion of Africa* 6:123–139.

—— 1978, *The Nizari Ismaili Tradition in the Indo-Pakistan Subcontinet* (New York: Caravan Books).

—— 1983, "The Nizari Ismaili Muslim Community in North America: Background and Development," in E. H. Waugh, B. Abu-Laban, B. Qureshi, eds, *The Muslim Community in North America* (Alberta: The University of Alberta Press): 149–164.

Nejima, S., 2002, *Islam and Development. The Transformation of the Ismaili Community in Karakorum* (Kyoto: Nakanishiya Shuppan) [in Japanese].

Papanek, H., 1962, *Leadership and Social Change in the Khoja Ismaili Community* (PhD thesis, Harvard University).

Rattansi, D., 1987, *Islamization and the Khojah Ismaili Community in Pakistan* (PhD thesis, McGill University).

Schimmel, A., 1993, *Make a Shield from Wisdom. Selected Verses from Nasir-i Khusraw's Divan* (London: Kegan Paul International) [IIS].

Schomberg, R. C. F., 1938, *Kafirs and Glaciers. Travels in Chitral* (London: Martin Hopkins).

Shahrani, M. N. M., 1979, *The Kirghiz and Wakhi of Afghanistan. Adaptation to Closed Frontiers* (Seattle, WA: University of Washington Press).

Stellrecht, I., ed., 1998, *The Past in Present. Horizons of Remembering in the Pakistani Himalaya* (Köln: Rüdiger Köppe Verlag).

Stellrecht, I. and Bohle, H., eds, 1998, *Transformation of Social and Economic Relationship in Northern Pakistan* (Köln: Rüdiger Köppe Verlag).

Stellrecht, I. and Winiger, M., eds, 1997, *Perspectives on History and Change in the Karakorum, Hindukush, and Himalaya* (Köln: Rüdiger Köppe Verlag).

Walji, S. R., 1974, *A History of the Ismaili Community in Tanzania* (PhD thesis, University of Wisconsin).

[IIS] means the title is published in association with the Institute of Ismaili Studies.

12

ISLAM ON THE WINGS OF NATIONALISM

The case of Muslim intellectuals in Republican China

Françoise Aubin

Unceasing convulsions, chaos and troubles have shaken China, as it is well known, during the first half of the twentieth century: the Boxer rebellion in 1900, the overthrow of the Qing dynasty at the turn of 1912, the xenophobic anti-Christian (more precisely anti-Protestant) outburst in 1925, the breaking of a tactical alliance between Guomindang[1] and Communists in 1927, the rapid militarization of the politics and so on.[2] While intellectuals were contending without end about the significance of the past, the throwing out of their so-called ossified spiritual legacy, the invention of a new way of life and thought, their political commitment, there were other groups of intellectuals who unostentatiously and unnoticed were conducting their own revolution, on the fringe of the main currents, especially in the coastal big cities. These intellectuals were Chinese believers in Islam.[3]

How Muslim intellectuals reacted to the surrounding turmoil

With cultural associations

The basis of their social activity was the creation of numerous cultural associations, whose program focused on the modernization and the expansion of popular religious education, on the improvement of higher religious formation, on the promotion of Islamic culture, and whose leaders were often the imams in charge of the cult (*zhangjiao* 掌教), usually called in China the *ahong*s.[4] Associations had too the merit of being a remedy for the dispersion of local communities, each of them congregated round a mosque, without links between one another. And, doing so, the activists were convinced that they put into practice their love of the Chinese motherland and their wish to help it, although without taking political stand, they say. But, from the names chosen for these associations and for the schools they supported, it is obvious that a very important point then was at stake: the identity of the Chinese Muslims, that is Muslims whose everyday and literary language is Chinese. Did they constitute a religious or an ethnic minority? That is a problem which was new at the turn of the twentieth century and during the following decades, linked with the diffusion of Western ideas (often thanks to a Japanese intermediary) about religion, ethnicity, nationality and citizenship.

Actually there are several Chinese expressions for rendering the concept of Islam and Muslim according to the point of view of the speaker, and each of them appears somehow in one or another designation of these associations. The traditional wording of self-designation was to be a follower of "the Religion of the Pure and the True" or of "the Pure and True Religion", *Qingzhenjiao* 清真教, a statement still very appreciated at the turn of the twenty-first century for it stresses the believers' purity as a special marker of their superiority. They could also be called *Mumin* 穆民, "the Mu[slim] people," an abbreviation of the word now currently in use, *Mu-si-lin* 穆斯林.[5] During the first half of the twentieth century they were more and more often named—and they called themselves more and more often—members of the *Huijiao* 回教 "the religion of the Hui," or *Huimin* 回民, "the Hui people," it being understood that Hui had then the meaning of the world-wide Islam,[6] an equivalent of the word now common, *Yi-si-lan* 伊斯蘭, Chinese transliteration of "Islam." They also frequently called themselves the *Hui Hanzi* 回漢子, "the Muslim Han." Later on, history has decided: under the People's Republic, the Chinese Muslims have been registered as a specific "nationality" or *minzu* 民族, as the *Huizu* 回族.[7] In the following list I shall draw from the main cultural associations created during the first decades of the twentieth century; I shall translate their names as closely as possible to their original meaning, unfortunately at the expense of elegance, because such names were not chosen at random, and each of the words forming them bore in itself the weight of an emotionally heavy tradition.

Since the very beginning, the appearance of associations of their own is unmistakably a reply the Muslim modernists gave to the pervasive atmosphere surrounding them. Indeed the earliest association just followed, at the end of the Qing dynasty, the official reform of the educational system, culminating in September 1905 in the abolition of the thousand year old civil service examinations and of the Confucian schooling. It was founded in 1906 (Guangxu 32)[8] at Zhenjiang 鎮江 (Jiangsu),[9] under the appellation of the "General Association for the Religious Education of the Muslim People (*Mumin*) of Eastern Asia" (*Dongya Mumin jiaoyu zonghui* 東亞穆民教育總會). Its initiator, Tong Cong 童琮,[10] was a local Muslim in his forties, having recently graduated in the Confucianist system, so a man well integrated in the surrounding society. The interesting point is that he was then in touch with a group of thirty-six young Muslim Chinese sent for studying in Tokyo, because Japan was, after its victory over Russia in 1905, the favorite place where one could be introduced into modernity.[11] These young men in their turn founded in 1907, on the model drawn by Tong Cong, an "Association for the Pure and True [i.e. Muslim] Education of the Students in To[kyo]/or in the East"—with a play on the word *dong*, 東 "East," and the first syllable of Tokyo, 'the Eastern Capital' (*Liudong Qingzhen jiaoyu hui* 留東清真教育會). And then, so important was, in the Chinese tradition, the correct naming of any enterprise, that Tong Cong, at these students' instigation, changed the name of his society to "General Association for the Pure and True Education of East Asia" (*Dongya Qingzhen jiaoyu zonghui* 東亞清真教育總會), a formulation which stressed at the same time the religious and the Chinese characters of his program. The aim of Tong Cong's association was the promotion of a good Muslim education, so many Muslim notables backed him. He had actually opened in 1905 one of the first "modernized" Islamic schools in China—if not the first one—, a "School of Muslim sources" (*Muyuan xuetang* 穆源學堂), fit out with a printing house for presenting his pedagogical ideas in a journal "To develop us" (the *Yiwobao* 益我). As early as in 1908, he called in the school a meeting of his supporters and encouraged the creation of branches of his association everywhere. But this still remained a provincial venture.

Merchants of Shanghai, during the troubles accompanying the fall of the imperial dynasty in the last weeks of 1911, constituted for protecting citizens a militia directed by a future journalist, Sha Shanyu 沙善餘,[12] and they were proclaiming to be adepts of the "Pure and True" using the name itself chosen for their group, *Qingzhen shangtuan* 清真商團 [Militia of Merchants of the Pure and True].[13] The need for a common local organization of the believers was then strongly felt. For example, shortly before the overthrow of the dynasty, in 1910, a group of Muslim merchants and students of Shanghai elected (through a genuine vote, *toupiao* 投票, with ballot papers) a marine officer as a general administrator with two assistants, to make up for the lack of a central authority heading their community; and they came to the office of the representative of the throne, the head of the *xian* 縣, begging for an official registration: this has been immortalized by an inscription on stone.[14] Shortly after the beginning of the new era in 1912, Muslim intellectuals of the major centers of coastal China felt more and more the acute need for associations promoting Islamic (*Hui*) culture and education. Pekingese launched in this very year 1912 a progressive movement with the long-lasting "Society for the Advance of the Hui Religion of China" (*Zhongguo Huijiao jujin hui* 中國回教俱進會 or *al-Ǧam'iyyat al-taqaddum al-islāmiyya al-sīniyya*),[15] which has been the first nationwide association of the believers, endowed with subsidiary associations (*fenhui* 分會) in each province, and, since 1934, subsidiary groups in the mosques too. Very fine scholars were among its members, such as the *ahong* Ma Songting 馬松亭[16] and its first director, the *ahong* Wang Haoran 王浩然.[17] The principle for naming this association, which was to be followed by several others, was to use the word *Huijiao*, meaning Islam as a whole, and to add the specification of *Zhongguo*, "China."

The movement extended to Shanghai later. In the full burst of xenophobic manifestations and of large strikes in 1925, appeared, in the foreground of Muslim revival, Ha Decheng 哈德成.[18] He was both a religious personality—an *ahong* at a Shanghai mosque—, and since 1913 one of the managers of an international commercial society, whose benefits were earmarked to finance the schooling of future *ahong* and to buy Islamic books overseas. In 1925, back to Shanghai after several years spent abroad, he was struck by the still low level of religious teaching. In order to remedy to this situation, he gathered ten or so co-religionists of Shanghai, among others Sha Shanyu, a teacher and journalist,[19] and Wu Tegong 伍特公, a journalist;[20] and on the 25th of June he created with them a specifically nonpolitical "Learned Society of the Hui Religion of China" (*Zhongguo Huijiao xuehui* 中國回教學會, or *al-Ǧamʿiyyat al-ʿilmiyya al-islāmiyya al-sīniyya*).[21] Its aim was the promotion of religious education, of the collective good, of friendship with foreign co-religionists; the practical actions were the creation of an Islamic school, of an Arabic school and of elementary schools, of a library, the diffusion of foreign Muslim scholarship, the translation of the Qurʾan, the publication of handbooks, of a journal, and so on. Such it remained, till the Japanese took over Shanghai, the most efficient society in the field of Muslim scholarship.

Some years later, in October 1929, still in Shanghai, some distinguished Muslim personalities, who were not professionals of religion, initiated a "Guild of the Hui Religion of China" (*Zhongguo Huijiao gonghui* 中國回教公會).[22] Its main leaders were again Sha Shanyu, Wu Tegong and Da Pusheng 達浦生,[23] an elderly man who had graduated some years before at the Cairo University of al-Azhar and who was to play a prominent part in the relation of the Muslim community with the Guomindang and the Communist governments. The aim of this association was to help the country and to plan the public good; the means to reach it was the formation of *ahong*s of the highest grade, the construction of numerous schools, hospitals and libraries, and the introduction of a technical training. However, the association could not carry it off, a failure due to a lack of organization, of talented helpers, and to some inner resistance, which shows that the task was not easy.

Two years after this one, in 1931, another scholarly society was created by young Muslims, in Nanking this time: the "Learned Society of the Youth for the Hui Religion of China" (*Zhongguo Huijiao qingnian xuehui* 中國回教青年學會), whose program was to meet together on a friendly footing, to study in a scholarly way, and finally to help the society as a whole, the means of action being meetings of young people, vocational orientation of the youth, various publications, contribution to an improvement of believers' life. A new step was passed, which showed that young Muslims had begun to feel concerned by the political atmosphere, especially in Nanking, then the capital of the Guomindang government: they have added to their program a study of Sun Yatsen's "Triple Demism" or Three People Principles (*Sanmin zhuyi* 三民主義) to check if it did not contradict Islam. They complemented their association in 1936 by an "Association for Scientific Research of the Hui People" (*Huimin xueshu yanjiu hui* 回民學術研究會)[24] which was aimed at realizing specific scholarly studies.

By that time, in 1934 a "Cultural Friendly Association of the Hui Religion of China" (*Zhongguo Huijiao wenhua xiehui* 中國回教文化學會)[25] was launched at

Shanghai. One of its founding members was Fu Tongxian 傅統先,[26] a modernist and the future author of a history of Chinese Islam which remains our best source of information for the evolution of Islam in the Republican era. The objective of the group was to upgrade the level of Chinese Islam, felt as too low, its tools being publication of new researches or of old classical studies in the field of Chinese Islam. The list of Muslim associations with a purely cultural aim, which started in the late twenties and early thirties, could be expanded with provincial initiatives too. We may quote, for example, a "Society for the diffusion of Chinese Islam" (*Zhongguo Yi-si-lan budao hui* 中國伊斯蘭佈道會),[27] introduced in 1933 into Taiyuan 太原, the capital city of Shanxi, whose program was to spread broadly the Muslim doctrine, through a translation of the Qur'an, various publications and news about the Religion in the local newspaper, the Daily of Taiyuan (*Taiyuan ribao* 太原日報). This time the name of the association showed it referred not just to Hui religion but Islam (*Yi-si-lan*) itself.

In the thirties, the Islamic associations were beginning to feel the weight of politics, as testified by the Nanking students' concern for the official ideology of the Guomindang as conveyed by Sun Yatsen's program. A new stage was passed when Muslim military personalities of Western China, while becoming warlords, were heartily supporting a revival of Islamic culture in its sinicized and confucianized version and adhered to Muslim cultural associations of the coastal regions. It was in May 1933, when Ma Hongkui 馬鴻逵,[28] just appointed governor of Ningxia, at the door of Tibet, entered into the administrative committee (*weiyuan* 委員) of a new "Society for the Promotion of Education of the Hui People" (*Huimin jiaoyu cujin hui* 回民教育促進會),[29] and served in this capacity till 1948. The program was a straight education for everybody. But a new preoccupation was added to the usual promise of establishing a lot of good schools: to push forward Chinese Islam to the western part of the country by proselytizing in border regions and applying to the government for bringing together Uighurs and Muslim Han and giving them a common education. The name of another association, started once more in the capital Nanking in 1934, the "Confederation of the Hui religion in China" (*Zhonghua Huijiao zonghui* 中華回教總會),[30] indicated a certain display of support for the government, as the term *Zhonghua* has been selected by Sun Yatsen, and after him by the Guomindang, for referring to China, instead of the usual *Zhongguo*. One of its subsidiary association (*fenhui* 分會), the one settled in Western China, in Lanzhou 蘭州 the capital of Gansu, was led by military and political figures belonging to the circle of warlords, Ma Lin 馬麟,[31] his nephew Ma Buqing 馬步青,[32] Ma Hongbin 馬鴻賓,[33] the nephew of the famous Ma Fuxiang 馬福祥,[34] and a cousin of Ma Hongkui—himself Ma Fuxiang's son.

The starting point of a general mobilization of believers for a political move was the shock of the so-called Marco Polo Bridge Incident, on 7 July 1937, the day Japan began to invade China. In the following months, a political personality of Tianjin, who was busy promoting a Muslim lobby inside the Guomindang, Shi Zizhou 時子周,[35] and an influential *ahong* of the same town, Wang Jingzhai

王靜齋,[36] initiated a "Friendly Association of the Hui People of China for the Resistance to Japan and the Salvation of the Country" (*Zhongguo Huimin kangri jiuguo xiehui* 中國回民抗日救國協會—with the term "Hui People" and no longer the "Hui Religion"). At about the same time, the higher Muslim member of the Guomindang government, the General Bai Chongxi 白崇禧,[37] wishing to unite the efforts of the cohort of Muslim voluntary associations, with Chiang Kai-shek (Jiang Jieshi)'s support, invited the most influential Muslim personalities of the hour to meet at Wuchang 武昌 (one of the three cities forming Wuhan 武漢 in Central China)[38] where the government had withdrawn after the fall of Nanking. So he gathered the so-called "Four Great *Ahong*s" (*si da ahong* 四大阿訇), Wang Jingzhai (who was then 66 years old), Da Pusheng[39] (63 years), Ha Decheng[40] (49 years), Ma Songting[41] (42 years), and activists of the education, as Tang Kesan 唐柯三 of Shandong.[42] After discussion, these men, at Bai Chongxi's instigation and with Chiang Kai-shek's approval, founded a "Friendly Association of the Hui People of China for the Salvation of the Country" (*Zhongguo Huimin jiuguo xiehui* 中國回民救國協會, later called, as we will see, "Friendly Association of the Hui Religion of China for the Salvation of the Country"),[43] which, under General Bai Chongxi, Tang Kesan and Shi Zizhou's joint leadership, began to make itself known at the beginning of 1938 and held its first general meeting in May 1938. Among the overabundant boards of trustees (thirty-two persons), were present the representatives of Muslim military power of the West, the cousins Ma Hongkui and Ma Hongbin, the brothers Ma Bufang and Ma Buqing; and among the eight "observers" (*jianshi* 監事) Da Pusheng and Wang Jingzhai. Inner departments (*bu* 部) were set up for organization, propaganda, investigation; and committees (*weiyuanhui* 委員會) were formed for dealing with specific questions such as education, youth, training, relief, and so on.[44] The aims of the association were: enlistment of Muslim citizens, especially youth, side by side with unbelievers, in the struggle against the invader, purge of "running dogs" of the enemy, and help to co-religionists who had fallen into misfortune, particularly in regions lost to the conquerors. During the summer of 1938, under threat of the progress of the front, the headquarters of the association moved to Chongqing 重慶, in Sichuan, shortly before the government and the intellectuals of the whole country.[45] There, in the cramped and boiling world of the wartime capital, Muslim intellectuals met with as never before the leaders of literature and scholarship, who in their turn became interested in Islam.

During that epoch, which saw in the country more than ever a blossoming of various kinds of associations among intellectuals of all convictions, an "Association for Studying the Culture of the Hui Religion" (*Huijiao wenhua yanjiu hui* 回教文化研究會 was established, at the beginning of 1939, chaired by the General Bai, co-chaired by Tang Kesan, and counting among its members famous scholars or writers such as Guo Moruo (better known as Kuo Mo-jo) and Lao She, sitting alongside Muslim intellectuals, totally 123 persons. The discussion about the meaning and limits of the concepts "Hui People/Hui Religion" (*Huimin/Huijiao*) was then fierce. So that finally, at Bai Chongxi's suggestion, the name of the main association was changed into "Association of the Hui Religion (*Huijiao* instead of *Huimin*) of China for the Salvation of the Country," to show that it concerned all the adherents to Islam, even recent converts[46] and not only members of what was more and more considered as a special ethnic group (it seems that Muslims from Xinjiang were not included in the scope of the project).

In the emergency of the age, an association like this was bound to encounter a great success, opening subsidiary associations (*fenhui* 分會) in the provinces—even in Hong Kong, in Tibet and, curiously enough, in Yan'an under the leadership of the Communist Party—, branches (*zhihui* 支會) in the *xian*, sections (*quhui* 區會) in the market towns, each of them subordinate to the local mosque. It launched periodicals too, which reached a large audience; it created other derived associations, one "for the Youth" (*Yi-si-lan qingnian hui* 伊斯蘭青年會) in February 1940, another "for the Study of Questions of the World of Islam" (*Yi-si-lan shijie wenti yanjiu hui* 伊斯蘭世界問題研究會 or "for the Study of Questions of the Northwest" (*Xibei wenti yanjiu hui* 西北問題研究會) both in April 1943. The assessment of its activity is diversified. Within the scope of its vast cultural and religious influence, it worked for organizing a company of Hui singers who had to popularize anti-Japanese songs; it asked the great writer Lao She 老舍 to write a play about the common front of Hui and Han facing the enemy: the result was "The Acme of the Nation" (*Guojia chishang* 國家至上), performed for the first time in Chongqing in Spring 1940. The patriotic awareness of Muslim citizens has been stirred up by the *ahong*s' sermons and collective prayers made through its impetus. Moreover, it led to the enrolment of volunteers to fight the enemy, in all sixty-one detachments. It succeeded in creating a kind of anti-Japanese pro-Chinese lobby in Muslim countries, from Egypt and the Near-East till South and Southeast Asia, paving the way for the role the future official Islamic association of the People's Republic would play as a link between the Chinese government and the Gulf countries. In 1946, the headquarters of the association followed the government to Nanking under Tang Kesan's leadership; and in May 1948, an assembly of delegates of all the branches installed everywhere since 1938, announced as a new program a return to specifically cultural and religious concerns. But 1949 was already the year of the withdrawal to Taiwan, where the association kept up its program.[47]

With educational institutions

In harmony with a motto popular in China since the late Qing, "Save the Country by Education" (*jiaoyu jiuguo* 教育救國),[48] every Muslim cultural association and its supporters advocated, as main practical action, the establishment of primary schools everywhere, and afterwards, as far as possible, of secondary schools. The aim was twofold: to increase the network of schooling in order to reach all the sons from believers' families—and, with the passing of years, the girls too; and to introduce a so-called "New Style of Education" (*xinshi jiaoyu* 新式教育). But here was concealed a crucial question: what exactly was the content of this new-style education, especially at its beginning, before it became rather well theorized in the late twenties and the thirties?

Its main ground appears to be a reaction of repulsion against the traditional system of mosque instruction, named the "Scriptural Hall education" (*jingtang jiaoyu* 經堂教育)[49]—which was in fact a madrasa system, that is a form of higher education, while the common new-style schools were at a primary or a secondary level. This standpoint of denial of the past was well in the line of rejection that the surrounding cultured society inflicted on the immemorial system of thought, Confucianism. It was also in the line of the traditional attitude of the Chinese ulama, who from century to century were overwhelmed with the feeling of an alleged decay of their religion, due to its distance from its origins in space and time, and who were convinced that a correct religious education was the absolute remedy for all the evils of the time. Anyway the introduction of the system of the "Scriptural Hall education" at the end of the sixteenth century had been celebrated as the most significant innovation in the history of Chinese Islam. Three centuries later, this system was repudiated and, in order to replace it, the Muslim elite had to face a much more complex agenda than the ordinary anti-Confucian modernists. It was still agreed that the education of the youth would remain under the tutelage of mosques: it is a fact that, so far as I am aware, new schools regularly settled within the mosque precincts, often in a special structure built on the backyard of the edifice. But the stake was the content of the teaching, a hard bone of contention between various Muslim allegiances during the first decades of the twentieth century.

The first part of the program of renovation concerned, of course, the teaching of Arabic and of religious matters (there was no more question of Persian, which had been, in its written form, more or less mastered by *ahong*s, and which would remain till the post-Maoist period the literary written language of female *ahong*s).[50] The first initiators of the modernist movement brought back from their trips to Mecca, Egypt, Turkey, India, in the early twentieth century, new teaching materials in Arabic, and, in the thirties even Western studies in islamology. In addition, on the model of public education in the country, the method of making the children drone by heart an incomprehensible classical text (in the case in point the Qur'an in Arabic) was given up. The first question to solve was how should Arabic be taught and pronounced by the schoolboys? In the late Qing, the elementary schools appended to mosques used manuals in which Qur'anic extracts were transcribed by Chinese characters sounding, in the standard Northern reading, roughly as the corresponding Arabic phonemes; and the believers remained all their lives accustomed to recite Surats from the Sacred Book according to such a distorted way: for example the *šahāda*, "*lā ilāha illā'llāh*," used to become in the mouth of a traditional Chinese Muslim "*la-yi-la-ho yin-lang-la-ho*." Reformers were adamant: Chinese transcription of Arabic phoneme was an evil to get rid of, and Arabic should be pronounced as correctly as possible. However, grassroots *ahong*s in charge of teaching in mosques not affiliated to a modernist trend continued being content with the traditional way of reading.

The next problem to resolve was the language in which to give the classes: Arabic or Chinese? At its beginning during the last years of the nineteenth century, the Ikhwani movement in China (there called *Yi-hei-wa-ni* 依黑瓦尼), inspired by the Wahhabi reformism, pleaded for a complete arabization of the teaching as well of the practice of religion, and for an utter prohibition of any Chinese and Sufi influence.[51] But very soon, already by the second generation of leaders of the movement, Islam as taught by the Ikhwani adepts, though it remained anti-Sufi, became more than ever a Chinese religion; and it was so well integrated into the social and political surroundings that it was since the mid-twenties a staunch supporter of every constituted military or civil power, that of the Muslim warlords of the Northwest as much as that of the Guomindang and later, paradoxically, that of the Communist Party.[52] The fundamentalism which remained firmly entrenched in an Arabian orthodoxy and in the refusal of political and social commitment was then the prerogative of the last wave of Muslim reformism reaching China, the Salafiyya movement, which has been endowed with its own personality since 1937 and has been really active since the founding of the People's Republic in 1949.[53]

So, in the twenties, when the move towards inner modernization of Islam was well set on its way, particularly endorsed by the advocates of the Ikhwan, one wish was nearly general among cultivated Muslim: it was that their children, who will graduate from new schools, be perfectly proficient in written, colloquial and literary Chinese, and in Chinese classics. The third side of their pedagogical program was to follow the full curriculum of the official schools, first not to be outdone by them—and later, in the thirties, because the Nationalist government has made it more or less compulsory for religious schools—, that is to have the children study arithmetic, geography, history, science, modern Chinese literature, often English too, and to practise physical education, handicrafts, music and so on; without forgetting the most important parts of the teaching, Arabic and religion, a very heavy program indeed. The final goal of these efforts was to give perfect citizens to the motherland, the underlying idea being that a good Muslim was intrinsically a perfect citizen.

The very first new-styled Muslim school appeared, so far as I am aware, already in 1898, and it would not have been by sheer chance that this happened in Hunan (in Southern central China), as this province has been at the forefront of the short-lived reforms of the last years of the nineteenth century—reformist spirit of the Muslim elite ought not to be dissociated from the reformist spirit at work in the surrounding society. It must be noted that this first reformed school, organized at the initiative of the mosque of Changde 常德 (in the North of the province), received sons of unbelievers as well as of believers;[54] as did Tong Cong in the new-style school he started to manage in 1905 (one year before initiating the first Muslim cultural association of modern times), the *Muyuan xuetang* 穆源學堂 (the "Teaching Hall of the Source of the Mu[slim]"—*xuetang* being the old generic name for school, before the new word *xuexiao* 學校 was introduced from Japan).[55] Of the many schools opened between 1898 and 1937,[56] some have rapidly disappeared due to the scarcity of financial means, to a bad organization, to a lack of suitable management, and to the scarcity of qualified teachers. Many were destroyed during the war. But some were reconstructed and have survived till the Communist time, and even till today, as for example the Muyan school of Tong Cong, which has recovered its original name of "Muyuan" in 1984. The schools which have left the most lasting memory are the "Sino-Arabic Schools" (*Zhong-A xuexiao* 中阿學校), that is, schools teaching Chinese language and literature (*zhongwen* 中文) and Arabic language (*awen* 阿文), in Western China under the tutelage of adherents to the Ikhwan, as the Mingde 明德 ("Luminous Virtue," a fundamental Neo-Confucian concept) School of Kunming 昆明, the capital city of Yunnan.[57]

The formation of both religious and teaching professionals at a good level has early become a deep concern for the activists. In 1907, the *ahong*s Wang Haoran and Da Pusheng initiated a "Pedagogical Institute of the Hui Religion" (*Huijiao shifan xuetang* 回教師範學堂)[58] at the famous Peking mosque of Ox Street (*Niujie libaisi* 牛街禮拜寺) for spreading knowledge of Qur'anic studies in Arabic and the history of Chinese literature, according to a genuine Islamo-Chinese design. This first normal school is still respected for the broad influence it had at this time, but it collapsed rather fast.

Later on, some normal schools were established in the 1920s and 1930s. The one, which has had the most far-reaching impact and which is celebrated by present-day Muslims like a kind of founding icon of modern Chinese Muslim identity, is the Chengda Normal School (*Chengda shifan xuexiao* 成達師範學校),[59] opened during the most bustling year of the Republic, on April 1925, at Jinan 濟南, the capital of Shandong, for "Perfecting [Virtue] and Manifesting [Talent]," *cheng[de] da[cai]* 成德達才, as was suggested by its name. Its main initiator was a young man of 30 years, Ma Songting[60] *ahong* of a mosque in the town, who was the head of studies, while the director of the school was Tang Kesan[61] who partly financed the institution. At that time, it was a limited experiment, as the first enrolment was only of ten students. Soon the unpleasant political events of May 1928 in the town led to its closure. However, in spring 1929 help came from a side which, seen from afar, would seem quite unexpected: from a Muslim general, native of Ningxia, in Western China, a weighty arbiter in the conflicts opposing Chiang Kaishek to Northern warlords, Ma Fuxiang,[62] in fact a fine connoisseur of Confucianism, a warm supporter of a sinicized version of Islam as of a modernized Muslim education, and a sympathizer of the new trend of the Ikhwani movement. He struck up a friendship with Tang Kesan as an approval of his endeavor, and therefore handled the Chengda case as his own affair: he pushed for reopening the school at Beiping (Peking) which became prosperous thanks to his money and to his personal involvement.

In 1932, Ma Songting traveled to Egypt and other Islamic countries, to find out how pedagogy should be organized. With the backing of the Egyptian king Fu'ad, he invited two Egyptian scholars to take in hand the teaching at Chengda. He also brought home a collection of Arabic books, given by the king and by the director of al-Azhar; so that he could undertake the establishment of a large Muslim library which he called the "Fu'ad Library" (*Fude*[63] *tushuguan* 福德圖書館), supported in 1936 by some leading personalities of the cultural national world, such as Cai Yuanpei 蔡元培, Chen Yuan 陳垣, Gu Jiegang 顧頡剛. On the eve of the Japanese invasion, Muslim elites had definitely enlarged to include non-Muslims in the circle of their sympathizers, at least in Peking. In 1937, the Chengda School was evacuated to Guilin 桂林, in Southern China. In 1945, when re-established at Peking, it was merged with another pedagogical school, first promoted in Ningxia by Ma Fuxiang's son, Ma Hongkui,[64] also a military and political leader of North Western China—Ma Fuxiang having died in 1932. The new school took the name of "High Institute of the Hui People" (*Huimin xueyuan* 回民學院), a name which it kept till its end, in 1958, under Communist rule.

Still another normal school was created in Eastern China in 1928, the "Normal Islamic School of Shanghai" (*Shanghai Yi-si-lan shifan xuexiao* 上海伊斯蘭師範學校),[65] which was successful thanks to Ma Fuxiang's financial support, once more, and was directed by Da Pusheng and Ha Decheng. Closed in 1937, it came to life again in Western China, in Gansu, under Da Pusheng's leadership, as the "Normal Islamic School of Pingliang" (*Pingliang* 平涼 *Yi-si-lan shifan xuexiao*).[66] Another normal school of the pre-war time in Eastern China was installed in Northern Hebei, not very far from Peking: the "Normal Islamic School of Wanxian" (*Wanxian* 萬縣 *Yi-si-lan shifan xuexiao*).[67] Opened in 1929, its curriculum has a modern tone, as subjects of the official program were taught along with Arabic grammar and Qur'anic theology; but it still taught traditional classical literature and written Chinese language, so disparaged by the young iconoclasts, heirs of the May Fourth movement. The school was short-lived, as it had closed in 1935, due to financial strain. The so-called "Sino-Arabic University" (*Zhong-A daxue* 中阿大學), founded in Ningxia by the warlord Ma Hongbin[68] in 1932, became in 1936, after various transformations, the "Yunting Provincial Normal School" (*Shengli Yunting shifan xuexiao* 省立雲亭師範學校)—Yunting being the courtesy name of the Ma Fuxiang,[69] and this school, the first Muslim normal school functioning with a provincial allocation of money, followed the official program of four years with the addition of a compulsory Arabic course.[70]

The ambitious educational programs, partly in Arabic, partly in Chinese, partly about modern topics, foreseen by the Muslim reformists since the last decades of the nineteenth century, have seen, in spite of many upheavals, interesting steps forward, the effects of which have made themselves felt even into the Communist period. However, it was obvious too that the movement which they implied could not reach all the places in such a broad land as China.

With the printed word

The activists, being aware of the difficulty of keeping in touch with the remote parts of the country, were willing to make use of the printed word in order to overcome the obstacles of distance and dispersal of their local communities, and to spread their ideas and programmes widely. They were particularly eager to exploit the new opportunities offered by the modern press, which had appeared in late Qing China first in foreign concessions of the treaty ports, and then slowly in the hinterland.[71] A total of 133 Muslim periodicals has been registered between 1904 and 1949[72]: more precisely 8 from 1904 to 1919, 22 from 1920 to 1929, 52 from 1930 to 1937, 49 from 1938 to 1949, the average being 1 new title every 2 years till the May Fourth movement of 1919, 3 every year for the decade finishing in 1929, and then about 5 every year till the Communists took control, with sizes going from a few to 80 pages. Statistics breaking down the figures according to places and turnover of publication show the leading role of coastal large towns and the instability of the press: 36 periodicals or so were launched in Peking, Tianjin and around, but 23 were already dead in 1937; 29 or so appeared in Shanghai, Nanking and around, but 10 were dead before 1937. In the South-Eastern province of Yunnan, the movement got a good footing too, but the political situation disturbed it rapidly: 6 journals were founded from 1915 till 1937, but they had already suspended their publication at the time of the general war; only one resumed in 1938. These total figures may seem not very significant by comparison with the publishing activity of modernist circles of China but, put in correlation with the small number of Muslim intellectuals actively participating in the modernist move, it is not bad at all.

The very first Muslim periodical publication had a title symptomatic of the interests of its founders: "The Journal of Correct Teaching and Love of the Country" (*Zhengzong aiguo bao* 正宗愛國報),[73] initiated already in 1904 in Peking and aimed at a popular Muslim readership, as it was written in spoken language; as was the next journal, born in the capital too, in 1906, the *Zhuyuan baihua bao* 竹園白話報 [The Journal of the Garden of Bamboos (in *baihua*, the colloquial language)].[74] The one which has most struck contemporary observers started in December 1908: it was the *Xing Hui pian* 醒回篇 [A Leaf for Awakening the Hui], due to the thirty-six Muslim students who had created in Tokyo, in 1907, the "Association for the Pure and True [=Muslim] Education of the Students in To[kyo]," quoted earlier.[75] The pamphlet was not for sale but for a free distribution, and, as the students soon returned to their motherland, it did not go beyond the first issue (or issues?).

Finally, the most durable and influential journal was the *Yuehua* 月華 [Moonlight] whose publishing house was established by the warlord Ma Fuxiang and others, in November 1929, in the precinct of the new Chengda School at Peking.[76] As a result of the war, the journal was compelled to close and to move several times (with the Chengda School at Guilin 桂林 in 1937, then at Chongqing 重慶, followed by a break from 1942 till 1946), nevertheless, when finally it closed in 1948, it had released a total of 418 issues in 18 volumes, with a circulation amounting to 3,000, and up to 4,000 copies in the most favorable year, 1931[77]—a notable figure by comparison with other Chinese Muslim publications of the time. It accepted articles in the old literary style as well as in the more fashionable colloquial language. It had the distinctive feature of turning its attention to social subjects, at least according to its initial program, which included in addition to religious subjects, such as modernization of Muslim doctrines and news from the Muslim world abroad, the improvement of the social status and standard of living of Muslims families. In tune with the times, patriotism was celebrated; and, a rare occurrence among the adepts of the Ikhwani movement of the capital, it stressed a reconciliation between and with the different Sufi allegiances. While after 1936 the program proposed mainly the diffusion of news: religious news from the field and from abroad, snatches of Muslim history.[78]

Books and booklets aimed, like the periodical press, at educating the believers and their most favorite topic was a minute description of correct ritual attitudes.[79] As formerly, in the imperial times, they were produced by printing houses appended to large mosques, the main one being the Ox Street mosque of Peking. When the first generation of young scholars produced by the reformed Muslim normal schools returned from their study trip to Egypt—a must in the 1930s—a literature of translations from Arabic became widespread, as well as some translations of European islamology, mainly thanks to the Yunnanese Ma Jian 馬堅.[80] The activists' most constant worry was to give to their co-religionists a reliable translation of the Qurʾan, initially in the form of serials in periodicals. Here, once again there was the problem of choosing the adequate language for translation (the Protestants have had to face the same dilemma when releasing new parts of the Bible in Chinese): whether to use the classical literary language, the *wenyan* 文言? Then at which level, a high or a low one (both were possible)? Or the colloquial language, the *baihua* 白話, which had been turned into the new literary language by the May Fourth movement in 1919? The choice was obviously a matter of personal sensibility, determined by the age of the translator. Ha Decheng, born in 1888, worked hard, till his last days in 1943, on a translation in *wenyan*, while his disciple Ma Jian, younger by 18 years, although helping him faithfully, was preparing by himself a *baihua* version (which was to appear posthumously as a book in 1981 only).[81]

The oddest editorial activity of the Muslim modernists was the multiple reprints and new editions they carried out, always in the printing houses of the mosques, of the masterpieces of their own literary tradition.[82] It is well known that some gifted ulama have produced, since the mid-seventeenth century, works which later shaped the spirit of every generation of cultivated Chinese Muslims. These books display a fascinating use of Confucian terminology and reasoning for expounding Islamic theology, Qurʾanic tenets and Sufi mysticism (without any affiliation to a particular brotherhood). Strangely enough, they have enjoyed batches of reprints, often with the same lithographic boards kept in mosques, or of new editions, at every time of crucial national crisis. The most striking example is the "Philosophy of Islam" (*Tianfang xingli* 天方性理) that one of the favorite ulama of the past, Liu Zhi 劉智, had composed in the early eighteenth century: since its first known edition in 1760, 17 new editions or reprints are attested,[83] 6 were released during the great turmoil of Muslim uprisings in mid-nineteenth century; while in the modernist crisis of the twenties and thirties, in spite of the condemnation of the old method of the "Scriptural Hall education," seven more editions were thrown on the market—and sometimes even on the general market through standard edition houses, not only for the Muslim audience of mosques. Nevertheless, the book was at that time largely out of date, owing to its literary style and to its Sufi content, while the modernist Islamic trend leaned towards an Ikhwani tendency. Even stranger is the personality of some sponsors. The general Ma Fuxiang financed between 1921 and 1931 the edition of almost all the most celebrated works of Chinese classical Islam from the seventeenth till nineteenth century, adding his own prefaces, often in his beautiful calligraphy.[84] Still stranger is the fact that these editions of the Republican time, with prefaces by Ma Fuxiang for example, were once more reprinted in post-Maoist China, sometimes in different kinds of editions, cheap or luxurious, whilst "translations" in colloquial language were undertaken. These classical works, using Confucianist terms, are a sort of symbol of the greatness of Chinese Muslim identity through the centuries.

Who were the intellectual modernizers of Islam?

It is rewarding to ask this question, because it helps to clear up the position of *ahong*s or imams in the Chinese Muslim society. It is certain that common *ahong*s are grouped together and receive negative judgments: they were those who delivered poor education to the children, those who were against any reform, those who came into conflict with local modernists, those who tried to wreck any new project. Such testimonies are numerous, though often veiled and diffuse. It is obvious too that the common *ahong* was not a highly respected personality, for his presence at the head of a mosque and his livelihood there were dependent on the committee of elders of the mosque: he was in the position of some high level employee. The prestige came only to *ahong*s with special talents and knowledge, who were, for this, invited to teach at a large mosque. We may suspect that more than once the source of their fame was their double expertise, in Qur'anic studies as well as in Chinese classics, as has been the case for almost all the personalities met in the present story.

We will now dwell upon men who have been considered as the main actors in the modernization of Chinese Islam, whether they were outside the field, as were politicians of various beliefs, or constituted the nucleus of the regeneration of Islamic education. The important point is that all these men have been recently, during the 1990s, the subject of many biographical notes, articles or books, even if they had chosen the Guomindang's side in the forties and had then migrated to Taiwan. If they have pertained to what we may call the hard core of religious activists, they are celebrated as venerated founding fathers of modern Chinese Islam.

The outer circle of modernists

The most conspicuous helpers of the modernist Muslim movement have been some Muslim generals, at the margin of warlordism before throwing in their lot with Chiang Kaishek and holding high positions in his government.

Bai Chongxi (1893–1966),[85] a native of the Southern province of Guangxi, received a traditional primary education in the Chinese classics, and then a modern schooling (in his biographies, there is no question of his Islamic education). He was a member of the so-called "Guangxi Clique,"[86] which accepted the authority of the Nationalist government at the end of 1936 only; in 1946, he was appointed minister of War. Defeated by the Communists, he finally fled to Taiwan in 1949 (his life has been the theme of a novel published in Mainland China, in his native province of Guangxi in 1988).[87] His support and leadership of the "Association for the Hui People/Hui Religion of China for the Salvation of the Country" was a warfare device in view of mobilizing his co-religionists in support of the Nationalist government in war and it had a definitely political orientation.

The two Generals Ma of Western China were born in Linxia 臨夏 (ancient Hezhou 河州), a stronghold of Islam where every denomination and trend has had a footing, on the boundary between Gansu and Qinghai (or Kökönōr); they are known as sympathizers of the Ikhwani movement. The elder brother was Ma Buqing (1901-?),[88] who received his primary education in the Chinese classics. The younger was Ma Bufang 馬步芳 (1902 or 1903–1975),[89] whose education was religious, preparing him to become an *ahong*. Both boys, however, chose a military career, which turned for Ma Bufang to be largely political and administrative: he was acting governor of Qinghai in 1936, with his uncle Ma Lin 馬麟 (1876–1945)[90] as titular head of the provincial government, and then nominal governor in 1938, and in 1943 member of the Guomindang's Central Executive Committee. He went to Egypt in the early 1950s, was Nationalist ambassador to Saudia Arabia in 1961 and ended his days in Islamic countries. His administration was reputed to be one of the most efficient and modern in China at that time—authoritarian but benevolent. He used to pay a special attention to basic education for all children and young people in his province, of any ethnic or religious origin, supporting the schools financially as well as administratively. As a part of his educational program, he began to develop after the war a special Muslim system of schooling: in 1944, the Ruiwei Elementary School (*Ruiwei xiaoxue* 銳威小學),[91] with a military training, intended especially for his son and other young boys of his family, which afterwards expanded; a pedagogical school;[92] a Arabic-Chinese school for girls (*Beiguan A-Zhong nüxiao* 北關阿中女校; in 1945);[93] the Kunlun Secondary School (*Kunlun zhongxue* 昆侖中學; in 1946);[94] the Fanghui Kindergarten for young children from 4 to 6 (*Fanghui youzhiyuan* 芳惠幼稚園).[95]

Among Muslim generals who are counted as warlords, the most interesting is Ma Fuxiang (1876–1932),[96] a really fascinating figure. The top specialist of Chinese Islam in the nineteenth and twentieth centuries, Jonathan N. Lipman has already recounted his political career: first a loyal officer of the Qing dynasty, then an almost independent leader in Ningxia, propelled in the last 1920s into the national political arena. He was born in the deepest Muslim China, like the two generals Ma, near Lingxia (or Hezhou), to a father who chose in 1872 to side with the governmental army at the end of the bloody Muslim uprisings of the Tongzhi era in 1862–1873; he then received the typical education of a distinguished young Muslim, half Confucianist, half Qur'anic, which was representative of Muslim intellectuality in the first half of the twentieth century. He has left delicious snatches of his way of thinking about morality in letters, for example to Tang Kesan, in prefaces and post-faces to the numerous editions of *Han kitab* (i.e. Confuciano-Muslim books) he backed financially, and also in his own collection of exhortations to his sons and nephews.[97] His cultural activity beneficial to his co-religionists was multifarious, as we have noticed. From 1915 on, in Ningxia, a province of North Western China with a notable Muslim population, he founded a pedagogical secondary school, about sixty primary schools, where Qur'anic studies were taught together with Chinese classical literature and colloquial Chinese, history, geography, arithmetic, sciences, physical education, hygiene—subjects still revolutionary at that early time; interestingly, as there was a Mongolian public too, Mongolian language in addition to Arabic. He strongly supported the rebirth of the Chengda Normal School in Peking and the other higher Muslim schools, kicked off the successful periodical *Yuehua*, granted stipends to gifted young men for studying in China or at al-Azhar. After his death in August 1932, his son Ma Hongkui (1892 or 1893–1970)[98] carried on with his father's action, although in a less flamboyant style. The message delivered about both loyalty and service to the country through improvement of education fitted perfectly well with the ideas of cultivated believers.

An example of an early and deep engagement in politics comes from a young man educated in the new Muslim system, Su Baoqiao 蘇抱樵 (1895–1962).[99] A Hunanese as was Mao Zedong, he was also of about the same age (Mao was born in 1893). Su entered in 1905 into a mosque school of Changsha 長沙 which one year later became a new-styled primary school named Jiejin 偕進 [litt. "Advance together"], under the impulse of a pioneer of the new Muslim education, Ma Linyi 馬鄰翼 (known too as Ma Zhenwu 振五, 1864–1938),[100] just returned from a three year study period (1903–1905) in Japan and was filled with Sun Yatsen's revolutionary ideas. In 1908, Ma Linyi joined Wang Haoran in Peking and participated actively there in the adventure of the beginning of the modernization of Islam. Later, he took advantage of his good positions in the national educational system to help the development of new-style mosque schools: he is credited with the birth of some hundreds of them and was the author of two influential books, the most ancient reflection about modern schooling (*Xin jiaoyu xue* 新教育學, "Schools with the New Education") and a presentation of Islam (*Yi-si-lan-jiao gailun* 伊斯蘭教概論, "A Summary of Islam").

As for Su Baoqiao, after his first religious education and a pedagogical secondary one, he began commercial studies, still at Changsha, when in 1919 the national and xenophobic turmoil known under the generic term of the "May Fourth Movement" broke out. Then 24 years old, he appeared as one of the local agitators, along with Mao Zedong. From that time onwards, he kept collaborating with both Mao brothers—with Mao Zedong indeed, but even more with

Mao Zemin 毛澤民 (when Mao Zemin was executed in Xinjiang/Sinkiang in 1943, he said "I am finished"). In the early twenties, he managed the library which the young Communist Party had opened in Changsha in order to spread its propaganda and he himself joined the Party in 1926. However he remained a right Muslim, devoted to the propagation of a new mosque education; after the founding of the People's Republic, he held several actual and honorary functions, especially in the field of cultural promotion of the "Hui people." Till the late 1950s, Party and Islam were not at all exclusive one from the other.

Another example of collaboration, although beginning much later, between a Muslim activist and the Communist regime is that of Da Pusheng (1874–1965),[101] descendant of a Persian who had come to China under the Mongolian dynasty in the thirteenth century. A native from the region of Nanking (from Liuhe 六合 in Jiangsu), he followed a traditional mosque education which enabled him to master Arabic as well as Persian, and then pursued his education in 1894 at Peking, at the Ox Street mosque, under the guidance of a future modernist, Wang Haoran. How the master taught at that early time, we don't know. In 1896, Da Pusheng "wore the clothing [or the robe]" (*chuanyi* 穿衣), the usual term to mean that somebody become an *ahong*, recognized as a specialist of religion. And indeed, in 1905, he was invited to lead the prayers at the Ox Street mosque. Two years later, when Wang Haoran came back from an overseas trip and founded a new pedagogical school at this same mosque, he collaborated in this innovative work. At the beginning of the Republic in 1912, he followed his friend Ma Linyi in North-Western China and, in Gansu, holding a position in the official educational system, he promoted Muslim schooling too. In the early twenties, he was invited by a group of Muslim merchants of Shanghai to represent their interests in India. There he learned Urdu and English, opened his eyes to the outside world and probably also to Indian versions of Islam. After his return to China in 1925, he joined Muslim modernists of Shanghai. His knowledge of languages turned him after 1937 as a perfect messenger of the Nationalist government for pleading the cause of the invaded nation to the Indian subcontinent, Egypt and other countries. Apparently forgotten during the first years of the People's Republic, the old man—he was 78 years old in 1952—was suddenly discovered as an ideal representative of Islam under Communist rule. Honours piled up on his shoulders and he became a sort of precious showcase presented to the Afro-Asian world under the label of the freedom of religion. He died one year before the Cultural Revolution. He is styled, at least now in the post-Maoist literature, as one of the "Four Great *Ahong*s," a near institutional term to mark the main designers of modern Chinese Islam, though he seems to have held a secondary role, becoming a symbol only after the Communist take over—because of this I prefer to classify him among the outer circle of activists.

In this outer circle were also men who had not received a special religious training but who dedicated a part of their active life to the promotion of a modern Muslim education, more as organizers, fund-raisers and administrators than as religious teachers. Among them a notable personality was Tang Kesan, native of Shandong (active between 1925 and 1946),[102] who, apart from administrative charges in the government, was involved very closely in the creation of the Chengda Normal School after 1925 and of the Friendly Association of the Hui People for the Salvation of the Country after 1938. There is also the Shanghai man, Sha Shanyu (1879–1968),[103] who was proud of his Arab ancestor who allegedly had come as an astronomer to the Ming court. After having acquired a double training, as a child in classical Chinese and as a grown-up in English, he took up the headship of a militia constituted by Muslim merchants of Shanghai at the fall of the Qing dynasty, and then he entered into the world of journalism in 1914. Yet after 1909 he was fully associated to several enterprises for the modernization of Islam, as trustee of schools in Shanghai, as one of the founding members of the Learned Society of the Hui Religion of China in 1925, as sponsor of the school Dunhua 敦化 of Shanghai after the war, and so on. Despite the fact that he had retired on the arrival of the Communists, he was invited in 1954, at the age of 74, to contribute to the compilation of documents about Islam in Shanghai. Wu Tegong (?–1963),[104] journalist like Sha Shanyu at the *Shenbao* 申報—a journal of Shanghai, the most ancient of China—had been his close collaborator in some scholarly ventures in the Islamic field, such as the redaction, printing and diffusion of the monthly periodical of the Learned Society of the Hui Religion in China. Both friends had worked with Ha Decheng and Ma Jian on their translations of the Qurʾan. We must note that Wu Tegong, who adopted the pen-name of "The Virtue of the Way" (*daode* 道德), championed the point of view of a pure traditional scholar and was prone to resort to the most elegant style of classical Chinese in his proposals for translations, notwithstanding that Ma Jian had finally opted for a version in modern colloquial language.

Now who were the supporters of all the modernist enterprises of the great Muslim teachers of the Republican time, who gave their money, their time, their expertise, and whose names are only known in the best cases? As money was the sinews of the success and as merchants appear sometimes in the course of the story, we may infer that at least some sympathizers were traders and businessmen, some were journalists, while some others were certainly teachers and specialists of religion.

The inner circle

This is the group of men whose entire *raison d'être* was the fulfillment of a modern Islamic education in the reach of every young believer, preparing him to a fruitful life of compliant citizen and of pious worshipper. Among the first ones, were two genuine pioneers, breaking new ground. Tong Cong (1864–1923),[105] who graduated in the official system as Bachelor (*xiucai* 秀才) in 1904, was only active in his province of Jiangsu and, perheps for this reason, seems now to be somewhat forgotten. The notable point in his case is the role that co-religionists who studied in the Japan of Meiji time exerted on him.

In contrast, the *ahong* Wang Haoran (also called Wang Kuan, 1848–1919),[106] of Peking, has been respected since the twenties as the genuine founder of a modern

Islamic curriculum. His father was an *'ālim* too. The great experience of his life, fraught with far-reaching consequences, was his pilgrimage to Mecca in 1905, and a return trip through Turkey and Egypt, which enabled him to see an evolution in Islamic countries that he did not suspect. Back in Peking in 1907, he launched a revolutionary cultural movement with the creation, at the Ox Street mosque, of a Pedagogical Institute of the Hui Religion, which included Chinese culture in its curriculum: this experiment was short-lived due to financial inadequacies, but it stood out in the mentalities. Wang Haojan was the initiator of primary new-styled mosque schools too and, at the very beginning of the Republic in 1912, of a popular Society for the Advance of the Hui Religion in China, created certainly with an underlying patriotic aim, though non-political in its program.

The hard core of activists is constituted by three *ahong*s belonging to the group called the "Four Great *Ahong*s" (Da Pusheng being the fourth one). The oldest one was Wang Jingzhai (also known as Wang Wenqing, 1871 or 1879–1949),[107] a native from Tianjin who all his life kept the strong accent characteristic of his Eastern province. Besides his religious training for becoming an *ahong*, which made him proficient in Arabic and Persian, he studied alone classical Chinese and a diversified Qur'anic literature. As a *hai-li-fan* (i.e. *ḫalīfa*, in China the helper of an *ahong*) and since 1905 an *ahong* invited to teach in a mosque of Peking, his fame began to increase. His psychological evolution was marked by the influence of a journalist of Peking, Ding Baochen 丁寶臣,[108] an ardent defender of the colloquial Chinese language in literature, a man who would later adhere to the Communist Party and die for this cause. In 1921, rich sponsors like Ma Fuxiang and Ma Linyi financed his pilgrimage to Mecca and a visit to leading places of Islamic learning—Istanbul, al-Azhar and others. In 1924, he brought back to China a collection of six hundred Western books dealing mainly with Islamic and Arabic studies, an unprecedented step at that time. Till his last days, his main activity was concentrated on translations from Arabic, on the compilation of a Chinese-Arabic dictionary and, first and most important of all, on attempts to translate the Qur'an: after his first translation into the classical language, he made another one in colloquial language which was greatly praised by his co-religionists. In 1927, due to a disagreement about the quality and level required for rendering the Sacred Book into Chinese, he expounded his views on the subject: for example, he criticized the position of Yang Zhongming, who in his own translation of the Qur'an (which would be destroyed during the war) had chosen to follow the obscure style of the sutras, considering that Buddhism is the dominant religion of China. Wang Jingzhai opposed this, just as he opposed the idea of taking Protestant translations of the Bible as models. For him, the style ought to be clear and comprehensible to everybody. Though an austere man—in his room the only book was a Qur'an—, he did not keep aloof from politics when this appeared necessary. Thus he was among the first to initiate a Friendly Association of the Hui People of China for the Salvation of the Country in 1937, and to be a consultant of the Nationalist government in wartime.

The case of Yang Zhongming 楊仲明 (1870–1952),[109] just quoted, is interesting too, because, when he was a young man following the regular religious curriculum which led to his becoming a professional *ahong*, he studied Chinese classics by himself so well that, at the age of 19, he was able to pass the examination of Bachelor (*xiucai*), an occurrence which, rare among the Muslims, was even more extraordinary on the part of an *ahong*. At the age of twenty-nine (in 1898), he wrote "The Essential Content of the Four Religions" (*Sijiao yaogua* 四教要括), that is of Confucianism, Buddhism, Christianity and Islam. He was throughout his life an activist urging the modernization of the teaching of Islamic studies at, among other places, the Chengda Normal School and in his writings, so that now he is considered an important "historical figure."

Ha Decheng (1888–1943),[110] from Shanghai, one of the "Four Great *Ahong*s," was, like the *ahong* Yang Zhongming, an enlightened ulama who was educated in both Qur'anic and classical Chinese studies. His pilgrimage in 1913 provoked his rejection of the traditional Chinese mosque teaching. As said earlier, he engaged in commercial activities abroad, in a Muslim commercial society of course, and in countries with a majority of Muslims, mainly India, Ceylon, and Egypt (he could speak Arabic, Urdu and English): this enabled him to import religious books from these countries and from Turkey. Back in Shanghai in 1925, his name was henceforth linked to every endeavor of Islamic modernization in Shanghai and of help to his co-religionists.

The last so-called "Great *Ahong*" was Ma Songting (1895–1992),[111] from Peking who already belonged to the generation formed according to the new system of education; he was trained at the Ox Street mosque after Wang Haoran and Da Pusheng initiated a Sino-Arabic curriculum there, and from 1925 on, his name was linked to the experiment of the Chengda Normal School. His exploratory trip to Egypt in 1932–1933 has already been mentioned here; it was followed by another in 1935–1936, from which resulted the foundation of a specialized library. In the fifties, he was one of those recognized Muslim intellectuals who were given functions and titles in the official Muslim association and who were representative of the "minorities" of the People's Republic. He taught Arabic at Peking University until he was dismissed during the Cultural Revolution; afterwards rehabilitated, he died at a very advanced age, venerated as one of the most glorious cases of the progressive Islam of the past.

Many other figures should be mentioned. One who cannot be overlooked is typical and important on several grounds: Ma Jian (1906–1978),[112] a Yunnanese from a small Muslim town sadly known for having been a martyr town during the Cultural Revolution, Shadian 沙甸, in the far South Eastern China, almost on the Vietnamese boundary, a town which for long was perceived as a center of vivid Muslim intellectual life. It was possible for Ma Jian to take advantage in 1922 of the new Sino-Arabic schooling, at a secondary school which was recently opened in a mosque of the provincial capital, Kunming 昆明. After his graduation, he taught in 1926–1927 in a primary Sino-Arabic school of Shadian. But he could not help feeling disappointed with the turn taken by the Muslim new-styled education: this inner view gives us a useful balance about the alleged tremendous success of the reform. So he went to the North-West of the country, in the homeland of brotherhoods, to be in 1927–1928 the disciple of the second generation leader of the anti-Sufi Ikhwan, Hu Songshan 虎嵩山 (1880–1956). This man had then recently (in 1925) returned from a pilgrimage to Mecca, where he was deeply hurt by the prejudices he encountered, merely because he was a Chinese. In consequence, he became convinced of the duty of any good Muslim to help China enforce its national and international stature. With this aim in mind, he transformed the Ikhwani teaching, which had been introduced into North-Western China in the last decade of the nineteenth century as an anti-Sufi and anti-Chinese undertaking, into a pro-Chinese and modernist movement.[113] This move adopted by Hu Songshan gives the main clue for understanding the modernization of Chinese Islam in the first half of the twentieth century and its apparently easy adaptation to the Communist rule.

The Muslim warlords of Western China, Ma Fuxiang, Ma Bufang and others, were full supporters of Hu Songshan's theories; the Four Great *Ahong*s and other main Muslim intellectuals of the coastal China also were his adepts. They concentrated on the pedagogical and cultural work, sure of bringing in that way their contribution to the motherland's greatness; and they placed their trust in the current government. When finally the Communist Party obtained the power after years of trouble, they rejoiced, as did many other patriots of the country, at the restoration of the national pride; and they were eager to collaborate to the reconstruction in doing what they have always done: to write books and articles, and to teach Arabic.

Ma Jian's case is exemplary in this respect. After his education in the Ikhwani convictions, he spent three years, in 1929–1931, in the new Normal Islamic School of Shanghai,[114] thanks to a stipend which may have been provided by Ma Fuxiang; and then eight years at al-Azhar, in 1932–1939, with Yunnanese financial help. There he began to act as an intermediary between Arabic modernism (incidentally modernism was not so much at work at al-Azhar itself, to Chinese students' great disappointment) and the Confucianist culture. Thus his first translation into Arabic was the Confucian Analects, the *Lunyu* 論語.[115] In wartime China and afterwards under the Communist rule, he remained without respite a hard worker, writing translation after translation in a clear colloquial Chinese. After 1949, he kept his position of professor at Peking University, and he was also a eulogist of the regime, with some honorary political positions. His role as official interpreter for Arabic in international relations spared him the worst of the Cultural Revolution; but he still bitterly suffered and lost a great part of the manuscripts of his works. Less compliant Muslim intellectuals lost their life during the Cultural revolution, as did Chen Keli 陳克禮 (1924–executed in 1970),[116] an Ikhwani militant, who had been a student of Wang Jingzhai, Ma Songting and Ma Jian himself, and a very prolific translator.

Conclusion

A wide range of figures involved in the propagation and teaching of Islam, from the late Qing to the beginning of the Communist era, has been met in the course of this short survey. Other names have been left aside for the fruit of their action has been of a different kind. So it has been for leaders of Sufi brotherhoods, notably the head of a Jahriyya *menhuan* 門宦 (a sub-branch of the Naqshbandiyya), Ma Yuanzhang 馬元章 (1853–1920)[117] who too cultivated Chinese classical literature along with religious endeavours; or for the leader of a Sino-Islamic collective movement, the *Xidaotang* 西道堂.[118] Muslim literate women could have been mentioned, so also collaborators to the Japanese occupying forces. Let us leave these questions for a later publication.

Despite the variety of particular cases, the whole story has a consistent background. All the intellectuals who have been here mentioned strongly believed in the power of a correct education as a royal way of entering into the modern and happy world of the future. All of them, at a certain time in their life, as a child or as a teenager or as an adult, received a double education, Arabic and Qurʾanic on the one side, Chinese on the other. Of course, local colloquial Chinese was for everybody the everyday language, as all of them were undivided sinophones. Their spoken language was only, for an inner intercommunication, interspersed with some special words generally of a Persian origin, like a kind of domestic slang. What they called an education in Chinese language meant, first, the command of the script for reading and writing; second, the regular use of the Chinese language, not only of the Arabic one, for explaining orally and in writing religious questions. The third part of an educational Chinese program was the mastery of the Chinese Confucian classics, of the Chinese classical literature, and, since the 1930s or later, of the colloquial Chinese as a form of modern literary language. The unavoidable modernization of thought and techniques meant for the Muslim intellectuals not a complete rejection of the past, but the comprehension of the Chinese literary language, which remained for them the classical written language, the *wenyan*, which lasted very much longer than for the commonalty of Chinese intellectuals. For this very reason, the masterpieces of the great Chinese ulama of the last three centuries, Confucian and Sufi though, far from being obsolete, remained or became—it depended on the reader's personality—favorite readings. Thus Muslim activists of the Republican times, particularly those who pursued their career under the Communist rule, have been the transmitters to their heirs of the post-Maoist times of the so-called *Han kitab*: these Islamic books written in Chinese since the mid-seventeenth century are definitely among the most enduring constituent of the Muslim intellectuals' feeling of identity, that is the very expression of their "Chineseness" with the necessary point of otherness.

Another way of voicing their Chineseness was their assertion that they loved their motherland and that they contributed in every possible way to its prestige in peacetime and to its integrity in wartime. It is significant that during the war the Japanese occupying forces, in spite of their propaganda and of their financial outlay for the young generation, could not create a separatist movement among the Chinese Muslims as they succeeded doing so among the Mongols of Eastern Inner Mongolia.[119] Now that the concepts of citizenship[120] and of a Han homogeneous ethnic group (or "nationality," *minzu*) are questions which have come to the foreground in the field of sociological studies on modern China, it is urgent to take account of the Chinese Muslims' experience in the Republican context. In 1925 for example, they could still contend that "Hui is the name of a religion, it is not the name of a race, *Hui yi ming jiao, fei yi ming zu ye* 回以名教, 非以名族也";[121] and that to quote in a single list "*Hui, Meng, Zang, Miao* 回蒙藏苗"—as was officially done under the Guomindang rule—is exact for the Mongols (*Meng*), the Tibetans (*Zang*), the Miao, but not at all for the Muslims. Are the Buddhists named a "*Fomin* 佛民" [Buddhist people] though Buddhism came from India? Are the Christians called a "*Jidumin* 基督民" [Christian people, *Jidu* being the Protestant appellation of Christianity], though Christianity came from Europe and America? Islam, as Christianity is a world religion,[122] but in the 1930s already, the Muslims themselves began to admit that they were a distinctive people, a *Huimin*, as shown in the names they chose for their associations. Specialists of this problem such as Jonathan N. Lipman, Dru Gladney, Matsumoto Masumi suspect that the crystallization of the idea of a Han nationality is indissolubly linked to the assertion of a Hui nationality, *Huimin*, becoming in the Communist times a *Huizu* 回族—a term which implies a criterion of genealogical descent. As Jonathan N. Lipman puts it: "We may ask how the presence of the Muslim as a familiar other has contributed to the formation of Chinese majority identity. How does Sino-Muslim history challenge the hegemonic narrative of monolithic, culturally homogeneous China? What modifications to our notions of Confucianism, of symbolic exchange must we make if some neo-Confucians are also Muslims?"[123]

The last question seeks to know from which side the Muslim activists received the impulse towards modernization in the way they took it. It is unthinkable to single out one influence to the exclusion of others. Potential applicants are the Japanese Meiji peaceful revolution, then the Chinese iconoclast atmosphere, and also anti-colonial and anti-Western feelings in India, Egypt, Turkey, and the revolutionary spirit widely held: all these trends were certainly combined. But a hidden hand from a Tatar Jadidist origin has little chance of being discovered in coastal China which was turned towards sea route, nor in Yunnan which was oriented towards the traffic through a Burmese route, unlike Sufi Brotherhoods which were concentrated in North Western China and were sensitive to Inner Asia's fragrance, but not to modernism. In the career of a typical Muslim intellectual of the twentieth century the great event was the opportunity of travel overseas, or at least, if unable to do better, of direct contact with travellers. Also, the best occasion for a discovery of the outside world was the pilgrimage to Mecca, usually followed, on the way back, by more or less lengthy stops in various Muslim countries.

In the course of the twentieth century more than ever, Sino-Islam was an integral part of the worlds of Islam as well as of Chinese culture. From an intellectual point of view, its literary tradition till nowadays goes back to the mid-seventeenth century without any real severance, through the mediation of the Republican times.

Acknowledgments

I wish to express my deepest gratitude to Prof. Donald D. Leslie who kindly, cleverly and speedily polished my English. It goes without saying that any remaining inaccuracies in the facts or in the style are my own.

Notes

1 The system of transcription followed for the Chinese is the now official pinyin, which, *inter alia*, renders *ts'* with a *c, hs* with an *x*.

2 For an overall picture of the situation during this period see for example, *The Cambridge History of China*, 11, *Late Ch'ing, 1800–1911*, Part 2, 1980; 12, *Republican China, 1912–1949*, Part 1, 1983; 13, *Republican China, 1912–1949*, Part 2 (Cambridge: Cambridge University Press, 1986); Marie-Claire Bergère, Lucien Bianco, and Jürgen Domes, eds, *La Chine au xxe siècle, d'une révolution à l'autre, 1895–1949*, 1, 1st ed. (Paris: Fayard, 1989), 3rd ed. (Paris: Armand Colin, 2000); Arthur Waldron, *From War to Nationalism: China's Turning Point, 1924–1925* (Cambridge: Cambridge University Press, 1995) and the bibliography included in these works.

3 For recent studies dealing with Chinese Islam and its believers: Françoise Aubin, "L'islam, une religion chinoise," forthcoming in *Revue bibliographique de Sinologie*.

4 *Ahong* 阿衡 / 訇 [< Persian *āḫūnd*] offers the rare case of a word pronounced differently from one of the characters transcribing it down (衡 is generally read *heng*). For the *ahong*'s functions: *Zhongguo Huizu dacidian* 中國回族大詞典 [Great Dictionary of the Hui Nationality in China], ed. Qiu Shusen 邱樹森 (Jiangsu guji chubanshe 江蘇古籍出版社 [Publishing House of Ancient Books in Jiangsu], 1992), 761.

5 Chinese words which are plain transliterations of Arabic-Persian originals are here by convention hyphenated (except *ahong*, which long ago became for Chinese Muslims an everyday word).

6 Although Huijiao indicated at that time, the worldwide Islam, we will keep a literal translation "Hui Religion" in the names of the associations where it occurs, to let speak by itself the terminological choice made by the Muslim activists.

7 The reification of the concepts of *Hanzu*, "Han nationality" and *minzu* 民族, "nationality," "ethnic group," during the Republican time till its official acceptance by the Communist regime, is being detected more and more subtly by a whole series of excellent studies, the most recent being: Susan D. Blum, *Portraits of 'Primitives': Ordering Human Kinds in the Chinese Nation* (Oxford: Roman and Littlefield, 2001); Jonathan N. Lipman, "How Many *Minzu* in a Nation? Modern Travellers Meet China's Frontier Peoples," *Inner Asia*, 4/1 (2002): 113–130; Dru Gladney, *Muslim Chinese. Ethnic Nationalism in the People's Republic* (Cambridge, MA: Harvard University Press, 1st ed. 1991, 2nd ed. 1996).

8 Guangxu 32, that is, 32nd year of the Guangxu era, is the date according to the Chinese calendar of the time.

9 Zhenjiang: a town of Eastern Central China, about 60 km east of Nanjing.

10 For Tong Cong [pron. Tong Ts'ong] (1864–1923) and his actions: *Zhongguo Huizu dacidian*, 704–705, 993.

11 For the cultural leadership of Japan in Asia after its victory over Russia, see Françoise Aubin, "Le Japon en terre d'islam chinois et au pays de Gengis-khan (fin XIXe-début XXe siècle)," *Études orientales*, 21–22 (2004), Special issue on *Le Japon et l'islam. L'islam au Japon*, pp. 36–79 and Japanese summary pp. 80–87. See a recent (anonymous) article about "Historical Materials on the Unrest of [Chinese] Students Staying in Japan in 1905": "Guangxu sanshiyinian liuri xuesheng fengchaoshiliao 光緒三十一年留日學生風潮史料," *Lishi dang'an* 歷史檔案, 2001/3: 62–67. About the action of the Muslim students who went to Japan in 1905: Matsumoto Masumi 松本ますみ, *Chūgoku minzoku seisaku no kenkyū. Shinmatsu kara 1945 nen made no 'minzokuron' wo chūshin ni* 中国民族政策の研究：清末から年までの「民族論」を中心に [Study about the Politic of Nationalities of China, Centred on the Theory of the Nationalities from the Late Qing to 1945] (Tokyo: Taga shuppan 多賀出版, 1999), 292–296.

12 For Sha Shanyu (Shanyu being his courtesy name, *zi*, while his given name, *ming*, is Qing 慶, 1879–1968): see Ma Zhongde 馬仲德 and Yang Zhenghua 楊振華, "Huizu aiguorenshi Sha Shanyu 回族愛國人士沙善餘 [A Hui Patriot, Sha Shanyu]," *Huizu yanjiu* 回族研究, 1993/4: 95–96; *Zhongguo Huizu dacidian*, 726. We must stress that a special feature of Muslim personal names is that many personalities are called by their courtesy name, *zi* 字 (*yi zi xing* 以字行), instead of their given name, *ming* 名.

13 *Huizu yanjiu*, 1993/4: 95.

14 A. Vissière, "Association culturelle mahométane de Chang-hai," forming "Etudes sino-mahométanes," 2e série, 4, *Revue du Monde musulman*, 19 (1912): 228–240.

15 The basic documentation about the *Zhongguo Huijiao jujin hui* (as about all the following associations) is due to a contemporary of the events, Fu Tongxian 傅統先, *Zhongguo Huijiaoshi* 中國回教史 [History of Islam in China] (Shanghai: Commercial Press, 1940, reprint Taibei: Commercial Press, 1969), 199–200. A detailed study is: Zhang Juling 張巨齡, "Zhongguo Huijiao jujin hui chuchuang jiping 中國回教俱進會初創記評 [First Stages of the Association for the Progress of the Hui Religion of China]," *Huizu yanjiu*, 1997/4: 1–11, 1998/1: 10–22, 1998/2: 14–16. About the branch founded in Yunnan: Sha Feiya 沙非亞, "1911–1951 nian de Yunnan Huizu Yi-si-lan-jiao zuzhi, 1911–1951 年的雲南回族伊斯蘭教組織 [Organization of Islam among the Hui of Yunnan in the Years 1911–1951]," *Huizu yanjiu*, 1992/4 (49–61): 49–53.

16 Among the numerous notices devoted to the *ahong* 'Abd al-Raḥīm Ma Songting (1895–1992), who is considered by the believers as one of the "Four Great *Ahong*s" and who has had a long career under the communist regime, see Sai Shengbao 賽生寶, "Aiguo zhuyizhe, yisilan jingxue jiaoyujia Ma Songting da ahong 愛國主義者, 伊斯蘭經學教育家馬松亭大阿訇 [The Nationalist and Qur'anic Teacher, the Great *Ahong* Ma Songting]," *Huizu yanjiu*, 1992/2: 98–100; *Zhongguo Huizu dacidian*, 969.

17 The given name of the *ahong* famous under the name of 'Abd al-Raḥmān Wang Haoran (1848–1919) is Kuan 寬, a Chinese translation of Raḥmān, "Merciful," while Haoran is his courtesy name; he enjoys many notices, for example in *Zhongguo Huizu dacidian*, 951; Bai Shouyi 白壽彝, "Ma Lianyuan, Wang Kuan, Ma Wanfu 馬聯元, 王寬, 馬萬福," in *Zhongguo Musilin* 中國穆斯林; Matsumoto Masumi, *Chūgoku minzoku seisaku no kenkyū* (see *supra*, note 11), 300–303.

18 Ha Decheng (given name: Guozhen 國鎮—Decheng being his courtesy name used as a given name, 1888–1943) is counted too as one of the "Four Great *Ahong*s"; see his notice (in French) by Leila Cherif, "Ha Te-ch'eng/Ha Decheng," in Marc Gaborieau, Nicole Grandin, Pierre Labrousse and Alexandre Popovic, eds, *Dictionnaire biographique des savants et grandes figures du monde musulman périphérique, du XIXe siècle à nos jours* (Paris: EHESS), 1 (1992): 39; *Zhongguo Huizu dacidian*, 966.

19 For Sha Shanyu: see note 12.

20 For Wu Tegong (?–1963): *Zhongguo Huizu dacidian*, 717.

21 For the *Zhongguo Huijiao xuehui*: Zhang Zhicheng 張志誠, "Ershi shijichu Shanghai Yisilanjiao xueshu wenhua tuanti: Zhongguo Huijiao xuehui 二十世紀初上海伊斯蘭教學術文化團體：中國回教學會 [A Cultural and Scholarly Islamic Organization in Shanghai at the Beginning of the Twentieth Century: The Learned Society of the Hui Religion of China]," *Huizu yanjiu*, 1992/3: 81–86; Fu Tongxian, *Zhongguo Huijiaoshi*, 201.

22 About the *Zhongguo Huijiao gonghui*: Fu Tongxian, *Zhongguo Huijiaoshi*, 200.

23 For Nūr Muḥammad Da Pusheng (given name: Fengxuan 鳳軒, Pusheng being his courtesy name, 1874–1965): Donald W. Klein and Anne B. Clark, *Biographic Dictionary of Chinese Communism, 1921–1965*, 2 vols (Cambridge, MA: Harvard University Press, 1971), 2: 794–796; Da Jie 達杰, "Da Pusheng ahong zhuanlüe 達浦生阿訇傳略 [Short Biography of the *Ahong* Da Pusheng]," *Zhongguo Musilin*, 1984/1: 18–26; *Zhongguo Huizu dacidian*, 960.

24 For the *Zhongguo Huijiao qingnian xuehui* and the *Huimin xuehui yanjiu hui*: Fu Tongxian, *Zhongguo Huijiaoshi*, 202–203.

25 For the *Zhongguo Huijiao wenhua xiehui*: Fu Tongxian, *Zhongguo Huijiaoshi*, 205.

26 For Fu Tongxian (1905–1985): *Zhongguo Huizu dacidian*, 739.

27 For the *Zhongguo Yi-si-lan budao hui:* Fu Tongxian, *Zhongguo Huijiaoshi*, 205.

28 For Ma Hongkui (*zi:* Shaoyun 少雲, 1892 or 1893–1970): Howard L. Boorman and Richard C. Howard, eds, *Biographical Dictionary of Republican China*, 4 vols (New York: Columbia University Press, 1967–1971), 2 (1968): 468–469 (date of birth: 1893); *Zhongguo Huizu dacidian*, 328. About the various Ma warlords of Gansu in Republican times: Jonathan N. Lipman, "Ethnicity and Politics in Republican China: The Ma Family Warlords of Gansu," *Modern China* 10/3 (1984): 285–316 (family lineages: 291); *Ningxia san Ma* 寧夏三馬 [The Three Ma of Ningxia] (Beijing: Zhongguo wenshi chubanshe, 1988)—about Ma Hongkui: 149–366.

29 For the *Huimin jiaoyu cujin hui:* Fu Tongxian, *Zhongguo Huijiaoshi*, 204.

30 For the *Zhonghua Huijiao zonghui:* Fu Tongxian, *Zhongguo Huijiaoshi*, 201.

31 For Ma Lin (*zi :* Xunchen 勛臣, 1876–1945): *Zhongguo Huizu dacidian*, 312.

32 For Ma Buqing (*zi:* Ziyun 子雲, 1901–?): Boorman and Howard, eds, *Biographical Dictionary of Republican China*, 2 (1968): 473–474; *Zhongguo Huizu dacidian*, 340.

33 For Ma Hongbin (*zi:* Ziyin 子寅, 1884–1960): Boorman and Howard, eds, *Biographical Dictionary of Republican China*, 2 (1968): 469–470; *Ningxia san Ma*, 49–143; *Zhongguo Huizu dacidian*, 321.

34 For Ma Fuxiang (*zi:* Yunting 雲亭, the name of his library being his pen-name: *Jishantang* 積善堂, 1876–1932): Boorman and Howard, eds, *Biographical Dictionary of Republican China*, 2 (1968): 464–465; *Ningxia san Ma*, 3–45; Jonathan N. Lipman, *Familiar Strangers. A History of Muslim in Northwest China* (Seattle, WA: University of Washington Press, 1997), 167–177; Ding Mingjun 丁明俊, "Lun Ma Fuxiang zaixiandai Huizu wenhua jiaoyusheshang de diwei 論馬福祥在現代回族文化教育史上的地位 [Ma Fuxiang's Position in the History of Culture and Education of the Hui]," *Huizu yanjiu* 1998/4: 58–69.

35 For Shi Zizhou (given name: Zuoxin 做新—Zizhou being his courtesy name—, 1879–d. in Taiwan 1967): *Zhongguo Huizu dacidian*, 315.

36 For Wang Jingzhai (first given name: Wenqing 文清, called too Hajj Sheykh, or Wang *lao* 老, "Old Wang," 1871 or 1879?–1949): *Zhongguo Huizu dacidian*, 962; *Zhongguo Musilin*, 1989/2: 2–6; Saguchi Tōru 佐口透, "Chūgoku Isuramu no kindai shugi 中国イスラムの近代主義 [The Modernism of Chinese Islam]," *Kanazawa daigaku hōbun gakubu ronshū. Shigakuhen* 金澤大學法文學部論集史學篇, 16 (1969): 37–40.

37 About Bai Chongxi (Qur'anic name: 'Umar, 1893–1966): Boorman and Howards, eds, *Biographical Dictionary* (*supra* note 34), 3 (1970): 51–56.

38 About Wuhan/Wuchang as a temporary wartime capital: Stephen R. MacKinnon, "Wuhan's Search for Identity in the Republican Period," in Joseph W. Esherick, ed., *Remaking the Chinese City. Modernity and National Identity, 1900–1950* (Honolulu: University of Hawai'i Press, 2000): 161–173, especially 168–170.

39 For Da Pusheng: see note 23.

40 For Ha Decheng: see note 18.

41 For Ma Songting: see note 16.

42 For Tang Kesan (whose dates are unknown): *Zhongguo Huizu dacidian*, 347.

43 For the *Zhongguo Huimin/Huijiao jiuguo xiehui*: see Bai Youtao 白友濤, "Zhongguo Huijiao jiuguo xiehui shulun 中國回教救國協會述論 [Account of the Friendly Association of the Hui People of China for the Salvation of the Country]," *Huizu yanjiu*, 1995/4: 48–55. About its branch in Yunnan: Sha Feiya, "1911–1951 nia..." (article quoted under note 15), 53–54.

44 According to the *Xinhua ribao* 新華日報 of 1938, June 19th, March 10th, November 24th, as quoted by *Huizu yanjiu*, 1995/4: 49.

45 For Chongqing during the war: Lee McIsaac, "The City as Nation. Creating a Wartime Capital in Chongqing," in *Remaking the Chinese City* (quoted *supra* note 38), 174–191.

46 This means that conversions to Islam occurred in the Republican time, a fact which is sometimes overlooked.

47 Information here given about the Association of the Hui Religion of China for the Salvation of the Country is entirely extracted from the Chinese article quoted in note 43.

48 Cf. for example Guan Wei, "Jiaoyu jiuguo sichao yu jindai shehui bianqian 教育救國思潮與近代社會變遷 [The Stream of Thoughts for Saving the Country by Education and the Changes of Modern Society]," *Lishi dang'an* 歷史檔案, 2002/3: 90–96. About the major educational debates during the late Qing and the early Republic: Paul Bailey, *Reform the People. Changing Attitudes towards Popular Education in Early 20th Century China* (Edinburgh: Edinburgh University, 1990, x–296). Among the numerous works dealing with Chinese education in the twentieth century, let us quote an article noticeable for its succinct survey of the main relevant questions: Colin MacKerras, "Education in the Guomindang Period, 1928–1949," in David Pong and Edmund S. K. Fung, eds, *Ideal and Realities: Social and Political Change in Modern China, 1860–1949* (Lanham, MD: University Press of America, 1985), 153–183.

49 See F. Aubin, "L'enseignement dans la Chine islamique pré-communiste (du xvie siècle au milieu du xxe). Entre affirmation identitaire et modernisme," in Nicole Grandin and Marc Gaborieau, eds, *Madrasa. La transmission du savoir dans le monde musulman* (Paris: Arguments, 1997): 373–401; Fu Tongxian, *Zhongguo Huijiaoshi* (1940: quoted *supra* note 15), 205–209. About the formation of a Chinese Muslim intellectual through education since the seventeenth century: Zvi Ben-Dor, *The 'Dao of Muhammad': Scholarship, Education, and Chinese Muslim Literati Identity in Late Imperial China* (Dissertation presented at University of California, Los Angeles, 2000), 51–107.

50 About the *nü* 女 (female) *ahong*s and their mosques, the *Qingzhen nüsi* 清真女寺: Elisabeth Allès, *Musulmans de Chine. Une anthropologie des Hui du Henan* (Paris: Editions de l'Ecole des Hautes Etudes en Sciences sociales, 2000), 235–287; about the ability of the female *ahong* to read Persian: Allès, *Musulmans de Chine*, 286.

51 Jonathan N. Lipman, "Hyphenated Chinese: Sino-Muslim Identity on Modern China," in Gail Hershatter, Emily Honig, Jonathan N. Lipman and Randall Stross, eds, *Remapping China. Fissures in Historical Terrain* (Stanford, CA: Stanford University Press, 1996), 97–112, 296–299—about what the author soundly calls the "scripturalist fundamentalism" of the founder of the Chinese Ikhwan: 105–106.

52 About the first anti-Chinese trend of the Ikhwan in China in late Qing time: Lipman, 'Hyphenated Chinese," 105–106; Leila Cherif-Chebbi, 'Ma Wanfu, Nūh, Zixi, surnommé Hāj Guoyuan ou Ma Guoyuan (1853–1934)', in Gaborieau *et al.*, eds, *Dictionnaire biographique des savants et grandes figures du monde musulman périphérique, du xixe siècle à nos jours* (Paris: EHESS, 1998), 2: 33–34. About the political conformity of the second trend of the Ikhwan: Lipman, "Hyphenated Chinese," 106–112; Lipman, "The Third Wave: Establishment and Transformation of the Muslim Brotherhood in China," *Etudes Orientales* 13–14 (1994): 89–105, especially 96–103; Leïla Cherif-Chebbi, "L'Yihewani, une machine de guerre contre le soufisme en Chine?," in Frederick de Jong and Bernd Radtke, eds, *Islamic Mysticism Contested. Thirteen Centuries of Controversies and Polemics* (Leiden: Brill, 1999): 576–602.

53 Dru C. Gladney, "The Salafiyya Movement in Northwest China: Islamic Fundamentalism among the Muslim Chinese?," in Leif Manger, ed., *Muslim Diversity. Local Islam in Global Context* (Richmond, UK: Curzon, 1999): 102–149, especially 130–135.

54 *Zhongguo Huizu dacidian*, 505.

55 Ibid., 507, 704–705.

56 See in the *Zhongguo Huizu dacidian*, a list with description of Muslim schools of different levels opened in late Qing times (505–509), in early Republican times (509–512), in the twenties (513–517), in the thirties and during the war (517–524), in the last years before the Communist taking of power (524–527), in the early Communist time (527–528), after the Cultural Revolution till 1989 (528–531).

57 About the School Mingde: *Zhongguo Huizu dacidian*, 515; Sha Feiya, "1911–1951 nia..." (quoted in note 15), 56, 59–61.

58 *Zhongguo Huizu dacidian*, 507; Sha Feiya, "1911–1951 nia..." (see note 15), 57.

59 About the Chengda School, among others, a presentation of the institution, of its aims, of its organization, by Ma Songting himself: "Zhongguo Huijiao yu Chengda shifan xuexiao 中國回教與成達師範學校 [The Hui Religion of China and the Chengda Normal School]," *Yugong banyuekan* 禹貢半月刊 [The Bimonthly Tribute of Yu] 5/11 (1937), *Huijiao zhuanhao* 回教專號 [Special Issue about the Hui Religion]: 1–14; Liu Dongsheng, "Chengda shifan xuexiao shuyao 成達師範學校史要 [Summary of the History of the Chengda Normal School]," *Huizu yanjiu* 1993/2: 61–75; 1993/3: 71–78; Saguchi, "Chūgoku Isuram...": 19–44 [see *supra* note 36]; Matsumoto, *Chūgoku minzoku*...(see note 11), 303–307.

60 For Ma Songting: see note 16.

61 For Tang Kesan: see note 42.

62 For Ma Fuxiang: see note 34. About his links with the Chengda School: Ding Mingjun 丁明俊, "Lun Ma Fuxiang zai xiandai Huizu wenhua jiaoyu shishang de diwei 論馬福祥在現代回族文化教育史上的地位 [Ma Fuxiang's Position in the History of Culture and Education of the Hui]," *Huizu yanjiu*, 1998/4: 58–69.

63 The Chinese characters used for transliterating the syllables of Fu'ad are noteworthy: *fu* "good fortune, prosperity," and *de* "Virtue."

64 For Ma Hongkui: see note 28.

65 For the Normal Islamic School of Shanghai: Fu Tongxian, *Zhongguo Huijiaoshi* (1940), 211–212; *Zhongguo Huizu dacidian*, 514.

66 For the Normal School of Pingliang: *Zhongguo Huizu dacidian*, 521.

67 For the Normal School of Wanxian: Fu Tongxian, *Zhongguo Huijiaoshi* (1940), 212; *Zhongguo Huizu dacidian*, 516.

68 For Ma Hongbin: see note 33.

69 For Ma Fuxiang: see notes 34 and 62.

70 According to Fu Tongxian, *Zhongguo Huijiaoshi*, 212–213.

71 See a recent article about the subject (and references given there): Natascha Vittinghoff, "Readers, Publishers and Officials in the Contest for a Public Voice and the Rise of a Modern Press in Late Qing China (1860–1880)," *T'oung Pao*, 87/3–4: 393–455.

72 The main references about the Muslim press in Republican China are: Rudolph Löwenthal (or Loewenthal), *The Religious Periodical Press in China*, 2 vols (Peking: The Synodal Commission in China, 1940, reprint San Francisco, CA: Chinese Materials Centre, Inc., 1996), 211–249+Chart VII in two parts; the same, "Djarīda [Press]/Japan," *EI*[2], 2/30–34 (1963), "China and Japan" (or French edition, 2/30–34 (1963), "Chine et Japon," 490–491). For a list of the 133 periodicals: Lei Xiaojing 雷曉靜, "Zhongguo jinxiandai Huizu, Yi-si-lan-jiao baokan de jueqi 中國近現代回族, 伊斯蘭教報刊的崛起 [Eminence of the Modern and Contemporary Press of the Hui Nationality and of Islam in China]," *Huizu yanjiu* 1997/1: 16–33.

73 According to Lei Xiaojing, "Zhongguo jinxianda..." (see note 72): 19.

74 Lei Xiaojing, "Zhongguo jinxianda...": 19. About the beginning of a Muslim press in China: Zhang Juling 張巨齡, "20 shijichu Zhongguo Huizu Yi-si-lan yanjiu shubu jiping 20世紀初中國回族伊斯蘭研究述補及評 [A Survey of the Study on the Hui Nationality and of Islam at the Beginning of the Twentieth Century]," *Huizu yanjiu* 2000/1: 10–15; 2000/2: 26–32.

75 See a facsimile of the first page and of the table of contents of the *Xing Hui bao* in Marshall Broomhall, *Islam in China. A Neglected Problem* (London: Morgan and Scott, and China Inland Mission, 1910), opposite p. 283 and 283–284. See also Yao Jide 姚繼德, "Huizu liuxuesheng yu Yunnan xiandai Yi-si-lan wenhua 回族留學生與雲南現代伊斯蘭文化 [Muslim Students Staying Abroad and the Contemporary Muslim Culture of Yunnan]," *Huizu yanjiu* 1996/3 (10–21): 11–12.

76 About the *Yuehua*: Löwenthal, *The Religious Periodical Press*, 226–228; *Huizu dacidian*, 619; Lei Xiaojing 雷曉靜, "Yuehua yu shehui diaocha 月華與社會調查 [The *Yuehua* and Social Investigation]," *Huizu yanjiu* 2000/2: 95–96; Matsumoto Masumi 松本ますみ, *Kingendai Chūgoku no kokumin tōgō genri to Chūgoku Isurāmu kaikaku-ha no seijiteki shokankei ni tsuite no rekishigaku teki kenkyū* 近現代中國の國民統合原理と中國イスラーム改革派の政治的諸關係についての歴史的研究 [Historical Study on the Relationship between National Integration of Modern China and Islamic Reformers' Roles in Politics] (Shibatashi, Niigata: Keiwa Gakuen Daigaku JinbunGakubu, 2003), ch. 2, "Kai aikokushugi no konkyo: *Gekka* ni miru Isurāmu kaikaku-ha no ronri 回愛國主義の根據：『月華』にみるイスラム改革派の論理 [The Logic of the Party of Islamic Reformers as seen in the *Yuehua*—The base of the Nationalism Hui]," 19–36. See also the paper by Matsumoto Masumi in the present volume.

77 Löwenthal, *The Religious Periodical Press*, 227.

78 Ibid., 226.

79 Some American Protestant missionaries in China who specialized in the apostolate amongst Muslims bought all these publications. Thanks to them two collections can be consulted in United States: one in the New York Public Library (Isaac Mason fund), the other in the Harvard-Yenching Library (Claude L. Pickens fund). There is an analytical catalogue of the Pickens fund by Matsumoto Masumi 松本ますみ, in *Chūgoku kenkyū geppō* 中國研究月報/*Monthly Journal of Chinese Affairs* 54/12 (2000): 28–42. For I. Mason, C. Pickens, and other Protestant missionaries, and their influence on the evolution of Islam in remote places of China: Françoise Aubin, "L'apostolat protestant en milieu musulman chinois," in *Chine et Europe: évolution et particularités des rapports est-ouest du xvi*[e] *au xx*[e] *siècle. Actes du IV*[e] *colloque international de sinologie de Chantilly* (Taipei, Paris and Hong Kong: Institut Ricci/Ricci Institute, 1991), 12–74.

80 For Ma Jian (or Muḥammad Ma Jian al-Sīnī, courtesy name Zishi 子實, 1906–1978), one of the greatest figures of the Sino-Muslim intellectual history of the twentieth

century, there are several detailed studies: Françoise Aubin, "L'islam chinois face à sa modernisation. Le cas de Ma Jian (Ma Chien) (1906–1978)," *Etudes Orientales* 19–20 (2003); Li Zhenzhong 李振中, *Xuezhe de zhuiqiu. Ma Jian zhuan* 學者的追求—馬堅傳 [The Research of a Scholar. A Biography of Ma Jian] (Yinchuan: Ningxia renmin chubanshe, 2000)—a part of this book (chapters 8 to 11 and some pages of chapter 12) being simultaneously published as an article, under the same title, in *Huizu yanjiu* 2000/1: 64—102.

81 For translations of the Qur'an: Françoise Aubin, "Les traductions du Coran en chinois," *Etudes Orientales* 13–14 (1994): 81–88.

82 A bibliographical analysis of these beloved masterpieces of the past is found in Donald Daniel Leslie, *Islamic Literature in Chinese, Late Ming and Early Ch'ing: Books, Authors and Associates* (Belconnen, ACT: Canberra College of Advanced Education, 1981).

83 For the Philosophy of Islam of Liuzhi and its editions: Leslie, *Islamic Literature*, 46 and chart p. 143.

84 For a survey of several of the publications sponsored by Ma Fuxiang and translations (in French) of his moral exhortations: A. Vissière, "Les musulmans chinois et la République. Littérature islamique chinoise," *Revue des Etudes islamiques* 3 (1927): 309–319, esp. 313–319.

85 For Bai Chongxi: see note 37; and *passim* in *The Cambridge History of China*, Volume 12 and 13, *Republican China* (quoted in note 2).

86 For the Guangxi Clique: *The Cambridge History of China*, 12: 293 *sq*., 13: 124 *et seq. passim*; and in the detailed biography of Bai Chongxi in Boorman and Howard's *Biographical Dictionary*, 3: (51–55) 52–55.

87 It is "The Storybook of Bai Chongxi" (*Bai Chongxi chuanqi* 白崇禧傳奇), by Su Liwen 蘇理文 (Nanning: Guangxi renmin chubanshe 廣西人民出版社, 1988).

88 For Ma Buqing: see note 32.

89 For Ma Bufang (*zi*: Zixiang 子香, Qur'anic name Husein): Boorman and Howard, eds, *Biographical Dictionary of Republican China*, 2 (1968): 474–475 (giving as date of birth 1903); *Zhongguo Huizu dacidian*, 341–342 (giving as date of birth 1902).

90 For Ma Lin: *Zhongguo Huizu dacidian*, 312.

91 For the Ruiwei Elementary School: Ibid., 524.

92 Ibid.

93 Ibid., 523.

94 Ibid.

95 Ibid.

96 For Ma Fuxiang: see notes 34 and 84.

97 Cf. note 84.

98 For Ma Hongkui: see note 28.

99 For Su Baoqiao: Su Yao 蘇瑤, "Su Baoqiao shilue 蘇抱樵事略 [Biographical Notice of Su Baoqiao]," *Huizu yanjiu* 1995/1: 82–88.

100 For Ma Linyi (*zi* Zhenwu): *Zhongguo Huizu dacidian*, 705.

101 About Da Pusheng: note 23.

102 For Tang Kesan: note 42.

103 For Sha Shanyu: note 12.

104 For Wu Tegong: note 20.

105 For Tong Cong: note 10.

106 For Wang Haoran: note 17.

107 For Wang Jingzhai: note 36.

108 For Ding Baochen: *Zhonguo Huizu dacidian*, 317, and *Zhongguo Huizu dacidian*, 705, under the notice about his elder brother, Ding Ziliang 丁子良 (*ming*: Guorui 國瑞, 1870–1935), who collaborated with him.

109 For Yang Zhongming (given name Jingxiu 敬修—Zhongming being his courtesy name, appellation Xiuzhen, Qur'anic name Salih): Yang Daye 楊大業, "Yang Zhongming shengping 楊仲明生平 [Yang Zhongming's Whole Life]," *Zhongguo Musilin/Muslims of China* 1990/1: 12–16; *Zhongguo Huizu Musilin*, 959.
110 For Ha Decheng: note 18.
111 About Ma Songting: note 16.
112 For Ma Jian: see note 80.
113 Jonathan N. Lipman and Leila Cherif-Chebbi have already dealt in detail with the transformation of the Chinese Ikhwan: see note 52.
114 For the Normal Islamic School of Shanghai: see note 65.
115 For Ma Jian's translation of the *Lunyu*: Giovanni and Virginia Vacca, "La prima traduzione araba del Lun yü (Dialoghi) di Confucio," *Oriente Moderno* 18 (1938): 184–190. Ma Jian's lectures in Arabic about Chinese Islam, held in Cairo in 1934, were translated into Italian by Virginia Vacca, "Notizie d'un Musulmano sui Musulmani Cinesi," *Oriente Moderno* 15 (1935): 353–364, 425–434, 483–487.
116 About Chen Keli: Leila Cherif-Chebbi, "Chen Keli, Yūsuf," in Gaborieau *et al.*, eds, *Dictionnaire biographique des savants et grandes figures du monde musulman périphérique* (Paris: EHESS, 1998), 2: 31; *Zhongguo Huizu dacidian*, 978–979.
117 For the Jahriyya in China, the sub-groups called *menhuan* and Ma Yuanzhang see Françoise Aubin, "En islam chinois: quels Naqshbandis?," in Marc Gaborieau, Alexandre Popovic and Thierry Zarcone, eds, *Naqshbandis. Cheminements et situation actuelle d'un ordre mystique musulman* (Istanbul: Isis—Institut Français d'Etudes Anatoliennes, 1990) : 491–572 (about Ma Yuanzhang: 562); Françoise Aubin, "Chine," in Henri Chambert-Loir and Claude Guillot, eds, *Le culte des saints dans le monde musulman* (Paris: Ecole française d'Extrême-Orient, 1995) : 367–388 (about Ma Yuanzhang: 376–380, 387–388); Jonathan N. Lipman, "Ma Yuanzhang and the Revival of the Jahrīya," in *Familiar Strangers* (Seattle, WA: University of Washington, 1997) : 177–186. A biography of Ma Yuanzhang can be found in *Zhongguo Huizu yanjiu*, 955.
118 Jonathan N. Lipman, "Ma Qixi (1857–1914)," in *Familiar Strangers*: 186–199.
119 For a brief survey of the politics of Japan in occupied China and Inner Mongolia see Françoise Aubin, "Le Japon en terre d'islam chinois et au pays de Gengis-khan" (forthcoming, see note 11).
120 See for example a collective work which has a symptomatic title: Joshua A. Fogel and Peter G. Zarrow, eds, *Imagine the People. Chinese Intellectuals and the Concept of Citizenship* (Armonk, NY: M. E. Sharpe, 1997).
121 Excerpt from the *Xing Hui pian zhaiyao* 醒回篇摘要 [Summary of "A Leaf for Awakening the Hui"—the journal started in Tokyo in 1908] (Peking: Chinese Islamic Book Co at Ox Street Mosque, 1925, publication kept in the New York Public Library), appendix *Lun Hui min* 論回民 [Discussion of the People Hui], 25a–27a.
122 Ibid., 26a–26b.
123 Lipman, "Hyphenated Chinese" (quoted note 51), 111. See also Gladney, *Muslim Chinese* (quoted note 7), 306 and *et seq.*

Main reference titles

Boorman, Howard and Howard, Richard C., eds, *Bibliographical Dictionary of Republican China* (New York: Columbia University Press, 4 vols, 1967–1971 + Index volume 1979).

Fu Tongxian 傅統先, *Zhongguo Huijiaoshi* 中國回教史 [History of Islam in China] (Shanghai: Commercial Press, 1940, republication Taibei: Commercial Press, 1969).

Huizu yanjiu 回族研究 /*Researches on Hui Nationality*, periodical (No. 1: 1990), Yinchuan: Ningxia shehuike xueyuan [Academy of Social Science of Ningxia].
Zhongguo Huizu dacidian 中國回族大詞典 [Great Dictionary of the Hui nationality in China], ed. Qiu Shusen 邱樹森 (Jiangsu guji chubanshe 江蘇古籍出版社 [Publishing House of Ancient Books in Jiangsu], 1992).
Zhongguo Musilin 中國穆斯林 /*China Muslims*, periodical (issue 28: 1981), Beijing: Zhongguo yisilanjiao xiehui [Islamic Association of China].

13

MUSLIM INTELLECTUALS AND JAPAN

A Pan-Islamist mediator, Abdurreshid Ibrahim

Komatsu Hisao

Since the end of the nineteenth century, especially after the Russo-Japanese War in 1904–1905, Muslim intellectuals began to take substantial interest in the emergence of modern Japan, and to develop a positive image of Japan and the Japanese people. In general, they supposed that Japan adopted Western civilization without abandoning its traditional culture, becoming one of the most developed countries in the world within a short period after the Meiji revolution. Of these Muslim intellectuals interested in Japan, Abdurreshid Ibrahim (1857–1944) was among the most outstanding.[1] He not only introduced Japan and Japanese people in detail to the broad Turkic Muslim audience through his extensive travels, by means of his journal, *Âlem-i İslâm: Japonya'da intişar-ı İslâmiyet* [The World of Islam: The Spread of Islam in Japan],[2] but also made efforts later in his life to establish a close relationship between the Muslim world and Japan based on his Pan-Islamic (*İttihad-ı İslâm*) ideology and strategy. This essay is a preliminary survey of his vision of modern Japan and aims to present basic information for further research on a comprehensive subject, Islam and Japan, the significance of which is clearly growing in the contemporary world.

A leading Pan-Islamist in Russia

We will begin with an overview of Ibrahim's activities before his arrival in Japan in 1909.[3] He was born in Tara, a city in the Tobol'sk governorate, Western Siberia. According to his autobiography, his Tatar family came from the descendants of Bukharans who had migrated from Central Asia to Western Siberia. Being an ardent student of Islamic learning, he traveled through Odessa and Istanbul to Mecca and Medina in 1879, just after the Russo-Ottoman War (1877–1878). There, he mastered Islamic learning. After returning to his country in 1885 to engage in reforming outdated madrasas, he was appointed a qadi in the Spiritual Assembly of the Muslim law located in Ufa. Established by order of Catherine II

(r. 1762–1796) to supervise "Muslim clergymen" such as the imams or *mudarris*es (madrasa teachers) in Russia proper and Siberia, this official institution enjoyed great authority among the Russian Muslims, who constituted at least 13% of the total population of the Empire at the beginning of the twentieth century. Ibrahim's esteemed position as a qadi caused Japanese journalism to introduce him in later years as "the former president of Muslims in Russia,"[4] even though such an office never existed. However, after a few years of protesting against the stagnation and collapse of the Assembly leaders under full control of the Russian government, Ibrahim resigned from his office to move to Istanbul in 1894.

Outside Russia, he published articles that criticized Russia's oppressive policy toward her Muslim subjects. For example, in his essay *Muslims in Russia* published in Cairo in 1900, he exposed various measures of forced conversion and assimilation applied by Orthodox missionaries toward Tatar Muslims, as well as obstacles that the Russian authorities imposed on the Muslim educational reform movement. Among Russian Muslims, he was the first to openly criticize Russian policies toward Muslims. Nonetheless, he had to acknowledge the overwhelming power of Czarism as well as the incapability and ignorance of Russia's Muslim population. Remembering that the Muslim revolts against Qing rule in Xinjiang in the nineteenth century brought about only the great tragedy of a massacre, he urged his fellow Muslims to engage in educational reform and development instead of direct opposition to the ruling power.[5]

During his travels in Europe, Ibrahim came into contact with Russian revolutionaries and socialists in exile. Probably due to his apparent anti-Czarist discourses and activities, he was surrendered to Russian authorities by the Ottoman government on the former's insistence and for a time was in jail in Odessa. According to Russian authorities, he was nothing less than a dangerous Pan-Islamist who advocated the awakening and mutual integration of Muslims inside and outside the borders of the Russian Empire. In addition to this, it is said that during the Russo-Japanese War Ibrahim had made the close acquaintance of General Akashi Motojirō (1864–1919), a leading Japanese intelligence agent in Europe.[6]

When the Russian revolution in 1905 brought about relative freedom of speech and of the press, Ibrahim published Tatar and Arabic newspapers and journals such as the *Ulfat* and *al-Tilmid* in St Petersburg, and otherwise contributed to the development of Muslim journalism in Russia. At the same time, in order to unite Muslim peoples in the direction of reform and progress he endeavored to convene Russian Muslim congresses (which were held three times) and bring into existence the first Muslim political organization, the *Ittifāq al-Muslimīn* [Union of (Russia's) Muslims]. As one of the most active leaders in the Muslim national movement in Russia, he published an interesting essay, *Avtonomija* [Autonomy], in 1907 that discussed the possible forms of autonomy for Muslim peoples in Russia. He envisaged territorial autonomy for the Qazaqs and Turkestanis as well as cultural autonomy for the Tatars and other Muslim minorities scattered among the Russian majority.[7] At any rate, his energetic activities in the political sphere during the revolutionary years caused later Japanese journalism to introduce him as "a former representative in the Russian parliament."[8]

The reaction of Czarism after 1907 put an end to the first Muslim political movement, however, and many Muslim intellectuals in Russia were obliged to migrate to Istanbul, where the Young Turks revolution in 1908 made their political and journalistic activities secure. Unlike them, Ibrahim traveled first in Russian Turkestan and Bukhara[9] to witness negative aspects of Russian colonial rule, and then at the end of September 1909 set out on a great journey from Kazan through Siberia, Manchuria, Japan, Korea, China, Southeast Asia, India, and Arabia to Istanbul. On his travels, he continued to send his reports and essays to the Tatar newspaper *Bäyanul-hak* in Kazan and the Ottoman journal *Sırat-ı müstakim* in Istanbul.[10] He was not, however, merely a journalist traveling in Eurasia. His travel account, *The World of Islam*, shows that his great journey had at least two major aims: first to awaken and enlighten Muslim peoples by describing real situations in the Muslim world that extends into Eurasia, and second to elaborate a strategy for the liberation of Muslim peoples under the rule of Western great powers. According to Ibrahim, Japan would play a decisive role in this strategy. Arriving in Vladivostok in January 1909, he waited for a steamship bound for Japan. Given that he visited the Japanese consulate in Vladivostok to consult with the officials, it is reasonable to think that Japanese authorities obtained considerable information about this famous Muslim activist in Russia.

Ibrahim in Japan

In February 2, 1909, Ibrahim arrived in Tsuruga harbor, where he observed on land the huge Russian cannon made in St. Petersburg and captured by the Japanese army during the previous war. In Japan, he observed considerable reminiscence about the war. After settling in Yokohama, he began to study Japan and the Japanese people with unlimited interest. Although he did not know the Japanese language, his acquaintance with Nakayama Itsuzō, who had a good command of Russian and was probably a member of the Kokuryūkai (Black Dragon Society),[11] enabled Ibrahim to communicate with many Japanese people by way of the Russian language. Ibrahim notes, however, that "after discovering that the grammatical structure of Japanese is similar to Turkish, my desire to learn Japanese was stimulated so much." He was proud of learning Japanese, and it helped his everyday life in Japan. In this way he began his field survey to study Japanese political, socioeconomic, military, and cultural systems, as well as customs and manners.

He stayed in Japan until June 1909. This long stay, exceptional in his great journey, underlines his strong interest in Japan. Indeed, he visited a variety of places: villages around Yokohama, the Parliament in session, the Sugamo prison, hospitals, shrines, temples, the Kabuki Theater, and a cherry blossom party. He preferred to visit schools such as Waseda University, the Tokyo Imperial University, the Tokyo Institute of Arts, and schools for girls. He even attended classes, as well as graduations. He was obviously impressed by a Japanese educational system that made rapid progress during the Meiji era (1868–1912). Underlying his admiration for Japanese education are the sentiments of a *Jadid*-Reformist intellectual who has not yet witnessed the full achievements of educational reform among Russian Muslims.

Another favorite place of his was the press bureaus. As soon as he arrived in Japan he visited the *Kokumin shinbun*, directed by a leading journalist, Tokutomi Sohō (1863–1957), and the *Hōchi shinbun*, which took pride in its daily 350,000 copies. The *Hōchi shinbun* of February 16, 1909 reported on "an unusual giant" who is nothing but "an ex-representative in the Russian Parliament and head of the recently banned revolutionary newspaper *Ulfat*, Mr Rashid Ibrahim (60 years old) himself." During his stay in Japan, major newspapers reported his activities and the aims of his journey with some curiosity. In other words, Ibrahim succeeded in introducing himself to the Japanese audience, who had hardly any knowledge about Muslims in Russia.

He tried to meet every kind of Japanese in order to study Japan and the Japanese people. His meeting list extends from ordinary people to ex-prime ministers, as well as university professors and notables. Among them we find such leading figures as Itō Hirobumi (1841–1909: one of the most eminent statesmen during the Meiji era, ex-prime minister), Ōkuma Shigenobu (1838–1922: ex-prime minister and ex-minister of foreign affairs, later once again prime minister), Inukai Tsuyoshi (1855–1932: later prime minister), Ōyama Iwao (1842–1916: Marshal, ex-general commander in Manchuria), and two ultranationalist leaders who advocated Pan-Asianist ideology for the sake of Japanese interests, Tōyama Mitsuru (1855–1944)[12] and Uchida Ryōhei (1874–1937).[13] Probably by their introduction, he was sometimes invited to give lectures, which were in Russian. In these meetings and lectures he used to stress three points, as described later.

First, he commented in every talk that Japanese should keep their "national spirit (*ahlak-ı milliye*)." Comparing Japanese characteristics—such as virtue, a sense of equality among people who are not divided into classes, and respectable manners—with characteristics of the European and Muslim worlds, he spares no word of admiration for Japanese virtue. Of all Japanese characteristics, he considered "national spirit" (sometimes translated into Japanese as "*Yamato damashii*") to be the most important. According to him the reason for the rapid progress of the Japanese was an intensive acceptance of Western science and technology while nonetheless keeping Japanese spiritual values—in other words, not losing their own tradition and identity. Although he clearly overestimates a spiritual factor in Japanese development, at the base of his argument we can recognize the deep anxieties of a Muslim intellectual who witnessed the decline of Islamic tradition in the Ottoman Empire due to rapid Westernization after the Tanzimat reforms, as well as the great changes in Muslim societies threatened by powerful Western influences.

Second, he never forgot to criticize any attitude of blind Westernization, especially the activities of Christian missionaries in Japan. This criticism is simply another aspect of his first argument. On every occasion he raised an alarm against the trend of superficial Westernization among the people, the so-called "*haikara*" phenomena (derived from the "high collar" used in Western clothes, a symbol of Westernization), and pointed out political motives of the great powers behind the missionary activities, including the Russian Orthodox Church. Here we should recognize the Muslim intellectual who confronts threats of cultural imperialism in the guise of missionary activities, not merely a Pan-Islamist with a simple irritation and opposition to Christianity. He was of course aware that the new method of conversion and assimilation through education by the native languages of *inorodcy* (non-Russian and non-Orthodox peoples in the Russian Empire), introduced by N. Il'minskij (1822–1891), was a crucial threat to Tatar Muslims in the Volga-Ural region. We consider that Ibrahim overestimated missionary activities in Japan due to his experiences in Russia.

Third, he stressed the geopolitical importance of the Muslim world extending from North Africa to East Asia and Southeast Asia, especially in his conversations with statesmen and military agents. It is worth noting that he tried to draw their attention to Chinese Muslims (present-day *Hui*s). According to him, Chinese Muslims could be the best partners for Japanese who wanted to penetrate into China. Such a partnership was planned as one of the rings of his great strategy, which envisaged the union of Asian peoples by joining the Muslim world with Japan and aimed to resist to the great powers' rule in Asia by this strong union. To join the Muslim world with Japan, he saw the best solution to be Japanese acceptance of Islam. Although he believed that Japanese virtue is in total accord with the doctrine of Islam, he was also convinced that the Japanese would never accept Islam if political and economical interests were lacking.

Ibrahim's vision is clearly presented in a speech published later in the journal *Gaikō Jihō* [Foreign Affairs], as follows:

> In short, my purpose in visiting Japan is to investigate Japanese affairs in detail. Frankly, before the Russo-Japanese War I knew almost nothing about Japan. Japan's great success in this war affected me so much that I decided to come to Japan. I am sure we can learn many things in Japan, which is developing day by day like the rising sun. As to our Tatar people, words cannot describe the various kinds of oppression that we suffered during 450 years under Russian rule. The Russian government has not permitted us to learn our own history. They do not want to have enlightened Muslim subjects; for example, last year alone 15 Tatar schools, built by the people's own efforts and expense, were closed down by order of the government. You can understand everything by this simple example. I will repeat once more that, as a whole, Asians are disgusted by the Europeans. From this point of view, I am sure that bringing about the union of Asian countries to stand up to Europe is our legitimate means of self-defense. We Tatars do not hesitate to respect Japan as our senior, and we hope to send our youth to study in Japan. I will never believe that our independence can be achieved by ordinary means. It will become possible for us to carry out the independence movement only when the world order transforms all at once and great changes come about in the balance of power.[14]

The *Ajia Gikai* [The Society for the Asian Cause]

Ibrahim's eloquent argument emphasizing the significance of the "rising sun" in world politics could not fail to attract the attention of Japanese nationalists and Pan-Asianists in the late Meiji era. As he was considered the most eminent political leader among Russian Muslims, his convincing words must have stimulated Japanese intellectuals. Ibrahim's Pan-Islamist vision of a union of Asian peoples coincided with their Pan-Asianist ideology. In fact, he became acquainted with Nakano Jōtarō (1866–1928), an agent of the General Staff Office and ardent Pan-Asianist, and Ōhara Bukei (1865–1933), a former General Staff officer and member of the *Tōa Dōbunkai*[15] who received his Muslim name Abu Bakr from Ibrahim. Introduced by these men, he cultivated close acquaintance with Tōyama, the charismatic master of Pan-Asianists, and statesmen with the same ideology such as Inukai Tsuyoshi and Kōno Hironaka (1849–1921: ex-president of the Diet). Their common objectives were to pave the way for joining the Muslim world with Japan and to bring about the union of Asian peoples. As a first step, they planned to construct a mosque in Tokyo as a symbol of cooperation.

Finally, they agreed to establish a political society, *Ajia Gikai*, aimed at the union and defense of Asian peoples. According to Ibrahim it was established in Tokyo on June 7, 1909, and the initiators swore an oath to keep their agreement.[16] The prospectus of the society says as follows:

> Our Asia, being full of sublime and sacred thought, occupies the most important place in the world. Asia is superior to any other continent in its wide space, vast landscape, huge population, and abundant products. Therefore the first civilization was born in Asia, and the greatest thought spread from Asia. However, it is a great pity for us that Asian peoples not only lack communication within them, but also do not hesitate to oppose each other. It was this opposition among Asian peoples that enabled Western powers to invade the East. Without being aware of this defect and putting an end to internal opposition, Asian peoples will have no future. Being confident in their capability, Asian peoples with superior ethics and manners as well as sound character and thought should endeavor after the reform and development of Asia. It is for this cause that we established the *Ajia Gikai*. We would like to address our proposal to a large audience in Asia and to call for their participation and assistance.

The prospectus referred to the following four directions of activities:

1. For the sake of the development of Asian countries, the society studies religion, education, economy, geography, colonization, international affairs, politics and military affairs in Asia.
2. Research results are to be published in our journal.

3. Our society gradually opens its branches in China, Thailand, India, Persia, Afghanistan, Turkey and other areas of importance.
4. Our society dispatches its members to Asian countries for field surveys.[17]

It is not certain to what extent the program was realized, because the society was short-lived. It is true, however, that according to Ibrahim's proposal the president of the society, Ōhara, sent a letter to the *şeyhülislam* [the chief of the ulama in the Ottoman Empire] in September 1910 asking for the dispatch of ulama to Japan and financial assistance. It is said that at the beginning of 1911 membership was more than 100, and three Turkish graduates were learning Japanese at the temporary dormitory of the society in Tokyo.[18] Although the group failed to construct a mosque due to lack of money, their prospectus and programs were published in an Ottoman Turkish translation by the major Islamist journal in Istanbul, *Sırat-ı müstakim*.[19] Since this journal circulated not only in the Ottoman Empire but also in Russia, we can suppose that the vision of the *Ajia Gikai* was popular among Turkic Muslim intellectuals.

Even after leaving Japan, Ibrahim continued to work in accordance with the program of the society. When he was in China, noting the rising waves of boycotting Japanese goods, he dared to call for the union and liberation of Asian peoples. He writes in his account of his travels that he contributed an article, "The East for the Eastern Peoples" to the Muslim journal published in Beijing, *Zhengzong aiguo bao* [*The Journal of Correct Teaching and Love of the Country*]. In this article, referring to Russian ambition in Inner Asia, the British invasion of Tibet, the French occupation of Tonkin, and the division of the Near-East and Iran by great powers, he pointed out that without a union of Eastern peoples they have no way to survive against merciless Western invasion, and anticipated the leading role of Japan that established her hegemony in Korea and Manchuria. Although this argument was not paradoxical for the author, who went so far as to advocate a Chino-Japanese union, he failed to consider how his argument for Japanese expansion in East Asia would affect a Chinese audience. Ibrahim probably told the program of the *Ajia Gikai* to Chinese Muslim leaders such as Wang Haoran (1848–1919).[20] A few decades later, however, they followed an alleged but popular hadith, "Love of one's country is part of religion." In other words, they participated intensely in anti-Japanese protest movements.[21]

In March 1910, just after a long journey, Ibrahim and his companion from India Yamaoka Kōtarō (1880–1959), the first Japanese hajji, were invited to give lectures by the Society of Muslim Students from Russia in Istanbul. Ibrahim's speech, which presented the prosperous future of the *Ajia Gikai*, won great applause from the audience. A young Bukharan student, Abdurauf Fitrat (1886–1938), may have attended this conference or read the *Âlem-i İslâm* carefully. In his Persian work, *Munāẓara* [The Debate], which became the manifesto of the *Jadid*-Reformist movements in Bukhara and Turkestan, Fitrat describes

Ibrahim's activities in Japan as follows:

> The Venerable Abdurreshid Ibrahim, leaving his home with only 12 rubles, did not mind the trouble of visiting as far as China and Japan in order to establish the union of Islam. In the capital of Japan, Tokyo, he succeeded in converting some notables to Islam and even setting up an Islamic society. This is nothing else than sincere service to Islam. One of the Japanese ministers is said to have dedicated his spare time for teaching children of the common people. Although he is a so-called school manager, he does not receive any money from anybody. It seems that he pays all expenses out of his own pocket.[22]

Of course, here Fitrat mentions the *Ajia Gikai*. The "school manager" may be marshal Ōyama, who according to Ibrahim was living in a school as a supervisor after retiring from the army. By the way, when Fitrat's work was translated into Uzbek in Russian Turkistan, this passage praising the devoted activities of Ibrahim was totally omitted, replaced by an account of humanistic activities of Tolstoy, due to Russian censors. However, positive images of Japan introduced by Ibrahim are found in other works of Fitrat such as *Bayānāt-i sayyāh-i hindī* [Tales of an Indian Traveler (Istanbul, 1912)], and *Rahbar-i nağāt* [The Guide to Salvation (Petrograd, 1915)].

Despite Ibrahim's personal efforts, clearly his vision of uniting Japan and the Ottoman Empire remained unrealized in real politics. When he visited Kamil Paşa (1832–1913) to consult about his project, this experienced Ottoman statesman told him:

> You are a little bit late to come. If you had come in the reign of Abdülaziz (1861–76), you would have enjoyed his favor. The late sultan was very fond of such projects. In those days, our mighty navy could serve to send you with special equipment. Sultan Abdülhamit (1876–1909) also intended to send a delegation of ulama; unfortunately, our ship Ertuğrul sank near the Japanese coast. Although the sultan had a goal, he had no power to realize it.[23]

Indeed, the Ottoman Empire, confronted with a series of fatal problems since the Young Turks revolution in 1908, could not afford to elaborate an Eastern policy as Ibrahim desired. At the same time, a new nationalist ideology of Turkism began to gain a broader audience among Muslim intellectuals in the Empire.

Ibrahim in war and revolution

Despite unfavorable conditions, Ibrahim worked actively as a Pan-Islamist journalist in Istanbul. His extensive travels as reported in *Âlem-i İslâm* made him widely known among Turkic-speaking Muslims. It is not, however, merely a travel journal. It is a unique work that reads the early twentieth century world from the viewpoint of a Pan-Islamist ideology based on his direct observations in Eurasia. While denouncing the great powers' colonial rule in Asia, the author does not hesitate to also criticize the weakness and contradictions that prevailed within the Muslim world. He describes at every opportunity the heavy damage caused by sectarian antagonism, corruption, and ignorance among Muslims. In other words, he is carrying out the duties of ulama, who should be responsible for the development of the Muslim community. This work is an example of enlightenment literature that aimed at awakening Muslim peoples in Asia. At the same time, it should not be missed that his detailed and overstated narration about Japan and the Japanese contributed to the formation of a long-lasting pro-Japanese image in modern Turkey.[24] For example, the poem *Japonlar* [Japanese], written by Mehmet Akif (1873–1936), who was inspired by the *Âlem-i İslâm*, introduced to fellow Muslims a "Japanese virtue" that is completely in accord with Islamic teachings. According to him, the Japanese could be the most perfect Muslims in the world.

Along with the publication of his travel narrative, Ibrahim started to publish Ottoman journals such as the *Teârüf-i müslimin* [Acquaintance of Muslims: 1910–1911] and *İslâm dünyası* [The World of Islam: 1913] to give information about the recent events in the Muslim world as well as to exchange opinions and information among Muslim intellectuals throughout the world.[25] In the former journal, an article by a member of the *Ajia Gikai* appeared. Ibrahim also published the Ottoman translation of a Japanese treatise that exposed Western oppressions against Asian peoples. In this treatise the author says:

> Once a Tatar colleague [Ibrahim] visited Japan, and made a very important attempt. That is he asked Japanese government supports to recover their independence. According to him, if the Japanese government carries out seriously its mission of leading Asian peoples, it will succeed in uniting Asian peoples within three or five years.[26]

Ibrahim's activism was also distinguished in the following war years. In 1911, when Italians invaded Libya under Ottoman rule, despite his advanced age he visited the front to encourage the defense army. Calling Ottoman Muslims for the jihad, he asked spiritual and material supports from Japan, Java, and India through his extensive networks of fellowship cultivated during his great travel. His Pan-Islamist activities were repeated during the Balkan war in 1912. In these war years, Ibrahim gained acquaintance with an eminent leader of the Young Turks, Enver Paşa (1881–1922). When the Ottoman Empire entered the First World War in 1914, at Enver Paşa's request Ibrahim went to Berlin and, from a great number of Russian war prisoners captured by the German Army,[27] recruited Tatar Muslim soldiers who could fight on the Ottoman front. By publishing the newspaper *Cihad-ı İslâm* [The Holy war of Islam] and working as an imam in the prisoner camps, he endeavored to form the Asian Battalion. Later on it was dispatched to the Iraqi front and fought against the British army. In 1918 he worked for the *Teşkilat-ı Mahsusa* (Intelligence Department of the Ottoman Army) and helped Ottoman citizens returning from Russia to their homeland.[28]

In October 1918, after the defeat of the Ottoman Empire, he decided to go back to his native country, where the civil war had continued since the October revolution in the previous year. He may have expected that the revolution had put an end to the Czarist oppressions and brought about favorable conditions for Russia's Muslims. On the way to Tobol'sk, however, he found miserable people suffering from a famine that prevailed in the Volga-Ural region. In his native city, Tara, he taught Muslim young people for two years. When Bolshevik repression toward Muslims obliged him to leave Tara, he traveled through Xinjiang, China, and Manchuria to Moscow. On the way, he heard news of the victorious Turkish National Army recovering Izmir from the Greeks. In Moscow he made acquaintance with the highest leaders of the Bolsheviks, such as Lenin and Stalin, and worked to ensure the existence of Muslim communities in Russia as well as to help Muslim peoples suffering from great famines. According to Zeki Validov [Togan (1890–1970)], who hosted Ibrahim and his Indian companions in the South Urals in March 1920, they planned to unite the Muslim world with Soviet Russia for the liberation of Muslims under Western colonial rule.[29] However, recognizing that compromise with the Bolsheviks could not be possible, in the spring of 1923 Ibrahim decided to go back to Turkey.[30]

Once again in Japan

However Ibrahim found that the new political conditions in the Republic of Turkey would never be favorable for him. First, his Pan-Islamist ideology was not allowable under Mustafa Kemal [Atatürk (1880–1938)]'s new regime, which had abolished the caliphate and aimed to be a secular national state. Second, Ibrahim's anti-Soviet speaking and behavior was also intolerable for a Turkish government that cultivated close relations with Soviet Russia after the difficult years of the Turkish war for independence. Consequently, after 1925 Ibrahim was obliged to live in retirement in Konya, where a number of Muslim migrants from Russia were now living. This "home arrest" may have promised him a peaceful old age. Starting in the latter part of the 1920s, however, Japanese military attachés in Ankara came to invite him to Japan. Although the details of this invitation remain to be unearthed, cooperation with eminent Muslim leaders must have been indispensable for Japanese authorities that understood the strategic importance of the Muslim world spreading in Asia. Ibrahim once again came to Japan in October 1933.

Ibrahim was warmly welcomed by Tokyo's Muslim community, headed by the Bashkir imam Muhammad Qurban-'Aliyeff (Kurbangaliev, 1890–1972),[31] as well as by Japanese dignitaries in a reception held on November 5, 1933.[32] According to his talk published in the *Yomiuri shinbun*, he had a set of projects to be realized in Japan: first, to promote cooperation between the Muslim world and Japan, which had withdrawn from the League of Nations; second, to study the current state of affairs in Japan that he was visiting once again after a twenty-five years' absence; third, to correct misunderstandings about Islam among the Japanese people, who got all their information about Islam from biased Western publications. The third project included the publication of his autobiography, which could instruct the Japanese as to the modern history of the Muslim world and the Japanese translation of the Qur'an.[33] Clearly, he was eager to realize his long-cherished plan to bring the Muslim world together with Japan in the post-war world order.

In Tokyo he was esteemed as the most respectable elder in a Muslim community that was established by Muslim émigrés, mostly Tatars, from the Russian Empire after the revolution. Especially after Kurbangaliev was deported to Manchuria in 1938, it was Ibrahim who presided in the community. When a long-desired mosque was set up in Tokyo in May 12, 1938, he was elected imam, thus securing a key position for his grand idea. At the same time he continued to work as an active journalist and contributed several articles to the *Yani Yapon muhbiri* [New Japanese Correspondent], a monthly Tatar-Ottoman journal founded by Kurbangaliev in February 1932. It aimed "to introduce Muslim peoples to social thought and movements important for both Japan and the Japanese people and for Muslims." The journal's nameplate is followed by these words: "a unique journal that introduces Japan to Muslim countries in the world." In fact, it contains a number of anonymous articles informing Muslim readers about the state of affairs in Japan as well as pro-Japanese articles written by Muslim intellectuals. Considering its contents and the high quality of its publication, it is likely that the Japanese authorities gave both moral and material support to the publisher, the Tokyo Muslim Community headed by Kurbangaliev.

It is worth noting that Ibrahim contributed his articles before arriving in Japan. For example, in his article, "The Eastern World," he thinks highly of the Japanese withdrawal from the League of Nations in March 1933. According to his interpretation, the League of Nations was nothing else than a trap set by Western great powers for putting Japan under their control and preventing Japan from playing a leading role in liberating Eastern peoples under Western rule. Therefore the day of Japanese withdrawal, March 10 [*sic*],[34] should be celebrated not only by Japanese people but also Eastern peoples, among others the Muslim peoples.[35] We find that his argument was totally in accordance with the hard-line foreign policy supported by Japanese right-wing thinkers.

The "el-Cihad [Holy war]," probably his first article written in Tokyo, is outstanding for its comprehensive and radical arguments. He reasons as follows:

> In the recent World War, Muslim peoples have made great mistakes. Despite their great losses and suffering, Muslim peoples were deceived by the Western powers and could not gain anything after the war. Even today, these powers are conducting oppressive policies in Muslim countries. Muslim peoples seem to have lost every hope as to the future of Islam. However, they must grow out of their present miserable situations.

> When great changes in the world and an unprecedented war are expected soon, Muslims should not make mistakes again. They should be careful and not be deceived. In this situation, they should pay attention to Japan and the Japanese people who, like us, give great importance to moral and spiritual matters, and do not spare sincere support to Muslims in Manchuria and Japan. Recently Japan announced its own worldview, different from the Western one, and declared its intention to put an end to the Bolsheviks' inhuman policies [*sic*]. This statement was addressed to the 30 million Muslims living in Soviet Russia. Therefore all Muslims should participate on the Japanese side for their liberation, and fight for the sake of Islam in the forthcoming war. Regarding this important matter, the ulama should consider what is right and lawful according to the directions of the Prophet, the sacred hadith.[36]

The argument can be considered the leitmotiv throughout his last activities in Japan.

In another article, "The Relationship between Japan and Islam," Ibrahim again raises the alarm as to Christian missionary activities in that country.[37] According to him, Christianity and Western rule in general threaten the "national spirit" and patriotism of oppressed peoples, as seen in the history of Asian peoples. Christianity deprives them of a natural spirit of bravery and brings about religious disputes among them. It is Islam that secures their survival against Western threats through Christianity. Despite the fall of the Ottoman Empire, Turkish people can live thanks to the spiritual force of Islam. From this point of view, the Japanese people also came to think about being acquainted with Islam. Protecting Japanese from the threats of Christianity is the most important for Asian peoples, especially Muslims.[38] Although his argument is rather subjective, he clearly shared a basic idea with the Japanese right wing that called for the revival of a martial spirit among Japanese people, in other words for the protection of the pure spirit of the Japanese. It is true that his arguments in the *Yani Yapon muhbiri* are consistent with those in the *Âlem-i İslâm*. However, his arguments in the former are more radicalized and militarized than in the latter. This change may reflect political and intellectual trends in Japan in the 1930s, as well as Ibrahim's sense of urgency as he anticipated a great change in the world.

Ibrahim participated in the organization of the Dai Nippon Kaikyō Kyōkai [Great Japan Islamic Society]. In 1938, four months after the opening of the Tokyo mosque, this society came into existence under the presidency of General Hayashi Senjūrō (1876–1943: ex-War Minister and Prime Minister). It aimed to establish close relations between Japan and 300 million Muslims in the course of building up the *Tōa shin chitsujo* [New Order in East Asia]. While introducing the state of affairs in the Muslim world to a Japanese audience through the monthly journal *Kaikyō sekai* [The Muslim World], the society also supervised Muslim organizations in the occupied territories in China and Manchuria.[39] Cooperation with influential Muslim intellectuals such as Ibrahim must have been indispensable for

Japanese authorities that worked to secure support from Muslim countries and populations in Asia. Mutual agreement existed between Ibrahim's Pan-Islamist strategy and Japanese expansionist strategies. It is not certain to what extent Ibrahim believed in the successful future of Japan. As far as this old Pan-Islamist was concerned, he had only a small-sized Tatar Muslim community in Tokyo and a journal with limited circulation. It is possible to raise a question: was not the Muslim world, to which Ibrahim addressed his work, an imagined community? He died in Tokyo on August 31, 1944, when Japanese defeat seemed certain.

Conclusion

This paper presents an overview of the activities and ideas of Abdurreshid Ibrahim, who worked for Pan-Islamic causes throughout his life. The paper focuses on his relations with Japan. His checkered career is worth examining, not only from the viewpoint of the modern history of the Muslim world but also from that of the modern history of Japan. Japanese approaches to Ibrahim and the world of Islam as a whole remain to be studied. Finally, we would like to mention a legacy of Ibrahim in Japan. The late professor Izutsu Toshihiko (1914–1993) has described an interesting personal episode regarding his meeting with Ibrahim: when he was a young assistant, he took private lessons in the Arabic language from Ibrahim in Tokyo and was encouraged to study Islam.[40] Given that Izutsu later made a great contribution to Islamic studies in the world, Ibrahim's name should be retained in the historiography of Islamic studies in Japan.

Notes

1 In the last decade a number of studies of Abdurreshid Ibrahim's life and activities have been published. As to the bibliography, see one of the most comprehensive works: İsmail Türkoğlu, *Sibiryalı Meşhur Seyyah Abdürreşid İbrahim* (Ankara: Türkiye Diyanet Vakfı, 1997), 172. Among other places, intensive studies have been conducted in Turkey. For example, see the special issues of *Toplumsal Tarih* (4/19, 4/20) published in 1995. In Japan also, several works have been published. For example, see: Komatsu Hisao, "Senkyūhyakugo nen zengo no sekai: Roshia musurimu no shiten kara [The World around 1905: From the Viewpoint of Russian Muslims]," in *Kyōshano sekai: Teikokushugino jidai* (*Kōza sekaishi 5*) [The Age of Imperialism (A Course of the World History: 5)], ed. Rekishigaku Kenkyūkai (Tokyo: University of Tokyo Press, 1995): 117–146; Komatsu Hisao, *Kakumeino chūō ajia: Aru jadīdono shōzō* [Revolutionary Central Asia: A Portrait of Abdurauf Fitrat] (Tokyo: University of Tokyo Press, 1996), 312; Sakamoto Tsutomu, "Yamaoka Kōtarōno Mekka junreito Abudeyurureshito Iburahimu [Yamaoka Kōtarō's Hajj and Abdurreshid Ibrahim]," in Ikei Osamu and Sakamoto Tsutomu, eds, *Kindai nihonto toruko sekai* [Modern Japan and the Turkic World] (Tokyo: Keisō Shobō, 1999): 157–217. See also Selçuk Esenbel and Inaba Chiharu, eds, *The Rising Sun and the Turkish Crescent: New Perspective on the History of Japanese Turkish Relations* (Istanbul: Boğaziçi University Press, 2003).

2 Abdürreşid İbrahim, *Âlem-i İslâm: Japonya'da intişar-ı İslâmiyet*, 2 vols (Istanbul: vol. 1: Ahmed Saki Bey Matbaası, vol. 2: Kadar Matbaası, 1910–1913), 620 + 243. As a Japanese translation of the chapter on Japan: Abudeyurureshito Iburahimu, *Japonya: isuramukei*

roshiajin no mita Meiji Nihon [Japonya: Meiji Japan Seen by a Russian Muslim], trans. Komatsu Kaori and Komatsu Hisao (Tokyo: Daisan Shokan, 1991), 412.

3 As to his early life, see Abdürreşid İbrahim, *Tercüme-i hâlim yâke başıma gelenler* (St. Petersburg, n.d.), 128. Some sources inform us that he prepared an autobiography during his second stay in Japan. However, it remains unpublished.

4 For example, see "Iburahimushito kataru," in the *Yomiuri Shinbun* (June 11, 1909): 2.

5 [Abdürreşid İbrahim], *Rusya'da Müslümanlar yahut Tatar Akvamının Tarihçesi* ([Cairo], 1900), 88. Later on its Tatar version was published: *Chulpan Yoldizi* (St. Petersburg, 1907), 58.

6 Wakabayashi Han, *Kaikyō sekai to Nihon* [The Muslim World and Japan] (Tokyo: Dainichisha, 1937): 9.

7 Abdurreshid Ibrahim, *Aftonomiya yake Idare-i Muhtariye* (St. Petersburg, [1907]), 35.

8 For example, see "Iburahimushito kataru," in the *Yomiuri Shinbun* (June 11, 1909): 2. In fact, on the occasion of the Third Conference of Russian Muslims held in Nizhnii Novgorod in August 1906, Ibrahim was elected a member of the Central Committee of the Union of Russian Muslims (Musul'manskaja konstitucionno-narodnaja partija) by the greatest majority; however, this party was not authorized by the Russian government. See *Nijni Novgorod'da vaki olan Rusya Müslümanları üçüncü nedvesinin muqarriratı: 16–21 August 1906* (Kazan: Matbaa-i Kerimiye, 1906): 16–19.

9 For an annotated English translation of Ibrahim's travel accounts in Bukhara see Kimura Satoru, "Bukhara-yi Sharif as Witnessed by a Tatar Intellectual in the Early 20th Century," *Iz istorii kul'turnogo nasledija Buhary* 7 (Bukhara: Izdatel'stvo Bukhara, 2001): 95–111.

10 The first part of his travels, describing his journey from Kazan to Vladivostok, was published in Tatar: Abdurreshid Ibrahim, *Devr-i Alem* (Kazan: Bäyanul-Hak, 1909), 160.

11 Kokuryūkai: A leading ultranationalist society founded in 1901 under the direction of Uchida Ryōhei (see later) succeeded to the ideas and strategy of the Genyōsha (see later). It advocated expelling Russia from Asia and Japanese expansion into Manchuria, Mongolia, and Siberia, as well as a hard-line foreign policy. The members were engaged in Russian and Chinese studies, and worked in close contact with the army. During the Russo-Japanese War, it provided the army with intelligence agents and translators. After the war, it supported the annexation of Korea and the Chinese revolutionary movement against the Qing dynasty. After the First World War it advocated the independence of Asian peoples under the guidance of Japan until the defeat in the Second World War.

12 Tōyama Mitsuru: charismatic leader of the first ultranationalist society Genyōsha (1877–1946), which advocated Japanese advance on the continent and a hard-line foreign policy. Until his death, he maintained a strong influence among nationalist groups. His close relationship with Ibrahim continued all his life.

13 Uchida Ryōhei: active leader of the ultranationalist society Kokuryūkai. He advocated war against Russia after the triple intervention in 1895, after the Sino-Japanese War. When Ibrahim visited Uchida, he was engaged in preparatory works for the annexation of Korea to Japan.

14 Abudorashitto Iburahimu, "Dattanjin dokuritsuno kibō [Tatars' Aspiration for Independence]," *Gaikō Jihō* 137 (1909): 212–219.

15 The *Tōa Dōbunkai* [East Asian Friendship Society] was a nongovernmental society established in 1898 for the purpose of promoting friendship between Japan and China.

16 The written oath is not found in the *Âlem-i İslâm*, but in Wakabayashi, *Kaikyō sekai to Nihon*.

17 The prospectus of the *Ajia Gikai* was published on every issue of the journal *Daitō* [Great East]. A preliminary survey of this journal is conducted in Japan. See Misawa Nobuo, "Ajia Gikai kikanshi *Daitō* ni shoshūsareru nijusseiki shotō no Nihonniokeru

isurāmu kankei jōhō [Introduction of Primary Sources Regarding Relations between Late Meiji Era Japan and the Islamic World: Information about the Islamic World in Early Twentieth-Century Japan Contained in the Journal of the Society for the Asian Cause, the *Great Orient*]," *Tōyō Daigaku Ajia Ahurika Bunka Kenkyūsho (Kenkyū nenpō)* 36 (2001): 60–75.

18 "Ajia Gikai," in the *Nihon oyobi nihonjin* 550 (1911): 8.

19 "Japonya'da *Dayto* mecellesi ve *Âsya Gikay* cemiyetinin beyannamesi," *Sırat-ı müstakim* 6/133 (March 23, 1910): 42–44; "*Âsya Gikay* cemiyetinin maksad-ı tesisi," *Sırat-ı müstakim*, 7/162 (October 5, 1911): 89.

20 In the *Âlem-i İslâm*: 428, Ibrahim put a document bearing signatures of some initiators of the *Ajia Gikai* as well as of three Chinese Muslim leaders including Wang Haoran.

21 For the details of sociopolitical movements of Chinese Muslims, see Matsumoto Masumi and Françoise Aubin's papers in this volume.

22 Fiṭrat Buḫārāyī, *Munāẓara-yi mudarris-i buḫārāyī bā yak nafar Farangī dar Hindustān dar bāra-yi makātib-i ğadīda (ḥaqīqat natīğa-yi tasādum-i afkār ast)* (Istanbul: Maṭba'a-i islāmiyya, 1911): 14. As to the details of the *Munāẓara* see Komatsu Hisao, "Bukhara and Istanbul: A Consideration about the Background of the *Munāzara*," in Stéphane A. Dudoignon and Komatsu Hisao, eds, *Islam in Politics in Russia and Central Asia (Early Eighteenth to Late Twentieth Centuries)* (London, New York, and Bahrain: Kegan Paul, 2001): 167–180.

23 Reşid Efendi İbrahim, *Tarihin Unutulmuş Sahifeleri* [Forgotten Pages of History] (Berlin, n.d.): 8.

24 We can suppose that Ibrahim's admiration for Japan had another aspect. The Japanese image was used as a mirror reflecting the defects of the Muslim societies.

25 Ibrahim's idea presented in these journals is well analyzed in Nadir Özbek, "Abdürreşid İbrahim'in ikinci Meşrutiyet yılları: Teârüf-i Müslimin ve İslâm Dünyası," *Toplumsal Tarih* 4/20 (1995): 18–23.

26 Hatano [Hatano Uhō], *Asya Tehlikede* [Asia in Crisis], translated by Japonyalı Mehmed Hilmi Nakava and Abdürreşid İbrahim (Istanbul, 1912): 13–14.

27 According to Ibrahim's talk, about 84,000 Muslim soldiers were in German prison camps. "Torukokara Nihon'e [From Turkey to Japan] (1)," *Yomiuri shinbun* (December 10, 1933): 4.

28 Türkoğlu, *Sibiryalı*: 70–81.

29 Validov, a leader of the Bashkir national movement, pointed out that their idea is nothing but an illusion, and tried to persuade them to give up the alliance with Communists. Zeki Velidi Togan, *Hâtıralar: Türkistan ve Diğer Müslüman Doğu Türklerinin Millî Varlık ve Kültür Mücadeleleri* (Istanbul: TAN Matbaası, 1969): 301–302. Cf. Şerif Mardin, "Abdurreshid Ibrahim and Zeki Velidi Togan in the History of the Muslims of Russia," in Korkt A. Ertürk, ed., *Rethinking Central Asia: Non-Eurocentric Studies in History, Social Structure and Identity* (Reading: Ithaca Press: 1999): 111–128.

30 Türkoğlu, *Sibiryalı*: 81–94.

31 As to Kurbangaliev, see: Nishiyama Katsunori, "Kurubangalī ryakuden: Senkanki zairyū kaikyōtono mondaini yosete" [Short Biography of Kurbangali: Émigré Muslims in Japan during the Inter-War Period], *Roshia kakumeishi kenkyū shiryō* 3 (1996): 1–26; Ajslu Junusova, "Velikij imam Dal'nego Vostoka Muhammed-Gabdulhaj Kurbangaliev," *Vestnik Evrazii* 2001/4[15]: 83–116.

32 As to the details of the reception see, *Yani Yapon muhbiri*, 12 (1933): 41–45. I am very grateful to Dr İsmail Türkoğlu for providing me this rare journal.

33 "Toruko kara Nihon e (1–4)," in the *Yomiuri shinbun* (December 10, 12–14, 1933).

34 Precisely on February 24, 1933, the Japanese delegation left its seats, protesting against the report of the Lytton commission that pointed out Japanese acts of aggression in Manchuria.

35 Abdürreşid İbrahim, "Şark âlemi," *Yani Yapon muhbiri* 8 (1933): 4–7. As to Ibrahim's argument, of course, we find opposite ones among contemporary Muslim intellectuals. For example Miyan Abdul Aziz, the ex-president of the All-India Muslim League, says as follows:

> Now it is quite clear... that Japan was contemplating aggression instead of achieving her object successfully by enlisting the goodwill of those concerned. For this reason it is impossible for Islam to sympathize with Japan's present mood. Adjustment between nations there must be from time to time, but adjustment by force and violence is not the way of Islam. At this late time in the history of the world the moral sentiment must count, and a country that outrages it must expect general condemnation. Violence is the negation of Islam, which means peace.

M. Abdul Aziz, *The Crescent in the Land of the Rising Sun* (London: Blades, East and Blades Ltd., 1941): 69. The author was requested to visit Japan to perform the opening ceremony of the Kobe mosque on behalf of the Islamic world in 1935, and during his long stay had ample opportunity of coming into contact with Japanese people and state of affairs. It should be noticed that he never refers to Ibrahim, while describing the inside story of the Tatar Muslim community in Tokyo in detail. According to the author he obtained a lot of information "regarding the real situation of Muslims in that country, which is full of spies and suspicious people." Abdul Aziz, *The Crescent in the Land of the Rising Sun*, 25.

36 Abdürreşid İbrahim, "el-Cihad," *Yani Yapon muhbiri* 12 (1933): 29–33. See also Türkoğlu, *Sibiryalı*: 97.

37 Ibrahim was critical of the Japanese law that authorized Christianity as one of Japan's official religions but excluded Islam. For example, see his speech at the celebration of the publication of the Qur'an in Tokyo: *Yani Yapon muhbiri* 19 (1934): 43. A number of Japanese dignitaries participated in this reception.

38 Abdürreşid İbrahim, "Yapon ve İslâm münasebeti," *Yani Yapon Muhbiri* 13 (1934): 37–41.

39 For the details, see Office of Strategic Services, Research and Analysis Branch, *Japanese Infiltration among Muslims in Russia and Her Borderlands*, August 1944 (R&A No. 890. 2). I am very grateful to Prof. Edward J. Lazzerini for providing me this important material.

40 Shiba Ryōtarō, *Shiba Ryōtarō rekishi kandan* [Shiba Ryōtarō's Conversations on History] (Tokyo: Chūō kōronsha, 2000, first published in the *Chūō kōron*, 1993/1): 479–484.

14

CLASH OF CULTURES?

Intellectuals, their publics, and Islam

Dale F. Eickelman

A new sense of public is emerging throughout Muslim-majority states and Muslim communities elsewhere. Joined with this new sense of public are new intellectual styles and messages, disseminated in increasingly diverse yet overlapping fields of communication and understanding. The influence of state authorities and intellectuals trained in the formal religious sciences remain strong, but their authority is increasingly displaced by intellectuals with increasingly disparate backgrounds. The idea of "intellectual" implies an individual claiming or imputed to possess an especially intense awareness of the sacred center of social and spiritual values and the ability to reflect and explain valued categories of knowledge.[1] In the present era, people have increased latitude in choosing who can most effectively articulate core social and spiritual values. In the contemporary Muslim majority world, those with training in the formal religious sciences remain important but are increasingly complemented by lawyers, engineers, and others lacking formal religious training. Indeed, formal education is often less significant than an ability to communicate effectively in different media and across social classes. As Olivier Roy pointed out in the early 1990s, modernist Muslim intellectuals can often choose among audiences and languages.[2] A Moroccan religious intellectual can choose to write in French or Arabic, or to record a cassette in colloquial Moroccan Arabic or in one of Morocco's Berber languages. His South Asian counterpart can choose between Urdu and English, and a Qazaq might switch between Russian and Qazaq. At the present, men remain foregrounded as communicators of religious ideas and practices, although women are playing increasingly important roles.[3] Books remain an important and valued means of communication, but pamphlets, newspaper and magazine articles, audio cassettes, videos, and the ability to master (and have access to) the broadcast media play an increasingly significant role. The book may remain the apex of valued knowledge, but its role is multiplied by discussion in other media and by word of mouth.

In language, audience, and style, messages—and those who create them—have become increasingly diverse. In the religious domain, both intellectuals and audiences are shaped by increasingly open contests over the authoritative use of the symbolic language of Islam. New and increasingly accessible modes of communication have made these contests increasingly global, making even local disputes take on transnational dimensions. Islam and thinkers within the Islamic tradition have always been transregional or transnational, but increasingly open and accessible forms of communication play a significant role in fragmenting and contesting political and religious authority.

In one respect, recognition of the role of religion in shaping intellectuals and intellectual life in Muslim societies shows a remarkable continuity with the West. Open societies claim to respect religion and religious worship. At the same time, however, in the words of the philosopher Richard Rorty, religion usually functions as a "conversation-stopper" outside of circles of believers.[4] The role of religion in public life has fared no better. This is because prevailing social theories have marginalized religion and the role of religious intellectuals. To the extent that many Muslim majority societies have failed to construct open and civil societies, the role of religion in them is often almost automatically invoked as a cause for this failure. Yet for such Muslim-majority countries as Indonesia and Turkey, religious intellectuals play a major role in furthering the goals of civil society, religious pluralism, and tolerance.[5]

Islam, modernity, and modernization theory

Ernest Gellner was characteristically blunt in his views of Islam, and his writings offer an exemplar of how religion in general, and Islam in particular, figure in much thinking about modernity. With the collapse of Marxist regimes, only Islam, Gellner argued, continued to resist the universal trend toward secularization and nationalism. As a faith, he regarded Islam as imposing "essential" constraints on the conduct and thought of those committed to it.[6] It offered a "closed system" of thought.[7] For Gellner, the "essence" of nationalism in the West is that a "high—literacy-linked—culture becomes the pervasive, membership-defining culture of the total society." In Islam, in contrast, fundamentalism becomes the essence of total society. As a consequence, regimes are judged by "the religious norms of sacred law, rather than the secular principles of a Civil Society." For Gellner, Islam "exemplifies a social order which seems to lack much capacity to provide political countervailing institutions or associations" and "operates effectively without intellectual pluralism."[8]

Contrary to such assumptions, the Muslim majority world is demonstrating a vigorous and increasing diverse intellectual pluralism. Such debates and awareness of alternative interpretations of Islam and its role in society do not translate directly into political and social practice. However, the proliferation and increased accessibility of the means of communication in today's global society, together with the rise of mass education, has increased the power of intellectuals to communicate and of audiences to listen and discuss. Religious intellectuals, like their secularly minded counterparts, tacitly compete for increasingly fragmented publics. Moreover, far from constituting an exception to worldwide trends, the role of religious intellectuals in the Muslim majority world increasingly reflects the spectrum of debate and public discussion prevalent in other parts of the world. Some religious leaders and intellectuals claim a privileged position for religious voices, but many more accept the pluralism of competing voices. In addition, the line between religious and secular voices is increasingly blurred.

Just as modern conditions facilitate a fragmentation of religious and political authority, they create diverse publics who understand ideas and messages in various ways. Some Muslim intellectuals increasingly form part of a transnational elite, but effectiveness on the global stage comes at a price. With globalization, mobility increases for a small segment of the elite but it increases polarities with the more localized rest. As a consequence, religious intellectuals like Iran's 'Abdolkarim Soroush becomes more in tune with Edward Said and accessible at a multilingual website (www.seraj.org), but at the risk of losing touch with more localized audiences.

The conventional wisdom of social thought remains profoundly informed by modernization theory, the single most important social theory to influence both academic and policy approaches to the Third World from the 1950s to the late 1970s, and with continued significance today. The secular bias of modernization theory had its specific echo in analyses of the Islamic world. In the early 1960s, modernization theorists saw the Muslim world as facing an unpalatable choice: either a "neo-Islamic totalitarianism" intent on "resurrecting the past," or a "reformist Islam" which would open "the sluice gates and [be] swamped by the deluge."[9] In Daniel Lerner's memorable phrase, Middle Eastern societies faced a stark choice—"Mecca or mechanization."[10] At the least, such views suggest an intensely negative view of the possibilities of evolution in Muslim societies and an inherent preference for militantly secularizing reformers such as Turkey's Mustafa Kemal Atatürk (1881–1938) and the Pahlavi Shahs of Iran, Reza Shah (1878–1944) and his son, Mohammad Reza Shah (1919–1980).

In such formulations, Islam is merely a particularly salient example of the hindering roles of religion and religious thinkers in modern society. Edward Shils offers a kinder, gentler, variant of the role of intellectuals in modern thought. For him, intellectuals possess an "innate need" to be in "frequent communication with symbols which are more general than the immediate concrete situations of everyday life."[11] Although intellectual work originally arose from religious occupations, Shils writes that religious orientations in modern times attract "a diminishing share of the creative capacities of the oncoming intellectual elite." In Shils's view, among Western intellectuals in earlier periods, and Asian and African intellectuals since the nineteenth century, "the tradition of distrust of secular and ecclesiastical authority—and in fact of tradition as such—has become the chief secondary tradition of the intellectuals."[12] The notion of the sacred has shifted in his view from religious concerns to a focus on and mastery of the technological, organizational, and political skills most useful in forging a modern state in the face of congeries of supposedly primordial loyalties. In modernization theory, the present thus belongs to the liberals and the technocrats, found primarily in the differentiated "modern" class. Shils argues that only intellectuals attached to "modern" values have the vision to rise above parochial identities and to attach themselves to the notion of a modern nation-state.

How disconcerting, then, for this view of modernization theory and the role of the nation-state to see no less a committed political leader than Václav Havel declare that "human rights, human freedoms, and human dignity have their deepest roots outside the perceptible world."[13] On the state and its probable role in the future, writes Havel, "while the state is a human creation, human beings are the creation of God."

Havel's statement serves as a poignant reminder that religious belief and practice are not necessarily inimical to modernity and can play a vital role in public life. Nonetheless, common to all variants of modernization theory is the declining role of religion, except as a private matter, as modernization takes hold. To move toward modernity, political leaders must displace the authority of religious leaders and devalue the importance of traditional religious institutions. "Modernity" is seen as an "enlargement of human freedoms" and an "enhancement of the range of choices" as people began to "take charge" of themselves.[14] "Secularization" thus refers to the fact that religious, and religious intellectuals, come to have a less prominent or influential position in modern societies. Religion can retain its influence only by conforming to such norms as "rationality" and relativism, or by making compromises with science, economic concerns, and the state.

Transnational religion and religious intellectuals

By the late 1970s this prevalent view of the declining role of religion began to erode. Several nearly simultaneous but independent developments indicated the continuing central role of religion in public life: the Iranian revolution, the rise of the Solidarity movement in Poland, the role of liberation theology in Latin American political movements, and the return of Protestant fundamentalism as a force in American politics.[15] Ignored by modernization theory, these developments and others suggest how religious ideas and practices sometimes act as a transnational force, at other times in highly locality- and historically specific contexts, and most often in an unstable and evanescent combination of the local and the global.

Even locally rooted movements benefit significantly with transnational sponsors or supporters, whether emigrants, states, or others sharing a group's objectives. Opposition to the Shah's regime was firmly rooted in Iran, but the safe haven provided for opposition leaders in exile, particularly Ayatollah Khomeini, and the transnational ties and freedom of movement and action of opposition leaders, were integral to the revolution's success. After the Second Vatican Council (1962–1965), the long-standing vertical transnationalism of the Roman Catholic Church was increasingly complemented by the horizontal transnationalism of decentralized grassroots networks and organizations created for purposes as diverse as Bible study, evangelicalism, and social and political action. Many of these organizations have direct and significant ties to the Church hierarchy, while others operate autonomously. Sometimes with direct Vatican encouragement but often without, such groups have played a significant role in sustaining resistance to authoritarianism and political repression and freely make tactical alliances with other like-minded groups. These groups, and their leaders, give concrete form to the ideas and practice of transnational civil society and suggest the changing framework within which ideas, movements, and practices spread.

Muslim religious intellectuals, and movements associated with them, operate in a significantly different context than Christian ones. Islam lacks a central organizational hierarchy. In certain limited contexts, Muslim intellectuals and organizations create formal institutions to "represent" Islam for various purposes. Thus in France since the 1930s, the imam of the grand mosque of Paris has been either an Algerian or Moroccan, presumed by the French state to represent "all" Muslim communities in France. In Germany, the Central Council of Muslims (*Zentral Rat der Muslime in Deutschland*) "represents" Islam in such functions as the 2000 World's Fair in Hannover. There are also transnational organizations such as the Organization of the Islamic Conference and numerous nongovernmental organizations. Yet of themselves, such organizations do not form centers of intellectual organization, although fragmented and loosely linked networks of like-minded groups and individuals play a major role in disseminating ideas.

Contemporary religious transnationalism and the diffusion of ideas facilitated by it take many forms. Some are highly structured, while others are only informally organized and related primarily by affinity of goals. Informality and the lack of formal structure can be an organizational strength in contexts of political and religious oppression.

Paradoxically, however, it is easy to see formidable challenges to modernization theory. Of all the countries of the Third World, Iran was a society that had undergone enormous modernization prior to 1978–1979. Nonetheless, revolution ensued and not political stability, with the greatest challenge emanating from the growing urban middle classes, those who had benefited the most from modernization. Moreover, it was religious sentiment and leadership, not the secular intelligentsia that gave the revolution its coherence and force.

An Iranian born French political scientist, Fariba Adelkhah goes even further. She argues that the major transformations of the Iranian revolution took place since the 1990s. A new generation of Iranians, not even born at the time of the revolution, came of age and had a significantly different interpretation of social context than the preceding generation. Adelkhah argues that a "religious public sphere" (*espace public confessionnel*) has emerged in Iran in which politics and religion are subtly intertwined in ways not anticipated by Iran's established religious leaders.[16]

The emergence of this public sphere has also been accompanied by a greater sense of personal autonomy for both women and men, and debates over core issues of politics and society that would have been difficult to imagine in an earlier era.[17] Others make the argument on a more general scale. Olivier Roy, one of the first to use the term "post-Islamism" in 1992, notes the proliferation of various types of Islamic movements. The fragmented and protean nature of these movements limits state efforts to control or channel them. Roy argues that the growing numbers of "centrist" Muslims largely support openings for democratization, while secular conservatives, often fearful about losing their special relationship with state authorities, often oppose efforts to open up the political system. Public religion, reminding the faithful of their commitment to higher values and contributing to shaping public and policy goals, has returned with force to the center stage of social and political life in the Muslim world and elsewhere.[18]

The return of religion to public life

The initial force and imagery of Samuel Huntington's "West vs. Rest" argument has largely dissipated. One lasting value, however, has been to spur a realization that there is no arbitrary division between "tradition" and modernity.[19] Huntington's article indirectly pointed out that "tradition" co-exists with the modern and that a number of traditions may co-exist in any given society. There may be clashes, but the fault lines along which sides are divided are rarely clear and often shifting. Thus ethnicity, caste, clientelism, and religion can be distinctly modern or can at least co-exist with it. In a word, Huntington reintroduced the concept of culture to international relations theory. Unfortunately, having reintroduced culture and religion to thinking about politics, Huntington overstated their coherence and force. Culture is composed of more than explicit ideas and ideologies, but it consists of ideas that are debated, argued, often fought about, and re-formed in practice. Thus ideas and their articulation in political practice count, and cannot be reduced to objects that wiggle when the strings are pulled by political and economic forces.

The role of religious ideas and practices in the public life of Muslim majority societies can be seen as less exceptional if the European experience with secularism is reassessed. As historian Dominique Colas argues, religious discourse was a basic precondition for the rise of the early modern public sphere in Europe and strong Christian traces remain in such matters as blasphemy laws, religious holidays, and public prayers.[20] Contemporary defenders of secularism often exaggerate the durability and open-mindedness of thoroughly secular institutions in the United States, Turkey, India, and elsewhere. Indeed, in many contexts, a militant secularism seems to have an affinity with authoritarianism and intolerance.

The role of religious intellectuals in the Muslim-majority world remains suspect by many secularists, although many religious movements and leaders contribute significantly to an emerging public sphere, calling for mutual respect among religious traditions. Turkey's Fethullah Gülen, Iran's Muhammad Khatami and ʻAbdolkarim Soroush, and Syria's Muhammad Shahrur each make such appeals to their respective audiences. Over the past half century, there has been a rapid growth in mass education throughout the Muslim world. In country after country since mid-century, educational systems have vastly expanded.[21] Even where educational expansion has not kept up with population growth, large numbers of citizens now speak a common language that crosses localities, and think of religion and other aspects of their society as systems and objects. This makes them more capable of adapting and incorporating new elements. Education contributes to systematizing religious belief and practice, eroding intellectual and physical boundaries, and facilitating connections across formerly impenetrable boundaries of class, locality, language, and ethnic group.

Both mass education and mass communications, particularly the proliferation of types of media and access to them, profoundly influence how people think about religious and political authority throughout the Muslim world. We are still in the early stages of understanding how different media—print, television, radio, cassettes, music, and the Internet—influence groups and individuals, encouraging unity in some contexts and fragmentation in others. Taken together, these various means of communication have multiplied the means by which ideas and practices are shaped and shared. For many persons, the availability and rapidly declining cost of many new media have vastly accelerated the pace at which ideas and practices can be shaped and shared throughout the world.

Turkey's Nurculuk movement and its successors

A salient indication of the ways in which new forms of communication and rising levels of education contribute to new ideas of political and religious authority is to follow the development of the Nurculuk movement. It began in Turkey in the early twentieth century and today has followers throughout Europe, Central Asia, and North America. The teachings of its founder, Said Nursi (1873–1960), were originally written and passed on in *samizdat* form because of state hostility toward religious expression in the first decades of the Turkish republic. Since the 1950s, Nursi's writings have been published in books and pamphlets with titles such as *The Miracles of Muhammad, Belief and Man*, and *Resurrection in the Hereafter*.[22] These pamphlets have "the function of explaining, in accordance with the understanding of the age, the truths of the Qur'an."[23] Nursi insisted that books, not people, "have waged a battle against unbelief," thus distinguishing his teachings in principle from the master–disciple relationship at the core of most Sufi orders.[24]

Nursi stressed the importance of direct contact with texts and encouraged his followers to adopt his own approach. He emphasized exploring multiple combinations of knowledge, including learning outside the Islamic tradition. In 1910 a policeman in Tiflis, asking Nursi about his plans for building a religious school, said that it was hopeless to envision a unity of the "broken up and fragmented" Muslim world. Nursi replied:

> They have gone to study. It is like this: India is an able son of Islam; it is studying in the high school of the British. Egypt is a clever son of Islam; it is taking lessons in the British school for civil servants. Caucasia and Turkestan are two valiant sons of Islam; they are training in the Russian war academy. And so on.[25]

In 1911, a half century earlier than the Second Vatican Council urged Christians and Muslims to resolve their differences and move beyond the conflicts of the past, Nursi advocated such a dialogue, and his successors have taken significant steps to engage in interfaith discussions.[26]

Another element in Nursi's writing sets him apart from religious intellectuals such as Muhammad ʻAbduh (1849–1905) and Jamal al-Din al-Afghani (1838/9–1897). As much as these two predecessors appealed to the learned classes throughout the Muslim world and sought to popularize their message, their primary audience remained the educated, urban cadres. Nursi, in contrast, never lost his rural roots and often employed the metaphors and imagery of Turkey's rural population. Other religious modernists, in contrast, distanced themselves from popular belief and rhetorical styles. Nursi was familiar with the structure and content of modern scientific knowledge, but he also recognized the value of fable and metaphor in shaping his message. They facilitated understandings of his message in different social and historical contexts. Thus in the early part of Nursi's career, his writings and messages were listened to by audiences rather than read, either directly by Nursi to his disciples or by "persons who had already acquired religious prestige." Moreover, in spite of the "official terror and persecution" carried out against those caught reading and teaching books in the old (Arabic) alphabet in the 1920s and 1930s, the practices continued.[27] The *Risale-i Nur*, the collection of Nursi's principal writings, was first disseminated by "thousands" of women and men, young and old, making copies by hand, and by 1946 or 1947 through the use of a duplicating machine.[28] After 1956, when Nursi's books were taken off the banned list and published in modern Turkish, *readers* were added to his audience—those whose primary contact with the *Risale-i Nur* was not necessarily the face-to-face or hand-to-hand contact of an earlier era.[29]

The *Risale-i Nur* is modern in the sense that its texts encourage reflection on ideas of society and nation. In countries other than Turkey, religious intellectuals also spoke of constitutionalism, justice, and the relation of Islamic belief to modern science, morality, public responsibilities, and the application of faith to public life and spiritual development. Moreover, Said Nursi made a distinctive contribution to the sense of public space in his post-1923 writings. The Syrian translator of his writings, Said Ramadan al-Buti, uses exegesis to reach this conclusion, reflecting on the disjunction in Said's career between his early political activism and his post-1923 writings and activities. These writings encouraged reasoned reflection and action on core ethical and religious values without prescribing particular, context-specific political action.[30] More so than many of his contemporaries, Nursi's message was accessible not only to religiously oriented educated cadres but also to the less educated, who saw in Said's message a means of integrating faith with modernity, nationalism, and social revitalization.

The other defining feature of his message, especially in the earlier part of this century, was its success in articulating with the conditions of Turkish society, especially rural Turkish society, when the hold of local leaders was rapidly giving way to an increasingly effective state apparatus, improved communications, and centralization. The message was sufficiently adaptable in structure and content, however, so that it subsequently articulated with the Turkey of later eras and, increasingly, to an international audience. Nursi's work is now communicated in multiple languages and publications and through a multilingual website (www.nesil.com.tr/). Nursi's style is readily accessible to these multiple audiences, and women are taking an increasingly active role in promoting the message. For some readers, the specifics of Turkish historical development help explain the nuances of certain passages and the context for which they were originally intended. For others, however, the rich metaphors and imagery offer a point of departure for religious understanding that requires only minimal familiarity with the specifics of the times and places in Turkey where the various elements of the *Risale-i Nur* first came into existence.

In the current era, the Nurculuk movement has succeeded in attracting significant followers from all social classes in Turkey. Fethullah Gülen (b. 1938), a leading contemporary disciple of Nursi, articulates the views of one of the two major clusters of those inspired by Nursi's teachings. Like Nursi, Gülen's interpretation of Islamic values offers a union between religion and science, and tradition and modernity, stressing the compatibility of Islamic ideas and practices with Turkish nationalism, education, and the market economy.[31] Gülen's followers control a complex web of businesses and broadcast and print media. The movement has over 550 schools in Turkey and the countries of the Commonwealth of Independent States, especially Central Asia. Within Turkey, the only religious classes are those prescribed by the Turkish national curriculum. The schools do not promote any particular interpretation of Islam, but rather instill a morality and sense of discipline intended to pervade private conduct and public life. In Turkey, the curriculum strictly follows state guidelines. Elsewhere, English is the language of instruction and religion is not taught at all. Gülen also advocates a public role for women in society. To the consternation both of conservative Muslims and Turkey's secular elite, he has stated that the wearing of the headscarf by women is a matter of personal choice, not one prescribed by faith. One need not visit Turkey to learn more about Gülen's views, for they are available on websites in English and Turkish (www.fgulen.org and www.m-fgulen.org).

The businessmen, teachers, journalists, students, and others to whom his message appeals stress the combination of knowledge and discipline for spiritual and personal growth. Less a centralized network than loosely affiliated clusters of organizations, those inspired by Gülen's ideas stress discipline and dialogue.[32] The use of reason and acquisition of knowledge is stressed within Turkey itself, and this is combined with highly publicized and sustained dialogues with Christian and Jewish religious leaders, stressing tolerance, electoral politics, moderation, and participation in a market economy.

In spite of efforts of some elements of Turkey's militantly secularist elite to consider all those who advocate a public role for religious expression as antidemocratic "fundamentalists," most Turks consider Islam an integral part of their social identity. Indeed, the "background" understandings of Islam are on the side of Gülen and others who see Islam as a religion of dialogue, tolerance, and reason. In televised chat shows, interviews, and occasional sermons, Gülen has spoken about Islam and science, democracy, modernity, religious and ideological tolerance, the importance of education, and current events. In this respect, rising educational levels, strengthened ties between Turks living in Turkey and in Europe, and the proliferation of media and the means of communication favor these more open interpretations. Public opinion polling is still in its infancy in Turkey and the Middle East, but available data suggest a growing openness of interpretation. For example, in 1992, 1993, and 1994 a sample of rural and urban Turks (N = 1,363) was asked whether Turkey was "Muslim," "European," or "both." Roughly the same number, 20–21%, said "European" in all three years. The number who said that Turkey was primarily Muslim, however, declined from 37% in 1992 to 25% in 1994, while the number who answered "both" increased from 25% to 36%.[33]

More recently, a survey conducted by Tesev, a Turkish think tank, found that 97% of those questioned identified themselves as Muslim, 92% said they fasted during the holy month of Ramadan, and 46% claimed to pray five times a day. But 91% also said different religious beliefs should be respected, and clear majorities thought it did not matter if Muslims consumed alcohol, failed to fast or pray or, if they were women, went outside without covering their heads. Only 21% called for an Islamic state, and once the implications were pointed out to them, some were not so sure.[34]

The Turkish experience does not represent the entire Muslim world, but it serves as a reminder of the diversity of the Muslim experience, both among intellectual formulations of Islamic thought, and the practical, implicit shared understandings of large numbers of people.

Islamic modernity, Syrian style

Civil engineer Muhammad Shahrur's 800-page long first book, *al-Kitāb wa al-Qurʾān: Qirāʾa muʿā ṣira* [The Book and the Qurʾan: A Contemporary Interpretation], has sold tens of thousands of copies throughout the Arab world in both authorized (Damascus and Beirut) and pirate (Cairo) editions.[35] The book is widely circulated by photocopy elsewhere (including Saudi Arabia), in spite of the fact that its circulation has been banned or discouraged.

Books such as Shahrur's could not have been imagined before there were large numbers of people able to read it and understand its advocacy of the need to reinterpret ideas of religious authority and tradition and apply Islamic precepts to contemporary society. Yet resistance to such challenges to established authority has also been intense.

Shahrur draws an analogy between the Copernican revolution and Qurʾanic interpretation, which he says has been shackled for centuries by the conventions of medieval jurists, who had mastered the craft of chaining authoritative commentaries to prior authoritative ones and of creating chains (*silsila*s), of traditions of authoritative learning:

> People believed for a long time that the sun revolved around the earth, but they were unable to explain some phenomena derived from this assumption until one person, human like themselves, said, "The opposite is true: The earth revolves around the sun."...After a quarter of a century of study and reflection, it dawned on me that we Muslims are shackled by prejudices (*musallimāt*), some of which are completely opposite the [correct perspective].[36]

Shahrur's ideas directly challenge the authoritative tradition of Qur'anic exegesis (*tafsīr*) and Islamic jurisprudence (*fiqh*). The subtitle of his first book—"a contemporary interpretation"—uses the term *qirā'a*, which can mean either reading or interpretation, rather than the term *tafsīr*, which directly evokes the established conventions of traditional Islamic learning from which Shahrur advocates a decisive break. For many Muslims and established men of religious learning, Shahrur argues that traditional disciplines of learning such as *tafsīr* have implicitly acquired an authority equal to that of the Qur'an itself, except that the juridical tradition says little about tyranny, absolutism, and democracy.[37] Such ideas are at the center of an emerging social imaginary.

Because Shahrur's ideas pose such basic challenges to existing authority, he has been attacked in Friday sermons in Damascus and elsewhere, even though one leading legal scholar, Wael Hallaq, recently wrote that Shahrur's efforts to reformulate Islamic jurisprudence are the "most convincing" of all contemporary thinkers.[38] The appeal of Shahrur's ideas and the speed at which knowledge of his first book spread in the early 1990s is remarkable. Prior to 1998, his primary means of communication was the book, an unadorned means of persuasion that appeals to a growing educated middle class and continues to represent the pinnacle of knowledge to others. Beginning in 1997, he spoke on several public occasions in Syria, spoke several times in the US, and more recently (January–May 2000), participated in a weekly religious program on an Egyptian satellite channel, Nile TV, that discussed *The Book and the Qur'an* chapter by chapter.

Shahrur is not alone in attacking conventional religious wisdom and the intolerant certainties of religious radicals. Others also argue for a constant and open reinterpretation of how sacred texts apply to social and political life. Another Syrian thinker, the secularist Sadiq Jalal al-'Azm, for instance, does the same. A debate between al-'Azm and Shaykh Yusuf al-Qaradawi, a conservative religious intellectual, was broadcast on al-Jazeera Satellite TV (Qatar) on May 27, 1997. For the first time in the memory of many viewers, the religious conservative came across as the weaker, more defensive voice. A similar debate took place in December 1997 on the same program between Nasir Hamid Abu Zayd and the Egyptian religious thinker, Muhammad 'Imara. Such discussions are unlikely to be rebroadcast on state-controlled television in most Arab nations, where programming on religious and political themes is generally cautious. Nevertheless, satellite technology and videotape render traditional censorship ineffective. Tapes of these broadcasts circulate from hand to hand in Morocco, Oman, Syria, Egypt, and elsewhere. Indeed, the format of satellite technology has begun to influence the format of books, in which scholars with contrasting views present their ideas. Recent titles in this style include *Islam and Modernity* and *What is Globalism?*[39]

Conclusion

As a result of direct and broad access to the printed, broadcast, and taped word, more and more Muslims take it upon themselves to interpret Islam's classical and modern texts. Much has been made of the "opening up" (*infitāh*) of the economies of many Muslim countries, allowing "market forces" to reshape economies, no matter how painful the consequences in the short run. In a similar way, intellectual market forces support some forms of religious innovation and activity over others. The result is a collapse of earlier, hierarchical notions of religious authority based on claims to the mastery of fixed bodies of religious texts. Even when there are state-appointed religious authorities—as in Oman, Saudi Arabia, Iran, Egypt, Malaysia, and some of the Central Asian republics—there no longer is any guarantee that their word will be heeded, or even that the religious authorities themselves will follow the lead of the regime.

Thinkers such as Fethullah Gülen, Muhammad Shahrur, and others are redrawing the boundaries of public and religious life in the Muslim-majority world by challenging religious authority, yet the replacement they suggest is a constructive fragmentation. With the advent of mass higher education has come an objectification of Islamic tradition in the eyes of many believers, so that questions such as "What is Islam?" "How does it apply to the conduct of my life?" and "What are the principles of faith?" are foregrounded in the consciousness of many believers and explicitly discussed. These objectified understandings have irrevocably transformed Muslim relations to sacred authority. Of crucial importance in this process has been a "democratization" of the politics of religious authority and the development of a standardized language inculcated by mass higher education, the mass media, travel, and labor migration. This has led to an opening up of the political process and heightened competition for the mantles of political and religious authority.

The impact of modern mass education is pervasive, but not necessarily in the ways intended by state authorities. Students are taught about the unity of Muslim thought and practice in a set national curriculum that includes Islamic studies as one subject among many. Even while teaching that Islam permeates all aspects of life, the formal principles of Islamic doctrine and practice are compartmentalized and made an object of study. The traditionally educated religious authorities sometimes adapt to this form of education, but some resist it. Without fanfare, the notion of Islam as dialogue, tolerance, and civil debate is gaining ground.

A new sense of public is emerging throughout Muslim-majority states and Muslim communities elsewhere. It is shaped by increasingly open contests over the use of the symbolic language of Islam. New and accessible modes of communication have made these contests increasingly global, so that even local issues take on trans-national dimensions. Muslims, of course, act not just as Muslims but according to class interests, out of a sense of nationalism, on behalf of tribal or family networks, and from all the diverse motives which characterize human endeavor. Increasingly, however, large numbers of Muslims explain their goals in terms of the normative language of Islam, and look to those intellectuals who can frame arguments in these terms.

This distinctly public sphere exists at the intersections of religious, political, and social life and contributes to the creation of civil society. People in Muslim majority societies have access to contemporary forms of communication that range from the press and broadcast media to fax machines, audio and video cassettes, from the telephone to the Internet. Like Christians, Hindus, Jews, Sikhs, and others, thinkers and activists in Muslim majority societies have more rapid and flexible ways of building and sustaining contact with constituencies than was available in earlier decades. These new media in new hands reverse the asymmetries of the earlier mass media revolution, when state authorities initially dominated radio and television. This combination of new media and new contributors to religious and political debates fosters awareness on the part of all actors of the diverse ways in which Islam and Islamic values can be created. It feeds into new senses of a public space that is discursive, performative, and participative, and not confined to formal institutions recognized by state authorities.

Publicly shared ideas of community, identity, and leadership take new shapes in such engagements, even as many communities and authorities claim an unchanged continuity with the past. Mass education, so important in the development of nationalism in an earlier era, and a proliferation of media and means of communication have multiplied the possibilities for creating communities and networks among them, dissolving prior barriers of space and distance and opening new grounds for interaction and mutual recognition.

In the present era, to paraphrase the Sudanese religious intellectual Hasan Turabi, an *'ālim* or religious intellectual is as likely to be an engineer or doctor as a religious scholar. Just as the new media have blurred the line between public and private, so has the modern era blurred the assumed hard and fast line between religion and politics. The prevailing secularist bias of prevalent theories of society has alternatively marginalized religious forces and religious intellectuals or has demonized them. Far from being resistant to modernity, the Muslim-majority world is as open to it as any other region of the world, even if the paths to modernity are multiple.[40] We live in a world in which an Islamic intellectual such as Fethullah Gülen meets popes and patriarchs, advocating diversity and tolerance in the public sphere more than many of his secular counterparts, and yet at the same time arguing that Islam is thoroughly compatible with an enlightened Turkish nationalism. Far from compromising the public sphere, religious movements and religious intellectuals can advocate compromise and a mutual agreement to persuade by words rather than by force. Contemporary religious intellectuals may claim strong links with the past, but their practice conveys significantly modern ideas of person, authority, and responsibility.

Notes

1 Edward Shils, *The Intellectuals and the Powers* (Chicago, IL: University of Chicago Press, 1973), 3.
2 Olivier Roy, *L'Échec de l'islam politique* (Paris: Éditions du Seuil, 1992), 37.
3 Azam Torab, "Piety as Gendered Agency: A Study of *Jalaseh* Ritual Discourse in an Urban Neighbourhood in Iran," *Journal of the Royal Anthropological Institute* (N.S.) 2/2 (1996): 235–252.
4 Richard Rorty, cited in John Keane, "The Limits of Secularism," *Times Literary Supplement*, January 9, 1998: 12.
5 For Indonesia, see Robert W. Hefner, *Civil Islam: Muslims and Democratization in Indonesia* (Princeton, NJ: Princeton University Press, 2000). For Turkey, see Bülent Aras, "Turkish Islam's Moderate Face," *Middle East Quarterly* 5/3 (September 1998): 23–30.
6 Cited in John Davis, "An Interview with Ernest Gellner," *Current Anthropology* 12/1 (1991), 71.
7 Ibid., 69.
8 Ernest Gellner, *Conditions of Liberty: Civil Society and Its Rivals* (London: Hamish Hamilton, 1994), especially 22, 29. For a further discussion of Gellner's views, see Dale F. Eickelman, "From Here to Modernity: Ernest Gellner on Nationalism and Islamic Fundamentalism," in John A. Hall, ed., *Ernest Gellner and the Theory of Nationalism* (Cambridge: Cambridge University Press, 1998): 258–271. In contrast, Augustus Richard Norton, "Introduction," in Augustus R. Norton, ed., *Civil Society in the Middle East* (Leiden: Brill, 1994), 25, argues vigorously that civil society is "theoretically, conceptually, normatively, and ontologically" as much a part of political discourse in the Middle East as it is elsewhere in the world.
9 Manfred Halpern, *The Politics of Social Change in the Middle East and North Africa* (Princeton, NJ: Princeton University Press, 1963), 129.
10 Daniel Lerner, *The Passing of Traditional Society: Modernizing the Middle East* (New York: Free Press, 1964 [orig. 1958]), 405.
11 Shils, *Intellectuals*, 16.
12 Ibid., 17.
13 Václav Havel, "Kosovo and the End of the Nation-State," *New York Review of Books*, June 10, 1999, 4–6.
14 Triloki N. Madan, "Secularism in Its Place," *Journal of Asian Studies* 6 (1987), 748.
15 José Casanova, *Public Religions in the Modern World* (Chicago, IL: University of Chicago Press, 1994).
16 Fariba Adelkhah, *Être moderne en Iran* (Paris: Karthala, 1998), 152–247, and Farhad Khosrokhavar and Olivier Roy, *Iran: comment sortir d'une révolution religieuse* (Paris: Éditions du Seuil, 1999), 143–205.
17 See Ziba Mir-Hosseini, *Islam and Gender: The Religious Debate in Contemporary Iran* (Princeton, NJ: Princeton University Press, 1999).
18 Robert Wuthnow, *Producing the Sacred: An Essay on Public Religion* (Urbana, IL: University of Illinois Press, 1994).
19 Samuel Huntington, "The Clash of Civilizations?" *Foreign Affairs* 72/3 (1993): 22–49. See Dale F. Eickelman, "Muslim Politics: The Prospects for Democracy in

North Africa and the Middle East," in John Entelis, ed., *Islam, Democracy, and the State in North Africa* (Bloomington, IN: Indiana University Press, 1997), 35–38, for a critique of Huntington's approach.

20 Dominique Colas, *Civil Society and Fanaticism: Conjoined Histories*, trans. Amy Jacobs (Stanford, CA: Stanford University Press, 1997), and Keane, "Limits of Secularism," 12.

21 Dale F. Eickelman, "Mass Higher Education and the Religious Imagination in Contemporary Arab Societies," *American Ethnologist* 19/4: 643–655; and Dale F. Eickelman, "Islam and the Languages of Modernity," *Daedalus* 129/1 (2000): 119–135.

22 Said Nursi, *The Miracles of Muhammad*, translated from the Turkish by Ümit Şimşek (Istanbul: Yeni Asya Yayınları, 1985); Said Nursi, *Belief and Man*, translated from the Turkish by Ümit Şimşek (Istanbul: Yeni Asya Yayınları, 1985); and Said Nursi, *Resurrection and the Hereafter*, translated from the Turkish by Ümit Şimşek (Istanbul: Yeni Asya Yayınları, 1985).

23 Said Nursi, *Nature: Cause or Effect?* translated from the Turkish by Ümit Şimşek (Istanbul: Yeni Asya Yayınları, 1985).

24 Cited in Şerif Mardin, *Religion and Social Change in Modern Turkey: The Case of Bediüzzaman Said Nursi* (Albany, NY: State University of New York Press, 1989), 4.

25 Şükran Vahide, *Bediuzzaman Said Nursi: The Author of the Risale-i Nur* (Istanbul: Sölzer Publications, 1992), 89–90. For a further discussion of the structure of Nursi's ideas and their appeal to different audiences, see Dale F. Eickelman, "Qur'anic Commentary, Public Space, and Religious Intellectuals in the Writings of Said Nursi," *Muslim World* 89/3–4 (1999): 260–269, from which part of this section is adapted.

26 Thomas Michel, "Muslim–Christian Dialogue and Cooperation in the Thought of Bediuzzaman Said Nursi," *Muslim World* 86/3–4 (1999), 325.

27 Vahide, *Author*, 217.

28 Ibid., 219.

29 Mardin, *Religion and Social Change*, 6.

30 Muhammad Said Ramadan al-Buti, "Bediuzzaman Said Nursi's Experience of Serving Islam by Means of Politics," in *Third International Symposium on Bediüzzaman Said Nursi: The Reconstruction of Islamic Thought in the Twentieth Century and Bediüzzaman Said Nursi, 24th–25th September 1995*, vol. 1, 111–121. Al-Buti is a prominent Syrian religious scholar who broadcasts a popular weekly television program in Damascus.

31 For an excellent overview of the significance of the movement, see M. Hakan Yavuz, "Towards an Islamic Liberalism? The Nurcu Movement and Fethullah Gülen," *Middle East Journal* 53/4 (1999): 584–605. See also Bülent Araş, "Turkish Islam's Moderate Face," *Middle East Quarterly* 5/3 (1998): 23–29.

32 Yavuz, "Islamic Liberalism," 600.

33 See David Pollock and Elaine El Assal, eds, *In the Eye of the Beholder: Muslim and Non-Muslim Views of Islam, Islamic Politics, and Each Other* (Washington, DC: USIA Office of Research and Media Reaction, 1995).

34 Cited in "Fundamental Separation," *The Economist*, June 10, 2000, "Ataturk's Long Shadow: A Survey of Turkey," 11.

35 Muhammad Šahrūr, *al-Kitāb wa al-Qur'ān: Qirā'a mu'ā ṣira* [The Book and the Qur'an: A Contemporary Interpretation] (Damascus: Dār al-Ahālī, 1992). For a description and analysis of the book, see Dale F. Eickelman, "Islamic Liberalism Strikes Back," *Middle East Studies Association Bulletin* 27/2 (1993): 163–168. For an example of his style of writing in English translation, see Muhammad Shahrur, *Proposal for an Islamic Covenant*, trans. Dale F. Eickelman and Ismail S. Abu Shehadeh (Damascus: al-Ahali, 2000). Shahrur's *Proposal* is also available at http://www.islam21.org/pages/charter/may-1.htm

36 Šahrūr, *Kitāb*, 29.
37 Muhammad Šahrūr, *Dirāsāt islāmiyya al-mu'ā ṣira fī al-dawla wa al-muǧtāma'a* [Contemporary Islamic Studies on State and Society] (Damascus: al-Ahālī li al-ṭabā'a wa al-našr, 1994, 23.
38 Wael B. Hallaq, *A History of Islamic Legal Theories* (Cambridge: Cambridge University Press, 1997), 253.
39 *Al-Islām wa al-'aṣr* [Islam and Modernity], ed. 'Abd al-Wāhid 'Alwanī (Damascus: Dār al-Fikr, 1998). In this book, Tayyib Tizini, a Marxist philosopher, presents his views alongside the television preacher Sa'id Ramadan al-Buti. *Ma al-'ulūmiyya* [What is Globalism] (Damascus: Dār al-Fikr, 1999) juxtaposes the views of a modernist Egyptian religious scholar, Hasan Hanafi, to those of the Syrian secularist philosopher, Sadiq Jalal al-'Azm.
40 S. N. Eisenstadt, "Multiple Modernities," *Daedalus* 129/1 (2000): 1–129.

GLOSSARY—INDEX

'ABBAS II HILMI (Egyptian Khedive from 1892 to 1914): **40** (Abdülhamid II's hostility to him, because of his alleged support to *al-Manār*)

'ABD AL-'AZIZ (Moroccan sultan from 1895 to 1907): **165** (his convocation of an "assembly of notables" in 1904–1905, and the opposition of Moroccan ulama to the ruler)

'ABD AL-FATTAH B. 'ABD AL-QAYYUM (the teacher of Riza al-Din in Nizhnye Chelchely, Southern Urals): **98** (his role in R.D.'s initiation to Islamic reform)

'ABD AL-HAFIZ (Moroccan sultan from 1907 to 1912): **165** (his succession to his brother 'Abd al-'Aziz, and his reception of the *bay'a* of the ulama of Fez in 1908)

'ABD AL-HAFIZ AL-FASI (d. 1963–1964, constitutionalist ulama from Fez): **166** (pupil of 'Abd al-Karim Murad)

'ABD AL-KARIM (1882–1963, leader of the Rif Mountains revolt in 1925): **182** (coincidence of his uprising with the Syrian revolt)

'ABD AL-KARIM MURAD (or al-Muradi, d. 1926 [or 1928], Lebanese-born visiting scholar and traveler): **161–175** (article by S. Reichmuth, esp. **165–171**)

'ABD AL-QADIR AL-JAZA'IRI (1808–1883, Algerian community leader and Sufi shaykh): **45** (his intellectual influence in Syria)

'ABDUH, MUHAMMAD (1849–1905, prominent Egyptian reformist thinker, *Shaykh al-Azhar*): **5** (his historical role in facilitating secular reform), **8–11** (his role and audience as the editor of *al-'Urwa al-Wuṯqā*), **12–14** (his stature as a paramount leader for the Islamic world), **17–20** (his authorship of the *Tafsīr al-Manār*), **26** (his reformist understanding of Islam), **27** (his rural origins, alien to the ulama aristocracy of the urban notables), **28** (his tradition of issuing fatwas on contemporary questions, as continued by al-Qaradawi), **47** (answer by al-Qasimi to an idea expressed in *al-Manār*), **55**, **56** ('A.'s connection with the early development of the Salafiyya), **57** ('A. on the independence of religious scholars from rulers), **58** ('A.'s answer to Renan on the question of the "rigidity" of Islam), **60** (his idea of modernism entailing Arab cultural revival), **67–68** (European views of his *Epistle of Unicity*), **74** ('A.'s ideas as a root of Islamism in Ottoman Turkey), **77** (interest of the Ottoman Westernist journal *İctihad* in 'A.'s ideas), **79–80**, **81** ('A.'s impact on Mehmed Âkif), **85**, **90**, **94**, **95**, **98–99**, **104** (his influence in Russia), **130** (translation of the *Risāla al-tawḥīd* into Chinese in 1933), **145** (reference to 'Abduh in the Malay-Indonesian writer Shaykh al-Hadi's novel *Farīda Ḥānum*), **146–147** (attendance of 'Abduh's lessons by Shaykh Muhammad Tahir from Sumatra), **176**, **178**, **202** (lessons given by 'Abduh to Sh. Arslan in the Madrasa al-Sultaniyya during his exile in Beirut), **296** (educated, urban cadres as the primary audience of his message—contrary to the broader public of present-day religious intellectuals)

Circassians of Egypt in the Ottoman Consultation Society), **61**, **161** (early twentieth-century constitutionalism as a model for the world of Islam), **65** (Rida's denunciation of early twentieth-century Westernization trends), **66** (edition by the Egyptian press of Italian and British texts urging women to return to decency in dress), **79** (Egypt as a refuge to Mehmed Âkif in 1926), **85** (fascination for Egypt among Muslim literati in late Imperial Russia), **86** (Egypt as a major destination for Muslim travellers from the Russian Empire), **122–123**, **259** (influence of Wang Haoran's travels to Turkey and Egypt on his reformist thought), **127** (information on Egypt in Hui periodicals of the 1930s), **128**, **253** (Chinese translations from Egyptian Salafi journals in the 1930s), **131** (relations between al-Azhar and the Chengda Normal School), **145** (description of Egypt in Shaykh al-Hadi's novel *Farīda Ḫānum*), **148** (Sayyid Shaykh b. Ahmad al-Hadi accompanying the Sultan and Raja Muda of Riau to the hajj and to Egypt), **163** (nineteenth-century constitutional initiatives by Egyptian sovereigns), **164** (support of Syrian Islamic reformists to Young Ottomans and Young Turks), **177** (Arslan's Egyptian network), **187** (the British occupation of Egypt since 1882), **250–251**, **260** (Ma Songting's travel to Egypt and other Islamic countries, in 1932–1933, to find out new pedagogical methods), **255** (Ma Bufang's travel to Egypt in the early 1950s), **260** (Ha Decheng's travels to India, Ceylon, and Egypt on behalf of his commercial society), **260** (Ha Decheng's importation of Islamic literature from Egypt, India, and Turkey), **300** (resistance to the challenges to their authority by state-appointed hierarchies in Oman, Saudi Arabia, Iran, Egypt, Malaysia, and ex-Soviet Central Asia), *see also* al-Azhar; Cairo

ENGINEERING: **46** (as a discipline to be caught up from Europeans)

ENGLISH LANGUAGE: **178** (its study by Arslan), **193** (E. as one of the languages of the European Muslim Congress of Geneva in 1935), **237** (the central place of E. in modern Isma'ilis' education and literacy), **249** (E. as a matter of teaching in Chinese Muslim reformed religious schools), **257** (Da Pusheng's learning of English language in India), **260** (Ha Decheng's fluency in Arabic language, Urdu, and English), **297** (E. language as the language of instruction in F. Gülen's schools outside Turkey)

ENVER PAŞA (1881–1922, Young Turk leader and Ottoman Turkish statesman): **179** (his first meeting with Sh. Arslan during the Cyrenaica campaign, and origin of their lasting friendship), **180–181** (his deeds in the former Russian Empire and his death in Eastern Bukhara), **181** (his foundation of the Islamic International as an extension of the CUP), **188** (his sending of Arslan to Berlin to negotiate problems regarding the Caucasus), **281** (his acquaintance with 'Abd al-Rashid Ibrahim during the Balkan War of 1912)

ESCORIAL: **200** (Sh. Arslan's consultation of manuscripts on the history of Muslim Spain)

ETHICS (Arabic: *aḫlāq*): **90** (role of ethics literature in the reform of Russia's madrasas), **100** ("women question" in the ethical debates of the 1900 to 1910s in Russia), **296** (relation of Islamic belief to modern science in the work of twentieth-century Muslim religious intellectuals), **297** (instillation by F. Gülen's movement of a morality and sense of discipline intended to pervade private conduct and public life), *see also* alcohol and alcoholism; clothing; education; women and the "women question"

ETOILE NORD-AFRICAINE (political organization created by Messali al-Hajj): **201** (its affinities with the French Communist Party)

EUROPE: **187** (on representations of Europe as an imperial threat since the 1880s), **295** (expansion of the Nurcu movement outside Turkey)

EUROPEAN MUSLIM CONGRESS OF GENEVA (in 1935): **191** (debates on the Italian administration of Libya), **193** (composition of the congress and Arslan's personal role), **194** (mobilization by the

LIBRARIES: **47** (al-Qasimi's library in Damascus), **94** (Russia's Muslim reformists' concern on the need for public libraries), **133** (Fude Library in the Chengda Normal School), **133**, **250–251**, **260** (creation of the Fude Library in 1936, in memory of King Fu'ad of Egypt), **244** (creation of an Islamic library in Shanghai after 1925 by the Learned Society of the Hui Religion in China), **244** (construction of libraries as an aim of the Guild of the Hui Religion of China), **250** (purchase of Islamic books in Egypt by Ma Songting, in 1932, for the future library of the Chengda Normal School), **256–257** (Su Baoqiao's administration of the library created by the Communist Party in Changsha), *see also* books and book trading; madrasa; sponsorship

LIBYA: **190–191** (Sh. Arslan's attacks against Mussolini's policy in Libya), **201** (Arslan's friendship with Ahmad al-Sharif al-Sanusi), **281** ('Abd al-Rashid Ibrahim's encouragement of Ottoman resistance against the Italian invasion of Libya in 1911)

LINSXIA: **255** (birthplace of the Ma warlords of Western China)

LISĀN AL-'ARAB ("The Arabic Language," an early twentieth-century journal of Tangier): **165** (its publication of a second draft constitution for Morocco in 1908)

LITERACY: *see* education

LIU ZHI (late Ming—early Qing Muslim Chinese scholar): **119–120** (his role in the elaboration of the Islamic thought through Chinese characters), **253–254** (successive reprint of his *Tianfang xingli*, and its modern Ikhwani criticism for its Sufi content)

LIUTONG QINGZHEN JIAOYUHUI (Association for Islamic Education in Tokyo): **121** (its creation by Hui expatriates in 1907)

LJUBOVIĆ, AMIR (b. 1945, Bosnian-Herzegovinian historian of local Ottoman literature): **218** (representative of the traditional secular intelligentsia)

LONGUET, JEAN (French socialist politician): **187–188** (his relations with Sh. Arslan)

LUNYU (the Confucian "Analects"): **260** (its translation into Arabic by Ma Jian)

LUTFALLAH, MICHEL (Syrian political activist, Chairman of the Syrian-Palestinian Congress): **182** (his alliance with Shahbandar against Arslan, Rida and al-Husayni), **183** (his and Shahbandar's opposition to Palestinians on the questions of territorial nationalism, compromise with Zionism, and allegiance to the Hashemites), **184** (challenge posed to M. L. by the creation by young Istiqlalists of the Finance Committee of the Syrian-Palestinian Congress, in 1925), **184–185** (M. L.'s ousting from the chairmanship of the Syrian-Palestinian Congress in 1927 by Rida and the Istiqlalists), **185** (conciliatory positions of the Lutfallah—Shahbandar faction regarding the British Mandate and creation of a Greater Lebanon), **185–186** (his and Shahbandar's intrigues against Arslan's negotiations with French officials)

MA BUFANG (1902/3–1975, nephew of Ma Lin: Chinese Muslim warlord, governor of Qinghai, and member of the Guomindang's Central Executive Committee): **246** (his membership in the board of trustees of the Friendly Association of the Hui Religion of China for the Salvation of the Country), **255** (support to the Ikhwani movement by the Ma warlords of Western China), **255** (his travel to Egypt in the early 1950s, and his term as a Nationalist ambassador to Saudi Arabia in 1961), **255** (his work in favor of reformed Muslim education)

MA BUQING (1901–?, Muslim warlord of Lanzhou, in Gansu, a nephew of Ma Lin's): **245** (his family's role in the creation, in Lanzhou, of a subsidiary association of the Confederation of the Hui Religion in China), **246** (his membership in the board of trustees of the Friendly Association of the Hui Religion of China for the Salvation of the Country), **255** (support to the Ikhwani movement by the Ma warlords of Western China)

MA FUXIANG (1876–1932, powerful Hui warlord of Ningxia): **124**, **125**, **250**, **256** (his role in the foundation and in the financing of the Chengda Normal School, during its Beijing period), **125** (his being a follower of *laojiao* Islam),

For Product Safety Concerns and Information please contact our EU representative GPSR@taylorandfrancis.com
Taylor & Francis Verlag GmbH, Kaufingerstraße 24, 80331 München, Germany

www.ingramcontent.com/pod-product-compliance
Lightning Source LLC
Chambersburg PA
CBHW071144100726
47908CB00002B/243

* 9 7 8 0 4 1 5 5 4 9 7 9 0 *